Dmitrij Dobrovol'skij, Elisabeth Piirainen
Figurative Language

Trends in Linguistics
Studies and Monographs

Editors
Chiara Gianollo
Daniël Van Olmen

Editorial Board
Walter Bisang
Tine Breban
Volker Gast
Hans Henrich Hock
Karen Lahousse
Natalia Levshina
Caterina Mauri
Heiko Narrog
Salvador Pons
Niina Ning Zhang
Amir Zeldes

Editors responsible for this volume
Daniël Van Olmen

Volume 350

Dmitrij Dobrovol'skij, Elisabeth Piirainen

Figurative Language

Cross-Cultural and Cross-Linguistic Perspectives

2nd edition, revised and updated

DE GRUYTER
MOUTON

ISBN 978-3-11-125560-6
e-ISBN (PDF) 978-3-11-070253-8
e-ISBN (EPUB) 978-3-11-070260-6

Library of Congress Control Number: 2021947889

Bibliographic information published by the Deutsche Nationalbibliothek
The Deutsche Nationalbibliothek lists this publication in the Deutsche Nationalbibliografie; detailed bibliographic data are available on the Internet at http://dnb.dnb.de.

© 2023 Walter de Gruyter GmbH, Berlin/Boston
This volume is text- and page-identical with the hardback published in 2022.
Typesetting: Integra Software Services Pvt. Ltd.
Printing and binding: CPI books GmbH, Leck

www.degruyter.com

Preface

This book is the second edition of *Figurative Language: Cross-Cultural and Cross-Linguistic Perspectives*, which was first published in 2005. It appeared within the Elsevier series Current Research in the Semantics/Pragmatics Interface. The book's popularity meant we needed to prepare a new edition. Since the Elsevier series had closed, we decided to publish the book with Mouton de Gruyter.

In the sixteen years between the first and second editions of this book, considerable changes in figurative language research made revision necessary. We updated the chapters in light of the latest research, and introduced new concepts. The theoretical part has been significantly revised and expanded, and now forms a greater proportion of the book. For example, Chapter 4, while retaining its title, has been significantly restructured and now includes completely new content. Major changes have also been made in chapters 1, 2, 6, 8 and 10.

In December 2017 Elisabeth Piirainen unexpectedly passed away, which made further revision extremely difficult. She collected invaluable empirical material, and I have largely tried to preserve it in this second edition.

What is this book about?

There are parts of the language system that cannot be analysed and described without addressing issues outside linguistics proper. The subject of our study belongs to this sphere. Any attempt to analyse figurative language by itself, without the inclusion of extralinguistic knowledge, is doomed to failure. The relevant differences between figurative units of language and their non-figurative near-synonyms can only be captured if we extend our data and methods and move into fields beyond linguistics in the narrower sense of the word. They cannot be exhaustively described or, more importantly, explained by means of purely linguistic methods. Instead, we have to address various types of extralinguistic knowledge, including knowledge that is culture-based.

The focus of our study is on conventional figurative units, i.e. not on novel metaphors, ad hoc metonymies, or various types of rhetorical figures, but on units such as idioms and lexicalised metaphors. The most important linguistic feature of these conventional figurative units is that they record and preserve relevant knowledge (as image traces) as part of their content plane, including, above all, reflections of the respective culture. The aim of this study is to develop a linguistic theory that is capable of taking this feature into account.

One of the most intriguing questions in the field of lexical analysis is the problem of the relationship between the figurative meaning of a lexical unit (idiom, proverb, one-word metaphor, etc.) and the mental image that forms its conceptual basis. For example, the word *web* denotes not only a spider's web but also a particular part of the Internet; the expression *a turn of the screw* stands not only for a technical procedure, but also for intense pressure, constraint, or extortion.

A theory designed to analyse units of figurative language has to answer, at a minimum, the following questions: Are there any regular relationships between the literal, image-based reading fixed in the lexical structure of a given figurative unit and its lexicalised figurative meaning, i.e. its actual meaning? In other words, are such relations part of the more or less systematically organised structure of the lexicon? Can they be regarded as a relevant dimension of the structure of the lexicon, comparable to lexical relations such as synonymy and antonymy, or are they, rather, accidental and unable to be accounted for in terms of semantic regularities? Furthermore, if the relations between the literal and figurative meanings are systematic in nature, are they ruled by basic principles of human cognition, in which case they would have to be near-universals? Or do they vary from language to language to such an extent that it would not be reasonable to attempt to derive them from universal cognitive principles? What role does culture play in this domain? Is it possible to verify the assumption that some basic principles of human cognition are responsible for the creation of figurative units on the basis of literal units, and would such principles be modified by relevant cultural factors? Is the mental image underlying the actual meaning of a given conventional figurative expression only an "etymological" phenomenon, or is it (at least partly) a component of the content plane of the given expression? If it is the latter, what position in the semantic structure does the image component occupy? Does it have to be readily apparent in the meaning in the semantic representation of the given expression?

The general aim of our study is to develop a theoretical framework that makes it possible to analyse different types of conventional figurative expressions from different languages on a basis of consistent parameters and criteria, so that the potential findings will be fundamentally comparable. Such a framework will allow us to find at least tentative answers to some of the questions listed above. We refer to this theory as *Conventional Figurative Language Theory*. Accordingly, the proper subject of our study is *conventional figurative language*, i.e. a subsystem of the lexicon, as opposed to figurative ad hoc expressions produced in discourse.

We are convinced that an efficient discussion of this subject will only be possible if it is based on large-scale empirical work. Without a thorough analysis of hundreds of conventional figurative units from different languages, it would be futile even to try to discover relevant conceptual and semantic relationships in the domain of linguistic figurativeness.

We assume that figurative units differ from non-figurative units with respect to their semantic structure. A relevant element of the content plane of figurative units is the so-called image component, a specific conceptual structure mediating between the lexical structure which triggers the corresponding mental image and the actual meaning of a figurative unit. One important consequence for a fine-grained linguistic analysis which follows from this assumption is that the traces of the literal meaning inherited by the figurative meaning have to be taken into account while describing the content plane of figurative units. This will help us not only to understand better the semantic and conceptual structuring of this part of the lexicon, but also to give an accurate lexicographic description of figurative units.

The conceptual nature of the image component can be roughly described as follows: mental images associated with figurative expressions are basically individual phenomena, but there are also intersubjective aspects to these mental images. The image component assumes the function of a semantic bridge between "what is said" and "what is meant", i.e. between the lexical structure and the actual meaning.

In order to achieve our goal, it is crucial to uncover the types of knowledge that are involved in the creation of motivating links between the two conceptual levels of figurative units, i.e. between the underlying mental image and the actual meaning. Even at first glance, our empirical data from different languages suggest that many significant properties of figurative language can only be explained on the basis of specific conceptual structures that we generally refer to as *cultural knowledge*. Furthermore, we assume that many phenomena found in figurative language can only be properly described if we address cultural codes other than natural language (folk beliefs, customs, literature, the fine arts, etc.). An appropriate theoretical framework should provide explanations for cases like these.

In summary, we would like to discuss in this study an array of questions that arise in the domain of figurative language, from both a cross-linguistic and a cross-cultural perspective. Instead of suggesting a global theoretical idea serving as a foundation for the description of figurative phenomena, we attempt to find an appropriate theoretical framework for all the individual aspects of figurative language. In our opinion, no global and abstract theoretical approach can capture all the relevant facets of this phenomenon and the links it has with other conceptual, cultural, and linguistic domains. As a whole, our approach (labelled here the Conventional Figurative Language Theory) can be qualified as cognitive because it addresses different types of knowledge as an explanatory basis for linguistic phenomena. The general task of this theory is not to predict particular expressions, but to explain their meanings and functions in connection with other conceptual and semiotic phenomena.

This book is both practical and theoretical. It is based on a large amount of empirical data from various languages, and certain parts of it can be used as an aid to the lexicographic description and contrastive analysis necessary for foreign language teaching. Theoretically, it offers a framework (including a metalanguage) within which units of figurative language can be effectively explored and explained.

Another crucial feature of conventional figurative language lies in the fact that a rigid application of the Saussurian distinction between synchrony and diachrony is of little value here. This is because many characteristics of the contextual behaviour of conventional figurative units can only be explained by means of their etymologies; that is, certain traces of original readings function as "etymological memories" and, as such, have an effect on synchronically observable linguistic behaviour.

This book presents a further development of these ideas and a synthesis of all our individual and joint work. It combines our quest for cognitive approaches to the phenomenon of idioms appropriate to better explain their special quality, our interest in language comparison and rich empirical data from different languages, and our interest in the semiotics of culture and the far-reaching cultural foundations of figurative language. Accordingly, the theory presented in this study is an attempt to develop a framework that makes it possible to integrate single observations and results and create a common explanatory basis for these individual phenomena.

The Conventional Figurative Language Theory is a set of principles which aims to answer questions such as

- What is the difference between *literal language* and *figurative language*?
- Are there any operational criteria for distinguishing between them?
- What are the specifics of *conventional figurative language* as compared to *non-conventional figurativeness*?
- Which kinds of lexical units belong to the field of *conventional figurativeness*?
- Are there any specific analytical instruments for investigating the crucial properties of conventional figurative units?

The intention of this second edition of our book is to discuss these questions and to provide clear and convincing answers.

Dmitrij Dobrovol'skij					Moscow, June 2021

Acknowledgements

The revised and updated version of this book is recommended for publication by the Academic Council of the Institute of Linguistics of the Russian Academy of Sciences. It is partially based on work supported by the Russian Science Foundation (RSF) under Grant 16-48-03006 "Semantic Analysis of Translated Texts for Comparative Cultural Studies and Cultural Specificity in Language Learning".

We would like to thank all the people who have assisted in doing this work. Our very special gratitude is due to Dr. Julia Miller (The University of Adelaide).

Contents

Preface —— V

Acknowledgements —— IX

1 **General issues** —— 1
1.1 Working hypotheses —— 1
1.2 Empirical data —— 2
1.2.1 The languages analysed in the present study —— 2
1.2.2 Sources used for the analysed languages —— 4
1.2.3 Languages analysed and the role of culture in figurative language —— 6
1.2.4 Arrangement of the linguistic data and typographical conventions —— 8
1.3 Criteria for figurativeness —— 9
1.3.1 Literal – non-literal – figurative —— 9
1.3.2 Image requirement —— 13
1.3.3 Additional naming —— 21
1.4 Figurative language and related phenomena —— 24
1.4.1 Indirect language —— 25
1.4.2 Non-figurative metaphors and metonymies —— 28
1.4.3 Phraseology —— 31

2 **Conventional figurative language and phraseology** —— 36
2.1 Research on phraseology: A brief outline —— 36
2.1.1 Terminology and main topics —— 36
2.1.2 Written vs. oral language as research topic —— 39
2.1.3 Anglo-American research tradition —— 40
2.2 One-word figurative lexical units —— 42
2.3 Types of phrasemes and their constitutive criteria —— 49
2.3.1 Idioms —— 51
2.3.2 Similes —— 58
2.3.3 Restricted collocations —— 62
2.3.4 Proverbs —— 66
2.4 Summary —— 71

3 **On the cross-linguistic equivalence of idioms** —— 73
3.1 Preliminary remarks —— 73
3.2 On the scope of cross-linguistic idiom analysis —— 77
3.3 Cross-linguistic equivalents of idioms from a functional perspective —— 83

3.4 Parameters of idiom comparison — 88
3.4.1 Semantics — 89
3.4.2 Syntactics — 95
3.4.3 Pragmatics — 98
3.4.4 Conclusion — 100
3.5 Summary — 101

4 Motivation of conventional figurative units — 103
4.1 Motivation and etymology — 103
4.2 Motivation and related phenomena — 109
4.2.1 Motivation vs. analysability — 109
4.2.2 Motivation vs. semantic ambiguity — 111
4.3 Unmotivated lexical units — 111
4.4 Types of motivation — 114
4.5 Metaphoric motivation — 116
4.5.1 Preliminaries — 116
4.5.2 Conceptual metaphor — 117
4.5.3 Frame-based metaphor and rich image — 122
4.6 Symbol-based motivation — 127
4.7 Coercion as a type of motivation — 132
4.8 Syntactic motivation — 136
4.9 Motivation based on textual knowledge — 137
4.10 Index-based motivation — 140
4.11 Interaction of motivation types — 143
4.12 Summary — 145

5 "False friends" and paronyms — 146
5.1 False friends of the translator — 146
5.2 False friends in conventional figurative language — 147
5.3 False friends in different types of conventional figurative units — 150
5.4 Paronyms and homonyms — 154
5.5 Factors relating to origin — 155
5.5.1 Idioms as false friends based on different conceptual metaphors — 156
5.5.2 Idioms as false friends based on different rich images — 159
5.5.3 Idioms as false friends based on different meanings of their constituents — 162
5.6 Summary — 164

6 The Cognitive Theory of Metaphor —— 165
- 6.1 Basic principles of the Cognitive Theory of Metaphor —— 166
- 6.2 Discussion: Are all postulates of the Cognitive Theory of Metaphor consistent with linguistic data? —— 168
- 6.2.1 Conceptual metaphors, the humoural doctrine or something else? —— 169
- 6.2.2 Levels of mappings and their linguistic relevance —— 175
- 6.2.3 Japanese culture, anger, and emotions as cultural constructs? —— 179
- 6.2.4 Do anthropological data fit into the Cognitive Theory of Metaphor? —— 184
- 6.2.5 What do conceptual metaphors really explain? —— 187
- 6.2.6 Idioms and conceptual metaphors —— 191
- 6.3 Conclusions —— 193

7 Idioms of FEAR: A cognitive approach —— 197
- 7.1 Introduction —— 197
- 7.2 Idiom semantics in cognitive perspective —— 198
- 7.3 Source domains of FEAR —— 200
- 7.3.1 Kövecses' proposal —— 201
- 7.3.2 FEAR in Russian, English, German and Dutch —— 205
- 7.4 Structure of the semantic field of FEAR —— 207
- 7.5 Does the imagery influence the meaning? —— 209
- 7.6 Concluding remarks —— 215

8 Cognitive modelling of figurative semantics —— 217
- 8.1 General aspects —— 217
- 8.2 Cognitive approach to semantic explanation —— 223
- 8.3 Addressing implicit elements of conceptual structures —— 226
- 8.4 Literal readings: Conceptual structures vs. "referential reality" —— 227
- 8.5 Cognitive modelling vs. conceptual metaphor —— 229
- 8.6 Metaphoric inference and cultural knowledge —— 232
- 8.7 Conclusion —— 235

9 Specific frames: The concept HOUSE in language and culture —— 239
- 9.1 Preliminary remarks —— 239
- 9.2 The concept HOUSE in English, German, Dutch, Swedish and Finnish —— 241
- 9.2.1 The multiple-room urban building as a source frame —— 241

9.2.2	Traditional dwelling houses as source concepts —— **246**	
9.3	The concept HOUSE in Japanese —— **247**	
9.3.1	The traditional Japanese dwelling house: Main elements of architecture and interior —— **247**	
9.3.2	Conventional figurative units containing HOUSE-frame constituents —— **248**	
9.3.3	Conclusions —— **252**	
9.4	The concept HOUSE in a Low German dialect —— **253**	
9.4.1	The "Low German one-room hall-house" —— **253**	
9.4.2	The concept HOUSE in conventional figurative units —— **255**	
9.4.3	Summary —— **261**	

10 Culture and figurative language —— 262

10.1	On the notions of culture —— **262**	
10.1.1	Introduction —— **262**	
10.1.2	Cultural anthropology —— **263**	
10.1.3	Semiotics of culture —— **265**	
10.1.4	Philosophy of language and linguistics —— **267**	
10.1.5	"Culture" in the field of figurative language: A working definition —— **272**	
10.2	Cultural phenomena in conventional figurative units —— **273**	
10.3	Social interaction —— **275**	
10.3.1	"Cultural models" —— **275**	
10.3.2	Social conventions, taboos and bans —— **279**	
10.3.3	Gestures —— **281**	
10.3.4	Gender-specifics —— **283**	
10.4	Phenomena relating to material culture —— **287**	
10.4.1	Preliminaries —— **287**	
10.4.2	Culture-specific artefacts —— **288**	
10.5	Textual dependence —— **296**	
10.5.1	Preliminary remarks —— **296**	
10.5.2	Quotations —— **297**	
10.5.3	Allusions —— **301**	
10.6	Fictive conceptual domains —— **303**	
10.7	Cultural symbols —— **307**	
10.8	Combining of cultural phenomena in figurative units —— **309**	
10.9	Cultural connotations —— **314**	
10.9.1	Preliminary notes —— **314**	
10.9.2	Proper nouns —— **317**	
10.9.3	Idioethnic realia —— **320**	

10.9.4	Culture-specifics in the target concept —— 322	
10.10	Concluding remarks —— 323	

11 Cultural symbolism in figurative language —— 325
11.1 The semiotics of culture —— 325
11.1.1 The Moscow-Tartu School —— 326
11.1.2 Semiotics of culture and figurative language —— 327
11.2 Concepts of the symbol in non-linguistic paradigms —— 330
11.2.1 Symbol research and research on conventional figurative units —— 330
11.2.2 Attempts to define "symbol" —— 333
11.2.3 Concepts of the symbol in various disciplines —— 335
11.3 Concepts of the symbol in linguistics and semiotics —— 337
11.3.1 Introduction —— 337
11.3.2 The symbol as analogical thinking —— 338
11.3.3 The symbol as an arbitrary sign —— 339
11.3.4 The symbol as connotative meaning —— 340
11.3.5 The symbol as a culture-semiotic phenomenon —— 341
11.3.6 Summary —— 346
11.4 Cultural symbols in figurative language —— 347
11.4.1 Metaphor vs. symbol —— 347
11.4.2 Symbols: Transparent vs. opaque —— 354
11.4.3 Cultural context of symbols —— 359
11.4.4 Cultural codes —— 365

12 Numeral words and number symbols in culture and language: Case studies —— 367
12.1 General remarks —— 367
12.1.1 Linguistic aspects of numerals and number symbols —— 367
12.1.2 Cultural aspects of number symbols —— 371
12.1.3 Numbers in conventional figurative units and culture: Special cases —— 373
12.2 Four: The special case of French —— 374
12.2.1 Four in conventional figurative units of different languages —— 374
12.2.2 Four in French conventional figurative units —— 380
12.2.3 Four in culture —— 383
12.2.4 Conclusions —— 384
12.3 Nine in figurative language and culture: Finnish, Lithuanian and English —— 384
12.3.1 Nine as a marginal numeral in some languages —— 385
12.3.2 Nine in Finnish conventional figurative language and culture —— 386

12.3.3　NINE in Lithuanian conventional figurative language and culture —— 390
12.3.4　NINE in English conventional figurative language and culture —— 394
12.3.5　The rivalry of NINE and SEVEN in languages and cultures —— 397
12.4　Eleven: The "crazy number" in Dutch figurative units —— 398
12.4.1　Iconic functions and textual dependence —— 398
12.4.2　Symbolic functions —— 400
12.4.3　ELEVEN in culture —— 402
12.4.4　Results —— 403

13　Animal metaphors and animal symbols: Case studies —— 404
13.1　Animals in conventional figurative language —— 404
13.2　SNAKE —— 409
13.2.1　Iconic functions of SNAKE —— 409
13.2.2　Symbolic functions of SNAKE —— 411
13.2.3　SNAKE in cultural codes —— 415
13.2.4　Results —— 417
13.3　WOLF —— 418
13.3.1　Iconic functions of WOLF —— 418
13.3.2　Symbolic functions of WOLF —— 420
13.3.3　WOLF in cultural codes —— 426
13.3.4　Results —— 429
13.4　BEAR —— 429
13.4.1　Iconic functions of BEAR —— 430
13.4.2　Symbolic functions of BEAR —— 431
13.4.3　BEAR in cultural codes —— 433
13.4.4　Results —— 434

14　Conclusions —— 435
14.1　Basic principles of the Conventional Figurative Language Theory —— 436
14.1.1　Basic postulates of the Conventional Figurative Language Theory —— 436
14.1.2　Tools of the Conventional Figurative Language Theory —— 438
14.2　The essence of the Conventional Figurative Language Theory —— 441

References —— 445

Abbreviations —— 483

Subject index —— 485

1 General issues

1.1 Working hypotheses

The present study is based on empirical data drawn from various languages (cf. 1.2). Numerous conventional figurative expressions are analysed in relation to their cultural background. While developing a number of theoretical ideas about the essence of figurative language, we let ourselves be guided by these empirical data, not by *a priori* models or conceptions.

Central to our study is the following idea: a specific conceptual structure underlies the meaning of a figurative unit. This conceptual structure contains traces of the image underlying the lexicalised meaning. These traces provide motivational links. These semantic elements constitute a special part of the content plane of a given figurative unit, based on mental imagery. We call this the *image component*.

The basic assumption of our study can be formulated as follows:

> The image component, i.e. a specific conceptual structure linking the lexical structure and the actual meaning of a figurative unit, is an important element of its content plane.

We derive the following hypotheses from this assumption:
1. Many restrictions on the use of figurative units are due to specifics of their image components.
2. Semantic and/or pragmatic differences between figurative expressions with similar actual meanings often originate from specifics of the image component.
3. Near-equivalent figurative units in different languages are never identical with regard to their semantics and/or pragmatics if their image components reveal substantial differences.
4. Even if an image component does not directly influence the way in which a given figurative unit is used, it is still a potential part of its content plane, which can be activated in specific contexts such as plays on words.
5. Since the specific features of the image component are often historically grounded (i.e. the component preserves knowledge structures relevant at the time when the figurative unit originated), some elements of the user's etymological knowledge may influence the image component's semantic and/or pragmatic properties.
6. Since the specific features of the image component are often culturally grounded, the specifics of a given culture can influence linguistic structures in the field of conventional figurative language. Hence, different kinds of cultural phenomena can have linguistic relevance.

To test these hypotheses against empirical data from different languages and different cultures, various tools of analysis have to be developed, among them selection criteria, classifications and taxonomies of relevant phenomena, a metalanguage for their description and the like. These can be regarded as metalinguistic components of the theory that we develop in this study. Elements of diachronic description must be included in the synchronic analysis if they help to capture the specifics of the image component.

All these ideas, assumptions and metalinguistic devices will be introduced, illustrated with rich empirical data, and discussed in detail in the following chapters.

1.2 Empirical data

The goals of this study are to investigate conventional figurative language. Although there are many innovative and/or ad hoc expressions which are strongly figurative, we are for the most part concerned with those conventional figurative units that are part of the lexical system of a given language. These figurative units are words or multiword expressions which are fixed, i.e. conventionalised. Accordingly, the empirical basis of this study consists of conventional expressions (idioms, proverbs, figurative collocations or one-word metaphors).

1.2.1 The languages analysed in the present study

Since our study is oriented not only towards cross-linguistic but also towards cross-cultural research, we had to select a range of languages that are (a priori) expected to reveal both linguistic and cultural differences. In selecting a suitable number of languages, we let ourselves be guided by the following oppositions: (i) standard literary languages vs. varieties without, or with only a late, written tradition, (ii) genetically and typologically affiliated languages vs. unrelated languages, and (iii) languages of more or less the same cultural area vs. languages of distant cultural areas. In addition to these oppositions, we took into account (iv) the differences between large and small linguistic (and cultural) communities (i.e. between widespread and lesser-used languages) and (v) the degree of geographical and cultural contacts of languages (geographically neighbouring vs. isolated languages).

Our empirical data were drawn from one dialect and ten standard languages and their respective cultural areas. We are fully aware of the fact that language communities and culture communities are almost never congruent (let alone the fact that a nation is never congruent with one language and one cultural community). Almost nowhere in Europe can we find a speech community that is identical to a cultural community. An extreme case of cultural diversity of people speaking the same language is English. But even a small dialect is not totally congruent with the corresponding culture because its speakers normally use a different standard language and are involved in various cultural codes.

Five Germanic language varieties are considered here, namely four standard languages and one dialect. We analyse the West Germanic standard languages *English*, *German* and *Dutch*, the North Germanic standard language *Swedish*, and a *Low German dialect*. This dialect, called "Westmünsterländisch" (WML), is located in a small area of Germany at the edge of the German-speaking region near the Netherlands (see below for details).

All the five Germanic languages are genetically related by definition. In addition, some of them (German, Dutch and the WML dialect) are geographically connected. While English, German, Dutch and Swedish are written languages, used by large linguistic communities (with English being the greatest international language of communication), the WML dialect is regionally bound and used only in oral form in some mostly private and informal domains of a mainly agrarian society. So, the question is which value subsumes all the pairs? Is, for example, the geographical closeness more important than the opposition between written vs. oral? Or vice versa?

The other languages analysed in the present study are also standard or literary languages. Besides the Germanic group of languages, four other main groups of the Indo-European language family are represented: *French* as a Romance language, and – regionally and genetically less closely related to the above-mentioned languages – *Russian* (as a Slavonic language), *Lithuanian* (as a Baltic language) and *Modern Greek*. Lithuanian is a lesser-used language with a late written tradition, in contrast to the large Francophone and Russian linguistic communities and to Greek, all of which look back on long literary traditions.

Furthermore, two non-Indo-European languages have been included in the research, namely *Finnish* and *Japanese*. Both languages are agglutinative. Thus, they are, to a high degree, typologically different from the other languages. Nevertheless, Finnish has had much influence from Germanic languages. Swedish was the official language of Finland up to the 19th century and linguistic contacts were natural in the bilingual regions of West Finland. What is more important, however, is that Finnish has shared the common European historical, religious, and cultural traditions and thus belongs to the same cultural area as the Indo-European languages named above.

Japanese has been chosen because it is not only geographically and linguistically very distant from the other languages but also represents an original culture, one that is largely independent of influences from Euro-American cultural areas. Japanese ranks sixth in the world with more than 125 million speakers in Japan. Its genetic relation is still a topic of discussion. Japanese has a long written tradition, which goes back to the eighth century AD. Because of Japan's self-imposed isolation until 1853, it was not until the 19th century that Japan's culture met European culture. Thus, there had been virtually no contact between Japanese and Western languages and cultures before that time. Consequently, Japanese society can be observed over time as a relatively coherent cultural entity, at least in contrast to English or French speaking societies.

We hope that these languages will provide a reliable empirical basis for testing our hypotheses.

1.2.2 Sources used for the analysed languages

For the most part, the empirical data for the standard languages were drawn from dictionaries, text corpora, or other written sources. In several cases, our data were completed by survey results. As speakers of Russian, German and Finnish, we could also refer to our own linguistic competence for these languages.

The situation we were faced with when collecting material for the WML dialect was far different from compiling the conventional figurative units of the ten standard languages. Dictionaries, idiom collections, or text corpora did not exist. Instead, the empirical data originate from our own questionnaire survey. In the following passages, we will first outline in brief the situation of this dialect and the conditions of the data collection, before we go into detail about the sources used for the analysis of the standard languages.

The Low German dialect "Westmünsterländisch". The dialect (located, as its name suggests, "west of the city of Münster") belongs to the family of Westphalian dialects of North West Germany. It refers to a well-defined dialect area that is relatively easy to distinguish from adjoining Westphalian areas through a number of isoglosses (cf. Kremer 1993, 1996). The dialect was spoken until recently in a small region adjacent to the Netherlands. Whereas in former times a dialect continuum extended over both sides of the Dutch-German border, this border became increasingly fluid after World War II. Due to the border location, WML was preserved as an archaic dialect, used in some private domains of an agrarian community, almost exclusively in oral form. On the whole, these were favourable conditions for the study of this dialect.

Between 1986 and 1992, when there were still a sufficient number of competent speakers of this old basic dialect available, intensive field research was carried out in the Westmünsterland region.[1] The dialectal idioms of WML were empirically collected with the help of numerous dialect experts of the older generation. Most of them had spent their childhood on farms and had acquired the dialect as their first language.

Two different types of methods were used to amass a vast amount of dialectal material: "indirect" methods (onomasiological and semasiological questionnaires) and "direct" methods (interviews, talk circles, participant observation). The topics addressed during this systematic collection of linguistic data are new for dialectology. They include, among other things, semantic classes such as APPEARANCE AND CHARACTERISTICS OF HUMAN BEINGS, PEOPLE'S SUBJECTIVE VIEWS OF THE WORLD, INTERPERSONAL RELATIONS, EXPERIENCES, and HUMAN ACTIONS. More than 4,500 dialectal idioms were compiled through the field research methods mentioned above. The collected idioms were constantly checked for accuracy by many other native speakers. In addition, the remaining WML speakers were asked about their knowledge of idioms and the mental images evoked by specific figurative units. A database was developed to facilitate queries on the entire phraseology of WML; this facilitates fast access to all sorts of questions and data combinations.

The standard languages. In what follows, we will enumerate the main sources used for compiling the conventional figurative units of the standard languages. Since the first edition of this book, several new idiom dictionaries have been published. In addition, there are now a number of online idiom dictionaries and text corpora available to verify our data. Nevertheless, the most important idiom dictionaries that we consulted should be mentioned here. For the sake of space, we cannot list all other (mono- and bilingual) dictionaries that we also referred to from time to time.[2]

There are a number of publications available for the study of *English* conventional figurative units. The following idiom dictionaries were consulted frequently: Cowie, Mackin, and McCaig (1993), Ammer (1997), Longman ID (1998), Speake (1999), Gulland and Hinds-Howell (2001), McCarthy (2002). For American idioms we also referred to Makkai, Boatner, and Gates (1995) and Spears (1997, 1999). We mainly used Duden (2013) for *German*, and additionally Schemann (1989). *Dutch* idioms were looked up, for the most part, in Van Dale IW (1999), and in some

---

[1] There are several studies on WML and its phraseology, see e.g. Piirainen (2000) for details.
[2] Several other publications, especially on proverbs, have also to be mentioned. The most important among them are Cox (1988), Mieder (1992), Paczolay (1994, 1997), Simpson (1992), and for Japanese proverbs Takashima (1981).

cases in Huizinga (1994). For *Swedish* we mostly referred to Schottmann (2012) and general dictionaries and asked native speakers.

The dictionary by Rey and Chantreau (2003) served as a basis for *French* conventional figurative units, supplemented by Pilard et al. (2012). With regard to *Russian* idioms, we made use of Lubensky's (2013) dictionary, the "Thesaurus of Modern Russian Idioms" (Baranov and Dobrovol'skij 2007), the "Academy Dictionary of Russian Phraseology" (Baranov and Dobrovol'skij 2020), the "Thesaurus of Russian Idioms: Semantic Groups and Contexts" (Baranov and Dobrovol'skij 2018), and the databases of "Modern Russian Idioms" (Russian Academy of Sciences, Russian Language Institute, Department of Experimental Lexicography, Moscow).

The situation with *Lithuanian* figurative units turned out to be more difficult. Besides the small phraseological dictionary by Galnaitytė, Pikčilingis, and Sivickienė (1989), there is the detailed but incomplete work by Grigas (2000, 2008). In addition, we had the "WordSmith Tools" database at our disposal. In many cases, we got valuable information from our respondents. We collected the bulk of our *Greek* empirical data from Antoniadou and Kaltsas (1994) and Brillouët and Kokkinidou-Maxime (2008). For special purposes (such as animal constituents), Chrissou (2000) and various general dictionaries were also consulted.

When selecting our *Finnish* examples, we sought advice from the publications of Kari (1993), Korhonen (2001, 2008), and Mauranen and Raudaskoski (2006). The following *Japanese* idiom dictionaries were consulted: Sasaki (1993), Maynard and Maynard (1993), Corwin (1994), Wallace and Kimiya (1994, 1995), Akiyama and Akiyama (1996), Garrison and Goshi (1996), Murakami (1997), Sanseido (2002), and Garrison et al. (2002). Several native speakers of Japanese also helped us with our data.

1.2.3 Languages analysed and the role of culture in figurative language

As outlined above, these languages were chosen in view of the oppositions (i–v) which enabled us to gain an insight into similarities and differences concerning the role of culture in conventional figurative language. Until now, much of idiom research has been concerned with standard literary languages, and thus almost exclusively with written forms of language, while minor languages with less developed literary traditions and dialects, in predominantly oral forms, have largely been ignored. However, the differences between standard languages and a basic dialect like WML, which has no written tradition, play a decisive role for figurative language.

Comparing figurative units of languages, literacy is a relevant parameter. WML speakers learnt to read and write Standard German only, and they never read or wrote their dialect. Thus, the dialect did not undergo changes through writing, such as standardisation or borrowings from written texts. Although WML is located in Central Europe, figurative units of this dialect are little affected by phenomena due to "intertextuality". There is no place for references to, for example, classical antiquity, or to the achievements of modern material and social culture as source concepts (e.g. technology, movies or sports). Instead, conventional figurative units of this dialect reveal their own cultural elements, rooted in the everyday experience of the rural dialect speaker community [cf. oppositions (i) and (v)]. Some peculiarities of Lithuanian (in comparison with the other European languages) might also be ascribed to the late development of the written language and literary tradition.

In contrast to the WML dialect, the nine standard European languages (English, German, Dutch, Swedish, French, Russian, Lithuanian, Greek and Finnish) are quite close to each other with regard to their conventional figurative expressions. It is a well-known fact that the languages of Europe show far-reaching similarities in the figurative lexicon. In fact, the term *widespread idiom* (*WI* for short) was recently introduced into linguistics. This refers to idioms that occur in a large number of languages and have almost identical lexical and semantic structures.[3] There are several WIs among the data of the present book.

Similar discoveries come from typology research. Fairly recently, linguists have recognised that there are great syntactic, morphological and semantic similarities between the languages of Europe; these similarities are called *Euroversals*. The languages of Europe are seen as a particular group with a remarkable uniformity, especially in contrast to non-European languages. Initially, the term *European Sprachbund* ("linguistic area") was used for this discovery; later the term *Standard Average European* (*SAE* for short) gained more acceptance. Up to now, the term has been used for mainly structural convergences that cannot be explained by genetic relationships.[4]

---

[3] To date, about 500 idioms have been identified using intensive research (cf. Piirainen 2012, 2016). Earlier terms such as *Europeanisms* or *internationalisms* are considered unsuitable for the phenomenon of widespread use of figurative units.

[4] Whorf ([1941] 1956) coined the term *SAE* when he compared structures of Native American languages with European languages. The term met with criticism much later because of ideological, hegemonic connotations. Whorf used it, among other things, to describe a way of thinking of Europeans as opposed to that of the Hopi people, and not primarily as a term for common grammatical properties. Typology research, on the other hand, embraced this term, and it became generally established through the project "Typology of Languages in Europe" (EUROTYP), where it is used in the sense of the term *European Sprachbund* or *European linguistic area* (e.g. Dahl 1990, 2001; van der Auwera 1998; König and Haspelmath 1999; Haspelmath and König 2001).

Explanations of how these typological "Euroversals" came into being have much in common with the evaluation of the "widespread idioms" in conventional figurative language. Both phenomena are attributed to far-reaching common historical, religious, and cultural traditions, from Greek antiquity, medieval Latin literature, the Renaissance and Humanism, when Latin was the scholarly lingua franca, to many other cultural contacts in Europe over the centuries. The European standard languages tend to grow closer together as far as their imagery in figurative language is concerned. This is paralleled by the extent to which modern urban societies converge culturally. Moreover, as the analysis of Finnish figurative units shows, genetic affiliation or linguistic typology is of no importance to conventional figurative language [cf. oppositions (ii), (iii) and (iv)].[5]

Finally, Japanese, an East Asian language, is particularly well suited for researching the role of culture in figurative language. Japanese, once completely isolated from Western cultural influences, serves as a contrast to the increasingly unified Euro-American languages. Japanese figurative language reveals its own original cultural components, rooted in the very different cultural traditions of Japan [oppositions (iii) and (v)].

In sum, Japanese as well as the Low German WML dialect turn out to be the most distant from all standard European languages and most likely to reveal idiosyncratic factors as far as their figurative foundations are concerned. With regard to their conventional figurative units, the uniformity of the European languages stands directly opposed to the idiosyncratic factors discovered in the WML dialect and in Japanese. This is grounded in various cultural aspects underlying the imagery of figurative units. In order to compare figurative phenomena across a great variety of languages and dialects, a typology of aspects of culture in figurative language will be suggested (see chapter 10).

1.2.4 Arrangement of the linguistic data and typographical conventions

The insufficiencies of idiom dictionaries, above all with regard to the semantic description of conventional figurative units, are well known (cf. Burger 1992; Dobrovol'skij 2015). Nevertheless, for several foreign languages in this study we have to rely on information given in dictionaries. Thus, the semantic paraphrases of some individual figurative units can only be approximations of their actual

---

[5] Similar results come from Arabic languages (Owens 1996). Structurally, Nigerian Arabic is a variant of Arabic, but idiomatically it belongs to what is termed a Chad basin idiomatic type, which includes languages of different genetic affiliation.

semantic potential and should not be regarded as adequate meaning definitions. For figurative units of our native languages, however, we will use a linguistically tenable metalanguage.

We used the following typing conventions: Linguistic units are given in italics, literal translations are enclosed in double quotation marks, and actual meanings are enclosed in single quotation marks. The underlying concepts appear in small capitals. In some cases, words have been added in the literal translations of linguistic units in order to facilitate comprehension; these additional words are given in round brackets. Grammatical explanations as well as additional, more readable translations are given in square brackets. Verbal idioms are normally given in the infinitive form, except where pragmatic or syntactic reasons render a citation form in the infinitive impossible. According to the custom, we cite Greek verbal idioms in the first person singular. For the Japanese linguistic units, we use the original writing and the Hepburn Romanisation in brackets. Chinese items are given in the Pinyin transcription.

1.3 Criteria for figurativeness

1.3.1 Literal – non-literal – figurative

Many studies on figurative language, especially on metaphors, start with historical remarks on the ancient Greek philosophers, above all on Aristotle.[6] Most authors regard Aristotle as the first to outline a theory of metaphor and as responsible for initiating a Western tradition that treats metaphors not only in terms of similarity but also in terms of deviation from literal language. Thus, on the one hand, "hardly a single twentieth-century study of metaphor passes over Aristotle in silence" (Leezenberg 2001: 31). On the other hand, recent studies draw attention to problematic misunderstandings of Aristotle in present-day research. Lloyd (2003: 101) points out that "[o]ur notions of metaphor have a history, one that ultimately goes back to the Greeks. It is well known that μεταφορά, transfer, is far from being an exact equivalent to our 'metaphor'."

We will not go deeper into the various concepts of *metaphor* in the history of philosophy and linguistics here, nor into the extensive discussions on this matter in present-day linguistics. However, we need to take a critical look at some notions

---

[6] Various researchers mention classic Greek philosophers in the context of research on figurative language (e.g. Black 1955; Johnson 1981, 1987; Ortony 1993; Ross 1993; Gibbs 1994: 121–122; Katz 1998: 20–22).

of *metaphor* in order to delineate our concept of figurative language. The central question is how the subject of our study, "figurative language", can be defined, and how it can be contrasted with other types of "non-figurative language". It is only from this angle that we approach metaphors.

There is a long tradition in linguistics concerning semantic change and the question of how novel expressions come into being through "similarity" or "analogy", i.e. via metaphors. In the late 19th century, the Neogrammarians published profound studies on this subject. Many of their examples have been taken up by later studies on metaphors. In his "Principles of Language History" from 1880, Hermann Paul deals with different cases where the "new" (occasional) meaning of a lexical unit becomes "usual" (conventional, lexicalised) and begins to lose its metaphorical character (Paul [1880] 1920: 94–96). For the most part, the lexicalisation of the "new" meaning is preceded by a period of polysemy (with the original and the new meaning used side by side).

There are examples where a former metaphor cannot be recognised except through the etymology (e.g. German *Rappe* 'black horse', metaphorically derived from *Rabe* 'raven (black bird)'). In other cases, the metaphor is easier to comprehend, as in units like *neck of a bottle, leg of a chair, foot of a mountain*. The analogy between spatial and temporal extensions also belongs to this group, manifesting itself in large portions of the lexicon, cf. German *die Zeit kommt, vergeht* "the time comes, goes by", or prepositions like German *in, an, zu, bis, durch, über*, etc. In addition, Neogrammarians have thoroughly described orientational metaphors connected with 'quantity', 'morality', etc. (e.g. German *die Preise steigen*, "the prices are rising", *er steigt in meiner Achtung* "he rises in my respect") or "CONTAINER metaphors" with MIND, HEART, as well as other well-known metaphors (later labelled "conceptual metaphors") such as UNDERSTANDING IS GRASPING (cf. Paul 1920: 96).

All these examples have been discussed continually in subsequent studies on metaphor. Compare the discussions on "metaphoric" prepositions by Lakoff and Johnson (1980) and Lakoff (1987b), or on spatial motion verbs in "metaphoric" temporal use (*winter comes*)[7] or other conceptual metaphors. In many studies, these cases are labelled "dead metaphors", "frozen metaphors" or "conventional metaphors". Let us look at an example:

---

[7] There is a rich literature on spatio-temporal relations in language (cf. Traugott 1978; Traugott and Dasher 2002; Lakoff and Johnson 1999; Boroditsky 2000, 2001; Radden 2003; Núñez, Motz, and Teuscher 2006; Casasanto and Boroditsky 2008; Evans 2013; Dancygier and Sweetser 2014: 168–177; Moore 2014; Athanasopoulos, Samuel, and Bylund 2017; Pamies-Bertrán and Yuan 2020 among others).

Poetic language is often considered to be a likely context for innovative metaphors, so let us consider first the following quotation from Shelley:

> If Winter comes, can Spring be far behind?
> Here we can recognize *comes* as a conventional metaphor exemplifying a peripheral meaning of the core spatial term designating motion. *Behind*, however, is higher on the reference scale, i.e. is more strongly metaphorical, since it is less conventional.
> (Traugott 1985: 33)

Metaphoricity is a matter of degree: *Winter comes* is a conventional metaphor, whereas *can Spring be far behind* is less conventional and more poetic. What Traugott calls "conventional" is labelled "non-literal, but not figurative" in our study.

The question that is relevant to the present study is whether or not we are dealing with figurative lexical units. As will be explained below, we regard dead or frozen metaphors (like *Rappe, neck of a bottle, in winter* or *the taxes are high*) as non-figurative. Therefore, these lexical units do not fall into the scope of our study. In order to differentiate the subject of our study from the "conventional metaphors" discussed above, we use the term *conventional figurative metaphor*.

To define "figurative language", we need to find criteria for the differentiation between "figurativeness" and the various kinds of "non-figurativeness". Let us first consider the well-known distinction between the *literal, non-literal* (but *non-figurative*) and *figurative* use of lexical units. Dirven (2002: 337–339) illustrates this trichotomy by the adjective *sweet* in *sweet apple* (literal use), *sweet water* 'non-salty water' (non-literal but non-figurative use) and *sweet child* (figurative use). Dirven points out that there are degrees in figurativeness, so that one can distinguish between low and high figurativeness (or "figurativity" in Dirven's terms).

Dirven analyses three main cognitive strategies to create non-literal and figurative meanings: *synaesthesia, metonymy* and *metaphor*. With regard to parts of speech, it is more or less predictable that synaesthesia will occur especially with adjectives and metonymy with nouns, while metaphor occurs with all parts of speech.

According to Dirven (2002: 339–340), metonymy, just like synaesthesia, may lead to non-literal extensions that are non-figurative. He exemplifies this with the word *heart*, literally meaning 'the central blood-pumping organ in the animal or human body'. All the expressions with *heart* in the sense of 'seat of emotions, mind, memory, etc.' or 'mental faculties' (e.g. *from the bottom of my heart; to know by heart*) are considered non-literal but at the same time non-figurative. The reason for the "non-figurativeness" of these expressions is that the heart was once believed to be the seat (the real location) of life, mind, memory, etc. (which is now in Western cultures more commonly attributed to the brain).[8] In Dirven's opinion, the figurative use of the word begins when *heart* comes to stand for single emotions (e.g. *My heart sank into my shoes*, where *heart* stands for 'courage'). Dirven (2002: 341) sums it up as follows:

> The figurative use of language in its various manifestations is then but a consequence of simultaneous mental operations of the sensory organs in synaesthesia, contiguity in metonymy, and similarity in metaphor. In all of these, the tension between one element and the other is built upon a different interaction of likeness and difference, of similarity and contrast. The greater the contrast between the two elements, the greater also the degree of figurativity, or in its higher realisation, the higher the degree of metaphoricity.

The extent of the conceptual contrast between literal and non-literal reading is decisive: if this contrast is minimal, the non-literal use is not perceived as figurative. Furthermore, in cases where the categorical shift is not evident synchronically, and especially if the speaker has no other way to denote the concept in question than to use an expression that is historically a metaphor, we are dealing with non-literal but not figurative expressions. Another question arising in this connection is whether it is useful to refer to such linguistic expressions as metaphors (cf. e.g. Stern 2000: 176).

We use the term *figurative* for a wide range of linguistic phenomena, including both conventional and ad hoc expressions. In this regard, our understanding of figurativeness differs from the interpretation by Lakoff and Johnson (1980). Using the example of the conceptual metaphor THEORIES ARE BUILDINGS, Lakoff and Johnson (1980: 52–53) point to the difference between conventional expressions like *construct a theory* or *foundation of a theory*, on the one hand, and novel metaphors such as *His theory has thousands of little rooms and long, winding corridors*.[9] The authors describe the former as based on the "used part" of the conceptual metaphor and, therefore, "normal" and "literal", whereas the latter is viewed as based on the "unused part" of the conceptual metaphor and, hence, "figurative": "These sentences fall outside the domain of normal literal language and are

---

[8] Here is not the place to discuss the semiotisations of HEART which have often changed. Nevertheless, there is extensive literature on this subject (cf. Foolen 2008; Geeraerts and Gevaert 2008 among others).

[9] Since the publication of the first edition of this book, several studies have emerged dealing in particular with the difference between *conventional* metaphors and *novel* metaphors. Cf. also the notions of *linguistic* metaphors, that is, those that exist in language, and *dynamic* metaphors (Hanks 2007), or the opposition of deliberate and non-deliberate metaphor (Steen 2008). See also the discussion of this issue in Gibbs (2011, 2015) and Steen (2015).

part of what is usually called 'figurative' or 'imaginative' language". (Lakoff and Johnson 1980: 53). Although Lakoff and Johnson's argumentation is convincing, and distinguishing between used and unused parts of a conceptual metaphor makes a lot of sense, we still do not agree with the authors' interpretation of figurativeness. From our point of view, many conventional metaphors are figurative units even if they do not fall outside the used parts of the metaphoric model in question. What is crucial is whether they possess (more or less) clearly perceivable image components and whether they are additional names (for more details, see sections 1.3.2 and 1.3.3). Thus, examples like *construct a theory* or *foundation of a theory* are really not figurative, but this is not because they are based upon the used part of the conceptual metaphor. They are perceived as literal expressions because nobody would interpret the words *construct* and *foundation* in the given combinations as entities from the BUILDING domain. These links are not part of the shared knowledge of the speech community. In the course of history, the words *construct* and *foundation* have developed abstract senses, which allow us to understand them without addressing images of building or construction. Therefore, they can hardly even be considered non-literal, let alone figurative. There are, however, many other metaphors based on the "used parts" that are still figurative in our sense, i.e. having a relevant image component in their semantic structure.

In order to define the subject of our investigation, we have to distinguish between figurative language and phenomena that are related but not identical. To be able to do so, we need some heuristic criteria for at least approximately identifying figurative units of language. We are aware of the fact that other interpretations of the phenomenon of figurative language are possible (cf. e.g. Bergen 2007); the interpretation we favour here is influenced by our purposes and our data. We put forward two heuristic criteria for distinguishing between figurative and non-figurative units. We call them
- Image requirement
- Additional naming

Let us discuss these two criteria.

1.3.2 Image requirement

The criterion of *image requirement* is conceptual in nature and can be operationalised by taking into account contextual properties. Let us introduce the term *image component*. By *image component* we understand a specific conceptual structure mediating between the lexical structure which triggers the corresponding mental image and the actual meaning[10] of figurative units. Hence, the content plane of a figurative unit not only consists of a pure "meaning", i.e. actual sense denoting an entity in the world, but also includes traces of the literal reading underlying the actual meaning. This distinguishes figurative units from non-figurative ones. Figurative units possess a second conceptual level at which they are associated with the sense denoted by their literal form.

The conceptual nature of the image component can be roughly described as follows: mental images associated with figurative expressions are basically individual phenomena, but there are also intersubjective aspects to these mental images. The image component assumes the function of a semantic bridge between "what is said" and "what is meant", i.e. between the lexical structure and the actual meaning.

From this heuristic stance, additional questions arise, and we will address some of these: Is the image component predominantly a semantic or a pragmatic phenomenon? Does it influence the actual usage of figurative expressions? Can the image component always be explained in terms of metaphorical mapping, or can it also be based on other semiotic phenomena? Are there significant cross-linguistic differences in the choice of image basis for figurative expressions, i.e. in the way in which certain concepts are linguistically fixed in figurative expressions? If so, how can they be explained? Are they due to coincidence, to different principles according to which certain domains of experience are structured, or to cultural phenomena? In other words, are the relevant cross-linguistic differences (if any) a matter of the specifics of the languages in question, or are they due to conceptual and/or cultural specifics behind the linguistic structures?

As the most salient feature of figurative language is its image component, the traces of the literal meaning inherited by the figurative meaning have to be taken into account, cf. (1).

(1) *(to be caught) between a rock and a hard place*
     '(to be) in a very difficult position; facing a hard decision' (Spears 1997: 15)

The explanation of the meaning given here is not sufficient because it neither involves the images connected with the individual constituents nor the metaphor as a whole. The constituent *rock*, as well as *hard place*, evokes an image of something very solid, heavy, and immovable that hurts when one attempts to move it. The underlying literal reading (i.e. the source concept), on the other hand,

---

[10] The term *actual meaning* is ambiguous and is used also in the sense of contextual or situational meaning. We use the term in the sense of 'lexicalised figurative meaning'.

is to be described as 'lack of freedom of movement'. When mapped on the target concept 'difficult position', idiom (1) appears as a realisation of the well-known conceptual metaphor DIFFICULTIES ARE IMPEDIMENTS TO MOTION (Lakoff 1993: 20).

The presence of such an image component in the actual, i.e. figurative, meaning of the idiom seems to be psychologically real because of relevant usage restrictions. Thus, the speaker perceives the difference between *to be in a very difficult position* and *to be between a rock and a hard place* due to the mental images evoked by the literal interpretation. Consider the following example.

(2) *When he had to submit the article by Friday and did not get the material in time he was in a very difficult position.*

In (2) it is not possible to replace *to be in a very difficult position* by *to be between a rock and a hard place* because the context does not involve the mental image of being between two obstacles, i.e. the idea of a 'lack of freedom of movement'. The concrete image fixed in the lexical structure of (1) presupposes that the subject finds himself/herself in a situation where he/she has to choose between two possibilities which both entail difficulties and failure. Therefore, idiom (1) should be defined as (3).

(3) 'facing a situation of choice between two possibilities that both entail difficulties and failure, as if the person pursuing his/her goals is not able to move away freely'.

This definition seems to be more appropriate not only than the definition given in (1) but also than the following definitions (4) taken from other idiom dictionaries, which are more elaborate than (1).

(4) 'in a difficult situation in which any choice that you make will have bad results' (Longman ID 1998: 286)
'in a situation where one is faced with two equally difficult or unpleasant alternatives' (Speake 1999: 297)
'nothing to choose between two difficult situations' (Gulland and Hinds-Howell 2001: 17)
'you have to make a difficult decision between two things that are equally unpleasant' (McCarthy 2002: 327)

Although (4) points to the fact that an important part of the meaning of this idiom is the existence of a choice between different ways to manage a situation, it does not take the image component itself into account, which provides relevant links between the lexical form of the idiom and its actual meaning.

To find out whether or not the plane of content contains an image component, we can carry out a kind of contextual substitution test. If some special semantic effects, which are entailments of the image component, can be found, the expression in question will qualify as figurative. The use of figurative expressions is also connected with special pragmatic effects (such as intended expressivity), which can result from their imagery. Checking for semantic and pragmatic effects can be applied as an operational criterion for figurativeness. Let us once more consider the meaning definition in (3) 'facing a situation of choice between two possibilities which both entail difficulties and failure, as if the person pursuing his/her goals is not able to move away freely'. The part of the definition starting with *as if* is responsible for the image component, which is crucial for distinguishing between the meaning of this idiom and the meaning of the near-equivalent word combination *in a very difficult position*.

The presence of the idea of choice between two possibilities, both of which are perceived as disadvantageous for the subject, as well as the image-based reference to a 'lack of freedom of movement', can be exemplified by the following contexts taken from the British National Corpus (5–7):

(5) She wanted to scream the words back at him, but they log-jammed in her throat. To reveal the truth would be to render herself still more vulnerable to him, and she couldn't allow that to happen. But the alternative – to have him believing her poor showing had been caused by drugs – was equally untenable. She was *caught between a rock and a hard place* – with no obvious way out.

(6) "[. . .] If you produce the right designs I'll use them. And be only too happy to give you full credit." He paused. "But, if you fail, I'll show no mercy. You can absolutely bank on that." That scarcely needed saying. Lisa felt a chill go through her. Suddenly she was *caught between a rock and a hard place*. "So, I would advise you", he added, nodding at her folder, "to make a bonfire with those sketches and start again from scratch."

(7) "[. . .] But if this is what love does to you, it's perhaps just as well you've never suffered from the malady before." Rory shook her head, sending her long wheat-coloured curls tumbling about her face. "Don't be ridiculous", she said adamantly, then bit her lip. She was *caught between a rock and a hard place* here, she realised with grim humour. Since Adam had been monopolising practically all her time, she couldn't protest her dislike of him too vehemently. Candy would pounce on that like a terrier, demanding to know why she didn't just tell him to get lost. But she'd given her promise, albeit with great reluctance, not to confide the truth to her friend.

Semantic and pragmatic effects of this kind may find expression in the form of combinatorial restrictions on the lexical unit in question (which is the case in these examples). Thus, if in certain contexts the image component, even as a peripheral part of the semantic structure, can be responsible for combinatorial restrictions, there is linguistic evidence for its relevance. In such cases the criterion of *image requirement* can be regarded as an important operational criterion because the relevant traces of a given image are obvious. We will deal with this phenomenon in more detail in section 8.2.

Another way of proving the existence of an image component is to look for contexts containing plays on words, as for example (8) and (9):

(8) She's an angel . . . always *up in the air* and *harping on things*.

(9) Customer: "Waitress, why is my doughnut all smashed?" – Waitress: "You said you wanted a cup of coffee and a doughnut, *and step on it*."

The literal readings of *up in the air* and *harping (on something)* in (8) evoke images that can be connected with the concept of an angel. The word play lies in the fact that the figurative meanings ('to be furious, angry' and 'to speak about something time and time again, to moan, complain about something', respectively) are activated simultaneously so that the expression is semantically ambiguous. The joke (9) makes use of the same pattern: *Step on it!* is a colloquial expression meaning 'Hurry up, move it, make it snappy!' The image component from car driving (to put one's foot down onto the accelerator pedal) is taken literally in the word combination *and step on it* (i.e. on the doughnut). Plays on words prove that it is always possible to make us aware of image components. Word play is only possible when the lexical unit in question has an additional meaning component that can be activated in this way.

Of course, not every play on words is based on the actualisation of the image. Compare slogans like *Sea-ing is believing* (based on homophony of *sea* and *see* in an advertisement for boat trips) or *The only thing we overlook is our river* (based on the homonymy of the verb *overlook*,[11] advertising a hotel on the Mississippi). Thus, this test is irreversible: it can be used to prove the existence of the image component, but it does not mean that every word that is used in two different senses in the context of a word play is figurative.

---

[11] Dictionaries often treat this kind of homonymy as polysemy, which is, from a linguistic viewpoint, inaccurate, because there is no nontrivial common semantic component for the two senses 'ignore' and 'have a view of'.

We can say that word play contexts are exceptions, but even the rare possibility of realising a certain semantic component as the central one proves that this meaning component is latently present. In principle, therefore, contexts of this type can be used as operational tests for proving the linguistic relevance of the image component, especially in cases in which there are no combinational constraints due to the image.

The essence of the image requirement criterion is the synchronically identifiable ability of a linguistic unit to denote its referent not directly but via another concept. A unit of figurative language differs from a literal unit, first of all, through this ability to combine two different conceptual levels in its semantic structure. In semiotic terms, a unit of figurative language is not just a linguistic sign having form and content and denoting something outside itself. It is a sign that uses the content of another sign as a form filled with new content (called an *inner form* in the Russian linguistic tradition following Potebnja), so that additional associations arising from interaction between the two signifieds of the one signifier come into existence. Thus, a figurative unit can be considered a secondary sign.

Let us briefly discuss the specifics of the image component among similar notions that have been developed within the linguistic theories of lexical semantics, especially within the conceptions having to do with processing figurative units of language (for more details, see Dobrovol'skij 2016b). In addition to the image component, three basic notions that provide our theoretical foundation are
– *inner form*,
– *mental image* and
– *etymological memory*.

The term *inner form* (*внутренняя форма*) in the sense discussed here was coined by the well-known 19th century Russian philologist and philosopher of language, Potebnja (1892). This term initially goes back to Humboldt, who introduced the notion of the *inner form of language* (*innere Sprachform*), and understood it in a completely different sense, as referring to something like "national spirit" reflected in a language, i.e. the specific ways of conceptualising reality characteristic of every language community (cf. Humboldt [1836] 1979).[12]

---

[12] "In Russian thought, with its marked interest in *logos*, many philosophers and linguists were interested in inner form (Aleksei Losev, Pavel Florenskii, Sergei Bulgakov, and Aleksandr Potebnia). However, the concept begins a new life thanks to Shpet's interpretation of Humboldt and his own original perspective on inner form that combines Western and Russian approaches to the question seen through the prism of hermeneutical logic" (Lyanda-Geller 2018: 61). Lyanda-Geller (2018: 73) points out that "for Gustav Shpet inner form is a locus of sense [. . .]. Inner form as a logical form has inspired developing new ideas in various fields of Russian and

Potebnja speaks of the *inner form of a word* (*внутренняя форма слова*) and defines it as the relationship of the thought's content to consciousness («отношение содержания мысли к сознанию»). The inner form shows the way in which people reflect their thoughts (Potebnja 1892: 102). Potebnja connected the inner form of the word both with its etymology and with the psychological side of its motivation.

Typical of 19th century philological studies, Potebnja's definition is rather vague and difficult to operationalise. Nevertheless, the notion of the inner form has become an important research instrument in Russian linguistics. Compare e.g. Zaliznjak (2013: 41–50).

It might seem that the term *inner form* is justified only as part of the Russian linguistic tradition and can easily be replaced by such terms as *source domain, source frame, mental image, background categorisation* (cf. *фоновая категоризация* in Baranov and Dobrovol'skij 2008), at least in figurative language research in Frame Semantics or Cognitive Linguistics. But this is not quite true, for the meanings of all these terms are not completely identical.

In terms of present-day linguistics, the inner form of a lexical unit (word or idiom) can be defined as a kind of semantic paradigmatic relation between the target lexeme and the meanings associated with its constituent parts and/or the underlying mental image.

Generally, the term *mental image* is a near-synonym of the *inner form*. The difference between *inner form* and *mental image* is that the former term points to the primary reading of the figurative sign in question, whereas the latter is conceptual rather than semantic in nature. Both notions differ from the *image component*, which denotes a part of the lexicalised meaning of a given figurative unit.

In other words, the inner form of a lexical item is a combination of the mental image fixed in its content plane and the motivation of its lexicalised meaning. Speakers derive the inner form of a lexical item from the meanings of its constituent morphemes or words.

As for the notion of *etymological memory* (also known as *cultural memory*), this can be defined as traces of the figurative past of a given lexical unit that are accessible in the present.[13] The synchronic motivation of a conventional fig-

---

West-European thought, and anticipated or influenced further development of Structuralism and semiotics, in particular, the traditions of "deep semiotics" (*glubinnaia semiotika*, represented by V. Vinogradov, G. Vinokur), Russian linguistics and the Prague School of linguistics, neurolinguistics (L. Vygotsky, A. Luriia), ethic psychology (C. Levi-Strauss, R. Jakobson)."

13 Elements of etymological memory can influence the use of lexical items of all types, not only units of figurative language (cf. Apresjan 1995 in this regard). Apresjan points to the study of Abaev (1948) in which this notion was introduced. Here we concentrate on conventional figurative units as the main subject of this study.

urative unit often does not coincide with the "true" etymology of that unit. In most cases, what is important for the functioning of a figurative expression is synchronic motivation, i.e. how most speakers intuitively construct the motivational "bridges". However, in some rare cases a given unit of figurative language may exhibit restrictions on its use that can only be explained by addressing its history, i.e. this figurative unit cannot be used in contexts that are not compatible with its etymological origin, even where speakers do not know the etymology. In such cases, the etymological memory of a given conventional figurative unit is extremely important. For more details, see chapter 4.

The specific feature of the image component, as compared to similar notions, is that it takes on the role of a semantic bridge between two levels of the figurative unit's conceptual structure, i.e. between its meaning proper (that is the actual or lexicalised figurative) and the literal interpretation of the underlying lexical structure which triggers the corresponding mental image. The image component consists of linguistically relevant traces of an image that are comprehensible to the majority of speakers.

The basic difference between the inner form and the image component can be illustrated with an example. Idioms such as English *to use a sledgehammer to crack a nut,* Russian *стрелять из пушек по воробьям* and German *mit Kanonen nach/ auf Spatzen schießen* (both literally "to shoot with cannons at sparrows") have very similar actual meanings that can be roughly described as 'to try to achieve a goal by investing a great deal of effort and using a means that is too powerful for achieving this goal, which obviously does not require such effort; the consequence is that the results are insignificant when compared to the wasted effort'. The image component provides conceptual material that is used in constructing the actual meaning, namely the idea that the means is fully inappropriate for achieving a given goal, in that it is too powerful, so that the subject of this action is wasting energy. Thus, traces of the underlying image can be found in all parts of the semantic definition.

An important feature of the image component is that it does not point to all details of the "rich image" but exploits only those traces of the source concept that are relevant for the actual meaning. This enables us to concentrate on the conceptual structures which provide the semantic bridge between source and target concepts. On the level of "rich images" there is, of course, a great difference between "cracking a nut with a sledgehammer" and "shooting with cannons at sparrows". All relevant conceptual details are part of the inner form rather than of the image component. These different images are used to convey the same general idea fixed in the semantic definition. However, since native speakers are aware of these details of mental imagery while processing the idiom, the conceptual details have to be described as relevant parts of the idiom's content plane.

Not all the features of the "rich images" have to be addressed in a semantic definition of every conventional figurative unit. Nevertheless, conceptual details of this kind are psychologically real. Being a part of the inner form, they can be addressed in non-standard contexts, i.e. in puns and contexts that include intentional plays on words.

The criterion of image requirement is connected with the notion of motivation (see chapter 4 for details) but does not depend on it directly. It is obvious that figurative units that are fully motivated from the synchronic perspective (like *to burn one's boats*) have a more salient image component than idioms, which are more opaque synchronically (like *to kick the bucket*). Yet, it would be wrong to say that *to kick the bucket* is not figurative and has no image component or inner form.

Even if speakers do not reflect on the motivating links between the mental image fixed in the lexical structure of an expression and its actual meaning, they are certainly aware of the specifics of the expression that make it different from literal expressions. Lexical units with no transparent motivating links, such as *to kick the bucket*, are perceived as figurative because they clearly refer to their denotata by using other concepts, and their secondary nature is obvious. Speakers are certainly aware of the fact that this idiom means something different from what is said literally. This discrepancy, and the possibility of a literal interpretation of the word string in question, provide speakers with the knowledge that they are speaking figuratively when using such an idiom. Besides, even opaque structures can become motivated in special contexts or sometimes individually, as speakers may have their own explanations for the relevant motivating links other than the original etymology, or even possess etymological knowledge.

1.3.3 Additional naming

The second criterion can be called *additional naming*. A unit of figurative language is not the only way to say what is meant. Normally, there is already a more direct and cognitively simple expression denoting approximately the same entity (compare, for instance, *to reveal a secret* vs. *to spill the beans*, *to become angry* vs. *to hit the ceiling* or *to deal successfully with a problem* vs. *to clear a hurdle*). The figurative units are, so to speak, additional (not primary) means for naming things, properties, actions, states, events, and the like.

The semantic surplus value of figurative units has often been stressed; we have illustrated this by the idiom *(to be caught) between a rock and a hard place* in (1–7). This criterion seems to be evident, and it is consistent with the "traditional" view of figurative language as a secondary, not obligatory or even ornamental part of the linguistic system. However, the practical application of this criterion meets certain difficulties. Firstly, there are many lexical units that have synonyms, some of which may look more basic (compare e.g. *to tell* vs. *to communicate, to happen* vs. *to occur, aim* vs. *purpose*). In such cases, the existence of different ways to say nearly the same thing does not allow us to conclude that one of the (near-)synonyms is literal and another one is figurative.

The second problem with this criterion arises from the fact that there are lexical units that may intuitively be perceived as figurative although they have no literal counterparts, at least not in the realm of everyday language. A good example is *seahorse*. Although there is no other English word for this kind of fish (the Latin term *hippocampus* belongs to the technical language of biological taxonomy and is, therefore, not a real literal counterpart), this expression may evoke associations based on the image that is fixed in its lexical structure. Due to its transparent constituent structure (*sea* + *horse*), it has a synchronically identifiable image component and is perceived as a conventional but metaphorically based lexical unit. However, this is not a decisive argument for qualifying *seahorse* as a figurative unit. Compare the word *hippocampus*, the Latin equivalent of *seahorse*, one element of which goes back to Greek *hippos* 'horse', the other to Greek *kampos* 'sea monster'. Hence, considered from the viewpoint of its origin, *hippocampus* is also a metaphorically based lexical item. However, nobody would argue that *hippocampus* is a figurative unit. There are many expressions in any language that are not really literal but not figurative either; *seahorse* is one of them. We do not consider this expression to be figurative, above all because it does not fulfil the criterion of additional naming. As mentioned above, there is no other possibility to name this animal within the scope of non-technical language. Of course, cases like this may be subject to discussion. This is due to certain image traces in the content plane of such expressions. We consider this understanding of figurativeness as appropriate for our purposes.

The two heuristic criteria for distinguishing between figurative and non-figurative units, *image requirement* and *additional naming*, occur in different combinations and can be developed to different degrees. The following combinations are possible:

(i) An expression has no *image* but can take on the function of an *additional naming*. Such an expression is non-figurative, without any doubt (all synonyms are additional namings).

(ii) An expression has an *image* but does not function as an *additional naming*. Such an expression is non-figurative as well. However, some borderline cases can be found in this domain. Compare the above-mentioned example, *seahorse*, which we regard as non-figurative. Strictly speaking, the reason for this is not only that this expression is not a real additional naming but also that the image traces have no linguistic consequences.

The word *mouse* as a term for the handheld computer device (cf. *mouse click, mouse pointer*) can serve as another example of this kind. The underlying image can easily be traced back, and we can even imagine contexts in which it could be exploited (e.g. when people make puns using *mouse* in the 'animal' sense and as a name of the computer device). Nevertheless, the word *mouse* in the latter sense is not figurative, because it is the only naming for this sort of input computer device, not an additional one.[14]

However, in some cases the image may be so clear, strong, and active that there could be linguistic consequences in the sense that the expression is perceived as being figurative, even though there is no "normal" synonym. The treatment of such cases depends much more on concrete research tasks than on the ontological properties of figurative language.

(iii) An expression has a (more or less strong) *image* and "normal" synonyms, i.e. it functions as an *additional naming*. Thus, both criteria are fulfilled. Many common (non-technical) names of plants, birds, or insects belong to this group. Let us look at the lexical unit *old man's beard*, also called *clematis*. This is a kind of climbing shrub growing on walls. The first criterion is fulfilled because there is a clear image: it is a plant that looks *as if it were the beard of an old man*. In view of the second criterion, we are dealing with a borderline case, depending on the speaker's familiarity with the second, more technical name, the quasi-synonym *clematis*. For speakers who do not know (or do not use) the name *clematis*, the expression *old man's beard* seems to be non-figurative because in this case it is only a "naming" like many others. If the speaker has the choice to say either *clematis* or *old man's beard*, however, the latter expression must be considered figurative. In such cases, the question of whether we are dealing with a figurative lexical unit or not depends on the degree to which the underlying image is linguistically relevant. The stronger the image, the more likely it is that the given lexical item will be perceived as a figurative unit. It is difficult to provide a strict definition of the notion of *figurativeness* before we have analysed the different kinds of figurative language in detail. What we can do at this point is just to use the heuristic criteria suggested above and point to the extension of this notion, i.e. list the kinds of lexical units expected to be figurative.

Figurative expressions include, firstly, all novel, nontrivial metaphors and metonymies used in poetic language, and then all the conventional figurative metaphors

---

14 The plural can be *mice* or *mouses*. This fact indicates that *mouse* as the name of a computer accessory has become independent from the "animal mouse".

and metonymies (words, idioms, proverbs and the like) that point to a denotatum not directly but via other concepts while there is another, simpler and more direct way to point to this denotatum. Only the latter are part of the present study.

We restrict our analysis to *conventional figurative expressions* because conventional figurative language has priority for linguistic theory.[15] From a theoretical perspective, it is more important to describe the lexicon with all its specifics as a part of the language system. There are still many gaps in the linguistic description of the lexicon. The novel, poetic use of language can be basically traced back to the systemic properties of the lexicon, and thus is of secondary importance for our study.

In our analysis, we will speak of *figurative expressions* or *figurative lexical units* or *units of figurative language*, using the terms interchangeably.

We use the following abbreviations:

CFL   conventional figurative language
CFLT   Conventional Figurative Language Theory
CFU   conventional figurative unit

1.4 Figurative language and related phenomena

In the previous sections, we encountered the trichotomy of *literal language – non-literal (but also non-figurative) language – figurative language*. In this section, we would like to shed some light on the second of these terms, *non-literal (but also non-figurative) linguistic units*. These units are related to figurative language but must be separated from it. What most figurative and non-literal utterances have in common is the existence of at least two readings, which are anchored in different conceptual levels and mostly need additional interpretation, i.e. additional cognitive operations for processing the non-literal readings.

First of all, two different phenomena have to be distinguished within the domain of non-literal yet non-figurative expressions: these expressions are either located on the level of discourse (on the text level) or grounded in the lexicon, i.e. in the language system itself.

The former group (non-figurative expressions located on the level of discourse) includes a variety of non-direct ways of speaking (indirect speech acts, irony, self-mocking, parody, sarcasm, play on words, etc.). In addition, this domain

---

[15] Since we limit ourselves to the investigation of the figurative lexicon, linguistic analysis of literary texts, discussions of cognitive poetics (cf. Tsur 1992, 2002; Gavins and Steen 2003 among others) and cognitive stylistics (cf. e.g. Semino 2002, 2008; Naciscione 2010; Deignan, Littlemore, and Semino 2013) do not belong to the scope of our study.

includes various kinds of "classical" figures of speech (litotes, hyperbole, zeugma, oxymoron and related tropes). All linguistic units of this kind are located on the pragmatic level and have to be studied mainly within the domain of linguistic pragmatics rather than semantics.

The latter group (non-figurative expressions grounded in the lexicon) includes non-figurative metaphors and metonymies. These linguistic units (as well as conventional figurative units, i.e. figurative metaphors, metonymies, idioms etc.) must be considered within the framework of lexical semantics. It is crucial for the present study to separate *non-figurative* metaphors, metonymies and *non-figurative* phrasemes from conventional *figurative* units. Only the latter are the subject of investigation in the present study.

Our study is concerned with units of the *language system*, and not with elements located on the level of texts. The main interest of our study concentrates on the semantics of figurative units and their relation to other domains such as pragmatics (above all, connotations and relevant cultural phenomena). The subject of analysis is CFUs of the lexicon, i.e. elements of the language system, rather than figurative utterances, i.e. elements of discourse.

A problem we are facing here is that certain indirect utterances are very common and show a tendency towards conventionalisation, so that they bear a resemblance to conventional lexical units (cf. indirect speech acts such as *Can I help you?*). However, even if it is reasonable to regard these types of utterances as cognitive units (i.e. utterances that are processed holistically), they still remain units of discourse (i.e. *textual units*) rather than units of the lexicon (i.e. *lexical units*). Even so, there is not always a clear borderline between such frequent utterances and other prefabricated conventionalised units (e.g. speech formulae). Let us consider phrases like *Have a nice day; Take a seat, please; Don't mention it; How do you do? You shouldn't have!* Obviously, we are dealing with gradual differences between textual units and lexical units.

What we are concerned with in this study is the level of the lexicon at which conventional figurative lexical units can be found. With the help of the heuristic criteria proposed above, we will try to distinguish units of figurative language from related phenomena. A differentiation of this kind is necessary to identify the issues for further analysis.

1.4.1 Indirect language

A number of authors concerned with metaphors and figurative language occupy themselves with phenomena related to figurative language (e.g. Norrick 1980; Gibbs 1994; Fass 1997: 28–30; Katz 1998). Not everyone in this domain makes a distinction between *non-literal* and *figurative expressions*, cf. Sperber and Wilson (1981: 259): "An ironical utterance is traditionally analysed as literally saying one thing and figuratively meaning the opposite". Psycholinguistic studies pay much attention to the issues of how non-literal meanings are processed and understood (see, for example, Cacciari and Glucksberg 1994; Gibbs 2001a; Gibbs and Colston 2012; Häcki Buhofer 2004 for a survey). Analysing the comprehension of irony, metaphors, idioms and proverbs can raise the same questions and lead to similar results, cf. Gibb's *direct access view* (the non-literal, "figurative" meaning is accessed first if there is enough contextual information; Gibbs 2002) and the *graded salience hypothesis* (literal and figurative language use is ruled by the same principles of salience; Giora 1997, 1999, 2002; Giora, Fein, and Schwartz 1998). All findings in this field are supported by numerous experiments. With regard to the rich literature on these topics, we restrict ourselves to a short outline.

Indirect speech acts: As has been mentioned, indirect speech acts have to be separated from units of figurative language for the purpose of our study. Utterances like (10) and (11) are questions from the formal viewpoint, but expressions of gratitude and request, respectively, from the illocutionary viewpoint (cf. e.g. Austin 1962; Searle 1969, 1975; Morgan 1978). In this sense, they are indirect (non-literal), but their indirectness is not based on mental imagery. It is rooted in the form of the utterance, and not in the semantics of its parts (i.e. not in the semantics of lexical units).

(10) *How can I express my thanks to you?*

(11) *Will you shut the door?*

Thus, the indirectness of such speech acts develops at the level of the utterance. It is a matter of intention whether one says things directly or in an alternative way. It is the *conversational implicatures* in the sense of Grice (1975) that allow us to interpret indirect speech acts in the right way. Even if indirect speech acts are accessed directly (cf. Gibbs 2002), they must be perceived as indirect ways of denoting a given situation.

Cross-linguistic analyses show that these implicatures, or the ways of expressing things indirectly, are not language independent. Even the classical example of an indirect speech act, *Can you pass the salt?*, is not just a question interpreted as a request on the basis of the relevant conversational implicature, but rather a conventionalised way of expressing a request typical of English, but maybe not of other languages. Pragmatic conventions effective in Russian demand that the negative subjunctive form of the modal verb should be used in cases like this;

cf. *Вы не могли бы передать соль?* "Couldn't you pass the salt?" instead of *Вы можете передать соль?* "Can you pass the salt?" which is – although possible – not the conventional way of expressing this idea. We deal with *conventional implicatures* here using Grice's (1975) terms. *Conventional implicatures* are conventions that have come into being more or less by chance and cannot be attributed to general pragmatic principles originating from the relevance principle in the sense of Sperber and Wilson (1986). Morgan (1978) explicitly distinguishes semantic and pragmatic set phrases and sources of idiomaticity. He proposes "usage conventions" to account for the illocutionary force of *I bet* as an indirect affirmation or *Is the Pope a Catholic?* as a standard retort to a question deemed too obvious to require an answer (cf. section 4.10).

The functioning of a certain pragmatic convention can be a matter of degree. Although strong in one language, the same pragmatic convention may have less weight in another language and operate only in contexts that support ambiguity of interpretation. Similar observations have been made by Wierzbicka (1985) and Dobrovol'skij (2001).

Irony: One phenomenon related to indirect speech acts is irony. The special position of irony in the field of non-literal language has often been stressed (cf. e.g. Sperber and Wilson 1981; Katz 2000; Dynel 2013; Athanasiadou and Colston 2017; Attardo 2017). Irony depends not only on what is said but also on how it is said and who says it. Various experiments have tested the understanding and processing of irony and related phenomena (e.g. Colston 1997, 2002; Giora 1995; Giora, Fein, and Schwartz 1998; Dews and Winner 1999; Kreuz et al. 1999; Giora and Fein 1999a; Colston and Gibbs 2002, 2007).

Irony involves discrepancy between the speaker's literal statement and his/her attitude or intent. Although Gibbs (1994: 365) holds that irony reflects the "figurative mode of thinking", we exclude ironic utterances from the scope of our study. When someone says *What lovely weather* in the midst of a rainstorm, this does not change the meaning of the adjective *lovely*. Although it is possible to ascribe the secondary meaning 'bad' to the word *lovely*, this would contradict the economy principle of linguistic description, because readings of this kind do not result from a profound semantic change but from universal conversational implicatures. Irony and sarcasm are closely linked, since sarcasm is a form of ironic criticism (cf. Kreuz and Glucksberg 1989; Lee and Katz 1998; Katz 2000).

Ironical and sarcastic utterances are non-literal because they point to a given situation by using linguistic signs that normally have a different meaning. However, since we restrict the scope of our study to units of the lexicon and assume that every kind of indirectness produced at the level of utterance is a phenomenon of a different nature, we will not address ironic or sarcastic use of words in this study.

Tropes and figures of speech: Tropes and figures of speech must also be seen from this perspective. They can be figurative, but they do not have to be. For example, litotes, which is a figure of speech based on conscious understatement and negation as a means of emphasis, is never figurative as such; cf. *It doesn't sound bad* instead of *It sounds good*, or *It's no fun being sick* instead of *It's miserable being sick*. Similarly, hyperbole (*A thousand thanks!*), paradox (*Less is more*), oxymoron (*loud silence*), euphemism (*rest room*), and zeugma (*In that year and that room he wrote many texts*) do not need to be figurative. Consider also other figures of speech like rhetorical questions, climaxes, and antitheses, or so-called figures of sound, such as alliteration, repetition or onomatopoeia (imitation of natural sounds by words). They are somehow deviant from what may be called the "normal", "neutral" or "standard" mode of speaking because they are indirect and/or expressive to a certain extent, but they are not figurative in our sense.

Many of these cases are examples of "indirect speech" in the sense that the same intention can be expressed in an alternative, easier and/or more explicit way; but this does not mean that they are figurative. Their indirectness is rooted in a special combination of lexical units and not so much in the combination of different readings of the same sign. Here we see the difference between the phenomenon of indirect language and the phenomenon of figurative language, which is a special case of indirect language. As for the expressiveness of some of these word combinations, it arises from the necessity of the additional cognitive effort involved in understanding them (cf. *less is more* or *loud silence*). Thus, expressivity, too, is a much broader phenomenon than figurativeness.

The traditional classification of tropes and figures of speech is based on their "technical" properties, rather than any criteria of figurativeness. Therefore, they include both figurative and non-figurative expressions. If they are based on mental images and include an image component in their semantic structure, they have to be considered figurative expressions, regardless of the type of trope or figure to which they traditionally belong. Since the present study intends to investigate the cross-cultural and cross-linguistic aspects of conventional figurative language, we will concentrate only on those expressions that are simultaneously both figurative and conventional.

1.4.2 Non-figurative metaphors and metonymies

Another fact that is crucial to our study is that not all metaphors and metonymies belong to the realm of figurative language. The difference between metaphor and metonymy has often been explained: *metonymy* is usually seen as something that "stands for" another thing, e.g. *a glove* standing for 'a baseball player'. This traditional view of metonymy points to the claim that two entities are close to each other in conceptual space or contiguously related. That is, the two entities belong to one and the same domain. In contrast to this, *metaphors* consist of elements from two different domains which are related by some kind of similarity (for the notion of metonymy and the differentiation between metaphor and metonymy see among others Croft 1993, Goossens at al. 1995; Papafragou 1996; Fass 1997; Kövecses and Radden 1998; Panther and Radden 1999; Barcelona 2000; Dirven and Pörings 2002; Deignan 2005: 53–71). In many cases, metaphor and metonymy cannot be differentiated clearly. Goossens (1990), for example, coined the term *metaphtonymy*, a corrupted form of the Greek words *meta-phora* and *met-onymy*.

According to the Cognitive Theory of Metaphor, metaphor and metonymy are omnipresent in natural language. It is not only lexical units with a salient imagery basis, perceived as marked items, that are metaphoric. There are many "dead metaphors" such as *table legs* (cf. 1.3.1).[16] Words like *fruitful* in the sense of 'productive' or *fruitless* meaning 'unprofitable' also contain metaphors pointing to the conceptual mapping RESULTS ARE FRUITS, or more generally, ACTIVITIES ARE PLANTS. Metaphors of this kind can be considered non-literal, in the sense that they do not point to a concept directly but through using another concept (so we are dealing with both source and target domain here). Being non-literal, such metaphors cannot be qualified as figurative units and do not belong to the scope of our study.

The debate surrounding "metaphoric" prepositions has been mentioned in 1.3.1. Supporters of the Cognitive Theory of Metaphor link, for example, the conceptual metaphor AN ACTIVITY IS A CONTAINER to expressions like *to put effort into a certain activity* (Lakoff 1987b: 434). Many spatial prepositions are conventionally used in the temporal sense and therefore are regarded as "metaphors" (e.g. *in this year* or *in the summer* are regarded as conceptualising periods of time as containers). Spatial motion verbs in the "metaphoric" or "metonymic" temporal meaning have also been mentioned.

Supporters of the Cognitive Theory of Metaphor developed a theoretical framework in which different linguistic phenomena, e.g. novel metaphors, idioms, dead metaphors (as described above) and the like, can be analysed in the same terms because they refer to things which are not encoded in their primary semantic structure. In other words, the same cognitive mechanisms are responsible for all these linguistic phenomena.

---

[16] Moreover, certain shifts in the predicate-argument structure can also be regarded as metaphoric phenomena (cf. David 2016).

In this sense, all these expressions are metaphors, but it would be wrong to qualify them as figurative. Not all metaphors are figurative. In order to be figurative, a metaphor has to possess a more or less salient image component in its meaning structure (cf. the criterion of image requirement). In addition, it has to be perceived as an indirect way of expressing the given entity. If a certain way of speaking or thinking about a given entity is the most frequent or even the only possible one, the degree of its figurativeness decreases considerably (cf. our criterion of additional naming).

What has been said about the metaphor holds for metonymy as well. There are many examples of metonymic figurative units (*a helping hand* or *to keep an eye on someone/ something*), but cases like *He ate the whole plate* are not figurative. The metonymic transfer from 'vessels' to their content is completely regular; it does not evoke any images. The use of this kind of metonymic expression does not imply any additional pragmatic effects. This linguistic phenomenon is known as *systematic* or *regular polysemy* (cf. Apresjan 1974a, 1974b; Padučeva 1988, 2004a; Nunberg and Zaenen 1992; Kustova 2002; Dobrovol'skij 2006; Taylor 2006; Zaliznjak 2006, 2013; Dölling 2021) and works as a powerful and near-universal mechanism for denoting conceptually related entities in a most economical and natural way.[17] Consider further well-known examples like *school, university, academy* and other nouns from the same semantic domain, which all have the following readings: (12) 'an institution', (13) 'a building', (14) 'an ensemble of people', (15) 'certain activities', (16) 'a type of institution'.

(12) *Bill left school ten years ago.*

(13) *Bill's school is just across the street.*

(14) *Bill's school is having a trip to the seaside.*

(15) *School annoys him.*

(16) *School is one of the most important inventions of modern times.*

It would be counter-intuitive to regard only the first reading as literal and all the others as figurative. For more details, see Bierwisch (1983) and Kiefer (1990: 3–4). An even more striking example of non-figurative metonymy is the so-called

---

[17] The phenomenon of regular polysemy can also be found (at least to a certain extent) in the domain of idioms (cf. Dobrovol'skij 2004).

meaning extension typical of the English verb system, cf. *John opened the door – The door opened*. The result of this kind of metonymic transfer is a restructuring of the verb's argument frame, called a diathetical shift, i.e. a semantic and syntactic transformation that is grammatical rather than lexical by nature.

It is obvious that transformations like this differ profoundly from metonymies such as *a helping hand*. The non-literalness and at the same time non-figurativeness of the former, and the figurativeness of the latter, have many significant linguistic consequences. Whereas regular, non-figurative metonymic expressions can be used without any combinatorial restrictions in all types of contexts, figurative expressions based on metonymy are restricted in their usage. Thus, even if there is a kind of shared knowledge in the English speech community that *hand* can metonymically stand for ACTIVITY, it is not possible to replace the word *activity* with the word *hand* in all contexts. Cf. *I find my recent activities very exciting* vs. **I find my recent hands very exciting*.

1.4.3 Phraseology

Phraseology will be the topic of chapter 2. Since phraseology and figurative language overlap to a great extent, we have to anticipate briefly here some aspects of phraseology which will be discussed in detail later. The aim is to separate figurative units from non-figurative ones.

We start with the assumption that idioms are the core category of phraseology and that they are prototypical examples of conventional *figurative* units. This does not mean, however, that the figurativeness of every single idiom is perceptible in the same way. Rather, we can observe a *gradual figurativeness*. Some borderline cases have to be discussed where the label *figurative* is not so obvious. We further assume that various proverbs are figurative, although there are also a number of non-figurative units in this class (cf. example (22) below). This section aims at discovering some possibly non-figurative idioms and proverbs.

Unmotivated (or opaque) idioms like *to pull someone's leg* 'to play a joke on someone, to tease someone playfully' are still figurative (see chapter 4 on motivation). The lexical structure of the idiom reveals a clear image component. What is "opaque" is the link between this lexical structure and the actual meaning of the idiom. The *motivation* of an idiom has to be separated from its *figurativeness*.

In view of idioms suspected of being non-figurative, we have to pay attention to one special group, namely expressions containing "unique constituents", i.e. words which do not function outside the structure of a given conventional expression. As strongly irregular expressions, we will count them among the class of idioms. As for their figurativeness, they might be regarded as borderline cases. Still, we do not exclude this group of expressions from the scope of our analysis.

This special group of idioms is significant in view of CFUs in general and has attracted the interest of linguists of various languages for a long time. In the Anglo-Saxon linguistic tradition, the term *cranberry collocation* is known for the phenomenon of "expressions containing unique constituents" (e.g. Moon 1998: 21).[18] The term goes back to the *cranberry morph*, a unique and opaque word element, like *cran-* in the compound *cranberry* (cf. Makkai 1972: 43). In the earlier Russian and German tradition, terms like некротизмы (*nekrotizmy*) 'necrotisms' or уникальные компоненты (*unikal'nye komponenty*) 'unique components' and *unikale Elemente / Unikalia* 'unique elements' or *unikale Komponenten* 'unique components' have been used (e.g. Rajxštejn 1980; Mel'čuk and Reuther 1984; Fleischer 1997; Stumpf 2015).

Other studies in this field – written in German (Feyaerts 1994; Dobrovol'skij and Piirainen 1994) – prefer the term *phraseologisch gebundenes Formativ* ('phraseologically bound formative') because not every "unique constituent" is restricted to one single idiom; some of them can be encountered in several idioms although they are never used as free words. They are therefore not unique, in the strict sense, but are bound to certain phrasemes. Compare similar arguments in Holzinger (2018). For example, German *Hucke* is a phraseologically bound constituent, even though it occurs in three or more idioms, cf. (17–19).

(17) *jmdm. die Hucke voll lügen* "to lie someone's *Hucke* full"
      'to tell (someone) a pack of lies'

(18) *jmdm. die Hucke voll hauen* "to beat someone's *Hucke* full"
      'to give someone a good beating'

(19) *sich die Hucke vollsaufen* "to drink one's *Hucke* full"
      'to drink a lot of alcohol, to get drunk'

Although no actual meaning can be attached to the word *Hucke* synchronically, these idioms are motivated by the other parts of the construction (*voll* 'full' and *lügen* 'to lie', *hauen*' to beat', *saufen* 'to drink/booze'). The question whether or not these idioms are figurative cannot be answered unequivocally. However, several factors can be listed that partly meet our criteria of figurativeness, though these factors are not immediately obvious. On the one hand, the word *Hucke* is

---

18 Stumpf (2018) prefers the term *unique components*.

semantically empty and does not provide a clear mental image. We can call this *constituent opacity*, which is an additional factor of irregularity. On the other hand, speakers perceive idioms (17–19) as non-literal units, based on semantic reinterpretation. We define this phenomenon as a *hidden image component*. Finally, idioms of this kind are instances of additional naming, a factor that fulfils one of our criteria of figurativeness. We postulate a broader peripheral zone for such cases. Cf. also (20).

(20) *(to be) in high (deep/great) dudgeon*
    '(to be) very angry because someone has treated one badly; (to be) in a state of deep resentment'

The constituent *dudgeon* is unique and is restricted to expression (20); the modifying adjective varies to some extent. The origin of *dudgeon* in the sense of 'resentment' is unknown; thus, this word as well as the whole expression can be considered opaque. Idioms (17–19) are motivated while idiom (20) is not: it has no literal reading based on other constituents [cf. German *lügen, hauen, saufen* in (17–19)]. Therefore, examples (17–19) can be related to certain conceptual structures that can take on the role of mental images, whereas (20) cannot. No image component can be directly extracted from its lexicalised meaning. The criterion of additional naming, however, applies to (20) as well. If we assume a graduation of figurativeness with a peripheral zone between figurative and non-figurative idioms, cases like (20) are located on the outermost border of this area.

The number of examples like (20), revealing a low degree of figurativeness, varies from one language to another (compared with e.g. Russian, the English language provides only a few such cases); see section 2.3.1 for more details. However, many idioms containing a unique constituent are figurative insofar as the unique constituents allows the discovery of image components on the basis of a literal reading of their individual elements, cf. (21).

(21) German *jmdm. den Laufpass geben* "to give someone the run-passport"
    'to dismiss someone (a partner in a relationship or the like)'

The word *Laufpass* does not exist outside the lexical structure of (21), but it is still interpretable due to its parts *Lauf-* 'run' and *-pass* 'passport'. Therefore, the image of giving a "run-passport" to someone can be regarded as a motivating link between the lexical structure and the actual meaning of this idiom. The idiom is also an additional name, so that both criteria of figurativeness are fulfilled.

As far as the languages analysed in this study are concerned, the phenomenon of *constituent opacity* is confined to the classes of idioms and restricted collocations.[19] Unique constituents, however, exist within the class of proverbs as well, but most of them are semantically transparent. Therefore, they have to be considered figurative in any case and are of no significance for this discussion.

Concerning proverbs, there are several lexical units that consist of words taken in their literal meaning. The phraseological character of this type of proverb is not based on figurativeness but on the stability of their form and the prescriptive illocutionary force. This means that a proverb always recommends a certain way of behaviour. Non-figurative proverbs are to be distinguished from figurative ones, cf. (22–23). Only the second type of proverb (23) belongs to the scope of our study.

(22) *every beginning is hard*
'it is always difficult at the beginning'

(23) *a new broom sweeps clean*
'those new in office are generally very zealous at first, and sometimes ruthless in making changes'

Non-figurative proverbs are of no importance for research in the field of figurative language. However, they may be interesting in some cases of cross-linguistic (and cross-cultural) analysis starting from target concepts in paremiology. There are, for instance, some non-figurative proverbs that match figurative ones expressing precisely the same idea. These examples may be worth considering in view of the pragmatic function of such expressions; cf. (24–25).

(24) German *kleine Ursache, große Wirkung* "small cause, great effect"

(25) English *great oaks from little acorns grow*
both meaning 'great effects can result from small causes'

The two proverbs are regarded as equivalent, despite the fact that one is non-figurative and the other is highly figurative. Both proverbs are isomorphic in their structure: *great oaks* standing for 'great effects' (oaks being the biggest trees in the climatic zone of Central Europe) and *little acorns* (the small fruits of the oak

---

19 The German constituent *Hinblick* is unique to the restricted collocation *im Hinblick auf* 'with regard to', but it is fully transparent, due to the verb *hinblicken* 'to look (across)', see 2.3.3. Unique constituents in proverbs mainly occur in languages that tend to use compounds as a means of word formation, e.g. *Müßiggang* in the German proverb *Müßiggang ist aller Laster Anfang* "Idleness is the beginning of all vices".

tree) standing for 'small causes'. However, proverb (24) does not belong to the scope of our study because it is not figurative.

All the linguistic phenomena considered in this chapter are related to the phenomenon of figurativeness in one sense or another. In what follows, we will restrict the subject of analysis to conventional units of figurative language, above all to those which belong to the core of this domain, i.e. idioms, idiomatic similes, figurative proverbs and restricted figurative collocations, as well as one-word metaphors and metonymies with a strong image component.

2 Conventional figurative language and phraseology

The main topic of this chapter is a discussion of the most important types of conventional figurative units (CFUs). Since most of these types – such as idioms, restricted collocations, proverbs, etc. (2.3) – belong to the field of phraseology in a wider sense, it seems reasonable to discuss these issues against the background of phraseology. To begin with, we must clarify two problems: first, we want to take stock of our position within the field of "phraseological research" (or "idiom research"). Therefore, it is necessary to take a short look at the main trends of phraseological research and the problems of terminology that have accompanied this field (2.1). Since the topic of our study is the figurative lexicon (conventional figurative units), *polylexicality*, one of the definition criteria of the *phraseme*, is of no importance. See section 2.2 on one-word metaphors (*single words* used with a conventionalised figurative meaning).

2.1 Research on phraseology: A brief outline

2.1.1 Terminology and main topics

In this section, we will briefly outline the essential results of phraseological research in Europe over the past decades and touch on the main terminological problems. For a long time, research into phraseology in different countries used somewhat inconsistent terminology.[1] At present, however, the term *phraseme* is well known in international phraseological research and there is a broad consensus that *phraseme* (or *phraseologism* in older terminology) is the appropriate term (cf. Burger et al. 2007b: 12). We follow this European tradition and use *phraseme* as a hyperonym that is suitable for all kinds of conventional multiword units, figurative as well as non-figurative. The term *phraseme* needs further explanation in English, where it is still not common (whereas *Phrasem* and *phrasème* are common in German and French respectively). The term *phraseme* has the following advantages over other terms:

---

[1] Wray (2002: 9) published a list of about 70 terms, for example *co-ordinate constructions, collocations, complex lexemes, fixed expressions, formulaic language, lexical(ised) phrases, multiword lexical phenomena, ready-made expressions, set phrases, stock utterances*, and many more. These terms appear in different fields of research to describe phrasemes and related phenomena. Some of these terms have more than one meaning.

2.1 Research on phraseology: A brief outline

- it is to be preferred over terms with *fixed* (like *fixed expressions, fixed units*), because most idioms, collocations etc. are not absolutely fixed but flexible to some extent
- *phraseologism* and *phraseological unit* (calques from the Russian term *фразеологизм* and *фразеологическая единица*) sound strange in English
- individual researchers, especially outside the European tradition, have often used *idiom* in the sense of 'phraseme'. However, *idiom* is unsuitable as an umbrella term.[2]

Charles Bally ([1909] 1951) is often considered the precursor of modern research on phraseology, and this tradition was further developed by Vinogradov ([1946] 1977b, [1947] 1977a, 1953). The beginning of scientific research on phraseology in the framework of a consistent linguistic theory, i.e. the Meaning-Text-Theory, can be ascribed to Mel'čuk (1960).

The main topics of phraseological research in Europe during the past four decades have been
1. the syntax of idioms
2. the semantics of idioms
3. the stylistic aspects and pragmatics of idioms (including text-related modifications)
4. cognitive approaches to idioms
5. cross-linguistic research on idioms including typological and areal aspects
6. the cultural specifics and cross-cultural comparison of idioms.

For research in both theory development and the empirical analysis of phraseology, cf. e.g. Amosova (1963), Černyševa (1975, 1980), Burger (1973, 2015), Häusermann (1977), Rajxštejn (1980), Burger, Buhofer, and Sialm (1982), Fleischer (1997), Gréciano (1983), Telija (1996), Moon (1998), Wray (2002, 2013), Filatkina (2005, 2018), Burger et al. (2007a), Baranov and Dobrovol'skij (2008, 2013), Wulff (2008, 2013), Dobrovol'skij and Piirainen (2009), Piirainen (2012), Dobrovol'skij (2016a). For lexicographic aspects of phraseology, see Fellbaum (2007) and the special issue of the International Journal of Lexicography "Phraseology and Dictionaries" (Dobrovol'skij 2015). An important field of the recent research is the investigation of phraseology and Construction Grammar.

---

[2] It contradicts the usage of the term *Idiom* in German or *идиома* in Russian (see 2.3.1). 'Idiom' is more commonly used in a narrow sense for units that are highly irregular, i.e. for units that show a high degree of idiomaticity and stability.

The terminology varied considerably across European phraseological studies, with terms like *phraseologisms, phrasemes, phraseological items, fixed expressions* or *multiword lexical units* among the most common (cf. footnote 1). Nevertheless, there was a consensus about the main features. According to the most general definition, phrasemes are considered conventional polylexical units of the lexicon which display various kinds of formal and semantic irregularity.

Phrasemes are stable by definition: as soon as an expression has become conventionalised, it will be reproduced in discourse as a prefabricated unit of language. In other words, phrasemes are multiword units of the lexicon, and as such they are, like all lexical units, relatively stable in form and meaning. The constitutive properties of phrasemes, which have been generally agreed upon, have been summarised as follows:

> Phraseologisch ist eine Verbindung von zwei oder mehr Wörtern dann, wenn (1) die Wörter eine durch die syntaktischen und semantischen Regularitäten der Verknüpfung nicht voll erklärbare Einheit bilden, und wenn (2) die Wortverbindung in der Sprachgemeinschaft, ähnlich wie ein Lexem, gebräuchlich ist. (Burger, Buhofer, and Sialm 1982: 1)
>
> [A combination of two or more words is phraseological if (1) the words form a unit that cannot be fully explained by the syntactic and semantic regularities of the combination and (2) the word combination is commonly used by the speech community, similar to the use of a lexeme.]

There is a long tradition in the scope of lexical research of classifying phrasemes into classes such as *restricted collocations, phrasal verbs, routine formulae, idioms, proverbs* and the like (see 2.3). The consensus here is that the central group of phrasemes is that of *idioms*. A crucial property of idioms is their semantic irregularity (or idiomaticity), which is closely related to the property of figurativeness. Furthermore, it is generally agreed that idioms, for the most part, are not frozen elements of a language, and that they are usually arbitrary only from the point of view of their production, but not from the perspective of their understanding, because most of them are clearly motivated by underlying knowledge structures.

Idiom research has paid much attention to the topic of idiom motivation (cf. Vinogradov 1977a; Gréciano 1993, 2002; Dobrovol'skij and Piirainen 2010, 2018, 2019). Different types of motivation have been postulated and analysed. This may be relevant in revealing different bases of figurativeness. If we know which phenomenon makes up the relevant motivating link between the lexical structure of an idiom and its actual meaning, we also know which linguistic and/or conceptual elements are responsible for the figurative nature of this expression (see chapter 4 for details).

2.1.2 Written vs. oral language as research topic

From its beginning, phraseological research has focused on the examination of major European standard languages. Initially, Russian was the central object of investigation (cf. Vinogradov's works in the 1940s). Back in the 1970s and 1980s, it was scholars of Russian and other Slavonic languages, among them Serbo-Croatian, Czech and Slovak, who dominated European phraseological research. They were followed by Germanists and Romanists. Thanks to the Hungarian and Finnish Germanists, these two Finno-Ugric languages were also present almost from the outset. Today's phraseological research is quite different from the situation at the start of this discipline. Almost all of the 40 standard European languages are now represented by larger or smaller phraseological studies. In addition, several non-European major languages have entered the field (e.g. Arabic, Chinese and Japanese).

All these studies have one thing in common – they are based on standard languages with a rich literary tradition and a high degree of written norms. In the past, phraseological research consistently excluded the exploration of linguistic varieties which exist only in oral communication. Only in recent times have a few studies been added which investigated dialects, on the one hand, and lesser-used languages that existed primarily in oral form, on the other. For an overview of the dialects, see Piirainen (2007). Phraseological work on two lesser-used languages, both belonging to the oldest linguistic layers of Europe, is to be emphasized, namely *Inari Saami* to the Far North of Europe (Idström 2012) and *Basque*, a language isolate spoken in the Western Pyrenees (Ibarretxe-Antuñano 2008, 2012). Finally, an initial approach has been made to researching figurative lexical units of lesser-used non-European languages within linguistic theories (cf. Idström and Piirainen 2012a; Piirainen and Sherris 2015).

It should be noted that international research has not taken note of various studies on the phraseology of languages without a long written tradition, most of which are lesser-used languages. On the European side, the rich literature on Kashubian and Upper and Lower Sorbian idioms was scarcely noticed by traditional phraseology. It is significant that in the two-volume *Handbook of Phraseology* (Burger et al. 2007a) these studies do not exist. By contrast, comparable investigations into the lesser-used languages of other continents exist in large numbers, as evidenced, for example, by the International Bibliography of Phraseology and Paremiology (Mieder 2009). Work on indigenous languages has been carried out mainly in the framework of anthropology and ethnology, usually dealing with metaphors and proverbs, along with magic formulas, rites, spells and incantations, among other things. This work did not meet the interest of phraseological researchers, although it belongs to the realm of formulaicity and figurativeness in general.

2.1.3 Anglo-American research tradition

In contrast to the prosperous phraseological research that has taken place in Eastern and Western Europe since the 1970s (only small parts of which are mentioned above), there is no comparable tradition in Anglo-American linguistics. This gap in English language research has, however, been recognised. Cowie summarises the situation as follows (introducing his 1998 edition of "Phraseology. Theory, analysis, and applications"): "[. . .] there is to date no book-length account in English of the various theoretical currents which inform present-day phraseological studies, nor one which takes account of the associated disciplines, such as computational analysis, language-learning, stylistics, and lexicography, to which those studies are making such a vital and invigorating contribution" (Cowie 1998a: 2).[3]

For a long time, Anglo-American linguists closed their eyes to the findings of the research on phraseology in the tradition of Bally. Whereas the early publications from Eastern Europe (mainly from Russia) were not accessible due to the Iron Curtain, publications from Western Europe, at least since e.g. Burger (1973), Häusermann (1977), Jaksche, Sialm, and Burger (1981), Burger, Buhofer, and Sialm (1982), were available worldwide. There may have been a language barrier for English-speaking linguists, however, because the most important books on phraseology were written in Russian, German or French.

In the Anglo-American tradition, phraseology as a distinct field has never occupied an important place. Phraseological phenomena have been regarded as marginal, as exceptions to the rule. This view was probably due to the once dominant Generative Transformational Grammar, which, at least in its early version, did not pay much attention to the structure of the lexicon (Chomsky 1965). This attitude may have obscured the perception of the abundance of phrasemes in any language. In Makkai's (1972) opinion, there exists only a small set of idioms. Under the impact of linguistic corpus analysis, however, the omnipresence of prefabricated, reproducible lexical items could no longer be concealed or played down. Thus, Sinclair's (1991) statement that there are many word combinations that are not completely compositional was considered a surprising finding: "The overwhelming nature of this evidence leads us to elevate the principle of idiom from being a rather minor feature, compared with grammar, to being at least as

---

[3] An important article on English idioms by Nunberg, Sag, and Wasow (1994) should be mentioned. The book-length study by Moon (1998) appeared in the same year as Cowie's book, thus could not be quoted there.

important as grammar in the explanation of how meaning arises in text" (Sinclair 1991: 112).[4]

Earlier Anglo-American studies on metaphors and related phenomena almost invariably referred to the so-called "traditional view" or "classical view" on idioms. According to this "traditional view", idioms are considered to be "long words". Hence, the only difference between idioms and words is their morphosyntactic structure, because idioms by definition consist of more than one word. Semantically, idioms were identified with non-metaphorical words, according to a line of reasoning that if it is possible to express the same idea (say 'to die') by means of idioms (e.g. *kick the bucket*) and by means of words (*die*), they would reveal no significant difference in their actual meaning.[5] Idioms were often regarded as completely "frozen" expressions, which are non-compositional and have arbitrary (non-motivated) meanings. Later research clearly showed that the formal stability of idioms is a matter of degree and that even fixed idioms can be varied (see e.g. Moon 1998).

As far as we know, this "traditional view" is actually the exception in the field of idiom research, and can mainly be found in American psycholinguistic approaches in the early 1970s (cf. Bobrow and Bell 1973). This "traditional view" has been singled out by many authors, mostly in order to contrast their own approaches against this background. Let us look at Gibbs and O'Brien's summary of this view, deputising for a number of similar studies.

> American English has thousands of idiomatic expressions whose meanings diverge in various ways from their literal interpretations, such as *spill the beans, button your lips, blow off steam, lose your marbles*, and *shoot the breeze*. Traditional theories of idiomaticity assume that idioms once had metaphorical origins, but have lost their metaphoricity over time and now exist as "dead" metaphors with their figurative meanings being directly stipulated in the mental lexicon [. . .]. Idioms are thought to be non-compositional since the figurative meanings of these phrases are not functions of the meanings of their individual parts. (Gibbs and O'Brien 1990: 36)

In the European research tradition, such "classical" views were never prominent. As early as the 1970s, there was general agreement that most idioms are semantically motivated, i.e. at least partly transparent with regard to conceptual links between their lexical structure and their actual meaning (often being based on a

---

[4] Contrary to the open-choice principle, the idiom principle implies that the speaker has a number of semi-preconstructed chunks at his or her disposal.
[5] Cf. Glucksberg's (2001: 68) criticism of the fact that linguistic data were restricted to a few idioms like *kick the bucket*: "Examples such as *kick the bucket* have led to the deceptively simple view that idioms are simply memorized expressions, nothing more than long words, and so require no further analysis or explanation." See also Jackendoff (2002: 167–168).

comprehensible metaphor). At the same time, there is a wide consensus about the linguistic status of idioms and other types of phrasemes, otherwise they would not be lexical items. That is to say, acceptance in the lexicon and semantic motivation are two different, complementary properties of phrasemes. This postulate seems to be agreed upon by most linguists working in this research domain, thus it will not be discussed further.

2.2 One-word figurative lexical units

Before starting to describe the different types of conventional figurative units, we must answer one basic question in order to find an appropriate framework for the empirical data, namely, how should one-word metaphors (or one-word figurative lexical units) be treated?[6]

In traditional lexicology, one-word metaphors and phrasemes are described separately, both in the domain of lexicology proper and in the domain of phraseology. However, there is no dividing line between words and phrasemes from the perspective of figurative language. Both types of expressions can be figurative, and they can even make use of the same images. Besides, there is a great similarity between idioms and compounds: both consist of more than one auto-semantic lexical constituent. The boundary between idioms and compounds may be due to orthography, morphosyntax, or (looked at from a cross-linguistic angle) linguistic typology.[7]

First, let us consider words with simple morphological structures, for example in utterances like (1) and (2):

(1)   *Would you be an angel and help me?*

(2)   *Accident clouds festival* (a headline)

The words *angel* and *to cloud* clearly have metaphorical senses in these contexts. They are both figurative and conventional. From this perspective, all words such as *angel* in (1) or *to cloud* in (2) should belong to the scope of our analysis and

---

[6] We use *one-word figurative lexical units* and *one-word metaphors* as synonyms.
[7] Finkbeiner and Schlücker (2019: 2) point to the fact that a cross-linguistically valid demarcation line between compounds and multiword expressions "may be impossible, given that languages vary greatly in their defining properties and in the number and productivity of compound and MWE subpatterns". For more details on the relationship between word formation and phraseology, see also Hüning and Schlücker (2016).

ought to be taken into consideration. However, the central topic of our study is multiword CFUs, idioms in the first place, and, to a certain extent, figurative proverbs. Figurative compounds are also included: although they are single words in form, they differ from metaphorical root words by their two-part structure (see below for more detail).

There are both technical and theoretical reasons why we restrict the scope of our analysis to expressions which are not only both figurative and conventional but also complex. First, a specific technical reason is the need for the context to determine one-word metaphors. Conventional figurative units such as idioms, figurative compounds and the like assume their figurative interpretations often (but not always) without a context. In order to formulate adequate semantic definitions, one always has to study the contextual behaviour of a given lexical unit. However, in order to decide whether or not we are dealing with a figurative lexical unit, we need less semantic information if we only consider complex conventional figurative expressions. For instance, a decision whether or not the word *angel* is used figuratively requires either a semantic definition or a context like (1). Likewise, the verb *to cloud* is in principle semantically ambiguous, though the literal sense is denoted by *to cloud over* rather than by *to cloud*. At any rate, some additional requirements must be fulfilled in order to determine the degree of figurativeness of single words that are used metaphorically (especially if they are not compounds or, at least, derivatives with affixes, such as *snaky* or *fishy*).

By contrast, no additional definitions and/or contexts are required in order to decide if an expression like *to jump out of one's skin* is figurative. Nevertheless, there are some cases (though rare) in which an idiom without context could coincide with an expression in its literal reading (e.g. *to drive someone into a corner*). However, even in such cases, the figurative reading seems to be more salient. For example, the meaning 'to put someone into a difficult situation so that they do not have any choice as to what to do' is more salient and, therefore, less context-sensitive for the word string *to drive someone into a corner* than is its interpretation as a physical action. In order to conduct an extended cross-linguistic analysis, it is technically simpler to take as empirical data only those lexical items which are figurative *per se* and can be regarded as such without preliminary work (such as analysing textual corpora, attending observations, or comparing lexicographic entries).

When we consult dictionaries of the languages analysed here, we often face a situation where a certain L1 word is included in both its literal and its figurative meaning, whereas the corresponding L2 word, which actually carries both meanings as well, is lexicographically represented as having only the literal meaning. Let us look at the entries of Dutch *haas* 'hare' and German *Hase* in two standard dictionaries, where the figurative meaning of HARE, 'coward', is treated differently:

(3) haas [...]
 1 grijsbruin knaagdier *(Lepus europaeus)* met lange achterpoten, korte staart en gespleten bovenlip [...]; 2 (stofn.) vlees van een haas of van hazen: (uitdr., soldatent.) *haas vreten* haasvreten; 3 naam van een sterrenbeeld ten zuiden van Orion *(Lepus)*; 4 (fig.) bangerik, lafaard; [...] (Van Dale GWNT 1992: 1078)
 [1 grey-brown rodent *(Lepus europaeus)* with long hind legs, short tail and split upper lip [...]; 2 (mass noun) meat of a hare or of hares: (expression, soldiers' slang) *to eat hare* to be or become anxious, afraid; 3 name of a constellation to the south of Orion *(Lepus)*; 4 (fig.) anxious person, coward' [...]]

Here the meaning 'coward' is listed among the four major meanings of HARE and marked *fig.* ('figurative'). Strangely enough, a figurative expression is also given under meaning 2, 'meat of a hare', provided with a paraphrase just as figurative (*haasvreten* 'to be or become anxious, afraid'). The German word *Hase* actually has the same literal and figurative meanings:

(4) *Hase* [...]
 1.a) wild lebendes Nagetier mit langen Ohren, einem dichten, weichen, bräunlichen Fell und langen Hinterbeinen. *er ist furchtsam wie ein Hase* [...]; **b)** männlicher Hase (1a); **c)** Hasenbraten, -gericht [...] (Duden 2015: 801)
 [**1.a)** undomesticated rodent with long ears, a thick, soft, brownish fur and long hind legs. *he is anxious as a hare* [...]; **b)** male hare (1a); **c)** roast hare, dish of hare [...]]

However, the German "Duden" only presents the literal meanings (by means of "encyclopaedic" paraphrases, similar to that of Dutch *haas*), whereas the figurative meaning 'coward' is mentioned only in the example sentence *er ist furchtsam wie ein Hase*, including the idiomatic simile *furchtsam wie ein Hase*. This is another reason why we exclude one-word metaphors from our investigation.

Secondly, there is a theoretical reason why we have reduced the bulk of our empirical data to complex figurative units. There is sufficient linguistic evidence (see below) to prove that complex linguistic structures, such as idioms, figurative proverbs or figurative compounds, accumulate more culturally and semiotically significant information than simple structures. Note, for example, idiom (5):

(5) English *something is no/not a bed of roses*
 'a situation or activity is sometimes difficult or unpleasant'

The motivating link between the lexical structure of this idiom and its actual meaning is provided by the association of *roses* with something very pleasant. This view of *roses* is supported by various cultural phenomena. First, idiom (5) is a borrowing from Latin *iacere in rosa* "to be lying in (the) rose" 'to indulge in constant pleasure'. The Latin expression originates from a tradition in late ancient Rome – during their banquets (*symposia*), Roman men used to lie on a kind of bed covered with rose petals. Therefore, the Latin saying could also be interpreted literally. Secondly, idiom (5) and some other CFUs with *rose* as a key constituent (*roses all the way* 'very successful or pleasant', *to come up roses* 'to develop in a very favourable way', *it's not all roses* 'there are difficulties to be overcome, as well as pleasure to be enjoyed', *No rose without a thorn* 'even in the most beautiful things there are some small disadvantages') suggest an interpretation of ROSE as 'the perfect flower' or as a kind of symbol standing for 'something very pleasant'.[8]

This kind of cultural knowledge is not present in the semantic structure of the word *rose*, even if taken in a metaphorical sense. There is no dictionary, to our knowledge, that would ascribe to the word *rose* meanings like 'the perfect flower' or 'a symbol of something pleasant'. Thus, the complex of conventional expressions with figurative senses provides more empirical evidence for analysing the specifics of figurative language, especially from a cross-cultural perspective. Analysis along these lines allows for contrasting languages and cultures. In Japanese culture, for example, the chrysanthemum has a similar symbolic function. Therefore, ROSE is not a universal symbol.

At this point, we must discuss the question of why we include a certain group of compounds in our research. Some conventional figurative units are, semantically and pragmatically, very close to conventional figurative multiword units, such as idioms, although they are not polylexical themselves. For the most part, these are compounds. It is obvious that many compounds have nothing to do with figurativeness (e.g. *tablecloth* or *housekeeper*, in contrast to *fence-sitting*). We will only consider those compounds that have a clear image component. We call these *figurative compounds*.

For certain compounds, the figurative meanings are much more salient than the literal meanings. The literal readings, e.g. "the speed of a roof" (6), "the

---

[8] In Western cultures, a rich cultural symbolism is connected with the ROSE. Various symbolic interpretations of this flower occur in classical antiquity (in connection with the Roman festival "Rosalia", with the Dionysian festivals or the myth of Adonis). In Christian tradition, the ROSE stands for God's love, for the blood shed by Jesus on the cross (Jesus was imagined as a rose, rooted in the prophetic words of Jesaja, verse 12). One should also note the well-known Shakespearean quotation about the *name of the rose* (Romeo and Juliet, II, 2) and similar allegories and judgements about the rose in heraldry, alchemy, and other domains (Biedermann 1994: 289–291).

licking of a cat" / "the washing of a cat" (7) or "a black guard (a guard coloured black)" (8), may occur, at best, in special (and more or less constructed) contexts like word plays, whereas the figurative reading is available context-free.

(6) Finnish *kattonopeus* "roof-speed/ceiling-speed"
'maximum permissible speed'

(7) a. English *catlick*
b. German *Katzenwäsche* "cat-wash"
both meaning 'a perfunctory wash'

(8) English *blackguard*
'a man of bad character, without honour'

What compounds (6–8) have in common with other conventional figurative units is that they reveal the same well-known types of motivation (see chapter 4). In example (6), this is the conceptual metaphor MUCH IS UP. Within the frame[9] BUILDING, the roof or ceiling marks the highest point (the upper limit), providing the source concept UP. This can be mapped onto more abstract target concepts involving scalable arrangements, as is the case with the concept of (low or high) SPEED. Thus, the Finnish compound *kattonopeus* can be understood without any problem as 'maximum permissible speed' (cf. 4.5.2).

The two expressions (7) are motivated at the level of the "rich image", through common knowledge about cats. Cats give the impression that they are scared of water, and wash themselves only perfunctorily by licking their fur. Within the frame CAT, this special kind of "body care" is a salient feature that can be mapped onto the body care of a human being (cf. 4.5.3).

Compound (8), on the other hand, is motivated by symbolic knowledge. *Black-* does not signify the colour 'black' but is related to symbolic functions of BLACK such as 'bad', 'illegal', 'dishonourable', as they emerge in many other CFUs with BLACK and in cultural codes(cf. 4.6; see also 10.7 and 11.3.5).

All these examples fulfil the criteria of figurativeness: (i) they have image components, and (ii) they are instances of additional naming. Instead of using compound (6), one could easily say *suurin sallittu nopeus* "(the) highest permissible speed". The same holds for compounds (7) and particularly for compound (8),

---

[9] For the notion of *frame* see chapter 8. Compare also Fillmore et al. (2003: 305) where the frame is defined as "a schematic presentation of a situation type that underlies the meaning of a word (or of the members of sets of words) along with named participant roles or aspects of the situation".

which is one of many near-synonyms such as *rogue, villain, rascal, crook, scoundrel, baddy* etc.

Being morphologically complex, these expressions are situated at the borderline between simple words and multiword lexical units. Figurative compounds belong to the scope of this study because, in contrast to one-word metaphors, their figurative meaning has been conventionalised. Hardly ever do they permit any choice between activating a literal or a figurative reading.

Lexical units can be largely parallel in different languages with regard to their meanings, image components and lexical structures, and yet appear, at the morphosyntactic level, as an idiom in one language and as a figurative compound in another language.

Figurative compounds have only occasionally been an object of research, not for their own sake but, rather, in the context of *polylexicality* as one of the postulated defining criteria of phrasemes. The fact that a polylexical unit in one language may have a compound equivalent in another language has been noted since the beginning of cross-linguistic studies. In her comparison of German and Hungarian phrasemes, Regina Hessky (1987: 62) refers to cases like German *unter vier Augen* "under four eyes" vs. Hungarian *négyszemközt* "four-eye-between", both meaning figuratively 'among the two of us, without the presence of other people'. At a complete loss for how to tackle this problem theoretically, researchers have even proposed excluding such cases from cross-linguistic works, especially from bilingual phraseological dictionaries. Let us look at examples (9–13).

(9) German *der Löwenanteil* "the lionshare"

(10) Finnish *leijonanosa* "lionshare" (*leijona* 'lion' – *osa* 'part')

(11) English *the lion's share*

(12) French *la part du lion* "the share of the lion"

(13) Russian *львиная доля* "lion [adjective] share/part"
all meaning 'the biggest part of something, especially money, food or work that is taken or done by one person instead of being shared fairly with other people'

All these figurative units are regular, following the morphosyntactic rules of the given languages. Units with a compound structure in one language (the more synthetic languages (9) German and (10) Finnish) correspond to idioms with a genitive construction ((11) English and (12) French) or adjective-noun structure ((13)

Russian).[10] It would seem odd to exclude the figurative units (9) and (10) from our research – even if they would have been analysed separately in traditional phraseology. This explains why CFU (*conventional figurative unit*) is much more suitable as a superordinate term for our study than the term *phraseme*.

A single word most often occurs as an equivalent of a word string when the agglutinative language Finnish is involved: Finnish *kädenkääänteessä* "in turning round (the) hand" is equivalent to German *im Handumdrehen* "in hand-turning", both meaning 'in very little time, very quickly'. Idioms and compounds cannot always be easily discriminated, even within the same language. Let us consider expression (14), derived from idiom (15), a derivational case typical of English, which is morphologically organised as a compound.

(14) *fence-sitting* 'remaining neutral'

(15) *to sit on the fence*
'to be unwilling to make a decision or commit oneself to one party in a dispute'

As far as Japanese is concerned, the figurative units called 四字熟語 (*yoji-jukugo*) should be mentioned here. Usually the term *yoji-jukugo* is translated as "four-character compounds", meaning expressions that are made up of four meaningful characters (*kanji*) joined without any synsemantic element (*kana*) between them. Maybe "four-character compounds" is a misleading translation, since *yoji-jukugo* are either proverbs, provided that they contain classical wisdom or a moral, or idioms. Most of them come from ancient China, cf. (16).

(16) Japanese 我田引水 (*ga-den-in-sui*) "self-ricefield-pull-water [(to) my ricefield (I) draw/carry water]"
'self-centred, self-seeking, promoting one's own interests, turning every argument to one's own advantage'

The distinguishing features of an idiom, its semantic irregularity and reinterpretation, clearly emerge here. A differentiation of such "four-character compounds" from other polylexical figurative units based only on specifics of the "orthography" would be artificial.

---

10 We also want to stress the similarity between certain similes and figurative compounds, e.g. German *hungrig wie ein Bär* "hungry as a bear" 'very hungry' and *Bärenhunger* "bear's-hunger" 'a great hunger'. There is no difference between these expressions from the viewpoint of figurativeness. Cf. the term *dephraseologische Derivation* in Fleischer (1997: 185–189).

Finally, the following word could be interpreted in a more or less non-figurative sense. On the basis of its elements, however, the more salient reading is a figurative one:

(17)   German *jmdn. anschwärzen* "to blacken someone"
       'to denigrate or denounce someone, to bring someone into discredit'

A literal interpretation of (17) on the basis of BLACK is impossible (except when used e.g. in puns). The verb does not signify 'to make someone black, e.g. by paint'. It is solely the symbolic interpretation of BLACK that makes up its meaning (obviously, *anschwärzen* is a loan translation from Latin *denigrare* 'to slander', where the same symbolic function of BLACK (*niger*) existed, just as in the etymological structure of English *denigrate*).

2.3 Types of phrasemes and their constitutive criteria

The category of conventional figurative units includes very heterogeneous entities, divided into smaller, more or less homogeneous subclasses. Here we will address the more or less commonly accepted types and give a short description of them in view of their figurativeness.

All phrasemes are "fixed expressions" by definition (cf. 2.1). However, not all types of phrasemes are figurative. In what follows, we will describe in more detail those types which – in most cases – belong to the scope of figurative language. *Idioms* constitute a central class of figurative units (2.3.1). This is the reason why the linguistic data of the present study consist for the most part of idioms. Another type of phraseme that has to be discussed here are *similes*. From the traditional point of view, these are regarded as belonging to the class of idioms, but the group of similes is in fact heterogeneous (2.3.2). A certain degree of figurativeness can be found in expressions belonging to other phraseme types; there are some *restricted collocations*, for example, that can be regarded as partly figurative (2.3.3). Another central class of figurative units, next to idioms, are *proverbs*. It is estimated that about half of all proverbs are figurative. The task of section 2.3.4 will be to show what points proverbs have in common with idioms and in what way the two classes are different.

In this section, we will discuss only those types of phrasemes which are relevant with respect to figurative language. Let us first mention four groups of multiword expressions which also have the criterion of fixedness but not necessarily that of figurativeness: (i) situational phrasemes, (ii) grammatical phrasemes, (iii) phrasal verbs, (iv) constructional phrasemes.

Situational phrasemes (traditionally called *routine formulae*) like *Nice to meet you, How do you do, I beg your pardon* or *Would you be so kind as to give me* do not belong to the scope of this study.[11] They are conventionalised multiword units, and they are non-literal for the most part, but they are hardly figurative (cf. Coulmas 1981).

Another group of phrasemes is that of *grammatical phrasemes*. These are prefabricated multiword units as well, but they do not reveal any kind of figurativeness. A good example is English *not only – but also*. This grammatical phraseme that functions as a connector is not figurative, but highly formulaic. The structure consists of four words. Nothing can be changed: *only not – but also; *not only – however also. The central feature is its absolute fixedness. Similar word groups exist in the other languages analysed here (German *nach und nach; wie dem auch sei*, Dutch *niet alleen – maar ook; tot nader order*; Russian *не только – но и*, etc.).

Especially with regard to English, the group of *phrasal verbs* should be mentioned. The multiword character of phrasal verbs exists through the combination of a verb and a particle (or adverb). Most of them are not, or are only weakly, figurative, e.g. *to hold together, to carry away, to shop around*. However, there are no clear borderlines: dictionaries of phrasal verbs (e.g. Cowie and Mackin 1998) list them together with idioms and other word strings resembling idioms (e.g. *shoot down – shoot one's mouth off; hold to – not hold a candle to*, etc.).

Another major topic which will be ignored here is linguistic units that can be better examined in the framework of Construction Grammar,[12] although they are closely related to phraseology. Most of them are not figurative in the sense discussed here. A particularly relevant subclass of constructions, in the sense of Fillmore, Kay, and O'Connor (1988), Fillmore (1990, 2008), Goldberg (1995, 2006), Hoffmann and Trousdale (2013) or Ziem and Lasch (2013), is the so-called *constructional phrasemes*. These are syntactic structures which have a lexical meaning as a whole. Only certain positions in their lexical structure are filled. Other positions represent slots that must be satisfied. The lexical filling is not entirely free, but subject to semantic restrictions (for more details, see Dobrovol'skij 2011b, 2016c; cf. also Steyer 2015, 2018; Mellado Blanco 2019, 2021; Mellado Blanco, Mollica, and Schafroth in press). Various terms have been used to describe these phenomena. Some of them are known as *Phraseoschablonen* in the German research tradition (cf. Fleischer 1997: 130–134). The English-speaking world uses terms like *lexically* or *formal open idioms* (Fillmore, Kay, and O'Con-

---

[11] Mel'čuk (2015: 73–77) labels this phraseme class as *formulemes* and describes it as "clichés with a specific abstract referent" (2015: 73). Cf. also the class of *pragmatemes*, i.e. pragmatically constrained clichés (Mel'čuk 2012: 41–42), such as *Hold the line!* or *Watch your step!*.
[12] For more detail, see, above all, Hoffmann and Trousdale (2013).

nor 1988: 505), *syntactic idioms* (Nunberg, Sag, and Wasow 1994), *constructional idioms* (Booij 2002), *schematic idioms* (Croft and Cruse 2004: 248), etc., some of them resembling constructional phrasemes, as they are defined in (Dobrovol'skij 2011b). An example is the English construction *the simplest/best/most natural/ most normal/... thing in the world*. The pattern has the superlative of an adjective as an open slot, while the lexical-syntactic template correlates with the intensification of the meaning of the adjective, 'very, particularly'. Compare also verb constructions such as *to go and V* or *to take and V*: "Now you tell me how Bob Tanner done it, Huck." "Why, he took and dipped his hand in a rotten stump where the rain-water was." (Mark Twain. The Adventures of Tom Sawyer).

These four types of phrasemes can be disregarded insofar as they are not figurative.[13]

Finally, there is no need to regard *aphorisms, maxims, winged words, slogans, quotations* and the like as independent phraseme types. Such linguistic items are either conventionalised (lexicalised) and thus belong to the lexicon (e.g. as members of the classes of idioms or proverbs), or they are not lexicalised. In the latter case they remain free quotations, slogans etc. and do not belong to the scope of linguistics (they can, however, be the subject of literary studies and other disciplines). There are borderline cases where it is difficult to decide whether a given text fragment has already been conventionalised and entered the lexicon or not. (For example, it could be asked whether *brave new world* is an idiom, used in order to comment on a certain situation, or merely an allusion to a well-known title).

2.3.1 Idioms

The central and most important class of phrasemes is made up of idioms. In order to explain the crucial criteria for separating idioms from other kinds of phrasemes, we need to engage in a concise theoretical discussion.

There are many contradictory approaches to definitions of the term *idiom*. Yet all attempts to define the notion of *idiom* can be reduced to two fundamental approaches: the definition of an idiom is based either on very general statements about its image-bearing and expressive functions (this approach makes any operationalisation impossible), or on a system of strict oppositions (e.g. Mel'čuk 1960). As a result of the latter approach, well-defined classes of phrasemes (among

---

[13] In certain rare cases, constructional phrasemes can be weakly figurative. Single instances of this type should be included in the domain of conventional figurativeness.

them also the class of idioms, often called *phraseologisms* or *phraseological units proper*) were delineated, but the borders between these classes were counter-intuitive. The approach that is presented here can be regarded as an attempt to reduce these contradictions. In what follows, we will give a brief outline of the idiomaticity theory as presented, among other things, in Baranov and Dobrovol'skij (2005, 2008).

Human memory has its limits. This is why establishing units like (18) as three separate words in the lexicon (to *tilt, at,* and *windmills*), with specific meanings which become explicit only in the given idiom, is not only uneconomical as far as the descriptive task is concerned, but also hardly optimal for the functioning of the human cognitive system.

(18) *to tilt at windmills*
 'to squander one's energy; to waste time on ideas that are not practical or not important; as if one were fighting imaginary enemies or evils'

Thus, the singling out of the phraseological system by traditional descriptions is well grounded – it is more economical to "store" these expressions as something indivisible, as integral lexical units, without producing them each time anew in the process of communication. Charles Bally (1932) pointed to the fact that a specific and arbitrary rule demands a greater effort than a general and rational one.[14] Therefore, there is an ontological foundation to distinguishing the class of phrasemes as a whole. The fundamental irregularity of phrasemes makes them lexical units (rather than "free" combinations of lexical units).

What place do idioms occupy in the large class of phrasemes? It is desirable for the theoretical model of idioms to be constructed as closely as possible to the "natural" way most linguists understand this category. Their understanding is based on the idea that idioms are a central class among a number of phrasemes. In other words, idioms are the most irregular category. Since, in terms of the Idiomaticity Theory, irregularity manifests itself through *idiomaticity* and *stability*, these features must be more salient and represented more explicitly in idioms than in other phrasemes.

- *Idiomaticity* is understood as a semantic reinterpretation and/or opacity and as being closely related to the notion of figurativeness.
- *Stability* is understood here as an expression's frozenness or lack of combinatorial freedom.

---

14 Cf.: "une règle spéciale et arbitraire demande plus d'effort qu'une règle générale et rationelle" (Bally 1932: 156).

Another important criterion of idioms is that that they are multiword units. These three criteria of the idiom are listed, among other things, in Černyševa (1975, 1980), Fleischer (1997), and Burger, Buhofer, and Sialm (1982), Burger et al. (2007b). Examples (19–20) show the phenomenon of semantic reinterpretation, whereas idiom (21) provides some kind of opacity.

(19)   *to make a silk purse out of a sow's ear*
       'to produce something refined, admirable, or valuable from something which is unrefined, unpleasant, or of little or no value; to completely change something from bad to good'

(20)   *when hell freezes over*
       'never; when one does not believe something will ever happen'

(21)   *to eat crow*
       'to be humiliated by one's defeats or mistakes, to be forced to admit that one is wrong or say that one is sorry, especially when this is embarrassing'

Idioms (19–20) are reinterpreted on the basis of shared cultural knowledge. The knowledge of SILK as something very valuable and of a SOW (or PIG) as something inferior or dirty (as a contrast to SILK) allows the reinterpretation of idiom (19). Both SILK and SOW/PIG evoke some tacit cultural knowledge, since both concepts are supported by cultural codes other than language (cf. e.g. the role of Solomon's silk or of the swine in biblical texts). At the same time, the idiom can be interpreted on the basis of the two frames: a purse being more valuable than the ear of an animal.[15]

Idiom (20) is reinterpreted on the basis of cultural knowledge about HELL, namely the mythological knowledge of hell as a hot place (see chapters 10 and 11 for details about aspects of culture in figurative language). Idiom (21) may be opaque for most speakers who have no knowledge of the fact that 'boiled crow' used to be a metaphor for something extremely disagreeable in the US. However, for other speakers, the idiom may be motivated by its inner form. BLACK, the prototypical colour of the crow, may have contributed to the negative associations.

There is a clear idea, shared by all members of the speech community, that what is literally said in (19) and (20) differs from what is meant, and that there is a link between the two concepts; the source concept has been semantically reinterpreted in order to denote the target concept. In such cases, the impression that

---

[15] Compare Sabban (2008: 233–234).

a given lexical unit is idiomatic is based on semantic reinterpretation. In other cases, the impression of idiomaticity can arise from the fact that a given lexical unit contains both semantic and/or formal elements which are unexplainable in a given context. Therefore, the connection between the concept of CROW in (21), on the one hand, and the actual meaning of this expression, on the other, lacks a clearly comprehensible motivating link.

Idioms can thus be defined as phrasemes with a high degree of idiomaticity and stability. In other words, idioms must be fixed in their lexical structure (within a certain standard variability), and they must be, at the same time, semantically reinterpreted units (i.e. they do not point to the target concept directly but via a source concept) and/or semantically opaque. Proceeding from this definition, it becomes obvious that there is no fixed borderline between idioms and other classes of phrasemes (restricted collocations, grammatical phrasemes etc.), since other groups of conventionalised multiword units also have to be stable and can possess a certain degree of idiomaticity (either opacity or reinterpretation).

Idioms are different from other classes only in that they show a higher degree of irregularity. Thus, it is necessary to find a way of measuring the degree of irregularity. Measuring the degree of irregularity means singling out discrete factors of irregularity, on the one hand, and setting the bottom limit of irregularity (we will use the term *irregularity barrier* here) on the other. It can be assumed that the more factors of irregularity are characteristic of a given phraseme, the higher its degree of irregularity, i.e. the more reasons there are to regard it as an idiom.

Let us turn to the concept of an irregularity barrier and to the relevant factors of irregularity with regard to their role in defining an idiom. Traditional phraseology does not give any adequate answer to the question of how to discriminate idioms from other types of phrasemes, i.e. to the question of how to define the irregularity barrier for idioms. Any attempt to rely on a single feature to be decisive for qualifying a phraseme as an idiom would not be successful, because none of these features is absolutely necessary and sufficient for the whole range of idioms. The quantitative strategy in solving this problem – i.e. establishing a "scale" for each irregularity factor – has also proved unsuccessful: the combination of several factors is not equal to the sum of these factors, and the effect of such a combination is hard to predict. Since idioms are quite a heterogeneous class, neither of these two strategies works. It makes more sense to work with groups of idioms, each of these groups possessing its own set of characteristics which determine their own irregularity barrier (i.e. the barrier of idiomaticity and stability).

Thus, the main idea of the approach advocated by Baranov and Dobrovol'skij (2005, 2008) and adopted here is that it is impossible to lay down a set of necessary and sufficient irregularity features for the whole class of what is intuitively perceived as idioms. However, if we are dealing with a rather homogeneous group of expressions, all of which possess a certain degree of irregularity, we can more easily decide which ones are idioms and which ones are not. In cases where the degree of irregularity is relatively low, we are dealing with other types of phrasemes, mostly restricted collocations (see below). In cases where the degree of irregularity is considerably higher as compared to other members of the same group, we are dealing with idioms. Within every group, there may be special criteria for operationalising the degree of irregularity. In other words, a number of factors can be singled out which must be taken into account when deciding whether or not a phraseme can be classified as an idiom. Let us briefly discuss some of these factors and the groups of idioms correlated with them.

Factor 1. The metaphoric model type. A considerable number of what we call 'phrasemes' in the broad sense contain nouns, some of which are used in many figurative expressions. There is a long tradition of phraseological research on idioms which contain different constituents of one thematic field, such as animals or parts of the body (cf. Rajxštejn 1980: 68–72, 91–94; Fleischer 1997: 173–178; Gréciano 1997: 104–105 among others). For example, constituents like *heart, head, hand, arm, way, day* are used very frequently. Let us call them *key constituents*. From the beginning of phraseological research, there has been a long tradition of analysing idioms containing body part constituents, so-called *somatisms* or *somatic phrasemes*, and it has been well-known for a long time that the human body with its parts is an extensive source domain of the figurative lexicon of many languages. Somatisms have been a favourite topic of cross-linguistic studies and the concept HEAD in idioms has been examined in many ways, in view of its metonymic and metaphoric potential and on the basis of the strongly elaborated semiotisation of HEAD as the location of reason and intellectual activities in Western cultures (cf. the rich literature on the dualism between "cerebrocentrism" and "cardiocentrism").

The question emerges as to what criteria we must rely upon in referring to such expressions as idioms. It is hardly reasonable to consider all these expressions as idioms, because expressions of this kind often show regular semantic (metaphoric and/or metonymic) transformations of the key constituents, which are usually described in dictionaries as secondary meanings of a given noun. In such cases, the whole expression is a regular, compositionally constructed word string.

Thus, it is more natural to regard an expression like *to be not quite right in the head* 'to be a bit stupid' as a free word combination, since the interpretation of the word *head* as 'mind container' is a typical example of a regular and predictable semantic shift. The well-known principle of least effort (Zipf 1949) requires that only those units be qualified as idioms whose metaphoric model (in the sense of

Lakoff 1987b, see chapter 6 for details) is not typical of the given key constituent within the chosen group of phrasemes.

To exemplify this idea, let us take a group of expressions with the key constituent *mind*. There are many expressions in which *mind* operates metaphorically as a kind of instrument with which people can think, make decisions etc., cf. (22). We can hardly regard all expressions of this type as idioms, because the TOOL metaphor is absolutely natural and common for understanding the characteristics of *mind*.

(22)　*to have a mind of his/her own*
　　　'to do what one wants to do, instead of doing or thinking what one is told'

In (23), we are dealing with a different case. The inner form of this idiom presupposes that *mind* is interpreted as a kind of CONTAINER external to a human being, i.e. a container in which people can be located or which they can leave. In such cases, we can speak of an EXTERNAL CONTAINER. This kind of metaphor is not common for understanding the nature of the mind. Therefore, the degree of irregularity is much higher in this case than in (22), and expression (23) must be considered an idiom.

(23)　*to go out of your mind*
　　　'to become so confused, worried, frightened etc. that one feels like becoming crazy'

This factor can be regarded as an operational criterion for distinguishing idioms from other types of phrasemes in the group of conventional figurative units with the constituent *mind*. Based on the idea of the typicality/non-typicality of the underlying metaphoric model, this criterion helps to determine the irregularity barrier for conventional figurative expressions of a phraseme group with a given key constituent.

The next factor which allows a determination of idioms on the basis of the irregularity barrier is based on the idea of measuring the degree of opacity of single phraseme constituents.

Factor 2. The degree of opacity of the constituents. In the phraseological system, there are many expressions with a unique constituent which are by no means all idioms. It would hardly make sense, for example, to regard the Russian expressions (24–26) as idioms.

(24)　*грецкий орех* literally "*грецкий* [an obsolete (synchronically unique) form meaning 'Greek'] nut" 'walnut'

(25)   *перочинный нож* literally "*перочинный* [a unique form meaning 'pen-sharpening'] knife" 'penknife'

(26)   *одержать победу* literally "*одержать* [a unique form meaning 'to gain/score'] victory" 'to gain/score victory, to win'

On the other hand, it is reasonable to consider the English expression *to get down to the nitty-gritty* or the German *keinen Deut besser sein als jmd.* "to be not a *Deut* [an obsolete word meaning 'a small coin'] better than someone" 'to be not one bit better than someone') as idioms. The degree of opacity differs for the former and the latter group of phrasemes. Let us look at some further examples, such as the German expression *keinen Hehl aus etwas machen* "to make no *Hehl* of something" 'to make no secret of something' (the root morpheme of the word-form *Hehl* is not unique in view of words like *verhehlen* 'to conceal, to hide' and *Hehler* 'receiver of stolen goods'). Expressions with such constituents possess a lower degree of irregularity than expressions containing components whose root morphemes are unique, as is the case with the English *get down to the nitty-gritty*, *to and fro* or *kith and kin*.

This does not mean, of course, that expressions like *keinen Hehl aus etwas machen, jemandem den Laufpass geben* (see section 1.4.3) are not idioms. The morphemes of these expressions are not unique, but the word combinations are reinterpreted, which in this case turns out to be a stronger factor of idiomaticity. Factor 2 is relevant only in cases of doubt.

Factor 3. The denotational significance of the opaque constituent. If we implemented only factor 2, disregarding all other factors, the following German expression would not belong to the class of idioms because it is reasonably transparent (English does not provide these kinds of unique nouns): *im Anzug sein* 'to be imminent, approaching, advancing'. Nevertheless, we consider it to be an idiom because another factor plays a role: opaque constituents can vary considerably in their degree of the denoting significance. The semantic focus of this expression lies in its noun constituent, not in the prepositions.

On the other hand, in order to understand word combinations like the Russian examples (8–10), the transparent constituent – that is, *орех* "nut", *нож* "knife" and *победу* "victory[acc]", respectively – is more important for denoting a given concept. Thus, whenever the denotatively important part of an expression is transparent and not reinterpreted, the corresponding word combination is not an idiom, even if the constituent which is less significant for denoting the given concept is opaque.

Factor 3 is also not sufficient for discriminating the class of idioms from other phraseme types. According to this factor, the Russian *не видно ни зги* "one does not even see *zgi*" 'it is too dark to see anything, it is pitch-dark' would not be an idiom, since the constituents *ne vidno* carry most of the actual meaning. Nevertheless, *не видно ни зги* is an idiom, because the lexical function MAGN of *не видно* is not expressed by a single word but by a word combination, namely *ни зги*. Strictly speaking, the real idiom here is *ни зги*, where *ни* ('not even') modifies *зги*, which is a lexical unit that has no autonomous meaning in contemporary Russian.

Factor 4. Non-standard comparatum. The entire class of similes was traditionally grouped under idioms. This is not correct, because there are many similes in every language which are regular to a large extent (cf. *as white as snow*), so that there is no reason to describe them as idioms. However, all conventional similes are figurative units of language and, therefore, belong to the scope of our study. For this reason, we discuss similes (both idioms and non-idioms) in a separate section (see 2.3.2). Here we confine ourselves to the fact that the subtype of idiomatic similes is a fairly homogeneous group, within which one special factor of irregularity is relevant, namely the factor of the basis of comparison. If the comparatum (for example *snow* in *as white as snow*) is a standard, in a certain sense, even prototypical, basis of comparison, the whole expression looks regular and compositional. If the comparatum is absolutely arbitrary and cannot be considered a prototypical example of the given property (cf. *as dead as a doornail*), the whole expression is likely to be understood as an idiom.

To sum up, we would like to point out two facts: first, there are no clear boundaries between idioms and other phrasemes, e.g. restricted collocations or proverbs. Borderline cases can be found in every language, and in every thematic or semantic domain. Second, it is practical and convenient for every investigation concerned with conventional figurative units to have some operational criteria for discriminating between idioms, which are the central class of the phraseological system, and other types of phrasemes. So it is important, for the purposes of our study, to know how to single out idioms when collecting empirical data because among all the types of conventional expressions that make up the empirical basis of the further analysis, idioms form the only class in which members are figurative *per se*.

2.3.2 Similes

As already mentioned, we will discuss similes separately from the class of idioms, though many of them satisfy all the relevant criteria of idioms. Similes can be singled out by their specific structure of comparison, consisting of the nomination of the relevant features, *tertium comparationis* (the topic of comparison, *white* in example 27) and the *comparatum* (the vehicle of comparison, *snow* in this example, a noun phrase in most cases). The two parts are connected via a conjunction or particle (*as* and *like*). Within a given context, the *comparandum* as the third part must also be considered (*shirt* in *the shirt is white as snow*) (see e.g. Žukov 1978; Grzybek 1994c; Norrick 1986, 1987). The entire class of similes was traditionally considered to belong to the category of idioms. However, there is a marked difference between similes like (27), on the one hand, and (28), on the other.

(27) *as white as snow*
      'very clearly white'

(28) *(as) dead as a doornail*
      'dead beyond any doubt; no longer effective, valid or interesting; something has failed completely'

The conjunction *as* (or *such as/like*) makes explicit the crucial component of the reinterpretation procedure (pointing to the syntactic factors as motivating links; for more detail, see section 4.8), which results in a decrease in the degree of idiomaticity as compared to metaphors (including metaphoric idioms).

There is extensive discussion about the relationship between similes and metaphors. In the "traditional view" (according to Aristotle's so-called "Comparison Theory"),[16] metaphors are "elliptical similes" – the metaphor *Achilles is a lion* is seen as a short version of the simile *Achilles is like a lion*. In contrast to this, it has been put forward that "metaphors are stronger than similes" and therefore cannot be short forms of similes. These findings were supported by various experiments. Cf. e.g. Glucksberg and Keysar (1993); Kennedy and Chiappe (1999); Chiappe and Kennedy (2000, 2001). We will not go deeper into these questions here.

The relatively low degree of idiomaticity characteristic of similes leads to the fact that some additional factors of idiomaticity and/or stability are needed to classify similes with the conjunctions *as*, *like* or *as if* as idioms. Hence, it seems to be unreasonable to regard (27) as an idiom, because each of its constituents is used in its literal meaning. The only feature which makes (27) a kind of phraseme, and not just a free word combination, is its stability. This expression is "fixed", which is to say that its usage is conventionalised. Although people can refer to other white things as prototypical specimens of something very white, the usual

---

[16] There is a voluminous literature discussing the "Comparison Theory", now attacking Aristotle (e.g. Black 1962: 35–37, 1993: 31; Searle 1979; Johnson 1981, 1987), now defending him (Fogelin 1994). See also Ross (1993), for an overview.

way of expressing this idea would be to use (27) as a conventional, prefabricated expression. Thus, similes such as (27) belong to the group of phrasemes, but they are not irregular enough to be considered idioms.

In contrast to this, we are dealing with an idiom in (28) because the choice of *doornail* as the prototype of dead beings is completely unpredictable. Assigning the reading 'something absolutely dead' to the word *doornail* violates, strictly speaking, the combinatorial rules, because artefacts can be neither alive nor dead. The entire simile gives the impression of a rather irregular word combination; it is highly idiosyncratic and arbitrary. Maybe the choice of *doornail* as the prototypical dead being is, at least partly, based on the phonetic structure, i.e. the alliteration of *d-* in *dead* and *doornail* may have been the decisive criterion for this choice. There are similar alliterative phrases, e.g. *deaf as a doornail*, *dour as a doornail* or *dead as a dodo*, etc. There are also many other examples among English similes (as well as among similes of other languages) in which the phonetic structure plays an important part, cf., for example, rhythm and rhyme in *drunk as a skunk* 'very drunk', or *kl-*alliteration in Dutch *klaar als een klontje* "clear as a piece of rock candy" 'very clear'. Being additional factors of stability, such specific features of phonetic structure contribute to the irregularity of the word combination in question. The complexity of the form is a factor in its stability.

Simile (28) contains an additional semantic factor of irregularity, namely the possibility of being understood in two different ways, as referring to people or to things (campaigns, projects, etc.). An additional semantic procedure is necessary for interpretation in the second reading. Not only does the word *doornail* appear in a unique reading, but the word *dead* also has to be reinterpreted if the reading 'something has failed completely' is activated. This kind of additional reinterpretation is a strong irregularity factor, which make similes idiomatic. As a contrast, we may examine example (29).

(29)   *as pure as the driven snow*
       'absolutely pure in one's moral character and behaviour; innocent, virginal, without any sexual experiences'

In example (29), the whole expression is reinterpreted, including its "left part" – the adjective *pure* does not mean a physical state, the sense suggested by *snow*. The interpretation of *driven snow* is twofold: this kind of snow is really fresh and clean; it has not become polluted yet. Therefore, there is a similarity between the untouched snow and an "untouched", virginal, innocent person. Furthermore, SNOW evokes the concept WHITE, the symbolic functions of which are 'innocence, chastity, virginity', directly corresponding to the meaning of *pure* in this simile.

Expression (30) contains the unique constituent *Honigkuchenpferd* "honey-cake-horse"; this word exists only in this simile.

(30) German *grinsen wie ein Honigkuchenpferd* "to grin like a honeycake-horse [gingerbread-horse]"
'to have a big smile on one's face, so that one looks silly or too pleased with oneself'

In such cases, we can speak of constituent opacity. This is an additional irregularity factor. Not only do speakers have to create a motivating link between the intensity of smiling and the word "honeycake-horse" – a link that does not exist in reality; they also have to memorise a non-existing word, namely *Honigkuchenpferd*. Although all its components – *Honig* 'honey', *Kuchen* 'cake' and *Pferd* 'horse' (and the compound *Honigkuchen* 'honeycake') – are normal German words (which makes the word *Honigkuchenpferd* understandable), they never usually appear in such a combination. Therefore, idiom (30) is evidently figurative and belongs to the class of idioms.

The degree of opacity is a powerful classificatory criterion within the structurally homogenous class of similes. According to Burger (2015: 56), the comparatum is transparent in an idiom such as German *flink wie ein Wiesel* "nimble as a weasel" 'very nimble, agile, quick'. Therefore, this simile is a collocation rather than an idiom. In contrast, the expression *dumm wie Bohnenstroh* "stupid as bean-straw" 'very stupid' is partly an idiom because the comparatum is not transparent in connection with *dumm* 'stupid'.

The discrimination between similes which are idioms and similes which are not is crucial for the theory of phraseology. As for the aims of our analysis and its theoretical implications, this discrimination is less decisive. From our point of view, non-idiomatic similes, like *as white as snow*, are situated on the borderline of the domain of figurative language and, therefore, belong to the periphery of the domain under investigation. As phrasemes, i.e. conventional expressions, they resemble certain restricted collocations (see below). Their conventional nature is based only on factors of stability, not on those of idiomaticity. Still, there is a mental image standing behind these linguistic expressions (in the form of an explicit reference to the entity lexically fixed in the comparatum) which we consider a crucial criterion for regarding them as figurative units of language.

In this connection, we would also like to point to the problem of describing similes with a constituent denoting an animal (cf. case studies in chapter 13).

Often the "left part" of a simile[17] explicates a feature of the animal in question which is supported by cultural traditions. In such cases the simile in question is strongly idiomatic because the choice of the animal is arbitrary, grounded not in reality but in cultural conventions (cf. *as wise as an owl* 'very wise').

Similes are good examples of the difference between "metaphoric motivation" and "symbolic motivation" (see chapter 4 for detail), though sometimes it is only a matter of degree, cf. (31–32).

(31) English *to eat like a horse*
'to overeat, to eat without restraint, to eat a huge quantity'

(32) French *manger comme un loup*
"to eat like a wolf"
'to eat very much and in a greedy manner, to eat voraciously'

Simile (31) may be regarded as based on the observation that horses really do need a lot of fodder. Compared with people, they give the impression of eating incessantly, without restraint. By contrast, the image that a wolf eats voraciously is not supported by observing the animal (32). This image is strongly supported by cultural symbolism. It goes back to the semiotisation of the wolf in various cultural codes, from the Bible to fairy tales and modern comics. All of them establish the conventional knowledge of the gluttonous animal, one which even devours human beings (cf. chapter 13). The Dutch verb *wolven* 'to eat voraciously' provides the same symbolic knowledge.

Discussing such issues in detail is interesting from the perspective of linguistic theory, as it shows that phenomena like figurativeness and phraseology, or figurativeness and idiomaticity, are of different natures, in spite of their relationship.

2.3.3 Restricted collocations

Traditionally, the term *collocation* (also *habitual collocation* or, more commonly, *restricted collocation*) has been regarded as an umbrella term which covers a

---

[17] The terms "left part" and "right part" are colloquial technical expressions that we use here for reasons of convenience. Strictly speaking, these expressions can only be applied to similes in some European languages. Japanese similes have the inverse word order, where the feature in question follows the comparatum. *yō* is the particle 'as, like', *no yō ni* means 'in this way'. Cf. 貝のようにをつぐむ (*kai no yō ni kuchi wo tsugumu*) "shellfish – in the way of/like – mouth – to close [to close the mouth like a shellfish]" 'to keep one's mouth shut, saying nothing'.

group of quite heterogeneous phrasemes. The term is commonly used to refer to word combinations that co-occur habitually[18] but are fully transparent. Normally one element of the collocation has a specialised meaning that occurs only in combination with the other element, cf. (33).

(33) *in broad daylight*

It is assumed that in most cases there is a *(collocative) base*, used in its literal sense (cf. *daylight* in example 33), and a *collocator* (or *collocate*), which is arbitrary to a certain extent: *broad* is the only appropriate adjective here (and not *large/huge/wide*). On the one hand, especially in language learning, great store is set on the phenomenon that one of the constituents of a given word string is more or less unpredictable and does not follow regular rules of semantic combinatorics (cases like French *se brosser les dents* "to brush one's teeth" vs. German *sich die Zähne putzen* "to clean one's teeth", Lithuanian *dantis plauti* "to wash the teeth" or Japanese 歯を磨く *(ha wo migaku)* "to polish the teeth" (cf. e.g. Hausmann 2004: 309–310). On the other hand, restricted collocations are an important matter of linguistic theory (especially with regard to phraseology and lexicography, cf. e.g. Mel'čuk 1998 and Fontenelle 1998).[19]

Of all collocations, a structurally homogeneous type is traditionally singled out, namely the so-called *light verb constructions* or *support verb constructions* (called *Funktionsverbgefüge* in German), such as examples (34–36).

(34) English *to make/take a decision*

(35) German *eine Entscheidung treffen/fällen*
      "to meet/to fell a decision"

(36) a. French *prendre une décision* "to take a decision"
      b. Greek *παίρνω μια απόφαση* "to take a decision" all meaning 'to decide something'

---

[18] The term *collocation* is also used in a very different sense, e.g. in computational linguistics. In several studies, *collocation* is primarily understood as the occurrence of two or more words within a short space of ezach other in a text; i.e. the term is equated with the co-occurrence of words in general, irrespective of their recurrence (their fixedness or convention of use) (e.g. Sinclair 1991).
[19] There are also dictionaries of collocations such as Crowther, Dignen, and Lea (2002) and Häcki Buhofer et al. (2014).

The stability of this kind of collocation results, above all, from the fact that the semantically "empty" element is chosen arbitrarily. It is, for instance, hardly possible to explain why the English verbs *make* or *take*, the German verbs *treffen* and *fällen*, the French verb *prendre* or the Greek verb παίρνω, respectively, have been chosen from the great number of verbs which are able to express the same general idea, namely 'to initiate something', such as English *do, produce*, German *machen* 'to make', *nehmen* 'to take', etc.[20]

With regard to the German example (35), *eine Entscheidung fällen*, we should point out that the verb *fällen* 'to fell' is not "empty". A decision that is "felled" is made deliberately; it is irreversible, as if it were a tree that had been struck with an axe and felled.

It is the arbitrary nature of the verb that determines the irregularity of a restricted collocation (cf. Bally's term *conditionnement arbitraire* "arbitrary conditioning", Bally 1932: 125). Nevertheless, certain "post factum combinatorial tendencies" can be revealed even in this domain (for more detail, see Apresjan 2004).

Some collocations contain unique constituents, which make them quite irregular. However, this irregularity is not strong enough to qualify these units as idioms. Here, the unique constituents contribute to stability rather than to figurativeness. Let us recall the Russian expressions (24–26) *грецкий орех*, *перочинный нож* and *одержать победу*.

Restricted collocations often contain reinterpreted elements, cf. (34–36) or the Russian collocations (37–39), where support verbs are semantically transformed, in the sense that their semantic structures are strongly reduced.

(37) Russian *принимать во внимание* "to receive/take into consideration"
'to take into consideration'

(38) Russian *дать знать* "to give to know"
'to let know'

---

20 Since our cross-linguistically oriented study includes two non-Indo-European languages, Finnish and Japanese, it is interesting to note that these two languages possess a similar type of verb structure. The support verb, however, does not show the same irregularity (and diversity) as in examples (36–38). Finnish uses the verb *tehdä* 'to make' in by far the most cases (*tehdä ratkaisu* "to make [a] decision"). Things are different in Japanese insofar as in many cases there is no choice between single verbs and constructions with a functional verb (the so-called *suru-verbs*; *suru* can be translated by 'to do, to give'), cf. 決定する (*kettei suru*) "decision – do" 'to decide'. Of the Indo-European languages analysed here, it is only the Low German dialect WML that does not make use of this type of restricted collocations.

(39) не давать в обиду кого-л. "not to give someone into offence"
      'not to let someone be offended'

The well-known apparatus of lexical functions is used for the linguistic description of the irregularity of a collocation resulting from the arbitrary choice of its constituents (cf. Žolkovskij and Mel'čuk 1967). The fact that a huge number of collocations can be constructed with the help of a limited set of lexical functions shows that the degree of irregularity of a collocation is fairly low in comparison to the irregularity of an idiom. Most collocations of this type are not figurative at all. This is the reason why we do not analyse this type of phraseme except in a few individual cases.

There are some collocations with a VP structure similar to (34–36) in which a certain degree of figurativeness can be found, e.g. *to set aside something*. The word *aside* can be traced back to *side* and may evoke certain spatial associations. Taken in its actual meaning, this collocation refers to an abstract action and can be regarded as motivated via the image of a physical action. However, its figurativeness is very weak.

There is still another structural type of collocation which has to be regarded as figurative. Consider (40–42).

(40) German *blöde Kuh* "stupid cow" 'a stupid woman'

(41) English *a busy bee* 'a very busy person'

(42) English *a sly fox* 'a very sly person'

These expressions are situated on the borderline between restricted collocations and idioms. What makes them similar to idioms is that they are based on semantic reinterpretation. Because they denote an animal in their literal reading, they are reinterpreted in the sense of denoting a person. They are, however, not entirely idiomatic, because their adjectival constituents, which carry the most salient part of the meaning, pointing to the relevant characteristic feature of the denoted person, are used in their literal sense ('stupid', 'busy' or 'sly' in the examples above). As a whole, they are hardly the result of an overall reinterpretation of an expression taken literally, but the result of adding a literally interpreted adjective to a reinterpreted noun. The reinterpreted noun can often also be used with the same meaning without the accompanying adjective, cf. German *sie ist eine Kuh* "she is a cow" 'she is very stupid' or English *he is a fox* 'he is very sly'.

Cases like these will be partly taken into account when analysing the empirical data. The crucial criterion is that the collocations under consideration contain an element which fits into the overall picture of the specifics of figurativeness in a given language and culture. We are dealing with gradual differences of cultural impact here. A cow may give the impression of being 'stupid', which can lead to a collocation like (40). However, this estimation of the animal is culturally bound; it would have no place, for instance, in the traditional culture of India, where bovine animals are considered holy beings. Cultural interrelations emerge more clearly in example (41). Since antiquity, bees have been used as a base of comparison for 'diligence' and 'busyness', which has left traces e.g. in literature (cf. Waldemar Bonsels' successful tale "Die Biene Maja und ihre Abenteuer", 1912, and its cartoon version). Finally, the FOX in (42) can be regarded as a cultural symbol, standing for 'cunning'. The knowledge of the link between FOX as a symbol in cultural codes (in fables or beast epics as well as in various kinds of everyday symbolisations, cf. section 4.6) and figurative language seems to be even more present than is the case in (41). Collocations containing cultural symbols are of especially great interest for the aims of our study (see chapter 11 for more details).

2.3.4 Proverbs

From the viewpoint of folklore studies, proverbs are elements of a code of folk culture; they are the subjects of paremiology. From the viewpoint of linguistics, proverbs are phrasemes, and, as such, elements of the lexicon; studies on the linguistic properties of proverbs belong to the field of phraseology. There is a considerable amount of literature which attempts to find an adequate definition that can cover all the specifics of the proverb: a generally acknowledged definition, however, has not yet been arrived at. For a survey of the wide variety of scientific approaches to the proverb, see e.g. Mieder (1982–1993, 2009), Cram (1983), Norrick (1985), Kleiber (1989), Grzybek (1994a, 1994b), Hrisztova-Gotthardt and Varga (2016). For a cognitive view on proverbs, based on the tenets of cognitive science, see e.g. Gibbs and Beitel (1995), Gibbs, Colston, and Johnson (1996), Gibbs (2001b), Honeck and Temple (1996), Katz and Feretti (2001). Cross-linguistic aspects of proverb research and corpus-based approaches are discussed e.g. in Steyer (2012, 2019), Ďurčo, Steyer, and Hein (2017). Some features of the proverb will be discussed in this section. Firstly, we attempt to discover the properties in regard to which proverbs are different from other phrasemes, mainly from idioms. Secondly, we want to show that proverbs have some points in common with other phrasemes.

The existence of non-figurative proverbs has been mentioned in section 1.4.3, e.g. *Every beginning is hard* 'it is always difficult at the beginning'. The discrimination of proverbs and idioms is relevant for the theory of phraseology. For the CFLT, however, the distinction between figurative and non-figurative units is of more importance.

The parameters of stability and idiomaticity established above (2.3.1) make it possible to distinguish idioms from many other groups of phrasemes, but they are not applicable to differentiating between idioms and proverbs because the latter are current in a more or less stable form and are also idiomatic in most cases. Attempts to find distinguishing features between proverbs and idioms often give priority to the formal side. The main structural property of proverbs, their sentence structure,[21] is compared with structural properties of many idioms. Most idioms are phrases (component parts of a sentence) and can be classified as either verb phrases, noun phrases or prepositional phrases. In the traditional interpretation, only phrases and sentence-like predicative units such as *someone's heart is in the right place* (propositional forms) are considered to be idioms.

Patterns similar to sentences in their form and functions have traditionally been excluded from the class of idioms and referred to the domain of paremiology. There are, however, some borderline cases, since proverbs can also be used to comment on a very specific situation. For example, we could say *the devil is/lies in the detail* while struggling with serious problems caused by apparently small, harmless things that are often overlooked. Therefore, this figurative unit could be classified as an idiom with the function of an utterance. Because it expresses a kind of folk wisdom or universal truth, however, it must be classified as a proverb as well.

A phraseme like *the coast is clear*, used in order to tell someone that there is no danger of interference from the authorities, is certainly not a proverb but an idiom, in spite of its sentence structure. The same holds for examples like (45–46) and similar expressions. The differentiation between such phrasemes with sentence structure ("sentence idioms" or "speech formulae") and proverbs does not take place on the syntactic level but is mainly based on semiotic, semantic and pragmatic parameters (cf. Dobrovol'skij 2011a). Let us look at the major distinguishing features with the help of some examples:

(43) *every dog has its day*
 'even the most unimportant person has a time in his/her life when he/she is successful and being noticed'

---

[21] Japanese is an exception in this regard. There are some Japanese proverbs that do not qualify as sentences in their narrow definition (Takeda 1995: 336).

(44) *beggars can't be choosers*
'in a bad situation in which you are limited to only one or two choices of things to do, you have to accept that you cannot have what you would like most'

(45) *tell that to the horse marines*
'that is incredible; don't expect me to believe that!'

(46) *the die is cast*
'an event has happened or an important decision has been taken that cannot be reversed'

The distinguishing features are to be found on different levels – in the plane of content, in pragmatics, and in the semiotic status of the proverb, although there is overlap between these features.[22] We propose the following parameters in order to distinguish proverbs (43–44) from the group of idioms with sentence structure (45–46).

(i) The first distinguishing criterion is the existence of a *universal quantifier* (or *all-operator*) in the content plane of the phraseme in question. Proverbs are general statements that are believed to express a universal truth (sometimes called "folk wisdom").[23] This is expressed on the surface level by words like *every* (cf. example 43), *all, any, each, always, never, no*. Proverbs refer to shared knowledge about rules governing social behaviour and human co-existence. In contrast to this, sentence idioms do not have a generalising function.

(ii) The second criterion is the presence of the illocutionary force of "recommendation/ recommending or explanation" in the semantics of proverbs and the lack of such force in the illocutionary semantics of sentence idioms or speech formulae. Proverbs recommend how to behave in certain situations or comment on relevant properties of a given situation. They provide moral support for an argument or action by reference to a generalised proposition. Speech formulae only comment on an ongoing, individual situation.

---

[22] Parameters of the plane of expression, often quoted in discussing the differences between idioms and proverbs, can be passed over here. Factors of stabilisation by means of common poetic devices like metre, rhyme, alliteration, assonance, are often ascribed to proverbs proper, but they can also be found in other classes of conventional figurative units, e.g. in similes and binomials (belonging to the class of idioms).

[23] The assumption that a proverb is generally "true" does not conflict with the existence of antonymous proverbs (cf. Kleiber 1999).

2.3 Types of phrasemes and their constitutive criteria — 69

(iii) The third criterion is a greater discourse dependence of sentence idioms as compared to proverbs. In this sense, we can speak of a discursive autonomy of proverbs and a discursive embedding of idioms. The discursive embedding of sentence idioms (some of which are traditionally labelled "sayings") is often, but not always, marked with the help of deictic elements, cf. *that* in idiom (45). In contrast to this, even if applied to a particular situation, proverbs, being general statements and impersonal in meaning, avoid using deictic elements, which tie an utterance to a current situation. The discourse dependence of sentence idioms consists in the fact that they are illocutionary, evoked either by the communicant's preceding remark or by any other, not necessarily verbalised, aspect of the situation.

Some sentence idioms are accompanied by a nearly identically worded VP idiom (cf. *The battle lines are drawn* 'people involved in an argument, competition, election etc. are ready to start and have decided on the best plan to achieve their aims' vs. *to draw the battle lines* or *to mark out the battle lines* 'to state one's intentions very clearly, to name one's supporters and opponents, who can be politicians, businessmen etc.'). This is another argument in favour of including such expressions in the class of idioms. A description of the corresponding pairs as units belonging to different classes would hardly be reasonable.

On the other hand, there are many proverbs that are accompanied by correlating idioms. Such correlates are mostly formed via a reduction of the proverb's lexical elements. It is not necessary to realise the whole proverb; some elements of the proverb are used allusively and evoke the whole proverb and its main idea, cf. proverb (47a) and its shortened idiom version (47b).

(47) a. *a watched pot never boils*
'if you are impatient and want something to happen too eagerly, it seems to take a long time or does not happen at all'
b. *a watched pot*
'something you want to happen too eagerly, which seems to take a long time or does not happen at all'

These cases are quite frequent. Many idioms have their origin in a proverb that is possibly obsolete, following the same schema and? reducing some elements. The idiom *the last straw* 'a slight addition to a difficulty or annoyance that ultimately makes it unbearable', for example, is a reduced version of the proverb *it is the last straw that breaks the camel's back*. Furthermore, the reduced version may result in a sentence idiom (similar to *The die is cast*) which comments on a special situation (cf. (48). In some cases, there are no clear borderlines; a lexical item may be both an idiom and a proverb.

(48) a. *when the cat is away, the mice will play*
'When someone in authority is not there, people can enjoy themselves or do what they want'
b. *the cat is away*
'someone in authority is not there'. For example: *We ought to do a bit of work this afternoon, even though the cat's away.* (Longman ID 1998: 54).

To sum up, proverbs have to be distinguished from idioms, on the one hand, but they have to be regarded as a class of phrasemes closely related to idioms, on the other. In terms of figurativeness, it is less important to decide whether we are dealing with a proverb or a sentence idiom in every case. It is significant, however, to determine to what extent the unit in question is image based. In all the languages analysed here, there are proverbs and similar kinds of paremias (commonplaces and the like) that are not figurative but present a good deal of regularity in their structure. Thus, it is important for further investigations to distinguish the following units, and establish whether they are types of *routine formula* (49) or *tautological commonplaces* (50):

(49) *it's a small world*
'said when you are surprised because you have met someone you know and it was very unlikely that you would meet them, or when you have found out that someone is connected to you in a way that you did not expect'

(50) *boys will be boys*
'it is natural for boys to be noisy and untidy, or to behave badly and do things that are not sensible'

Gibbs (1994: 345–347) calls cases like (50) *colloquial tautologies*.[24] Wierzbicka (2003) even speaks of "truisms" and shows that they are not based on pragmatic implicatures but are largely culturally based.

Proverbs reveal all types of cultural phenomena in figurative language (see chapter 10). In addition to aspects of material culture (e.g. by means of constitu-

---

[24] Gibbs (1994: 345) maintains that the tautology *Boys will be boys* has no equivalent in German and other languages, but he fails to see that the original version *Sunt pueri* is well known by traditionally educated middle-class intellectuals.

ents denoting idioethnic or other culture-specific realia), their intertextual relations are particularly important. This is because many proverbs (being simple texts themselves) are directly interrelated with other culturally relevant texts. Above all, proverbs are cultural models, giving information about how to behave or which values are upheld in a given culture. This property of the proverb is not shared by the members of any other class of conventional figurative units.

For example, the proverb *spare the rod and spoil the child*, "[a] Victorian adage which has been rejected by later generations of parents" (Gulland and Hinds-Howell 2001: 142), is one such model that reveals socio-cultural concepts of former times. However, we can even examine changes in such cultural models through the modern reinterpretations of traditional proverbs. For instance, the Japanese proverb かわいい子には旅をさせよ (*kawaii ko ni wa tabi wo saseyo*) "send your beloved child travelling" (cf. Takashima 1981: 292) once meant roughly the same as *spare the rod and spoil the child* 'a child's character will be ruined by his parents' indulgence', or, to be more precise: 'a child (a boy) should go through bitter experiences, experience the hardships of society, far away from home'. Nowadays, the proverb is used in the sense of *travel broadens the mind* 'parents have to make every effort to make foreign travels possible for their children'.

Proverbs play an important role in the present study for two reasons: firstly, because many of them are figurative and show various kinds of motivation, and secondly, because of their far-reaching cultural significance.

2.4 Summary

The results of the analysis presented in this chapter are summarised in Table 1.

Table 1: Types of lexical units with regard to figurativeness

	Term	Examples	Not figurative	Weakly figurative	Figurative
1	Figurative compound	*scapegoat* *fig leaf*			+
2	Figurative simplex	*to blacken (someone's reputation)* *snaky*			+
3	Figurative idiom	*to lose one's head* *the calm before the storm* *full steam ahead*			+
	Non-figurative idiom	*to and fro* *by and large*	+		

Table 1 (continued)

	Term	Examples	Not figurative	Weakly figurative	Figurative
4	Idiomatic simile	to eat like a horse as pure as the driven snow (as) dead as a doornail			+
	Non-idiomatic simile	(as) white as snow		+	
5	Figurative proverb	beggars can't be choosers when the cat is away, the mice will play no rose without a thorn			+
	Non-figurative proverb	every beginning is hard opposites attract each other tastes differ	+		
6	Restricted collocation	in broad daylight to lay the table a busy bee		+	
7	Constructional phraseme	the ADJ$_{superl}$ (simplest etc.) thing in the world for the sake of N to take and V to go and V	+		
8	Grammatical phraseme	not only..., but also and so on of course	+		
9	Phrasal verb	to carry away to shop around	+		
10	Situational phraseme	nice to meet you how do you do beg your pardon	+		

3 On the cross-linguistic equivalence of idioms

3.1 Preliminary remarks

Cross-linguistic and cross-cultural analysis of conventional figurative units is central to the present study. We prefer to use idioms as our empirical data for two reasons. First, idioms belong to the core of conventional figurative units (cf. 2.3.1). They are therefore well suited to exemplify relevant ideas concerning cross-linguistic equivalence in the domain of CFL. Secondly, there is a rich tradition in cross-linguistic idiom analysis, which can be made use of (cf. Rajxštejn 1980; Hessky 1987; Gréciano 1989; Ďurčo 1994; Korhonen 1995, 1996, 2007; Földes 1996; Dobrovol'skij 1999a, 2002; Šichová 2013b; Mellado Blanco 2015; Mellado Blanco, Berty, and Olza 2017; Cotta Ramusino and Mollica 2020 among others).

Questions regarding the cross-linguistic equivalence of idioms are relevant for both theoretical and practical tasks. The similarities and contrasts found in this domain need explanation in terms of their linguistic and/or conceptual structure. These similarities and contrasts are often grounded in culture.

This chapter discusses some general issues of cross-linguistic idiom analysis. Although the term *cross-linguistic* competes with terms like *contrastive, confrontative* or even *comparative*, we prefer the common English term *cross-linguistic* to the other terms (see below). To discover all the types of cross-linguistic differences between idioms which are intuitively perceived as being semantically similar is the most important aim of cross-linguistic idiom analysis. Achieving this aim helps to distinguish real cross-linguistic equivalents from pseudo-equivalents and to explain the nature of idiom semantics, syntactics, and pragmatics (three well-known semiotic dimensions).

Methods and tools of cross-linguistic idiom analysis vary widely, depending on their aims. Previous studies focused on general and fundamental questions about the nature of idioms, such as questions about the relations between idiosyncratic phenomena and universal idiom features (compare, for example, Dobrovol'skij 1988, 1992; Abraham 1989). In recent decades, the cognitive and cultural aspects of these relationships have become especially crucial (Dobrovol'skij and Piirainen 2009; Dobrovolo'skij 2016a).

Various questions arise from this field of research. We will briefly look at possible causes of cross-linguistic similarities and then focus on subtle cross-linguistic contrasts between seemingly identical idioms. Cross-linguistic similarities in the area of figurative expressions have attracted the attention of researchers for a long time. Attempts at explaining cross-linguistic similarities of all kinds (including non-figurative elements) usually either highlight the *contact linguistic model* (which explains restricted regional borrowings, often due to bilingualism, and includes the increasing *influence of English* in the context of globalisation) or *polygenesis*, which can apply to idioms based on common human experience. However, it seems reasonable to assume that there is no mono-causality; rather, various factors must have come together in producing parallel (equivalent) idioms, leading to polygenesis (including independent recourse to the same ideas) and monogenesis (including diverse kinds of borrowing processes).

Cross-linguistic contrasts must also be questioned. They can go back to coincidences of metaphorisation, to consistent preferences of certain conceptual metaphors (in the sense of Lakoff) by the linguistic communities in question, i.e. to cognitive factors, or to relevant differences in the given cultures. It is evident that answering these questions requires an interdisciplinary approach. Research of this kind would contribute not only to the theory of phraseology but also to Cognitive Linguistics and the semiotics of culture.

However, there are also more practically oriented tasks in the field of cross-linguistic idiom analysis, that is, to develop appropriate descriptive tools for evaluating semantically similar idioms of both source language (L1) and target language (L2) in terms of their *functional equivalence*. Using empirical data from Russian and German, we will discuss relevant issues of cross-linguistic equivalence and, in particular, focus on factors which have to be taken into account while looking for an L2-equivalent of a given L1-idiom (see 3.3 and 3.4 below).

Functionally adequate equivalents are defined here as lexical items of both source and target language (L1 and L2) which can be used in the same situations. We claim that in spite of obvious progress in the description of Russian and German phraseology, there are still major difficulties to overcome in solving both the theoretical and practical problems of comparison between idioms in these two languages. Existing dictionaries and available cross-linguistic ("contrastive") descriptions of German and Russian idioms (e.g. Graf 1954; Edlička and Rubinštejn 1959; Binovič and Grišin 1975; Škljarov, Eckert, and Engelke 1977; Petermann, Hansen-Kokoruš, and Bill 1995; Šekasjuk 2010; Mal'ceva 2011; Semenova 2011)[1] do not allow us to find parallel expressions which can be used equally in all the relevant cases, i.e. the question of functional equivalence has not been answered so far (for a detailed survey and some recent developments, see Dobrovol'skij 1999b and 2013). To find functionally adequate equivalents, we

---

[1] There are also some online resources containing German phrasemes and their Russian (pseudo)counterparts; cf. e.g. http://de.wiktionary.org/wiki/Kategorie:Sprichwort. German and Russian idiom can sporadically also be found in corpus-based internet resources such as https://de.glosbe.com.

need additional empirical data concerning the actual usage of idioms and their thorough interpretation against a sound theoretical background.

The main problem in this field comes from the fact that most idioms which have traditionally been regarded as absolute parallels are, in reality, far from being equivalent. There are several possible explanations for this phenomenon. First of all, the further we progress in semantic analysis, the more items of the lexicon we find that are language-specific, because "every language draws semantic distinctions which other languages do not" (Wierzbicka 1996: 15) (cf. section 10.1).

Let us first look at bilingual idiom dictionaries. The German idiom *Eulen nach Athen tragen* "to carry owls to Athens" is traditionally described as an equivalent of the Russian idiom *ехать в Тулу со своим самоваром* "to go to Tula with one's own samovar" and of the English idiom *to carry coals to Newcastle*. Although the cultural specifics of the Russian idiom (due to the constituents *Tula* and *samovar*) as well as that of the English idiom (due to the constituent *Newcastle*) have often been pointed out, the semantic equivalence of these idioms has never been questioned. Compare the dictionary entrances (1–3).

(1) *Eulen nach Athen tragen* 'везти что-л. туда, где этого имеется в избытке' [to bring something to a place where it exists in abundance]; wörtlich „везти сов в Афины"; vgl. *ехать в Тулу со своим самоваром* (Binovič and Grišin 1975: 160)

(2) *Eulen nach Athen tragen* (*fig.*) to carry coals to Newcastle; to take milk to the cow (Taylor and Gottschalk 1978: 121)

(3) *carry coals to Newcastle* [...] 'возить что-л. туда, где этого и так достаточно' [to bring something to a place where it is sufficiently available] vgl. *ехать в Тулу со своим самоваром* (Kunin 1984: 156)

These lexicographical descriptions are based on the principal semantic equivalence of these idioms. However, Lubensky's (2013) dictionary deals with this pair of idioms in a different way. The Russian and English idioms are not presented as equivalents; instead, the sign ≈ is used to point out that there is a certain semantic similarity between them.

(4) *в Тулу со своим самоваром не ездят* [...] 'there is no need to bring sth. to a place that already has an abundance of it': ≈ why <don't> carry water to the river. Cf. it's useless to carry <it would be like carrying> coals to Newcastle (Lubensky 2013: 654)

The assumption of an equivalence [dictionary entries (1–3)] is therefore incorrect, as can be easily proved by taking into consideration the contextual embedding of these idioms.

The question arises, first of all, as to why in most cases cross-linguistic equivalents can be found in dictionaries but cannot normally be used in translation situations. In general, this is due to the fact that phraseology is full of pseudo-equivalents. This has been shown by text examples of the three idioms, cf. Dobrovol'skij and Piirainen (2009). Here, we merely highlight two text examples from the British National Corpus where it is not possible to translate the idiom *to carry coals to Newcastle* with the help of the Russian idiom *ехать в Тулу со своим самоваром*.

> The artists themselves sometimes had a Jekyll-and-Hyde career, the prime example being the Australian bass-baritone Peter Dawson, who for many years dressed up as a Scotsman and hijacked Sir Harry Lauder's songs, touring Scottish music-halls under the name Hector Grant. He was evidently so successful at "*carrying the coals to Newcastle*", making a ten-year career out of the impersonation and rerecording Sir Harry's repertoire for Sir Harry's record company, that when the pair met at the recording studio in 1920 and their producer told Sir Harry about the deception, he simply refused to believe it. Another form of deception which affected the consumer occurred in the early days of LPs. (B2Y)
>
> When Bunny clicked his fingers, signifying the rise of the curtain, Geoffrey, the student, was supposed to imitate the sound of a gun being fired. Given his military background, such a task should have been in the nature of *coals to Newcastle*, but in the event he was scrutinising his reflection in the mirror above the fireplace. Bunny banged on a table instead and the new girl gave a convincing scream. (FNU)

The reason is that the Russian idiom *ехать в Тулу со своим самоваром* "to go to Tula with one's own samovar" means something like 'to bring or send certain objects to a place where there are already many objects of that kind',[2] whereas the German idiom *Eulen nach Athen tragen* "to carry owls to Athens" and the English idiom *to carry coals to Newcastle* can also be used to point out that it is not reasonable to present certain mental entities (ideas, artistic achievements, etc.) as being new if they are already well known in a given place. These differences seem to be connected with the image component of the semantic structure of the idiom: *samovar* as an artefact predisposes the usage conditions to a certain extent. It is also significant that the noun *samovar* is used here in the singular form, combined with a possessive. This impedes the interpretation of the Russian idiom in the abstract sense.

---

[2] In certain contexts, this Russian idiom can also be used in the sense of 'to bring somebody to a place where there are many people of that kind'.

This example also shows the role of the pragmatic component of the idiom's plane of content. Even in those contexts in which the semantic differences mentioned above are neutralised, it is not possible to translate the idiom *ездить в Тулу со своим самоваром* as *Eulen nach Athen tragen* (or into *to carry coals to Newcastle*) because of significant differences in cultural specifics. See also chapter 10 for detail.

3.2 On the scope of cross-linguistic idiom analysis

Different interpretations of the term *cross-linguistic* (or *contrastive*, see below) can be encountered in the linguistic literature. First, cross-linguistic idiom analysis can be understood in its most general sense, i.e. any kind of comparison of idioms taken from different languages can be considered to be cross-linguistic. It does not matter how many languages are involved, which aspects are focused on, or which methods of analysis are made use of. The term *cross-linguistic* used in this sense embraces, among other things, linguistic typology, translation analysis and cross-cultural aspects of idiom comparison. The term *contrastive* is used as a synonym for *cross-linguistic* (cf. Burger, Buhofer, and Sialm 1982: 274–276). In some older studies, the term *confrontative*, German *konfrontativ* (primarily applied by scholars in the former GDR) and Russian *конфронтативный* are used in a similar sense (cf. Fleischer 1997: 25–26; Wotjak 1992b: 197–199).

It is remarkable that the traditional cross-linguistic (contrastive) analysis of idioms has not paid sufficient attention to theoretical and practical issues as they are considered here. Traditionally, cross-linguistic idiom research has focused on the following three domains:
(i) description and comparison of structural types of idioms (e.g. idioms with verb-phrase-structure, idioms with noun-phrase-structure, idioms with sentence structure)
(ii) description of the so-called *Sachgruppen* (*thematic groups*), i.e. of idioms with constituents referring to aspects of the same thematic field (e.g. idioms with constituents denoting parts of the human body, animals, colours, etc.)
(iii) typology of cross-linguistic equivalents.

In what follows, we will show that these approaches do not help us solve the key problems of cross-linguistic idiom analysis.
(i) Dividing idioms into structural types for purposes of comparison means ignoring the well-known fact that the morphosyntactic structure of an idiom does not necessarily reflect its functional properties and that it depends

primarily on factors which are external to idioms and their imagery system.[3] So, for example, the German idiom (5) can be most adequately translated into English by using idiom (6):

(5) German *die Ratten verlassen das sinkende Schiff*
 "the rats leave the sinking ship"

(6) English *like rats leaving a sinking ship*

As the example shows, the morphosyntactic structures (an idiom with sentence structure vs. an adverbial idiom) do not uncover the deep semantic and functional properties of the idiom. In general, any structural parallels or non-parallels are of no importance for the functional properties of idioms.

(ii) As for "thematic groups", they may be instructive in certain cases if taken as a starting-point for analysis; compare the study of conventional figurative units from different languages containing number symbols, colour symbols and animal symbols in Dobrovol'skij and Piirainen (1997).[4] Yet, if words denoting the same concept and exploited as idiom constituents in L1 and L2 make a different semantic contribution to the meaning of a given idiom as a whole, then it means that the same entity has been conceptualised in different ways by the linguistic and cultural communities of L1 and L2. Solving problems of this kind is one of the most crucial aims of conceptual analysis and the semiotics of culture. The necessary prerequisites for a successful implementation of this approach are, first, a classification of the idioms in question according to their motivation types (see chapter 4).

This means that we have to investigate what kind of knowledge is involved in the processing of the idiom, and, secondly, measure the degree of analysability involved in a given case, otherwise it is not possible to describe the semantic function of single constituents in operational terms. However, all known traditional descriptions of idioms on the basis of so-called "thematic groups" have not even begun to touch upon these problems (cf. the well-

---

[3] Of course, the image – to be more precise, the highlighted slots of the source frame (see chapter 8 for details) – can be significant in certain cases (particularly in contexts highlighting the idiom). Translators of literary texts are often confronted with this problem. Here, however, we only discuss functional equivalence with regard to ordinary, neutral linguistic usage.

[4] The "symbolic domains" investigated in Dobrovol'skij and Piirainen (1997, 1998) and frame-based domains (see chapter 9) are not identical to "thematic groups" because the former are based on underlying concepts, and the latter on lexical constituents. Therefore, "thematic groups" can be considered only a starting-point for research in this field.

known German idiom dictionary by Friederich 1966), the macrostructure of which is based on this grouping principle, or numerous dissertations on phraseology describing groups of idioms with key constituents from the same thematic field. Grouping idioms according to their key constituents, as practiced in traditional research into phraseology, has no theoretical value whatsoever. As for the practical value of the *Sachgruppen* approach, this is also very questionable, because from the practical point of view it is more promising to take semantic fields as a starting-point for analysis.

The grouping of idioms on the basis of their key lexical constituents into "thematic groups" (ANIMALS, PLANTS, COLORS, GARMENTS, etc.) cannot be used for explaining relevant similarities and contrasts between L1 and L2. Such classifications have often led to unstructured collections of idioms of most diverse origins, failing to take into account their essential feature, which is their culture-based nature.

Let us look at a few extreme cases taken from some traditional sources, for example when the idiom *to carry **owls** to Athens* is subsumed under BIRDS and the idioms *God's **lamb*** and *to worship the golden **calf*** under FARM ANIMALS, or when equivalents of *to weep/shed **crocodile** tears*, which go back to old legends, are merely grouped under WILD ANIMALS, or when the idioms with the constituent *laurels* (e.g. *to gain one's **laurels***, which originates from a popular custom in antiquity) are considered to belong to the thematic group of PLANTS because LAUREL is a plant. Along the same lines, the French idiom *jeter le gant* (a widespread idiom, cf. English *to throw down the **gauntlet***) is classified as belonging to the thematic group of GARMENT, together with COAT, SHIRT, SHOES, etc., instead of taking its cultural historic background into account (where it refers to a gesture of medieval knighthood, a sign of issuing a challenge).

(iii) The types of traditionally postulated cross-linguistic equivalents in the field of phraseology (cf. Eckert and Günther 1992: 153 and many subsequent studies) can be reduced to the following three main classes:
  (a) "full equivalents" (or "absolute equivalents"), i.e. idioms of L1 and L2 which are identical with regard to meaning, syntactic and lexical structure, and imagery basis
  (b) "partial equivalents", i.e. idioms of L1 and L2 which have identical or near-identical meanings, but do not fully correspond in syntactic and lexical structure, or imagery basis
  (c) "non-equivalents", i.e. a given L1-idiom has no idiomatic correspondences in L2

In what follows, we will show that this typology must be replaced by a functional one in order to enable the speaker to find real, functionally adequate

L2-equivalents to given L1-idioms. We claim that the traditional typology is of no significance, either for linguistic theory or for a practically oriented description of idiomatic expressions. Let us illustrate this by some examples.

It is possible to imagine a pair of languages L1 and L2 which would not have a single "full equivalent" in the traditional sense; that is, there are no idioms in L1 and L2 which would have absolutely the same meaning and, at the same time, correspond to each other as word-for-word translations. However, this means very little for a systematic comparison of these two languages with regard to their idiomatic expressions. If the idioms in question have the same conceptual foundations, they can be traced back to the same cognitive structures, and their seeming non-equivalence is only due to the surface structure. Cf. the German idiom (7) and the Russian idiom (8).

(7) German *jmdn. in die Enge treiben* "to drive someone into the narrowness"
'to stalemate someone to put someone in trouble (through questions, threats, etc.)'

(8) Russian *припереть/прижать к стене/стенке кого-л.* "to press someone to the wall; to place someone firmly against the wall"
'to stalemate someone'
Cf. also English *to drive someone into a corner, to drive someone against/to the wall, to push someone to the wall*

Within a cognitively oriented theoretical framework, examples like (7) and (8) are interpreted as basically similar units. This does not mean, of course, that they are absolutely identical in terms of all their semantic, syntactic and pragmatic properties (see 3.4), but regarding them as being not equivalent at all would be counterintuitive. One of the main ideas of this book is the importance of "rich images" for explaining most linguistically relevant features of idioms. However, this does not mean that the underlying conceptual metaphor (DIFFICULTIES ARE IMPEDIMENTS TO MOTION in this case) does not play any role for the semantic and pragmatic analysis of idioms (see section 6.3).

Two different tasks have to be distinguished in this regard. On the one hand, the specifics of semantic, syntactic and pragmatic behaviour of every single idiom can only be explained on the basis of individual images. On the other hand, to discover conceptual similarity between idioms which seem to have nothing in common, if only their lexical structures are taken into account, we need instruments such as conceptual metaphors.

The imagery-based cross-linguistic contrasts are cognitively relevant if the underlying conceptual structures (either on the superordinate level of metaphoric models or on the level of single metaphors, see section 4.5 for details) also differ from each other. This does not mean, of course, that "surface" contrasts in the lexical structure are never significant for cross-linguistic idiom analysis, cf. idiom usage in word plays where the literal meanings of the constituent parts are intensively exploited. But in terms of basic cross-linguistic equivalence vs. non-equivalence, conceptual similarity prevails over lexical contrasts.

On the other hand, some idioms of L1 and L2 may be "full equivalents" in traditional terms, but if, for example, they differ with regard to the degree of their familiarity and textual frequency or the possibility to modify their structure according to relevant contextual conditions, they are not functionally equivalent to each other.

The analysis of idiom functioning in different languages shows that there are very few really full equivalents. As a rule, instances of "absolute equivalents" as they can be found in traditional descriptions turn out to be lexicographic fictions which result from inaccurate semantic analysis. Truly full equivalents can mostly be found in cases in which idioms from different languages go back to the same text source, for example, German *im Schweiße seines Angesichts* "in the sweat of his face" and Russian *в поте лица своего* "in (the) sweat of one's face" (both going back to the Bible and meaning 'through hard work or effort', compare also English *by the sweat of one's brow*).

The research methods currently available do not allow us to make exact statements about whether there is "full equivalence" at all. This would require hundreds of texts from the two languages under comparison. First, all texts that use the idiom in an ironic, playful, author-specific, faulty (non-prototypical) manner would have to be rejected. Next, competent translators would have to check whether the idiom can be translated in all texts without exception by the parallel idiom from the other language. Such work would be more effective using parallel text corpora, provided that the relevant idiom could be found in sufficient numbers. However, parallel corpora of this size do not yet exist. Therefore, such research goes beyond the scope of this book.

Contexts such as (9) can be translated into Russian (or into English) literally, at least with regard to the idiom in question.

(9) Im Museum gibt es gut 1.000 Exponate zur bäuerlichen Tradition. „Ich will darauf hinweisen, wie unsere Vorfahren *im Schweiße ihres Angesichts* ihr Brot verdienten", so Müllner. (NON12/AUG.03427 Niederösterreichische Nachrichten, 02.08.2012)
[In the museum, there are more than 1,000 exhibits on the peasant tradition. "I want to point out how our ancestors deserved their bread *in the sweat of their faces*," says Müllner.]

Cases like this seem to be exceptions rather than typical phenomena. In most cases, relevant semantic, syntactic or pragmatic differences between a given L1-idiom and the corresponding L2-idiom can be found. Hence, the traditional typology of cross-linguistic equivalents in the field of phraseology makes some irrelevant distinctions and fails to make some relevant ones.

From a functional point of view, relevant distinctions do not depend on formal criteria (for example, idiom vs. compound), but on usage-based parameters. In fact, all *diasystematic* criteria must be taken into account, in order to label two idioms "full equivalents". The main diasystematic features in cross-linguistic phraseology are *diastratic, diachronic* and *diatopic* aspects.

First, the potential "diastratic", i.e. stylistic or pragmatic, aspect is ignored in cases where the L1-idiom is stylistically elevated or coarse and that of L2 is stylistically neutral. Examples are German *einen/eins auf den Sack kriegen* "to get on one's sack/scrotum" as an equivalent of Finnish *saada takkiinsa* "to get on one's jacket" (Korhonen 2001: 353) or Finnish *tunnustaa väriä* "to admit/confess colour" as an equivalent of German *die Hose(n) runterlassen* "to let down the trousers" (Korhonen 2001: 677).

Let us illustrate the "diachronic aspect" with the following example. The German compound *Hundewetter* and the Russian idiom *собачья погода* (both literally "dog's weather") are not fully equivalent to each other, not because they exhibit differences in their morphosyntactic structure, but because the Russian expression is outdated whereas the German word is quite common. Many cases of such asymmetries can be encountered in bilingual dictionaries.

As for the "diatopic", i.e. regional aspect of idiom use, bilingual dictionaries of idioms disregard completely the fact that some idioms are common only in particular regions of a given speech community, not in the whole area where the language is spoken. An example is the German regionalism *es regnet Schusterjungen* "it's raining shoemaker's boys", which emerges in several dictionaries as an equivalent of idioms meaning 'it is pouring with rain'. Many examples of this kind can be found in the German-Russian dictionary of Binovič and Grišin (1975). There are various regionalisms from Upper-Saxonia (a region located in the former GDR) which can often be found in idiom dictionaries of GDR provenance, such as *sich ein Bewerbchen machen, seinen Dreier dazugeben, etwas in die Esse schreiben, Fettlebe machen, Habchen und Babchen, Schliff backen.*

To be able to achieve some progress in functionally based cross-linguistic idiom analysis, we have to develop tools other than the traditional typology of cross-linguistic equivalents.

3.3 Cross-linguistic equivalents of idioms from a functional perspective

The main prerequisite for a reasonable comparison of idioms with semantically parallel constituents is their underlying semantic resemblance, as in the case of (10) and (11):

(10) Russian *ударить как обухом по голове кого-л.* ≈ "to strike someone's head with a butt"[5]

(11) German *wie vor den Kopf geschlagen sein* "to be as if struck on/against one's head"

If we set aside the differences in the diathesis of (10) and (11), both idioms can be regarded as equivalents – they mean something very close to the semantics of the English expression *to be thunderstruck*. The contexts that we have at our disposal show that both the Russian and the German idiom denote a mental and emotional state caused mostly by a message containing information about some trouble affecting the subject.

Let us consider another pair of idioms:

(12) German *den Bock zum Gärtner machen* "to make the ram/he-goat into the gardener"
'to allow a person who seems to be able to do much harm in a given field of activities to do just these things'[6]

(13) Russian *пускать козла в огород* "to let the he-goat into the kitchen-garden"
'to allow a person, who seems to be able to do much harm in a given field of activities and to derive benefit for himself/herself to do just these things'

Subtle semantic differences, which become evident as a result of contrasting idioms such as (12) and (13), need to be analysed in more detail. The semantic interpretations of (12) and (13) differ with regard to the semantic element 'to derive

---

[5] Explanations marked with "≈" are not semantic definitions, but only rough English paraphrases (sometimes in combination with English near-equivalent units of figurative language, i.e. idioms or metaphors) which are intended to provide the reader with a first impression of the meaning of the German and Russian idiom discussed, but not to cover the whole range of use.
[6] Müller (1984: 447) has already pointed to the fact that the dictionaries were not able to adequately explain the meaning of this idiom.

benefit for himself/herself', which is part of the meaning of the Russian idiom (13) but not part of the meaning of the German idiom (12). Semantic differences like these are of prime importance for both bilingual lexicography and translation. However, research along these lines is only possible if the starting-point of analysis is a semantic field, i.e. a group of lexical items having much in common semantically, and not merely a group of idioms having parallel constituents. The lack of research findings in this area is responsible for the fact that so far no one has compiled a bilingual dictionary of idioms which pays enough attention to the semantic differences between nearly equivalent idioms, as discussed above.

Compare also the idiom pair (14–15), which is considered to be equivalent in (Škljarov, Eckert, and Engelke 1977).

(14) Russian *раз-два и обчелся чего-л.* ≈ "one-two (of something) and you have to stop counting"
'very few, not enough'

(15) German *etwas kann man an den (fünf) Fingern abzählen* "one can count something on one's (five) fingers"
'it is a very small number, there are surprisingly few of certain things'

Both idioms mean, roughly speaking, 'very few', but (14), in contrast to (15), also focuses on the idea of the lack of the entities in question ('being not enough for something'), which is based on the underlying mental image, namely the failure of the counting procedure, i.e. something like 'I started counting the things I needed, assuming that there was a sufficient amount of these things, but after counting two of them I had to stop this procedure because there were no more things of this kind, so I had to rethink my assumption and to change my plans'. Idiom (15) is a "widespread idiom"; it exists in more than 50 European languages, cf. English *one can count something on the fingers (of one hand)* and Russian *по пальцам можно пересчитать что-л.*, among others. This idiom is also based on the idea of the counting procedure, but focuses on the point that one is able to count the things in question very easily because the amount is small. The idea of a failure is therefore not part of the semantic structure of these idioms. For subtle differences between apparently closely related idioms and the importance of their discrimination, compare also Cowie (1998b).

Parallels in the "core meaning" do not necessarily mean perfect equivalence in language use. This accounts especially for lexical items denoting non-physical entities (e.g. emotion concepts or mental predicates), which tend to depend much more on linguistic factors than words denoting physical entities (e.g. artefacts or natural kinds), because the latter have a different ontological status from the former. Since most idioms are predicates with regard to their semantics (i.e. lexical items denoting properties, states, actions, events and the like), they display a high degree of linguistic specificity.

It is also important to mention another, more important, factor of the tendency towards idiosyncratic configurations in the semantic structure of an idiom – the image component of the idiom's plane of content. As an essential part of the conceptual structure (cf. Lakoff 1987b: 450–452; Gibbs 1993), mental images evoked by idioms influence their actual meanings. Furthermore, the image component is often responsible for relevant restrictions in the usage of idioms (see Dobrovol'skij 2007; Baranov and Dobrovol'skij 2008, 2013). On the other hand, it should be emphasized that it is not possible to predict the actual meaning of an idiom on the basis of its image, i.e. its literal meaning. The same image can often be traced back to different conceptual metaphors; that is to say, the lexical structure of an idiom does not tell us which conceptual metaphor should be taken as a framework within which this idiom must interpreted (see chapter 6 for more details).

The result is that – both within the same language and cross-linguistically – semantic differences between idioms cannot be predicted. To reveal those differences is a purely empirical endeavour, i.e. they can be discovered mainly through research into their range of use. Hence, given an L1-idiom and some L2-idioms which are considered near-equivalent to the L1-idiom, the only way to find out possible differences between them is to inquire into their functioning in authentic texts. This accounts not only for cross-linguistic non-parallelism in the meaning of idioms in question (idiom semantics), but also for relevant differences in their combinatorial and transformational properties (idiom syntactics) as well as for the specifics of the situation in which they can be used (idiom pragmatics). For both theoretical and practical issues, it is much more important to discover non-trivial differences between lexical units of L1 and L2 than to point to their similarities. A systematic empirical search for relevant cross-linguistic differences in idiom semantics, syntactics and pragmatics needs certain theoretical guidelines, which would ensure its systematic character. To provide these guidelines is a task for the theory of cross-linguistic idiom analysis, which must elaborate parameters and procedures of comparison.

The procedure of finding functionally adequate equivalents, as we see it, breaks down into three stages. In stage one, we have to group the idioms from both L1 and L2 into semantic fields postulated on the same principles, in order to get semantically comparable groups which can then be analysed in more detail. In stage two, we have to identify near-equivalent idioms in those languages. To be able to do this, we must not stop at the lexical structure (looking for idioms with similar key constituents) but should focus on the shared conceptual metaphors, "rich images", and/or culturally relevant symbols. In stage three, we have to investigate the combinatorial properties of the near-equivalent idioms discovered in stage two. Even when we have identified the shared underlying metaphors (like BAD IS DOWN) and/or "rich images" [like "a he-goat being the gardener", cf. (12) and (13)] and/or shared symbols (like SNAKE for 'evil' or BLACK for 'bad'), the most we can hope for is small groups of near-equivalents in L1, none of which can precisely translate all of a group of near-equivalents in L2. We therefore have to go a step further and identify the combinatorial possibilities of each item. Only if these are identical may we speak of fully equivalent idioms in L1 and L2.

The task of cross-linguistic idiom analysis obviously serves the needs of bilingual lexicography, translation and second language acquisition. In the end, it has to answer the following question: given an L1-idiom, which L2-equivalents (if more than one) are possible under which contextual conditions? As we have shown above, traditional analysis with its types of equivalence does not even try to answer this question. To find alternative descriptive tools, it seems advisable to divide the relevant tasks into those that are primarily theoretical and those that are primarily practical.

If we consider the tasks of functionally based cross-linguistic idiom analysis from a purely practical perspective, we should first look for equivalents which can be used in the translation of L1-texts containing idioms into L2. If an L1-text containing an idiom is to be translated into L2, some ad hoc solutions must, as a rule, be found, because equivalents provided by dictionaries (i.e. L2-idioms which semantically correspond to a given L1-idiom to a certain extent) in many cases do not meet relevant contextual conditions. Whereas bilingual dictionaries of idioms mostly try to find an L2-idiom (but not a single word or a free word combination) to explain the meaning of the corresponding L1-idiom, for translation adequacy it is not so important whether a given L1-idiom is translated into L2 by an idiom, a word or a free word combination.

Some phraseological studies start from the assumption that an adequate translation should have the same number of idioms in the target text as in the source text. Compared to other lexical units, idioms have no special value; they can be translated by any possible means. A word of L2 having the same functional properties as the L1-idiom in question is a much better translation equivalent than an L2-idiom which, for one reason or another, sounds strange in the given context. As mentioned above, such factors as frequency are also important in this regard.

Moreover, not only is the translation of idioms by idioms an unrealistic ideal, but the equivalence of isolated lexical items (no matter whether they are idioms or single words) is also of no relevance to the quality of translation. The only point that matters is the translation adequacy of the whole text. As Jakobson

(1959) pointed out, most lexical units are untranslatable, but every utterance can be translated. Hence, an experienced translator should not pay too much attention to single lexical items, trying to find L2-expressions that are as similar as possible to elements of a given L1-text; instead, they should concentrate on the text as a whole. As to why translators often prefer formally similar lexical units to functionally adequate ones, see, for example, Doherty (1996: 443–444).

This attempt to reproduce single lexical items is mostly due to a prejudice interfering with our target-language competence: we feel bound to the forms of the original in every detail, as each form seems to manifest the author's choice. We therefore try to find as many similar forms as possible and ignore our target-language intuition, which would often lead us to prefer different forms. Trying to stick to formally similar L2-units is especially dangerous in the field of phraseology. Cf. the Russian context (16) and its translation into German (17).

(16) [...] так што ш ты гонишь мне опять про своих Пикассо шмикассо Утрилло шмутрилло, я ш *в гробу видел* твоего Ван Гога там шмангога [...]. (В. Сорокин. Дорожное происшествие)[7]
[[...] why are you talking again about your Picasso shmicasso, Utrillo shmutrillo, I saw your Van Gogh kind of shmangogh in the coffin, you know [...].]

(17) [...] also was quatschst du mich wieder voll mit deinem Picasso Schmikasso Utrillo Schmutrillo, ich *hab* ja deinen Gogh dings Schmangoch [...] *im Sarg gesehen* (V. Sorokin. Vorfall auf der Straße)

Context (16) contains the idiom *видеть в гробу кого-л.* "to see someone in the coffin" 'somebody is of no interest to someone, so that this person does not want to have anything in common with somebody or even hear of him/her'. Since in German there are no lexical units based on the same conceptual metaphor, context (17) is not understandable to native German speakers.

This does not mean that word-for-word translations of idioms are impossible. On the contrary, it is a well-known fact that in some cases a literal translation is the best way to reflect the semantic and pragmatic specifics of the corresponding L1-idiom. However, the necessary prerequisite for a literal translation of idioms is a common conceptual basis.

Since all possible contextual conditions, including conversational implicatures, cannot be predicted, bilingual dictionaries of idioms are basically incapable

---

[7] The author's spelling is preserved.

of registering all L2-equivalents of a given L1-idiom which might be preferable in all potential translations from L1 into L2. Thus, the best instruments to serve the needs of a translator are parallel text corpora[8] and other text-oriented tools. The comparison of original texts and their translations into other languages reveals a broad range of potential translations with regard to idioms, from word-for-word translations to the use of other types of lexical units. From the point of view of translation, it is probably more important to know all the syntactic, semantic and pragmatic properties of the L1-idioms in question than to have a list of possible L2-equivalents, because the choice of equivalents depends on contextual conditions each time and cannot be predicted.

For bilingual lexicography and second language acquisition, in addition to the aim of finding the most precise translation in every context, there remains the aim of comparing all similar idioms (i.e. idioms that are intuitively perceived as equivalents) and describing all relevant differences between them. For a systematic comparison of this kind, a typology of contrasts between intuitively near-identical idioms is needed.

Such a typology raises a theoretical question. For a theory of cross-linguistic idiom analysis, it is crucial to elaborate on the question of which idioms are at the speakers' disposal in L1 and L2 for denoting certain concepts. This first requires a description of L1- and L2-idioms according to their semantic fields, i.e. those L1- and L2-idioms which are closest in meaning and function must first be discovered. As a second step, an apparatus for indicating parameters of non-equivalence has to be developed in order to distinguish between semantically similar idioms. To sum up, a typology of relevant differences between heuristically similar idioms of L1 and L2 is needed both for practically oriented tasks (especially in the field of bilingual lexicography and second language acquisition) and for the theoretical aims of cross-linguistic idiom analysis.

3.4 Parameters of idiom comparison

The following section will concentrate on some parameters of cross-linguistic comparison, in order to offer a typology of non-parallel features between L1- and L2-idioms. On the one hand, a typology of this kind can help to distinguish real cross-linguistic equivalents from pseudo-equivalents and, in this way, improve bilingual dictionaries. On the other hand, it could help to explain the nature

---

[8] Compare in this regard the project on parallel corpora of various languages conducted in the framework of the Russian National Corpora in Moscow, e.g. Dobrovol'skij (in press).

of idiom syntactics, semantics and pragmatics, because, being concerned with relevant differences in idiom functioning, comparison is an instrument of investigation not only into cross-linguistic issues, but also into intralinguistic features and properties of the items in question.

Relevant parameters can be roughly divided into three groups according to three well-known semiotic dimensions – semantics (axis "sign – world"), syntactics (axis "sign – sign") and pragmatics (axis "sign – speaker/hearer").

Although it is scarcely possible to draw a clear borderline in every concrete case (because, for example, nearly all syntactic transformations have certain semantic and/or pragmatic consequences), it seems reasonable to group relevant parameters of comparison according to their fundamental semiotic and linguistic features. The primary aim is not to classify concrete cases of cross-linguistic near-equivalence, but to offer a typology of parameters which would allow us to describe all idioms under consideration more consistently.

3.4.1 Semantics

Basically, the content plane of idioms consists of two macrocomponents – (i) actual meaning, and (ii) mental image – being both a starting-point and conceptual foundation for semantic reinterpretation. These two macrocomponents are independent of each other to a certain extent. One consequence of this fact is the existence of idioms which have (nearly) the same image, but differ with regard to their actual meanings, as well as the existence of idioms which have (nearly) the same actual meaning, but differ with regard to their images. Hence, these two major types of non-equivalence and their different combinations can be distinguished. It goes without saying that a certain degree of similarity between the idioms under consideration is a crucial precondition of their analysis in terms of cross-linguistic equivalence vs. non-equivalence. If we take two idioms which significantly differ in both actual meaning and image component, there is no reason to compare them at all, much less to regard them as possible candidates for cross-linguistic equivalence.

Contrasts in actual meaning. Let us first consider the types of non-equivalence which are characterised by a similarity of images and non-parallel features of actual meaning. Here at least the following types can be distinguished:
(a) idiomatic "false friends"
(b) cross-linguistic near-synonyms
(c) "asymmetrical polysemy"

(a) The most striking cases of semantic non-equivalence are the so-called "false friends". This phenomenon will be discussed in chapter 5 in detail. Let us consider only a couple of examples here. Compare the English idiom (18) and its Russian pseudo-equivalent (19).

(18)   English *to throw dust in/into someone's eyes*
'to confuse (someone) or take his attention away from something that one does not wish him to see or know about'

(19)   Russian *пускать пыль в глаза кому-л.* "to throw dust in/into one's eyes" 'trying to impress other people, show oneself or his/her position in a much better light than it really is'

Both idioms consist of analogous constituents and have an identical image basis. Nevertheless, they reveal significant differences in actual meaning.

From a linguistic viewpoint, phraseological "false friends" present a more sophisticated problem than "one-word false friends". The latter are words of L1 and L2 which sound similar and often go back to the same etymological roots, such as German *eventuell* 'possible; possibly, perhaps', *Fabrik* 'factory' and English *eventual, fabric*. Such cases are fairly well described and can be found in every good bilingual dictionary. On the other hand, the idioms which are classified here as "false friends" resemble each other not on the phonetic and/or graphic level, but on the level of lexical constituent parts and mental images, i.e. on the level of a literal reading. Hence research into this problem requires a semantic and conceptual analysis of given idioms, using the metalinguistic apparatus developed by the Cognitive Theory of Metaphor.

(b) Another type of semantically based non-equivalence can be exemplified by the German idiom (12) and its Russian counterpart (13) discussed above. Let us go back to these idioms, (12) German *den Bock zum Gärtner machen* and (13) Russian *пускать козла в огород*. The subtle semantic differences were evident. As has been shown, the semantic explanations of (12) and (13) differ with regard to the semantic element 'to derive benefit for oneself', which is part of the meaning of the Russian idiom (13); compare also the English idioms *to put the cow to mind the corn, to put the wolf in charge of the sheep, to set/put the fox to guard the henhouse/the chickens,*[9] which are equivalent

---

[9] There are various (quasi-)equivalents in other languages, e.g. Greek βάζω το λύκο να φυλάει τα πρόβατα) "to engage the wolf to guard the sheep". There is also a Japanese idiom similar

to the Russian idiom (13) rather than to the German idiom (12). The meaning of the corresponding German idiom (12) does not include this semantic element. Therefore idiom (12) can be used in a broader range of contexts than (13). Cf. example (20), which cannot be translated into Russian with the help of idiom (13).

(20) [...] einige Zeit später stieß er [...] darauf, daß er sozusagen *den Bock zum Gärtner gemacht hatte,* denn es stellte sich heraus, daß bei der Planung der Flachdächer der Architekt fehlerhaft gearbeitet hatte. (Mannheimer Morgen, 26.04.1986)
[[...] some time later [...] he found out that he, so to speak, *had made the ram/he-goat a gardener,* since it turned out that the architect had made a mistake in planning the flat roofs]

This type is rather similar to type (a) – the so-called "false friends" – in the sense that being based on very similar mental images, which go back to the same conceptual structure, the actual meanings of these two idioms are not completely identical. However, there is an important difference between type (a) and type (b). Whereas the "false friends" display significant semantic differences, often developing meanings which have nothing in common [cf. (18) and (19)], the idioms subsumed under (b) have the same core meaning. The meanings of such idioms only differ slightly, and these differences, as a rule, concern peripheral elements of their semantics [cf. (12) and (13)].

Since near-equivalents of this kind have traditionally been treated as "full equivalents", it seems especially important to draw attention to them from both a theoretical and a practical point of view. For a semantic theory, it is a reasonable task to single out all ostensible cross-linguistic equivalents which, from a functional perspective, are not fully equivalent, and to describe all relevant semantic differences. It would also help to find out the function of nontrivial semantic components, such as presuppositions, semantic consequences, the speaker's attitude, and the like. From the point of view of bilingual lexicography and second language acquisition, there is a need to develop metalinguistic tools which would enable the user to get access to the functional properties of the idioms in question.

---

to (13): 猫に鰹節(を預ける) – *neko ni katsuobushi (wo azukeru)* "(to entrust) a cat with a dried bonito-fish". Garrison et al. (2002: 431) regard this idiom as an equivalent of English *to trust a wolf to watch over sheep* and *to leave a fox to guard the henhouse.*

(c) The next type of non-equivalence is based on a semantic property which can be called "asymmetrical polysemy". This semantic property is apparent in all cases in which a given L1-idiom has more than one meaning, but the corresponding L2-idiom only has one meaning. This monosemous L2-idiom may fully correlate with one of the meanings of the polysemous L1-idiom, but even in this case both idioms, taken as a whole, are not fully equivalent. Their cross-linguistic description and relevant dictionary entries have to contain information about such cross-linguistic semantic asymmetry.

Examples of this kind can be taken from the semantic field 'death/to die'. Besides the meaning of 'death/ to die', many German idioms of this field have a second meaning, akin to 'dysfunction'. For example, the German idiom (21), according to (Duden 2013: 261), has two meanings (it is a widespread idiom, compare the English idiom *to give up the ghost*). The Russian idiom (22), which fully corresponds to this German idiom in terms of lexical constituent parts and image basis, has three meanings (according to Baranov and Dobrovol'skij 2020).[10]

(21) German *den Geist aufgeben* "to give up the mind/spirit"
1. (ironic, obsolete) 'to die', and 2. (colloquial, jocular) 'to be broken/ functioning'

(22) Russian *испутить дух* "to give up the mind/spirit"
1. (elevated) 'to die', 2. (journ.) 'to stop existing' (with institutions, organisations and political subjects), and 3. (colloquial) 'to stop working/ functioning'

Thus, all bilingual dictionaries which consider these two idioms absolute equivalents (cf., for example, Binovič and Grišin 1975: 207) give the user misleading information. As a matter of fact, these idioms are far from being equivalent. Even taken in the corresponding meaning 'to die', they are not fully equivalent from the functional point of view. This is because the German idiom (21) is hardly ever used in the sense of 'to die', while this is the central meaning of the Russian idiom.

The phenomenon of "asymmetrical polysemy" has to be analysed in a systematic way. The first impression we get while looking at examples from the semantic field 'death' is that the cross-linguistic non-coincidence of polysemous

---

[10] Compare in this regard investigations into the phenomenon of regular polysemy in the field of idioms, e.g. Dobrovol'skij (2004). Regularities of this kind in the semantic field 'to die' in Dutch are expounded in Piirainen (2003b).

structure is normal. This finding is of vital importance, especially because we are dealing here with regular polysemy. It is well known that regular polysemy is based on systematic conceptual correspondences between certain domains. Most cases of regular polysemy are based on metonymic shifts, but cases of metaphorically based regular polysemy can also be found. For example, idioms with the actual meaning 'to die' often develop a secondary meaning, such as 'to vanish, to disappear, to fail' (about quite different things like organisations, ideas, devices, etc.). The underlying cognitive mechanism is the metaphor of personification, which is very general in nature. Therefore, theoretically, it can be expected that every expression denoting DYING sooner or later develops the secondary meaning of EXTINCTION or FADING.

This is just the conceptual potential of the expressions from this semantic field, including idioms. But not all idioms realise this conceptual potential. Whereas some idioms with both meanings can be found in various languages, there are also idioms from the same semantic field which resist developing a secondary meaning. The selection criteria used by different languages to implement this kind of semantic derivation are yet unknown. It is likely that they are usage-based only.

As we have shown, the German idiom *den Geist aufgeben* "to give up the ghost" can be used almost exclusively in combination with mechanical devices, compare (21). The primary meaning 'to die' is perceived as obsolete today. Conversely, its Russian counterpart *испустить дух* has preserved the primary meaning 'to die', and has also developed a secondary meaning, which, however, primarily combines with institutions, organisations and ideas rather than with devices, as in German, compare (21).

In principle, the idea of finding explanations in terms of underlying images appears very attractive, especially against the background of our theoretical assumptions. Maybe there are certain restrictions to regular semantic derivation which can be formulated as image governed phenomena, but this is only possible to a certain extent. Counterexamples can be found in several languages.

It is obvious that motivation is a matter of degree. The stronger the image is, the more image-based restrictions can be discovered. Idioms with faded motivation demonstrate more derivational freedom. All in all, our observations in the field of "asymmetrical polysemy" bear out the thesis that idioms are irregular units of the lexicon. Every attempt to find regularities in this domain has its natural limits.

Contrasts in images. Now let us consider the idioms of L1 and L2 which are similar with regard to their actual meanings, but differ with regard to their images. In such cases we are dealing with semantic similarity of a high degree, since idioms with identical actual meanings and similar syntactic and pragmatic features can basically be treated as real equivalents. But in certain contexts, the image component of the plane of content of a given idiom plays a crucial role in its functioning. In such cases the idiom cannot be translated into L2 by the corresponding idiom, which differs with regard to its imagery.

For example, in standard contexts the German idiom (23) can be translated into Russian by idiom (24).

(23) German *nicht alle Tassen im Schrank haben* "not to have all cups in the cupboard"

(24) Russian *не все дома у кого-л.* "not all people at home with someone" evoking a mental image of a situation of "not all people being at home at someone's place"
both idioms meaning 'to be mad'

Although both images can be traced back to the same basic conceptual structure, which is something like "absence of completeness or absence of entities which have to be there in a standard case", as a source concept for the target idea of 'madness', they reveal significant differences on the "rich" conceptual level (the image of cups being in the cupboard vs. people at home).[11]

Combined semantic contrasts. Concluding the description of semantically based types of cross-linguistic non-equivalence, we would like to add that many different combinations of the types discussed in this section are possible. Let us consider an example. Although the German idiom (25), the English idiom (26) and the Russian idiom (27) are traditionally regarded as full equivalents (cf. Binovič and Grišin 1975: 377), they differ with regard to both actual meaning and image component.

(25) German *mit einem silbernen Löffel im Mund geboren sein* "to be born with a silver spoon in the mouth"

(26) English *(to be) born with a silver spoon in one's mouth*

(27) Russian *родиться в рубашке/сорочке* "to be born in (a) shirt"

---

[11] Here we are dealing with a pattern that can be filled with various elements. Burger (1979: 96) describes this pattern for Swiss German idioms as "not to have all X in (the) Y". Vernacular varieties of German show a number of expressions which follow this pattern, e.g. *nicht alle Steine auf der Schleuder/nicht alle Speichen im Rad/nicht alle Schindeln auf dem Dach haben* "not to have all stones at the sling/all spokes on the wheel/all shingles on the roof", and the like (material drawn from the project "Survey on the Common Knowledge of Idioms in Colloquial German", Piirainen 2003a).

Whereas the German idiom (like the English idiom, which has the same lexical structure and is based on the same mental image) means '(to be) born into a wealthy family with all the advantages that can be given to a child', the Russian idiom means something akin to 'to be lucky, esp. to escape a dangerous situation which seemed to be inevitable, or to achieve something desired that seemed to be unattainable' (cf. Gurevič and Dozorec 1995: 403).

The images behind these idioms are also not identical, although, from a cognitive point of view, there is a certain similarity between them. In terms of the Cognitive Theory of Metaphor, both mental images can be traced back to a similar conceptual structure, namely the idea of being born with a special facility (and, therefore, to be something special, not like other people). This conceptual structure serves as a source domain for the metaphoric inference in both cases. This seems to be the reason for treating these idioms as equivalents in bilingual dictionaries.

From the perspective of linguistic theory, cases like this are of prime interest, because they demonstrate the need for an additional tool for analysing the image component of the content plane of idioms. In Dobrovol'skij and Piirainen (1997) we suggested that the so-called "symbolic component" should be included in the description of conventional figurative language, as it helps to explain phenomena that cannot be explained on the basis of conceptual metaphors. Compare, in the case above, SILVER as a symbol of wealth. The corresponding constituents in the lexical structure of the German idiom (25) and the English idiom (26) activate this "symbolic" knowledge, which in its turn correlates with the actual meaning '(to be) born into a wealthy family with all the advantages that that can give a child'. The absence of such a constituent in the lexical structure of the Russian idiom (27) accounts for the absence of the sense 'wealth' in its semantic structure. Idiom (27) can be traced back to an ancient folk belief – a child that was born with the remains of the amniotic sac (here referred to as *в рубашке/сорочке*) was believed to be protected from misfortune. This leads to the specific features of the actual meaning of idiom (27), which is different from the actual meaning of both (25) and (26). Hence, the relevant semantic differences are based on symbolic knowledge, on the one hand, and on "etymological memory", on the other (for further details, see sections 1.3.2 and 4.1).

3.4.2 Syntactics

In order to describe the syntactic properties of an idiom, we basically have to answer the following three questions:
(a) Which words does it combine with?
(b) In which syntactic patterns can it be embedded?
(c) What kinds of transformations does it undergo?

We will briefly mention the relevant types of non-equivalence before giving a few examples.

(a) Idioms which are very close semantically can sometimes be found in L1 and L2. Compare, for instance, the German idiom (28) and the semantically equivalent Russian idiom (29).

(28) German *in aller Munde* "in everyone's mouth"

(29) Russian *у всех на устах* "on everyone's mouth"
both idioms meaning 'being said or discussed by many people'; cf. English *on everyone's lips*

However, these idioms are not fully equivalent from a functional perspective, because the Russian idiom mostly combines with words from the semantic field SPEECH (*имя* 'name', *цитата* 'quotation', *высказывание* 'utterance', *речь* 'speech', *история* 'story', *новость* 'news', *вопрос* 'question'), whereas the German idiom combines with words denoting a wide variety of entities.

(30) Der demografische Wandel ist *in aller Munde* – doch was bedeutet er für die Menschen in der Metropolregion? (Mannheimer Morgen, 21.01.2012) [demographic changes are *on everyone's lips* – however, what does it mean for people in densely populated areas?]

Context (30) cannot be translated into Russian while using idiom (29). An appropriate translation would be *все говорят о демографических изменениях* 'everybody speaks about demographic changes'. Observations of this kind can be used as additional proof of the psychological reality of the mental image underlying the figurative (actual) meaning of idioms and its crucial role for real usage. What is extremely important here is the fact that the image component inherited by the actual meaning can be profiled in varying degrees and with different intensity. Although, from the point of view of the underlying mental image, idioms (28) and (29) are nearly identical, the traces of this image are profiled in Russian so strongly that they constrain the co-occurrence with nouns from semantic fields other than SPEECH.

(b) Often the L1-idiom differs from its L2-near-equivalent in that its valencies are saturated in different ways. In most cases an adequate result for the translation can be obtained by a transformation of the diathesis. Therefore, these cross-linguistic contrasts can also be regarded as differences in the syntactic embedding. Let us illustrate this by an example from German and Russian. The German idiom *sich keinen abbrechen* "not to break off anything for oneself" 'not to try too hard' is very often used in the form *jmd. bricht sich keinen ab, wenn ...* "someone does not break anything off for himself if ...". A reasonable Russian translation is *от кого-л. не убудет, если* literally ≈ "it would to decrease from someone if ..." both roughly meaning 'you do not lose anything if ...'. The free subject valency of the German expression corresponds to the *от кого-л.*-valency "from someone" in Russian.

(c) We are dealing with transformational factors of non-equivalence in cases in which a given L1-idiom and the corresponding L2-idiom are equivalent along all parameters but one, namely the L1-idiom does not undergo the same transformations as the L2-idiom: e.g. the L1-idiom can be nominalised, and the L2-idiom cannot. In other words, the ability to modify the idiom structure according to relevant contextual conditions can differ, even if the idioms in question are "fully equivalent" in the traditional sense.

This can be illustrated by German idiom (31) and its Russian counterpart (32). Whereas (31) can easily be passivised, (32), which is semantically equivalent to (31), cannot; cf. (33) and (34). The only way to translate sentence (33) into Russian, preserving the same topic-comment-structure, is to use the indefinite-personal construction (36), which, strictly speaking, corresponds not to (33), but to (35).

(31) German *jmdm. das Fell über die Ohren ziehen* "to pull someone the skin over the ears"

(32) Russian *драть/содрать три шкуры с кого-л.* "to take off three skins from someone"
both idioms meaning 'to exploit someone pitilessly by making him pay large taxes, very high interest, exorbitant prices etc.'

(33) German *ihm wurde das Fell über die Ohren gezogen* "the skin was pulled him over the ears"

(34) Russian ??*с него были содраны три шкуры* "three skins were taken off from him"

(35) German *man hat ihm das Fell über die Ohren gezogen* "one pulled him the skin over the ears"

(36) Russian *с него содрали три шкуры* "one took off three skins from him"

There are many similar cases in every language. They prove the importance of transformational factors for questions of cross-linguistic functional equivalence.

3.4.3 Pragmatics

Since, among all the factors of non-equivalence, pragmatic factors have been investigated most intensively (cf., for example, Burger 1991), we will simply enumerate them here and give a few examples. The pragmatically based differences between semantically and syntactically similar idioms of L1 and L2 can be traced to:
(a) differences in their stylistic properties
(b) differences with regard to their degree of familiarity and/or textual frequency
(c) differences in the cultural component of their plane of content
(d) differences in their illocutionary function

(a and b) Differences in stylistic properties and in the familiarity degree can be exemplified by idioms (37) and (38).

>   (37) German *einen Bock schießen* "to shoot a ram/he-goat"
>   'to make a bad mistake'
>
>   (38) Russian *убить бобра* "to kill a beaver"
>   'to make a bad mistake'
>
>   Idioms (37) and (38) are not equivalent, as erroneously assumed in many bilingual dictionaries, because (37) is familiar and widely known in current German, whereas (38) is absolutely obsolete. Most of today's native speakers of Russian do not even know the meaning of this idiom, and anyone using it would achieve a special stylistic effect which would be totally different from the stylistic properties of the corresponding German idiom (37).

(c) Differences in the cultural component of the content plane of near-equivalent idioms can be exemplified by (39) and (40).

>   (39) Spanish *el chino de la esquina* "the Chinese at the corner"
>
>   (40) German *Tante-Emma-Laden* "aunt-Emma-shop"
>   both meaning 'a small shop of traditional type'

Idiom (39), which is common in Peru, is not fully equivalent to (40), though both idioms have identical actual meanings. The reason is that (39) is culture-specific in comparison to (40), and vice versa. See for more details Segura García (1997: 224). We describe phenomena of this kind as "cultural connotations" (see section 10.9).

(d) In every language that has been analysed in this regard there are idioms whose illocutionary potential is more or less fixed and bound to certain speech act types. For example, Burger (1991: 21) points out that idiom (41) is normally used in utterances with the illocutionary function of warning or threat, such as (42).

(41) German *blaues Wunder* "blue miracle"
'a big unpleasant surprise'

(42) German *Da kannst/wirst du dein blaues Wunder erleben.* "Then you can/will see your blue miracle."
≈ 'you will get what's coming to you'

If a given L1-idiom tends to be used in certain speech acts, and its near-equivalent L2-correspondent does not, or is bound to speech acts of different types, the idioms in question cannot be considered absolute equivalents. Compare idioms (43) and (44), which have the same semantics (with regard to both actual meaning and image component) and a very similar lexical structure.

(43) German *im Klartext* "in the clear-text"

(44) Russian *открытым текстом* "with (an) open text" both idioms meaning 'in a very clear and explicit way'

The German idiom (43) is mostly used to introduce an utterance which reformulates the previous utterance in a more explicit and exact way, i.e. in the function of "self-correction", something like (45), whereas the Russian idiom (44) is normally used in statements like (46).

(45) German *im Klartext heißt es...* "in the clear-text, it means..."
um das noch einmal im Klartext zu sagen... "To say it once more in the clear-text..."
das bedeutet also im Klartext... "Hence, this means in the clear-text..."
'to put it more clearly...'

(46) Russian *она сказала ему открытым текстом, что*... "she told him with (an) open text that..."
'she let him explicitly and clearly understand that...'

Some important pragmatic properties of idioms become evident only when analysing large text corpora. At first glance, the German idiom (47) seems to be easy to translate in every language by means of corresponding idioms, because in all languages investigated from the point of view of figurative lexical units, there are many idioms having the core meaning 'to be mad'.

(47) German *von allen guten Geistern verlassen sein* "to be left by all good spirits/genii"
'to be mad'; ≈ to have taken leave of one's senses'

However, research into the text corpora of the Institute of the German language in Mannheim (DeReKo) has shown that (47) is predominantly used in hypothetical utterances, such as (48).

(48) Zugleich sprach sich der Finanzminister deutlich gegen Forderungen [...] nach einem Sonderopfer der Bundesbürger für die DDR in Form von Abgabenerhöhungen oder als Verzicht auf die Steuerreform aus. "<u>Wir wären</u> *von allen guten Geistern verlassen,* <u>wenn</u> über den Umweg der Deutschlandpolitik sozialistische Vorstellungen eingebracht würden", kommentierte Waigel dazu. (Mannheimer Morgen, 15.11.1989)
[At the same time, the Minister of Finance clearly expressed himself against claims [...] for a special sacrifice by the citizens of the Federal Republic for the GDR in the form of increased payments or abandoning the tax reform. "<u>We would be</u> *left by all good spirits/genii* <u>if</u> we indirectly brought in socialist ideas by way of the German policy", commented Waigel.]

In Russian, no single idiom with the same illocutionary potential could be found among idioms denoting abnormal mental states. Consequently, no Russian idiom from the semantic field 'abnormal mental states' can be regarded as fully equivalent to (47).

3.4.4 Conclusion

A systematic description of functionally relevant factors in the use of idioms allows us to develop a typology of parameters for their cross-linguistic comparison. First of all, such a typology aims at improving the theoretical background of cross-linguistic idiom analysis. In practice, such a typology helps to uncover all subtle differences in the semantic, syntactic and pragmatic properties of L1- and L2-idioms. This is especially important in those cases where traditional analysis and bilingual dictionaries postulate a relation of "full equivalence" between a given pair of idioms, failing to take into account their functional non-parallelism.

3.5 Summary

In this chapter, we have discussed some specific aspects of conventional figurative language from a cross-linguistic perspective. Using idioms from different languages (chiefly German, English and Russian) as empirical data, we have focused particularly on factors which have to be taken into account while looking for an L2-equivalent of a given L1-idiom. Our analysis has aimed at uncovering all types of cross-linguistic differences between idioms which are intuitively perceived as being semantically similar. Achieving this aim helps distinguish real cross-linguistic equivalents from pseudo-equivalents (cf. the so-called "types of cross-linguistic equivalents" in the traditional cross-linguistic analysis of idioms) and to explain the nature of idiom semantics, syntactics, and pragmatics (being three well-known semiotic axes: "sign – world", "sign – sign" and "sign – speaker/listener").

The analysis has shown that there are several factors responsible for semantic, syntactic and/or pragmatic differences between similar idioms in different languages. These factors can arise from the internal structure of a given language (cf., above all, the syntactic behaviour of idioms), or they can be motivated cognitively and/or culturally.

The image component – a central notion of the Conventional Figurative Language Theory – is one of the relevant factors in cross-linguistic semantic contrast. Pseudo-equivalent figurative units of different languages are never identical with regard to their semantics and/or pragmatics if they reveal substantial differences in their image components (although minor differences may be important in specifically designed contexts, such as puns). However, not all the relevant cross-linguistic differences analysed here are due to the specifics of the image component, and not all the pseudo-equivalent figurative units of different languages which have identical images are identical with regard to their semantics and/or pragmatics. That is to say, the same image cannot guarantee the semantic identity of the actual meanings of the idioms in question. This can be considered to be one of the main findings of cross-linguistic idiom analysis carried out in the framework of the CFLT.

A fine-grained context-based cross-linguistic analysis of idioms shows that there are few really full equivalents. As a rule, instances of "absolute equivalents", as they are known in traditional descriptions, are actually lexicographic fictions which result from inaccurate semantic analysis. Truly full equivalents can mostly be found in cases in which idioms from different languages go back to the same source, but even in this case they may have developed different features.

For these reasons, we have introduced the notion of *functional equivalence*. To find functionally adequate equivalents is the only reasonable aim of cross-linguistic idiom analysis if it is really to serve the needs of bilingual lexicography, translation and second language acquisition. In the end, cross-linguistic idiom analysis has to answer the following question: given an L1-idiom, which L2-equivalents (if more than one) are possible under which contextual conditions? To achieve this aim, large-scale empirical data concerning the actual usage of idioms are needed, as well as an appropriate theoretical background, which has been provided in this chapter.

A systematic description of functionally relevant factors in the use of idioms allows us to develop a typology of parameters for their cross-linguistic comparison. First of all, such a typology aims at improving the theoretical background of cross-linguistic idiom analysis. In practice, such a typology helps to uncover all subtle differences in the semantic, syntactic and pragmatic properties of L1- and L2-idioms. This is especially important in those cases where traditional analysis and bilingual dictionaries postulate a relation of "full equivalence" between a given pair of idioms, failing to take into account their functional non-parallelism.

4 Motivation of conventional figurative units

One aim of this study is to differentiate between specific types of conventional figurative units. Some CFUs seem to be intuitively and naturally regarded as belonging to a particular type of figurativeness, and the reasons for this lie, to a large extent, in the kind of motivation the unit has. The relevant conceptual links between the mental image associated with the lexical structure and the actual meaning of a figurative unit can be of different natures, involving different types of knowledge. In this chapter, the phenomenon of motivation will be discussed in detail. The main topics of this chapter are the correlation between etymology and motivation (4.1), motivation and related phenomena (4.2) and, after a brief look at unmotivated idioms (4.3), a typology of motivation (4.4–4.10).

4.1 Motivation and etymology

The discussion of the notion of motivation has a long tradition in lexicological research. Since Vinogradov's pioneering work (1977a) all serious studies on CFUs, especially idioms and figurative phrasemes of other types, consider motivation a central parameter because of its relevant linguistic consequences, although motivation is partly a matter of subjectivity (cf. e.g. Gréciano 1993, 2002; Burger 2015: 67–69). Vinogradov (1977a) distinguishes two classes of phrasemes by means of the criterion of motivation, interpreted in the tradition of Saussure:
- *фразеологические сращения* (*frazeologičeskie sraščenija*) "phraseological entireties" (opaque phrasemes, phrasemes that are not motivated) and
- *фразеологические единства* (*frazeologičeskie edinstva*) "phraseological units" (motivated phrasemes which have a comprehensible image basis)

The criterion of motivation has been criticised from different points of view, above all because it is a subjective criterion that is hard to verify. It has for a long time been excluded from the linguistic description of CFUs (idioms in particular). Seen from the cognitive viewpoint, however, this criterion is a relevant parameter, because the motivation of an idiom influences its cognitive processing. Experiments carried out by Häcki Buhofer and Burger (1994) have shown that people are often unable to distinguish between the literal and the figurative meaning of an idiom.[1] This means that the literal sense is often mentally present for speakers,

---

[1] Cf. also the experimental findings within the *interference hypothesis* (Cacciari and Glucksberg 1991; Cacciari, Rumiati, and Glucksberg 1992), the *graded salience hypothesis* (Giora

even if they use an idiom only in its figurative meaning. Hence, the relevant mental image of a motivated idiom must be regarded as part of its content plane in a broad sense. In certain cases, some relevant traces of the mental image that is fixed in the lexical structure of an idiom must be regarded as part of its actual meaning (we call it the *image component of the actual meaning*).[2] As a rule, the image component is involved in the cognitive processing of the idiom in question. What this means for the semantic description of idioms is that relevant elements of the inner form have to be included in the structure of the semantic explanation.

Within Cognitive Linguistics (cf. e.g. Sweetser 1999, 2000; Taylor 2006), any word combination that an adult speaker intuitively regards as semantically interpretable is either motivated or transparent. In most cases, this has nothing to do with the right or "true" etymology of a given CFU. Therefore, word combinations can make sense even if they do not literally mean what they appear to say. This may be because idiom etymologies are, in fact, often folk etymologies (Lakoff 1987b: 451–452). As Lakoff points out, only these folk etymologies are relevant to the speaker.

> Motivating links for idioms – that is, cases where there is some link (L) of the form *conventional image + knowledge + metaphors* relating the idiom to its meaning – have traditionally been called *folk etymologies*. The term arose in historical linguistics, where the goal was to come as close as possible to the "real" etymology, the real history, of each word and idiom. Folk etymologies are, to historical linguists, things to avoid, things students are warned against. But since the real history of an idiom is hardly ever known, folk etymologies are just about all there is for a historical linguist to go on. Moreover, since hardly any ordinary person ever really knows for sure the real origin of an expression, the folk etymologies that people automatically – and unconsciously – come up with are real for them, not historically, but psychologically.

For the European tradition of phraseological research, this has already been pointed out (Burger, Buhofer, and Sialm 1982: 219). In these authors' opinion, the subjective motivation of an idiom is in most cases neither a product of conclusive historical reflection nor the sum of the meanings of the individual words, following the laws of semantic composition (or "abstract logical thinking" as they describe it). Instead, the motivation of an idiom is the result of strategies used for understanding the imagery of the idiom. These strategies seem to stabilise the understanding of the idiom. They make the idiom plausible and conceivable to

---

2002; Laurent et al. 2006) and the *superlemma theory of idiom production* (Sprenger, Levelt, and Kempen 2006).

2 In Cognitive Grammar, this is an essential element of a profile's "base".

the hearer/speaker by virtue of providing additional information on the actual meaning. Let us consider an example:

(1) German *jmdm. den Brotkorb höher hängen* "to hang the bread basket higher for someone/to hang someone's bread basket higher"
'to put someone on short rations; to keep someone short (financially), to reduce someone's salary etc.'

The "true" etymology of this idiom goes back to an item connected to horse keeping, the "bread basket", which is a basket for feed in the stable. In order to keep a horse from eating too much, this basket can be raised a little (Duden 2013). Even though this is the "true" historical origin, the understanding of the idiom is not disturbed if a speaker connects its inner form with a "bread basket for people" that can be moved a little so that one cannot reach it. The concept BREAD (a cultural symbol often meaning 'livelihood, the money one earns', see 4.6) provides sufficient motivating links to actual meanings like 'cutting rations' or 'reduction of salary'.

In this study, motivation is understood as the possibility of an interpretation of the mental image in a way that makes sense of the use of a given word or word combination in the meaning conventionally ascribed to it. In other terms, a motivated lexical unit includes in its underlying conceptual structure not only the actual meaning and the image component but also conceptual links between them. Although there can be no doubt about the cognitive reality of motivation (see e.g. Gibbs 1990, 1994), this notion cannot be operationalised in a strict sense. There is no way to prove how every individual speaker processes a given lexical unit; only certain trends can be revealed, by means of psycholinguistic experiments. However, this is not our aim. We can only claim that a given expression correlates with a conceptual structure, which reveals a potential coherence between the elements of the imagery and those of the semantics proper. Still, the analysis of the usage of the expression provides a powerful heuristic for the development of a cognitively based theory of figurative language such as the Conventional Figurative Language Theory.

The motivation of idioms is an autonomous phenomenon that cannot be traced back to other semantic properties of idioms. The fact that one idiom can be motivated in different ways for different individual speakers makes investigations into this phenomenon more difficult. The motivation of an idiom can be based on everyday experience or on some knowledge of an educational and cultural background [as in idiom (1)]. The latter kind of motivation depends on the extent to which the speaker is familiar with certain specific areas, for example historical circumstances, cf. idiom (2).

(2) *to put a screw/the screws on someone*
'to put pressure on someone, usually with the intent of extracting money; to exert strong psychological pressure on someone; to force someone to do what you want by intimidating them into doing something or making things difficult for them'

The literal reading of idiom (2) can be traced back to methods of torture in the Middle Ages. By turning the thumbscrew, torturers could increase pressure on their victims until the pain became unbearable. Nevertheless, the idiom may be comprehensible independent of this historical knowledge of the medieval inquisition. It can be processed on the basis of individual association as well as by imagining other types of screwing tools (such as a screw clamp).[3] The lack of a clear borderline between different types of motivation does not mean that it is useless to distinguish such types. The existence of different motivational types does not contradict the fact that some of them often occur in combination in natural language use.

Traditional structuralist approaches to figurative language made a strong distinction between "diachronic" (etymological) and "synchronic" factors. In general, the differentiation between "etymological derivation" and "synchronic motivation" is not so important from the viewpoint of Cognitive Linguistics because they are based on comparable conceptual operations.[4]

Hence, from our point of view, research on the motivation of figurative units cannot but include etymological description as a constituent part. This does not mean that etymology always influences actual meanings and brings about relevant usage restrictions, but it cannot be excluded a priori. There are sufficient examples to show how the "etymological memory" of a lexical unit determines its behaviour in current discourse. Once the etymology of a given figurative unit has been clarified, the second task is to check for possible linguistic consequences, i.e. for certain usage restrictions, traceable to the etymology.

Obviously, such linguistic consequences can be detected in the field of gender-specific usage restrictions. There are various cases of such restrictions in all the languages considered in our study. These kinds of usage restrictions may be traced back to relevant etymological phenomena if the following conditions are fulfilled:

---

[3] We do not want to go into detail about the question of how every single speaker activates his or her etymological knowledge. We start from the assumption that there are some intersubjective features in the motivation of many idioms, which can be linguistically relevant.
[4] Cf. similar ideas in Traugott (1985), Sweetser (1990) or Geeraerts (1997). With respect to idioms see also Dobrovol'skij and Piirainen (2010).

- The inner form of the figurative unit in question points to a concept that was once prototypically and exclusively related to either females or males (e.g. a garment, a gesture).
- The significance of the concept in question has now been lost.

As an analysis of large text corpora[5] reveals, even at present these lexical units may be restricted to either women or men (apart from all kinds of ironic or jocular use). Thus, the gender restrictions that originate from the inner form of an idiom are stable components of their semantic structure. A suitable example is the following idiom (3).

(3) German *seinen Hut nehmen* "to take one's hat"
 'to resign from one's post, office, to step down (referring to men)'

The inner form of this idiom is based on a physical action. In former times, middle class men used to wear a hat in public, which they had to take off when they entered a room. When a man was leaving, he took his hat, and the expression denoting this action developed into the meaning 'to leave a group, to say goodbye' (cf. Röhrich 1991: 776). Of course, women also wore hats in public, but they were not obliged to take them off upon entering a room. Therefore, a woman who was going to leave did not have to take her hat. The consequence is that this idiom was originally restricted in its use and referred exclusively to males.

Although the custom of wearing a hat in public has changed and the action of "taking one's hat" is no longer of any importance today, the gender-specific restriction of this expression still has an impact on its usage, even if it is rather limited. Frequency analysis clearly testifies to the restriction to males. Among more than 500 text examples drawn from the Internet, only one example referring to a woman was found, more precisely to a female minister. Furthermore, the text examples reveal another peculiarity of this idiom: the person resigning has to be socially important, and their resignation has to have some consequences for a given social group. Either they come from a higher occupational group, such as ministers, directors, managers, chairpeople and the like, or they are otherwise popular, e.g. a popular sportsperson leaving a club. This usage restriction can be interpreted as correlating with the etymology. The etymologically relevant feature 'belonging to the middle class' (wearing a hat was left to middle class men) corresponds to the social importance of the resigning person. Thus, the

---

[5] We are aware of the fact that there are problems with finding corpora which provide enough evidence of idiom use, but we use just what is available (cf. e.g. Colson 2003).

elements of etymological knowledge (labelled here "etymological memory") may have synchronic relevance.

However, there is a gradual scale, from the clear relevance of etymologically anchored traces for the actual meaning and/or usage to cases where etymology is not important any more. A good example is the German idiom (4).

(4) German *unter die Haube kommen* "to get under the bonnet"
     'to get married (reference to women)'

First, let us look at the etymological description. The bonnet (*Haube*) was the headgear that belonged to the traditional costume of the married woman. A significant gesture was involved when the bride, on her wedding day, donned the bonnet for the first time (Röhrich 1991: 674). Secondly, the socio-cultural aspects connected with the concept BONNET (a sign of being married; a married woman had to wear this headgear) have completely lost their familiarity in the present. It could be assumed that the "etymological memory" of the idiom preserved traces of this historical origin in the form of usage restrictions, but an Internet enquiry shows the contrary. About one third of the examples refer to males (*Kronprinz Frederik kommt unter die Haube* "Crown prince Frederik comes under the bonnet"; *Boris Becker schon wieder unter der Haube?* "Boris Becker once more under the bonnet?", and the like). Obviously, there is a trend to weaken the gender-specific usage restrictions, but it would be wrong to say that they have disappeared completely. We cannot decide whether a real meaning shift has taken place here (i.e. the abandonment of one element of the semantic structure of the idiom). Corpora alone cannot answer the question of whether a usage restriction is in the process of being abandoned. We need also the relevant knowledge of speakers to be able to answer this question. However, empirical research along these lines would go beyond the scope of our study.[6]

In short, we do not argue that all motivation is based on the knowledge of a CFU's true etymology, but we do argue against the postulate that only "folk etymology" is relevant for the processing and the usage of conventional figurative language whereas knowledge of the real etymology is never relevant for explaining motivational phenomena. The result of these reflections is that the investigation of motivation must include an etymological description. Only at the

---

[6] Both Dutch and German CFL provide about 100 gender-marked examples of this kind, many of them revealing restrictions on the level of usage (cf. Piirainen 2001a). Gender-restriction became a current topic of phraseology research: see Dobrovol'skij and Piirainen (2010) for German idioms, and later similarly for idioms of other languages, e.g. Czech (Šichová 2013a), Estonian (Baran 2015), etc. See also section 10.3.4.

next stage of analysis can we decide whether the data obtained via etymological analysis are consistent with the specifics of usage and whether they are suitable for explaining the structure of the image component. Even if the true etymology does not influence the usage, it is important for describing the cultural context in which a given figurative unit came about. This aspect of research on figurative language is, to be sure, not central to linguistically dominated approaches, but it is significant from the viewpoint of cultural semiotics.

4.2 Motivation and related phenomena

In order to use the notion of motivation efficiently, we have to distinguish it from related phenomena, above all from *analysability* and *semantic ambiguity*.

4.2.1 Motivation vs. analysability

We assume here that the "analysability" (or "decomposability") of the semantic structure of CFUs is a well-known phenomenon. The notions of *analysability* or *decomposability* have often been debated. See e.g. Rajxštejn (1980), Dobrovol'skij (1982, 2011c, 2014), Gibbs, Nayak, and Cutting (1989), Cacciari and Tabossi (1993), Nunberg, Sag, and Wasow (1994), Titone and Connine (1999), Abel (2003), Langlotz (2006), Cacciari (2014), Cserép (2017a, 2017b). Analysable idioms are expressions in which certain constituents have more or less autonomous meanings in the scope of the actual meaning, cf. (6) below.

Nunberg, Sag, and Wasow (1994) distinguish "idiomatically combining expressions" (i.e. motivated and analysable expressions) like *to pull strings*, which distribute their meaning among their parts, from "idiomatic phrases" (i.e. unmotivated and non-analysable expressions) like *to kick the bucket*, which do not. On this basis, they discover regularities in the grammatical and semantic behaviour of idioms.

Some cognitively oriented studies equate the motivation of an idiom with the *analysability* of its semantic structure (cf. e.g. Gibbs 1990). This equation, however, cannot be justified. The motivation of an idiom does not necessarily result from its analysability. Two examples may serve to illustrate this:

(5) *to split hairs*
    'to make insignificant and overly fine distinctions; to worry about unimportant differences between things as if they were important; to argue with exaggerated subtlety'

(6) *to throw the baby out with the bath (water)*
  1. 'to discard something valuable along with something not wanted'
  2. 'to proceed too radically, destroying what is good or important by mistake while trying to change and improve it'

Idiom (5) is non-analysable (non-compositional), since neither *split* nor *hairs* has an autonomous meaning in this phraseological context. Idiom (6), on the other hand, is clearly analysable: autonomous meanings can be ascribed to *baby* (meaning roughly 'the good'), *throw out* ('get rid of') and *bath water* ('a substance not needed anymore'). In this case, we are dealing with a kind of homomorphism between the structure of the actual meaning and the structure of the underlying metaphor. This is the clearest case of semantic analysability, which has also syntactic consequences and can be tested via syntactic transformations (cf. *that was the baby that was thrown out with the bath water*). However, there are also cases where the relative semantic autonomy of idiom constituents cannot be clearly tested syntactically. This type of semantic analysability will play an important role in chapter 11.

Though (5) and (6) differ with regard to the analysability of their semantic structures, both idioms are motivated. Motivation and analysability are not identical, because it is not only the meanings of the constituent parts that make up the meaning of the whole. There are also other factors that provide links between the underlying image and the actual meaning. The analysability of the semantic structure of the idiom is just one reason why the idiom in question is perceived as being motivated. There are many idioms which are not semantically analysable, in the sense that it is not possible to ascribe autonomous meanings to their constituent parts, and yet they are motivated, cf. (7).

(7) *to rattle someone's cage*
  'to do something that annoys or frightens someone; to make someone angry, usually deliberately'

Idiom (7) is not analysable, since its constituents *rattle* and *cage* cannot be regarded as (more or less) autonomous metaphors. On the contrary, they can only be plausibly interpreted in combination. Nevertheless, idiom (7) is motivated because the sense encoded in its lexical structure provides a clear basis for the metaphoric understanding of the idiom, i.e. for its actual meaning: 'as if one were sitting in a cage like a bird and somebody else rattled the bird's cage'. One of the consequences would be that the bird would become annoyed or frightened.

4.2.2 Motivation vs. semantic ambiguity

Another phenomenon which is related but not identical to motivation is the so-called semantic ambiguity of a lexical item. Thus, idioms with a literal reading that is just as current as the figurative one are semantically ambiguous, as example (8) illustrates. However, the motivation must not be equated with its semantic ambiguity. Taken literally, many idioms consist of word combinations that are semantically incompatible (*ill-formed strings*). Idiom (9), for instance, has no literal reading, only a figurative one.

(8) English *to keep one's head above water*
   1. literal 'to keep one's head above water (e.g. while swimming)'
   2. figurative 'to manage to deal with all one's problems, work, debts etc. when this is difficult and almost unfeasible; to earn enough money to be able to live or pay one's debts'

(9) German *die Oberhand gewinnen über jmdn.* "to gain the upper-hand above someone"
   'to get into a superior position, to obtain a decisive advantage or control over someone'

There is no *Oberhand* "upper-hand" in the literal sense; the combination of *Ober-* and *-hand* violates the norms of semantic compatibility. Nevertheless, idiom (9) is quite well motivated due to the standard meaning of *Ober-* 'higher (in rank)' and the secondary meaning of HAND, standing for 'power' and 'control' in this context.[7]

4.3 Unmotivated lexical units

It is important to be able to separate CFUs which are not motivated (at least, from our point of view) from those that are motivated, if we are to develop an appropriate instrument. We consider such an instrument an important part of the CFLT because motivation is one of the central notions of this theory.

---

[7] Compare the English *upper hand*, meaning figuratively 'a dominating or controlling position', in idioms like *to get/to gain the upper hand over someone* 'to get the better of someone'. Etymologically, *upper hand* comes from an ancient game in which each player in turn grasps a stick with one hand (https://idioms.thefreedictionary.com/upper). Because of the space between the words *upper* and *hand*, the compound is not perceived as a unique constituent.

Idioms can be unmotivated for different reasons. There are some idioms which, from a synchronic point of view, are semantically opaque. From the cognitive viewpoint, most idioms are considered motivated in some way or other because the speaker intuitively looks for an interpretation that makes sense. Yet, there are gradual differences. There are some idioms which are strongly motivated, in the sense that the conceptual links between the actual meaning and the image component are immediately comprehensible. There are other idioms whose motivating links are not so evident but can still be (re)constructed on a somewhat subjective basis. Finally, there are idioms for which most speakers do not see any motivation, as in idioms (10–11).

(10) *to go bananas*
   1. 'to get crazy, to go mad'
   2. 'to become extremely angry or excited, to get enraged, to lose control'

(11) *spick and span*
   'very clean, neat, tidy'

Idiom (10) shows no metaphoric inference, neither on the abstract level of a conceptual metaphor nor on the level of rich images (see below). The word string *to go bananas* is "ill-formed" and incomprehensible; it makes no sense in itself. There is no element which points to the figurative meaning of the idiom – neither a similarity between the image fixed in the idiom's lexical structure and its actual meaning nor any other parallel.

Idiom (11) does not contain any element which would allow an interpretation on the basis of the literal reading (both constituents *spick* and *span* being semantically empty, unique constituents).[8] We can say that this idiom is entirely opaque. Thus, in view of the first criterion of figurativeness (the requirement of an image component), idioms of this type have to be regarded as borderline cases, i.e. as weakly figurative units. It is hardly possible to find any traces of the image in their plane of content, i.e. the semantic structure of such idioms does not possess any kind of image component. The meaning is not expressed directly but in a roundabout way, through images that are no longer understandable and yet these idioms are still perceived as image-based, at least etymologically.

---

8 Although the word form *span* also exists outside this idiom, it can be regarded as unique because this word, as it enters the idiom, has semantically nothing in common with other, not bound, meanings of *span*.

Let us look at two other examples:

(12) *(to be) at sixes and sevens*
'(to be) in a state of total confusion or disarray, in a situation that is disorganised or hopelessly confused'

(13) *to beat about the bush*
'to broach a subject indirectly, to delay coming to the point, to hesitate to answer a question'

There are several idioms in European languages where the number SEVEN (less often the number SIX) occurs in a "symbolic function" (see chapter 12). However, a symbolic motivation cannot apply to the numerals in (12) as this idiom is completely opaque.[9] It is not possible to find out on which basis the numerals *sixes* and *sevens* have to be interpreted, although we are dealing with a non-literal but nonetheless figurative unit here. Neither does example (13) provide any link between the mental image and the actual meaning, although there is a clear mental image evoked by the lexical structure of the idiom. Thus, this idiom qualifies as a figurative unit.[10]

These examples show that motivation must not be mixed up with figurativeness. Even opaque idioms like (10–13) are figurative to some extent, because they meet our criteria (cf. section 1.3). The idiom *to beat about the bush*, for instance, is figurative, because it takes an indirect way of expressing the denotatum 'to broach a subject indirectly, to delay coming to the point, to hesitate to answer a question'. That is, there is another, simpler and more direct way to denote this concept. We maintain that almost all idioms are figurative to a certain extent and that even the presence of unique elements is one possible means of creating figurativeness. It might be possible, therefore, that idiom (13) is motivated for some speakers.

Motivation is a matter of degree in two senses. First, it varies from absolutely obvious cases of motivation to absolutely opaque, unmotivated figurative units. Secondly, the perception of a CFU as motivated varies from speaker to speaker.

---

9 Etymological studies derive the idiom from gamblers' jargon; it may be a corruption of Old French *cinque* and *sice*, the highest numbers on the dice. "From the idea of hazarding all one's goods on the two highest numbers came the idea of carelessness and neglect of one's possessions and hence the modern usage" (Speake 1999: 323).

10 It is not necessary to know the historically "true" etymology (originating from hunting or netting of birds); hunters used to beat the undergrowth with long sticks to force birds out of the bushes into the open (Speake 1999: 21).

In this sense, motivated units are neither wholly arbitrary nor fully predictable (Langacker 1987: 48). There are levels of predictability and motivation, both from the perspective of a speaker and from the perspective of the semantic structure of a given unit.

4.4 Types of motivation

Apart from the quite small number of conventional figurative units looked at in the former section, where no comprehensible link can be found between the literal reading and the figurative meaning that would allow a meaningful interpretation of the conventional figurative unit, all other CFUs have to be considered transparent or motivated. In this chapter, we will present a typology of motivation that captures all types of transparent idioms and other lexical figurative units.[11]

In general, four types of motivation can be distinguished:
(i) semantic motivation
(ii) syntactic motivation
(iii) motivation based on textual knowledge
(iv) index-based motivation

These four types of motivation differ quantitatively. Most motivated idioms belong to type (i), *semantic idiom motivation*. The semantic nature of this type manifests itself in the relation between literal and figurative readings (both of the whole word string and of one single constituent or parts of the constituent). Idioms of this type can be divided into three subtypes, which are also quantitatively different, namely (a) *metaphors*, (b) *symbols*, and (c) *coercion* (see below).

In contrast to the three semantically motivated types, there are also some groups of idioms whose motivation is based on the properties of their syntactic structure. Type (ii), *syntactic motivation*, is based on the speaker's knowledge that certain syntactic structures have their own typical semantics. We found only a few outstanding groups of this type in the languages we studied (cf. section 4.8 below).

Motivation type (iii) is of a different kind. It seems to be close to the first type, but differs in that it is not solely of semantic (metaphoric and symbolic) nature. Here, certain additional knowledge structures are involved, i.e. the knowledge

---

[11] Our typology of motivation applies to all categories of conventional figurative unit. For the sake of simplicity, we will focus on idioms as exemplary representatives of the category: idioms are particularly complex CFUs; they have not only a figurative meaning but also an inner syntactic structure. For details on idiom motivation, see e.g. Pamies (2011).

of a pre-fabricated text that underlies the interpretation of a given idiom.[12] This knowledge type motivates a considerable number of instances in the literary languages we analysed (section 4.9).

Type (iv), *index-based motivation*, is very rare. Here, we deal with features encoded (*indicated*) by certain features of the structure of the idiom: it is either its phonological or its conceptual features which point to the idiom's actual meaning as a whole (section 4.10).

As already mentioned, the large group of semantic idiom motivation can be divided into three subtypes, which are also quantitatively different, namely:
(a) metaphors
(b) symbols
(c) coercion

The largest group (a) consists of all kinds of idioms which are motivated on the basis of metaphors.[13] On a superordinate, more abstract level of description, there are the conceptual metaphors; on a subordinate and more concrete level, the frame-based metaphors that have to be traced back to rich images. Motivation type (b) can clearly be separated from type (a). Idioms of this type are also semantically motivated, not by a metaphoric re-interpretation of the whole phrase but by the symbolic functions of certain constituents. Type (c), coercion, is neither metaphoric nor symbolic in nature. It is based on the polysemy of a single constituent which is responsible for the motivation link between the lexical structure of the idiom and its lexicalised meaning.

In the following, we will discuss each type of motivation in turn. See sections 4.5 *Metaphoric motivation*, 4.6 *Symbol-based motivation*, 4.7 *Coercion as a type of motivation*, 4.8 *Syntactic motivation*, 4.9 *Motivation based on textual knowledge*, and 4.10 *Index-based motivation*. In each subsection, the specifics of motivation will be explained, with a view to validating the Conventional Figurative Language

---

12 The motivation type based on textual knowledge must not be confused with "etymological knowledge" about the origin of an idiom from a certain well-known text.
13 The literature on metaphor is vast and growing rapidly (cf. Gibbs 2008). See also chapter 6. Subjects of research are, among other things, types of metaphor (Hanks 2007; Steen 2008; Haught 2013), metaphor processing (Lai, Curran, and Menn 2009; Mashal and Faust 2009; Cuccio 2018), metaphor in context (Hanks 2004; Ritchie 2006; Thibodeau and Durgin 2007; Turney et al. 2011), metaphor in grammar (Apresjan 2019), metaphor in discourse (Cameron and Stelma 2004; Cameron 2008; Campbell and Katz 2006; Harris, Friel, and Mickelson 2006; Hidalgo-Downing and Kraljevic Mujic 2020), metaphor in corpora (Charteris-Black 2004; Deignan 2005, 2007, 2009; Stefanowitsch 2007; Hanks 2010), metaphor in Construction Grammar (Sullivan 2007), the Cognitive Theory of Metaphor and its criticism (Takada et al. 2000; McGlone 2007; Kövecses 2010, 2011; Ibarretxe-Antuñano 2012; Kessler 2013).

Theory. As for the role of the image component of idiom semantics, there are considerable differences between motivation types (i) and (iii), on the one hand, and (ii) and (iv), on the other. The image component has the most important function in idioms motivated by semantic factors and by textual knowledge. In cases of syntactic and index-based motivation, other conceptual processes are involved which can be understood as image components only in a broad sense.

All these types of motivation rarely exist in pure form; they overlap in most cases. The purpose of the present typology is to postulate types rather than to describe individual units of figurative language. The typology of motivation outlined here provides a framework for a fine-grained description of possible ways of conceptual re-interpretation for conventional figurative units.

4.5 Metaphoric motivation

4.5.1 Preliminaries

Metaphoric motivation of idioms means that the image component extends to the comparison between source and target concept. The source concept can be considered to be similar to the target concept, to a certain extent. Therefore, one conceptual domain can be mapped onto the other. We use the term *metaphoric* for those kinds of motivation that are based on similarity between the entity reflected by the underlying image and the entity denoted by the idiom taken in its actual meaning.

The metaphoric motivation can be analysed on two different levels of abstraction. The links that are relevant to metaphorically motivated idioms, i.e. the similarity between source and target domain, can be explained either on the superordinate level of the *conceptual metaphor* in the sense of the Cognitive Theory of Metaphor[14] (Lakoff and Johnson 1980; Lakoff 1987b; 1993) or on the subordinate level or the *frame-based level of categorisation*. On this level, the motivating link is provided by a conceptual structure that we call the *rich* or *conventional image* (after Lakoff 1987a; 1987b). The rich image is encoded in the lexical structure of an idiom.

Before we go into more detail concerning various types of metaphors or different levels of their analysis, some remarks are in order. Rich images are nearly always crucial for providing a motivation link. Often, the conceptual met-

---

[14] We use the abbreviation CTM for the Cognitive Theory of Metaphor. This theory is also referred to as Conceptual Metaphor Theory.

aphor as a general framework of interpretation is also involved, since idiom motivation mostly arises from a combination of conventional images and conceptual metaphors. However, this is not always the case. Sometimes it is not possible to connect the idiom with a certain conceptual metaphor, because idioms are highly conventional and their semantic re-interpretation does not follow a certain established path in all cases.

Crucial for our analysis is the fact that the rich image and conceptual metaphors are not separate subtypes of metaphoric motivation, but different levels of abstraction from which relevant motivating links can be viewed. Cases in which the idiom is motivated only by the underlying conceptual metaphor without addressing the rich image simultaneously are extremely rare. The conceptual metaphor, for the most part, is too abstract to be involved in motivation as one single factor. This can be illustrated by a simple, often quoted example – the conceptual metaphor HAPPY IS UP. An idiom such as *to be in seventh heaven* fits this metaphor; however, its basic motivation will be ascribed to its rich image – for example, to ideas about paradise.

4.5.2 Conceptual metaphor

Our empirical data include only a very few idioms which are motivated on a rather abstract level alone. So far, we have only discovered a couple of idioms (out of hundreds) which point to the abstract motivation "directly", without a frame-based image being evoked. Cf. the idiom *to be slow on the uptake* 'to lack the ability of understanding quickly, especially of understanding something new' and its antonym *to be quick on the uptake*. The motivation of the actual meaning of these idioms is based on the conceptual metaphor UNDERSTANDING IS GRASPING, which links them to other expressions of this metaphoric model, e. g. *she got a grip on it; his grasp of this subject is remarkable*, etc. Though *uptake* is comprehensible by its word formation, it is a kind of (quasi) unique constituent that makes little sense outside of the idiom. There is no need to refer to an explicit frame that can be assigned to the idiom in order to understand how the actual meaning came about.

Significant numbers of metaphorical expressions are grouped into *metaphoric models* according to rather abstract conceptual correspondences between groups of source and target domains.[15] The principal advantage of the CTM is that it

---

[15] Conceptual metaphors can be postulated at different levels of abstraction. Compare the notions of "generic metaphors" and "basic-level metaphors" in Lakoff (1987b: 397 and 406).

reveals common features of metaphorical expressions that could not be discovered otherwise. There are various concrete rich images (as well as "dead", i.e. non-figurative, metaphors) that seem to have nothing in common at first glance but, from the viewpoint of the CTM, fit into one or more patterns already present in the speaker's conceptual system.

Along these lines, one particular conceptual metaphor (metaphoric model), UNDERSTANDING IS GRASPING, serves to bring together not only conventional expressions such as *to be slow on the uptake, to be quick on the uptake, to get a grasp of something* or German *schwer von Begriff sein* "to be hard of concept (grasping)", but also many other expressions that can be classified as non-figurative metaphors belonging to this metaphoric model (cf. utterances like *I can't get it* 'I don't understand', *I grasped the main points of his speech* or *she was quick to catch on to the new program*). From an etymological point of view, even the English words *comprehend* or *concept* are examples of the conceptual metaphor UNDERSTANDING IS GRASPING.[16] Of course, this does not mean that these expressions are figurative, even though they go back to metaphors.

Finally, the same conceptual metaphor can be found in unrelated languages from culturally different areas. So, the Finnish verb *käsittää* 'to comprehend, understand' is also related to the conceptual metaphor UNDERSTANDING IS GRASPING. It can be traced back to *käsi* 'hand', the prototypical instrument of grasping (the word may be a loan-formation under the influence of Latin and German philosophical literature).

There is also a Japanese conventional figurative unit where no such influence of alien cultures is likely: 手に取るように分かる (*te ni toru yō ni wakaru*) "to understand as if picking up something with one's own hand" 'to understand something very clearly', which is going back to the metaphor UNDERSTANDING IS GRASPING. It can be assumed that a "near-universal" (culturally independent, body-based) conceptual metaphor could be discovered if many further languages from widely different cultural areas were analysed in this respect. According to Lakoff (1987b: 267), the "conceptual structure is meaningful because it is *embodied*, that is, it arises from, and is tied to, our preconceptual bodily experiences."[17]

---

16 The words originate from Latin *comprehendere* 'to get, take, understand' and *concipere* 'to grasp, catch, understand', respectively. There are various loanwords and loan translations containing the same metaphor, which is "dead" now, e.g. German *begreifen, erfassen* or *auffassen* 'to understand, comprehend' (affixations of the verbs *greifen* and *fassen*, both meaning 'to grasp, take hold of'). Cf. similar observations in Jäkel (1988).
17 The historical emergence of new word senses based on metaphors of this kind has followed a set of universal psychological and cognitive principles (cf. Ramiro et al. 2018).

4.5 Metaphoric motivation

An exhaustive description of every single figurative unit is not central to the CTM, which therefore cannot be a universal instrument for investigating figurative language. It can be used successfully only for certain tasks, such as answering the question of what regular cognitive mechanisms are implemented in generating and processing various expressions. However, it does not answer questions about the specific linguistic features of every single expression and the ways they can be explained in motivational terms. What is even more important is the fact that only a small number of figurative units – by no means all CFUs that are motivated on a purely metaphoric basis – can be grouped into metaphoric models in line with the corresponding conceptual metaphor.

As pointed out above, we can group metaphorically motivated figurative units into clusters according to their motivational bases, while applying the CTM ideas as an instrument of analysis. Such a grouping or clustering can yield many non-trivial results. Firstly, it may be a way to discover systematic, regular features in the field of figurative language. There is some plausibility to the idea that relatively few metaphoric models stand behind large numbers of figurative units across all languages. Secondly, the inventory of figurative expressions grouped according to underlying metaphoric models could provide empirical evidence for testing some hypotheses about the structure of the mental lexicon. We would like to illustrate the formation of such clusters by the orientational metaphors UP and DOWN (cf. Lakoff and Johnson 1980: 14–16). These metaphors motivate a number of figurative units, and there emerge several related metaphoric models, for example:

MORE/MUCH IS UP VS. LESS/FEW IS DOWN
SUCCESSFUL IS UP VS. UNSUCCESSFUL IS DOWN
GOOD IS UP VS. BAD IS DOWN
HAPPY IS UP VS. UNHAPPY/SAD IS DOWN.

Conceptual connections between these metaphoric models explain why some of the idioms in this domain are polysemous or have a vague meaning covering a wide range of uses, cf. (14–16).

(14) *to be on the up*
 1. 'to be increasing, improving'
 2. 'to become more successful'

(15) *to hit/reach rock bottom*
 1. 'to be at a very low level, especially of prices'
 2. 'to be in a very bad situation, which you think could not possibly be worse'

(16) *to be down in the dumps*
   1. 'to feel very sad and have no interest in life'
   2. 'to work unsuccessfully (of a business or the economy)'

The meanings of (14) correspond to two conceptual metaphors at the same time: the first meaning is based on the metaphor MORE/MUCH IS UP, and the second one on the metaphor SUCCESSFUL IS UP. The meanings of idiom (15) also correspond to two conceptual metaphors: LESS/FEW IS DOWN and BAD IS DOWN. There is a similar case of metaphorically based polysemy in idiom (16). Here the two different meanings go back to the conceptual metaphors UNHAPPY IS DOWN and UNSUCCESSFUL IS DOWN. Let us illustrate these metaphors with some further figurative units.

The metaphors MORE/MUCH IS UP and LESS/FEW IS DOWN appear in various figurative expressions (conventional as well as novel ones), cf. e.g. *rock-bottom prices* 'very low prices' [a derivation of idiom (16)], *to go into freefall* 'falling very quickly', *astronomical prices* 'extremely high prices'; German *etwas (z.B. der Dollarkurs) macht eine Berg- und Talfahrt*[18] "something (e.g. the dollar) makes a mountain and valley trip" 'something (e.g. the dollar) is worth more one moment and less the next', German *in den Keller gehen* "to go into the cellar" 'to decrease, to fall (prices, shares etc.)' or English *to fall through the floor* 'to be greatly reduced in price' and *to hit the roof/go through the roof* 'to rise very sharply, reach extreme heights'.[19] Cf. also the *monetary snake* 'margin of fluctuation of a currency' named in 13.2.1. or concepts like *yo-yo dieting, yo-yo effect* 'alternating weight loss (down) and weight gain (up)'.

The conceptual metaphors SUCCESSFUL IS UP and UNSUCCESSFUL IS DOWN manifest themselves in idioms like *to push someone over the top* 'to make someone more successful than other people, especially in a game or contest'; *to come out on top* 'to win or succeed at something you were trying to do'; *to be riding high* 'to be very successful'; *the highest rung of a ladder, the top of the heap/pile* 'the highest, most powerful, or richest position in a society, a company, an organisation etc.'; *the top of the tree* 'the highest position in a profession'; *to sink or swim* 'to fail or succeed' or *to fall flat on your face* 'to fail or make a mistake in an embarrassing way'. Another illustrative example is the English *glass ceiling* 'an obstacle, caused by people's attitudes and traditional practices, that prevents women from being successful and reaching top levels of their profession'. This

---

[18] Compare Jäkel's (2003: 218–220) term *Gebirgs-Topologie* "mountain topology" for this metaphoric model.
[19] Cf. also idiom (7) in chapter 9, meaning 'to suddenly become very angry, to be furiously angry'.

metaphoric model has equivalents in Japanese CFUs as well, since structures of social hierarchy in Japan are similar to those in Western countries (cf. examples (2–5) in chapter 10).

The metaphors GOOD IS UP and BAD IS DOWN come into view in novel metaphors or in idioms like the English *the ups and downs* 'good or bad luck befalling someone' or the German *es geht bergauf mit jmdm.* "it is going 'uphill' with someone" 'things are looking up for someone' and the English *things are going downhill* or *he is on the downhill path*,[20] often connected with aspects of morality. Thus, MORAL IS UP and IMMORAL IS DOWN can be called submodels of the metaphors GOOD IS UP and BAD IS DOWN. Cf. *a life of high morality*.

There are also many expressions based on the conceptual metaphors HAPPY IS UP and UNHAPPY IS DOWN, like the English expressions *to be low, to be beaten to the ground, one's spirits reach rock bottom* 'to be very depressed, unhappy' and *to be on top of the world, to be walking on air* or Dutch *boven de huizen zijn* "to be above the houses", all meaning 'to feel extremely happy, often so that you do not notice anything else'. Compare also German *Hochstimmung* 'high spirits' which reveals the same metaphor. Finally, the metaphoric model HAPPY IS UP can be encountered in the culturally distant Japanese language. Idioms meaning '(to be) very happy' include e.g. 飛び上がって喜ぶ (*tobiagatte yorokobu*) "to be glad (as if) jumping" or 天にも昇る心地 (*ten ni mo noboru kokochi*) "feeling elated (up) even to heaven [(as if) one ascends to heaven]". Nevertheless, the concept of HEAVEN must not be equated with that occurring in the English idiom *to be in seventh heaven* (cf. Corwin 1994: 246–247).

An analysis along these lines shows that not only are expressions from the same semantic field connected with each other via their metaphoric foundations, but even expressions from such different semantic fields as 'prices, currency rates', 'professional success', 'morality', and 'happiness' can be related to each other, albeit on a deeper conceptual level.

From the perspective of semantic theory, cases like these are especially instructive. They show a mechanism for the creation of regular polysemy. It is a well-known fact that lexical units from certain semantic classes can easily develop a common secondary meaning (Apresjan 1974a). This semantic potential is often based on a conceptual vicinity of the two senses in question. For example, the regular polysemy of the type "action → time of the action" can be explained in this way. In the

---

[20] There is no symmetry between *uphill* and *downhill*, since *uphill* in expressions like *an uphill task* 'a difficult task' has no counterpart in *downhill*. The underlying concept of *uphill* is associated with a steep road, arduous to walk. *Downhill*, however, is not associated with things that are easy.

field of figurativeness, however, we often deal with another mechanism responsible for regular polysemy. The link between the two meanings is provided by a close relationship between the motivating conceptual metaphors.

In conclusion, we have to stress that only parts of the motivation of many idioms and other figurative units can be described exclusively on the basis of conceptual metaphors. In numerous cases, other types of motivating links are activated as well.

4.5.3 Frame-based metaphor and rich image

As motivational basis of CFUs, metaphors show different levels of abstraction. Let us once again consider the idioms (6–7) discussed above, *to split hairs* and *to throw the baby out with the bath water*. The relevant motivating links are provided at the level of rich images, evoked by the lexical structure of the idioms. We can picture the situation when someone behaves or acts *as if* he or she was splitting hairs or *as if* he or she was throwing a baby out with the bath water, the images serving as bases for inference, i.e. we refer to a certain frame. In cases like these, it would be hard to formulate an abstract metaphoric correspondence in the sense of a conceptual metaphor at the superordinate level.

The dichotomy between the *conceptual metaphor* and the so-called *rich image* is crucial for describing the iconic motivation of CFUs. In order to describe various kinds of figurative units, we need different tools, namely the apparatus of the Cognitive Theory of Metaphor, on the one hand, and the apparatus of frames and scripts that is well-known in Cognitive Linguistics, on the other. This approach to metaphor analysis on the level of rich images (frame-based metaphors) will be discussed in chapter 8.

An important assumption of the CFLT is that the central metaphor type in the field of conventional figurative language is the frame-based metaphor. Lakoff (1987a: 194–195) distinguishes four general types of metaphor:

(i) *complex schema mappings*, where the source ontology is mapped onto the target ontology;
(ii) *image-schema mappings* such as containers, paths, linear scales, centre-periphery, force, links, balance, contact/noncontact, cycles, front/back;
(iii) *one-shot rich-image mappings*, where there is no system of concepts being mapped;
(iv) *Aristotle's metaphor*, following the principle SOMETHING IS WHAT IT HAS SALIENT PROPERTIES OF.

Lakoff (1987a: 195) points out that these types of metaphor are not mutually exclusive, and mixed cases are common. This is true also for the field of conventional figurativeness. However, the leading type in this domain is type (iii). The term *one-shot rich-image mappings* points to two significant features of this metaphor type. On the one hand it is an elaborated image based on a concrete frames with all its participants and properties; that is why it is *rich*, rather than schematic. On the other hand, this image is, as a single entity, based on convention and not on regular ontological mappings from source to target.[21]

If an idiom is constituted by a conceptual metaphor, there is also almost always a more concrete motivation that points simultaneously to the underlying rich image. This means that, in most cases, the figurative semantics of an idiom is comprehensible on the basis of its correspondences with the underlying image partly fixed in the idiom's lexical and syntactic structure. The following example (17) shows how the two levels of metaphoric motivation coexist and can be distinguished for an analysis of motivating links.[22]

(17) *to throw dust in someone's eyes*
      'to deceive or mislead someone by distracting him/her willfully; to make an opponent temporarily unable to assess the situation'

On the one hand, idiom (17) is motivated by a conceptual metaphor.[23] The abstract source concept DISTURBANCE OF SEEING (indicated by *to throw dust in someone's eyes*) can be mapped onto the target concept DECEPTION (denoted by the lexicalised meaning of the idiom), due to the similarity of the source and target concepts. We encounter the conceptual metaphor DECEPTION IS DISTURBANCE OF SEEING which can be found in several figurative expressions (see below). On the other hand, the idiom is motivated by its rich imagery. The literal reading of the idiom's lexical structure evokes a concrete image: one can imagine how someone throws dust in another person's eyes (as practiced for example in unfair competitions in

---

21 Type (iv) *Aristotle's metaphor* may also be based on convention to a certain extent. Cf. Lakoff's examples such as *Man is a wolf, Harry is a pig*. Metaphors of this type have variable domains and possess elements of metonymy. Lakoff (1987a: 195) points out that "little of a systematic nature is known about this metaphor (e.g. whether there are restrictions on its domains)". This type of metaphor is encountered in the field of conventional figurativeness rather often, especially in cases of symbol-based motivation, where metonymy plays a leading role.
22 We speak here of two levels of metaphor analysis: *conceptual metaphor* including types (i) and (ii) distigished by Lakoff, and *frame-based metaphor* revealing one-shot rich-image mappings (iii) and in certain cases also traces of Aristotle's metaphor (iv).
23 Compare type (i) *complex schema mappings* in the classification of metaphors developed in Lakoff (1987a: 195).

earlier times). This source frame provides a basis for comparing a person's physical action with the action of deceiving another person. Therefore, the figurative meaning of the idiom should be formulated as 'to deceive or mislead someone by distracting him/her willfully; to make an opponent temporarily unable to assess the situation, which is regarded as an intentional attempt to effect his/her organ of vision in order to distract his/her perception of reality'.

In cases of this type, using the Lakoffian metalanguage of conceptual metaphors has clear advantages. Figurative expressions such as (17) can be brought together with conceptually similar expressions which otherwise would be analysed separately in the framework of traditional lexicology. Together with idioms like *to pull the wool over someone's eyes* 'to deceive, mislead someone', *to muddy the waters* 'to make things more confused by obscuring them', etc., the metaphor underlying idiom (17) forms a well-developed metaphoric model. The idioms belong also to wider metaphoric models such as KNOWING IS SEEING or NOT KNOWING IS DARKNESS. There are clusters of the same metaphor, built up not only by idioms but by all kinds of figurative expressions, across boundaries between taxonomic classes. This enables us to compare idioms with all other metaphoric units, even "dead metaphors" fixed in words like *evident, obvious* (from Latin *videre* 'to see'), because all of them go back to the conceptual metaphor KNOWING IS SEEING. However, an attempt to interpret idiom (17) exclusively on the basis of the relevant conceptual metaphor fails. To reveal relevant motivating links we have to address, first of all, the conventional or rich image which can possibly be interpreted in the next stage of analysis in terms of conceptual metaphors.[24]

Attempts to explain every possible figurative expression on the basis of conceptual metaphors are doomed to failure. Compare, for example, the analysis of the idiom *don't throw the baby out with the bath water* in terms of alleged abstract metaphors like FAITH RELATES TO CHILDREN and IDEAS ARE OBJECTS (Kispál 2004: 136). In this case, such an abstract metaphoric correspondence can hardly have psychological reality. It can be assumed that the majority of metaphorically motivated idioms are based on a concrete "rich" imagery, even if in certain cases they can be traced back to a conceptual metaphor. Often, however, there is no association with a conceptual metaphor whatsoever. Compare idiom (18).

(18) *the ball is in your court*
 'it is your turn to take the next step (in a negotiation, dispute, etc.)'

---

[24] Cf. the well-known interpretation of conceptual correspondences motivating idioms as links "of the form *conventional image + knowledge + metaphors* relating the idiom to its meaning" (Lakoff 1987b: 451).

For this idiom (and for most other metaphorically motivated idioms), it is impossible to formulate an abstract metaphor at the superordinate level. Instead, the idiom is fully motivated by frame-based knowledge. To process the idiom adequately, relevant knowledge of the frame TENNIS is required. When the tennis ball falls on a player's court, it is their turn to hit the ball back. There is a metaphoric similarity between the actual meaning and the inner form (the imagery evoked by the lexical structure; see for detail Dobrovol'skij 2016b). The situation denoted by the actual meaning resembles the situation encoded in the lexical structure, *as if* someone had to hit the ball back to the other one's court. The frame as a whole serves as the relevant metaphoric basis, and addressing the rich image allows for the correct interpretation of motivating links.

When we consider the notion of *rich image* in metaphorically motivated idioms, we will see that various types of knowledge are involved. First of all, a distinction can be made between knowledge that is more or less independent of culture and knowledge that is based on culture. The opposition between "natural experience" and "cultural knowledge" is one of the central dichotomies of our study. It also becomes apparent here in the context of metaphoric motivation. There is a relatively small group of idioms which are motivated by certain features of the outward appearance of something, where no particular cultural knowledge is required, as in idiom (19). The opposite can be illustrated by idiom (20). Its motivation is highly dependent on cultural knowledge (symbolic knowledge in this case). On the level of formal structure, the two idioms (19) and (20) seem to resemble one another.[25]

(19) French *avoir des yeux de hibou* "to have the eyes of a screech owl"
'to have big, round, fixed eyes'

(20) French *avoir des yeux de lynx* "to have the eyes of a lynx"
'to have very sharp eyesight, to have good powers of vision'

Since an owl really has big eyes, a salient property of the bird, one which everybody can identify, idiom (19) is primarily based on direct experience, i.e. immediate perception of the appearance of an owl. No other knowledge (for example of the symbolic value of the OWL) is required. Nevertheless, even here minimal elements

---

[25] Since specifics of figurative language can be successfully explained by examples containing "animal constituents", we will repeatedly return to this illustrative material. Several researchers have made use of "zoological metaphors"; cf. e.g. Black's (1962: 39–41) prominent example "Man is a wolf". Lakoff labels such cases as *Aristotle's metaphors*. A detailed case study on this topic will be given in chapter 13.

of culture appear, namely with respect to the reason why the linguistic community takes just this bird (rather than another animal) as the "best example" of a creature with big round eyes. By contrast, idiom (20) cannot be interpreted on the basis of "natural experience". The eyes of a lynx are not actually sharper than those of other animals belonging to the *Felidae* family. The meaning of idiom (20) came into being by cultural tradition alone. According to some medieval cultural codes, the LYNX was considered a symbol of 'watchfulness, vigilance' and 'sharp eyesight'. These alleged properties of the animal were spread by several authors and resulted in CFUs like (20) (see section 4.6 and 11.4.3).

The domain of animals in figurative language provides further examples of this kind. The SNAKE, for example, turns out to be a symbol in many CFUs. However, there are also a few expressions containing the concept SNAKE that can only be interpreted on the basis of natural experience, such as the outward appearance of the animal as 'something long' (e.g. German *Schlange stehen* "to stand snake" 'to queue up, to stand in line'). The same holds for other animal concepts in figurative language. This will be worked out in more detail in chapter 13.

For the adequate interpretation of the majority of idioms motivated on the level of rich imagery, however, it is necessary to address cultural knowledge. In many cases, aspects of material culture are dominant (cf. the typology of aspects of culture in chapter 10). We will consider once again an animal constituent: the concept HORSE is richly elaborated in the figurative languages cross-linguistically analysed here. Nevertheless, only a very few expressions refer to aspects of the outward appearance, for example English *horse laugh* 'a very noisy and stupid laugh', referring to a peculiarity of the horse, its "laughing" noise, which is similar to a human laugh. All the other CFUs with HORSE require some cultural knowledge, either of the horse as a draft animal, as a saddle horse, or as a race horse. Let us look at (21), where a special kind of knowledge about equestrian sport is involved in the interpretation.

(21) *to back the wrong horse*
      'to rely on a person who then lets you down'

There is a "metaphoric similarity" between the actual (figurative) meaning and the inner form (the imagery evoked by the lexical structure) of the idiom. The situation denoted by the actual meaning resembles the situation encoded in the lexical structure, *as if* someone was backing the wrong horse, or to be precise: as if someone was betting on a horse that will not win the races. Hence, some knowledge of the frame HORSE RACING is required to process this idiom adequately. Within this frame, relevant knowledge of the details of "backing a horse" (the procedure of betting on a horse) must be activated. In such cases, an approach merely based on conceptual metaphors is completely unsuitable for offering access to the correct interpretation, since the frame as a whole serves as the metaphoric basis here.

Such conceptual links motivating the lexicalised figurative meaning of idioms are often provided by metonymy, rather than by metaphor, or by both metonymy and metaphor in combination (cf. Goossens 1990; Geeraerts 2002; Radden 2002; Cserép 2009; Ruiz de Mendoza Ibañez and Galera-Masegosa 2011; Reda 2016). One special case of metonymic motivation is *symbol-based motivation*, the subject of the next section.

4.6 Symbol-based motivation

A second type of motivation, also based on semantics, differs from metaphoric motivation in that the focus is on the knowledge of certain cultural symbols. The meaning of a symbol motivates the actual meaning of the idiom. That is, knowledge of the meaning of the symbol makes the idiom transparent to the speaker/hearer and is the core of the image component of its meaning.

The image component extends to *one single constituent* (or more precisely, to the concept behind it) and not to the idiom as a whole. This constituent can be separated from other elements of the idiom's lexical structure; it shows relative semantic autonomy. The symbol-based motivation is brought about not by the comparison between source and target domain (as is the case with the metaphoric type of motivation) but by the coherence between the symbolic concept in the language and similar symbolic phenomena in relevant cultural codes other than language (such as mythology, religions, folk belief, popular customs, fairy tales, fine arts, etc.). This characteristic of symbols is accompanied by a high degree of culture-based *conventionalisation*. Therefore, we call these linguistic units *cultural symbols*. The symbolic type of motivation also appears in combination with other types of motivation in many cases.

Consider idiom (22), where we encounter two symbolic concepts (WOLF and DOOR) along with other types of motivation.

(22) *to keep the wolf from the door*
 'to ward off starvation or financial ruin; to maintain oneself at a minimal level'

Of the two symbols in idiom (22), WOLF is certainly the more important one. That is why we only want to briefly touch on the symbol door in the idiom. DOOR has developed several symbolic meanings in language and culture, among them the meaning of a 'strict distinction between inside and outside' which dominates here. This symbolic meaning came about as a result of a *metonymic semantic shift*. Thus, the symbolic concept DOOR has also preserved aspects of its literal meaning.

The other symbol in idiom (22), WOLF, is better suited to explain the symbol-based motivation type. Cultural symbols can show a kind of polysemy: DANGER is one of the central symbolic functions of the WOLF; in idiom (22), however, the symbolic meaning POVERTY, ECONOMIC DESPAIR plays the principal part in the motivation of the idiom. The wolf, from ancient times, has been noted for its greediness and ravenous appetite. These symbolic functions are recurrent in various idioms and proverbs and they agree with the symbolic functions of WOLF that are anchored in cultural codes other than language. The negative symbolisations of the wolf are not based on the speakers' experience with the animal but are due to age-old semiotisation, which mainly came about through literary and narrative traditions, from antiquity and the Bible up to fairy tales or nursery rhymes. These symbolisations are not based on similarity but on *convention*. In order to process the idiom, knowledge of the symbolic meaning behind the constituent *wolf* must be activated: this knowledge makes it possible to equate WOLF with POVERTY, ECONOMIC DESPAIR which leads to the semantic result as denoted by the lexical meaning.

Symbol-based motivation often appears together with other types of motivation. The lexical structure of idiom (22) also evokes an image: a house or residence (induced by the constituent *door*) which the wolf wants to invade. The concept WOLF does not belong to the frame of a house, so the symbolic motivation clearly dominates any frame-based metaphoric motivation. Yet another type of motivation is involved: motivation based on textual knowledge (cf. section 4.9). The image evoked by the literal meaning comes close to well-known fairy tale motifs. Particularly close to the idiom is the story of the Brothers Grimm "The Wolf and the Seven Young Kids" in which the mother goat warns her young *not to open the door for the wolf*. As in other cases, different motivating mechanisms work closely together.

In chapter 11, we will explain our notion of the cultural symbol in figurative language in detail. There we will discuss the operational criteria employed to discriminate symbol-based CFUs from units of other types. Here, we will only take a brief look at this topic from the motivation angle, which can be illustrated with some additional examples:

(23) a. *a sly old fox*
'a very shrewd person'
b. *foxy*
'sly, clever, crafty'

CFUs (23a) and (23b) cannot be understood on the basis of zoological knowledge about foxes. Rather, we deal with a semiotisation of the FOX in Western culture. Throughout the centuries, the concept FOX has absorbed and accumulated fragments of knowledge coming from sources quite different from "natural experience", namely from culturally relevant sign systems. Since antiquity, tales of animals, fables, beast epics, or bestiaries have had a large share in creating the picture of the 'sly, crafty, or deceitful fox', which has been personified and thought of as behaving like a human.

Although the significance of fables, once an important educational tool, has decreased since the last century, the vitality of the concept of the 'sly fox' has not diminished. This concept has been adapted and is supported by modern media, such as animated cartoons, computer games, and advertising. The picture of a fox is immediately understood as 'a clever person', someone who has an eye to his or her advantage. Compare also the derived adjective *foxy* (23b). So firmly is the concept rooted in culture that one might even take it for granted that the fox is a sly and crafty creature. However, the members of the European cultural communities did not obtain this concept of the FOX through confrontation with the real animal, but only through its symbolisation in different semiotic systems.

It is easy to recognise the difference between this "symbolic knowledge" (as with the FOX) and the "iconic" knowledge structures underlying idioms like *horse laugh* and *to back the wrong horse* (discussed above). A sentence like *Peter is an old fox* can be unambiguously decoded into its actual meaning 'Peter is a very shrewd person' because the symbolic meaning of FOX as 'a sly person' has been conventionalised and is so strongly present in Western culture. A sentence like *Peter is a horse*, however, would not be comprehensible without additional (contextual) information, as there is no conventionalised symbolic meaning of HORSE in English.

Currently, the cultural symbol FOX, once widespread in idioms and proverbs of European languages, is mainly present in idioms which are closely related to collocations and in similes (e.g. German *ein schlauer Fuchs*, Dutch *een sluwe vos* "a sly fox", Russian *старая лиса* "an old fox", Finnish *vanha kettu* "an old fox", Swedish *listig som en räv* "cunning as a fox", Greek *πονηρός σαν αλεπού* "crafty as a fox", etc.). However, there is also a somehow outdated Finnish idiom (24):

(24) Finnish *hänella on ketunhäntä kainalossa* "he has the fox tail under the armpit"
'he is very crafty, having an ulterior motive for something or having intrigues and deception in mind'

Here, the concept FOX (the personified FOX) is not indicated by the word *kettu* 'fox' but metonymically by the word *ketunhäntä* 'fox tail'. Idiom (24) would not be comprehensible without "symbolic knowledge", i.e. the knowledge, shared by members of this linguistic community, that words or word groups pointing to the concept FOX have secondary readings, referring to a 'a shrewd, crafty, cunning person'.

In sum, the concept FOX can be regarded as a symbol that is firmly established in both culture and figurative language. It is a salient symbol, not only from the viewpoint of cultural semiotics but also from the viewpoint of linguistics. Thus we can call it an *active symbol*.

There are also "less active" cultural symbols in figurative language, which can be classified as *inactive symbols* or *dead symbols*, according to their degree of linguistic and/or cultural-semiotic relevance. These groups include symbols that were active at the time when the CFUs in question came into being but are no longer comprehensible or linguistically effective today. We will discuss these groups of cultural symbols in more detail in chapter 11.

The semantic procedures underlying symbol-based motivation in most cases constitute a *metonymic shift*. This does not mean, of course, that symbol-motivated CFUs cannot be metaphoric at the same time. The difference between metaphoric motivation and symbol-based motivation is that the former involves the idea of similarity between the entity encoded in the inner form and the entity denoted by the actual meaning, whereas the latter exploits certain cultural conventions.

The interconnectedness between symbolic concepts in CFL and culture can be demonstrated by means of cross-linguistic and cross-cultural examples. What seems to be "natural" in a given language and unquestionable from the perspective of one's own culture may turn out to be idiosyncratic and conventional (culture-specific) from the perspective of another language and culture. For illustration, let us consider the concept BREAD in the idioms of European languages. The symbolic meanings of BREAD in these idioms are LIVING, LIVELIHOOD (25), or, closely related, more general senses like WORK or SOURCE FOR EARNING ONE'S LIVING (26) and MONEY, COSTS (27).

(25) English *to take the bread out of someone's mouth*
'to deprive someone of his/her living'

(26) German *das ist ein hartes Brot* "that is hard bread" or "that is a hard loaf"'
'it is a hard way to earn one's living'

(27) French *ça ne mange pas de pain* "this does not eat bread"
'this does not incur expenses'

There are dozens of CFUs in European standard languages that reveal the concept BREAD in such symbolic meanings. In some expressions, the aspect of LIVING, LIVELIHOOD is the central one, cf. English *the bread-winner* 'the person in the family whose wages provide what the family needs to live on' or Russian *заботиться о куске хлеба* "to care about (a) piece of bread" 'to care about how to earn the money you need in order to live'. Other idioms give priority to the aspect of LIVELIHOOD with a conceptual link to WORK providing the living (e.g. Finnish *olla jonkun leivissä* "to be in someone's breads" 'to be employed by someone, to work for someone') or to MONEY, cf. Swedish *en konst som icke ger bröd* "an art that does not give bread" 'an activity that does not bring any money with it'. However, these aspects mostly go together, cf. Lithuanian *duonos kąsnis* "(a) piece of bread" 'the money you earn to be able to live' or Greek *κάτι έχει ψωμί* "something has bread" 'it is a safe, promising, and lucrative matter'.

Even if most average speakers of these languages are unaware of the fact that this interpretation of BREAD is a nontrivial, culturally based artefact, it can be easily proved by looking at languages from other, non-European cultural areas. Japanese, for example, has some idioms with the constituent 飯 (*meshi*),[26] meaning both '(cooked) rice' and 'meal' and carrying symbolic functions similar to those of BREAD. The meaning WORK or SOURCE OF MONEY, LIVELIHOOD prevails in the idiom 無駄飯を食う (*muda meshi wo kuu*) "to eat useless (cooked) rice" 'to be unproductive, getting little work done, making an effort to no avail'.

The fact that bread (rather than another basic foodstuff, e.g. porridge) became so important in occidental languages and cultures is due to the central position of BREAD in Christianity and the extensive semiotic complex with which it is surrounded, cf. e.g. 'breaking the bread' in the Last Supper, BREAD in Eucharistic liturgies, or the prayer verse *give us today our daily bread*. This symbolic knowledge manifests itself in languages from various Christian cultural areas, irrespective of particular ecclesiastical or biblical traditions: not only in languages from the sphere of influence of the Roman Catholic church or the Lutheran Bible but also in the languages of the Russian and Greek Orthodox Churches.

Similarly, the concept RICE is central to Japanese culture. It has developed a rich symbolism and is seen as a symbol of Japanese identity (Ohnuki-Tierney

---

[26] *Meshi* (as well as *kuu* 'to eat, guzzle') is used in male language and somewhat rude. The neutral word, 御飯 (*gohan*), also meaning '(cooked) rice' and 'meal', does not carry any symbolic meanings.

1993). Mythology, folk-belief, annual festivals, and many other cultural activities are heavily related to the RICE concept. Every rice grain is thought to have a soul, and this soul is identified as being divine, a deity (Handelman 1998: 413). The enthroning of the Emperor is accompanied by splendid rice ceremonies. In Shintoistic shrines, rice is given to the deities as a sacrificial offering. In sum, the concept RICE has symbolic functions in the Japanese culture that are comparable to the symbolic functions of the concept BREAD in Christian cultures.

The symbol-based type of motivation differs significantly from the other types of motivation. Links between the literal reading and the actual meaning are provided by cultural conventions here (as the conceptual link between FOX and A SHREWD PERSON, or between BREAD and MONEY). Unlike metaphoric motivation, symbol-based motivation is metonymic for the most part. To uncover relevant motivating links in symbol-based CFUs, one has to address semiotic systems other than natural language. See chapter 11 for details.

What is especially important here for the CFLT? Symbol-based motivation shows that one of the central points of motivational phenomena is of a cultural nature. Symbols are based on highly conventionalised cultural codes, part of the tacit knowledge of speakers belonging to a given cultural landscape. Symbols show how important it is to compare different languages to discover general linguistic principles. The more languages we consider, the more cultures we can contrast. A thorough cross-linguistic analysis is the only way to discover cultural specifics, i.e. phenomena that are significant features of CFUs in purely linguistic terms. To understand the linguistic concept of motivation we have to address cultural codes as well.

4.7 Coercion as a type of motivation

The third type of semantic motivation is of a different nature. We label it *coercion*. The image component is based on a meaning shift of the idiom. The previous section has shown that symbolic motivation does not extend to the whole expression (as is the case with metaphoric idioms) but mainly to one of its constituents. In the case of coercion, the relationship between one constituent and the entire word string is different again. On the one hand, the potential polysemy of one of its constituents is a prerequisite. On the other hand, the construction semantics is important, i.e. the contrast between the literal interpretation of a given lexical structure and the figurative reading of the polysemous constituent within the idiom's semantic structure. The specific feature of coercion in terms of motivation is that the speaker/hearer has to realise two different meanings of the constituent: one induced by the semantics of the idiom and the other forced by the semantic coherence between this constituent and the construction in which it is embedded. The image component manifests itself in the semantic bridge between the two meanings of this polysemous constituent. Cf. (28).

(28) *to turn on the waterworks*
'to start crying, especially deliberately, in order to make someone do what you want'

The word *water* is polysemous: on the one hand, it refers to 'water in general' or 'stretch of water'. On the other hand, and more specifically, *water* can refer to tears. Normally, it is clear which reading of a polysemous word or word element must be activated in which context. In the case of idiom (28), we deal with an intended ambiguity. The actual meaning of the idiom, 'to start crying', requires the activation of the second reading of *water*, 'tears'. However, the lexical structure of the idiom, i.e. the underlying construction, forces the activation of the other meaning of *water*, namely 'water in general'. Thus, the literal reading of the word string *to turn on the waterworks* presupposes this *water*-meaning. At the same time, the actual meaning of the idiom presupposes the *tears*-reading. This leads to a double-take effect in semantic interpretation. The motivating link is based on the potential semantic ambiguity of the lexical element and on focusing the role that constructions play in resolving this ambiguity.

There is a similar German idiom, cf. (29):

(29) German *nahe am Wasser gebaut haben* "to have built close to the water"
'to be rather weepy, tearful, to cry often, frequently without any reason'

Like the English word *water*, the German word *Wasser* is polysemous: on the one hand, it refers to 'water in general' (as in a lake or river). On the other hand, and more specifically, *Wasser* can refer to body liquids, among them tears (cf. the German idiom *jmdm. tritt das Wasser in die Augen* "the water comes into someone's eyes" 'someone begins to cry'). When the second reading of *Wasser* is activated (which is necessary in order to use the idiom in its actual meaning), the image of 'being built close to the water' is re-interpreted in the sense of 'being close to tears'.

The contextual conditions of the idiom's literal reading force the realisation of one meaning of the constituent, while the figurative meaning of the whole idiom requires the realisation of the second (less frequent) meaning of this constituent. The motivation link is provided by the semantic links between these two readings. The motivation mechanism that initiates the semantic interpretation of the idiom is coercion.

Idiom (30) is a similar case.

(30) *if you pay peanuts, you get monkeys*
 'only stupid people will work for you if you do not pay very much'

The word *peanuts*, literally referring to small nuts, is also a modern slang expression for 'a very small amount of money'. In the first part of the idiom, *if you pay peanuts*, we deal with the meaning of this slang expression, indicated by the verb *to pay*, whereas the second part of the idiom activates the literal meaning of *peanuts* (indicated by *monkeys*, animals that are particularly fond of peanuts). Like (28–29), idiom (30) is a conventionalised play on words or punning cliché. It is based on an intended violation of the norm, namely on the lack of disambiguity, which is used in a humorous way in order to express the idea that the consequence of paying *peanuts* (i.e. low wages) to professionally skilled people will be that they leave their job and the only employees one will be able to find instead will be no better than *monkeys*.

Various conventionalised plays on words reveal this type of motivation. There is a special type of wordplay, including similes, which is less common in English or in Russian but abundant in German. The motivation is due to the lack of disambiguity of a polysemous constituent. An example is the German idiom *Einfälle haben wie ein altes Haus*. Literally, it means either "to have collapses like an old house" or "to have ideas of an old house", depending on which meaning of the polysemous constituent *Einfälle* (collapses or ideas) is activated. In view of the actual meaning, 'to have very strange ideas', only the second reading makes sense. When hearing the phrase *Er hat Einfälle* . . . "he has ideas" or "he has collapses", the addressee initially thinks of "ideas". After perceiving the rest of the sentence . . . *wie ein altes Haus* "like an old house" the addressee triggers the frame HOUSE at the same time. The initial reading of *Einfälle* as 'ideas' remains activated while the simultaneous processing of both readings of *Einfälle* induces a double-take effect. The idiom's actual meaning 'to have very strange ideas' is a result of the interplay of the construction taken literally and the polysemy of the word *Einfälle*.

Compare some more constructions which follow the same procedure: *jmdn. ausnehmen wie eine Weihnachtsgans* "to draw/to rob someone like a Christmas goose" 'to rob someone, to take something away from someone', *gerührt sein wie Apfelmus* "to be stirred/to be moved like apple purée" 'to be very moved', *gespannt sein wie ein Flitzebogen* "to be strained/to be curious like a toy bow" 'to be very curious', etc. Cf. also the French simile (31).

(31) French *beurré comme une tartine* "buttered like a slice of bread"
 'completely drunk'

The constituent *beurré* is the subject of the constructional coercion: it consists of the different meanings of *beurrer*, 'to butter' and 'to get terribly drunk'. The context of the literal reading, *une tartine* "a slice of bread" forces the realisation of the reading of *beurré* 'buttered', to meet the co-occurrence requirements, while the figurative meaning of the simile forces the speaker/hearer to realise the other reading, namely 'to get terribly drunk'. Both readings are actualised at the same time. This provides an *incongruity effect*. In order to trace the motivation, the speaker/hearer has to realise both meanings at the same time: 'buttered' to understand the construction how it is presented on the level of the lexical structure and 'to get terribly drunk' to understand the actual meaning. The motivation link is the bridge between the lexical structure and the actual meaning, i.e. to trace it, one has to realise the polysemy structure.

A basically similar case is idiom (32) that also displays a play on words.

(32) *for donkey's years*
'for a very long time'

What is specific about this case is that the constructional coercion affects paronyms rather that readings of a polysemous word. According to Speake (1999: 104), the idiom is a pun alluding to the length of a donkey's ears and playing on the incorrect pronunciation of *years* as *ears*. The concept TIME is indicated directly, by the constituent *years*, while the idea of VERY LONG is expressed in terms of space, using an object that is prototypically 'long' (such as the ears of a donkey in comparison to the ears of most other animals). Thus, the associated construction *donkey's ears* vaguely points to a long object whereas the word *years* instead of *ears* forces the shift from SPACE to TIME in the semantic interpretation of the whole expression. An additional motivating link is provided by the conceptual metaphor TIME IS SPACE.

These examples show that the constructional phenomenon of coercion, how it is applied to the analysis of conventional figurative expressions here, correlates with the blending of mental spaces at the conceptual level.[27]

What has been discussed in this section concludes a result that is completely new in the theory of phraseology. Idioms can be motivated not only be

---

27 Compare Blending Theory or Conceptual Integration Theory. For more details, see e.g. Fauconnier (1997), Fauconnier and Turner (1998, 2002), Oakley (1998), Grady, Oakley, and Coulson (1999), Coulson and Oakley (2000, 2005), Gibbs (2000), Sweetser (2000). In phraseology, the instruments developed in this theory were applied in Omazić (2005, 2008), Omazić and Delibegović Džanić (2009) and Jaki (2014) for analysis of idiom modifications as well as in Dobrovol'skij and Piirainen (2017) for studying constructional patterns in idioms.

well-known tropes such as metaphor or metonymy, but also by constructional coercion. So far, this motivational mechanism has not been taken into account. These ideas connect our theory to the Construction Grammar approaches.

4.8 Syntactic motivation

Motivation of the following type is based on some specific features of the idiom's syntactic structure. The syntax itself has no imagery in the strict sense. Rather, it is a kind of constructional component. This means that knowledge is required about the fact that certain syntactic structures have typical (almost default) conceptual interpretations.

Units of this type come close to the notion of *construction* in the sense of Construction Grammar (CxG), more precisely to the postulate that certain syntactic patterns themselves have a kind of lexical meaning. We restrict ourselves to two examples. The first group is *similes*, which are motivated by their structure. Cf. (33).

(33) a. *as plain as a pikestaff* 'very obvious'
 b. *as dead as a doornail* 'absolutely dead'
 c. *as drunk as a skunk* 'very drunk'
 d. *to eat like a horse* 'to eat very much', etc.

There is no need to look for the logical coherence of the comparison, because one knows that the simile *as plain as an X* always means 'very plain, obvious'. The same holds for many other similes. All constructions of this type [as Q as X] or [to V like X] have in common the intensification of the actual meaning. Therefore, the interpretation must contain an expression like 'very', 'absolutely', 'very much', etc. In addition, idioms like (33) can be characterised by alliteration, rhyme or rhythm and are often used jokingly.[28]

In contrast to wide-spread syntactic patterns such as similes, other syntactic patterns to which a figurative meaning can be attributed are few. Compare idioms (34) which reveal a pattern that seems to be limited to German and closely related

---

[28] Similes are a very common subgroup of idioms. They go far beyond one single language. Within the European languages studied so far, no language has been discovered that does not include similes. This is remarkable, especially with regard to CxG. This means that certain constructional patterns may be similar in different languages due neither to genetic affiliation nor to borrowings.

languages. The underlying pattern is [with X and Y] meaning 'with everything, all together, completely'.

(34) a. German *mit Kind und Kegel* "with child and (bowling) pin", etymologically: "with legitimate and illegitimate child"
   b. German *mit Sack und Pack* "with bag and stack/pack"
   c. German *mit Haut und Haar* "with skin and hair"

These idioms are by no means synonymous, but they share one common meaning aspect, that of 'with everything, all together, completely': while idiom (34a) emphasizes the idea 'with the whole family' and idiom (34b) 'with all one's belongings', idiom (34c) refers to 'totally, with all one's passion', in contexts such as *to deepen into one's field of interest "with skin and hair"*. Again, alliteration or end rhyme can be found as an additional factor of idiomaticity. Compare English *(with) bag and baggage* 'with all one's belongings; completely, totally' and *(with) kith and kin* 'with one's friends and relationship'. These idioms come close to pattern (34) but also occur without the preposition *with*.

Most syntactic constructions have no lexical meaning by themselves. They do not force the speaker/hearer to link the pattern with a meaning. Nevertheless, we have shown by the constructions [as Q as X], [to V like X] and [with X and Y] that a motivation due to syntactic patterns also exists, be it through very common similes or a small group of idioms in only a few languages.[29]

Specific of this motivation type is that the relevant motivating link is provided not by the image component in our interpretation proposed in chapter 1, but by the speaker's knowledge of the semantic properties of a given syntactic structure. As for the concrete imagery fixed in the inner form, it is there and may play an important role for the idiom's semantic, stylistic and pragmatic properties. Some traces of the inner form may influence the idiom's actual meaning.

4.9 Motivation based on textual knowledge

The subject of this section is a group of idioms (and other figurative lexical units) that partly escape semantic motivation based on metaphoric or symbolic elements. Compare the notion of *intertextual resonance* opposed to the concept of *lexical resonance* in Hanks (2016). The image component of this type connects the idiom with a well-known text or text passage. There are two basic requirements for

---

[29] Compare similar observations in Parina (2014).

the realisation of this motivation type. Firstly, the lexical structure of a given CFU is derived from an already existing text. Secondly, the speaker/hearer must have appropriate information about the text (i.e. a quotation, an allusion) in order to connect the text with the CFU. We call this type of motivation *textual dependence* or *text-based motivation*. In other words, what we understand by textual dependence is the relation between CFUs and other text fragments or passages of texts with an identifiable source. Compare idiom (35) based on a well-known allusion.

(35) *a/the Trojan Horse*
'a concealed danger; an enemy concealed within someone or something that attacks the group or organisation he/she belongs to'

The expression is nowadays popular in computing, more commonly known simply as a *Trojan*, which is a program with a concealed function that damages other programs on the computer to which it is downloaded. The idiom is either opaque to speakers or motivated by textual knowledge. A semantic motivation (i.e. a metaphoric or a symbolic motivation) can be excluded. The expression is motivated by a certain knowledge that there is a story behind it, even if this story may not be mentally present with all its details to every speaker.

To this group we only count idioms (and other CFUs) which are clearly motivated for all well-educated speakers, i.e. conventional figurative units like *to be someone's Achilles' heel, to open a Pandora's box, an ugly duckling, Open Sesame!, to run with seven-league boots*, while a connection to the text partly varies depending on the speaker.[30] It could be assumed that this kind of information is purely etymological in nature. In a synchronic description, however, etymology had no place for decades. Accordingly, these idioms were either declared "opaque", or an attempt was made to elicit a semantic, above all metaphoric, motivation. Our empirical data allow us to consider these idioms to be motivated not only in terms of etymology, but also synchronically. The reason is that speakers who perceive these idioms as explainable have to address the elements of their text knowledge, rather than look for metaphoric mappings or a symbolic foundation.

Textual dependence is an important factor in the development of conventional figurative units of standard languages with a literary tradition.[31] In most cases, textual dependence as a motivating link occurs in combination with other types of motivation (see section 4.11 for more details). However, textual

---

[30] Cf. idioms like *to change not an iota, to have feet of clay, to warm a viper in one's bosom*.
[31] As far as we know, it rarely occurs in dialects.

4.9 Motivation based on textual knowledge — 139

dependence is a special case, because it causes some irregularities in the realm of motivation. Let us look at an example.

(36) German *das (also) ist/war des Pudels Kern* "that (thus) is/was the poodle's core"
'that is what is behind it'

Educated speakers of German know that idiom (36) is a quotation from Goethe's drama "Faust" (part I, line 1323). There is a completely equivalent idiom in Finnish: *siinä on villakoiran ydin* "(in this) there is the poodle's core". Although the poodle is a rare breed of dog in Finland, the idiom is quite familiar. Most speakers of Finnish, however, seem not to be conscious of the fact that it is a loan translation (maybe mediated by the Swedish *vara pudelns kärna* "to be the poodle's core") and has its origins in a work of German literature. Hence, those speakers of Finnish who do not have appropriate knowledge about the relevant fragment from Goethe's "Faust" cannot connect the idiom *siinä on villakoiran ydin* with an identifiable textual source. In this case the motivating link remains unclear and the idiom is processed as an opaque figurative unit.

Example (36) shows that the typology of idiom motivation developed above can be thwarted by idioms that originate from pre-existing texts. Any attempt to explain the motivation of idiom (36) on the basis of the concept POODLE is bound to fail. The idiom is neither metaphorically nor symbolically motivated. The link between the lexical structure and the actual meaning of the idiom does not seem to be fully comprehensible without knowledge of the specific literary-historical connections. Without such relevant knowledge, the function of the word *Pudel* remains unclear: no conceptual metaphor can be constructed, nor is there any metaphoric image connected with *the poodle's core*. The 'poodle' as the devil is restricted to the drama "Faust". The concept POODLE itself is not a cultural symbol (POODLE has no equivalents in other cultural codes). The only way to make sense of this idiom is to address the literary source.

The phenomenon of text-based motivation has been underestimated so far. In fact, many CFUs that cannot be fully explained by the well-known patterns of motivation, above all by the metaphoric type, turn out to be quotations, such as German *Eulen nach Athen tragen* (cf. chapter 10) or *to be in seventh heaven* (see 12.3.3). We could enumerate many further idioms of this kind, mainly in the realm of "animal constituents", where a regular motivation (as it is known in the traditional theory of phraseology) is thwarted by intertextual origins. Several idioms that are translations of biblical verses display such specific properties, cf. e.g. the English expression *to cast pearls before swine* 'to waste gifts on those who are too uncultured to appreciate them'. There is no motivational explanation as to why the rather uncommon word *swine* is used instead of the more usual *pigs*, other than that it is "inherited" from the source text, an antiquated translation of verse 6 in Matthew 7. Interestingly, equivalents in other languages show this phenomenon as well. The Dutch *parels voor de zwijnen gooien* reveals the same irregularity (*zwijnen* 'swine' instead of the "normal" word *varkens*); in the French *des perles aux pourceaux/aux cochons*, the uncommon, antiquated constituent *pourceaux* exists side by side with the modern *cochons*.

The same holds for some CFUs originating from allusions to an entire text (with an identifiable source), e.g. to a fable or story. Compare the idiom *to shed/weep crocodile tears* 'to show sadness that is not sincere', which is an allusion to a legend. The idiom cannot be motivated by knowledge about crocodiles, neither in the form of natural experience nor of symbolic knowledge. However, many CFUs that are connected with literary texts can be motivated metaphorically or symbolically as well (examples are given in section 10.8).

The great number of proverbs which have emerged from well-known texts or quotations cannot be dealt with here in detail; cf. for example *The spirit is willing but the flesh is weak* (Matthew 26:41), *All that glisters is not gold* (popularised by Shakespeare's *The Merchant of Venice*, II, 7) or *A penny saved is a penny earned* which is attributed to Benjamin Franklin. However, it is not only idioms and proverbs which go back to well-known texts, but also one-word metaphors and figurative compounds.

For example, the biblical story of the Great Flood and Noah's Ark (Gen 6–8) has produced the idioms *before the flood* and *out of the ark*, both meaning figuratively 'very old or old-fashioned, a very long time ago'. At the same time, figurative single words have emerged from this story, such as the adjective *antediluvian* and its parallels in other languages (German *vorsintflutlich*, Russian *допотопный*, Greek *προκατακλυσμιαίος*). Literally, they mean "from before the flood", and they are used in a figurative sense similar to that of the idioms.

4.10 Index-based motivation

Idioms of this type provide a motivating link that does not take place on the semantic or syntactic level, but on the level of phonetic associations between parts of a given CFU and words pointing to its actual meaning or on the level of the knowledge of certain general principles of pragmatics.

It seems appropriate to call this motivation type "index-based". This is because the motivating links are provided neither by a similarity between certain elements of the conceptual structure represented by the literal reading and corresponding elements of the figurative reading (metaphoric motivation), nor by a culture-specific convention (symbol-based motivation). Instead, these motivating links are provided by an indexation of the notion in question. By *indexation* we mean something similar to Peirce's *index*. Remember his well-known example: If you see smoke, there must be fire somewhere. Hence, it is neither similarity nor convention which provides a motivating link, but rather the pointing to a symptom.[32]

We have to distinguish between *phonetic indexation* and *conceptual indexation*. In the case of phonetic indexation, some features of the sound structure point to the corresponding features of the actual meaning. In the case of conceptual indexation, it is not the meanings of the idiom constituents but the conceptual organisation of the given expression as a whole that underlies the actual meaning and influences the pragmatic aspects of the utterance.

Example (37) may serve to illustrate phonetic indexation.

(37) German *den heiligen Ulrich anrufen* "to call on the Holy Ulrich"
      'to vomit'

Example (37) is a humorous and euphemistic idiom which means 'to vomit'. Its inner form seems to point to an act of praying (although there is no Holy Ulrich). The name *Ulrich* must be regarded as an onomatopoetic imitation of the sound that one makes when vomiting. There is an equivalent in Austrian German tantamount to (37): *nach Melk gehen* "to go to Melk". *Melk* is the name of well-known town in Austria. The same onomatopoetic function is ascribed to *Melk* as to the name *Ulrich* in (37). Though the phonetic structures of *Ulrich* and *Melk* are quite different, both are considered to imitate the sound in question. Cf. also the Russian idiom *ехать в Ригу* "to go to Riga" and English idioms such as *talk to Huey on the big white telephone* or *meet my friends Ralph and Earl*. The examples show the high degree of conventionality of such indexations.

A similar type of motivation occurs in (38).

(38) Swedish *fy sjutton!* "ugh seventeen!"
      'ugh, how disgusting!

Swedish *fy sjutton* sounds like *fy tusan* "ugh devil!", a vulgar curse one is supposed to avoid. There are similar Swedish sayings like *det vete sjutton* "the seventeen may know this" instead of *det vete tusan* "the devil may know this". Therefore,

---

[32] In general, the term *index* is used here in accordance with Peirce (1960), but not exactly in the sense of the trichotomy *index-icon-symbol* in the Peircean semiotic paradigm.

the numeral *sjutton* 'seventeen' should not be interpreted as a culture-specific symbol fixed in Swedish as a 'bad number', like THIRTEEN in some CFUs. The only contribution of the numeral to the understanding and processing of the idiom is of an indexical nature. Comparable to this are functions of the Russian numerals *раз* 'one' and *два* 'two' in (39).

(39) Russian *раз два (и готово)*
"one-two (and ready)"
'very quick (about achieving a result); in great haste'

It is the speed at which these lexical units are pronounced and/or the counting function is fulfilled that point – like an index – to the actual meaning 'very quick'. Neither of the number constituents is used with a secondary meaning, be it metaphorically or symbolically.

Moreover, let us consider examples (40–42), in which the denotatum is referred to via conceptual indexation.

(40) Russian *в огороде бузина, а в Киеве дядька* "in the kitchen garden (there is) an elder bush, but in Kiev (there is) an uncle"
'what you are saying lacks any logical coherence in connection with what I've just said'

(41) English *How long is a piece of string?*
'a thing cannot be measured or quantified simply on the basis of its nature; used as a rejoinder to indicate that it is unreasonable for someone to expect the speaker to be more precise about something, as there could be several different answers'

(42) English *Is the Pope a Catholic?*
'used as an answer to a question to show that the answer is obvious and definitely "yes"'

The actual meaning of idiom (40) does not primarily result from the meaning of the single constituents but from the fact that there is no sensible coherence between the two parts of the idiom: "an elder bush in the kitchen garden" and "an uncle in Kiev". It is this lack of coherence that is indexically linked to the incoherence of the words someone has uttered. Similarly, the motivation of idiom (41) is index-based because of the parallelism between the question encoded lexically and the intended communication (your question is absurd). Idiom (42) is a question used in reply to answer another question. It is a standard retort to a question deemed too obvious to require an answer.[33]

What these idioms have in common is the violation of a certain kind of shared knowledge, namely some well-known pragmatic principles of communication, above all, the Gricean maxim of relation or the principle of relevance (Sperber and Wilson 1986).[34] This is, so to speak, the cognitive foundation of this type of motivation. For example, the question in (41) violates the Gricean cooperative principle, which states, among other things, that one must not ask questions which one knows have no answers. Idiom (42) is based on the violation of the same maxim: One must not ask questions which have only one obvious answer. Hence, in cases of *conceptual indexation,* the motivational basis is parallel to the violation of certain pragmatic principles at the level of the literal reading, which results in the actual meaning. In these examples, the core of the actual meaning points to the fact that somebody has violated the same pragmatic principle in the course of the previous conversation.

Index-based motivation is a semiotic and conceptual phenomenon totally different from the other motivation types. A special metalanguage has to be developed for analysing such expressions. This could be a task for future research in connection with the CFLT.

4.11 Interaction of motivation types

There are various forms of combinations among the types of motivation discussed in the previous sections, i.e. many CFUs comprise more than one type of motivation. We use the word *interaction* to refer to the overlap of different types of motivation in the content plane of one CFU, and to the combination of various cultural phenomena in the realm of conventional figurative language. Several cognitive mechanisms can contribute to the motivation of one particular CFU. First, we discuss the interaction of metaphoric and symbol-based motivation.

---

[33] Idioms of this kind have been the subject of several studies. Haas (2013) calls them *sarcastic interrogatives* while Doyle (2008) uses the terms *sarcastic interrogative affirmatives* and *sarcastic interrogatives*. There is a variety of similar idioms, e.g. *do chicken have lips?, can snakes do push-ups?, do frogs have watertight assholes?, does a bear shit in the woods?* .
[34] "To communicate is to claim an individual's attention; hence, to communicate is to imply that the information communicated is relevant. This fundamental idea, that communicated information comes with a guarantee of relevance, we call the principle of relevance. We argue that the principle of relevance is essential to explaining human communication." (Sperber and Wilson 1986: vii).

(43) a. German *noch grün hinter den Ohren sein* "to still be green behind the ears"
b. German *(noch) feucht/nicht trocken hinter den Ohren sein* "to (still) be wet/not dry behind the ears"
c. German *(noch) grün sein* "to (still) be green"
all meaning 'to be very young and inexperienced, to be too young to understand or know enough about certain things'

Etymologically, idiom (43a) is a contamination of (43b) *(noch) feucht/nicht trocken hinter den Ohren sein*, literally referring to the outward appearance of birds just hatched, and a predicative use of the adjective *grün* in (43c) *(noch) grün sein*, referring to the concept GREEN in its symbolic function 'inexperienced'. A combination of the metaphoric and the symbolic motivation is fixed in the lexical structure of (43a). There are many idioms that are motivated metaphorically as a whole and, at the same time, contain a constituent that must be interpreted in terms of its symbolic function. This is the case in the following idioms (44–45):

(44) Dutch *geen brood op de plank hebben* "to have no bread on the plank"
'not to have enough money or not to earn enough money to live on'

(45) Japanese 冷や飯を食わさる (*hiyameshi wo kuwasareru*) "to eat cold (cooked) rice"
'to be treated coldly by other people, to be kept in a low position, to be out of favour (with someone)'

Idiom (44) is motivated metaphorically, since there was a time when bread was really kept on planks, be it the planks of a cupboard in the kitchen or the planks in the bakery. At the same time, the symbolic reading of BREAD, 'money, source for living, etc.', is also relevant to the semantic interpretation of this idiom.

The symbolic significance of RICE in Japanese culture and language has already been mentioned. The concept MESHI/(COOKED) RICE (the prototypical meal) appears in several idioms, mostly in a metaphorically motivated context, as in (45). Sasaki (1993: 95) gives the following etymological explanation: the element 冷や飯 (*hiyameshi*) 'cold (cooked) rice' points to a person's dependence on other people living: it refers to a rice meal that has been brought over from another household and, therefore, cooled down. Thus, symbolic and iconic elements come together: (COOKED) RICE as a symbol of 'living' and the actual meal of cooked rice. The symbolic meaning of MESHI/(COOKED) RICE as 'the whole area of living conditions' is evident here, while *hiya* 'cold' also contributes to the actual meaning of 'people's callousness and harsh treatment'.

There are several Japanese idioms where MESHI, as in (45), occurs together with the concept of EATING, cf. 他人の飯を食う (*tanin no meshi wo kuu*) "to eat the (cooked) rice of another person/of other people"[35] 'to gain experience and to become mature by going abroad, leaving one's home' or 朝飯前 (*asameshi mae*) "before the morning rice/meal [breakfast]" 'an easy task, a small matter to attend to'. Cooked rice, as a prototypical meal, provides the person in question with energy; a morning's cooked rice (breakfast) is the first source of energy for the day. A task that can be completed even before one's first meal is something that requires next to no effort.

4.12 Summary

In summary, it is clear that a sophisticated metalinguistic apparatus is needed in order to achieve a thorough description of the structure and functioning of CFUs. Since figurative units form a very heterogeneous domain, it is not reasonable to put forward any universal instrument of analysis. Instead, different types of CFUs can be singled out, each of which demands its own approach. In this chapter, we have suggested a typology of motivation for CFUs. Such a typology seems to be useful heuristically. Starting from this typology, we will be able to analyse CFUs of different motivational types and describe them with the help of those metalinguistic tools which best suit the given type.

In the case studies below, we will analyse different approaches that can contribute to the development of such suitable metalinguistic tools.

---

35 Idiom (45) resembles the German *anderer Leute Brot essen* "to eat other people's bread" (meaning 'to be dependent on other people, being far from one's home') but seems to be a "false friend" in view of its different actual meaning (see chapter 5).

5 "False friends" and paronyms

5.1 False friends of the translator

In this chapter, we would like to verify the theory of motivation developed in chapter 4 and to illustrate with some examples how different types of motivation manifest themselves in conventional figurative language. A special sector of this complex field, namely that of the so-called "false friend", is suitable for this task. The phenomenon of false friends and paronyms in conventional figurative language is part of the CFLT proposed in this study.

"False friends", also called "faux amis" or "false friends of the translator", are a well-known problem in bilingual lexicography and in teaching and translating foreign languages. It has been studied very extensively (cf. e.g. Wandruszka 1979; Neuhaus 1988; Gorbahn-Orme and Hausmann 1991; Kroschewski 2000; Chamizo Domínguez and Nerlich 2002). Language learning theory and translation studies, in particular, show a great interest in this phenomenon, with the aim of avoiding possible translation errors. A simple general definition of the "false friends of the translator" phenomenon reads as follows:

> False friends are words which are formally similar or identical in two languages but do not mean the same thing.

Cross-linguistically, "false friend" word pairs abound in all languages. The main reason for this can be found in the various historical processes that affect word meanings and which manifest themselves in two main groups. One group consists of pairs of words in two closely related languages which can develop semantically in different directions, like the English word *gift* 'present' and the German word *Gift* 'poison', both derived from the Old-Germanic verb **geban* 'to give'. So *gift/Gift* is something you can *give* to another person (be it poison or a present). The same holds e.g. for many pairs of words of the closely related languages Estonian and Finnish. The Estonian word *rahvas*, 'folk', can be traced back to the same origin as the Finnish word *rahvas*, used derogatorily to signify the rural population or 'rabble, mob'.

The largest group, however, is made up of so-called "internationalisms" (Euro-Latin and Euro-Greek words), which have been borrowed repeatedly during different phases of language history. They often undergo different semantic developments in two or more languages, notwithstanding their genetic relationship. Similar processes lead to the development of polysemy and/or homonymy within one language. Good examples are words that can be traced back to the Latin word *concursus* but have different meanings today. One group of words means 'bankruptcy' (e.g. German *Konkurs*, Finnish *konkurssi* and one of two homonymous Slovakian words, *konkurz 1*). Another group of words denotes a 'competition, music or art contest' (French *concours*, Russian конкурс, Japanese コンコクール (*konkūru*), etc.). Slovakian *konkurz 2* 'public talk of application for a job' belongs to this group. Still other meanings can be found in English *concourse*, meaning 1. 'entrance hall', 2. 'crowd of people', 3. 'confluence', etc.

Another pair of lexical false friends is, for example, French *pamphlet* 'polemical defamatory treatise' and Japanese パンフレット (*panfuretto*) 'advertising brochure'. Both words have been borrowed from English *pamphlet*, which still has both meanings: 1. 'prospectus, advertising brochure, booklet, leaflet', and 2. 'polemical defamatory treatise, piece of invective'. This type of "false friend of the translator" (one-word false friends) has been well described and can be found in many bilingual dictionaries and special lists of faux amis.

5.2 False friends in conventional figurative language

False friends is a term from language teaching. In spite of the broad range of studies on "one-word false friends", little attention has been paid to idioms as false friends, also called "phraseological false friends". In what follows, we will briefly focus on the term *phraseological false friends* and refer to the literature in this field. In the present study, however, the phenomenon of false friends will be looked at from the viewpoint of conventional figurative language. This means that it is not only idioms (although they are the central group) but also all other kinds of CFUs that make up the empirical basis.

There are only a few studies on phraseological false friends. German and Russian phraseological false friends are discussed by Rajxštejn (1980: 23–56). Several detailed studies concern phraseological false friends in French and German (Ettinger 1994, 2012), English and Polish (Szpila 2000), English and Slovene (Vrbinc and Vrbinc 2014), and German and Dutch (Piirainen 1999), among others. Various languages are considered in Piirainen (2004a).

In other studies on phraseology, phraseological false friends are only mentioned marginally but not as an object of research in their own right. Examples of phraseological false friends, even in one single language, are discussed e.g. by Wotjak and Richter (1993: 9), such as the German idioms *über den Berg sein* and *über alle Berge sein* (see (13) below) or *die Augen schließen* vs. *die Augen verschließen (vor etwas)*; see (17–18). Obviously, such pairs of idioms are crucial for didactic and lexicographic purposes. In linguistic research, they are usually called *paronyms*.

Let us look at examples (1–2) discussed by Ettinger (1994: 129).

(1) German *jmdm. einen Floh ins Ohr setzen* "to put a flea into someone's ear"
'to arouse an unrealisable wish in someone'

(2) French *mettre la puce à l'oreille de qqn* "to put the flea into the ear of someone [into someone's ear]"
'to make someone mistrustful, suspicious'

As these examples show, phraseological false friends pose more subtle and complicated problems than one-word false friends. Idioms classified as false friends resemble each other on the level of mental images and lexical constituents, i.e. on the level of inner form, but they display significant differences on the semantic level.

Definitions of "phraseological false friends" (e.g. Burger 2015: 211–212; Wotjak 1992a: 105–107) usually correspond to the definition of "false friends of the translator". This definition has to be formulated more precisely for most false friends in the domain of conventional figurative language. It concerns, above all, motivated CFUs.[1] It has to be pointed out that the similarity or identity of the figurative units in question is not grounded in the plane of expression but in the image evoked by the figurative unit. The identity of idioms (1–2) does not concern the form (as was the case with *gift* vs. *Gift*, above) but relates to part of the content, the literal reading, which evokes certain images. It can be called "meaning level 1" or "source domain". In terms of cognitive semantics, false friends in conventional figurative language can be defined as follows:

> False friends in conventional figurative language are two or more expressions that evoke almost identical or very similar mental images but show significant differences in the actual meaning.

Thus, the knowledge structures of the source domain are mapped onto the knowledge structures of the target domain, so that it is possible to give an interpretation of the connection between the inner form and the actual meaning. Different salient features of the knowledge of the source domain can surface in each of the conventional figurative units in a "false-friend-relationship". The image evoked by the lexical structure *to put a flea into someone's ear* shows a great potential for being exploited for semantic reinterpretations. The actual meanings of the idioms depend on which elements of this source concept are highlighted.

---

[1] However, pairs or sets of false friends in conventional figurative language are also taken into account. In these, only one of the lexical units is motivated and the other ones may be opaque or have to be interpreted literally, see 5.5.3.

Hence, 'a flea in the ear' can be related to an unrealisable wish (1) because both cause trouble (in the person's head or mind), and both can dissolve into nothing. The ear is an organ which is able to perceive information that can be transformed into wishes. Other elements of the image 'to put the flea in someone's ear' are highlighted in idiom (2), so that this concept can be seen as corresponding to 'mistrust'. Here, the flea could be interpreted as a foreign body in the ear that gives secret information in order to alarm someone to be mistrustful. The flea could even be considered responsible for mistrust and suspicion. These examples will be discussed in more detail in section 8.4, examples (14–15).

The image 'to put a flea into someone's ear' or 'to have a flea/fleas in one's ear/in one's ears' has the conceptual potential to be used for several different target concepts. There are Italian and Greek idioms (3–4) with the actual meanings 'to make someone mistrustful' and 'to become mistrustful' respectively, which are close to that of the French idiom (2). Furthermore, there is still another German idiom, (5), meaning 'to be stupid' and a Dutch idiom, (6), meaning 'to be restless'. The word string *a flea in one's ear* in the English idiom (7a) signifies 'a sharp reproof or rebuke', cf. also (7b, 7c).

(3) Italian *mettere la/una pulce nell'orecchio a/di qcn* "to put the/a flea into the ear into someone's ear"
'to make someone mistrustful, suspicious'

(4) Greek *του μπαίνουν ψύλλοι στα αυτιά* "fleas go into someone's ears"
'someone becomes mistrustful, suspicious'

(5) German *einen Floh im Ohr haben* "to have a flea in one's ear"
'not to be in one's right mind, to be stupid'

(6) Dutch *een vlo in het oor hebben* "to have a flea in one's ear"
'to be very restless or fidgety'

(7) a. English *a flea in one's ear*
'a sharp reproof or rebuke; an annoying or surprisingly sharp reply; an idea or answer that is unwelcome'
b. English *to have/get a flea in one's ear*
'to be reprimanded, rejected or humiliated'
c. English *to send someone away with a flea in his/her ear*
'to angrily refuse what someone has come to ask you; to snub or rebuke a person'

As in idiom (5), a foreign body in the head, such as a flea, can lead to a disturbance of intellectual capacity; therefore, this image can be mapped on the target domain 'stupidity'. Furthermore, the situation of having a flea in one's ear denotes a noticeable 'restlessness' which makes up the target domain of idiom (6). Finally, the image of 'a flea in the ear' can be mapped on 'a reproof or rebuke' (7). Here the flea can again be interpreted as an agent that gives information to someone to make that person act. It has to be emphasised that all these interpretations (1–7) are inherent in the same image (source concept).

5.3 False friends in different types of conventional figurative units

Examples (1–7) already reveal the boundaries of the notion of false friends that are favoured here. It is a narrow concept, which only includes the type of invariance of the source concept accompanied by divergence of the target concepts, in contrast to a broader notion (see, for example, Ettinger 1994, 2012), which also includes "faux amis based on morphosyntactic differences" and "faux amis based on diasystematic differences".

False friends can be discovered in all types of conventional figurative units (see section 2.3), although idioms are the largest group. In what follows, the focus will be on idioms. For the sake of completeness, however, we will also look at other types of CFUs.

Proverbs prove to be false friends in some cases, mainly when they are borrowed from another language and culture and have undergone semantic transformations according to the respective cultural area. Let us look at examples (8–9) which can be traced back to a proverb of classical origin (Simpson 1992: 217; Mieder 1992: 565). The Japanese proverb is probably a translation from the English one (see Paczolay 1997: 100–102).

(8) English (outdated) *a rolling stone gathers no moss*
 'a restless person will not accumulate wealth, status, friends, etc. (a person leading an unsettled life will not be successful)'[2]

---

[2] This is the original meaning of the proverb. The new meaning, which seems to be the opposite of the original use, implies that a person who does not settle down does not accumulate hindrances, which can be a good thing.

(9) Japanese 転石苔をむさず (*tenseki koke wo musa-zu*) "(a) rolling stone will not be mossy"
(today's reading) 'one must keep on being in motion, being active (one must get experiences e.g. by travelling, by changing one's job, etc.)'

The interpretation of the English proverb quoted in (8) agrees with that handed down since antiquity, but there are also more recent reinterpretations (cf. varying meanings discussed in Lakoff (1987b: 451). This former meaning given in (8) also used to be very well suited to Japanese culture: according to aesthetic conceptions, e.g. of Buddhist gardens, a stone must be covered with moss to be beautiful. An earlier interpretation of the Japanese proverb (9) was in agreement with that of (8), reading as 'one must be settled and persistent (in order to be successful)'. However, Japanese socio-cultural conditions and attitudes have changed in modern times so that the meaning transformation quoted in (9) is preferred today. Cases like (8–9) can be considered "proverb false friends".

One-word-metaphors can also reveal false friends. There is a British English word *snaky* meaning 'winding'. Here we are dealing with the metaphoric interpretation of the concept SNAKE (something, e.g. a road, which has a form similar to that of a snake). In contrast, the American slang word *snaky* means 'false, evil, sly'. It is the symbolic knowledge of the concept SNAKE that is activated here. The SNAKE is a symbol of 'deceitfulness, evil, shrewdness etc.', which is strongly established in cultural codes (see chapters 11 and 13).

Restricted collocations are of marginal importance with regard to false friends. In our data there are only a few pairs of figurative collocations that could be regarded as false friends.

Similes (many of them belonging to the class of idioms, cf. 2.3.2) occur quite often in pairs or series of false friends. All similes revealing this phenomenon have to be included under idioms, because CFU false friends are figurative by nature. Let us have a look at a series of similes with the lexical structure "to speak/talk like a book":

(10) German *reden wie ein Buch* "to speak like a book"
'to talk a lot and very quickly, incessantly'

(11) English *to speak/talk like a book*
'to speak/talk in an affected or a pretentious manner'

(12) French *parler comme un livre* "to speak like a book"
'to speak elegantly, in a refined, scholarly and cultured manner'

Once again, different properties of the source concept are at the forefront. On the one hand, a book normally contains a long and continuous text. Mapped on a person who is speaking, the semantic result 'to talk a lot and very quickly, incessantly' is comprehensible (10). On the other hand, the written language of a book can differ from the spoken language and is often more elaborate or more scholarly. This leads to different actual meanings, since different aspects are highlighted – the violation of the norms of everyday communication in (11) and the quality of being 'well formulated, elegant' in (12). There are corresponding similes in other languages, most of them following either the actual meaning of (11) (e.g. Swedish *tala som en bok*) or that of (12) (e.g. Spanish *hablar como un libro*).

The previous examples show that CFU false friends occur not only in pairs but also in series of expressions that have similar image bases. Furthermore, they appear not only between two or more standard languages but also between CFUs of a standard language and a dialect or a regional colloquial language, as well as between a present-day language and a historic variety of the same language (see Burger 2015: 148 for examples). A pair of false friends between Standard German and a Low German dialect (WML) illustrates this well. Such examples are quite frequent.

(13) Standard German *über den Berg sein* "to be over the mountain/hill"
'to overcome a crisis, an illness; to be out of the greatest trouble or difficulty'

(14) WML *'n Barg öwwer wessen* "to be over the hill"
'to be dead'

The underlying image 'to be over the mountain/hill' has a conceptual potential that allows it to be mapped onto several different target concepts, cf., for example, the English idiom *to be over the hill* 'to be past one's most successful times; to be too old to do one's job well, or too old to be attractive', Japanese 山を越す (*yama wo kosu*) "to go over the mountain" 'to be past the critical point, to be over the worst (difficulties, etc.)', but also the German idiom *über alle Berge sein* "to be over all mountains/hills" 'to have escaped, got away (from an unpleasant situation) very quickly; to be already far away' – different from (13). There are many examples of this kind between closely related languages as well as between genetically non-related and culturally distant languages. Finally, there are also "false friends" within one single language (or *paronyms*, see above). Sometimes they are called *intralinguistic false friends* or *inner false friends* (e.g. Wotjak and Richter 1993). These concepts are used mainly for the purposes of language teaching. From the linguistic viewpoint, we are dealing with paronymy as well as with homonymy or polysemy.[3]

The following kind of false friends in two languages should be left out of consideration here. This is pairs of idioms whose literal translation seems to consist of almost identical words, despite significant differences in the cultural area behind the identical or similar word strings. Let us consider examples (15–16).

(15) a. German *den Löffel wegwerfen* "to throw away the spoon"
b. Finnish *heittää lusikka nurkkaan* "to throw the spoon into the corner"
both meaning 'to die'

(16) Japanese 匙を投げる (*saji wo nageru*) "to throw away the spoon"
'to give up in despair'

The images of idioms (15) and (16), evoked by the word string "to throw away the spoon", seem to be completely identical. Obviously, the difference in the actual meaning of both idioms is based on cultural phenomena. Here, SPOON is the most important concept. In European cultures, the spoon was used as a predominant eating implement, as MUSH or PORRIDGE were the prototypical kinds of food. In some rural areas of Europe, PORRIDGE as a staple food has been more important than BREAD up to the present day. This has left traces in two genetically non-related European languages, German (15a) and Finnish (15b): the person who has passed away will not eat any more; there is no need for a spoon. By contrast, the old Japanese word 匙 (*saji*) denotes a 'spoon to make medicine'. In ancient times, the doctor had to prepare a special mixture of ingredients that would cure the patient. When the patient did not feel better, the doctor would hurl the spoon into the air in despair (cf. Maynard and Maynard 1993: 202).

Idioms (15) and (16) are nearly identical on the lexical level but different with regard to their source concepts. According to our definition of CFU false friends, they are not false friends. However, in terms of their lexical structure they could be considered false friends. Therefore, we call them *near-false-friends*. Such pairs of figurative idioms in culturally very different languages have to be discussed mainly within the framework of cultural semiotics.

---

[3] Distinguishing between homonymy and polysemy is often a matter of theoretical interpretation of empirical data, see 5.4 below.

5.4 Paronyms and homonyms

Let us consider the so-called *intralinguistic false friends* or *inner false friends*. As has been mentioned, we are dealing with paronymy as well as with homonymy or polysemy here. In some cases "false friends" of this kind can be helpful in explaining similar looking pairs of idioms in different languages. Here is one example:

(17) German *die Augen schließen* "to close one's eyes"
 'to die'

(18) German *die Augen verschließen (vor etwas)* "to close one's eyes (to the subject)"
 'to ignore something; to pretend that something is not really happening'

These paronymic idioms have an identical morphosyntactic structure (apart from the fact that idiom (18) has an obligatory prepositional complement) and a similar lexical structure. They are also identical with regard to their images (source concepts). It is obvious that the English idiom (19) only corresponds to the German idiom (18) and is a false friend for idiom (17).

(19) *to close one's eyes (on the subject)/to shut one's eyes (to the subject)*
 'to ignore something; to pretend that something is not really happening'

Idioms (17) and (18) can be definitely set apart in terms of their lexical structures (*schließen* vs. *verschließen*) and actual meanings ('to die' vs. 'to ignore something'). However, there are cases where it is not even clear whether we are dealing with one (polysemous) idiom or with two (homonymous) idioms, cf. (20).

(20) German *jmdm. schwillt der Kamm* "someone's cockscomb swells up"[4]
 1. 'someone becomes very proud and arrogant'
 2. 'someone gets very angry and enraged'

As has been shown by examples (1–7) and (13–14), certain source concepts are predisposed to be used for more than one target domain. One such concept is

---

[4] The idiom shows gender-specific usage restrictions. Because of its image (the cock is seen as a prototypically male creature), the idiom is related mainly to the male gender (Piirainen 2001a: 300–301).

'someone's cockscomb swells up', underlying idiom (20). Two different salient elements of the knowledge structures regarding this source concept stand out; each of them is used for a completely different target domain.

On the one hand, the cock's upright way of walking with the head held high – the swollen comb makes the animal still taller – gives the impression of it behaving proudly and arrogantly. On the other hand, the red colouring and swelling of the cockscomb can be interpreted as a sign of rage.[5] Expression (20) seems to be a polysemous idiom in which the strongly divergent meanings 'pride' and 'anger' are connected by the same image. Nevertheless, it is possible that we are not dealing with polysemy in the strict sense, since in the case of PRIDE and ANGER the two images are not completely identical, but differ due to the accentuation of certain elements (the cock's posture or the red colouring of its comb). It therefore seems reasonable to consider both readings of (20) as homonyms: *jmdm. schwillt der Kamm 1* 'someone becomes very proud and arrogant' and *jmdm. schwillt der Kamm 2* 'someone becomes very angry and enraged'.

Idioms like (20) often provide a source for false friends. Compare the Swedish idiom *(tupp)kammen sväller/växer/reser sig på ngn.* "someone's cockscomb swells up/grows/rises", which has only one of the discussed readings, namely 'someone becomes very proud and arrogant'. Thus, this idiom corresponds to the German idiom *jmdm. schwillt der Kamm 1* but is a false friend for *jmdm. schwillt der Kamm 2*.

5.5 Factors relating to origin

As has been indicated, the reason for the existence of false friends in conventional figurative language is to be found mainly in the motivation of the idioms and, therefore, it requires a semantic and conceptual analysis. In what follows, some types of idiom-false-friends will be discussed to give an insight into some possible regularities of "false friend relationships". Most false friends can be ascribed to one of the three types (i–iii).
(i)   Idioms as false friends based on different conceptual metaphors
(ii) Idioms as false friends based on different rich images
(iii) Idioms as false friends based on different meanings of their constituents

---

[5] The last interpretation can be illustrated by the Dutch idiom *een rode kam krijgen* "to get a red cockscomb" 'to get very angry and enraged'. It is based on the similar image of the swelling cockscomb where there is more emphasis on its red colouring.

5.5.1 Idioms as false friends based on different conceptual metaphors

For this type of motivation, the divergence between the actual meanings of two idioms can be explained by different conceptual metaphors (see chapter 6 for details). In fact, the conceptualisation of PRIDE on the one hand and ANGER on the other, by means of the nearly identical image, is no isolated case; some regularities can be found. Consider idiom (21), a German regionalism, and (22), a Low German (WML) idiom, which are related to each other as false friends.

(21) German (regional) *auf Stelzen gehen* "to walk on stilts"
 'to be proud, self-confident and arrogant'

(22) WML *up Stölpen staon* "to stand on stilts"
 'to be very angry and enraged'

Here we are dealing with the following kind of semantic construal: the level of rich images (somebody puts himself/herself into a higher position than other people by walking/standing on stilts) induces the source concept UPWARDS, UP, HIGH ABOVE on a more abstract level of description. This is the invariant source concept of both idioms, which can be mapped onto the two different target domains, PRIDE and ANGER. Within the framework of cognitive semantics, we encounter two well-known conceptual metaphors (a) ARROGANCE IS ELEVATED POSTURE and (b) ANGER IS RISING INTERNAL PRESSURE.

(a) A salient trait of proud and arrogant people is their behavioural reflections of pride, which include a special form of walking, a way of holding their head high and a posture which is stretched and raised upwards. Hence the conceptualisation of PRIDE AS ELEVATED POSTURE that can be found in many idioms, for instance in English *to go around with one's nose in the air* 'to be haughty, to be stuck up' as well as in Japanese 鼻っ柱が高い (*hanappashira ga takai*) "(the) nose septum (is) high" 'someone is very proud, arrogant', and in Russian *задирать нос* "to raise (the) nose" 'to be stuck up'. Cf. also English *with his/head held high*, German *erhobenen Hauptes* "with one's head raised", and Russian *с (высоко) поднятой головой* "with one's head raised (high)" reflecting the meaning of 'pride of achievement, or refusal to be ashamed', or English *with his chest out*, German *mit geschwellter Brust* "with swelled chest" meaning 'very proudly', etc. Another image that can indicate the elevated posture is "walking on stilts" (the proud person gives the impression that he/she is higher than all other people, as if he/she were walking on stilts). Therefore, the image of idiom (21) is comprehensible.

(b) In conceptualising ANGER, the direction 'upwards' or the position 'high above' plays an important role, too. This image can also be found in many idioms, such as German *auf die Palme gehen* "to go (climb) up on the palm", *die Wände hochgehen* "to climb up the walls", Dutch *op de kast zitten* "to sit on the cupboard", *er op hoge poten heengaan* "to go on high paws", all meaning 'to be very angry'. The image of a person 'standing on stilts (being higher than in normal state)' such as in idiom (22) is another suitable rich image for denoting ANGER.

Another possibility to be higher than other people is to get on a horse. This image is also repeatedly used to conceptualise PRIDE, on the one hand, and ANGER, on the other. Let us consider two WML paronymic idioms (23–24):

(23) *sik up't hooge Peerd setten* "to get on the high horse"
 'to behave in an arrogant manner, be in a supercilious mood; to be proud and haughty'

(24) *(hoog) te Peerde wessen* "to be (high) on (the) horse"
 'to be very angry and enraged'

The same conceptualisations can be found in several standard languages where the invariant image "sit on a high horse/high on a horse" is used for the target domains PRIDE and ANGER. First, let us consider idioms denoting 'proud' (25).

(25) *to be/get on one's high horse*
 'to behave in an arrogant manner, be in a supercilious mood; to be proud and haughty'

There are several idioms in other languages similar to (25), e.g. German *auf dem hohen Ross sitzen/sich aufs hohe Ross setzen* "to sit on the high horse/to get on the high horse", Dutch *hoog te paard zitten* "to sit high on the horse", Swedish *sitta/sätta sig på sina höga hästar* "to sit on one's high horses/to get up on one's high horses", all meaning 'to behave in an arrogant manner, be in a supercilious mood; to be proud and haughty'.[6]

---

[6] At the same time there seems to be a kind of background motivation at the level of the rich image – someone behaves as if he or she was a noble, proudly sitting on their horse.

The French idiom (26) is similar with regard to its lexical structure. However, it signifies 'anger'.[7]

(26) French *monter/être sur ses grands chevaux* "to climb up/be up on one's great horses"
'to flare up, to be very angry and enraged; to get indignant and speak in a high-flown manner'

The last three groups of idioms, the "cockscomb-idioms" (20), the "stilt-idioms" (21–22), and the "high-horse-idioms" (23–26), have something in common; they show that the conceptualisation of PRIDE, on the one hand, and ANGER, on the other, by means of the same image is not an isolated case. The concrete images "someone's cockscomb swells", "to be walking on stilts" or "to sit on a high horse" reveal the same divergence in their actual meanings.

Another example of false friends based on diverging conceptual metaphors is provided by idioms (27–28).

(27) German *in den Keller gehen* "to go into the cellar"
'to become less, to fall (prices, shares etc.)'

(28) Dutch *naar de kelder gaan* "to go into the cellar"
'to become unusable, to perish, to go bust, to go to pieces'

There is no cultural difference between 'cellars' in Germany or in the Netherlands. The difference in the actual meanings of the idioms can only be explained by addressing the different conceptual metaphors behind them. Both idioms have the same source concept. Since the CELLAR is the lowest part of the building, this concept has the cognitive potential to indicate the lowest point on a scale.

According to a well-known metaphoric model, the quantity of shares, the amount of stock market prices etc. is arranged on a scale or on a chart, where MORE IS UP, and LESS IS DOWN (27). According to another widespread metaphor, the lowest part (of the scale or chart) is BAD, the upper part is GOOD (28). Thus, the German idiom and the Dutch idiom are based on the two different conceptual metaphors LESS IS DOWN and BAD IS DOWN respectively.

---

[7] Interestingly, Luxembourgish conventional figurative language has both versions: *um héich Päerd sinn 1* 'to be very proud and arrogant' and *um héich Päerd sinn 2* 'to be very angry and enraged' (Filatkina 2002: 33). Linguistically, Luxembourgish is a dialect based on the German Westmoselle Franconian dialect, it has been influenced both by Standard German and by French, which could be the reason for the existence of the two idioms.

Many pairs or series of idioms which look similar on the surface (with almost identical literal readings) can be explained by the observation that they are based on different conceptual metaphors.

5.5.2 Idioms as false friends based on different rich images

Other false friends in conventional figurative language cannot be captured on the rather abstract level of conceptual metaphor, but can be interpreted on the basic level of the so-called "rich image" (cf. chapter 8). It has already been shown that certain source concepts on the level of rich images are predisposed to be mapped onto different target domains (e.g. 'a flea in someone's ear' or 'to be over the hill').

The observation that insects tend to fly towards a light and die instantly when they are drawn into the flame of a candle serves as a further example. This fact of nature can be observed in different regions of the world, regardless of the respective culture. Therefore, this image can be used by culturally distant languages. Here are two examples (29–30).

(29)   Dutch *in de kaars vliegen* "to fly into the candle"
       'to be very naive, clueless or stupid (and to be the victim of one's naivety or stupidity)'

(30)   Japanese 飛んで火に入る夏の虫 (*tonde hi ni iru natsu no mushi*)
       "flying into (the) flame (a) summer insect [a summer insect that flies into the flame]"
       'to ask for trouble, to provoke difficulties in a self-destructive way'

Here we are dealing with a source concept ('an insect drawn into the flame') that has many slots. Different salient features of this image (different slots of the frame) can be highlighted (the insect flies unsuspectingly into the flame or it does so in a self-destructive way), and these can be exploited for different actual meanings. There are even further idioms that are similar with regard to this image (e.g. German *von etwas angezogen werden wie die Motten vom Licht* "to be attracted by something as moths by the light" 'to be irresistibly attracted by a person or a thing, to be under someone's spell').

For another example, let us look at the idioms whose underlying rich image is 'within the four walls'. This source concept can be exploited for semantic reinterpretation in quite different ways. First, there is a positively connoted version (31).

(31) a. German *in den/seinen eigenen vier Wänden (sein)* "(to be) within the/ one's own four walls"
b. Greek *μέσα στους τέσσερεις τοίχους* "inside the four walls"
c. Finnish *(olla) neljän seinän sisällä* "(to be) inside the four walls"
all meaning '(to be) in the privacy of one's (own) home, at home; in an atmosphere of confidence'

In other CFUs with a nearly identical lexical structure, negative aspects of the given situation are dominant. Dwelling between one's four walls, cut off from the outside world, may have a negative impact on the mood or mental state of the person, which finds expression in the actual meanings of idioms (32). The images of 'sitting' or 'living' within the four walls in these idioms entail semantic consequences – they have connotations of being isolated in one's own home, having no contact with the outside world, feeling shut in, being bored and depressed with (the sight of) these four walls (e.g. when someone is forced to stay at home, be it because of illness or unemployment).

(32) a. German *in seinen eigenen vier Wänden hocken* "to crouch in one's own four walls"
b. French *loger/être/rester entre quatre murs* "to be/stay between four walls"
c. Russian *сидеть в четырех стенах* "to sit within four walls"
all meaning something like 'to always stay at home, never go out, be isolated, be bored, feel hemmed in'

Idioms (31) and (32) may be considered a borderline case of false friends, since they have a similar "core meaning" (cf. the "cross-linguistic near-synonyms" in section 3.4.1). Finally, there is a Dutch and a French idiom which at first glance seem to be similar to the expressions listed under (31–32). The underlying images, however, are different. Examples (33) refer not to the walls of a room but to those of a prison cell. The idea 'to be in prison' is pointed out in a euphemistic way.

(33) a. Dutch *tussen de vier muren zitten*[8] "to sit between the four walls"
b. French *(être) entre quatre murs* "(to be) between four walls"
both meaning 'to be in prison'

---

[8] Further secondary meanings can be attributed to the Dutch idiom (33a), such as 'to be mentally retarded; to have no chance of escaping'. Some semantic specifics are due to the fact that there is no lexical differentiation between the "wall of a room" and an "external wall" in Dutch and French (unlike the distinction between German *Wand* and *Mauer*).

The examples show that the same lexical structure can evoke different frames (a house with dwelling rooms or a prison with cells). Let us look at another pair of false friends where one of the idioms (35) can also be labelled as a euphemistic circumlocution.

(34) a. Swedish *ställa ngn. mot väggen* "to put someone against the wall"
 b. Finnish *asettaa/panna jk. seinää vasten* "to put someone against the wall"
 both meaning 'to put someone in a difficult situation or predicament'

(35) a. German *jmdn. an die Wand stellen* "to put someone up against the wall"
 b. Russian *поставить к стенке кого-л.* "to put someone up against the wall"
 both meaning 'to execute someone by shooting'

The concrete image of a wall in idiom (34) induces a well-known conceptual metaphor, i.e. DIFFICULTIES ARE IMPEDIMENTS TO MOTION. The source concept IMPEDIMENTS TO MOTION (a person who is "put against the wall" cannot escape or move away) is mapped onto the target concept 'a difficult situation or predicament'. This conceptual metaphor can be seen in idioms like the German *mit dem Rücken zur Wand* "with the back to the wall" 'in a great predicament', the English *to have your back to/up against the wall* 'to be in a difficult situation that is very hard to change or to get out of'.[9]

By contrast, expressions (35) deal with a euphemistic intention, underspecifying in order to play down the facts. Some knowledge of the frame 'execution by shooting' is required to activate the actual meaning (the offender is actually put against the wall).

In (34) and in (35) different features of the image, i.e. different potential functions of the WALL, are focused on. The consequence is that this concept has to be interpreted as part of different frames: as a slot of the frame 'motion' ("wall as an impediment to motion") in (34), and as a slot of the frame 'execution by shooting' in (35).

---

9 The idioms allude to a situation of close combat, as in fencing or military actions. When fighters retreat to avoid being hit and finally reach a wall, they have no choice but to face the danger of the opponent's attack. They need to defend themselves since the wall behind them makes further retreat impossible.

5.5.3 Idioms as false friends based on different meanings of their constituents

In many cases, the reason for there being a pair or set of false friends is not based on the CFU as a whole, but on one single lexical constituent. Nevertheless, these are not one-word false friends (like English *gift* and German *Gift*).[10] On the contrary, these are words that are absolutely identical in two languages in terms of their semantic potential. It is the constituents that have several secondary readings besides their primary reading. Above all, these are very productive somatic constituents like *hand, heart, hand, eye*, etc.[11] Let us consider idioms (36–37).

(36) German *kein Herz (im Leibe) haben* "to have no heart (in one's body)"
'to have no sympathy, to be pitiless'

(37) Dutch *geen hart in zijn lijf hebben* "to have no heart in one's body"
'to have no courage, to be cowardly'

In both idioms, HEART does not occur in its primary reading ('organ of the blood circulation') but in its secondary reading as 'imaginary organ of (good) feelings'. The HEART concept affects several aspects, one of them being SYMPATHY, and another one COURAGE. There are also other aspects, such as LOVE, or AFFECTION.

In the German idiom (36) and the Dutch idiom (37), the HEART concept has two different functions. Both functions of HEART can be recognised in several other idioms belonging to European languages. The function SYMPATHY, for example, occurs in English *to have a heart for someone* 'to be sympathetic' or in Dutch *een hart van steen hebben* "to have a heart of stone" 'to have no sympathy, to be pitiless', whereas the function COURAGE occurs in German *sich ein Herz fassen* "to take a heart" 'to muster up all one's courage' or in Dutch *het hart hebben* "to have the heart" 'to have courage, to dare to do something' etc.

---

10 CFU false friends that are based on one-word false friends seem to be extremely rare; cf. English *to give someone a wink* 'to wink at someone' vs. German *jmdm. einen Wink geben* 'to give someone a hint'. These expressions are only poorly figurative; the semantic difference between both units is based on the words *wink* in English and *Wink* in German.

11 From the very beginning of phraseological research there has been a long tradition of analysing idioms containing "somatisms" (constituents denoting parts of the body), see e.g. Rajxštejn (1980: 91–92). This has also been a favourite topic of cross-linguistic studies. Many false friends based on somatic constituents can be found within the linguistic data of those studies, although the problem of false friends hardly attracted any attention; cf. recent studies on "somatisms" coming from Krohn (1994), Kim-Werner (1996), Čermák (1998), Davidou (1998), Zhu (1998), Farø (2002), Kotb (2002), Mejri (2003) or Budvytyte (2003).

5.5 Factors relating to origin — 163

As has been shown in section 5.5.1, many pairs or series of similar-looking idioms (with almost identical literal readings) can be explained by the observation that they are based on different conceptual metaphors. These metaphors can be induced by such frequent constituents as *hand* or *eyes*. The concept HAND reveals several secondary functions, such as HELP, LABOUR/WORK, ACTIVITY, or POWER, CONTROL. The function LABOUR/WORK can be recognised in idioms of various languages, regardless of their respective cultural area, as in (38) and (39).

(38) Japanese 手が空く (*te ga aku*) "hand(s) (to be) empty [one's hand becomes empty/one's hands become empty]"
'to be free, to have no work anymore, to have a minute, to have some time'

(39) English *to go/come away empty handed*
1. 'to return without anything [without bringing anything along]', 2. 'to return with nothing to show for one's efforts'

Idioms (38–39) are based on two different metaphors evoked by the HAND concept: (i) WORKING IS ACTING (WITH ONE'S HANDS) and (ii) POSSESSING IS HOLDING (IN ONE'S HANDS). The "empty hand" in (38) stands for 'having no work, being free (of work) and having some free time'. Obviously, idioms (38) and (39) are false friends. Idiom (39) in its first meaning connects HAND with HOLDING: empty hands do not bring anything with them. The second meaning, however, also contains an aspect of acting hands.

Let us remember the German paronyms (22) *die Augen schließen* 'to die' and (23) *die Augen (ver)schließen (vor etwas)* 'to ignore something; to pretend that something is not really happening'. Idiom (22), 'to die', has to be interpreted on the basis of the conceptual metaphor LIFE IS SEEING. The activity of seeing is finished (brought to an end) by death. In contrast to (22), idiom (23) *die Augen (ver)schließen (vor etwas)* and the English equivalent (24) *to close one's eyes (on the subject)/to shut one's eyes (to the subject)* are based on the conceptual metaphor CONTROL IS SEEING. This metaphor can be found in several other idioms, such as English *to keep an eye on someone* 'to watch or control someone carefully' or German *jmdn. nicht aus den Augen lassen* "not to let someone out of the eyes" 'to control, to observe someone strictly'. This metaphor, evoked by the EYE concept, does not seem to be culturally specific (cf. culturally based false friends in 5.3), because it can be found in languages of a very different cultural background, like the Japanese idiom 目をつぶる (*me wo tsuburu*) "to close one's eyes" 'to ignore something (e.g. incorrect behaviour); to pretend that something is not really happening', which is a false friend to the German idiom (22).

5.6 Summary

This chapter has focused upon a topic which has been given little attention in research into figurative language so far. We have shown that false friends in conventional figurative language, unlike the well-known "false friends of the translator", require a semantic and conceptual analysis. In the first place, research of this kind presupposes an analysis of metaphors within the framework of cognitive semantics. Differences between the actual meanings of two or more CFUs with false-friend properties can be explained either at the basic level or at the superordinate level of categorisation, i.e. via different rich images or via different conceptual metaphors. In addition, there are false friends in conventional figurative language caused by one single lexical constituent, their meanings emerging in different secondary readings in the two CFUs in question. Thus, the whole variety of paronyms in the domain of conventional figurative language can be reduced to these three factors and, from this point of view, reveals certain regular features.

6 The Cognitive Theory of Metaphor

The Cognitive Theory of Metaphor – initiated[1] by Reddy's (1979) study on the "conduit metaphor" – was developed mainly by Lakoff, Johnson and their colleagues (Lakoff and Johnson 1980, 1999; Lakoff 1987a, 1987b, 1990, 1993; Johnson 1981, 1987; Lakoff and Turner 1989). It met with widespread acceptance. The metalinguistic apparatus proposed in the framework of this theory (cf. the notions of conceptual metaphor, metaphoric model, source and target domain, mapping, conceptual correspondences, etc.) proved to be efficient for the analysis of all kinds of metaphorical expressions, from novel and/or poetic metaphors to near-universal SPACE-TIME-shifts in the semantics of prepositions. This metalinguistic apparatus has been adopted and emulated by many other linguists, cf. e.g. studies on metaphorical expressions in different languages (Baldauf 1997, 2003; Baranov and Dobrovol'skij 1996; Drewer 2003; Gibbs 2008; Jäkel 2003; Kövecses 1986, 1990, 1995a, 2010, 2011; Liebert 1992; McGlone 2007; Takada et al. 2000), and studies on psycholinguistic aspects of metaphor processing (Gibbs 1990; 1993; 1994; 1996; 2006; Kutas and Federmeier 2000; Gibbs and Colston 2012).[2] Despite the far-reaching appreciation, however, several points of criticism have been expressed;[3] many of these involve aspects of culture.

This chapter deals with some basic postulates of the Cognitive Theory of Metaphor (CTM). To put it briefly: It was not the goal of the CTM to analyse and describe conventional figurative units or to contribute to the theory of phraseology. The Cognitive Theory of Metaphor was developed for quite different purposes: it "is not simply the study of linguistic metaphors; it aims at tackling crucial cognitive problems: e.g., how do people understand abstract domains such as morality, politics, and mathematics? How are they able to understand language and each other?" (Fusaroli and Morgagni 2013: 2). Nevertheless, there are many points of intersection between CTM and theories of conventional figurative language.

---

[1] Some fundamental ideas similar to those of the CTM had been expressed earlier, although in different theoretical contexts. Precursors who developed similar ideas can be found throughout philosophy; see (Jäkel 1999, 2003) for details. Central principles of the generally cognitive approach to metaphor appear in studies of Weinrich from the late 1950s (collected in Weinrich 1976). Weinrich distinguishes also between the conceptual level of metaphor (called *Bildfeld* "image field") and the linguistic level of metaphor (called *Metapher*). Weinrich coined the terms *Bildspenderbereich* ("image donor field") and *Bildempfängerbereich* ("image recipient field"), the meanings of which are very similar to that of the Lakoffian *source domain* and *target domain*.
[2] There are also several new research directions. Cf., for example, research on the neural aspects of metaphoric conceptualisation (Lakoff 2008).
[3] For response to criticism see (Kövecses 2011).

Therefore, our aim is to find out to what extent the methods of analysis developed in this theory can be effectively applied to the analysis of figurative language, and, above all, at what points other tools of analysis have to be added in order to exhaustively describe the plane of content of figurative units.

6.1 Basic principles of the Cognitive Theory of Metaphor

In this section, we give a brief outline of the Cognitive Theory of Metaphor. The cognitive approach to metaphor research puts forward the following ideas:

1. Metaphor is a conceptual category. According to the classical theory of metaphor, from the time of Aristotle, the term "metaphor" was defined as a poetic linguistic expression in which a linguistic unit is used outside its normal conventional meaning. The Cognitive Theory of Metaphor revealed that metaphor is not a matter of language, but of thought. Metaphor is one of the basic principles of human cognition.
2. Metaphors are central to natural language semantics. The general principles which take the form of conceptual mappings apply not only to "novel" or "poetic" expressions, but also to large portions of ordinary language. A set of conceptual metaphors (i.e. of conceptual correspondences that are mapped) structures people's everyday experience, including most abstract concepts (like time, quantity, state, change, action, causation, purpose, means, modality, etc.). Likewise, most concepts relating to emotion are understood metaphorically.
3. The basis of the metaphor is the cross-conceptual mapping. A conventional conceptual metaphor is a (partial) mapping of one conceptual domain (the source domain) onto another conceptual domain (the target domain). The metaphor is structured by ontological, topological and logical correspondences. This means that metaphor is not based upon similarity between source and target concepts, but on people's ability to structure one conceptual domain in terms of another. What this implies for metaphoric mapping is that the target domain has to be structured according to the structure of the source domain (see below). The conceptual correspondences between source domain and target domain are reflected metalinguistically by the formula TARGET IS SOURCE (e.g. MIND IS A CONTAINER), used for representation of the metaphoric mapping.
4. Metaphoric mappings preserve the cognitive topology of the source domain, in a way that is consistent with the inherent structure of the target domain. For the CONTAINER schemas, this means that interiors will be mapped onto interiors, exteriors onto exteriors, and boundaries onto boundaries. Thus, the target concept is partially structured and constituted by the source concept, i.e. the target domain preserves the structure of the source domain.

The inherent target domain structure automatically sets limits on what can be mapped. This postulate is called the *Invariance Hypothesis* or *Invariance Principle* in later versions put forward by Lakoff (e.g. 1993: 251–252).[4]

5. Metaphors show different levels of abstraction. Compare the notions of "generic metaphors" and "basic-level metaphors" in Lakoff (1987b: 397, 406). Generic mappings take place on a very abstract level (such as orientation, space, motion, e.g. IDEAS ARE PHYSICAL ENTITIES or MORE IS UP VS. LESS IS DOWN). The generic level includes different basic-level categories. Cf. mappings such as ANGER IS INSANE BEHAVIOUR. In addition, there is a level of rich mental images and rich knowledge structure (Lakoff 1987b: 31–50). A mapping at the superordinate level maximises the possibilities for mapping rich conceptual structures of the source domain onto the target domain, since it permits many basic-level instances, each of which is information-rich and explains a variety of lexical units. For example, the conceptual metaphor LOVE IS A JOURNEY[5] explains the systemic nature of concrete metaphorical expressions, such as *we're spinning our wheels; our relationship has hit a dead-end street; look how far we've come* (Lakoff 1993: 206).

6. Since then, the literature on phraseology and cognitive semantics has examined a lot of conceptual metaphors, many of them idioms. Often, these idioms are used as evidence in favour of the hypothesis about the existence of conceptual mappings that are independent of language and govern the corresponding linguistic structures in their semantic and pragmatic behaviour. According to the so-called "classical view" (completely out-dated today, see below), idioms have arbitrary meanings; within Cognitive Linguistics, however, most idioms are considered to be motivated rather than arbitrary (cf. 4.1). This does not mean that idioms arise automatically through the implementation of productive rules, but that they tend to fit one or more patterns already present in the speaker's conceptual system. The actual meanings of idioms can be accounted for by their imagery, so to speak, *ex post factum* (see for further discussion 6.2.6).

---

4 According to the Invariance Principe, "metaphorical mappings preserve the cognitive topology (that is, the image-schema structure) of the source domain, in a way consistent with the inherent structure of the target domain" (Lakoff 1993: 215). Numerous idioms contradict this metaphor concept, since their lexicalised figurative meanings have come about by quite different, often complex cognitive procedures. In many cases, the function of figurativeness is not to explicate the target concept by the structure of the source concept, but rather to obscure it (by means of mental detours).

5 This mapping met with much criticism. See section 6.2.5 for detail.

One of the main goals of the CTM is to develop universal methods and tools for analysing metaphorical expressions of all kinds, including idioms. However, a central problem of the CTM literature on idioms is that it completely ignores the generally accepted results of idiom research in Europe from the last 50 years, as repeated quotations of the so-called "classical view" on idioms indicate. What is called the "classical view" in CTM-oriented works is a conception that must be regarded as completely out of date and standing in clear contradiction to the state of the art in contemporary idiom analysis (cf. section 2.1 for details). In the following sections, we will discuss the linguistic relevance of the basic principles of the CTM for the study of the figurative lexicon.

6.2 Discussion: Are all postulates of the Cognitive Theory of Metaphor consistent with linguistic data?

The Cognitive Theory of Metaphor met with much criticism, despite its popularity.[6] In this section, we summarise and elaborate some points of criticism that have been expressed in studies discussing metaphoric issues. Some critical remarks have stressed the overvaluation of the physical basis in the Lakoffian theory of metaphor, which disregards the cultural implications of many metaphors. This criticism concerns the analysis of metaphors denoting emotions (primarily ANGER) in Western languages (6.2.1), and the explanatory power of conceptual mappings postulated at rather an abstract level of categorisation (6.2.2), as well as the analysis of metaphors in languages that are very different, such as Japanese (6.2.3). Further critical remarks come from anthropologists, who question the role of culture in the formation of metaphoric models (6.2.4). Furthermore, we ask whether the assumed conceptual metaphors can claim psychological reality (6.2.5) and whether idioms can be used for testing CTM-hypotheses (6.2.6).

---

[6] We are not concerned with criticism of CTM as a whole but only with critical points that can help improve the Conventional Figurative Language Theory. There are several critical papers on CTM that do not deal with the problems of culture specific features of figurative units in single languages (which is what is primarily important for our purposes), but with some elements of this theory that are claimed to be inconsistent with general scientific requirements (cf. e.g. Vervaeke and Kennedy 1996; Vervaeke and Green 1997; Rakova 2003; Kessler 2013). Further criticism comes from Jackendoff and Aaron (1991), who point above all to the overlooked role of culture in poetic metaphors. Even supporters of the CTM believe some parts of this theory to be incorrect (e.g. Ritchie 2003; Kövecses 2011). Criticism also comes from psycholinguistics (cf. e.g. Glucksberg, Brown, and McGlone 1993; Onishi and Murphy 1993; McGlone 1996, 2001; Keysar et al. 2000), and corpus linguistics (Deignan 2005, 2007, 2009; Stefanowitsch 2007; Hanks 2010).

6.2.1 Conceptual metaphors, the humoural doctrine or something else?

One of the general – and seemingly very productive – conceptual metaphors, namely ANGER IS THE HEAT OF A FLUID IN A CONTAINER, has been found in many expressions in different languages (Lakoff and Kövecses 1987; Lakoff 1987b; Kövecses 1990; 1995a;, 1998; cf. also Gibbs 1990). Nevertheless, the assumed "universality" of this metaphor has been a target of criticism from different sides. According to Lakoff, Kövecses and Gibbs, this metaphor is based on physiological experience. The conceptualisation of ANGER as HEAT OF A FLUID IN A CONTAINER is supported by a physical explanation in terms of body heat and increasing internal pressure, based on shared ideas about the human body. Due to the essential sameness of human beings and their physiological functioning across cultures, this body-based conceptual metaphor has been regarded as ubiquitous in all cultures, if not "universal". In the following, we will concentrate on various objections that have been raised against this assumption of ubiquity.

One point of criticism comes from Geeraerts and Grondelaers (1995); cf. also Geeraerts (2006: 227–251). As the authors have shown, the body-based interpretation of the ANGER metaphor fails in some cases and does not apply to various metaphorical expressions that have been described in this way, because the relevant cultural background has been ignored, cf. idiom (1).

(1) German *jmdm. läuft die Galle über* "someone's gall/bile flows over"
    'someone gets very angry'

According to the physically motivated ANGER-metaphor, the "gall" could be any "container", randomly interchangeable with other hollow organs of the body, but this is just not the case. There is a motivating link between the literal reading "someone's gall is overflowing" and the actual meaning 'someone gets very angry' that is more convincing than the body-based conceptual metaphor ANGER IS THE HEAT OF A FLUID IN A CONTAINER.

The metaphor in (1) cannot be put down exclusively to bodily experience but has to be seen as a cultural product as well. It must be traced back to knowledge about the "humoural pathology" of ancient times. From classical Greek antiquity (Hippocrates) and medieval times up to the present, this doctrine is still effective in contemporary metaphorical expressions. The humoural theory is a typical medieval, analogical way of thinking (therefore, ancient beliefs in physiological effects of emotions can be regarded as "metaphorical" in a broad sense). Four humoural fluids were believed to regulate the vital processes in the human body. From this followed the doctrine of the four temperaments: the four fluids defined the four prototypical temperaments: choleric, melancholic, sanguine, and phlegmatic. The choleric temperament was said to manifest itself in the anger and irascibility of a person's character. This temperament was connected to one of the four fluids, namely to the yellow bile, as in idiom (1). Within this edifice of the humoural doctrine, ANGER was seen as overproduction of yellow bile (cf. Schöner 1964).

In the medieval way of thinking, this fourfold schema was an elaborated semiotic system. The four elements were also associated with the four seasons, four times of the day, four rivers of Hades and other groups comprising the same magic number and influential in several cultural domains. The old doctrine continued to exist in popular belief for much longer, and the theory of the four humours has influenced the vocabulary of emotions in several European languages, cf. idioms like (2).

(2) a. Dutch *geel zien van nijd/groen en geel worden van nijd* "to be looking yellow with envy/to become green and yellow with envy"
b. English *to go/be/turn green with envy*
both meaning 'to become or be very envious, very upset or annoyed because one wishes one had another person's possessions, abilities, success etc.'

For most average native speakers, the relation between YELLOW or GREEN and 'envy, jealousy' is not comprehensible anymore, but, since these expressions exist, maybe there are associative links after all. Connections between particular colours and emotions like 'envy' or 'anger' are to be traced back to knowledge about the ancient humoural doctrine, which ascribed the colours green, yellow and black to particular emotions (and temperaments).

Although this doctrine has become outdated as a result of modern medical science, traces of it have survived in contemporary words and idioms. There are many words like French *bilieux*, English *bilious* 'morose', French *cholérique*, English *choleric* 'splenetic, irascible' or Dutch *zwartgallig* "black-bile like" (a loan translation of Ancient Greek μελαγ-χολικός 'melancholic'), Swedish *svårtsjuk* "black-ill" 'jealous', Russian *желчный* "yellow-bile-like" 'irascible', and so on. Compare also equivalents of idiom (1) in various European languages, e.g. Polish *żółć się w kimś gotuje* "[the] gall boils in someone", Greek χύνω τη χολή μου "I pour out my gall/bile", Finnish *jkn sappi kiehuu/kiehahtaa* "someone's gall boils", all meaning 'to be or become very angry'.

All these examples show that various types of knowledge have to be taken into account when explaining the motivational basis of idioms, including knowledge types that are different from conceptual metaphor, such as tacit knowledge of cultural models that are remote in time. Therefore, there is reason for interpreting idioms such as (1) by means of traces of the humoural doctrine and not only by the HEATED FLUID IN A CONTAINER metaphor.[7]

In Geeraerts' and Grondelaers' opinion, the humoural hypothesis provides a better explanation of the motivation behind this particular subset of emotion concepts. The authors give the following summary:

> The fact that a number of contemporary emotional expressions have their historical origin in the theory of humours does not imply, to be sure, that the theory synchronically determines the interpretation of those expressions: though our vocabulary for the concept still bears the imprint of ancient (medical) theories, we no longer believe in the theory as such. (Geeraerts and Grondelaers 1995: 170–171)

In further articles, Kövecses (1995b, 1995c) deals with Geeraerts' and Grondelaers' criticism,[8] providing a kind of corrective according to which both opinions are right: ANGER IS A CONTAINER is a metaphor and, at the same time, it is also based on the pre-scientific humoural theory. These influences seem to operate at two different levels of abstraction: at the generic level that "gives us a sense of similarity in the conceptualisation of anger across [...] cultures", and at a less generic level where "significant differences in conceptualisation, concerning especially the causal and the expressive aspects of the concept" are focused (Kövecses 1995b: 143).

We think that the "conceptual metaphor explanation" is not substantiated in this case. Of course, it cannot be claimed that all speakers possess knowledge of the humoural doctrine and address this kind of knowledge while processing idioms like (1) – see the above-cited statement by Geeraerts and Grondelaers. However, speakers may have a vague idea of the (pseudo)-causal connection between "gall" and "bile" on the one hand and the concept of ANGER on the other. This means that the conceptual metaphor determines that ANGER is in a container while culture determines which container (i.e. which of several hollow organs) is chosen.

Even if this kind of connection contradicts modern scientific knowledge, it does not impede the processing of idioms like (1) and (2). There are many expressions in natural language that are conceptually based on ideas rejected in the course of the development of scientific knowledge (cf. *sunrise* or *sunset*).

---

[7] In general, one should not dismiss the possibility that since the humoural doctrine is not prominent in contemporary cultures, present-day speakers interpret expressions like (1) in terms of the conceptual metaphors of ANGER. Investigating this question may be a task for experimental psychology. What is much more relevant for linguistics is the question of the extent to which traces of the source concept influence the usage of a given figurative unit.

[8] Cf. also Stefanowitsch (2007: 71–78) for further points of criticism.

Nowadays they may be interpreted in terms of culture because all these old models of the world are part of our "cultural memory". These "wrong", "unscientific" ideas can provide motivating links for understanding such expressions. It is more reasonable to assume that people make a "wrong" connection between "bile" and ANGER, even while being aware of the absence of a real biological basis for this connection, than to assume that they try to explain this kind of metaphorical expression by looking for a container as a relevant image basis.

Thus, people are unlikely to regard the gallbladder as a closed container filled with heated bile, where the feeling of ANGER is located. Firstly, idioms like (1) say nothing about the temperature of the bile. Secondly, there is linguistic evidence in favour of the "humoural" interpretation, cf. words like *bilious* in English, *zwartgallig* "having a black gall" 'melancholic' in Dutch and so on, whereas there are no expressions in which the idea of a HEATED FLUID IN A CONTAINER is applied to the image of "gall" or "bile" as indicators of ANGER.

There are also other cases where the addressing of conceptual metaphors for discovering motivating links interacts with the addressing of other structures of knowledge. Several studies of the Cognitive Theory of Metaphor use the following idiom (3) as an example of the ANGER-AS-HEAT metaphor.

(3) English *to hit the ceiling*
    'to suddenly become very angry'

Analysing idioms like *to blow your stack, to flip your lid* and *to hit the ceiling*, Gibbs (1993: 66–68) put the motivation of these expressions down to two conceptual metaphors: ANGER IS PRESSURISED HEAT and THE MIND IS A CONTAINER. This can be true for idioms like *blow your stack* and *flip your lid*, but hardly for (3), "as if a person goes up as anger explodes". Rather, the motivation in (3) seems to be based on the behaviour of people in a state of strong emotions which lead them to jump or perform other unintended physical activities. There is some linguistic evidence for this assumption. The German idiom (4), which is lexically equivalent to (3), has the meaning JOY in addition to the meaning ANGER.

(4) German *an die Decke gehen* "to go to the ceiling"
    1. 'to suddenly become very happy', 2. 'to suddenly become very angry'

Thus, it seems more convincing to put the actual meaning of idioms like (3) and (4) down to not only the ANGER-AS-HEAT metaphor but at the same time some typical behavioural symptoms of strong emotions, i.e. a kind of metonymy. The CONTAINER metaphor does not seem to be relevant in this case, because the structure of the underlying mental image points to strange or insane behaviour rather than to processes inside the body or the mind.

It also remains unclear why, throughout the literature on ANGER, a clear distinction is drawn between the idiom *to climb the walls* (always assigned to the metaphor ANGER IS INSANE BEHAVIOUR) and *to hit the ceiling* (exclusively assigned to the CONTAINER metaphor) (cf. Lakoff 1987b: 390, 385). As result, two idioms sharing very similar image components are considered to be mutually exclusive with regard to their underlying conceptual metaphors.

Focussing on ANGER metaphors as the exclusive explanatory basis of motivation is not correct, since the German idiom (4) – whose lexical structure and imagery are nearly identical to the English idiom (3) – has an additional meaning, which does not contradict the underlying image. Assuming that these two closely related meanings are based on entirely different conceptual metaphors seems to be counter-intuitive.

Our general impression of some well-known applications of the Cognitive Theory of Metaphor for the analysis of concrete linguistic data is that in many cases the postulated conceptual links are arbitrary. Sometimes alternative explanations can be put forward. These explanations may be based on cultural knowledge [as in (1) and (2)] or direct experience [as in (3) and (4)], though even in these cases culture may be involved to a large extent, as is shown by traditional anthropological research dealing with emotions and their symptoms (both real and imagistic ones) across cultures.

The concept of LIVER used for denoting emotional states in many idioms in European languages is another example of a metaphor interpretation that is typical of the Cognitive Theory of Metaphor. Like many others, this interpretation seems to lack a cultural component crucial for explaining motivating links. Kövecses (1995a: 125) analyses the Hungarian idiom (5) only in terms of the CONTAINER metaphor.

(5) Hungarian *nagy mája van* "his liver is big"
    'he is angry'

Aware of the fact that Kövecses, as a native speaker of Hungarian, knows the meaning, functional properties and image basis of this idiom very well, we would still propose an alternative interpretation, including elements of relevant cultural knowledge that may provide crucial motivating links in this case. From the perspective of the Cognitive Theory of Metaphor, the LIVER is just a "container" like any other. If this were true, any other hollow organ could replace LIVER in this idiom. This is obviously not the case, and it seems worthwhile to emphasise the cultural status of LIVER.

In many European languages the LIVER is a culturally loaded part of the human body, the organ of vitality. Numerous idioms reveal these specifics of the LIVER, for example, English *to be lily livered* 'to be cowardly', Italian *avere del fegato* "to have liver" 'to have courage', *mangiarsi/rodersi il fegato* "to eat/swallow the liver" 'to be very angry', French *avoir les foies blancs* "to have the white livers" 'to have terrible fear, to be terribly worried',[9] *donner/ficher les foies à quelqu'un* "to give/make the livers to someone" 'to frighten someone, to make someone anxious; worried', Spanish *tener hígados* "to have livers" 'to have courage' (the corresponding English idiom is *to have the stomach*), Greek *μου κόπικαν τα ήπατα* "the livers cut me" 'I lose courage' (the English equivalent is *to lose heart, to be disheartened*), *μου κόβονται τα ήπατα* (*mu kóvonde ta ípata*) "the livers make me break down" 'I am frightened, horrified' and the like.

In all these idioms from languages that belong to the Central and Southern European cultural area, LIVER is just not replaceable by, for example, STOMACH or any other hollow organ. There is a long cultural and historical tradition as to why the LIVER represents a special place of emotions. Let us consider the ancient Greek myth of Prometheus being punished. In an act of vengeance, Zeus had him fettered to a pillar and sent an eagle to eat his immortal liver (i.e. the place of vital energy), which constantly replenished itself – the liver that the eagle consumed in the daytime grew again during the night. In antiquity as well as in medieval medicine, the liver was seen as the place of the juices of life and temperaments, especially of wrath. Therefore, the Hungarian idiom (5) *nagy mája van* must be primarily interpreted within the edifice of humoural pathology, and not merely as a CONTAINER metaphor.

The conceptual metaphor ANGER IS THE HEAT OF A FLUID IN A CONTAINER is often seen as being productive in many languages, if not universal. However, according to Kövecses (1995b) referring to Lutz (1988), there are some exceptions. There is one language (Ifaluk, spoken on an atoll in Micronesia), which does not provide this metaphor:

> [T]here are cultures in the world where the container metaphor for anger plays an insignificant role in comparison with folk conceptions that are very different from it; for example in Ifaluk, a Micronesian atoll, the folk conception of anger emphasizes the prosocial, moral, and ideological aspects of anger (Lutz 1988) – as opposed to the antisocial, individualistic, and physical aspects that the pressurized container metaphor emphasizes in Western cultures. (Kövecses 1995b: 194)

---

9 According to a pre-scientific belief, the liver was the organ that delivered the blood, and the seat of 'courage' (cf. 11.4.3). The liver was also thought of as the seat of love – a belief still present in Shakespeare's times (cf. Brewer 1992: 618).

In section 6.2.4, some data concerning emotions in the Ifaluk language will be considered. However, the lack of the conceptual metaphor ANGER IS THE HEAT OF A FLUID IN A CONTAINER can also be found in cultural communities in Central Europe. The WML dialect (the Low German dialect that has been chosen as a contrast to standard or literary languages, cf. 1.2.2) serves as an example. There are twelve WML idioms denoting ANGER, none of them based on this "universal" metaphoric model.

To summarise, we would like to stress that although the Cognitive Theory of Metaphor can explain significant portions of figurative language (primarily, the mechanisms providing the understanding of novel metaphors), it is not a universal instrument for revealing all possible motivating links in this domain. Many other kinds of knowledge, especially knowledge about facts of material culture or cultural conventions with historical roots, have to be taken into account more intensively in order to exhaustively describe the plane of content of idioms.[10]

6.2.2 Levels of mappings and their linguistic relevance

Let us have a look at one more example: Idiom (6) can be regarded as based on a version of the aforementioned conceptual metaphor ANGER or EXCITEMENT IS PRESSURISED HEATED FLUID (or: A HEATED SUBSTANCE IN A CONTAINER, STEAM pointing to a high degree of heating, metaphorically pointing to emotional intensity) and another conceptual metaphor, namely PEOPLE ARE CONTAINERS FOR EMOTIONS. The idioms and the understanding thereof as mapped onto ANGER are motivated and framed by the same generic metaphors.

(6) English *to let/blow off steam*
'to get rid of one's anger or excitement by doing something noisy or active'

Describing the German equivalent of idiom (6), *Dampf ablassen* "to let steam off", Burger (1998: 31–32) found that the most common explanation of the nature of motivating links is not based on these conceptual metaphors but on knowledge about steam engines. Asking speakers about their mental imagery leads to clear results. In cases like (6), interviewees refer to a steam engine, a steaming boiler,

---

[10] Within the CTM, the role of culture has been mentioned in other contexts (not from the viewpoint of idiom motivation), for example, to explain how people acquire cognitive models such as LIFE IS A JOURNEY: "This semantically autonomous understanding of journeys is grounded in what we experience of journeys and in what we learn of journeys through our culture." (Lakoff and Turner 1989: 66).

a pressure cooker and the like rather than to heated fluid in one's body. It seems as if there is a blending of at least two mental spaces here: on the one hand, the combination of the metaphoric mappings ANGER or EXCITEMENT IS PRESSURISED HEATED FLUID IN A CONTAINER and PEOPLE ARE CONTAINERS FOR EMOTIONS (which is a direct bodily experience), and, on the other hand, the relevant knowledge of material culture, in this case the knowledge about engines in old trains and factories working with steam.

In fact, the interaction of these mental spaces can be described as a variation of the same conceptual structure at different levels. What motivates the choice of expressions with 'steam' is, in general, the emotional and physiological sensation of INTERNAL PRESSURE predetermined by the folk theory of emotions. This feeling of internal pressure leads to the choice of a concept of one's body as a container (at the level of generic metaphors) or a concept of a specific container type (cf. notions like steam engine, steam boiler, pressure cooker, etc.). Rich cultural information about these objects (engines, cookers, etc.) is incorporated into our understanding of these idioms at the basic level. Therefore, ANGER-idioms of this image type are ultimately framed by the same generic metaphors ANGER IS A HEATED SUBSTANCE (FLUID, GAS, etc.) IN A CONTAINER and PEOPLE ARE CONTAINERS FOR EMOTIONS.

The basic-level metaphor PEOPLE ARE STEAM ENGINES is a kind of specification of this PEOPLE-CONTAINER metaphor. What is important from the purely linguistic point of view is that some specific features of the "rich image" are often relevant for the actual usage of these expressions in discourse, whereas the generic metaphors only make up a conceptual framework that guarantees the mapping from source to target. Therefore, the basic-level metaphor PEOPLE ARE STEAM ENGINES can be interpreted not only in the conceptual framework of CONTAINERS FOR EMOTIONS but also, for example, in terms of STRENGTH or EFFICIENCY. An utterance like *John is a steamroller* would normally be interpreted as meaning that John is ruthlessly efficient, that he stops at nothing to achieve his goals.

By activating all relevant kinds of knowledge at the same time, people can understand why idiom (6) means what it means. Not only is addressing the conceptual metaphors of HEATED FLUID and CONTAINER a necessary precondition for understanding e.g. idiom (6), but the "technical" knowledge about steam engines is also involved in the motivation process as a necessary conceptual element. Compare other English and German idioms: *all the steam has gone out of the idea; to get up steam; under its own steam; jmdm. Dampf machen; mit Dampf, mit Volldampf; unter Dampf stehen/sein; der Dampf ist raus aus etwas.*

What has been said so far does not mean that the assumptions of the Cognitive Theory of Metaphor are inadequate. However, we need an explanation for the fact that knowledge about steam engines is also involved in the metaphoric conceptualisation of emotions. For some reason, people of different speech communities see parallels between the domain of steam engines and the domain of emotions. Obviously, the link between them is an intuitively constructed conceptual mapping from our knowledge of a steam engine to our knowledge about the human body. In this regard, the CTM idea of conceptualising the human body as a container for all possible entities, including mental and emotional factors, seems to be effective. What has to be stressed here, however, is the general possibility to postulate various alternative conceptual metaphors for the same metaphorical expression. Thus, besides the conceptual metaphors of HEATED FLUID and CONTAINER, other conceptual metaphors could also be proposed, e.g. PEOPLE ARE ENGINES (a kind of anti-personification metaphor). Admittedly, this metaphor is less general, but it has more explanatory power, including a cultural component, i.e. the knowledge about relevant facts of the material culture.

This example shows that the CTM and the Conventional Figurative Language Theory pursue different goals. For the CTM, it is important to discover near-universal conceptual metaphors that underlie each single metaphorical expression (therefore, idioms based on a concept of STEAM ENGINES and the like are classified as belonging to the CONTAINER metaphor etc.). For the Conventional Figurative Language Theory, however, the level of a very general metaphor is mostly of no interest. The Conventional Figurative Language Theory has to explain how the characteristics of figurativeness (above all, the image component) influence semantic and pragmatic specifics of CFUs.

Pursuing this goal, we have to concentrate on the basic level of a figurative expression with its rich images. At this level, the kind of world knowledge that is involved makes a great difference. Such an approach is more relevant linguistically because the real behaviour of a given idiom is not governed by knowledge of a general kind (e.g. by knowledge about containers), but by more concrete, culture-specific knowledge.

Let us look at some further figurative units where STEAM has the meaning 'energy': English *to run out of steam* 'to lose energy, to have no drive anymore'; *all the steam has gone out of him* 'he has lost all his drive, energy (as if he were a steam engine)'; *to get up steam to do something* 'to find the energy necessary for doing something'; *under one's own steam* 'by one's own effort'; German *Dampf drauf haben* "to have steam on it" 'to be really moving, to be vital, full of life'; *Dampf dahinter/hinter etwas machen* "to make steam behind it" 'to get a move on; to get a move on with something, get things moving'. The reference to technology in these idioms influences the image component. The person in question is seen as a mechanism, as a container filled with steam. At the level of the CONTAINER metaphor, all expressions for ANGER are identical. However, they differ from each other in their linguistic behaviour: they may show different restrictions of use in one language, or, from a cross-linguistic viewpoint, they may not be considered full equivalents.

Another example in favour of the significance of the rich image can be drawn from the WML dialect. ANGER in WML is verbalised by using a number of animal metaphors. These idioms fit into the conceptual metaphor ANGER IS ANIMAL BEHAVIOUR. However, describing the idioms only on the level of this superordinate metaphor would not be sufficient to reveal their linguistic peculiarities.

The image components of WML expressions meaning ANGER consist mainly of the BREEDING-BULL. Idioms evoking this image refer either to the animal's eyes (e.g. *he verdräit de Oogen in'n Kopp* "he rolls the eyes in the head"; *he lött 't Witte van de Oogen sehn* "he shows the white of the eyes"[11]) or to the animal's posture (e.g. *he steck 'n Kopp in'n Nacken* "he puts the head to the neck"). Their source domains consist of particular fragments of knowledge of agrarian life and culture: WML speakers are acquainted with the motivating links between 'rolling the eyes' or 'putting the head to the neck' and ANGER, because it is precisely the behaviour of a breeding-bull, as it can be observed in the everyday environment of the WML speech community.

Traces of this "rich image" have an impact on the actual usage of the idioms, since the concept of the BREEDING-BULL entails a clear reference restriction to men. Conceptually different are ANGER idioms of the WML dialect that imply a reference restriction to women; their image components mainly consist of the BROOD-HEN, cf. *se stüff dr' up an as ne (olle) Kluckhenne* "she dashes/scatters on as an (old) brood-hen" 'she is very angry' (Piirainen 2000, 1: 392).

Thus, BREEDING-BULL or BROOD-HEN are not interchangeable by any other (even very similar) animal concept. The interpretation of these idioms on the basis of particular everyday cultural knowledge is more convincing than proposing only a "universal" but unspecific conceptual metaphor such as ANGER IS ANIMAL BEHAVIOUR. From the linguistic point of view, it is more important that describing idioms merely on the abstract level of conceptual metaphors does not reveal the relevant usage restrictions (like gender-marked restrictions in these cases), because they are located on the level of the "rich image".

The metaphoric mapping at the basic level of categorisation (not at the superordinate level) is much more relevant for investigating conventional figurative language because specific properties of the image component become salient if the analysis concentrates on the basic level.

---

[11] Compare a similar image in the Lithuanian *baltomis akimis žiurėti* "to look with white eyes" 'to look with anger'.

6.2.3 Japanese culture, anger, and emotions as cultural constructs?

Japanese linguists have raised further criticisms of the conceptual metaphor ANGER IS THE HEAT OF A FLUID IN A CONTAINER. Particularly, they argue against the assumption of a universality of this metaphor as presented in several nearly identical papers (e.g. Lakoff and Kövecses 1987; Lakoff 1987b; Kövecses 1986, 1990, 1995a). Here we single out three points of criticism, concerning (i) the empirical data, (ii) the cultural uniqueness of the concepts of HARA and MUSHI, and (iii) social factors.

(i) As comprehensive studies (Matsuki 1995; Tsuji 1996) on ANGER in Japanese show, the area of metaphoric cross-linguistic equivalence is insignificant. In particular, the criticism addresses the empirical data of Lakoff's and Kövecses' analysis of ANGER expressions in Japanese, which are not always correct or were interpreted in a wrong way: "To simplify the situation, it could be said that the cognitive linguists tend to gather data, extracted from the literature for example, that fit into their own hypothesized mould of conceptual metaphors" (Tsuji 1996: 27).

With regard to the issue of empirical data, we would like to mention a further shortcoming of this study. Arguing that there are "many" idioms that denote ANGER and are based on the HEATED-FLUID metaphor in Japanese, Kövecses (e.g. 1995a: 125–127) presents sixteen Japanese expressions containing this metaphor. On closer examination, however, the bulk of these examples is made up of one and the same idiom. This is the familiar Japanese idiom (7).

(7) Japanese 腹が立つ (*hara ga tatsu*) "(the) abdomen/belly rises up/stands"
    'to be/get angry'

The form *hara ga tatsu* is the neutral standard notation normally used as a dictionary entry, also called "infinitive form". The same idiom, however, is present in different morphosyntactic and/or lexical variations, such as *hara o tateru* "somebody raises (the) abdomen/belly" (with a transitive verb) or *haradatashii* "abdomen/belly-rising", but also in accidental example sentences such as *anmari hara ga tatta node hon wo nagetsuketa* "because (the) abdomen/belly rose up so much, I threw (the) book", *haradatatashisa ni mune wo shimetsukerareru* "feel straggled with (the) chest because of (the) rise of (the) abdomen/belly" or *haradachi magire ni* "rising (the) abdomen/belly in/with anger".[12]

---

[12] The translations we use here for explaining the forms of the idiom *hara ga tatsu* differ from the translations proposed by Kövecses.

Furthermore, the lexical unit *rippuku* (立腹) "standing abdomen/belly" 'anger' is given as an example for the variety of metaphorical expressions based on the HEATED-FLUID metaphor. However, this is the Sino-Japanese reading of the same characters that occur in 腹が立つ (*hara ga tatsu*), i.e. 立(つ) *ritsu/tatsu* 'to rise' and 腹 *fuku/hara* 'abdomen/ belly'. So we are dealing with an almost identical concept in another character reading here (cf. Corwin 1994: 85–86; Garrison et al. 2002: 96). To summarise, the empirical basis of the conceptual metaphor in Japanese is certainly not as comprehensive as a cursory glance at Kövesces' (e.g. 1995a) studies would suggest.

(ii) However, the main criticism of the interpretation of Japanese metaphorical expressions in terms of the Cognitive Theory of Metaphor, which comes from Matsuki (1995) and Tsuji (1996), does not concern the empirical data but the omission of cultural factors connected with Japan and Japanese society, that is, factors which foreign researchers are unlikely to comprehend. Both Matsuki and Tsuji point to the fact that there are only a few Japanese expressions for ANGER which seem to be based on similar conceptual metaphors and metonymies to those found in European languages.

At this point we would like to distinguish between factors that have to be interpreted within the framework of cultural semiotics and factors connected with contemporary Japanese society (for the latter see below). It is questionable if not downright false to consider HARA merely a kind of container, comparable with notions of bodily containers in European languages. As has often been stressed, HARA enjoys the status of a key concept in Japanese culture and has no equivalent in Western languages (e.g. Hashimoto 1953; Dürckheim 1956; Yamaoka 1976; Matsumoto 1988; McVeigh 1996; Hasada 2002). There are various Japanese conventional figurative units in which *hara* does not appear in its literal meaning (denoting a part of the human body, the lower abdomen)[13] but as a semiotised concept. In all these idioms, HARA is a positively connoted symbolisation rather than a "belly".[14] The concept HARA manifests itself in various semiotic systems other than language, e.g. in mythological and aesthetic symbolisations. Mention should be made of China's ancient traditional medical theories, with their way

---

13 *Hara* is used mainly in male speech; the female word for the same thing is *onaka*. Translations of *hara* as 'belly', 'abdomen', 'stomach', 'the inner of the belly', etc. are only makeshift.

14 As far as the estimation of these parts of the body (BELLY/LOWER ABDOMEN/THE ENTRAILS) is concerned, there are great differences between cultures, extending from very negative to very positive connotations. In Occidental cultures, influenced by Christian thought, the BELLY/LOWER ABDOMEN is related to the most negative connotations; it is seen as the place of carnal desires and sin. These diverging views are one reason why metaphors containing BELLY concepts cannot be cross-culturally similar or "universal".

of thinking in analogies, or of the concept of a BIG/FAT BELLY, connected with Buddha or with Hotei, one of the Shintoistic seven gods of luck, symbolising wellness and prosperity. HARA as the centre of vitality is also important in specific breathing techniques in Zen Buddhism, in sumo wrestling or in the ancient Japanese ceremonial rite of self-disembowelment, of cutting out the vital centre of life (*seppuko*, mistakenly also called *hara-kiri*).

In folk theory, HARA is considered the location of the mind, of a person's inner self, the centre of mental energy and emotions. There is no strict separation between intellectual thought and emotion in the East Asian way of thinking. Knowledge is not just a matter of the mind and of theoretical reasoning but rather an activity of a person as a whole; the instrument of thinking is not the head but the belly (HARA). Hashimoto (1953: 37) points to expressions like "to think with the belly", "this does not want to fall into my entrails".[15] HARA is considered the realm of vitality, the seat of mental energy and the like. What is "thought" in the HARA is taken as more fundamental than what is "thought" in the head (McVeigh 1996: 39). HARA contains some invisible, hidden truth. This culturally based concept emerges in many idioms, e.g. 腹を割る (*hara wo waru*) "to split the belly" 'to reveal one's thoughts, to tell the truth', 腹を決める (*hara wo kimeru*) "to decide the belly" 'to make a decision', 腹が黒い (*hara ga kuroi*) "(to have a) black belly" 'to be evil, underhand, deceitful, scheming', 太っ腹だ (*futoppara da*) "to have a thick belly" 'to be magnanimous, generous', 腹が大きい (*hara ga ōkii*) "belly (is) big" 'generous', 腹が見えすいている (*hara ga miesuite iru*) "(one's) belly is transparent" 'one's true intentions are obvious', 腹を見られる (*hara wo mirareru*) "(one's) belly being seen" 'to have one's thoughts found out', 腹がわからない (*hara ga wakaranai*) "to not understand (the) belly" 'I can't understand his intentions', etc. (cf. Dobrovol'skij and Piirainen 1997: 72–73).

The ANGER scenario in Japanese culture obviously differs from that in the USA. ANGER metaphors in Japanese include three body zones: ANGER has its source in the HARA, the region of the belly/abdomen; it may rise to MUNE, the chest region; or, at its most intense stage, it may reach ATAMA, the head. This leads to metaphors not found in American English. Even if in some cases the conceptual metaphor THE BODY IS A CONTAINER FOR EMOTIONS seems to be part of the physiological basis for processing these Japanese expressions, it is the culture-specific concepts that provide the bulk of motivating associations for speakers of Japanese. Therefore, Japanese metaphors and idioms denoting ANGER cannot

---

[15] This is mentioned in a short note by Lakoff (1987b: 312), who says that some "metaphorically defined concepts (e.g. the Western TIME IS MONEY or the traditional Japanese idea that THE BELLY [hara] is THE LOCUS OF THOUGHT AND FEELING)" cannot be universal.

be compared in principle with corresponding expressions in American English. The invisible, truthful content of HARA is called *honne* 'private self'. This word is usually used in contrast to *tatemae* 'social face'.

> The consideration of the sociocultural context in which these notions function is fundamental to understanding the prototypical scenario of Japanese anger. Even when a person gets angry, his *honne*, or anger, may be kept inside; he may smile while fighting increasing anger. *Hara, honne,* and *tatemae* are parts of the Japanese scenario of anger, structuring such emotions in conflict. (Matsuki 1995: 144)

There are further examples of misinterpretations of culturally relevant Japanese concepts by Western linguists. Let us investigate the Japanese idiom *hara no mushi ga osamaranai*, which is translated by Kövecses (1995a: 128 and 1995c: 59) as "stomach bug no calm down" (sic!)[16] meaning 'I can't calm down'. The author uses this example to illustrate the significance and ubiquity of the ANGER-CONTAINER metaphor across languages and cultures. It is not only the cultural significance of HARA but also that of MUSHI that is disregarded here. The word *mushi* is simply translated as *bug*.[17] However, the Japanese concept of MUSHI has no equivalent in Western cultures. It is sometimes translated in a makeshift way as "the inner worm" or "insect of the soul", i.e. by word combinations that do not represent this concept as a whole. There is a popular belief in Japan that the MUSHI dwells inside a person in the form of an alien, influencing his or her feelings. This MUSHI is attributed with the ability to make someone angry or to mollify someone, to like or dislike something. Many Japanese idioms employ the concept MUSHI, which is not simply a bug (nor an insect or a worm). Compare idioms such as 虫が好かない (*mushi ga sukanai*) "(one's) MUSHI does not like" 'to dislike for some reason, to just dislike someone', 虫いの居所が悪い (*mushi no idokoro ga warui*) "the location of the MUSHI is bad" 'to be in a bad mood', 虫がいい (*mushi ga ii*) "(one's) MUSHI (is) good" 'to push one's luck, to ask too much, to take too much for granted', or (see above): 腹の虫が結まる (*hara no mushi ga osamaru*) "(one's) stomach-MUSHI settles down", where MUSHI is the attributed cause of feeling of resentment (cf. Corwin 1994: 135, 182; Hasada 2002: 122–123; Garrison et al. 2002: 415–418).

---

[16] A better translation would read "(my) stomach worm/insect does not calm down" or "the *mushi* in one's belly will not calm down" (Hasada 2002: 122).

[17] The translation "bug" involves a concept very different from that of MUSHI, since English uses the word *bug* in various (negative) figurative meanings, such as 'bacillus', 'disease, infection', 'defect', 'quirk', and so on. In terms of CTM the MUSHI-in-the-HARA metaphor could be regarded as an instantiation of the conceptual metaphor ANGER IS A DANGEROUS ANIMAL, but it is counter-intuitive because the concept of MUSHI, as it is used in figurative expressions, is not categorised as a dangerous animal.

This example shows that it is not always possible to explain certain concepts involved in figurative units with (near)-universal, biologically based entities (i.e. THE BODY IS A CONTAINER FOR EMOTIONS). Many of the concepts are very idiosyncratic with respect to the traditional culture, which can be understood as a unique semiotic code. Although it would be possible, in principle and at a very abstract level, to say that MUSHI and HARA fit into this metaphoric model despite their cultural uniqueness, the explanatory power of such a generalisation seems very questionable. From the perspective of the relevant motivating links between source and target concepts, the MUSHI-in-the-HARA metaphor discussed here has nothing to do with a pseudo-universal ENTITY-in-a-CONTAINER metaphor. On the contrary, it is a very specific, Japanese way of thinking of emotional states. Describing figurative language, from this point of view, does not mean finding a universal framework for all possible conceptualisations of similar entities across cultures; rather, it seeks to reveal the culture-specific features that make every language and its corresponding model of the world more or less unique.

Several recent studies on emotion concepts in non-European languages clearly refute the idea of a "universality" of ANGER conceptualisations. In Chinese, the emotion of ANGER is structured by a HEAT or FIRE metaphor, though not by the HEATED FLUID metaphor (Yu 1998: 52–54). Taylor and Mbense (1998) show that FLUID-STEAM metaphors are completely absent in Zulu, which provides entirely different conceptualisations (when ignoring the influence of English on Zulu for a century and a half of colonialism). Furthermore, in Taylor's and Mbense's (1998) opinion, the word *anger* projects an Anglocentric and therefore inappropriate concept onto this foreign culture. The Tsou language also shows unique conceptualisations of emotions, although it makes limited use of the metaphor ANGER IS EXCESS OF BREATH IN THE BODY (Huang 2002: 174–176).

(iii) Both Matsuki (1995) and Tsuji (1996) point to the fact that there are only a few Japanese expressions for IKARI (the Japanese pseudo-equivalent of ANGER) that seem to be based on conceptual metaphors similar to those found in European languages. Yet there is another factor, the factor of contemporary Japanese society, which makes it impossible in principle to compare Japanese metaphorical expressions denoting ANGER with corresponding expressions from American English. In Japanese culture, anger is not expressed but kept under control, especially in the public domain, where the social hierarchy plays an important role. Many social factors (the gender role, the principle of face-saving etc.) are crucial for the manifestation of emotions and, therefore, for the conceptualisation of a given emotion as well as for the use of relevant metaphors. As a consequence, the conceptual target domain of ANGER itself is not exactly the same in Japanese culture on the one hand and Western cultures on the other. Consequently, the metaphors (even if they look similar) can never be identical, because they refer to different target domains (cf. Matsumoto 1996: 86–87, 122–124).

According to Hasada (2002: 122), anger should not be openly shown in Japanese society and consequently should be suppressed in the presence of others. Therefore, MUSHI is appropriately used when referring to anger, since a person can appeal to MUSHI as a cause.

To summarise, it should be emphasised that the stipulation of universal or near-universal metaphoric models is one of the most problematic postulates of the Cognitive Theory of Metaphor. In the absence of an analysis of a sufficiently wide range of empirical data from different languages, these metaphoric models are assumed to hold for all human beings just because they obviously correspond to biological features. However, languages often do not choose biological features as such for denoting abstract concepts, but instead make use of a kind of cultural filter which allows only a few biological features from a relevant set to pass through into the given conceptual domain. So, even in the field of "body-based" conceptual metaphors, culture-specific elements should not be neglected.

6.2.4 Do anthropological data fit into the Cognitive Theory of Metaphor?

Another criticism of Lakoff's metaphor theory comes from anthropologists, who insist on the role of culture in the formation of metaphoric models, proposing that metaphors simply reflect cultural models (Holland and Quinn 1987; Quinn 1987, 1991). One of their points of criticism concerns the fact that the Cognitive Theory of Metaphor is based on mere introspection and on knowledge of the contemporary American culture but has no real empirical basis, such as interviews, for example: "In this analysis Lakoff has used metaphorical clues together with his own competence as a member of American culture to reconstruct American's 'cognitive models' of the emotion of anger and its physiological, psychological, and social consequences" (Quinn 1991: 63).

Their main criticism, however, is that culture does not play an important enough role in the Cognitive Theory of Metaphor to reflect the real mechanism of conceptualisation. Quinn (1991: 65) speaks of "a missing level in Lakoff's and Johnson's analysis – that of culture."

> This is not to say that Lakoff and Johnson are unaware that culture plays some role in understanding: Lakoff [...] introduces assorted "folk theories" and "folk models" into his analysis, and although Johnson's concern is with "embodied" meaning, he takes care to include "cultural traditions", along with language, values, institutions, and history, in a list of factors that he repeatedly reminds his readers are part of the environment in which meaning is embedded. But culturally constituted meaning has no place of its own beside embodied

> meaning in Johnson's analysis and no systematically developed or well-articulated place in that of Lakoff. (Quinn 1991: 65)

Furthermore, Quinn claims that metaphors play a comparatively small role in constituting the understanding of the world and that cultural models of the world play a relatively large role in constituting this understanding. In her empirically based case study on metaphors ("tropes") for marriage, she reaches the conclusion that the target concept is always culturally based, e.g. attitudes and cultural views of marriage, and that the tropes in question reflect only the view of contemporary American society. From an anthropologist's point of view, the metaphors are shaped by this culture. Quinn seeks to probe the cultural foundations behind metaphors, and authentic contexts and cross-cultural perspectives are therefore required as an important corrective to the Cognitive Theory of Metaphor.

In contrast to the criticism coming from the linguistic perspective, the anthropologically based criticism of the Cognitive Theory of Metaphor is less concerned with the source domain, i.e. with the questions of what linguistic and conceptual material is taken for denoting a given target concept and of how far this choice is universal or culture-specific. The anthropologically based criticism focuses on the target concepts themselves, as, for example, the very idea that ANGER, FEAR or MARRIAGE is, at least to a certain extent, culturally and/or socially determined. Hence, the problem is not only that certain conceptual metaphors do not explain the motivating links between the lexical structure of a given expression and its actual meaning, but also that the actual meanings of seemingly parallel expressions in different languages are not the same. Thus, they cannot be compared in principle (cf. the Japanese concept of ANGER in contrast to "Western ANGER" in 6.2.3).

Pointing to the cultural specifics of certain target concepts, Quinn (1991: 57) defines the concept of culture as follows:

> By culture I mean the shared understandings that people hold and that are sometimes, but not always, realized, stored, and transmitted in their language. Unfortunately, the case of metaphor illustrates a uniform tendency for linguists and other cognitive scientists outside of anthropology to neglect altogether the organizing role of culture in human thought, or to grant culture, at best, a residual or epiphenomenal place in their accounts.

In the following chapters of this study, in which we will analyse empirical data from different languages revealing relevant cross-linguistic and cross-cultural contrasts, we will not only investigate the influence of the shared presuppositions (i.e. culture in the sense of Holland and Quinn 1987) on language functioning but also introduce and use a semiotically based concept of culture (our notion of culture will be developed in subchapter 10.1). Since in the empirical part of this study we will be concerned with, among other things, cultural symbols in figurative language, we will pay attention not only to cultural specifics of the target concepts but also to cultural specifics of the source concepts, which in many cases are rooted in a knowledge of semiotic systems that were significant in previous times.

The Cognitive Theory of Metaphor has been debated and criticised in other anthropological studies. Generally, the criticism concerns the universal concept of human experience as the pre-conceptual basis of (nearly all) metaphors and the claim that most metaphors are ruled by a relatively small inventory of underlying imagery concepts which determine metaphorical choice in terms of body-based imagery. The central point of criticism, however, concerns the absence of aspects of culture in the argumentation of the CTM. Such criticism comes not only from Quinn and Holland (1987) or Quinn (1987, 1991) but also from other researchers, for example from Alverson (1991). On the basis of several metaphors that go back to the game of poker, Alverson (1991: 101–102) states: "To me the motivation and force of these metaphors and probably of most novel, compelling, apt ones found in powerful use of language are irreducibly *cultural*."

What has been said so far about anthropologically based objections to some postulates of the Cognitive Theory of Metaphor finds independent support from an influential psychological approach called *social constructivism* (Harré 1986). For example, Lutz (1987, 1988) shows in her studies of emotions in the culture of Ifaluk (a community living on a Micronesian atoll) that it would be wrong to translate emotion words from Ifaluk directly into Western languages, e.g. into American English, because the emotions denoted by Ifaluk words have no direct equivalents in Western emotional experience.

An emotion concept called SONG in the Ifaluk language is considerably different from that associated with the English word *anger*. The folk conception of SONG emphasises the prosocial, moral, and ideological aspects of 'anger'. Therefore, any translation of the Ifaluk word *song* by *anger* will fail. Ifaluk SONG is considered a social-cultural construction, the properties of which depend on specifics of Ifaluk culture and society (Lutz 1988). One of the main conclusions of Lutz's study is that emotion concepts are cultural artefacts rather than biologically based phenomena.

> I conclude by rejecting one possible interpretation of the structure of this analysis. It is *not* meant to be a model of how the Ifaluk "really feel", nor is it intended as a model of how the Ifaluk "think about their feelings". I have argued elsewhere that the concern with "true, underlying feeling" is a local cultural preoccupation and that the dichotomous categories of "cognition" and "affect" are themselves Euroamerican cultural constructions, master symbols that participate in the fundamental organization of our ways of looking at ourselves and others [...], both in and outside of social science. (Lutz 1987: 308)

This statement holds also for other cultures and languages. From this point of view, almost nothing is "embodied" or biologically based.

Similar ideas can be found in Wierzbicka (1999). The author points out that almost everything in language reveals a certain degree of cultural specificity. In the same way, emotion concepts (emotion prototypes) are not "universal" but differ from culture to culture, whereas the semantic primitives with which these differences are expressed in the semantic metalanguage can, according to Wierzbicka, be universal. What people say about their emotional states or what metaphors they use are not part of a universal, innate way of conceptualising the world but part of a semiotic system that prescribes what signs (both verbal and nonverbal) must be used in what situation (cf. also Palmer 1996; Harkins and Wierzbicka 2001).

6.2.5 What do conceptual metaphors really explain?

Other points of criticism deal with the explanatory power of the notion of conceptual metaphor. The question raised by Murphy (1996, 1997) is: How real and psychologically plausible are conceptual metaphors? In other words, if people talk in a certain way, does it really mean that they conceptualise the world in such a way? Murphy's doubt is grounded, above all, in the fact that there are often many different source concepts for the same target concept. If, in accordance with the Cognitive Theory of Metaphor, the target concept often has only one metaphoric representation, and (according to the Invariance Hypothesis) if its structure inherits the structure of the source concept, how can we deal with cases in which there are many different sources for the same target? According to which source concept should it be structured? Murphy doubts that, for instance, the concept of LOVE can be structured simultaneously according to the concepts of A JOURNEY, A FINANCIAL TRANSACTION, AN OPPONENT, INSANITY, A VALUABLE COMMODITY, etc. In a case like this, we are dealing with a multiple metaphor, so to speak (cf. also Baldauf 2003).

Imagine that one person uses all these metaphors in his or her discourse.[18] How can his/her way of thinking and behaviour be influenced by many different metaphors at the same time? Lakoff and Johnson (1999) stress that multiple metaphors are not exceptions but the rule, although they do not explain how this is compatible with the "aptness of metaphor": "In philosophy, metaphorical

---

18 Cf. Lakoff's and Johnson's (1980: 3) observation that "[M]etaphor is pervasive in everyday life, not just in language but in thought and action."

pluralism is the norm. Our most important abstract philosophical concepts, including time, causation, morality, and the mind, are all conceptualized by multiple metaphors, sometimes as many as two dozen" (Lakoff and Johnson 1999: 71).

In order to maintain the hypothesis that the structure of the source concept influences the relevant features of the target concept, it must be assumed that the target concept (LOVE in this case) changes significantly according to the corresponding source concept. For example, the concept of LOVE in expressions based on the conceptual metaphor LOVE IS A JOURNEY highlights different aspects of the concept of LOVE in expressions based on the conceptual metaphor LOVE IS A FINANCIAL TRANSACTION. This assumption (vaguely put forward in Lakoff and Johnson 1980) seems to be too rigid to be accepted both linguistically and psychologically (cf. Engstrøm 1999).

In his answer to Murphy's criticism, Gibbs (1996: 313) formulated the following idea: "The so-called problem of multiple metaphors for identical target concepts can be easily handled if we view concepts not as fixed, static structures but as temporary representations that are dynamic and context-dependent. Under this view, concepts are temporary, independent constructions in working memory created on the spot from generic and episodic information in long-term memory".

This statement is obviously true. Target concepts are flexible and temporary entities. A very important consequence is that it would be wrong to assume that by using certain metaphors from time to time, speakers force themselves into a very specific, metaphorically based view of reality. The structuring of a target concept according to the structure of a source concept is valid and relevant just at the moment that speakers use a given metaphor. The next moment, when they use another metaphor, this structure is put aside.

As for multiple metaphors in general, there is nothing wrong with them from the viewpoint of known semantic theories, including the CTM. Every metaphor structures the target only partially. Various sources suggest different views of the same target. This is the major cognitive and linguistic role of metaphors, and it is the reason why there can be many different metaphorical expressions referring to the same object. What is wrong is the claim that the use of a given metaphor influences the construction of reality in a significant way.

Similar ideas can be found in European research on metaphors and idioms. Burger (1998: 36) stresses that the conceptual mappings reflected in German idioms are not relevant to their use in real texts:

> Where idioms are used on the grounds of their inherent metaphorical impact, their application in texts usually shows no coherent structure which could be used as an interpretative model of a reality construction. It rather serves as a kaleidoscopic interpretation of short reality cuts. Accidental context elements, be they linguistic or non-linguistic, evoke

certain idioms, or a speaker chooses certain metaphors in order intentionally to focus metaphorically on aspects of the spoken text. This usually happens unsteadily and with an ever changing perspective. Only rarely do authors aim to establish a continually coherent relation between the source domain and the target domain of the metaphor.

There are two versions of the Cognitive Theory of Metaphor – a strong one and a weak one. Even if we reject as too rigid the strong version, which claims that many concepts can be structured only via their metaphoric representation, and agree with the weak version, we will have some difficulties with cases like multiple metaphors or the use of conceptually inconsistent metaphors in the same text segment. According to the weak version, speakers possess well-developed structures for representing target concepts, which exist independently of any metaphors; Lakoff and Johnson (1999) seem to adopt this version. However, the existence of certain metaphors in a given language must have influenced the structure of these concepts so that they have to be consistent with the relevant metaphoric models. This seems to be one of the most ambitious postulates of the Cognitive Theory of Metaphor. So even the weak version claims that the source concept structures the target concept. Hence, if many well-known and linguistically strongly represented source concepts correspond to one target concept, the weak version has to admit that either such a target concept has no stable structure (cf. Gibbs' statement above) or that the general claim of source-target consistency must be reformulated in a more flexible way. Otherwise, if it is possible to speak of the same entity in terms of SOLDIERS and SOUP INGREDIENTS in one sentence, this means that the use of such metaphors does not influence the strategy of reasoning about a given topic.

In summary, one of the main postulates of the Cognitive Theory of Metaphor, namely the assumption that the metaphors we use influence our thoughts and behaviour, has to be reformulated in the sense that a given metaphor, in most cases, perhaps, does so only at the moment we use it.

Criticising the general principles that structure conceptual metaphors, Murphy indicates that, for example, the conceptual metaphor LOVE IS A FINANCIAL TRANSACTION shows that not all source domains are less abstract than their corresponding target domains, contrary to the rather general claim of every known theory of metaphor: "in fact, love is much more embodied than financial transactions are." (Murphy 1997: 99). Murphy addresses also the claim of the Cognitive Theory of Metaphor that the source concepts are more familiar to the speakers than the target concepts, and this not only because the former are concrete and the latter are abstract but also because the source concepts are accessible via direct experience. This may hold in cases like BAD IS DOWN or EVENT IS MOTION, where the source concepts are really embodied, i.e. given in a direct body-based experience.

However, trying to keep this claim up for cases like LOVE IS A FINANCIAL TRANSACTION would mean that one has to prove that FINANCIAL TRANSACTION is a more basic, directly experienced or even body-based concept than LOVE.

This objection by Murphy is not quite correct. The target concept, in this case, is not the concept of LOVE as a whole, but certain aspects of LOVE, i.e. only those aspects that can, in principle, be understood in terms of financial transaction. Here we are obviously dealing with emotional and social aspects of LOVE. They can hardly be represented in the form of visual images and the like. As compared with those aspects, the concept of FINANCIAL TRANSACTION is less abstract and more embodied in that it involves physical entities (e.g. money) rather than psychological ones. A financial transaction is a clearly structured scenario consisting of relatively simple operations.

Another example of this kind is the conceptual metaphor ARGUMENT IS WAR, often mentioned in discussions about the Cognitive Theory of Metaphor (see Baldauf 1997: 213–215; Ritchie 2003). Since everybody is involved in arguments from time to time, knowledge about arguments is more or less directly available. Fortunately, however, not everybody takes part in wars. One reason why language nevertheless produces metaphors based on the conceptual mapping ARGUMENT IS WAR is that cultural experience has just the same important position in people's cognitive systems as direct body-based experience. In this case, the historical perspective must be taken into account. At the time when many metaphors and idioms based on the conceptual mapping ARGUMENT IS WAR were created, wars and fights were much more common and directly available situations than now. This historical perspective is part of our cultural knowledge. Another reason for using WAR as a source domain in the conceptual correspondence ARGUMENT IS WAR is that the concept of WAR is more embodied than ARGUMENTS, because the former involves physical force while the latter involves only verbal force. Thus, the cultural aspects of both the origin and processing of metaphorical expressions have to be taken into account while analysing their conceptual foundations.

Another point of criticism, which is especially important in the context of our theoretical discussion, concerns the ontological status of conceptual metaphors. The Cognitive Theory of Metaphor assumes that the fact that mappings like LOVE IS A JOURNEY are a fixed part of the human conceptual system explains why new and imaginative uses of such mappings can be understood instantly, given the ontological correspondence and other knowledge about journeys. However, how do we know what is primary? Our knowledge about love or our knowledge about journeys? Does our knowledge about journeys really influence our knowledge about love? (This seems to be rather dubious; one reason is that a journey is a purposeful activity whereas love is not.) Or is the formula LOVE IS A JOURNEY just an "umbrella label" to cover some English expressions? There is enough linguistic evidence in favour of the latter assumption (cf., for example, Padučeva 2004b; Apresjan 2009: 420–421).

It is likely that the CTM protagonists did not intend this interpretation of conceptual metaphors. However, from the linguistic perspective it is that which makes this concept interesting and important. For solving linguistic problems (such as the problem of cross-linguistic parallels or contrasts in the field of figurative language), it is not important what is primary: the conceptual metaphor as a mental entity or the corresponding linguistic expression. What is important is to have a powerful metalinguistic tool for describing nontrivial properties of linguistic structures.

The last point of criticism which we would strongly support is that there are large portions of figurative language which cannot be captured with the help of the theoretical apparatus of conceptual metaphors. Thus, although a powerful metalinguistic tool, this apparatus still cannot be claimed to be a universal instrument for describing units of figurative language. Think of idioms like *to kick the bucket* – there is no larger conceptual metaphor of KICKING IS DYING or BUCKETS ARE DEATH that would explain this idiom. Thus, many idioms must be explained by historically opaque conventions (cf. Murphy 1997: 104).

Of course, in this case one could say that *to kick the bucket* is not motivated at all, but similar doubts arise when explaining clearly motivated idioms. In general, the question of the extent to which conceptual metaphors influence the understanding of idioms remains open. There are cases where it can easily be proved that understanding an idiom is based on a common conceptual metaphor, which creates many other expressions of the same type. There are, however, other cases where the connection to any conceptual metaphor is not so obvious because the relevant motivating link is provided at another level.

6.2.6 Idioms and conceptual metaphors

Some further points of criticism come from cognitive psychologists Keysar and Bly (1999). Their main ideas could be summarised as follows:

It is problematic to consider conceptual metaphors as primary entities that exist independently of language and govern corresponding linguistic structures in their semantic and pragmatic behaviour. Instead, it is rather our knowledge of the actual meaning of a given linguistic expression that predetermines our interpretation of conceptual mappings.

Idioms cannot, in principle, be used as evidence either in favour of or against the hypothesis about the existence of conceptual mappings, because there is no way to find potentially negative evidence. In other words, it is always possible to find a couple of idioms which would support the postulate of one or another conceptual mapping. However, this cannot be taken as evidence in favour of the hypothesis that such a conceptual mapping really exists because, if we cannot indicate which concrete findings prove that this conceptual mapping does not exist, we may not interpret any findings as evidence.

Native speakers' intuition that certain idioms are transparent is based, so to speak, on backward reasoning. An idiom is perceived as transparent not because speakers evoke their knowledge of conceptual metaphors and project it on the idiom's lexical structure. On the contrary, speakers know the actual meaning of the idiom because they have in fact learnt it. Then, they project this knowledge on the idiom's lexical structure and reconstruct the conceptual mapping. If a given idiom had a completely different meaning, it would also be possible to construct an explanation of this other meaning. Such an explanation would fit the relevant conditions just as well as in the case of the "real mapping".

Taking as example the idiom *to keep someone at arm's length*, Keysar and Bly first refer to Lakoff (1987b: 447–449). Lakoff describes the motivation of this idiom as an inference resulting, first, from an elaborate image of a person extending an arm forward. Secondly, two conceptual metaphors "provide the link between the idiom and its meaning", namely INTIMACY IS PHYSICAL CLOSENESS and SOCIAL (OR PSYCHOLOGICAL) HARM IS PHYSICAL HARM (Lakoff 1987b: 448). The main impetus of the Cognitive Theory of Metaphor in this field is pointing to the linguistically independent nature of conceptual mappings motivating the idioms: "What it means for an idiom to 'be natural' or to 'make sense' is that there are independently existing elements of the conceptual system that link the idiom to its meaning" (Lakoff 1987b: 449).

Keysar and Bly show convincingly that this idiom could also mean the opposite, namely 'to be very close to a person'. Our world knowledge allows us, in principle, to interpret the distance of an extending arm between two objects as a long one as well as a short one. And indeed, in other languages, idioms having nearly the same lexical structure mean something like 'to be available, to be at someone's disposal'. Keysar and Bly exemplify this by taking an idiom from Hebrew.

This does not mean that the ideas of the CTM cannot be effectively implemented while investigating the idioms. For purely linguistic aims, the ontological status of the conceptual metaphor is not as important as the possibility to use the metalinguistic apparatus of the CTM for describing motivation phenomena. Of course, other metalinguistic instruments are also necessary, especially those which are designed to analyse the individual features of idioms and cross-linguistic differences in this field. Idioms, by definition, are irregular units of the lexicon. Thus, the most salient features of their semantic structure cannot be captured by the metalinguistic tools aimed at finding regularities in the realm of metaphorical expressions.

6.3 Conclusions

The Cognitive Theory of Metaphor is important for investigations into the phenomenon of figurativeness because it provides the researcher with a well-developed metalinguistic apparatus, including heuristically significant concepts such as source domain, target domain, metaphoric model, conceptual mapping, conceptual correspondences, and metaphoric entailment. In many cases, applying this apparatus allows us to explain many real properties of figurative units which could not be captured in the framework of traditional approaches. The explanatory power of the CTM is especially high in cases where an explanation is needed as to how a particular novel metaphor works.

Speakers creating a new metaphor in order to be able to talk about a difficult, barely structured situation propose, by using such a metaphor, a way of structuring the given situation, i.e. an original view on it. The metaphor is therefore not just a means of naming, but an instrument of conceptualising the world. The CTM is the only theory which points to this fact and comes with appropriate tools of analysis.

However, conventionalised metaphors, idioms among them, have a different function and a different cognitive and communicative value. What they have in common with individual novel metaphors is their origin, i.e. they often use the same mappings; but their value in understanding a situation is not identical. This fact has not received enough attention so far. Conventional metaphors, especially idioms, contribute much less to the structuring of unstructured situations, but rather convey different kinds of knowledge that they have accumulated in the course of their functioning in the language. This does not mean that the metalinguistic apparatus of the CTM cannot be applied to the description of idioms and other conventional figurative units. But what is needed, in addition, is a theory specially designed to describe the irregularities in the realm of conventional figurative language. To develop such a theory is the main aim of this book.

It is evident that subsuming all possible metaphorical expressions of different languages under the same conceptual metaphor would be an important step of linguistic analysis. As for figurative language research, it would enable us to compare idioms, among other things, with other kinds of metaphorical expressions, and enlarge the explanatory basis. For example, expressions like *to be down*, *to be low* on the one hand and *beaten to the ground* on the other (all of them going back to the conceptual metaphor SAD/UNHAPPY IS DOWN) are analysed separately in the framework of traditional lexicology because of their different status in the taxonomy of lexical units. The CTM approach allows us to ignore taxonomic differences and analyse related lexical units semantically and pragmatically across boundaries between taxonomic classes. Compare, for example, the following metaphorical expressions based on the conceptual metaphor DIFFICULTIES ARE IMPEDIMENTS TO MOTION:

(8) English *to drive someone into a corner; to put a spoke in someone's wheel; in a bind; in a fix; in a jam; up the creek (without a paddle); in queer street; with one's back to the wall; to clear/knock over a hurdle; there is no way out; between a rock and a hard place; caught in a cleft stick; encirclement; bottleneck; logjam; strait*

(9) German *in der Klemme sitzen* "to sit in a clamp" 'to be in difficulties, in a great predicament'; *ein Klotz am Bein* "a block at the leg" 'a problem that is stopping someone from succeeding or progressing'; *keine großen Sprünge machen können* "not to be able to make big jumps" 'to be unable to afford many luxuries'; *ausweglos* "without way out" 'hopeless'; *Beklemmung* "clamping" 'oppressive feeling'; *Engpass* "narrow way" 'difficulties with supplying etc.'

(10) Dutch *tussen de deuren komen* "to come between the doors" 'to get into difficulties, in a great predicament'; *tussen (de) deur en (de) drempel zitten* "to sit between (the) door and (the) threshold" 'to be in a predicament, in a very embarrassing situation'; *in de nesten zitten* "to sit in a muddle" 'to be in great difficulties'; *in het gedrang komen* "to come into the crush" 'to get into difficulties, into a difficult position'; *in de puree zitten* "to sit in the puree" 'to be in trouble'; *nauw* "confinement; restriction" 'difficulties'

(11) Finnish *olla ahtaalla* "to be in [a/the] narrow" 'to be embarrassed, to be in great difficulties'; *olla pinteessä* "to be in [a/the] clamp" 'to be in a great predicament'; *(selkä) seinää vasten* "(back) against [a/the] wall" 'in a great predicament'; *olla puun ja kuoren välissä* "to be between [the] tree and [the] bark" 'to be in a hopeless situation, in a great predicament'; *heitellä jklle kapuloita rattaisiin* "to throw cudgels in someone's carriage/cart" 'to hinder someone violently'; *jku ei pääsee eteen eikä taakse* "someone does not come out at the front nor at the back" 'someone is in great difficulties'; *ahdingossa* "in the narrow" 'in great difficulties'; *pullonkaula* "bottleneck" 'difficulties with supplying etc.'

(12) Japanese 八方塞さがり (*happō fusagari*) "eight (all) directions being blocked/closed" 'in a great predicament'; 板挟みになる (*itabasami ni naru*) "to become squeezed between boards" 'in a dilemma, in a very difficult situation'; 厚い壁にぶっかる (*atsui kabe ni butsukaru*) "to collide with a thick wall" 'to be up against a problem'; 二進も三進も行かない (*nitchi mo satchi mo ikanai*) "not (able to) progress two nor three" 'to be in a great predicament'; 袋の鼠 (*fukuro no nezumi*) "mouse/rat in a sack/bag" 'trapped/surrounded, in a difficult position'; 道を遮る (*michi wo saegiru*) "to block the road" 'to hinder, obstruct'

Clusters like these provide a good basis for semantic analysis. From this point of view, the idea of conceptual metaphor as a cognitive foundation for different linguistic expressions is an efficient instrument of analysis, both within one language and cross-linguistically. On the other hand, it is obvious that we need a more sensitive tool of analysis than conceptual metaphor for explaining semantic differences between the expressions listed under (8–12). Idioms and other figurative expressions based on the same conceptual metaphor often reveal semantic differences that cannot be explained on the basis of rather abstract metaphoric models.

As for the discussion about the validity of certain postulates of the CTM, different points are of different value for our purposes. Thus, the extent metaphors influence thinking and behaviour is not so important for the issues investigated in this study. Much more important are purely linguistic questions, such as the question of an implicit presence of certain traces of the source concept in the structure of the target concept. If these conceptual traces can be found, do they influence the use of a given lexical unit? If so, do they belong to the semantic structure of this lexical unit? What metalanguage must be developed to capture the relevant specifics of the semantic structure? If the traces of the source concept do not influence the use of a given lexical unit (i.e. no relevant combinatorial constraints can be found), does it mean that there are none? Alternatively, could it be that they are implicitly present in the plane of content and play a certain role at the conceptual level, which is potentially significant for the actual meaning? Which is linguistically more salient – the abstract level of conceptual metaphors, at which very general correspondences between source and target can be stated, or the more concrete level of individual mappings (i.e. frame correspondences), at which individual lexical units can be distinguished from each other? What tasks of linguistic description are needed to address which parts of metaphor structure?

Our results suggest that for revealing the specific semantic and pragmatic features of every single CFU, i.e. for describing every conventional metaphor (be it an idiom or a word) as a lexical unit with a unique set of properties, the level of "rich images" is more promising. Often, concrete features of metaphor structure play a more important role in profiling the actual meaning of a CFU than does the metaphor's schematic structure fixed in the conceptual mapping.

The most important conclusion for our study that can be drawn from the discussion above is that the CTM in its present version does not cover all relevant aspects of the semantic and pragmatic behaviour of conventional figurative units. Knowledge of underlying conceptual metaphors is not the only type of knowledge which is linguistically relevant. In order to describe how conventional figurative units function, one has to take into account other, chiefly culturally based, concepts as well, which in many cases govern the transfer from literal to figurative.

7 Idioms of FEAR: A cognitive approach

7.1 Introduction

The aim of this chapter is the implementation of theoretical ideas already discussed, with particular reference to the Cognitive Theory of Metaphor investigated in the previous chapter. However, the conceptual correspondences we want to employ as an instrument of analysis here are not conceptual metaphors in the "classical" sense, but models that are based on both metaphors and metonymies (cf. Goossens 1990; Geeraerts 2002). We have chosen the semantic field FEAR because it is particularly suitable for investigating correspondences between semantic phenomena and conceptual properties, between the image component of the content plane and the actual meaning. Conventional figurative units meaning 'to be afraid', 'to be scared' and the like have been brought together to examine in depth this semantic domain as a whole.

In what follows, we will show that conventional figurative units referring to the same concept and forming a semantic field can be analysed according to their metaphorical nature in terms of relevant *metaphoric models* providing a link between a *source domain* and a *target domain* (in the sense of Lakoff 1987b, 1993). For FEAR as it appears in many European languages, such source domains as e.g. COLD or PHYSICAL WEAKNESS can be postulated.

People conceptualise FEAR (and other emotions) not only through observing relevant events and their biological or psychological reactions, but also via different mappings between source and target domains. For example, to conceptualise FEAR as PHYSICAL WEAKNESS one need not necessarily feel it. It is sufficient to think about the given emotional experience in terms of *my knees knocking together, having my heart in my mouth, being in a cold sweat, breathless with fear*, or *rooted to the spot*, etc.

The findings presented in this chapter also give credence to the growing idea in Cognitive Linguistics that conventional figurative units of language express certain underlying mental features which systematically contribute to the conceptualisation, and maybe even influence some fragments of our model of the world. Contrary to the traditional view, empirical results demonstrate that cognitively based semantic theories are compatible with the ideas of semantic decomposition developed in structural semantics.

7.2 Idiom semantics in cognitive perspective

In the Anglo-American tradition (Bobrow and Bell 1973), idioms were considered to be "long words", i.e. lexical units comparable in their nature with simple words (cf. section 2.1). According to this view, the only difference between idioms and words is their formal structure, because idioms by definition consist of more than one word. Semantically, idioms were identified with non-metaphorical words, following the line of reasoning that if it is possible to express the same idea (say, 'to die') by means of idioms (e.g. *to kick the bucket*) and by means of words (*die*), they reveal no significant difference in meaning.

From the practical point of view, this implies that for the purpose of finding an adequate equivalent in another language it does not matter which idioms or one-word equivalents are used in the target language for translating a given idiom from the source language.

Following the same line of reasoning put forward by structural semantics, some cognitively oriented theories first regarded idioms as being stored in the mental lexicon as non-analysable units, cf. the so-called "Lexical Representation Theory" mainly developed by Gibbs (1980) and (1986). Further investigations in this field showed that the alternative idiomatic units that are used to designate a given concept can, at least to a certain extent, modify it. These observations go along with our linguistic intuition that for example, the expressions *to kick the bucket* and *to die* do not signify exactly the same.

In his later papers on the conceptual structure of idioms (1990, 1993), Gibbs writes that even very close idiomatic synonyms reveal important specific features. Using experimental methods, he and his collaborators demonstrated that, for example, some idioms denoting ANGER can differ from each other so much that it is not even possible to use them in the same context without changing the sense of the utterance (Nayak and Gibbs 1990). For example. though both *to blow one's stack* and *to bite someone's head off* denote ANGER, their meanings are totally different and they cannot appear in analogous contexts.

In one experiment described in Gibbs (1993: 70–71) people were asked to read the two following stories and to decide which of the two idioms in question seems to be appropriate in each context.

(1) Mary was very tense about this evening's dinner party. The fact that Bob had not come home to help was making her fume. She was getting hotter with every passing minute. Dinner would not be ready before the guests arrived. As it got close to five o'clock the pressure was really building up. Mary's tolerance was reaching its limits. When Bob strolled in at ten minutes to five whistling and smiling, Mary . . .

(2) Mary was getting very grouchy about this evening's dinner party. She prowled around the house waiting for Bob to come home to help. She was growling under her breath about Bob's lateness. Her mood was becoming more savage with every passing minute. As it got closer to five o'clock Mary was ferociously angry with Bob. When Bob strolled in at 4:30 whistling and smiling, Mary ...

Participants in this experiment gave preference to the idiom *blew her stack* for context (1), and *bit his head off* for context (2). This can be explained on the basis of mental imagery that motivates different idioms in a different manner. As a metalinguistic device for taking the mental imagery into account, Gibbs proposed the apparatus of *conceptual metaphors* going back to Lakoff's Cognitive Theory of Metaphor (as has been outlined in the previous chapter).

In Lakoff's CTM, the model underlying the idiom *to blow one's stack* is described as ANGER IS THE HEAT OF A FLUID IN A CONTAINER, whereas *to bite someone's head off* is supposed to be based on the metaphoric model ANGER IS ANIMAL BEHAVIOUR. As has been shown in chapter 6, postulating such conceptual metaphors is not always convincing. Nevertheless, there is no doubt that conventional figurative units, the image components of which belong to different conceptual domains, differ with regard to some more or less relevant conceptual properties. Hence, idioms based on different metaphoric models designate different kinds of ANGER. That is why the two idioms are not freely interchangeable.

The judgments about the appropriateness of these idioms in contexts (1) and (2) were influenced by the metaphoric coherence of the two stories; cf. such expressions as *getting hotter, the pressure was really building up* in (1) and *prowled around the house, growling under her breath* in (2). But there are also purely semantic differences. ANGER expressed by the idiom *to bite someone's head off* is not only stronger, but it also evokes associations with the active aggressive behaviour of the subject who wants to let other people know how angry he or she is. "The phrase *bite his head off* implies that the angry person is demonstrating her anger in a more deliberate, intentional manner than is the case with the phrase *blow her stack*" (Gibbs 1993: 71).

Sometimes idioms reveal semantic differences which cannot be explained on the basis of abstract metaphoric models. There are idioms that belong to the same metaphoric model but nevertheless display specific semantic features.

> Thus, even though *spill the beans, let the cat out of the bag, blow the lid off,* and *blow the whistle* each roughly mean 'to reveal a secret', there exists some convention such that *spill the beans* might be appropriate to use in situations where a person is revealing some personal information about someone else, while *blow the lid off* might be used to talk of revealing secrets about, say, governmental corruption. (Gibbs 1990: 421)

Both the idioms *to spill the beans* and *to blow the lid off* activate the same two conceptual metaphors at the same time, namely MIND IS A CONTAINER and IDEAS ARE PHYSICAL ENTITIES, so the explanation of the above-mentioned differences in the meaning has to be looked for in another domain. Though Gibbs does not give the reasons for these differences, it is quite obvious that they are caused by mental images corresponding to the idioms under consideration. *To spill the beans* evokes an image of an unintentional action, whereas *to blow the lid off* involves the active role of an observer who makes an effort to look into a container where some secret process is taking place. Therefore, the explanatory power of metaphoric models increases if the corresponding source domains are formulated not in abstract terms like CONTAINER or PHYSICAL ENTITIES, but oriented to the *basic level of categorisation* (sensu Rosch 1975, 1978). This does not contradict the findings according to which, in general, mappings from a source domain to a target domain "are at the superordinate level rather than the basic level" (Lakoff 1993: 212). For the description of semantic properties of idioms inherited from the *image structure*, the level of primary conceptualisation where rich mental images can be found is more important than the superordinate level suitable for relevant generalisation.

A crucial problem in describing differences of this kind consists in putting it into practice, because traditional semantic metalanguages are incapable of referring to the image component of meaning. Structural semantics refuses even to recognise this component as a part of the linguistic meaning, with obvious consequences for the theory of lexicology and lexicography. One possible solution is the thesaural representation of idioms (Dobrovol'skij 2016a), which allows us to group idioms according to their semantic and conceptual resemblance, including the image component of meaning (see 7.3).

The necessity of taking mental images into account results from the fact that the image component not only has a connotative potential, modifying speakers' imaginative associations, but it also affects the meaning and usage of idioms. This means that a semantic theory which does not respond to these needs cannot be considered an adequate instrument for describing idioms.

7.3 Source domains of FEAR

On the basis of the evidence illustrated above, let us now consider idioms belonging to the conceptual domain of FEAR. If the metaphoric model influences the meaning of a given idiom, it can be helpful first to find out which source domains are represented in this field and then to investigate how the meaning depends on these metaphoric sources.

The metaphoric basis of FEAR has already been the subject of linguistic research. Uspenskij (1979) proposed the metaphor of HOSTILE BEING for the description of all important connotations of FEAR. In this, he was referring to Russian expressions like *страх душит/охватывает/парализует кого-л.* "fear strangles/grips/paralyses someone". Cf. in German *jmdn. würgt die Angst* "the fear strangles someone", *jmdm. sitzt die Angst im Nacken* "the fear is sitting in someone's neck" or *die Angst schnürt jmdm. die Kehle zu* "the fear constricts his/her throat/almost stops him/her from breathing".

Uspenskij (1979) labelled images like this *вещные коннотации* (≈ 'material connotations') and pointed out that these conceptual elements have a certain effect on our perception of "non-material" entities, such as FEAR.

In an article on metaphors in the realm of emotions, Apresjan and Apresjan (1993) pointed out that the model FEAR IS A HOSTILE BEING is a dead metaphor and suggested that the source domain of COLD should be considered the leading metaphoric foundation of FEAR. Cf. in English *to shiver with fright, to get/have cold feet*, in German *zittern vor Angst* "to tremble with fear", *schaudern vor Angst* "to shudder with fear", *zittern wie Espenlaub* "to tremble like an aspen leaf", *jmdm. stehen die Haare zu Berge* "someone's hair stands up to mountain", *jmdm. sträuben sich die Haare* "someone's hair bristles", *kalte Füße bekommen/kriegen* "to get cold feet". The interpretation of FEAR in terms of COLD has biological foundations and seems, in the opinion of Ekman, Levenson, and Friesen (1983), to be of a universal nature. Of course, the source domain of COLD does not cover all possible idioms denoting FEAR, cf. for example *frighten the shit out of someone*.

7.3.1 Kövecses' proposal

Descriptions of emotional concepts adopted in cognitive semantics are generally based on a very explicit interpretation of all kinds of metaphoric and metonymic expressions naming the concept under consideration in a given language. Kövecses (1990: 70–78) suggests several conceptual models reflecting different features of FEAR. First, Kövecses puts forward the following metonymic models for conceptualising FEAR in English.

> Physical agitation: *Our enemies must be trembling in their shoes.*
> Increase in heart rate: *My heart leapt into my throat.*
> Lapses in heartbeat: *His heart stopped when the animal jumped in front of him.*
> Blood leaves face: *She turned pale.*
> Skin shrinks: *A shriek from the dark gave me goosebumps.*
> Hair straightens out: *The story of the murder made my hair stand on end.*

Inability to move: *I was rooted to the spot.*
Drop in body temperature: *The blood turned to ice in his veins.*
Drop in body temperature and inability to move: *She was frozen in her boots.*
Inability to breathe: *She was breathless with fear.*
Inability to speak: *I was speechless with fear.* (see comment 1)
Inability to think: *You scared me out of my wits.*
Involuntary release of bowels or bladder: *You scared the shit out of me; I was almost wetting myself with fear.*
Sweating: *The cold sweat of fear broke out.*
Nervousness in the stomach: *He got butterflies in the stomach.* (see comment 2)
Dryness in the mouth: *My mouth was dry when it was my turn.*
Screaming: *She was screaming with fear.* (see comment 3)
Ways of looking: *There was fear in her eyes.*
Startle: *That noise nearly made me jump out of my skin!*
Flight: *When he heard the police coming, the thief took to his heels.* (see comment 4)

This list of quite heterogeneous "metonymic models" demands some comments. In the following points we think corrections are necessary:

- *Comment 1:* In view of the expression *I was speechless with fear*,[1] there is a colloquial, certainly jocular version (a modification punning cliché) in American English: *I was shitless with fear*, which shows, on the one hand, the importance of the source domain SPONTANEOUS DEFECATION for the conceptualisation of FEAR and, on the other hand, the possibility of contaminating different metaphoric models (see below) and converting the source-domain-concept into its opposite, in this case SPONTANEOUS DEFECATION into CONSTIPATION, without changing the meaning of the corresponding target-domain-concept. The result of such contamination is understandable, even if the word combination is absurd from the perspective of our everyday knowledge. There also exists the conventionalised figurative unit *to be scared shitless*.
- *Comment 2:* The example *He got butterflies in the stomach* is not a metonymic model but a metaphorically based idiom. This idiom can be sensibly interpreted only in the *as if*-modus. From the perspective of figurative language analysis, this fact is more important than the general metonymic link between NERVOUSNESS IN THE STOMACH and FEAR. In the following analysis we will subsume idioms of this kind under the metaphoric model PHYSICAL WEAKNESS. This leads to the following two points. First, the analysis

---

[1] Compare also *I was scared witless* and *I was scared out of my wits*.

in terms of conceptual models (be it conceptual metaphors sensu Lakoff or metonymic models such as those suggested by Kövecses) offers a variety of possible methods. The consequence is that models of this kind may not claim an ontological status (cf. 6.2.5). They are, to a certain extent, artefacts of analysis. Thus, their explanatory power has to be measured by their adequacy for the given research goals. Second, the aims of the analysis extending to capturing the relevant properties of figurative language differ from the aims of the cognitively based description of certain conceptual domains (such as emotion concepts in Kövecses 1990). Even though they are based on the same theoretical assumptions, these two kinds of analysis develop different metalinguistic instruments and make relevant distinctions at different points.

- Moreover, the idiom *to have butterflies in one's stomach/tummy* does not primarily signify 'fear' but more general states of nervousness or excitement. Idiom dictionaries define the meanings of this idiom as 'to feel very nervous, usually about something you are going to do' (McCarthy 2002: 55–56), 'to have an attack of nerves before an important event' (Gulland and Hinds-Howell 2001: 77) or 'to have a queasy feeling because one is nervous' (Speake 1999: 54). There are equivalents in other languages (e.g. Dutch *vlinders in zijn buik hebben* or German *Schmetterlinge im Bauch haben*), none of them meaning 'to be frightened'.
- *Comment 3:* Some expressions which Kövecses uses to exemplify his models are not figurative. Here, we can clearly see the difference between the aims of analysis suggested by Kövecses and the aims of researching figurative language. From the perspective of the latter, expressions like *She was screaming with fear* have to be excluded from the scope of analysis. It remains unclear why Kövecses labels expressions of this kind metonymy. The interpretation which immediately emerges as obvious is based on the assumption that the subject of the sentence really was *screaming*, rather than on the assumption that pointing to the *screaming* is just a metonymic, indirect description of 'being in the state of fear'.
- *Comment 4:* As for the expression *When he heard the police coming, the thief took to his heels*, we are again dealing with an idiom. It points to the concept RUNNING AWAY and could be analysed in terms of underlying image-based concepts in itself. The question concerning the degree to which RUNNING AWAY is associated with FEAR is not of prime interest for linguistic research. From a linguistic viewpoint it is much more important to uncover the links between the conceptual structure fixed in the lexical structure of the idiom *to take to one's heels* and its actual meaning 'to flee, to run away'. Conceptual links between RUNNING AWAY pointed out by Kövecses' analysis are not at issue in a sentence like *When he heard the police coming, the thief took to his heels*, because the concept of FEAR is not a part of the plane of content of this sentence, which focuses on the idea of RUNNING AWAY. The concept of FEAR

can, at best, be regarded as an element of possible semantic consequences which may be pragmatically inferred from this sentence.

Further, Kövecses puts forward the following metaphors of FEAR in English (cf. also Kövecses 1998: 128–129).

> Fear is a fluid in a container: *Fear was rising in him.*
> Fear is a vicious enemy (human or animal): *He was choked by fear.*
> Fear is a tormentor: *They were tortured by the fear of what was going to happen to their son.*
> Fear is an illness: *She was sick with fright.*
> Fear is a supernatural being (ghost, etc.): *It was a ghastly scene.*
> Fear is an opponent: *He was wrestling with his fear.*
> Fear (danger) is a burden: *Fear weighed heavily on them as they heard the bombers overhead.*
> Fear is a natural force (wind, storm, flood, etc.): *Fear swept over him.*
> `Fear is a superior: *Fear reigned in their hearts.*

In this list, the first metaphor construction, among other things, should be questioned. Why should the sentence *Fear was rising in him* be interpreted in terms of FLUID? Obviously, this metaphor points to a certain substance inside the body of the subject, but nothing is said about this substance being a fluid (the verb *rise* can collocate with smoke/vapour, voices, dough/paste, molten metal and many other things or substances).

On the one hand, the attempt to single out as many features of a concept as possible is of great value from the cognitive viewpoint. On the other hand, if the models are too concrete they cannot be used as a tool for describing different entities and finding their common features. The metaphoric model is an efficient instrument for analysing idioms of a certain semantic field in different languages only if it provides a basis for forming groups containing well-known expressions so that the processing of potentially possible occasional word combinations belonging to a given group can be also explained in cognitive terms, otherwise the predicting power of such a model is dubious.

The models suggested by Kövecses give an ad hoc impression and can hardly be used for generalisations (cf. e.g. Stefanowitsch 2007: 78–80 for several points of criticism). For example, it is not clear how the source domains of "a vicious enemy", "a tormentor", "an opponent", "a supernatural being", and "a superior" can be distinguished in practice. If I say, for example, that *I was gripped by fear*, how do I have to interpret the FEAR-metaphor: was it an opponent, a supernatural being, a vicious enemy, a tormentor or a superior who gripped me?

A further questionable point about this kind of conceptual modelling is the separation of metonymies and metaphors. Since most symptomatic expressions do not denote the symptoms as such but turn out to be conventional conceptualisations, they cannot be considered standard metonymies (cf. Dirven and Pörings 2002). In other words, since somebody who is *shaking in his boots* is as a rule not shaking literally, it does not make any sense to describe this expression in terms other than expressions like *he was wrestling with his fear*. In both cases the motivating link is provided by the metaphoric *as if*-modus, so Kövecses' "metonymies of fear" can be regarded as body-based metaphors.

7.3.2 FEAR in Russian, English, German and Dutch

The analysis of familiar idioms denoting FEAR in Russian, English, German and Dutch indicates that three relevant source domains can be put forward, namely (a) COLD, (b) SPONTANEOUS DEFECATION and (c) PHYSICAL WEAKNESS:

(a) COLD (freezing, chilling, symptomatic phenomena connected with cold)

Russian: *страх леденит кровь/сердце* "fear freezes the blood/heart", *кровь стынет/леденеет в жилах* "the blood freezes in the veins", *мороз по коже* "a chill went through the body", *мурашки бегут/ползут по спине/по коже* "it gives someone goose pimples", *волосы встали дыбом* "the hair stood on end"

English: *to curdle/chill/freeze someone's/the blood, someone's blood runs cold, the blood turned to ice in one's veins, to get/have the shivers/willies, to chill/ freeze someone's spine/ marrow, to send chills/a chill up/down (up and down) someone's spine, to send shivers/a shiver up/down (up and down) someone's back/spine, to get/have cold feet, to shake/tremble like a leaf, someone's hair stands on end*

German: *kalte Füße bekommen/kriegen* "to get cold feet", *es lief jmdm. eiskalt über den Rücken* "a cold shiver went down someone's spine", *das Blut stockte jmdm. in den Adern* "the blood curdled in someone's veins", *zittern wie Espenlaub* "to tremble like an aspen leaf", *jmdm. stehen die Haare zu Berge* "someone's hair stands on end", *jmdm. sträuben sich die Haare* "someone's hair bristles"

Dutch: *huiveren/een kippenvel krijgen van angst* "to shudder/to get goose pimples with fear", *met angst en beven* "with fear and tembling", *trillen als een espeblad* "to tremble like an aspen leaf", *zijn haren rijzen te berge* "his hair stands on end"

(b) SPONTANEOUS DEFECATION (involuntary release of the bowels)

Russian: *полные штаны (от страха) у кого-л.* "someone has the pants full (with fear)", *наложить/наделать в штаны (от страха)* "to do into his pants (with fear)"

English: *to frighten the shit out of someone, to have one's pants full, to shit bricks, to have/get the shits*

German: *die Hosen (gestrichen) voll haben* "to have the pants full (to the brim)", *sich in die Hosen machen/scheißen* "to make (a mess)/to shit in one's pants", *(vor jmdm./etwas) Schiss haben/kriegen* "to get shit of someone/something", *jmdm. geht der Arsch mit Grundeis/auf Grundeis* "someone's arse is going with/on ground ice"

Dutch: *het in zijn broek doen* "to make it in one's pants", *in zijn broek schijten* "to shit in one's pants", *het loopt hem dun door de broek* "it is running him thinly through the pants"

(c) PHYSICAL WEAKNESS (inability to stand on one's feet, inability to move, inability to breathe, increase in heart rate or lapses in heartbeat, sweating, etc.)

Russian: *коленки/колени дрожат/трясутся/подгибаются* "the knees tremble/shake/bend", *поджилки трясутся (от страха)* "the knees shake (with fear)", *душа ушла в пятки* "the soul sank in the heels", *холодный пот прошиб* "in a cold sweat"

English: *someone's knees knock (together), to shake in one's shoes, to be rooted to the spot/ ground, to catch one's breath, to have one's heart in one's boots, to have one's heart in one's mouth, in a cold sweat, he broke out in a cold sweat*

German: *mit schlotternden Knien* "with shaking/trembling knees", *in den Knien weich werden* "to get weak in the knees", *weiche Knie haben* "to have weak knees", *jmdm. werden die Knie weich* "someone's knees become weak", *jmdm. schlottern die Knie* "someone's knees are shaking/trembling", *zur Salzsäule erstarren* "to turn into a pillar of salt", *jmdm. bleibt das Herz stehen* "someone's heart stops beating", *jmdm. stockte der Atem* "someone caught his breath", *jmdm. rutscht das Herz in die Hose(n)* "someone's heart slips down in the pants"

Dutch: *met knikkende knieën* "with bending knees", *als aan de grond genageld staan* "to stand as nailed to the ground", *als een zoutpilaar staan* "to stand like a pillar of salt", *geen adem kunnen halen* "not to be able to draw breath (not to get one's breath back)", *de adem stokte in zijn keel* "the breath stopped in his throat", *zijn hart stond stil/klopte in de keel* "his heart stood still/beat in his throat", *de angst sloeg hem om het hart* "fear beat someone round the heart", *met bonzend hart* "with a pounding/beating heart", *het klamme zweet/angstzweet brak hem uit* "a cold damp sweat <the sweat of fear> broke out on someone".

The metaphoric model FEAR IS A HOSTILE BEING is hardly represented at all by the idioms proper. The expressions based on this model do not evoke real imaginative associations, so this metaphoric model can be ignored (cf. also the arguments of Apresjan and Apresjan 1993).

Three other models often appear in combination.
- German *jmdm. geht der Arsch mit Grundeis/auf Grundeis* "someone's arse is going with/on ground ice" combines COLD and SPONTANEOUS DEFECATION;
- German *zittern wie Espenlaub*, Dutch *sidderen als een espeblad* "to tremble like an aspen leaf", English *to get cold feet*; German *kalte Füße bekommen/kriegen* "to get cold feet", Russian *холодный пот прошиб* ≈ "in a cold sweat", English *in a cold sweat*, Dutch *het klamme zweet brak hem uit* "a cold damp sweat broke out on him" combine COLD and PHYSICAL WEAKNESS;
- German *jmdm. rutscht das Herz in die Hose(n)* "someone's heart slips down into their pants" combines PHYSICAL WEAKNESS and SPONTANEOUS DEFECATION.

Idioms of this kind are elements of more than one set. The overlap of these idiom sets is no argument against their appearing as separate domains of conceptualisation and confirms the idea that different metaphors can interact within one linguistic expression (cf. Lindner 1983: 146). The three metaphoric models postulated above are based on physiological symptoms which seem to be universal in nature.

If certain regular correlations between the source domain and the usage of expressions corresponding to this source domain can be found, the structure resulting from metaphoric modelling can be considered a useful heuristic for analysing idiom semantics. This structure can be used as a basis for compiling a multilingual idiom thesaurus. However, it only makes sense if metaphorically based thesaurus-taxa can predict relevant semantic features.

7.4 Structure of the semantic field of FEAR

Thus far, it has been shown that the idioms denoting FEAR are heterogeneous in terms of their metaphorical nature. Let us now consider the question of whether these metaphoric differences influence the usage of these idioms.

In order to answer this question we first have to analyse the structure of the semantic field of FEAR.

The languages that have been analysed in the field of FEAR (such as German, English, Dutch, French, Russian) have relatively large groups of synonyms denoting FEAR. This means that between these expressions some semantic differences have to be found, because normally different languages tend not to have absolute synonyms. Research on this topic has included material from different languages (cf. Iordanskaja 1973: 403–404; Bergenholtz 1980: 247–248; Iordanskaja and Mel'čuk 1990; Wierzbicka 1990, 1999; J. Apresjan 1995: 51–56; V. Apresjan 1997; Zaliznjak 2013: 68–78). According to their findings, the following *semantic oppositions* can be postulated:

(i) strong vs. not such a strong fear;
(ii) expectation of something bad vs. reaction to something bad (to something already in existence);
(iii) an especially "personal" feeling (concerning the subject as such or the subject's personal sphere) vs. an unspecified, "general" feeling;
(iv) control vs. lack of control (i.e. the subject does or does not have things under control);
(v) a sudden reaction vs. not necessarily sudden;
(vi) immediate danger vs. not immediate danger;
(vii) for a long time vs. for a short time.

Iordanskaja (1973: 404) explains the semantic differences between the Russian words *страх* 'fear' and *ужас* 'horror, terror' as follows:

> Thus, *užas* (horror, terror) is an emotional shock resulting from an encounter with something monstrous. In such a situation a person is very often gripped by a strong fear, which explains the very common definition of the word *užas* as a 'sil'nyj strax' (strong fear). At the same time, there are a number of important differences in the meaning of these words: *strax* (fear) is connected with an expectation of something bad, *užas* (horror, terror) is a reaction to something already in existence: *strax* is an especially 'personal' feeling: people expect something bad for themselves or for those dear to them, while *užas* is a reaction to something monstrous which may or may not concern the subject of the feeling.

Wierzbicka (1990) points out, for instance, that *to be scared* can be mistaken for a full synonym of *to be afraid*. In fact, however, there are important semantic differences between these two phrases: *to be scared* is personal [see opposition (iii)], whereas *to be afraid* (like the correlating noun *fear*) is unspecified in this respect. *To be scared* implies an immediate danger and *to be afraid* does not [see opposition (vi)], cf. *a woman who is scared of men* and *a women who is afraid of men*.

Analogous distinctions can be postulated for Russian *испугаться* vs. *бояться* or German *sich erschrecken* vs. *Angst haben* or *(sich) fürchten*.

The difference in usage between *panic* and *fear* can be explained on the basis of two semantic oppositions: (i) and (iv), i.e. *panic* is not only stronger than *fear*, but also reveals a lack of self-control in the subject's behaviour. German *Furcht* is stronger than *Angst*, and *Entsetzen* is stronger than *Furcht* (for further details, see Wierzbicka 1999). German *Schrecken* or Russian *ispug* indicate sudden reactions (v) to an immediate danger (vi) which cannot last for a long time (vii). Thus, all words indicating FEAR in the languages considered here can in principle be differentiated from each other by the semantic features contained in the seven oppositions presented above.

7.5 Does the imagery influence the meaning?

Let us now consider the idioms denoting FEAR in terms of these semantic oppositions. As a whole, idioms tend to express strong emotions, otherwise one would not use idiomatic language. Normally, the speaker uses an idiom if he/she feels that standard non-idiomatic linguistic means are not expressive enough. This does not mean that there are no differences in intensity between individual idioms, but it is very difficult to find stable correlations between metaphoric models and the degree of intensity. Therefore, it cannot be claimed that COLD-idioms, for example, denote a stronger feeling of fear than SPONTANEOUS DEFECATION-idioms or vice versa. As for the oppositions "expectation of something bad vs. reaction to something bad" and "personal vs. not necessarily personal feeling", only the idiom *someone's hair stands on end*[2] can be singled out, because typically it indicates HORROR, TERROR rather than mere FEAR, cf. (3–5).

(3) Steve and Jack gave a talk about their trek across the Polar ice cap. It was very interesting but it *made my hair stand on end* just to hear about the dangers they faced. (Cowie, Mackin, and McCaig 1993)

(4) The sight of him lying there on the floor *made my hair stand on end*. (Long and Summers 1979)

---

2 We are dealing here with a so-called *widespread idiom*. Equivalents are spread across at least 60 European and various non-European languages and evidence can be found from the oldest writings (Iliad, Old Testament), handing down the semiotised meaning of the bodily experience of fear.

(5) Kyle told remarkable stories on his tour, of experiences both he and the staff of Fort George had had over the years. Some will *make your hair stand up on end*. (www.hountigsresearchgroup.homestead.com)

In these examples the idiom is used to indicate a reaction to something bad that is already in existence and is not personal (the person in danger and the subject of emotion do not coincide). Cf. also German *jmdm. stehen die Haare zu Berge*, *jmdm. sträuben sich die Haare*, Dutch *zijn haren rijzen te berge* or Russian *волосы встали дыбом*.

Intuitively it could be assumed that other idioms which are based on the metaphoric model FEAR IS COLD behave in the same manner. Indeed, it is possible to use some COLD-idioms for denoting a retrospective emotional reaction to a phenomenon which does not necessarily involve the subject of the feeling, cf. (6). But there are also contexts where idioms of the same source domain indicate a prospective and "personal" emotion, cf. (7), or allow ambivalent interpretations, cf. (8) and (9).

(6) Wendy – who appears in 'Shadows', the series (TV) of children's *spine-chillers* – is far too down-to-earth to take ghosts seriously. (Cowie, Mackin, and McCaig 1993)

(7) When we got home the light was on in our flat. The idea that someone was in there waiting for us *sent a chill down my spine*. (Long and Summers 1979)

(8) There was a sudden scream from the building. We all *got the shivers* and came home as quickly as we could. (Long and Summers 1979)

(9) The news of the accident *sent a shiver down his back*. (Long and Summers 1979)

Idioms of other source domains do not show any stable correlations with these semantic features. Even the same idiom can indicate, depending on the context, a "personal" (10) and a "not personal" (11) feeling.

(10) I *had my heart in my mouth* when I went to ask the bank for more money. (Long and Summers 1979)

(11) All those watching the attempt to save the drowning child *had their hearts in their mouths*. (Long and Summers 1979)

As far as the opposition "control vs. lack of control" is concerned, the idioms of FEAR do not reveal any clear preferences, i.e. the meaning of a context-free idiom does not indicate whether or not the subject has the situation (and his or her own behaviour) under control.

The features "suddenly", "immediately", "for a long time" and their opposites can be clearly felt in certain contexts. For example, in (12) a sudden reaction to an immediate danger which cannot last for a long time is described, whereas the feeling described in (13) is not caused by an immediate danger, does not necessarily arise suddenly, and can last for a long time.

(12) He was *shaking in his shoes* as the large dog moved towards him. (Long and Summers 1979)

(13) The students *sweated blood* while waiting for the examination results. (Long and Summers 1979)[3]

Since the idioms *to shake in one's shoes* and *to sweat blood* belong to the same source domain of PHYSICAL WEAKNESS, it is not possible to claim that there are any correlations between these semantic features and a certain source domain. Furthermore, in different contexts the same idiom can reveal opposite features, e.g. the idiom *(to get) cold feet* explicitly indicates a sudden reaction in examples (14–16), is unspecified in this respect in example (17), and denotes a repeating, long lasting emotional state in (18).

(14) After weeks of preparation he suddenly *got cold feet* on the day of the wedding. (Long and Summers I 1979)

(15) He also fails to point out that if Mr Superman signs the policy and suddenly *gets cold feet* the next day, it is not too late to extricate himself. (The Sunday Times)

(16) I don't know how genuine that sudden bit of urgent business was; perhaps he just *got cold feet* and wanted me to go ahead and soften things up. (John Wain)

---

[3] This idiom is polysemous: 1. 'to work very intensely and diligently; to expend all of one's energy or effort doing something' and 2. 'to suffer intense distress, anxiety, worry, or fear'. Cf. also the corresponding German idiom *Blut und Wasser schwitzen* "to sweat blood and water".

(17) Make up your mind – now I decide to stay, you start *getting cold feet*. (Bernard Kops)

(18) All seemed set, and each day passed without any signs of *cold feet* on the part of my colleagues. (Field-Marshal Montgomery)

Cf. also German *Blut und Wasser schwitzen* (19) and English *to sweat blood* (13), which are equivalent semantically but behave differently conceptually with respect to the semantic oppositions "immediate danger vs. not immediate danger" and "for a long time vs. for a short time".

(19) German Sie *schwitzte Blut und Wasser*, als die Polizei das Fahrzeug kontrollierte. (Duden 2013: 125)
[She *sweated blood and water*, when the police controlled the vehicle]

In general, we have to conclude that there are no stable correlations between the metaphoric models postulated in section 7.3 and the semantic features singled out in section 7.4. This result seems to be disappointing, but, in fact, it does not mean that the metaphor has no influence on semantics. Hypothetically, it can be assumed that these correspondences lie in another realm, and the semantic oppositions based on the functional analysis of non-metaphorical words cannot be applied to idioms referring to the same conceptual domain. "In fact, one might think of the function of idioms in terms of specification of existing concepts in a way that is not already specified in semantic memory by existing lexical items" (Cacciari 1993: 40).

Let us now turn to some examples and try to find out what kind of semantic specification is connected with the imagery underlying the concept. Perhaps it will be possible to postulate other semantic oppositions to which the idioms of FEAR are more sensitive. Let us begin with examples that represent the metaphoric model FEAR IS COLD.

(20) The chemical industry, which is supposed to have bent the Minister's ear with *spine-chilling* stories about what would happen if [...] (New Statesman)

(21) It (quite) *chilled my blood* to hear the voice of a man who I thought had been dead for years. (Long and Summers 1979)

(22) Jane's gone rock climbing with her new boyfriend once or twice. She says that it *makes her hair stand on end* when she looks down at hundreds of feet of empty air. (Cowie, Mackin, and McCaig 1993)

What is so special about these idioms? Why is it very unlikely for idioms of other source domains to appear in these contexts? Though in principle it is possible, to replace, for example, *makes her hair stand on end* in (22) by *she has her pants full*, the sense of the utterance would not remain the same. In this case the subject of emotion would appear as a cowardly person who overestimates the real danger and whose feeling of anxiety is not to be taken seriously. However, the COLD-idioms seem to evoke associations with a feeling caused by an external factor which has nothing to do with the inherent cowardice of the subject of the feeling. Thus, the cause of fear has to be taken seriously, cf. (3–9) and (20–22).

So, COLD and SPONTANEOUS DEFECATION can be contrasted in this respect, whereas PHYSICAL WEAKNESS is somewhere in between. Idioms (23) and (24) behave practically in the same way as the COLD-idioms, whereas idioms (25) and (26) evoke associations similar to (32).

(23) The people who were watching *caught their breath* as the man almost slipped from the roof. (Long and Summers 1979)

(24) Mir *blieb das Herz stehen*, als ich die Kinder am Rand des Wasserfalls sah. (Duden 2013: 343)
[My *heart stopped beating* when I saw the children at the brink of the waterfall.]

(25) I *had my heart in my boots* when I went to see my boss. (Long and Summers 1979)

(26) I heard someone coming towards the door and *my knees were knocking together* as I quickly put the money back in the drawer and closed it. (Long and Summers 1979)

In the cases in which the source domain PHYSICAL WEAKNESS is combined with the source domain COLD, the idioms tend to indicate an acceptable, more reasonable feeling caused by external circumstances, cf. (27) through (29). The combination of PHYSICAL WEAKNESS and SPONTANEOUS DEFECATION tends to denote a less acceptable fear, cf. (30) where *die Fahrprüfung* cannot be accepted as a serious reason for being afraid if the subject of emotion wants to be considered a courageous, self-confident person.

(27) He woke up during the night *in a cold sweat*, thinking of the examination he was going to take in the morning. (Long and Summers 1979)

(28) Bij veel inwoners van de Bijlmer, die zich de vliegramp noch goed kunnen herinneren, *breekt* noch elke dag *het klamme zweet uit* als er een vliegtuig laag overvliegt. (Van Dale IW 1999)
[Many inhabitants of the Bijlmer, who still remember the plane crash well, *break out into a damp sweat* still every day when a plane is flying over low.]

(29) Nie zuvor hatten sie einen so grässlichen Schrei gehört; alle *zitterten wie Espenlaub*. (Duden 2013: 877)
[Never before had they heard such a horrible scream; they all shivered like an aspen leaf.]

(30) Wenn ich an die Fahrprüfung denke, *rutscht* mir gleich *das Herz in die Hose*. (Duden 2013: 343)
[When I think of the driving test, *my heart slips down in my pants* immediately.]

The difference between the idioms of the source domain PHYSICAL WEAKNESS and the source domain SPONTANEOUS DEFECATION consists, first of all, in the degree of unacceptability of the subject's emotional state from the perspective of the speaker, cf. (31) and (32).

(31) Als der Maskierte die Pistole auf ihn richtete, *wurden* dem Kassierer *die Knie weich*. (Duden 2013: 414)
[When the masked person pointed the pistol at him, the cashier *got weak knees*.]

(32) Natürlich *hatte* er dann *die Hosen gestrichen voll* vor Angst, ich würde ihn verpfeifen. (Duden 2013: 366)
[Of course, he *had* than *his pants full to the brim for fear* I would grass on him.]

The fear of the *Kassierer* in (31) is caused by more serious reasons than the fear of the subject in (32) because *der Maskierte mit der Pistole* is clearly dangerous for the *Kassierer*, who surely has a large amount of money on him.

Very often, PHYSICAL WEAKNESS-idioms (and also combinations of PHYSICAL WEAKNESS with other source domains) are neutral with respect to the acceptability of the fear that they express, especially if the subject of the emotion coincides with the speaker, cf. the Dutch idioms *met knikkende knieën* and *zijn hart klopte in de keel* in minimal contexts (33) and (34) or the English idiom *to sweat blood* in (35).

(33) Dutch *Met knikkende knieën* ga ik naar mijn baas.
 [I go to my boss *with bending knees*.]

(34) Dutch Ik voelde *mijn hart in mijn keel kloppen*.
 [I felt *my heart beating in my throat*.]

(35) English "You look frightfully composed and superior." "If I may say so, sir, that's just what struck me about you." "Good God! I*'ve been sweating blood* at the thought of this afternoon for a week." (Richard Gordon)

Thus, the following semantic oppositions can be postulated:
(i) acceptable vs. unacceptable fear
(ii) fear as a feeling caused by serious vs. not serious reasons
(iii) fear as an inherent quality of the person in question vs. as an emotional state conditioned by external factors

These semantic oppositions are connected with each other. Fear as an acceptable feeling caused by a serious reason does not display its subject as a cowardly, faint-hearted person, whereas the subject of the unacceptable fear caused by a less serious reason appears from the speaker's perspective as a coward, i.e. as a person whose state of being afraid is an inherent quality.

7.6 Concluding remarks

To sum up, within the field of conventional figurative language these findings are innovative in three ways: First, they combine the legacy of structural semantics with new insights from methods developed in the context of Cognitive Linguistics. The impetus of the cognitive approach is not a refusal to describe the meaning in terms of semantic components, but an efficient extension of this metalanguage. By means of the analysis of mental imagery, new, still undiscovered semantic features can be found.

Second, this approach allows us to consider the semantic relations between the conventional figurative units of a given target domain as a kind of network based on people's conceptual knowledge, and reveals some evidence of possible links between figurative units in the mental lexicon.

Third, it shows that conventional figurative units such as idioms play an important role in the linguistic ontologisation of emotions. The vocabulary of emotions has been the object of extensive investigation in many languages, but the idiomatic component of the lexicon still remains outside the main field of theoretical interest. Imaginative associations provided by idioms have to be taken into account when describing emotion concepts and improving the lexicographical representation of the corresponding lexical items.

The practical consequence of this analysis can be described as follows: While translating idioms of FEAR (and other emotions), one has to take into account not only their actual figurative meaning but also the conceptual structures behind them. As for the "invisible world", FEAR depends on the linguistic means involved, i.e. the same emotion expressed by different means can invoke different parts of people's conceptual knowledge and therefore does not remain completely the same emotion. This is strong evidence in favour of the basic assumption of the CFLT (see section 1.3). The findings presented in this chapter can be used for compiling multilingual idiom thesauri, which are efficient tools for linguistic research.

8 Cognitive modelling of figurative semantics

8.1 General aspects

This chapter discusses metalinguistic tools for describing motivation phenomena, particularly with regard to metaphoric motivation. One of the purposes of this is to develop an apparatus which enables us to register cases of frame-based metaphoric motivation and differentiate them clearly from the other motivation types, particularly symbol-based motivation (i.e. motivation based on cultural symbolism, see chapter 11). A metalinguistic apparatus of this kind is seen as an important component of the CFLT. For a theoretical discussion about figurative phenomena, it is necessary to possess an instrument which allows us to analyse and describe not only relevant linguistic structures but also their corresponding knowledge structures and the operations that can be applied to them.

As has already been pointed out, the specific character of the image basis of metaphorical expressions is primarily salient not at the rather abstract level of conceptual metaphor, but at the level of the so-called "rich image". As will be shown in the following sections, all relevant motivating links between the lexical structure of a conventional figurative unit and its actual meaning can be uncovered only if all parts of the image structure are taken into account. For instance, to be able to understand the motivational basis of idioms such as (1), one has to know at least some of the rules of baseball and/or have an overall impression of this game.

(1) American English *to get to first base, to be (way) off base, to touch base, to do something right off the bat, to go to bat for, to hit a home run*, etc. (cf. Longman ID 1998: 313)

In cases like this, an analysis that involves specific kinds of world knowledge is the only way to discover the relevant motivating links. It is not possible to construct conceptual metaphors which would be able to motivate the idioms in (1). For more details, see section 8.5.

To discover the mechanisms of frame-based metaphoric motivation, we should first analyse the metaphoric mapping from the source concepts (i.e. the image basis) onto the target concept, i.e. the actual meaning of the CFU in question. If we know how the metaphoric mapping works in every case, we will also know how figurative units of this kind are motivated, i.e. how speakers make sense of them. If we succeed in discovering certain regularities in the metaphoric mapping across different semantic domains and different languages, we might be able to determine which conceptual elements and cognitive procedures rule the mechanisms of frame-based metaphoric motivation.

In most cases, correspondence between two concrete concepts underlying the semantics of each metaphorical expression determines the relevant individual features of single figurative units, rather than a general correspondence between two conceptual domains involved in the metaphoric inference. Compare in this regard the contrasting of superordinate concepts such as ENTITY, INTENSITY, LIMIT, FORCE, and CONTROL, that function as source domains of conceptual metaphors, and concepts like HOT FLUID, INSANITY, FIRE, BURDEN, STRUGGLE, which "appear to be basic-level concepts, that is concepts that are linked more directly to experience, concepts that are information-rich and rich in conventional mental imagery" (Lakoff 1987b: 406). Lakoff calls metaphors based on such concepts "basic-level metaphors", and suggests that most of our understanding of certain target concepts comes via basic-level metaphors. What we understand by "rich images" are not always basic level concepts (sensu Rosch 1975, 1978). The conceptual structures underlying the motivation of many idioms are concrete, very specific source frames and have to be seen primarily as concepts at the subordinate level. What is decisive for modelling the semantic result of metaphoric inference in the domain of conventional figurative language is the conceptual richness of images providing a basis for relevant cognitive operations.

Conceptual correspondences at the level of rich images (*basic-level* or *subordinate level metaphors*), as compared to abstract conceptual metaphors (*metaphoric models*), are not abstract correlations between knowledge domains with a high degree of abstraction, like that for example, between EVENT and MOTION. On the contrary, the analysis of rich images addresses correspondences between concrete portions of knowledge captured in the semantic structure of concrete figurative units. Compare idiom (2).

(2) German *ins Wasser fallen* "to fall into the water"
     'to fail to take place, to be cancelled (about events, plans, projects, etc.)'

According to the Cognitive Theory of Metaphor, this idiom could be ascribed to metaphoric models like EVENT IS MOTION and BAD IS DOWN. Such metaphoric models do not contribute to discovering relevant motivational links. Although the verb *to fall* may evoke the image of DOWNWARDS (and the metaphor BAD IS DOWN), this is not a case of "MOTION" but a phenomenon due to gravity. The source domain consists of the rich image "to fall into the water" with all its relevant consequences (see below for more detail). An analysis using this apparatus would help to uncover connections between this idiom and all the other units of figurative language that are based on the same metaphoric models. In this way, conceptual parallels which are not obvious at first glance can be made transparent. Analysis at the level of the "rich image" of this idiom addresses concrete semantic and conceptual information evoked by the literal sense encoded in the lexical structure of (2). Hence, the concept of WATER is crucial for making world knowledge-based inferences that guarantee the consistency of the inner form with the actual meaning. For example, everyday knowledge that things which have fallen into the water are either lost or spoilt explains why the lexical structure of this idiom is able to denote a situation of failure. Thus, the knowledge of what happens to material objects falling into the water is mapped onto non-material entities like events, plans, projects, etc.

Cognitive procedures involved in the motivation can be both frame-based (i.e. based upon a more or less static conceptual structure) or script-based (i.e. based upon a dynamic, procedural knowledge structure). It would go beyond the scope of this study to go into detail about various versions of the frame-theory (cf. e.g. Abelson 1973, Schank 1975, Schank and Abelson 1977).[1] The version of the cognitive modelling of figurative semantics we present in this chapter can be regarded as a component of the frame-based theory of lexical semantics developed by Fillmore and his colleagues (see, for example, Fillmore, Johnson, and Petruck 2003; Fillmore et al. 2003). As compared to the FrameNet project, the peculiarity of our approach is that the apparatus of frames is, above all, applied to purely semantic and conceptual parameters, rather than to cognitive aspects of the argument structure of predicates.[2]

Let us point to some general ideas and explain the most important terms. According to Minsky (1985), a *frame* is a structure of data (or, to use another term, a conceptual structure) designed to represent a stereotypical situation. In cognitively oriented versions of lexical semantics, framelike structures are also used as a means of meaning explanation (cf. e.g. Fillmore 1977, 1985; Fillmore and Atkins 1992; Konerding 1993). Fillmore, Johnson, and Petruck (2003: 235) define *semantic frames* as "schematic representations of the conceptual structures and patterns of beliefs, practices, institutions, images, etc. that provide a foundation for meaningful interaction in a given speech community". Compare also Fillmore et al. (2003: 305), who define the frame as "a schematic presentation of a sit-

---

[1] For details on frame semantics, see e.g. Ziem (2008, 2015).
[2] In the FrameNet projects the frame is seen, primarily, as an interface between syntax and semantics. "Frame semantics is a theory that links the meanings of words very explicitly to the syntactic contexts in which those words occur" (Atkins, Fillmore, and Johnson 2003: 254).

uation type that underlies the meaning of a word (or of the members of sets of words) along with named participant roles or aspects of the situation". A *scenario* or *script* is a particular type of the frame.

> The specificity of a scenario derives from the fact that it is oriented towards the sphere of action described in an algorithmic form, or towards such types of knowledge, which are procedural in nature (i.e. composed of separate procedures or small actions). Declarative representation is, so to speak, descriptive. The linguistic analogue or declarative representation (metalanguage) is the traditional dictionary definition of a lexeme with a concrete meaning, i.e. the enumeration of the concrete properties of the denotatum, which are common for objects of the same class (for example the class of chairs) and specific when compared to objects of other classes (tables, sofas, cupboards). Procedural representation seems exotic from the point of view of traditional language theory: according to the procedural paradigm, knowledge is not interpreted as a set of characteristics (integral and specific) as it is in traditional theory; it is understood as a consequence of the procedures peculiar to the functioning of an object or typical of one action or another.
>
> (Baranov and Dobrovol'skij 1996: 416)

Framelike structures (frames, scenarios etc.) consist of *slots*, which correspond to relevant constituent parts and participants of a given situation. Compare also the notion of *frame elements*, which is similar to the notion of *slots* (see e.g. Fillmore, Johnson, and Petruck 2003).

To illustrate the difference between frames and scenarios, let us look at examples (3) and (4).

(3) German *eine Schraube ohne Ende* "a screw without an end"
 'a difficult, unpleasant state or activity that never seems to end'

(4) English *to take the wind out of someone's sails*
 'to embarrass or frustrate someone by unexpectedly anticipating their action or remark; to make someone feel much less confident about what they are doing and saying'

The imagery of idiom (3) is based on a static conceptual structure, i.e. on knowledge about screws. Since the fact that all screws have an end is part of shared knowledge, the concept presented in the lexical structure of this idiom is perceived as a kind of violation of physical laws. This conceptual structure, the frame of a screw with the highlighted slot "end", from which its filler (i.e. the conceptual content of the slot) is removed, maps onto the target frame of a state or an activity with the consequence that the slot of the target frame corresponding to the slot "end" of the source frame inherits its relevant features. As a result, the actual semantics of this idiom includes not only the "temporal" aspects of the denoted situation (it is lasting too long), but also a pragmatically significant attitudinal component, namely that the speaker thinks that the situation violates the relevant norms and is considered unnatural in this regard.

The imagery of idiom (4) is based on a dynamic, procedural conceptual structure, i.e. knowledge about sailing. Without going into detail, we can simply stress that for the successful processing of this idiom in terms of motivational inference, some knowledge about the scenario of sailing, i.e. about the structure and functioning of a sailing vessel and the position of the wind in relation to the vessel, is required.

In general, analysis at the level of "rich images" involves various operations with the slots of a given frame or script. In the case of metaphoric motivation – cf. (2–4), two frames or scripts (*source* and *target*, see above) are involved. In the case of metonymic motivation,[3] cognitive processing operates upon one frame or script. Compare (5).

(5) *to lend an ear to someone*
'to give someone the opportunity to tell you their ideas, feelings etc., especially if no one else will listen to them'

In this case we are dealing with a listening script. One of the slots, namely the instrumental slot "ear", is highlighted. This is, of course, only one of the conceptual procedures necessary for the motivational inference, but for our argumentation it is important that other conceptual operations leading to the semantic result of the actual meaning also involve only this single cognitive structure (i.e. the script of listening) rather than two or more cognitive structures (as in the case in metaphoric motivation).

To investigate and describe conceptual correspondences of this kind, a special metalanguage is needed. Such a metalanguage has been developed in a series of publications by Baranov and Dobrovol'skij (1996, 2008). The empirical data from different languages used for the designing and theoretical support of this metalanguage encompasses idioms, in the first place, but the results can also be applied to other kinds of figurative units. The main elements of this metalanguage are well-known formal devices for describing cognitive structures, namely frames and scripts. The actual meaning of idioms can be derived from frames or scripts with the help of a restricted set of conceptual operations. The implemen-

---

[3] The Cognitive Theory of Metaphor uses the term *metaphor* in a broader sense, covering *metonymy* among others. We therefore consider metonymically based idioms within the same theoretical framework as metaphorically based ones.

tation of these theoretical ideas and the application of the frame-based metalanguage is known as the *cognitive modelling of the actual meaning of idioms*.

In what follows, we outline the relevant ideas concerning the cognitive modelling of figurative semantics and illustrate them with the help of some examples from English, German and Russian. We use only idioms for our empirical data, because they give clear evidence of the role of motivational phenomena. We use the term *frame* in its general meaning, i.e. as an umbrella term for both frames proper (static knowledge structures) and scripts (dynamic knowledge structures). The reason for this lies in the irrelevance of distinguishing static and dynamic properties for explaining general principles of cognitive modelling.

Cognitive modelling achieves the best results in the field of frame-based metaphoric motivation (for details see section 4.5.3). To demonstrate what is understood by the notion of cognitive modelling, let us start with an example.

(6) *to be the fifth wheel on the carriage/coach*
traditionally defined as 'to be an unwelcome and unnecessary extra person; to be someone who is with a group of people even though that group does not want to be with them or does not feel comfortable with them'

General knowledge of carriages and coaches is involved in the interpretation of the idiom (6). In this case we can talk about similarity, because the situation denoted by the idiom taken in its actual (i.e. figurative) meaning resembles the situation encoded in its lexical structure.

Normally, coaches, carts and the like have four wheels.[4] A fifth wheel is superfluous and is, in fact, an obstacle to the functioning of a coach or a car. The interpretation of the procedures responsible for generating the actual meaning of this idiom proposed in Dobrovol'skij (2007: 793–794, 2016a: 185–198) is as follows. First, with the help of the lexical structure of the idiom, the frame COACH or CARRIAGE is activated. We call this the *source frame*. Within this frame, the filler of one slot is highlighted, namely the number of the wheels. The next cognitive operation involved in the construction of motivating links is replacing the filler of the slot [four wheels] (a characteristic filler, i.e. the usual number of wheels) by [five wheels] (a non-characteristic filler). Finally, the fillers of the

---

[4] Here we exclude the cart type with two wheels, which is irrelevant for the "rich image" of idiom (6). There are, however, idioms like American English *to be the third wheel*, Danish *være tredje hjul på vognen/en vogn* "to be the third wheel on the carriage/on a carriage", Albanian *të bëhesh rrota e tretë* "to be the third wheel" and Finnish *olla kolmantena pyöränä (vaunuissa)* "to be (like) the third wheel (on a/the wagon)".

relevant slots of the source frame are mapped onto the corresponding slots of the *target frame*, namely a "group of people". The person referred to as *the fifth wheel* is highlighted in relation to the highlighted slot of the source frame.

What is practicable for this interpretation of the underlying metaphoric inference is that the actual meaning of the idiom is seen as the result of sophisticated knowledge processing. In other words, the actual meaning of a metaphorically motivated figurative unit is always interpreted against the background of source-target-correspondence, from which people get comprehensible evidence about how the actual meaning presumably has come into being, rather than as the result of the semantic transfer of a given word combination from 'a wheel' to 'a person' (as is assumed in traditional lexicology).

The analysis along these lines aims at revealing all the relevant conceptual procedures that establish motivating links. What is important is that cognitive modelling in figurative semantics does not aim to describe psychological reality, but is much more oriented towards uncovering potential motivating links.

Cognitive modelling in figurative semantics should be seen as a theoretical approach based on the idea of the conceptual nature of semantic reinterpretation. The semantic reinterpretation which takes place in the process of creating figurative units is a result of the interaction of knowledge structures. One of the consequences of this postulate is the assumption that the knowledge structure, which is the source of semantic reinterpretation (i.e. the source frame), is relevant not only at the moment when a given figurative unit comes into being, but also while the conventional figurative units are being processed. In this sense, we can refer to the relevant traces of the source frame that we call the *image component* of the plane of content of CFUs.

8.2 Cognitive approach to semantic explanation

If we take the relevance of the image component seriously, we have to develop new principles of semantic explanation which would enable us to take the source frame into account. For example, the meaning explanation of idiom (6) *to be the fifth wheel on the carriage / coach* should not only paraphrase the main part of the actual meaning but also address the idea that people do not want their vehicles to have superfluous parts, which would be an obstacle to their normal functioning. This idea goes back to the image component and determines the relevant pragmatic features of the content plane of this idiom. An adequate meaning explanation of (6) constructed along these lines could be formulated as follows (7):

(7) *to be the fifth wheel on the carriage/coach*
'to be someone who is with a group of people, even though that group does not want to be with them or feel comfortable with them, *considering their presence as redundant, as an obstacle to the normal functioning of their group*'

The last part of this semantic explication (in italics) reflects the image component, which provides the relevant motivating link, and belongs, in our semantic theory, to the plane of content of the idiom. For more details on defining the meaning of idioms, see Dobrovol'skij (2013). That study outlines metalinguistic instruments that can be used for meaning explanation with regard to the image component. In principle, there are explicit and implicit ways of pointing to the image. The explicit strategy includes semantic operators which introduce the idea of comparison of the target concept with the relevant parts of the image, fixed associations and the like. Compare operators such as 'like X', 'is perceived as X', 'is associated with X', 'is analogous with X' etc. Such an operator introduces a special part of the meaning explanation, which is responsible for the image component. Example (7) can be considered an instance of the explicit strategy. The implicit strategy requires the distribution of relevant semantic information among various elements of the meaning explanation.

To illustrate the difference between the explicit strategy (as in example 7) and the implicit strategy, let us look at example (8).

(8) Russian *носить воду решетом/в решете* "to carry water with/in a sieve"
'to try to achieve a goal using a totally inappropriate means for achieving this goal, which inevitably leads to failure'

In terms of the cognitive modelling of figurative semantics, the motivation of this idiom can be described as follows. In the frame CARRYING WATER, the typical filler of the instrumental slot (some kind of container appropriate for carrying water) is replaced by something entirely unsuitable, i.e. [a sieve]. The semantic effect of this replacement is a kind of situational dysfunction (carrying out an action with an unsuitable instrument). This leads to a conclusion of the following kind: to carry water in a sieve means to try to achieve a goal in a manner that dooms the action to failure, using a totally inappropriate means for attaining this objective (cf. Dobrovol'skij 2007: 799). The conceptual structure evoked by the underlying mental image is mapped with all its relevant parts onto the class of situations which is referred to by the actual meaning of the idiom, i.e. onto the target frame. Thus, a semantically adequate definition of this idiom (such as that given in example 8) must reflect all relevant aspects of the source frame. So, the idea of using an inappropriate means while trying to achieve a goal, and that of failure

8.2 Cognitive approach to semantic explanation — 225

as a semantic consequence, are included in the semantic explanation. This is crucial from the perspective of the real usage of the idiom. Let us have a look at two textual examples from the current Russian Internet newspapers.

(9) К сожалению, внутри зданий фотографировать не разрешалось, а пересказывать экскурсию своими словами – это то же самое, что пытаться *носить воду решетом*. (Весенний IDF 2002 в Сан-Франциско) http://www.ixbt.com/editorial/idf-spring2k2.shtml retrieved October 2017

   [Unfortunately, it was not allowed to take pictures in the building, and to retell the excursion in one's own words is just the same as *carrying water with a sieve*.]

(10) [. . .] число правонарушений несовершеннолетних по сравнению с прошлым годом уменьшилось на 12%. [. . .] Главная задача – предупредить сам факт отсутствия надзора, при этом бороться только полицейскими методами – все равно, что *носить воду в решете*. (Публицистика Интернета)

   [[. . .] the number of delinquent acts committed by minors has come down by 12 percent, as compared to last year. [. . .] The main task is to prevent the children being neglected, but for all that, to struggle against it using police methods only is just the same as *carrying water in a sieve*.]

This idiom is often used in the context of a metalinguistic commentary, such as *это то же самое, что* or *все равно что* '≈ is just the same as'. In other words, this idiom is usually embedded in a comparative construction (a kind of simile) which normally highlights the image component making the mapping operation explicit.

In both contexts we are dealing with situations considered to be doomed to failure because, from the point of view of the writer, the agent of the situation would use a completely inappropriate means for achieving his goal – *retelling an exciting excursion in one's own words* in (9), and *trying to struggle against children being neglected using police methods only* in (10). So, in both cases, the parts of the given idiom's semantic structure which are inherited from the mental imagery and labelled here as "image component" are crucial to an adequate denoting of the situation. Any other idiom from the semantic field of FUTILE EFFORTS would not be appropriate in contexts of this type. Compare Russian idioms such as *толочь воду (в ступе)* "to pound water (in the mortar)" 'to waste effort and time on doing senseless or pointless things; to endeavour to do something without obtaining any result' (cf. the English idioms *to beat the air* and *to mill the wind*); *биться как рыба об лед* "≈ as the fish hits against the ice" 'to struggle desperately against something'. The reason why these idioms could not be used in the same situations as idiom (8) is obvious. Their image components focus conditions and circumstances of FUTILE EFFORTS different from (8). In *биться как рыба об лед*, for example, the idea of "persistence in a course of action" is the focus. The agent (*fish*) tries to struggle against forces and obstacles which are objectively not surmountable (*ice*), and the agent hurts itself in this hopeless struggle. So, on the level of the image component, this idiom has very little in common with (8), where the agent uses an inappropriate instrument (without hurting itself) without understanding.

8.3 Addressing implicit elements of conceptual structures

Compared to the traditional idea of "meaning transfer", the most important advantage of the use of the metalinguistic apparatus we have discussed consists in the possibility of taking into account not only explicit (that is, linguistically expressed) but also implicit elements of conceptual structures which are evoked by idioms. The importance of involving implicit elements in semantic analysis is a commonplace in present day linguistics. The fact that linguistic structures are knowledge-based by nature is relevant not only to the analysis of figurative language and has been pointed out many times in several regards. For instance, Strohner and Brose (1992: 66–67) stress that

> the meaning of a verbal expression is not only a function of the meanings of its constituents, but also of the relevant world knowledge. Without considering the environment of knowledge of the model, the constitution of the meaning of an utterance will fail in those cases where its intended total meaning is only partly connected to the meanings of the components of the expression.

Linguistically expressed elements (slots of a given frame) are not always relevant for revealing the inference and, hence, explaining the motivating links. Since the selection of denoting features is more or less arbitrary, it is not only explicit (i.e. linguistically expressed) elements of a given conceptual structure that may turn out to be important for a given semantic result, but also conceptual elements which are not expressed explicitly.

In Dobrovol'skij (2007, 2016b) much attention is paid to the fact that there exists a wide range of motivated and "transparent" idioms, which are not accounted for by any version of idiom theory. Consider, for example, idiom (11).

(11) American English *behind the eight ball*
'at a disadvantage, in a situation where you lack advantages, especially because you have been too slow in taking opportunities'

To process this idiom, some knowledge of the frame POOL (a U.S. pocket billiards game played with coloured balls and a cue on a table) is required. Within this frame, the knowledge of one detail, the "eight ball", has to be activated. The black ball is numbered "eight" in a variety of the game of pool. This eight ball must not be hit into any of the "pockets" (the holes at the side of the table) until all the other balls have been pocketed by the player. If the ball someone wants to hit is behind the eight ball, he/she is in a difficult position because the eight ball is likely to be pocketed together with the ball being played. According to this idiom, the person "behind the eight ball" is in a position similar to that in which the ball he/she wants to hit is behind the eight ball. This is a situation without advantages, because he/she was too slow in taking opportunities.

Thus, the actual meaning of (11) results not from the semantic reinterpretation of the lexical structure *behind the eight ball*, but from a whole complex of knowledge concerning this game. The conceptual material relevant for the semantic result (actual meaning) includes, above all, knowledge of the tactics one must employ during the game: e.g. one must be very attentive and react immediately to gain advantageous positions, to pocket the balls without getting behind the eight ball, etc.

8.4 Literal readings: Conceptual structures vs. "referential reality"

Another important idea arising from the postulate of the cognitive nature of figurative reinterpretation is that metaphoric mapping does not necessarily presuppose the existence of a "normal" literal reading of a figurative unit. The only necessary prerequisite is the existence of both source and target *concepts* (cf. the notion of *intensional reinterpretation* in Baranov and Dobrovol'skij 2008). The source concept that lends cognitive structures for metaphoric mapping can be based on knowledge which does not necessarily have any correspondence in our everyday life. Compare (12).

(12) German *jmdm. einen Floh ins Ohr setzen* "to put a flea in someone's ear"
 'to arouse an unrealisable wish in someone'

The source concept does not correspond to an action normally performed in our everyday life. Hence, the actual meaning of (12) is a result of various cognitive operations on heterogeneous knowledge structures, i.e. we are dealing with a kind of *conceptual blending*. These knowledge types relevant to the target concept can be approximately described in the following way.

(a) Normally, nobody puts a flea in someone's ear, but we can imagine this action (so, here we are dealing with a conceptual construction rather than with a concept based on experience).
(b) A flea bite is irksome. This is a kind of shared knowledge, which implicates (c).
(c) A flea in the ear constitutes a foreign body in a person's head, which causes trouble. This implication lends conceptual material for mapping: the flea in the ear can be linked to a wish that is unrealisable because both cause trouble.
(d) The flea is an insect that moves very quickly; therefore the flea can be mapped onto something desirable but unrealisable (as it could disappear at any time).
(e) The head of a human is the seat of thinking ("metonymic" knowledge). Therefore, the function of thinking is disrupted by the foreign body, so that one loses the ability to think realistically.

The same conceptual material could be regrouped in a different way with other elements highlighted. The result would be another kind of blending and, hence, a different actual meaning. The evidence for this can be found in French and English. Let us look at examples (13) and (14) – idioms using the same lexical structure, and, therefore, the same conceptual "raw stuff" as (12) and producing semantic results different from (13) and from each other. See the account of "false friends in conventional figurative language" in chapter 5 for details.

(13) French *mettre la puce à l'oreille de qqn* "to put the flea into the ear of someone [into someone's ear]"
'to make someone mistrustful, suspicious'

(14) English *to send someone away with a flea in his/her ear*
'to angrily refuse what someone has come to ask you; to snub or rebuke a person'

Let us have a look at another example.

(15) *to bite/snap someone's head off*
'to answer or speak to someone in a very angry way, especially without a good reason'

Even the biggest animal would not bite a person's off (some basically possible exotic exceptions can be ignored in this context). The source concept that lends cognitive structures for metaphoric mapping is based on knowledge which usually does not have any correspondence to everyday life and, therefore, the given lexical structure is almost never used in its literal sense. In reality, an animal or someone else would hardly bite a person's head off. Knowledge in this case therefore refers to a virtual situation. The knowledge about what would happen to a person whose head is bitten off, rather than a kind of "animal behaviour", makes up the source concept.

Nevertheless, this idiom is metaphorically motivated because it is not the real situation which is addressed during the processing of the idiom but the knowledge about virtual situations of a certain type. Our knowledge about what would happen to a person whose head was bitten off motivates the actual meaning. The relevant motivating link is provided by the semantic implication, hence by an implicit element of the given conceptual structure, rather than by an explicitly expressed element.

The main theoretical conclusion that can be drawn from the issue discussed here is that the metaphoric inference is based not on "meaning transfer" but on the activation of relevant knowledge. The literal reading of a given lexical structure (whether "normal" or "abnormal", i.e. constructed in terms of a possible world) activates the corresponding knowledge structures. The actual meaning emerges as a result of operations on these structures Cognitive modelling of figurative semantics is seen as a metalinguistic apparatus for capturing and formalising such operations. In this sense, cognitive modelling has aims similar to the aims of the metalinguistic apparatus of conceptual metaphor. Nevertheless, there are some relevant differences between both metalanguages. They will be discussed in the next section.

8.5 Cognitive modelling vs. conceptual metaphor

The advantages of the cognitive modelling of figurative semantics as a kind of analysis at the level of "rich images" can be demonstrated by an example. Compare the German idiom (3) *eine Schraube ohne Ende*, on the one hand, and (16–18), on the other.

(16) German *ein Fass ohne Boden* "a barrel without a bottom"
 'an endless drain on someone's resources'

(17) Russian *бездонная бочка* "(a) bottomless barrel"
 1. 'an endless drain on someone's resources'; 2. 'someone who can consume a lot of alcohol/food'

(18) Dutch *een bodemloos vat* "a bottomless barrel"
    1. 'an endless drain on someone's resources'; 2. 'someone who can consume a lot of alcohol/food'

Conceptually, the three idioms have much in common. They name an artefact which lacks an important part; this leads to its dysfunction. Nevertheless, there are significant differences in the actual meanings of these idioms. These are due to some important differences in the image structure, which can be captured by analysis along these lines. The CONTAINER-metaphor is involved in the interpretation of all three idioms (16–18). This evokes the concept of resources, which is a crucial part of the actual meanings of the idioms. In the Russian idiom (17) and in the Dutch idiom (18), even more parts of the image are used [as compared to (16)]: the idea that the content of the barrel must be a kind of fluid (or other substance) gives rise to the second reading of this idiom – 'someone who can consume a lot of alcohol/food'. In the source frame BARREL, the slot of the "bottom" is eliminated. The lack of a bottom results in invariably abortive attempts to fill the barrel with water or some other substance. Mapping the source frame onto the target frame also eliminates the filler of the corresponding "end" slot in the scenario "draining someone's resources" – cf. (16), (17.1) and (18.1) – or in the scenario "consuming alcohol/food", cf. (17.2) and (18.2).

This example shows the importance of cross-linguistic contrasts in this area. The widespread idiom "(to be) a bottomless pit/barrel" has developed a noticeable polysemy. Various languages use it to describe a situation, project, institution, etc. that is being funded with more and more money without any prospect of improvement. In other languages, it can also be said of a person's insatiability, a gluttonous eater or an excessive drinker. Idioms (16–18) are representatives of the differences between the figurative meanings of the idioms in individual languages. Idioms based on the same rich image and possessing (near) analogous lexical structures do not have to coincide semantically. Because they have the same conceptual potential concentrated in the image and encoded in the lexical structure, such idioms can unfold this conceptual potential in different ways. Observations of this kind verify one of the main postulates of the CFLT, namely that not all quasi-equivalent figurative units of different languages which have identical underlying images are identical with regard to their semantics and/or pragmatics. The same image can be utilised to denote the target concept in many different ways. If different parts of the conceptual structure of a given image are highlighted, the semantic result of the mapping in question has to be different. Hence, there is no predictability as to how the potential of a given source concept will be used in metaphoric inference; cf. in this regard also examples (12) to (14).

8.5 Cognitive modelling vs. conceptual metaphor — 231

Thus, two main tasks can be postulated in the field of metaphoric motivation of figurative units:
- describing the motivational peculiarities of every single figurative unit, and
- discovering general rules according to which (mainly frame-based) metaphorically motivated figurative units are processed.

To perform these two tasks, two different tools are needed. As has already been pointed out, these tools are metaphor analysis at the basic level, labelled here as cognitive modelling, and the apparatus of conceptual metaphor designed to describe metaphorical expressions at the superordinate level.

Both tools are often needed at the same time to enable us to explain the motivating links of a given figurative unit. Without addressing the notion of cognitive modelling, Lakoff (1993: 211) pointed to the role of different kinds of knowledge in the processing of figurative expressions.

> An idiom like "spinning one's wheels" comes with a conventional mental image, that of the wheels of a car stuck in some substance – mud, sand, snow, or on ice – so that the car cannot move when the motor is engaged and the wheels turn. Part of our knowledge about that image is [...] that it will take a lot of effort on the part of the occupants to get the vehicle moving again – and that may not even be possible. The LOVE IS A JOURNEY metaphor applies to this knowledge about the image. It maps this knowledge onto knowledge about love relationships: [...].

These ideas can be summarised in the following way. The conceptual metaphor (or metaphoric model) determines the direction of mapping (onto which target concept the given source concept will be mapped), whereas the "rich image" evoked by the given lexical structure provides semantic material for construing the actual meaning. However, this kind of alliance between both knowledge types (and, correspondingly, between both metalinguistic tools) is not always productive. In many cases, the mapping direction relevant to a given figurative unit cannot be described in terms of conceptual metaphors because it is not supported by other metaphorical expressions taking the same way of inference.

A further example of this kind is idiom (19).

(19) *to change the record*
'said when you want someone to stop talking about the same thing all the time'

Idiom (19) is motivated via knowledge that listening to a person talking about the same thing over and over again reminds us of listening to the same record repeatedly, i.e. this person keeps saying the same all the time as if their speech was recorded. In principle, this conceptual correspondence could be represented in the form of a metaphoric model, such as LISTENING TO SOMEONE TALKING ABOUT THE SAME THING ALL THE TIME IS LISTENING TO THE SAME RECORD. However, this does not seem reasonable, because the postulating of conceptual metaphors or metaphoric models is based on the fact that they can really function as models, i.e. serve to describe and explain various metaphorical expressions, and, by doing so, reveal some general mechanisms governing the production and reception of these expressions. Metaphor constructions that are ad hoc solutions and have a singular value are not metaphoric models. The explanation of relevant motivating links proceeds in cases like (19) on the basis of the cognitive modelling of a given image structure as a whole, i.e. on the basis of the "rich image". This knowledge involves the frame LISTENING TO A RECORD with highlighted slots such as "recorded sounds", "potential reiteration" and the like, entailing potential semantic implications like "rigid fixity", "tediousness", etc., which provide a "conceptual bridge" between the source and the target concept.

8.6 Metaphoric inference and cultural knowledge

In the semantic structure of some CFUs there are also relevant meaning components which are bound not to the interaction between the source frame and the target frame, but to the knowledge of other types, above all, the knowledge of various cultural phenomena. An important task of the CFLT is to explain all the relevant components of the actual meaning, including phenomena of this type. Let us look at some motivation aspects of idiom (20).

(20) *the black sheep (in the family)*
'an odd or disreputable member of a group; someone who is very different from the rest of his/her family, group or society and considered worthless by them because he/she is less successful or more contemptible than the rest'

This idiom originating from the Bible is widespread in many European languages, cf. for instance German *das schwarze Schaf (in der Familie)*, Dutch *het zwarte schaap (in de familie)*, Greek *το μαύρο πρόβατο (της οικογένειας)*, Finnish *(perheen) musta lammas* "the black sheep (in a family)".

Though the definition provided in (20) points to elements such as "less successful or more contemptible than the rest" and does not highlight the idea of being "more immoral than the rest", this idea is profiled in many authentic contexts and is absolutely central to the use of (20). Compare textual examples from BNC (21–22).

(21) He asserts that in the majority of businesses the moral standards have improved very significantly. But the media only pick out the failures, because that's what we as readers want to read. You can blame the media, but really you ought to blame the readers. No matter where you are, there are always a few *black sheep*. The snag today is that those *black sheep* will create much bigger problems than they could in the past.

(22) Gain all the well-established health advantages of eating meals high in dietary fibre content. Who says so? Not some earnest, eager and ignorant lady running a slimming clinic in Slough. Not some dubious doctor (all professions have their *black sheep*!) cashing in on some personal theory totally unsupported by scientific evidence.

The semantic components "less successful or more immoral than the rest" are to be explained via "symbolic knowledge", namely the knowledge shared by all members of a given linguistic community that words meaning BLACK have a secondary reading, which can be generally described as 'bad'.[5] This symbolically based conceptual component is responsible for the idea of being "less successful or more immoral than the rest" fixed in the structure of the actual meaning. That means that a *black sheep* is not only different from the other members of the relevant group of people (as logically follows from the mapping discovered by means of cognitive modelling). This property of being different is judged to be 'bad'.[6]

The conclusion from this is that the type of motivation based on symbolic knowledge is very different from the type of motivation based on metaphors. The relationship between the literal reading of the given word combination and its actual figurative meaning are not based on similarity (BLACK and BAD are not similar) but on certain conventions that are handed down by the given culture. See section 4.6 and chapter 11 for more details.

Figurative units that are motivated via cultural symbols cannot be analysed with the help of the same metalinguistic tools as metaphorically motivated expressions. The latter can be analysed by means of the cognitive modelling of

---

5 There is a huge movement away from using *black* negatively due to racial overtones.
6 SHEEP is also a salient cultural symbol playing a significant role in Christian tradition. Nevertheless, it is not necessary to turn towards "symbolic knowledge" of this kind (in contrast to the symbolic interpretation of BLACK) in order to reveal relevant conceptual links between the lexical structure of the idiom and its actual meaning (i.e. to comprehend relevant motivational links). In other words, to understand the meaning of the idiom *black sheep*, it is not essential to know about the symbolic status of the SHEEP in Christian symbolism.

individual mental images. Symbol-based motivation, however, requires a culture-semiotic approach. That is to say that there is a need for metalinguistic instruments which would allow us to analyse semiotic codes of various kinds along the same lines. Such tools are developed within the framework of the semiotics of culture (cf. e.g. Lotman 1990 and further development in Dobrovol'skij and Piirainen 1997, 1998). The cultural semiotics approach will be elaborated on in chapter 11.

Interestingly, idiom (20) has an additional culturally-based conceptual component, which can be described as part of its connotation and is language-specific, i.e. crucial to the English idiom discussed but not to its (near) equivalents in other languages. In English, there is a nursery rhyme *Baa, baa, black sheep, have you any wool*, which (as well as any other figurative expressions with *black* in the symbolic function of 'bad') may be repugnant to members of ethnic minority communities, and there are people who think that English speakers should be careful about its use. Consider (23).

(23) Let me give you an example of the misuse of the press. The Sun published a front page lead stating that a Labour London borough had banned the teaching of *Baa Baa Black Sheep* as racist. This had been replaced by Baa Baa Green Sheep. This story was completely untrue and was successfully challenged in front of the Press Council. The correction was printed in a small two centimetre box hidden well inside the paper.

This is a special feature of social culture, absolutely untypical of other languages such as German, Dutch, Greek, Finnish, etc.

Going further, the limits of the metalanguage of cognitive modelling can be illustrated with the help of figurative expressions which have a nearly identical structure in their source frames and involve nearly the same cognitive operations. Nevertheless, the actual meaning of these expressions may provide essential differences. This may be because the relevant features of the source frame are mapped onto a different target frame, or because (even if the interaction between relevant conceptual structures is very similar in terms of the basic principles of metaphoric inference) there are relevant differences of a cultural and intertextual nature (compare, for example, the idioms discussed in chapter 5).

The synchronic appearance of idioms in several languages may suggest a similarity which is not justified historically because different sources are involved. One example is idiom (20) *the black sheep (in the family)*, which has equivalents in a large number of European languages. According to lexicographic traditions, it is equated with idioms such as French *la brebis galeuse* and Russian *паршивая овца*.

Idiom (20) and its German, Dutch, Greek and Finnish correlates are connected with the Bible verse Gen 30:32, where Jacob wants to select the spotted and the brown sheep from Laban's flock in order to obtain them as his wage. The idioms *la brebis galeuse* and *паршивая овца*, however, must not be confused with (20), because they go back to a different textual source. This is the classical fable of the mangy sheep (Juvenal's "Satires" 2, 80), according to which the whole flock will die if the single sheep with infectious mange is not removed. The different texts have left traces in the lexical-semantic structures of the idioms. Firstly, the idioms *la brebis galeuse* and *паршивая овца* are not used together with the element "in/of the family" because the fable text does not include the aspect of a group of related individuals. Secondly, the underlying story which highlights the aspect of "being mangy" can still be recognised in the figurative meaning of these idioms (compare also German *ein räudiges Schaf*): the sick sheep is a severe threat to all the other sheep in the flock, which, by analogy, leads to the semantic result that a bad person in a team puts all the others at risk – semantic subtleties that are different from idiom (20). Even if the difference between BLACK and MANGY may be regarded as insignificant (from today's perspective) – both are undesirable qualities with respect to a sheep's wool/coat – the two groups of idioms differ fundamentally in their image components, which are based on two different textual sources.

8.7 Conclusion

One of the traditional tasks of lexicology is the description of the meaning derivation of linguistic units from the meanings of their constituent parts. Much effort has been invested in the development of semantic metalanguages which would permit the description of a relation between the literal meaning and its derivatives.

One of the central problems in the field of conventional figurative language is the formulation of rules according to which particular secondary meanings can be derived based on some initial semantic and conceptual material that is only partially given by the literal meaning of a particular expression. In spite of obvious spontaneity and unpredictability, the formation of figurative units is not completely arbitrary; it is partially governed by certain conceptual laws. To analyse and describe conceptual procedures, a specific, cognitively based metalanguage has to be developed. In this chapter, we have presented such a metalinguistic apparatus, labelled here "cognitive modelling of figurative semantics". Use of our metalanguage for the purpose of describing and explaining language phenomena makes it possible to bring to light cognitive structures hidden under the surface of linguistic facts.

Although the ontological status of frames remains uncertain, the metalinguistic apparatus of cognitive modelling based on frame semantics is very useful heuristically. In particular, this apparatus can be successfully applied in research on metaphorically motivated figurative units.

The question that remains is to what extent all these conceptual procedures are psychologically real. In other words, do speakers really process every metaphorically motivated figurative unit they use in such a way? Or do they just refer to the current situation by knowledge of the actual figurative meaning, which is stored in the mental lexicon? This question cannot be answered in the framework of linguistics. For plausible argumentation, results from research areas other than linguistics (above all, experimental psychology) are needed. Relying on what is known about the processing of idioms from experimental findings, we can assume with certainty that at least familiar idioms are accessed directly (cf. Schweigert 1986; Schweigert and Moates 1988; Giora and Fein 1999b; Giora 2002; Laurent et al. 2006). This is one of the main reasons why conventional figurative units must be regarded as stipulated in the lexicon, i.e. as lexical items. The cognitive modelling of figurative semantics (as has been presented and briefly exemplified here) does not aim to describe psychological reality but is much more oriented towards uncovering potential motivating links. The linguistic significance of this task is grounded in the overall theoretical assumption that most of the language is not completely arbitrary to its speakers.

In other words, cognitive modelling does not enable us to say what people really think while using conventional figurative expressions.[7] It does, however, provide the opportunity to analyse conceptual structures underlying a given figurative expression and to describe them lexicographically.

Evaluating the results of semantic analysis, we would like to stress that two different aspects of figurative semantic derivation have to be distinguished. On the one hand, the semantics of every figurative unit is unique. This is because the semantic result depends not only on regular and universal cognitive operations involved in constructing the actual meaning on the basis of initial conceptual material, but also on this conceptual material itself, which is unique in every given case. Moreover, many additional factors (such as cultural phenomena, "ety-

---

[7] We assume that even carefully designed psycholinguistic experiments cannot provide absolutely reliable data in this regard. Compare the experimental results gained by Gibbs and his associates and the results described by Cacciari and her colleagues. The data discussed e.g. in Gibbs (1986, 1990) suggest that people address the underlying conceptual metaphor while processing figurative expressions. Conversely, the experimental data gained e.g. by Cacciari and Tabossi (1988), Cacciari and Glucksberg (1991), Cacciari (1993, 2014) are consistent with the assumption that literal meanings of single constituents of an idiom are crucial to its imagery.

mological memory" of lexical items, etc.) influence the actual meaning. On the other hand, the principles according to which the initial conceptual material, i.e. the source frame, is processed are regular. The consequence is that the semantic result, i.e. the actual meaning of a given figurative unit, is predictable to a certain extent. Conventional figurative units are simultaneously arbitrary and not arbitrary. They are arbitrary in the sense that, given the initial conceptual structure only, the semantic result is not fully predictable – the degree of its predictability depends on the degree of motivational transparency. But they are not arbitrary in the sense that there are logical relations between conceptual input and output, i.e. motivating links between the source frame partially fixed in the lexical structure and the actual meaning. That is to say that, possessing knowledge about both the source frame and the actual meaning, we can figure out which cognitive operations have led to the given semantic result. That is why the figurative unit in question appears motivated.

It is obvious that cognitive modelling can only capture this "predictable" part of the actual meaning. It would be unrealistic to expect it (or any other instrument of analysis) to explain all the relevant meaning components of every figurative unit in terms of causal relations, or even to predict them. This metalinguistic instrument is designed to analyse regular cognitive mechanisms underlying motivational phenomena. Since conventional figurative units, per definitionem, are irregular linguistic structures, it is clear that cognitive modelling has certain limits. Nevertheless, cognitive modelling may be an efficient instrument of analysis because it provides data that show how the inference may take place.

Even if it is clear that overall significant systematisation is not possible in the domain of figurative language, every instrument that helps to bring some order into this "realm of disorder" is welcome. Generally, one of the most important tasks of linguistic theory is to extract whatever subregularities exist in domains that are predominantly organised irregularly.

The idea behind the apparatus of cognitive modelling must also be applied to the technique of meaning explanation. That is, while describing the semantics of a figurative unit we should also take into account the source frame. Some relevant components of the semantic structure can be traced back to the mental image and determine relevant features of the contextual behaviour of a given figurative expression.

Compared to the traditional idea of "meaning transfer", the most important advantage of the use of the metalinguistic apparatus discussed is the possibility of taking into account not only explicit (that is, linguistically expressed) but also implicit elements of conceptual structures which are evoked by conventional figurative expressions. Linguistically expressed elements (slots of a given frame) are not always relevant for revealing the inferences and, hence, explaining the motivating links. Since the selection of semantic features relevant for denoting the target concept is more or less arbitrary, it is not only explicit elements of a given conceptual structure that determine the semantic result, but also conceptual elements which are not expressed explicitly.

Another important idea arising from the postulate of the cognitive nature of figurative reinterpretation is that metaphoric mapping does not necessarily presuppose the existence of a "normal" literal reading of a figurative unit. The only necessary prerequisite is the existence of both source and target *concepts*. The source concept that lends cognitive structures for metaphoric mapping can be based on knowledge which does not necessarily have any correspondence in the real world.

9 Specific frames: The concept HOUSE in language and culture

9.1 Preliminary remarks

Theoretical explanations of the cognitive modelling expounded in the previous chapter will now be exemplified by a case study. A particular source frame, HOUSE, will be considered as a unit of cross-linguistic and cross-cultural description. We regard it as a basic requirement for any reliable study on conventional figurative language to examine in depth all conventional figurative units of a given domain as a whole, rather than to look at isolated examples that happen to attract attention (e.g. *to kick the bucket* or *to spill the beans* in the American works on idioms and their cognitive foundations). Therefore, the compilation of a potentially complete inventory of CFUs within a given domain is required.

The empirical basis of this case study extends mainly to Japanese and the Low German dialect WML. Some European languages will be used by way of comparison. Thus, reference will be made to languages belonging to both closely related and quite distant cultural areas. The frame HOUSE has been chosen because the "dwelling", a basic necessity for all people, reveals major differences in the light of social, material and even mental culture. As will be shown, it is essential to incorporate cultural knowledge into the cognitive modelling of figurative semantics.

Housing, food and clothing belong to the most elementary requirements of all human beings. Despite the biological sameness of all people and their basic needs, there is a wide spectrum of cultural diversity regarding how people build their homes, prepare their food or manufacture their clothes. It is obvious that peculiarities of these elementary domains of human culture have left traces in conventional figurative language. This chapter will investigate the question of how conceptualisations of the HOUSE (HOME, DWELLING HOUSE as source frames) manifest themselves in CFUs.

Since one of the basic ideas of the theory developed in this study is the assumption that the mental images fixed in the lexical structure of CFUs may reflect relevant features of a given culture, we expect that the differences between "dwelling cultures" will find equivalents in the image components of conventional figurative units in different languages. Likewise, the analysis of the image components in these CFUs will help to determine culture-specific features of the DWELLING HOUSE as it is understood, with its traditional associations, by the members of every linguistic community.

Furthermore, it can be assumed that in certain cases the conventional figurative units of different languages using virtually the same lexical structure will point to different source frames. Since it has been shown that the frames (rather than single constituents in their literal meanings) provide material for establishing motivating links, we can assume that CFUs based on different frames – even if they have an almost identical lexical structure – are motivated in different ways. Hence, their actual meanings may reveal relevant differences.

We speak about the *frame* of a DWELLING HOUSE because the conceptual structure as a whole is considered a source domain for many CFUs. The motivating links between the frame of a DWELLING HOUSE and the figurative meanings of many conventional expressions are provided not just by words denoting parts of the house's construction, but rather by the knowledge of the specifics and functions of these elements of a DWELLING HOUSE. The closely related Germanic standard languages such as English, German, Dutch and Swedish will be examined, as well as Finnish, which is not genetically related to the former but belongs to the same European cultural area. The concept HOUSE will also be investigated in CFUs of the culturally and genetically quite distant Japanese language. In addition, the Low German dialect WML will be examined; although located in Central Europe, WML shows its own specific cultural conceptualisation of HOUSE.

Our basis for the data in this chapter was made up as follows: all the conventional figurative units of the six languages and the WML dialect mentioned above were scrutinised in order to single out expressions which show image components belonging to the HOUSE concept. In most cases these are idioms and proverbs containing constituents that denote architectural elements (e.g. equivalents of 'post', 'pillar' or 'beam') and parts of the exterior of a house (e.g. 'wall', 'roof', 'chimney', 'threshold', 'veranda' etc.). Besides these, several constituents belonging to the domain of the interior of a house contribute to this concept in CFUs, for instance 'chamber', 'ceiling' and 'wallpaper' in European dwellings or 'straw mat' and 'sliding doors and windows' in Japanese homes.

In various cases it was necessary to ask native speakers about the mental images these conventional figurative units evoked for them. The aim was to exclude expressions whose constituents belong to the domain of architecture or the interior of a room, but which cannot be clearly assigned to the concept of a DWELLING HOUSE, and relate instead to buildings in general, for example, office blocks, castles, churches etc. Constituents of this kind are, among others, *door, wall* or *window*. There are, for example, idioms like *to meet behind closed/locked doors* 'in secrecy, without the press or public present', in which the concept DOOR does not necessarily belong to the frame of a private home, but to any kind of room or building. Thus, such idioms are not considered here because they do not contribute to the concept DWELLING HOUSE as a culturally relevant frame.

In other CFUs, these constituents point to more general metaphors (as in the often quoted conceptual metaphor DIFFICULTIES ARE IMPEDIMENTS TO MOTION, cf. idioms like *to have one's back to the wall* 'to be in a defensive position'; *all doors are open to him* 'he has many opportunities to do things'; *to close the door to something* 'to make something impossible'). Finally, these HOUSE constituents can take on metonymic meanings (e.g. German *vor der Tür stehen* "to stand at the door" 'just about to occur'; *a window of opportunity* 'a limited period of time in which to do something or the best time to do something') and are thus, in some cases, far from belonging to the frame of a real house. In all these idioms the image components of WALL, DOOR and WINDOW cannot be traced back exclusively to the frame of a DWELLING HOUSE. Therefore, cases like these are excluded here (for some functions of DOOR and THRESHOLD see below).

It was discovered that the conventional figurative units of the five European standard languages have almost the same HOUSE frame constituents. The similarity of CFUs is connected with the fact that the European standard languages tend to grow closer together, even if they are not genetically affiliated. This is a result of the cultural convergence of modern urban societies in Europe. We thus apply the term "Standard Average European" (SAE), well-known in the field of linguistic typology research, to contemporary research on conventional figurative language (see 1.2.3).

Thus, because of the uniformity of European standard languages, these data can be presented in one summarising section (9.2). In Japanese conventional figurative language, several constituents have been found which evoke the concept of the traditional dwelling culture in Japan (9.3). The WML dialect examined in depth here also provides plenty of CFUs which are based on the imagery of the ancient peasant house in this region of Germany, so that we have to restrict ourselves to presenting only the essential parts of this comprehensive material (9.4).

9.2 The concept HOUSE in English, German, Dutch, Swedish and Finnish

9.2.1 The multiple-room urban building as a source frame

A well-known HOUSE metaphor often quoted in political discussions is that of the "Common House of Europe", coined by Leonid Brezhnev and prominently adapted by Mikhail Gorbachev. This metaphor is based on the concept of a large urban building with many rooms or apartments, each of them inhabited by one person or one family (metaphorically compared with the nations of Europe). This concept of a HOUSE bears a great resemblance to the imagery basis which can be discovered in CFUs of the European standard languages considered in this section, but differs completely from those discovered in Japanese on the one hand, and in the WML dialect on the other.

The idea of living very close to other people, e.g. in a terraced house, in a semi-detached house or in a multiple dwelling with several apartment emerges in some less figurative idioms such as the English *one's next-door neighbours* or *live next door to someone*, the German *Tür an Tür wohnen mit jmdm.* "to live door to door with someone", as well as the Swedish *bo vägg i vägg med ngn.* "to live wall to wall with someone" 'to live in the house or flat next to someone'. The idea of living very close to other people is evoked either by the concept DOOR or by the concept WALL, both belonging to concepts of an urban house or a multiple-room dwelling in a residential block. By contrast, similar ideas are not found in Japanese conventional figurative units on the one hand, or in CFUs of the WML dialect on the other, since the imagery basis of conventional figurative language here is drawn from culturally very different HOUSE conceptualisations.

The conceptualisation of HOUSE in English, German, Dutch, Swedish and Finnish CFUs reveals far-reaching common features. In most cases we are dealing with the frame of a multiple-room urban house in which one dwells within the limits of (one's own) four walls, in single rooms, close to other people. The main phraseological constituents drawn from expressions which make up this source concept are equivalents of 'walls', 'wallpaper', 'ceiling' and 'door'. First, let us consider the role of the 'walls' as an image component in the idiom (1) (cf. examples (31) in chapter 5).

(1) German *in den eigenen vier Wänden* "within one's own four walls"
    'in the privacy of one's home, at home'

This kind of dwelling within one's own four walls, cut off from the outside world, can have negative effects on the mood or mental state of a person, which is the actual meaning of some further idioms of the languages considered here (2–3). Interestingly enough, the image components of these idioms consist of different elements of the HOUSE frame, i.e. WALLS (2) and CEILING (3). These idioms mean something like 'to feel or to get claustrophobic, to feel shut in, to be bored and depressed with the sight of these four walls' (e.g. when someone is forced to stay at home, whether it be because of bringing up children, illness or unemployment).

(2) a. Dutch *de muren komen af op iemand* "the walls come down on someone"
    b. Finnish *seinät kaatuvat jkn. päälle* "the walls fall upon someone"

(3) German *jmdm. fällt die Decke auf den Kopf* "the ceiling falls down on someone's head"

9.2 The concept HOUSE in English, German, Dutch, Swedish and Finnish — 243

There are some differences between the images of idioms (2) and (3), but these differences are not very significant. German *auf den Kopf* seems to be more expressive, with *Decke*, the ceiling, falling directly onto a person's head while the walls collapse sideways onto them. Finnish *päälle* 'upon', in postposition, is etymologically related with *pää* 'head'. The WALLPAPER is the most salient feature of the HOUSE frame in some further expressions (4–5). Idioms containing this constituent show the same concept as a four-walled living room. One has to "change the wallpaper" in order to change the scenery or residence (4). Furthermore, the wallpaper is the boundary of the living space which, in the case of sudden anger, becomes too narrow and cramped (5).

(4) German *die Tapeten wechseln* "to change the wallpaper"
'to have a change of scenery'

(5) Dutch *door het behang gaan* "to go through the wallpaper"
'not to be able to control oneself; to suddenly become very angry'

WALLPAPER in (4–5) is the slot which induces the frame ROOM. Idiom (5) shows a somehow absurd imagery. The contemporary Dutch word *behang* means 'wallpaper', but in the historical context it refers to a kind of fabric of woven material between two rooms; according to (Van Dale IW 1999: 47), however, the origin of this idiom is not clear. Another Dutch expression used in order to say that a person suddenly becomes very angry is *dan wordt het huis te klein* "then the house becomes too small", which alludes to the uncontrolled and abnormal behaviour of a furious person – a metaphor like ANGER IS UNCONTROLLED BEHAVIOUR may be found here, possibly also in idiom (5). The lexical field of ANGER is highly elaborated in the CFUs of the languages examined here. HOUSE is one of the predominant source concepts for metaphors indicating this target domain. Once again, constituents like 'walls' on the one hand (6) and 'roof' (7) or 'ceiling' (8) on the other hand have the same function.

(6) Finnish *hyppiä seinille* "to jump up the walls"

(7) English *to go through the roof/hit the roof*

(8) German *an die Decke gehen* "to jump to the ceiling"
all meaning 'to suddenly become very angry, to be furiously angry'

Here they only refer to those elements of the frame that can be interpreted as BOUNDARIES. ANGER is seen as a state in which a person goes beyond those boundaries or limits pre-determined by his/her culture.

The DOOR is also a significant component in the conceptualising of a HOME or HOUSE. In various CFUs the DOOR is used metonymically for the home in its entirety (9–12). Expressions like *to live next door to someone* have already been mentioned, where the concept DOOR indicates that people live close to each other. In one Swedish idiom, the HOUSE indicated by DOOR does not undergo any semantic reinterpretation (9). Being a metonymic expression, DOOR simply highlights one of the slots of this frame.

(9) Swedish *inte sticka näsan utom dörren* "not to put one's nose out of the door"
'not to leave the house or home'

In several expressions, however, this home or house, indicated by the explicitly named concept DOOR, has a more abstract meaning, something like 'one's own affairs', 'one's own private life'. Idiom (10a) and proverb (10b), alike in respect of their image components, reveal the concept of a single house, the door of which leads to the street or the like (rather than a concept of an apartment, the door of which leads to a corridor or similar).

(10) a. Swedish *sopa rent framför egen dörr* "to clean in front of one's own door"
'to put one's own affairs in order, to mind one's own business'
b. German *jeder kehre vor seiner eigenen Tür* "everyone has to sweep in front of his own door"
'everyone should put his/her own affairs in order, should mind his/her own business'

In other CFUs, DOOR has taken on the secondary function of a boundary between the inside and the outside of a house, the contrast between the private and the unknown area. Let us consider the idiom *to keep the wolf from the door* (example (45) in chapter 13). Here the concept DOOR reveals the reading 'border between the space inside the house and the space outside the house', whereas the frame HOUSE, indicated by the slot DOOR, has been reinterpreted in the sense of 'all circumstances of living, the whole of someone's existence'. This interpretation of the HOUSE as 'privacy, one's own private life' and 'all circumstances of living, the whole of someone's existence' can also be found in idioms (11–12).

(11) a. English *to show someone the door*
 b. German *jmdm. die Tür weisen* "to show someone the door"
 c. Swedish *visa ngn. på dörren* "to lead someone to the door"
 all meaning 'to call upon someone to leave one's home immediately, to expel someone from one's home; to dismiss or eject someone from a place'

(12) English *never darken my door again!*
 1. 'to call upon an unwelcome person to leave one's home immediately, to expel someone from one's home'; 2. 'not to want to see someone anymore because he/she has done something to make you angry and upset'

Here the image of using the door in order to leave the house is evoked. At the same time, this "real use of the door" is a conventionalised and culture-semiotic gesture. Idiom (12) can be regarded as polysemous, since it can be interpreted on a more concrete or a more abstract level.

In some conventional figurative units, the concept THRESHOLD is quite similar to that of DOOR in (11–12), because of the same salient feature: the boundary between the interior and the exterior of the house. Compare (13) and also a similar idiom (36) below.

(13) Dutch *iemand niet over zijn drempel laten komen* "not to let someone come over one's threshold"
 'to call upon someone to leave one's home immediately, to expel him from one's home'

Finally, particular elements of the frame HOUSE can be semiotised. These manifest themselves in culture as well as in conventional figurative units. In the European languages and their cultural areas, among the parts of the HOUSE frame the concepts DOOR and THRESHOLD have undergone the most significant semiotisation of this kind. In various cultural contexts, above all in architectural symbolism, the DOOR and the THRESHOLD are regarded as symbols of a borderline between two worlds and as symbols of transition and transcendence. In CFUs, both concepts can take on symbolic meanings such as 'border', 'transition, crossing a borderline', and 'limit', for example Finnish *jonkin kynnyksellä* "on someone's threshold" 'a very short time before (something)' and English *at death's door* 'near death', *to be on the threshold of something* (e.g. *Mankind is on the threshold of a new era*) or *pain threshold* 'the limit up to which pain can be borne'. As has been mentioned above, the imagery base is rather vague, and is scarcely connected with the image of a real house.

9.2.2 Traditional dwelling houses as source concepts

Most CFUs in English, German, Dutch, Swedish and Finnish containing HOUSE-frame constituents reveal a relatively uniform source concept, as either a kind of multiple-room urban building or a less specified dwelling house with rooms, walls, ceilings, doors, etc. Although there have been independent cultures of house building in different European areas, all of them steeped in tradition, only a very few conventional figurative units of these standard languages represent other concepts of a HOUSE than those described above. Only one Finnish idiom has been found which reflects elements of the former traditional dwelling house in Finland. It is the command *tuosta on viisi hirttä poikki!* "there, five (unhewn) beams are cut off!" 'Out with you, leave my home immediately!'. It has the same propositional meaning as the idioms in (11–13), but reveals a significantly different source-frame. Here it deals with quite another concept of a HOUSE: the traditional wooden house, built of beams or rough pieces of timber. The main elements of this HOUSE frame are the unhewn beams, Finnish *hirsi*. This house-type has lost its significance over the ages. Its concept, however, is still present in one standard Finnish expression (see example (29) in chapter 10 for more details).

Another example comes from Dutch conventional figurative language, where there are some expressions with the constituent *stoep*. This word denotes a specific element of the Dutch bourgeois town house in a street, roughly translated as 'front doorstep, big step at the entrance door'. In some CFUs, *stoep* is used metonymically for the house in its entirety or for the area of activity in question, cf. (14).

(14) Dutch *op de stoep staan bij iemand* "to stand on someone's doorstep"
  1. 'to stand in front of someone's door in order to be let in (for a visit, for example)';
  2. 'to go and see someone with whom one has to clarify something, in order to request or (especially) to demand something, to call him/her to account for something'

There are some other CFUs in which the concept of a former bourgeois town house emerges. One outdated British English expression is reminiscent of the former town house, where the kitchen and other equipment for the domestic servants were in the basement: *below stairs* 'among the domestic staff, in the rooms designated for housekeeping'. A similar type of urban bourgeois house with a separate kitchen where the servants work can be seen in expressions such as Swedish *gå köksvägen* "to go the kitchen-way (to go through the back door)" and Finnish *kyökin/keittiön kautta* "through the kitchen", both meaning 'not through the official entrance'. A German equivalent idiom *von hinten durch die kalte Küche* (*reinkommen*) (outdated, regional) "(to come in) from behind through the cold kitchen" is used with the figurative meaning 'using indirect or dishonest ways to achieve one's goals.'

Finally, constituents meaning 'chimney' or 'fireplace' point to particular HOUSE frames of earlier times. Idiom (15) originates in the concept of traditional houses with an open fireplace, a chimney breast and a flue over the fire. What is remarkable is that idiom (15) reveals many regional German variants for 'chimney'. All idiom variants belong to Standard German, though the given variants are more frequent in the areas where the variable constituents *Esse, Schlot, Kamin* etc. prevail.[1] The idea is that nobody will be able to read what has been written into the chimney, because the fire will wipe it out immediately.

(15) German *etwas in den Schornstein/Schlot/Kamin/Rauchfang/in die Esse schreiben* "to write something into the chimney"
'to write off something, to give up a plan, etc.'

Other examples are German *der Schornstein raucht* "the chimney is smoking" 'things are ticking over nicely; business is good', *Heimchen am Herd* "house cricket at the stove" 'little housewife, not emancipated housewife' or English *by one's own fireside* 'in one's own home and circumstances', all of them revealing the concept of an earlier dwelling house.

9.3 The concept HOUSE in Japanese

9.3.1 The traditional Japanese dwelling house: Main elements of architecture and interior

Due to the warmer climate in Japan (apart from the Northern parts of the country), traditional houses were of a very light wooden construction, and were generally airy structures. The typical Japanese dwelling house used to be a one-storey detached house with a garden. Salient elements of this type of house were the central wooden pillar, the sliding paper-covered lattice doors and the surrounding veranda. These elements were adapted by the urban dwelling culture several centuries ago from the type of construction found in the palaces of the nobility.

---

[1] *Esse* is most frequently used in Middle East Germany, *Schlot* in Middle East/South East Germany, *Kamin* in western Austria, Switzerland and South/Middle West Germany, *Rauchfang* in Middle and East Austria and *Schornstein* in northern Middle Germany.

The concept of rooms is quite different from Western houses. Traditional Japanese houses had no strict partitioning of rooms; the living area could be remodelled according to the requirements of the family. A Japanese room with *tatami*-straw mats[2] on the floor (see below) can serve many purposes – it can be used as a living room in the daytime and as a dining room at mealtimes, and it can be changed into a bedroom when the bedding is laid out at night. It is the custom to put away the bedding every morning, and the "furniture" (a low table with folding legs, cushions and bolsters, or the bedding) can be changed accordingly. All rooms in the traditional house, apart from the kitchen, were *tatami*-rooms and were used as a living space during the day and a sleeping space at night.

The rooms could be separated from each other by sliding partitions, and the room divisions could be removed if needed. The sliding room dividers are called either 襖 (*fusuma*) 'room dividers' (a solid paper partition on a wooden frame), or 障子 (*shōji*) 'sliding paper screens' (wooden lattice frames covered with a tough, translucent white paper). *Shōji* were traditionally outside doors opening onto the surrounding veranda, but are also used between rooms. In a traditional house, rooms have no locks. All supports are visible and all the units are modular. No paint or wallpaper is used in a typical Japanese house.

Traditionally there were no strict boundaries between the inside and the outside of the dwelling house, but there were some transitions. The interior area, the living space, which was only entered after removing outdoor footwear, was higher than ground level: the floors of these rooms were covered with thick straw-covered reed mats – 畳 (*tatami*) – giving this floor area an intimate quality. The surrounding veranda or open corridor – 縁側 (*engawa*) – formed the transition to the outer area. This veranda was covered with wooden floorboards. The sliding doors and paper windows opening onto the garden, gave an impression of great light. The lower room at the back of the house – the 奥 *oku* – was the housewife's domain. Hence, even today the wife is called 奥様 (*okusama*), "the person at the back of the house".

9.3.2 Conventional figurative units containing HOUSE-frame constituents

Although the dwelling culture in Japan has changed in many respects, the concept of the ancient traditional type of house is present in several Japanese conventional figurative units. One example of a supporting constructional element is the thick

---

[2] See Tohyama (1991: 202–204) for details about the Japanese "sitting culture" connected with the *tatami*-culture and the Japanese nonverbal behaviour produced by the *tatami*-room.

pillar in the middle of the traditional house (16). Another constructional element emerging in aCFU is the 敷居 (*shikii*), the step-high threshold at the entrance of the dwelling house (17). The porch or open corridor (*engawa*) has already been mentioned. One specific feature of the traditional house, the space between the veranda and the ground, 縁の下 (*en no shita* "below the veranda"), appears in one CFU (18). The sliding paper screens (*shōji*), a feature of the traditional dwelling house for the most part well-known outside Japan, have also been mentioned (19). Furthermore, some CFUs with *tatami* 'straw mats' as a constituent can be found in (20–21). In addition, one expression with 枕 (*makura*) 'pillow, bolster' (22) and one with 床 (*toko*) 'Japanese-style bed' (23) will be considered.

First, let us have a look at the figurative compound 大黒柱 (*daikoku-bashira*), which is a well-known metaphor in Japanese culture and language. When a wooden house was built, a thick pillar was erected in the centre to support the whole building. The compound *daikoku-bashira* describes a person who is a central figure (16). The actual meaning has to be interpreted in the *as if*-modus: 'someone supports something as if they were the central pillar of a house'.

(16) 大黒柱 (*daikoku-bashira*) "the central pillar"
      'the person who sustains a household, company, etc.'

The compound is used in expressions like 家の大黒柱になる (*ie/uchi no daikoku-bashira ni naru*) "to become the central pillar of a house" 'to become the wage earner in the house' or 彼はチームの大黒柱 (*kare wa chīmu no daikokubashira*) "he is the support of the team". The concept of the 'central pillar' or 'heavenly pillar' is connected with cultural features in various ways. The term 大黒 (*Daikoku*) originates from mythology. *Daikoku* is one of the *Shichi-fuku-jin*, the seven gods of luck, a group of seven popular Japanese deities, all of whom are associated with good fortune and happiness. He is said to be the father of 恵比寿 (*Ebisu*), another of the lucky seven, and is supposed to be the god of wealth, a great bearer of good luck and the guardian of farmers. *Ebisu* is usually depicted as a fat, prosperous-looking individual, standing or sitting on two rice bags (cf. Naumann 1981: 135–136). When building a house, special sacrifices were made to this central pillar in the topping-out ceremony. A small domestic altar dedicated to the god *Ebisu* was erected on the top of the pillar.

This 'central pillar' – a well-known metaphor itself up to the present day – is deeply anchored in Japanese mythology. The far-reaching symbolism of the *daikoku-bashira* can be traced back to the Japanese cosmologies dealt with in the "Kojiki" (712), when the god Izanagi and the goddess Izanami stirred the ocean with a spear from the heavens. When the spear was withdrawn, the brine dripping from the tip solidified in the form of an island. Izanagi and Izanami descended to this island, met each other by circling around the celestial pillar and began to procreate. They produced the eight islands which make up Japan (Kojiki I, 4, see Philippi 1969: 398–399). To sum up, there are profound associations between the image components of (16) and aspects of Japanese culture.

Idiom (17) evokes the image of a further constructional element of the traditional Japanese house. Since the living space of this house is a little higher than the ground, the house is entered by stepping up to the *shikii*, a kind of threshold or doorstep. Even today this feature of the HOUSE concept is present in the Japanese expression for 'to enter a room, house or building' which uses the verb 上がる (*agaru*) 'to go up, to climb, to step one step higher'. The equivalent speech formula for English *come in, please* is Japanese お上がり下さい (*oagari kudasai*) "go up [step one step higher], please" (as if there were still a step e.g. from the entrance hall to a room).

(17) 敷居が高い (*shikii ga takai*) "(the) threshold (is) high"
'to have inhibitions about visiting someone, to feel awkward about visiting someone'

Normally the threshold is not high, just the height of a step, and is easy to step up to. The image components of idiom (17), however, evoke the idea of a threshold that seems to be insurmountably high. The actual meaning of the idiom refers to not wanting to visit someone's house because one has failed to perform some social duty or because one is ashamed of something one has done (Sasaki 1993: 221). Hence, the *shikii* 'threshold of a house' appears in the secondary function of 'entering a house'. Although the *shikii* belongs to a different frame of a DWELLING HOUSE than a threshold in Western style houses, a parallelism between this function and the above-mentioned symbolic meanings of THRESHOLD in European languages, cf. (13), is obvious.

In the traditional dwelling house there is a space between the veranda (*en*) and the ground, its original purpose being to avoid dampness in the rooms. The veranda, which leads to the living space of the house, is slightly higher than the surrounding area outside. Thus this veranda is at the same height as the living space, but there is a space between the veranda and the ground.

(18) 縁の下の力持ち (*en no shita no chikara-mochi*) "a strong man under a veranda"
'a person whose work is not recognised, who works inconspicuously in the background and does all the thankless tasks'

The metaphor originating from this feature of the HOUSE concept has to be interpreted as follows: as the space under the veranda is hidden from sight, so is the work of a person who bears continuous hardship for the benefit of others, unnoticed by the outside world. Their work is unappreciated and unrecognised (Sasaki 1993: 46). Furthermore, a house without a veranda and the space below it would collapse.

As has been outlined above, Japanese *shōji* are the sliding outer partition doors and windows made of a wooden latticework frame and covered with thin white paper. When closed, they softly diffuse light throughout the house. In summer, they are often removed completely, opening the house to the outside – a desirable arrangement in Japan because of the extreme humidity.

(19) 壁に耳あり、障子に目あり (*kabe ni mimi ari, shōji ni me ari*) "the walls have ears, the paper sliding screens have eyes"
'a warning to be careful what one says because other people in the house could be listening and watching'

At first glance, expression (19) shows equivalents with idioms such as the English *walls have ears*, also a warning to be careful what one says because one can be overheard or the conversation can be taped. Mainly due to the word *shōji*, however, the image components in (19) are quite different from those of the English idiom. The Japanese expression evokes the image of the thin and lightly constructed wooden walls of a Japanese house with its paper sliding doors and screens which cannot contain a private space such as is found, for example, in rooms that have brick walls. Although the paper of the sliding screens cannot actually be seen through, due to their thinness the screens can be likened to "eyes" with the function of 'seeing', and the walls can be likened to "ears" with the function of 'hearing'. Hence, as far as the image base of the Japanese and the European expressions is concerned, we must emphasise the differences instead of the similarities.

Typical elements of the interior of a Japanese house are the *tatami* – rectangular mats used as a floor covering (see 9.3.1 above). The mats consist of a thick straw base and a soft, finely woven rush cover with cloth borders. To protect the floor and the tatami, shoes are left in the entrance hall before entering. Even today, every home has an area for removing shoes before entering the main home. Tatami are susceptible to wear and tear and must be replaced from time to time. In Japanese compounds the characters usually get the Sino-Japanese reading. Thus, in the compound 半畳 (*hanjō*) 'half a tatami mat' (20) the character 畳 does not have the Japanese reading *tatami* but the Sino-Japanese reading *shō*.

(20) 半畳を入れる (*hanjō wo ireru*) "half *tatami*-mat to put in [to throw in half a *tatami* mat]"
'to interrupt a conversation or discussion with derision'

The idea of 'half a tatami mat' is associated with a senseless unfinished matter and can therefore be used to denote a derisive or disturbing interruption when people are talking (Akiyama and Akiyama 1996: 70). Idiom (20) is less familiar at present than in the past.

Expression (21) is one of the proverbs which are felt to be of discriminatory origin, humiliating women and therefore somewhat rude. There are some resemblances to the English proverb *A new broom sweeps clean*. Here the *tatami*-straw mat appears as a prototypical object of everyday life, used mainly in the literal sense.

(21) 女房と畳は新しいほどよい (*nyōbō to tatami wa atarashii hodo yoi*) "women and tatami are good when new"

Traditional Japanese bedding, still in use in the late 20th century, consisted of quilted padding and coverlets or pallets (called *futons*) with a pillow (*makura*) arranged directly on the floor, which was covered with straw mats. During the day this bedding was stored in a cupboard and the multifunctional room used for other social activities. The image components of conventional figurative units (22–23) show some references to this former Japanese dwelling culture.

(22) 枕を高くして眠る (*makura wo takaku shite nemuru*) "to sleep by making one's pillow higher"
'to sleep peacefully'

(23) 万年床 (*mannen doko*) "ten thousand-year bed"
'a bed not tidied away for a long time; something untidy or in disorder'

The idea of the *makura* has changed completely. In ancient times it was a headrest consisting of a block of wood on which to lay a person's head while sleeping in order to protect their complicated hairstyle. This historical-etymological knowledge of the former headrest does not play a role in processing idiom (22). When the bedding has not been tidied away from the floor for "ten thousand years" the person in question is really very lazy, this creates a situation of great disorder (23).

9.3.3 Conclusions

Most of conventional figurative units (16) through to (23) are still familiar to Japanese native speakers. The image component underlying these expressions, the traditional Japanese dwelling house as it existed throughout the country in the rural areas and small villages and in the bigger towns as well, has lost its significance over time. Nowadays, the house construction has changed considerably. Many contemporary Japanese houses are significantly different from the traditional ones; they now have more modernistic shapes and use more colours, owing largely to the introduction of Western architectural forms and functions. Modern homes usually incorporate a mix of Western and traditional features, such as a formal *tatami*-matted living room alongside the more modern practice of separate bedrooms. The concept of the ancient traditional type of house, however, is present in the Japanese conventional figurative units considered here. In the European languages analysed with regard to the HOUSE as source-frames, this phenomenon is not so obvious.

9.4 The concept HOUSE in a Low German dialect

9.4.1 The "Low German one-room hall-house"

In this section we will look at the Low German dialect WML, located in a small area of the most western region of Germany, near the Netherlands (cf. 1.2.2). In the north-west of Germany another type of house was widespread. It was a half-timbered house constructed with large, tall beams, which used to contain the cowsheds, stables and the whole harvest all under one roof, and in one large room. The German technical term for this type of house is *Niederdeutsches Hallenhaus*, the "Low German hall-house". This term refers to the fact that the occurrence of this type of house is approximately congruent with the north-western regions of Germany where the Low German dialects were spoken. In this ancient hall-house no ceilings, no separate rooms or wallpaper could be found. For that reason, idioms like the English *to hit the ceiling* or Dutch *door het behang gaan* "to go through the wallpaper" (cf. examples 5 to 8), as a conceptualisation of sudden ANGER, would make no sense in the Low German dialects of these regions. However, in the dialects there are many conventional figurative units which can be traced back to the frame of this ancient hall-house.

This dwelling is a thing of the past, when people lived together with the livestock and the harvest in one big hall-house. Throughout the centuries, this type of ancient one-room farmhouse has been rebuilt, as alterations have been made for a more comfortable lifestyle. Over the years, a separation of the living space from the cowsheds, the introduction of central heating, brick walls instead of wattle and daub, and concave tiles instead of thatched roofs have become natural within the centuries-old fabric of this building (cf. Eiynck 1996: 80–82; Schepers 1995: 24–26). There is a conventional figurative unit in WML, used for members of a family who differ in certain respects, and throughout the generations, from other people – be it by a special gift or by a disease:

(24) *dat sitt in de Pöste* "that sits in the posts"

A common disposition shared by members of one family can be ascribed to the fact that they have grown up and live in the same house. Here the concept HOUSE, however, does not manifest itself in the same way as the above quoted concept of an urban building with many rooms or apartments (such as the "Common House of Europe"), but through the large open hall-house without walls and single rooms, which once united family and farmhands in one household. A massive framework of oak beams supports the half-timbered structure of this house type, and it is exactly these "posts" in the interior, on both sides of the long hall, that make up the image. Although living conditions in the rural area of Westmünsterland have since been brought into line with urban culture, there are various elements of the "Low German one-room hall-house" which keep the old HOUSE concept alive in conventional figurative units.

The HOUSE frame can be traced back to noun constituents (e.g. *Pöste* 'posts') which, partly as technical terms, refer to special constructional elements or spatial features of the house. A short description of the old farmhouse with its constructional elements is given below. In addition to the posts of the timber frame construction [*Pöste*, (25–27)], another important element of the wooden house appears as a constituent of CFUs, namely the large, strong peg or dowel [*Pinn*, (28–29)].

The working area, a large hallway or threshing floor [*Dääle*, (30–31)], was located in the front section of the farmhouse. Behind a row of wooden beams, lower than ground level, were the cow stalls on the right and the stables on the left. This working area could be entered through a large double door at the gable end (the front of the house), the entrance gate [*Nenndöre*, (32–34)] of the farmhouse. The threshold [*Drümpel*, (35–36)] appears in several CFUs.

Below the loft for the harvest was another small loft situated under the roof slant, roughly on an eye level with a tall person [*Hilde*, (37–38)]. High above the threshing floor was the loft for the harvest [*Balken*, 39–40)], which was used as a hayloft with wide wooden rafters and as a granary [*Solder*, (41)] with narrow rafters. The hay was loaded in and out through the hatch [*Balkenschlopp*, (42)] above the threshing floor. Furthermore, the ridge tiles [*Fosspannen*, (43)] occur as a constituent of many CFUs.

Without a partition wall on the inside of the hall-house, the main kitchen could be entered from the threshing floor with the stables at the side. The open fireplace at the end of the kitchen formed the centre of the living area. The picture of the open fireplace with the chimney breast [*Boosem*, (44–45)] over the fire up to the ceiling forms the basis of several idioms. Finally, the function of the chimney [*Schosteen*, (46)] will be examined (see Piirainen 2004b for details).

9.4.2 The concept HOUSE in conventional figurative units

In this section, conventional figurative units will be listed, the image components of which evoke the frame of the 'Low German hall-house', or special elements of this old type of farmhouse. The expressions are structured in the sequence of the above-named constituents. Firstly, idioms with the constituent *Pöste* will be considered, as in example (24).

(25) *binnen de Pöste* "between the posts"
'at home, in the privacy of one's own home'

(26) *dat bliff binnen de Pöste* "that stays between the posts"
'this stays between you and me, this will be treated confidentially'

(27) *he löpp an de Pöste* "he runs against the posts"
'he is very stubborn, pig-headed and unreasonable'

Idioms (25–27) evoke the concept of the wide hall-house with its massive oak beams to both sides of the threshing floor. Here, *Pöste* stands metonymically for the whole hall-room. The similarity between (1) *in den eigenen vier Wänden* "within one's own four walls" and (25) is obvious. Both idioms point to the target 'in the privacy of one's home, at home', while using different HOUSE concepts.

Another important element of the half-timbered construction is the large wooden dowel (*Pinn*) pegged into the beams, cf. idiom (28).

(28) *dat Huus wödd van de Pinne trocken* "the house is pulled from the dowels"
'the house is demolished'

If the large dowels were pulled out, the beam construction of the house would no longer have a firm support and would collapse. This source concept can be mapped onto the target concept 'slaughtering a pig' (29).

(29) *dat Farken wödd van de Pinne trocken* "the pig is pulled from the dowels"
'the pig is slaughtered'

This idiom can be understood from the interaction of both knowledge structures – 'demolition of a house' and 'slaughtering a pig'. Within the complete frame 'Low German hall-house' the large dowel is to the fore. A collapsing pig is actually similar to the collapsing beam construction of a house: when the pig collapses, its legs bend because they are no longer able to support the body. Thus slaughtering a pig is viewed as if the pig were a house from which the large dowels have been removed, as if the pig's legs were the posts, which can no longer support the stonework, etc.

The threshing floor (*Dääle*), the room between the stalls, takes up the largest part of the hall-house; it formed the focal point of the farmer's work. If someone says: *Wi häbbt noch up de Dääle te doon* "We still have work to do on the threshing floor" then he/she is talking about looking after the animals (feeding and milking them). The threshing floor is conceptualised as the essential point of all material value – comparable values are ascribed to no other part of the farm, neither to the stables and cowsheds nor to the barn or pasture. Proverb (30) shows the importance of the threshing floor for the farmer to make his living.

(30) *bi ne Buur mott't van de Dääle kommen* "for a farmer it has to come from the threshing floor"
'the farmer makes his living by working on the threshing floor'

Originally, the threshing floor was made of bare clay, stamped down hard enough to enable a loaded harvest wagon to roll over it. This is still alive in simile (31).

(31) *de Grund is so hatt as ne Dääle* "the ground is as hard as a threshing floor"
'the ground is very hard'

The large four-sectioned entrance door at the gable end of the farmhouse is called *Nenndööre*. It could even be parted horizontally so that the upper doors could also be opened when the fully loaded harvest wagon had to enter the threshing area. Bringing in the harvest guaranteed the living of the family for the whole year. This fact is clearly illustrated in a proverb which criticises the extravagance of women (32).

(32) *ne Frou kann met de Schlippe mähr uut de Sieddööre dräägen as de Buur met de Waage de Nenndööre in* "a woman can carry more out in her apron through the side door than the farmer can bring in with his wagon through the entrance door"
'women can be very wasteful'

Idiom (33) is based on the concept of only the two upper sections of the entrance door (*Nenndööre*) being open, with the two lower sections closed at about eye level. This idiom is used as a jocular insinuation when courtship starts for the young heiress of the farm.

(33) *daor kiekt de Jungs all froh öwwer de Nenndööre* "there the boys are looking over the entrance door early"
'when the heiress of a large farm reaches marriageable age'

Idioms (34) and (35) are euphemistic expressions alluding to a person's death. The idioms are ambiguous in the sense that the image components do not immediately enable conclusions to be drawn about the target concept. Some knowledge is required of the old customs surrounding death that were common even up to the first decades of the 20th century. The coffin with the corpse was only allowed to be carried out through the large entrance door (*Nenndööre*) through which the person entered the farm at their wedding. The line of sight is worth noting in (34); the event is described from the viewpoint of the deceased, who "walks" out of the door.

(34) *he geht et leste Maol döör de Nenndööre* "he walks out of the entrance door for the last time"
'he died recently'

The words *et leste Maol* 'the last time' in idiom (34) denote death. The function of the 'entrance door' can only be understood through cultural knowledge of earlier customs. Another important element of this HOUSE frame is the threshold (*Drümpel*). For the motivation of idiom (35), two types of cultural knowledge converge – knowledge of the old customs surrounding death as well as knowledge of the symbol THRESHOLD.

(35) *he kümp nich anders öwwer'n Drümpel as met de Fööte vöörup* "the only way he'll get over the threshold is feet first"
'he'll die soon'

The literal reading of idiom (35) is about carrying out the corpse in a closed coffin after the deceased had been lying in the open coffin for three days (see (42) below). This custom of carrying out the coffin on its final journey to the graveyard was subject to strict rules. The deceased was always carried out feet first through the entrance door. In idiom (35), this procedure is induced by a profiled element, the threshold. Further dimensions, based on the symbolic function of THRESHOLD, emerge on an abstract level. First, on the concrete level, *Drümpel* stands for the threshold of the entrance door, which is connected with the customs surrounding death by the words "feet first". The THRESHOLD also stands for a person coming in and leaving, ending in their death. At the same time, THRESHOLD is a symbol of the transition from this world to the next, from life to death.

The Dutch idiom (13) showed the significance of the threshold. It is an important symbol of the border between the inside and outside, between one's own private sphere and an unknown area. Not to let someone over the threshold means, on a concrete level, not to let them into one's own house, and on an abstract level total rejection (36).

(36) *ik lao em nich öwwer den Drümpel kommen* "I do not let him (come) over the threshold"
'I do not let him into my house; I do not like him, I do not want anything to do with him'

The small loft (*Hilde*) under the roof slant, mostly situated over the cow stalls and open towards the threshing floor, is only 1.70 meters high and much lower than the loft for the harvest (*Balken*). A proverb compares *Hilde* and *Balken*:

(37) *fall van'n Balken un häs kinn Nood, fall van de Hilde un büs dood* "fall from the harvest loft and nothing will happen, fall from the small loft and you will die"
'there are hidden dangers in small things'

A tall person can be called *Hildenkieker* "person who looks into the small loft (*Hilde*)" in the WML dialect. From the ground floor, one could reach this small loft without any effort (38). Somebody says directly that they can dispense with "thanks" expressed verbally, that is why such thanks should simply be put into the small loft.

(38) *den Dank, den legg män in de Hilde* "put the thanks into the small loft"
'thanks for the unpaid help (if somebody only gets a "thank you" instead of being paid for his help)'

Balken is the dialect word for the massive oak beams in the 'Low German hall-house' which form the main element supporting the loft construction. The whole loft for the harvest above the threshing floor is named after this beam, which is also called *Balken*, see (37). The height of this loft forms the basis for the motivation of idiom (39). On the other hand, (40) evokes the whole scenario of bringing in the harvest.

(39) *daor fall ik nich üm van'n Balken* "that is why I do not fall from the loft"
 'that does not upset me, that is only a trifle'

(40) *se häbbt 't Höi up'n Balken* "they have the hay in the loft"
 'they have happily finished something, they have made it'

The huge attic of the main house was principally used as a hayloft. The hay had to be brought in quickly, if possible on the same day it was harvested, because sudden rain could have destroyed the harvest. It was hard work to pitch the hay by the cartload through the hatch into the hayloft. Completion of this very hard work is used as the basis of comparison for 'to get something happily done' (40). The image component (concerted hard work of haymaking) is still effective in so far as idiom (40) shows a restriction to the plural; it cannot be used with reference to one single person but only to a group.

That part of the loft used as a storeroom for the granary is called *Solder* in the dialect. The granary is situated high above the threshing floor, similar to the hayloft but differing in its function. The wooden rafters are narrow in order to prevent the grain from falling through the slats. Townspeople might think that 'hayloft' and 'granary' are virtually the same, but this is not the case for people who speak the dialect and have knowledge of the old farmhouse. They know, for example, that there are mice in the granary but not in the hayloft, so that cats feel quite comfortable up in the granary. Idiom (41) only makes sense because of the constituent *Solder*, which cannot be exchanged for *Balken*.

(41) *lääwen as ne Katte up't Solder* "to live like a cat up in the granary"
 'to live a full life, live in luxury'

The hatch, through which the hay was pitched into the loft, is called *Balkenschlopp*. Idiom (42) as well as (34–35) refer to the previous customs surrounding death.

(42) *he kick et leste Maol döör't Balkenschlopp* "he looks through the hatch for the last time"
 'he died recently'

Three days before the funeral, the deceased was laid in the open coffin below the hatch on the threshing floor. This custom surrounding death is derived from the early Christian idea of the transmigration of souls. The soul can only be released through the open coffin and the open hatch in order to start its transmigration.

Here again, the deceased's line of vision is remarkable – he or she "looks" through the hatch. This also shows strong euphemism.

The ridge tiles on the house form the essential elements of roof construction as they hold the roof together; this produces the image component of idiom (43).

(43) *et geht üm de Fosspannen* "it affects the ridge tiles"
'it is important; it refers to an important decision'

Compared with the English expression *it's all or nothing*, which corresponds to idiom (43) in its actual meaning, the dialect shows a pictorial originality. Another WML idiom with the same actual meaning says *et geht üm Huus un Hoff* "it affects house and yard (the whole property)"; the ridge tiles are therefore equivalent to "house and yard", which emphasises their important function.

The focal point of the living area was the open fireplace, which was used for cooking and heating. In the 18th century, the open fireplace was replaced by the open chimney with a superstructure, which draws and exhausts the smoke. The chimney breast (*Boosem*) was as high as the roof and is therefore used to characterise a particularly tall person (44).

(44) *he is so groot as 'n Boosem hoog* "he is as tall as the chimney breast"
'he is very tall'

Idiom (45) reveals a neighbourhood custom during Shrovetide – the young and unmarried men of the neighbourhood would dress up smartly and go singing from farmhouse to farmhouse to ask for smoked sausages to enjoy together in the following. During this procedure, one man was lifted into the chimney breast to take down the sausages, which had been hung there for smoking. The collected sausages were shared at the meal (Sauermann 1996: 33).

(45) *könn' we nümms in'n Boosem böörn?* "can't we lift anybody into the chimney breast?"
'said when people are looking for a reason to stand around and celebrate'

Since the 18th century, the open smokehouses without any flues have been rebuilt with proper chimneys. The chimney above the cooking area with *dampen* 'to steam, smoke' (46) is regarded as a sign of well-being, the source of food and living.

(46) *he kann Mooders Schosteenken nich mähr sehn dampen* "he cannot see mother's (little) chimney smoking anymore"
'he is abroad, he is far from home'

Idiom (46) is only used with reference to young men (cf. section 10.3.4 for gender-specific usage restrictions revealing cultural models). The idiom shows the diminutive form *Schosteenken*. As it in fact refers to a large and not a small part of the house, the semantic consequences of the diminutive form can be assumed in the actual meaning of the idiom. They indicate a homely atmosphere, closeness, intimacy of the native fireplace, which would not be shown by the non-diminutive form. *Mooders Schosteenken* (48) symbolically stands for the sense of security in childhood and for a homely environment in general. Cf. the English *by one's own fireside* mentioned in 9.2.2.

9.4.3 Summary

Although dwelling culture has changed throughout the centuries, the concept of the old one-room hall-house (the "Low German hall-house") still seems to be present in the consciousness of speakers of WML. More than 60 conventional figurative units of the dialect were found to be based on the image of this ancient type of farmhouse. CFUs of this dialect, although located in Central Europe, reveal a very specific HOUSE concept, which is completely different from the HOUSE concepts emerging in the conventional figurative units of European standard languages. The dialect speakers do not associate HOUSE with the same ideas as Standard German speakers or speakers of other standard languages. Therefore, metaphors composed of elements of the HOUSE concept as their source frame also differ in the two varieties: dialect versus standard languages. This is a cognitive-semantic phenomenon. It is also a cultural phenomenon, as it can be ascribed to cultural differences. The concept of living in individual, separate rooms has no place in the world of the WML dialect, since neither "the four walls" of a room, nor its wallpaper, nor its ceiling are part of the old culture of Westmünsterland.

10 Culture and figurative language

10.1 On the notions of culture

10.1.1 Introduction

The significance of culture for figurative language has already been emphasised in the previous chapters. As has often been pointed out, "culture" seems to be a concept that evades a precise or unified definition (see below), so that it might in fact be simpler not to use the notion of culture at all. This is the case in many works on theoretical semantics, which try to avoid using metalinguistic concepts that are difficult to operationalise. It makes more sense, however, to start with concrete research tasks and then modify the notion of culture according to these tasks. This is useful for describing the conceptual foundations of certain semantic phenomena, because the relevant features of conceptual structures are often grounded in cultural specifics. Another argument in favour of using the notion of culture in linguistic research is that this notion is intuitively valid.

In this section, some of the concepts of culture that have been developed in various scientific paradigms will be discussed. Against this background, we will then work out a specific concept of culture relevant to the issues discussed in this book. One aim here will be to develop a working definition of "culture". This working definition can then provide an instrument with which it is possible to understand and examine figurative language.

Since "culture" is one of the most important analytic concepts (cf. Sebeok 1986a), presenting an exhaustive and adequate "definition" of culture would be beyond the scope of this study. Such a definition would have to include every conceivable code that has ever been created, and it should further emphasise our mental ability to think abstractly, to semiotise things and events, and so on. Such a "full definition" of culture, one that includes all of the heterogeneous aspects of this phenomenon, is not possible in principle (see also footnote 2).

Over the centuries, scholars of various academic disciplines have attempted to either investigate culture as a semiotic whole or describe all possible aspects of culture, in order to answer the question of what is understood by "culture". There have been many attempts to define "culture", but no definition has succeeded in covering this complex phenomenon as a whole. Most efforts to find an appropriate account of culture foundered on the impossibility of integrating all the various aspects in one definition, and therefore it must be approached from a different perspective.

First, we will have a cursory look at the different traditions that work with the concept of culture in linguistics and related fields. Certain human traits are taken as starting points for definitions, for example our *membership in society* (put forward mainly by *cultural anthropologists*) and our *ability to symbolise* (which is favoured, among others, in the works of *semioticians of culture*).

As examples, we will consider the notion of "culture" in both *cultural anthropology* and *semiotics of culture*, insofar as they are related to, or partly integrated into, linguistics. Subsequently we will discuss the notion of "culture" in relation to the recognised literature on *the philosophy of language* and *linguistics*. Against this background, we will present a working definition of culture, which we need in order to analyse figurative units and their underlying cultural phenomena.

10.1.2 Cultural anthropology

The notions of culture fluctuate depending on whether a wider or a narrower view is taken. A *wider concept* of culture is applied, for example, in the field of *cultural anthropology*. This concept mainly extends to social aspects of culture, including all phenomena of social experiences, interactions and behaviour. In this anthropological sense, the term *culture* refers to the wide areas of human behaviour, to a system of common values, attitudes and meanings (e.g. how people eat, drink, speak, celebrate, get married, etc.) insofar as they are determined by membership in a society. Let us have a look at Tylor's (1871) prominent definition of culture:

> Culture or Civilization, taken in its wide ethnographic sense, is that complex whole which includes knowledge, belief, art, morals, law, custom, and any other capabilities and habits acquired by man *as a member of society*. The condition of culture among the various *societies of mankind*, in so far as it is capable of being investigated on general principles, is a subject apt for the study of laws of human thought and action.
>
> (Tylor 1871: 1) [emphasis ours]

This definition was often quoted in the earlier anthropological tradition, for example in Lowie (1934: 3). According to Lowie's definition, culture does not mean "refinement or education, but the whole of social tradition". It includes "capabilities and habits acquired by man as a member of society. Culture includes *all* these capabilities and habits in contrast to those numerous traits acquired otherwise, namely biological heredity". One main aspect of these earlier conceptions of culture preferred by anthropologists was that culture is "an abstraction from behaviour" which is specifically human.[1] This "classic" anthropological conception of culture was criticised and has been modified and developed further over the last decades.[2]

Central to this conception of culture is the idea of "cultural models", which are shared by members of a given community and which make up their entire cultural knowledge. Shore (1996: 208) points to the dynamic structure of cultural models. "From the perspective of objectivist history, human culture might be said to be produced inside-out – from the mind into the world [. . .]. These external models become experiences only to the extent that they can be translated 'outside-in' into mental models – form the social world to the mind." According to Shore, cultural knowledge is distributed through many different kinds of models:

> Though cultural knowledge is, by definition, shared, the nature of this sharing is a complex matter. *Cultural knowledge is best thought of as a distributed system of models.* Cultural models are *socially distributed* in that not all members of a community will share all models or will have the same variant of a model. An adequate description of cultural models necessarily includes an account of which, or whose, perspective is being modelled. A player's model of baseball is not that of a spectator, and viewing a game through a television tube will engage yet another model of the game [. . .]. Cultural models may also be *contextually distributed*, such that different versions of a model represent different functional or rhetorical perspectives. (Shore 1996: 312–313)

The large field of cultural models consists of *non-linguistic cultural models* (e.g. dances, games, customs, etc.) and *linguistic cultural models*; the latter are of particular interest in this study. Linguistic cultural models, as they manifest themselves in figurative language (e.g. in "tropes", proverbs, and other linguistic empirical data), have repeatedly been the subject of studies by cultural anthropologists. Their methods and concepts are partly similar to those developed in the field of linguistics (cf. Quinn 1987, 1991; Holland and Quinn 1987; Geeraerts 2006: 272–306). For the purpose of our study, we would like to highlight the role of social interaction as one of the relevant aspects of culture in figurative language.

---

[1] However, the existence of patterns of behaviour that are transmitted by social rather than biologic heredity has also been established for animals.

[2] For an impression of the diversity of the concepts of culture let us point to another standard work: Kroeber and Kluckhohn (1952) list as many as 164 definitions of culture from popular and academic sources. They identify six principal understandings of culture, ranging from "learned behaviour" to "ideas in the mind", "a logical construct", "a statistical fiction", "a psychic defence mechanism", etc. According to Smith (2001: 3–5), these definitions have remained current until today, although there have been subtle shifts. For a survey of further developments see also Geertz (1973) and Payne (1996).

10.1.3 Semiotics of culture

Other principal characteristics of "culture" come to the fore in the field of *semiotics*, particularly in the so-called *semiotics of culture*. The notions of culture in this field include both a wide concept of culture (just as wide as the ones mentioned above) and a narrower one (cf. e.g. Portis-Winner and Winner 1976; Portis-Winner 1986, 1994). Central to all attempts at defining "culture" from a semiotic viewpoint is humankind's "symbolic activity", our predisposition to create "signs" and give significance to everything around us. Culture is viewed as a system of symbols or meaningful signs. Since the prototypical sign system is natural language, semiotics of culture can be regarded as a heterogeneous complex of research on cultural phenomena, extending from natural language to all other culturally relevant phenomena. Therefore, among the different paradigms of semiotics, it still remains a matter of interpretation what the term *culture* refers to in concrete contexts (cf. the discussions in Koch 1989).

For the aims of our study, one semiotic tradition is of particular interest, namely that of *semiotics of culture in the Moscow-Tartu school*. Since "cultural symbolism" belongs to the topic of figurative language, some ideas worked out by the Moscow-Tartu school can provide elements for the theoretical foundations of our study. In section 11.1 we will refer to the main characteristics of "culture" outlined by semioticians of the Moscow-Tartu school and then discuss those theoretical issues that we have adopted for our purposes (above all the idea of comparability between natural language and other cultural codes).

According to this school, culture is regarded as the totality of all non-inherited information, as a hierarchy of semiotic systems and the set of functions correlated with them. All cultural processes are seen as semiotic processes. Culture is considered to include the entirety of semiotic codes, by means of which particular groups of humans maintain their coherence. All codes are viewed as supplementary superstructures based on natural language, the only means by which cultural codes can be interpreted and stored in the collective memory. This perspective has been explicated by Uspenskij et al. (1973: 1) in their well-known "Theses on the semiotic study of cultures (as applied to Slavic texts)":

> In the study of culture the initial premise is that all human activity concerned with the processing, exchange, and storage of information possesses a certain unity. Individual sign systems, though they presuppose immanently organized structures, function only in unity, supported by one another. None of the sign systems possesses a mechanism, which would enable it to function culturally in isolation. Hence it follows that, together with an approach which permits us to construct a series of relatively autonomous sciences of the semiotic cycle, we shall also admit another approach, according to which all of them examine particular aspects of the *semiotics of culture*, of the study of the functional correlation of different sign systems.

> From this point of view particular importance is attached to questions of the hierarchical structure of the languages of culture, of the distribution of spheres among them, of cases in which these spheres intersect or merely border upon each other.

To summarise, the main aspects of culture in this semiotic tradition can be characterised by the interplay of sign systems, brought into existence by the human ability to symbolise (for more detail, see section 11.1).

In some Western studies, "culture" is viewed as superordinated to "nature", as humankind's transformation of the natural environment (e.g. Koch 1989a; Duranti 1997: 24–26). However, we would like to stress the fact that the notion of culture that includes an opposition of "culture" to "nature" is no more than just one of several possible views characterising culture. There is a long European tradition, going back to an anthropocentric world-view, which defines culture in contrast to nature. Culture is seen as something that humans have developed over and above nature. However, quite different conceptions of culture exist in other cultural areas, for example in East Asia.

In the Western tradition, the concept of "culture" is occasionally brought into relation with the etymology of the word *culture*, which can be traced back to the Latin verb *colere* 'to cultivate (the soil)'. Thus, culture is seen as the result of our *cultivation* of nature. There is nothing that could be compared with the concepts of *bunka* or *fūga* in Japanese, words that are used to roughly translate 'culture' but have a very different origin. Both terms have nothing to do with "cultivating nature": *bunka* originally was understood as 'education in writing and reading characters', as culture of literature, as written culture, whereas *fūga* is etymologically and culturally connected with concepts such as WIND, AIR, NATURE and NATURALNESS (cf. Ōhashi 1999). In Japan, and initially also in China, the character denoting 'wind', 風 (*fū*), was used as an expression for 'culture'. In that view, similarity with nature is the aim of education and culture, so it is the naturalness of the wind that establishes the connection to cultivation and education of the mind.

Researchers in the field of cultural semiotics in Japan have developed quite different notions of culture, in accordance with old Japanese traditions. According to Ikegami (1989a: 20–21), the relationship between culture and nature from this perspective is of another quality compared to the view of Western semioticians. Culture and nature are not to be contrasted but to be harmonised with each other. Both have in common the general laws of development and movement, which are universally effective. Human culture and society is not only a result but also an integral part of the common natural history:

> Contrary to the Western tradition, in which culture is customarily defined as something that stands in contrast to nature, something that 'man' produces by acting on (or *cultivat-*

ing) 'nature', the Japanese tradition leans heavily toward the opposite goal, namely, 'man' being incorporated into 'nature.' In fact, 'to be at one with nature' has been considered an important aspect of the philosophical, religious and artistic ideals.   (Ikegami 1991: 16)

Thus, a Western notion that "culture is everything but nature" will easily meet with counterarguments. For example, before presenting such a notion, the status of "nature" should be clarified. Culture can even be seen as subordinate to nature, both being fixed by a set of semiotic codes (cf. the genetic code, a sign system belonging to "nature"). However, reflections like these are beyond the interest of this study.

10.1.4 Philosophy of language and linguistics

The hypothesis that there is a relationship between language and culture has a long tradition. It was proposed as early as the end of the 18th century by Johann Gottfried von Herder, followed by similar ideas put forward by Wilhelm von Humboldt. In his study of the ancient Kawi language of Java and in further studies, Humboldt (1979) stressed the correlation between language differences and their influence on culture-specific ways of thinking.

This hypothesis was again formulated explicitly in the period before World War II: by German structural semioticians such as Jost Trier, Walter Porzig and Leo Weisgerber, on the one hand, and by the anthropological linguist Edward Sapir and his student Lee Benjamin Whorf on the other hand.

Similar to Humboldt's ideas, Trier (1931), Porzig (1950) and Weisgerber (1929, 1961, 1962) pointed out that many of the structural differences of the lexicon of different languages can be accounted for in terms of cultural differences. The lexical field of colour terms served as a prime example to illustrate that different languages impose different structures upon the world (i.e. in this case upon the continuum of colour). Weisgerber, who greatly contributed to coining the terms *Weltbild* and *sprachliche Zwischenwelt* (the world of ideas standing between the real world and language) is seen as the main supporter of the theory of "linguistic relativity" in Germany.

Edward Sapir's and Benjamin Whorf's studies of indigenous North American Indian languages led them to ideas about the relation between language and culture (cf. e.g. Sapir 1949, 1964; Whorf 1956) that were similar to those of Humboldt (or Porzig, Weisgerber and Trier). Sapir and Whorf developed the concept of an equation of culture and language, which became known as the "Sapir-Whorf hypothesis". Their hypothesis of "linguistic relativity" even extends to the assumption that the world is principally perceived through the medium of language. For them, the relation between language and cognition implies that the particular language that a person learns and speaks determines his or her world-view and ways of thinking (cf. Koerner 1984; Irvine 1994).

Although in the course of the last decades some of Sapir's and Whorf's postulates have been questioned (e.g. the non-existence of the concept of dimensional time in the Hopi language, cf. Malotki 1983), the idea of a crucial role of language in the conceptualisation of the world still has a considerable impact on the development of the philosophy of language, as well as on certain approaches in linguistics and cognitive sciences (see also Ikegami 1985).

Even though few linguists today would fully agree with a strict reading of the Sapir-Whorf hypothesis (or of concepts like "Weltbild" and "sprachliche Zwischenwelt" in the Weisgerberian philosophy of language), it is now generally accepted that a language influences its speakers' cultural patterns of thought. Sociolinguistics and language learning theory have created an awareness of the fact that language and culture are closely related.

Recent works in semantics, contrastive linguistics and related fields repeatedly come to the conclusion that language, especially the lexicon, is dependent on the culture of the speech community in question. Several linguists assume that almost everything fixed in the lexicon is "culture" in the widest sense. Extreme supporters of the idea that lexical units are idiosyncratic even claim that the meaning of natural kind words like *mice* or *horses* embodies a great deal of cultural knowledge (Haiman 1982). In principle, such an approach can be accepted because if a wide concept of culture is favoured, then the lexicon as a whole must be regarded as a cultural artefact. The lexicon (and even a language as a whole) is a product of (unconscious) human activity. From this perspective, every language (and especially its lexicon, which leads to the corresponding model of the world more directly than grammar) belongs to a given cultural community. Therefore, the lexical unit can be considered culture-specific. The question is how linguistic research can benefit from this conclusion.

Givón (1995: 18) emphasises within another theoretical context, i.e. the functionalist approach in linguistics, the fundamental idiosyncrasy of the lexicon: "Finally, we know that the lexicon represents the bulk of culture-specific cross-linguistic diversity. The diversity represented in the lexicon is that of world-view, i.e. a group's perspective on its relatively-stable conceptual universe".

Givón speaks of "culture-specific cross-linguistic diversity" in the sense of a uniqueness of the historically originated techniques of naming and structuring the world, not in the sense of handing down traditional values and attitudes (as is often the case in traditional research on figurative units). In this view, often to be encountered in works on Functionalist and Cognitive Linguistics, the idea is emphasised that there is a uniqueness of the model of the world that is fixed in a given language, and first of all in the lexicon.

Every language reflects and structures reality in its own way, and, therefore, creates its own world-view. Although there is support for this idea (which is crucial for every serious attempt at analysing lexical semantics), there is no reason to call these specifics "culture". It is not incorrect to use the term "culture" here if the notion of culture is broadly defined, but it makes this term almost semantically empty. The word *cultural* becomes a quasi-synonym for *conceptual*. In describing such phenomena as the uniqueness of the semantic structure of most lexical units, it is possibly more appropriate to speak of "conceptual" and not "cultural" specifics, leaving the term *cultural* for cases where specifics of this kind have to be traced back to other semiotic codes (see Dobrovol'skij 1997, 1998 for details).

It has been noted in relation to the science and praxis of translation that because of culture-specifics certain words have no full equivalents in another language. Numerous semantic researchers have also observed this feature of the lexicon and pointed to the untranslatability or unrenderability of many lexical units. A well-known example is Jakobson's (1959: 233) observation that even such a simple word as English *cheese* cannot be completely identified with the standard Russian word *сыр*, because *cottage cheese* is regarded (and named) in Russian not as a kind of cheese, but as a separate dairy product.

Certain explanations for this phenomenon can be put forward. First of all, through an increase of knowledge in semantic analysis, more items of the lexicon have turned out to be language-specific. Wierzbicka (1992, 1996, 1997, 1999) persistently points to the fact that many lexical units are cultural artefacts with a historical origin and are therefore not easily translatable. Although the elaboration of the vocabulary is undoubtedly a key indicator of the specific features of cultures, it is of course not the only one. In terms of her "Natural Semantic Metalanguage" (NSM), Wierzbicka regards all semantic units as "culture-specific", except for the hypothesised semantic primitives (the semantically indivisible *primes*). Wierzbicka states that the meanings of most words differ from language to language because they are cultural artefacts, reflecting aspects of the cultures in which they were created. According to Wierzbicka, the underlying concepts of, for example, German *Käse* and English *cheese*, or English *horse* and German *Pferd*, are not identical, because the cultural environments of the given speech communities are not the same. More obviously, the concept underlying a word like German *Seele* is not identical with the concept underlying the words English *soul* or Russian *душа*, etc. Let us look in more detail at some examples presented in (Wierzbicka 1996: 15).

> [. . .] I fully accept the Humboldtian view that despite the presence of universals, on the whole semantic systems embodied in different languages are unique and culture-specific; and second, that the presence of "embodied" (that is, lexicalized) universals does not mean perfect equivalence in language use. Both these points require some elaboration.

> As all translators know to their cost, every language has words which have no semantic equivalents in other languages, and every language draws semantic distinctions which other languages do not. For example, translating the classic texts of the Hindu cultural tradition into European languages one must face the fact that these languages do not have words coming even near in meaning to key Sanskrit terms such as *nirvana, brahman, atman,* or *karma* [...]. But even comparing languages which are genetically, geographically, and culturally very close, for example French and English, one constantly encounters examples of profound lexical differences. For example, the French word *malheur* has no counterpart in English [...]. In a sense, most words in all languages are like the French *malheur*, that is unrenderable (without distortion) in some other languages.

To a certain extent, this interpretation of lexical phenomena as culture-specific entities is similar to the above-mentioned ideas by Jakobson, Haiman or Givón (all of which go back to the Humboldtian philosophy of language and all of which are based on deep insights into the nature of the lexicon and on serious empirical studies). From the perspective of the importance of language specific principles of lexicon organisation, it is extremely important to regard every lexical unit as a unique configuration of semantic features. The aim of semantic analysis in the lexical field is to uncover fine-grained differences both between near-synonymous lexical units within the same language and between cross-linguistic near-equivalents. On the other hand, there are profound differences between concepts like NIRVANA or KARMA, concepts like MALHEUR, and concepts like HORSE. So qualifying all of them as cultural artefacts is not wrong in itself but creates the illusion of a fundamental homogeneity where in reality we are dealing with, at least, three different linguistic and conceptual categories, which should not be confused.

(i) Words like *nirvana, karma* etc. represent unique concepts. These concepts are products of a concrete culture; they can be understood and described only against the background of the knowledge of all the paradigms of this culture. Thus, these concepts are culturally bound. Their fundamental specifics do not lie in certain features of the language in question but represent a cultural paradigm.

(ii) Pairs of words like French *malheur* and English *mishap* are of a different nature. They do not differ against a cultural background, but show linguistic differences. Different languages generate different bundles of semantic components. The French word *malheur* differs from English *mishap* or German *Missgeschick* (if at all) by some peripheral semantic features. It can hardly be assumed that *malheur* is a salient concept of French culture (as *karma* is for Indian culture). Cross-linguistic meaning differences of this kind are a matter of lexical semantics, not of culture (at least, not of "culture" in a narrower, linguistically relevant sense).

(iii) Words like English *horse* and German *Pferd* are equivalent in every sense of the term "semantic equivalence" (i.e. no matter how one interprets the concept of semantic equivalence). They differ only, like many lexical units, in their associative aura. They probably evoke different associations for native speakers of different languages, but this does not mean that they reveal semantic differences. In order to prove that words such as *horse* and *mouse* are culturally bound and have no equivalents in other languages, one would have to prove that there are linguistically relevant differences between these words in different languages. Normally, this cannot be achieved. Only in certain cases are these vague, associative features relevant to language use. The only domain where the assumption about conceptual and linguistic specifics of words denoting natural kinds or artefacts seems to be reasonable is the field of figurative language (except for artefacts bound to a given cultural tradition, like, for example, the concept HOUSE in different cultures; see chapter 9). If words such as *horse* and *mouse* are used in their secondary, semantically reinterpreted meanings (e.g. in metaphors, idioms), they may reveal some culture-specific features.

Specific features of this kind, which appear in figurative use, can often be traced back to linguistically relevant connotations that these words have in their literal meaning. If there is something culturally based about these connotations, it is reasonable to speak about their cultural relevance.

Similar ideas have been expressed by Apresjan (1995). Words that form part of metaphorical expressions of different kinds, in folklore, popular beliefs, puns, etc., preserve the traces of the most salient additional senses that they take on in their figurative meanings. Apresjan calls them *cultural connotations* and illustrates this observation with the help of the Russian words *тёща* 'mother-in-law' and *тесть* 'father-in-law': only *тёща* is culturally connoted, since it appears repeatedly in puns, sayings, jokes etc., as a negatively connoted stereotype, whereas *тесть* is not. Here, we are dealing with "culture" in the sense that the additional meaning components are (at least partly) based on features outside of language, e.g. on social factors; that is, they do not originate exclusively from language. This phenomenon is very different from culturally bound concepts like *karma* or semantically specific lexemes like *malheur*. Thus, we are dealing here neither with culturally salient conceptual entities nor with problems of lexical semantics, but with purely pragmatic phenomena, i.e. with *cultural connotations*.

To sum up, if associative specifics of a given lexical unit are intersubjectively relevant, they acquire the status of pragmatically significant components of the content plane. If they prove to be culturally based as well, they have to be categorised as cultural connotations (see 10.9 for details). We would like to stress the following points:

Many words, taken in isolation, are language-specific in the sense that they are not translatable into other languages without distortion. On the other hand, all people have, in principle, the same ability to think and to conceptualise reality. The differences found in the lexicon are often due to the specifics of a given lexical system or to the specifics of pragmatic conventions. Both the structure of lexical systems and the conventional pragmatic implications are more or less unique and can be considered to be cultural artefacts. However, naming them "culture" does not help to improve the linguistic analysis. This phenomenon (even if we call it "cultural artefact") has to be distinguished from those cases in which a given word reflects a certain cultural "key concept". A comparison between words like *cheese* on the one hand and cultural symbols (e.g. words like *seven, rose, bread*; see chapter 11) on the other hand is significant here. For the purposes of our study, only the latter are relevant. This points to the necessity to define the notion of culture according to our specific task.

10.1.5 "Culture" in the field of figurative language: A working definition

The aim of this study is to investigate the nature of conventional figurative language. The relevance of culture for analysing CFUs has been stressed in the last chapters. It has been shown that our approach to conventional figurative language requires an orientation towards culturally relevant knowledge structures. From the discussion of the Cognitive Theory of Metaphor (chapter 6) it became clear that motivation phenomena in the realm of CFL cannot be exhaustively explained on the basis of near-universal conceptual correspondences.

When investigating conventional figurative language, a notion of culture is necessary for various reasons. One of the main goals is to explain motivation phenomena, i.e. to reveal the relevant links between the primary and the secondary readings of conventional figurative units. Other tasks include the description of specific image properties in CFUs of a given language in comparison to other languages, i.e. cross-linguistic and cross-cultural research. In order to achieve results in the fields of motivation and contrastive analysis that are both psychologically realistic and linguistically valuable, we need to address the native speakers' tacit knowledge of relevant facts of their culture.

A broad notion of culture (something like "everything that is not nature is culture") is not helpful for linguistics. In this notion, language as a whole is a part of culture. An overgeneralised concept of culture is of no use for the theoretical foundation of our study. An approach to language based on such a concept would be meaningless. If everything we examined were "culture", we would not need any concept of "culture" at all, since the entire lexicon would be "culture", and all conventional figurative units would be culture-based by definition. Furthermore, this notion of culture is identical with the notion of a model of the world, so that one of the two would be superfluous.

Our concept of culture focuses on the cognitive nature of culture and on collective conceptions as they are fixed in language. Crucial for the aims of this study are the various parts of cultural knowledge that stand behind figurative units. The focus will be restricted to those aspects of culture that are linguistically relevant. In this study, we advocate the following notion of culture:

> Culture is the sum of all ideas about the world (including fictional, mythological etc. ideas) that are characteristic of a given community.[3]

For the aims of our study, only those features of culture are essential that contribute to the uncovering of the nature of conventional figurative language. Therefore, we approach the notion of culture from different directions. Several aspects of cultural knowledge that underlie figurative language will be discussed in the following sections. Those aspects are, above all: (i) social aspects of culture, (ii) aspects of the material culture, (iii) textual dependence, (iv) fictive conceptual domains, and (v) cultural symbols.[4] Different to (i–v) are the cultural connotations, i.e. additional, associative features of a concept that is embedded in the culture in question. In all the cases that we describe here, addressing the notion of culture is necessary for an adequate modelling of how conventional figurative units are generated and how they are cognitively processed.

10.2 Cultural phenomena in conventional figurative units

In the following sections we attempt to create a classification of the principal cultural phenomena that occur in CFUs. Starting from the linguistic basis of this study, i.e. conventional figurative language, we would like to discuss in more

---

[3] Compare a definition of culture proposed in (Teliya et al. 1998: 57): "By culture, we understand the ability of members of a speech community to orientate themselves with respect to social, moral, political, and so on values in their empirical and mental experience. Cultural categories (such as Time and Space, Good and Evil, etc.) are conceptualized in the subconscious knowledge of standards, stereotypes, mythologies, rituals, general habits, and other cultural patterns."

[4] If we start exclusively from CFL, structures of cultural phenomena emerge that are similar (though not identical) to those established by semioticians. While attempts to define the notion of "culture" repeatedly resulted in a triad such as social, material and mental culture (cf. e.g. Posner 1991: 42–44), the category "mental culture" seems unsuitable for describing linguistic phenomena because language as a whole is a mental phenomenon.

detail the role of culture, or more technically the role of culture-specific features, in CFL. We have examined large portions of conventional figurative language (idioms, proverbs, figurative compounds, etc. drawn from various languages) in order to see what types of cultural knowledge[5] are involved in establishing motivated links between literal and figurative meanings. Obviously, only motivated figurative units can be considered here. Within our rich cross-linguistic empirical data, five main types of cultural phenomena have been found to underlie figurative language. It is, however, often difficult to draw sharp lines between these types, as they tend to overlap and be interrelated.[6]

The five types of culture-based knowledge that we consider crucial for describing figurative language will be discussed in the following sections.

(i) The first type is represented by conventional figurative units whose underlying cultural knowledge can mainly be traced back to knowledge of culture-based *social interaction* within a given community, including all aspects of social experiences and behaviour (10.3).

(ii) Conventional figurative units of the second type reveal image components that can be ascribed to *material culture*, primarily to artefacts of a given culture, including all aspects of material environment (10.4).

(iii) Conventional figurative units of the third type can be subsumed under the label *textual dependence*. Originally, they are quotations or allusions. Thus, they are related to certain texts that can be identified as their sources. (10.5). This type is similar to the next two types, although they should not be confused.

(iv) Type four is represented by conventional figurative units traced back to *fictive conceptual domains*, such as ancient folk theories and pre-scientific conceptions of the world. Here, the underlying image components come from "non-material conceptions" of the world (including religion, superstition, ancient beliefs etc.) (10.6).

(v) Type five deals with *cultural symbols* (10.7). In CFUs of this type, the relevant cultural knowledge extends to mainly one single constituent and not to

---

[5] We do not want to go into the question whether this is an active knowledge (shared by almost all speakers of the given speech communities) or rather a tacit knowledge. The individual knowledge of special cultural contexts varies individually, depending on biographical data such as experiences, education, interests etc.

[6] The progress of research on cultural phenomena within phraseology varies from language to language. Apart from some studies on smaller sub-areas on cultural specifics of individual phrasemes, there exist only a few comprehensive reference books, such as the historical and cultural work on German phraseology by Röhrich (1991) or the etymological dictionary on Russian phraseology by Birix, Mokienko, and Stepanova (2005).

the figurative unit as a whole. The motivational link between the literal and figurative readings is established by semiotic knowledge about the symbol in question, about its meaning in culturally relevant sign systems other than language. In order to describe figurative units of this type we apply metalinguistic tools developed in the framework of cultural semiotics (see chapter 11 for more details).

There are various connections between these five types of culture-based CFUs. There is certainly some connection between types (iii) and (iv), since CFUs originating from works of literature, for example, may contain symbols. Similarly, type (i), "social interaction", correlates with type (ii), "aspects of material cultural", and so on. Some overlaps of the five types will be considered in section 10.8. There is still another group of CFUs which is different from the former. It consists of expressions that native speakers realise as, or feel to belong to, specifics of their traditional culture. CFUs of this kind contain, for example, proper nouns and idioethnic realia. These expressions stand out for their *cultural connotations* (10.9).

The following dichotomy is important for describing culture in conventional figurative language. We have to distinguish between the terms (a) *culture-based* and (b) *culture-specific*.
(a) The term *culture-based* denotes a very general quality, including culture in a wide sense. Most figurative units belong to this type. Exceptions are figurative units that can be understood without any cultural knowledge, where the motivation is based merely on biological facts or on the outward appearance of something.
(b) The second term, *culture-specific*, presupposes a cross-linguistic perspective. A figurative unit can be regarded as culture-specific only in contrast to another language or to several other languages.

In the following sections we will refer back to the dichotomy between the notions *culture-based* and *culture-specific* in more detail.

10.3 Social interaction

10.3.1 "Cultural models"

In this section we will look at CFUs whose cultural components can mainly be ascribed to the conceptions of patterns of behaviour and social interaction. This means that a certain shared knowledge of culture-based and/or culture-specific phenomena in society is involved in the processing of these expressions. So-called *cultural models* (in anthropology formerly also called *social models*) are central here, as they can be uncovered on the basis of CFUs.

As far as cultural models are concerned, the cultural knowledge does not extend to the source concept but only to the target concept. Many *proverbs* belong to this category of culturally determined CFUs. It is in the nature of proverbs that they express general ideas, among them generally applicable rules governing (and utterances commenting on) social behaviour. Proverbs are therefore a part of social life. They are considered to represent "folk wisdom" or well-known truths in the sense of cultural models (see section 2.3.4).

Let us look at an example where the idea of the proverb is clearly based on conceptions of social interactions (of former times), i.e. on a (former) mode of thinking in a given society:

(1) German *Lange Haare, kurzer Verstand* "Long hair, short mind"
 'used by men to say that women are simple-minded and have less faculty of reason'

According to Paczolay (1997: 413–415) this proverb type is wide-spread in European and Oriental languages, for example Dutch *lange haren, kort verstand*, French *longs cheveux, courte cervelle* "long hair, short brain", English *women have long hair and short brains*, Slovakian *dlhé vlasy, krátky rozum* "long hairs, short reason", Russian *волос длинный – ум короткий* "long hair – short mind",[7] and the like. In present times, proverbs like (1) are presumably used in a joking or ironic, (self-)mocking way, although in past centuries they were understood and passed on as comments about social conditions.

"Long hair" itself is not necesserily a matter of culture. The choice of a certain hairstyle may in some cases be ascribed to semiotic reasons (for example, it may be a sign that indicates the membership of a particular group), or it may be ascribed to ornamental or practical reasons; all these reasons can be disregarded here. Rather, in proverbs like (1), "long hair" refers to the concept WOMAN, because former conventions in European societies forced women to wear long hairstyles, and this custom has left traces in the images fixed in these proverbs. Moreover, proverbs like (1) contain a play on words. In this context the adjectives *long* and *short* (or their German, French and Russian equivalents) are not used as

---

[7] According to Teliya et al. (1998: 63), such expressions "illustrate the general idea of how the cultural concept of gender is encoded in Russian". The spreading of proverbs like (1) over many languages, however, shows that such cultural concepts are not restricted to the culture of Russia.

antonyms in the strict sense. Only *long* refers to spatial extension; *short*, however, refers to something like 'small, weak'. The cultural background of proverb (1) is the idea that women have to accept subordinate positions in society because of their alleged intellectual deficiency. Thus, traces of patriarchal social concepts are handed down via certain CFUs. More examples of this kind are given in Petrova (2002) and Kochman-Haładyj (2020).

Although proverbs are the prototypical group of CFUs, often revealing cultural models as described in (1), CFUs referring to social concepts are by no means restricted to proverbs but also include many idioms and restricted collocations. Let us consider the well-known conceptual metaphor SUCCESSFUL IS UP, which produces several idioms like (2–5).

(2) *to climb (up) the ladder*
'to become more important and successful in one's work by being promoted'

(3) *the highest rung of a ladder* or *the top of the ladder*
'the highest level or position in a system or organisation, especially a very important job; the summit of one's career of profession'

(4) *to kick someone upstairs*
'to remove someone from an influential position in a business by giving them an ostensible promotion; to give someone a job at a higher level but with less power than before, usually because they are not effective any more'

(5) Japanese (outdated) 鯉の滝登り (*koi no takinobori*)
"a carp's climb up a waterfall / carp's waterfall climbing"
'a quick rise to the top (of one's profession or field); getting ahead succeeding vigorously in life'

The metaphor SUCCESSFUL IS UP seems to have experiential foundations. Especially in cases in which professional or political success is meant, an image of a ladder (2–3), a staircase (4) or a multi-storey building (cf. German *in die höhere Etage kommen* "to come to the higher floor" 'to get a higher position', Russian *высшие этажи власти* "(the) highest floors of power" 'the most important groups in the political hierarchy') seems to be responsible for the metaphoric mapping.

Idioms like (2–4) can be found in many other European languages, but also in genetically unrelated, non-European languages, as example (5) shows. Such expressions can occur only in cultures with particular social hierarchies and concepts of values, where SUCCESS correlates with occupational positions and where certain jobs are better paid and enjoy a higher reputation than others, so that the target concept SUCCESS can be expressed in spatial relation terms like UP and DOWN.

We would like to emphasise that the connection between idioms (2–5) and aspects of culture, i.e. of social conditions of modern society, is of more concern to the actual meanings than to the figurative background, cf. the paraphrases 'the highest level or position in a system or organisation', 'to give someone a job at a higher level but with less power than before', or 'a quick rise to the top (of one's profession or field)' and the very different figurative background (LADDERS and STAIRS in the English expressions (2–4) as well as the culturally loaded concept CARP in the Japanese expression (5)[8]). The source concept UP-DOWN, however, seems to be a very general and culturally unspecific idea. The superordinate level of the conceptual metaphor is very abstract and allows us to uncover nontrivial common features of such different expressions as (2–4) and (5). On the other hand, the specific features of the underlying mental images can be revealed at the basic level only. Features of this kind are linguistically and culturally more important than the conceptual metaphors, because the subtle cross-linguistic differences are crucial for the precise description of concrete CFUs. In view of the dichotomy between "culture-specific" and "culture-based" (cf. 10.2), the "specifics of culture" will emerge only in comparison with languages of other cultural areas, remote from contemporary industrialised societies.[9]

Similar implementations of social aspects of culture are at work in the so-called metaphoric model TIME IS MONEY.[10] In modern industrialised cultures, TIME is conceptualised as a limited resource. This limited resource is comparable, at least to a small extent, with money, which may also be 'limited'. However, limited resources may also comprise, for instance, foodstuffs, water, raw materials, etc. So we can say in English *to waste time, to save time, to spend time* etc. (just as one can waste, save, or spend materials, water, or money, etc.) in order to talk about different aspects of TIME.

---

8 The Japanese idiom is an allusion to a Chinese legend, according to which the carp alone among all fishes was able to swim up a waterfall on the upper reaches of the Yellow River (Garrison et al. 2002: 345). CARP (Japanese *koi*) is a symbol of strength, courage and patience. According to the Chinese legend, a carp that courageously climbed up waterfalls was turned into a dragon.
9 The same is true for some traces of the material culture that emerge at the basic level of images which are very common (artefacts like ladders or stairs), but this is of no interest in this context.
10 There is no reason, why this metaphoric model involves the concept TIME IS MONEY rather than more general concepts, like TIME IS A LIMITED RESOURCE or TIME IS A VALUABLE COMMODITY. *Time is precious* is an old, widespread proverb; Japanese 時は金なり (*Toki wa kane nari*) "Time becomes money" as a translation of *Time is money* came into use in Japan by the end of the 19th century. "Remember that Time is Money" is a quotation from Benjamin Franklin (Paczolay 1997: 429).

Similar collocations can be found e.g. in German: *die Zeit nutzen* "to utilise the time", *jmdm. Zeit schenken* "to give time to someone (as a present)" or *jmdm. die Zeit stehlen* "to steal the time from someone", in Russian: *тратить время* "to spend time", *экономить время* "to save time", *разбазаривать/транжирить время* or *тратить время впустую* "to waste time".

They exist, however, also in other languages of industrialised, business-oriented communities. There is a Japanese expression that is completely parallel to the English *to waste time*, 時間を浪費する (*jikan wo rōhi suru*) "to waste (the) time".

Nevertheless, it is not difficult to imagine other pre-industrialised cultures (societies that have remained outside the technological development of the "modern West"), where similar conceptualisations of TIME do not exist. Compare in this respect the Saami languages. Therefore, the role of culture in these expressions is primarily based on the conditions of a given society and manifests itself mainly on the level of the target concepts.

To summarise, the cultural components that underlie the target concepts of CFUs like (1–5) can, to a large extent, be equated with conditions of society. In these cases, a social concept of culture is addressed, including all aspects of social behaviour, experiences and circumstances (as opposed to, for example, biological conditions).

Here we would also like to point to metaphors of emotions in culturally distant languages. Target concepts that may seem identical at first glance may turn out to be considerably different, as can be illustrated, for example, by the concept of ANGER in Euro-American and Japanese culture and society. It is virtually impossible to compare English idioms referring to ANGER with corresponding expressions from Japanese (cf. 6.2.3). Similarly, let us reconsider what we said about the metaphors for marriage unearthed by anthropological research (6.2.4). As has been shown, the target concept MARRIAGE is always created by the culture and the society, and, accordingly, all CFUs referring to this concept are culturally based (in the sense of being social aspects of the cultural concept).

10.3.2 Social conventions, taboos and bans

The conventions of a given society can influence figurative units in many different ways. This includes the area of figurative circumlocutions, euphemisms and allusions used to avoid talking about something directly. There are various situations where saying a word openly is felt to offend common decency or violate behavioural norms. Compare conventionalised figurative utterances like *he is under the influence* for *he is drunk*, or *he has gone to a better place* for *he died*. The cultural foundation of these cases lies in the need of the speech community to avoid direct naming and employ strategies of glossing over instead.

In extreme cases there is not even a direct one-word expression available for denoting a given matter on which a ban on speaking has been placed. As an example, let us look at social conventions in the quite conservative community of speakers of the Low German dialect WML (see 1.2.2). According to one particular convention, 'pregnancy' is a topic that one must not talk about.[11] Consequently, there is no word with the denotation 'pregnant' in this dialect, although there are more than 30 idioms meaning something like 'to be pregnant, to expect a child'. Thus, particular cultural conventions can be said to cause an elaboration of a semantic field through the coinage of numerous CFUs. Here is a selection of some more or less euphemistic WML idioms (6–10):

(6) WML *se häff 't Gatt in de Netteln satt* "she has put the bottom into the stinging nettles"

(7) WML *se is met de Nösse an'n Näägel loopen* "she has run with the nose against the nail"

(8) WML *se häff 'n Kloss an't Been* "she has a block (of wood)/a log on the leg"

(9) WML *se häff 'n dick Knee* "she has a thick knee"

(10) WML *se häff all een under de Schlippe* "she has already one under the pinafore"

If WML speakers nonetheless want to talk about this subject (e.g. about a woman expecting a child), they have indirect ways of speaking at their disposal, and they can make use of the option to switch to one of the prefabricated figurative units. Many of these idioms are ambiguous in the sense that the word string of the literal reading does not immediately allow conclusions about the target concept. The literal readings of idioms like (6–10) refer to domains quite different from 'pregnancy' [the painful bodily experiences caused by stinging nettles or a nail (6–7), to a disability which makes walking difficult (8), to the shape of a part of the body (9), or a particular garment (10)], although they also allow some vague associations with 'pregnancy'. This indirectness of speaking can be chosen to

---

11 There are deeper cultural messages involved in such euphemisms used as an avoidance strategy, making use of vagueness and underspecification. According to a taboo within the larger taboo area associated with sexual intercourse, it was not acceptable to talk about 'pregnancy'. Knowledge of this area of language is therefore not merely linguistic but rather cultural.

avoid a violation of conventional rules or social norms. It is true, though, that this phenomenon manifests itself mainly in rather informal dialogue situations.

Obviously, the wide idiomatic extension of the semantic field 'pregnancy' in the WML dialect is embedded in a set of social conventions. Moreover, other conceptual target domains are also affected by this phenomenon. Further domains that trigger a need for circumlocution and therefore tend to produce euphemistic figurative units include 'drunkenness and alcoholism', 'mental illness', 'stupidity' and 'poverty', to name but a few (Piirainen 2000, 1: 360–362). To some extent, this phenomenon can also be observed with similar target concepts in standard or literary languages.

10.3.3 Gestures

Gestures are another form of social interaction, namely nonverbal utterances understood by members of a given community as signals or signs. Looking for further domains of conventional figurative language where aspects of social culture are apparent, we should pay attention to this complex of gestures. Several CFUs point to certain gestures on the level of their literal readings, cf. idiom (11), spread across 60 languages.

(11) *to roll up one's sleeves*
 'to be ready and willing to set about hard work; to prepare oneself for a difficult task or to fight someone'

The interpretation of idiom (11) is not based on the concrete imagery of "rolling up one's sleeves". Processing this idiom requires the knowledge that the gesture serves as a sign that stands for something else[12] – in this case, for 'announcing one's intention to set about hard work or to prepare oneself for a difficult task'. It does not matter whether the actual gesture (nonverbal behaviour) is still performed.

Equivalents of idiom (11) exist in other European languages as well, almost identical in respect to both their image components and actual meanings, for example German *die Ärmel hochkrempeln*, Dutch *de mouwen opstropen*, Swedish *kavla upp ärmarna*, French *retrousser ses manches*, Russian *засучить рукава*[13]

---

[12] Burger (1976) coined the term "Kinegramm" for gestures encoded in the lexical structure of idioms.
[13] Some Russian etymological sources point to the fact that the sleeves of garments typical of ancient times were very long, often down to the knees, meaning that it was not possible to do something without rolling up one's sleeves.

or Finnish *kääriä hihat ylös*. So the gesture of "rolling up one's sleeves" is culture-specific only from the viewpoint of very distant cultures.

A different gesture is familiar in Japan, where over centuries the kimono used to be the common garment. The Japanese idiom (12), seemingly similar to the English idiom (11), shows the semiotisation of a specific gesture originally performed by a Japanese man.

(12) Japanese 一脱肌ぐ (*hitohada nugu*) "to take off one skin/a layer of skin [to undress completely]"
'to help somebody, to offer help to someone who is in difficulties'

The kimono is an ankle-length gown with long, expansive sleeves, which get in the way of hard physical work. A man's gesture of taking off his kimono to uncover the whole upper part of his body can be regarded as a sign of both readiness to do hard physical work and willingness to help another person. Originally this was a lexical element of male language. This restriction to male language was due to the image component: women do not perform the gesture of taking off their kimonos. In present days the idiom is also used by younger females, as girls have been adopting aspects of the male rough speech style and are intentionally violating certain conventions.

In Japanese conventional figurative language, kimonos, or, to be more precise, the sleeves as the most salient parts of this garment, are involved in some other gestures: hiding one's hands in the sleeves can be understood as a sign that one does not want to get into contact with another person (13). Grasping another person's sleeve must be interpreted as begging for mercy (14).

(13) Japanese 袖にする (*sode ni suru*) "to put (hands) in (kimono) sleeves"
'to rebuff someone'

(14) Japanese 袖にすがる (*sode ni sugaru*) "to cling to someone's (kimono) sleeve"
'to appeal to someone for mercy'

As has already been pointed out, there is no need to picture the gestures underlying CFUs like (11–14). Rather, semiotic knowledge about the gestures is required to interpret these idioms. In traditional culture, gestures of this kind served as signs, regardless of whether such gestures are still performed or whether they can be traced back to traditional forms of behaviour in bygone times. However, various CFUs have handed down gestures that were traditionally executed in the past, although their semiotic meaning has been lost in the course of history, cf. (15).

(15) *to tear one's hair out*
'to be unbearably frustrated or worried about something; to show extreme desperation'

Idiom (15) has equivalents in a large number of European languages (e.g. German *sich die Haare raufen*, French *s'arracher les cheveux* "to tear one's hairs (off)", Slovakian *trhat' si vlasy* "to tear one's hair", Russian *рвать (на себе) волосы* "to tear one's hair", Greek *τραβώ τα μαλλιά μου* "I tear my hair", Finnish *raastaa/repiä hiukset päästään* "to tear the hairs from one's head"). All of these are quite familiar in the present, although the cultural dimension of the gesture is not understood anymore – tearing the hair was a sign of mourning in antiquity. From the viewpoint of history (etymology), the source concept of idiom (15) is the semiotisation of a gesture of mourning, anchored in the culture of antiquity. Synchronically, the idiom can be remotivated. One could imagine a person who inflicts themselves with pain or hurts themselves because of their despair. This view is favoured within the Cognitive Theory of Metaphor; cf. metaphoric models such as VIOLENT FRUSTRATED BEHAVIOUR STANDS FOR ANGER (Lakoff and Kövecses 1987: 204).

10.3.4 Gender-specifics

The Japanese example (12) clearly shows certain restrictions of use. Until recently, it has been used only with reference to men. Thus, there is still another aspect of social interaction to be observed in conventional figurative language – the aspect of "gender-specifics".[14] In what follows, we will look at CFUs showing socio-cultural aspects of this kind. Since speech communities normally consist of about fifty percent males and about fifty percent females, it can be assumed that this division into two groups of speakers is perceptible also in conventional figurative language (cf. also examples (3) and (4) in chapter 4).

This approach to conventional figurative language does not belong to gender linguistics in a strict sense, although it is clearly related to this discipline. The most general tasks of gender linguistics are investigating and describing differences between "male language" and "female language" (compare, for example, Coates 2016). In some speech communities, women use other elements of language

---

[14] Of course, examples (6–10) are gender-specific, too. Their restricted use is based on natural or biological facts. The actual meaning 'to be pregnant' normally excludes a reference to men. A wholly different case is proverb (1), where the restriction is based on a former cultural model.

than men without variation in meaning (cf. R. Lakoff 1975). The "gendering" of language, the fact that there are certain linguistic expressions that can be used exclusively by either female or male speakers, has already been the subject of early linguistic studies, above all of research into exotic languages. Wilhelm von Humboldt was interested in women's language. Similar observations have been made by Sapir (1964). Indeed, the best examples come from Japanese, a language that has developed a comprehensive system of men and women's language, deeply rooted in Japanese culture.

Another research goal is the discovery of gender-specific characteristics which are a stable component of certain linguistic expressions. Let us consider one of the prime examples of gender-marked idioms with restrictions on the level of usage (16).

(16) mainly British English *someone wears the trousers (at home, in the family)*
'it is the wife and not the husband or partner who makes decisions in the family; she is the dominant partner in a marriage or the dominant person in a household'

Usually, this idiom is applied only to women, or more exactly, to women who are married or live in a partnership. The question has not been posed whether a noun denoting a male would be possible as a subject here. Does a sentence like *Mr. Smith wears the trousers in that family* violate the norm? Any kind of ironical usage or jocular modification must be ruled out here, because an ironic use of the idiom would deliberately violate its semantic structure and/or the conventionalised social coherence. Let us look at another example:

(17) British English *mutton dressed as a lamb*
'a middle-aged or old woman who tries to look younger than she is or wears clothes that are suitable for a much younger person'

As far as the image component is concerned, there is no indication whether the referent is male or female person, since the words *mutton* and *lamb* are used to denote both male and female animals in English. Nevertheless, idiom (17) is understood as referring to women only. If we inquire about the causes for this restriction, we have to take into account that it is the actual meaning of the idiom that is grounded in cultural and social facts. Among current ideas in contemporary Middle-European cultures, for example, there is an idea about conforming to the standard that only a woman (but not a man) should look nice, attractive and youthful; yet at the same time, she must not go too far, may not wear clothes unsuitable for her age, not wear too much make-up, etc.[15]

Therefore, MUTTON has been chosen as an image component, not with reference to its property of a 'male animal' but to its property of an 'old animal' – clearly in contrast to LAMB, the younger representative of this kind of animal. So the reasons for the gender-specific restrictions of idiom (17) do not primarily lie in the image component but in the actual meaning, and this meaning is grounded in specifics of the contemporary cultural society.

Most gender-specific characteristics of CFUs are apparent at the level of the actual meaning. Cf. the idiom *to be left on the shelf*. This idiom refers to a woman who is past an age at which she might expect to get married. The idiom reveals the idea that only a woman should be married by a certain age. A man, however, must be strong, brave, and emotionally insensitive (cf. *a big/great girl's blouse* 'a weak, cowardly, emotionally over-sensitive man'); he must be self-confident, not influenced by others, especially not by his mother (*to be tied to someone's apron strings*). Even good naturedness is not a positive characteristic (cf. Dutch *een zijden sok* "a sock of silk", *een zacht ei* "a weak/soft egg" 'a weak man, not able to assert himself'). All these idioms have no counterparts for females; using them with reference to a girl or woman would make no sense. They clearly reveal cultural models of contemporary Central European societies. Deviations from these sociocultural norms are unfavourably commented on by the speech community via such idioms.[16]

The WML dialect possesses many gender-marked idioms (cf. Piirainen 2004b), most of which are restricted to male referents. In many cases, the usage restrictions are caused by the image sources. The working world of men and women is an example for a whole area of source concepts that function in restrictive ways, albeit in ways completely different from the standard language. Image sources like HORSE AND CARRIAGE (18) always restrict the usage of the idioms to men, while the image source KITCHEN, COOKING is associated with a restriction to women (19).

(18) WML *he häff met alle Schwöppen knappt* "he has cracked with all whips" 'he is crafty, ingenious, clever'

---

[15] Speake (1999: 238) points out that *mutton* occurs in various derogatory contexts relating to women, even as a slang term for a prostitute.
[16] For more detail on the role of sociocultural norms in phraseology, see, among other things, Meunier and Granger (2008).

(19) WML *se kockt up'n Kessling Suppe* "she cooks soup on a big stone"
'she does senseless or pointless things; she is confused, suffers from mental illness'

It would be unthinkable to use idiom (18) with reference to a woman, or idiom (19) with reference to a man. According to this perception of the world, women do not crack the whip, and men do not cook soup. This phenomenon allows insights into former value orders and socio-cultural conventions that used to govern the relatively conservative community of the dialect speakers. A strict role-specific behaviour of a once patriarchal society becomes visible through the conventional figurative units of the dialect, which differs noticeably from standard languages in this respect.

Gender-specific doublets are very rare in Standard German conventional figurative language, cf. a single doublet like *im Adamskostüm* "in Adam's suit" and *im Evaskostüm* "in Eva's suit", both meaning 'completely naked' (compare English *in one's birthday suit*). In the WML dialect, however, there are a number of doublets with conventionalised gender-specifics, cf. (20–21).

(20) WML *he höllt kinne Noppe up't Böis* "he keeps no woollen knop on the jacket"
'he is very poor'

(21) WML *se höllt kinne Noppe up'n Rock* "she keeps no woollen knop on the skirt"
'she is very poor'

Woollen knops (or loops) were a status symbol by which the wealth of a person or family was to be recognised from the outside. Idioms (20) and (21) are used either for females or males, depending on the context. The restriction is grounded in the image components, with SKIRT representing a garment for women and JACKET for men. In fact, it is not only a pragmatic difference but also a profound conceptual phenomenon, since the gender of the referential subject is always mentally present. This means that gender-specific characteristics are stable components of the semantic structure of these idioms. The gender in pairs of idioms like (20–21) is considered to be a salient feature. Other languages (namely, the standard languages that have so far been investigated) make little use of this potential differentiation, whereas this opposition is common in idioms of WML. The cause of this phenomenon, again, is the culture of this dialect speaking community.

In conclusion, it can be recorded that "social interactions" are significant as cultural foundations for many conventional figurative units.

10.4 Phenomena relating to material culture

10.4.1 Preliminaries

The vast majority of CFUs appear to be those whose cultural components can be ascribed to aspects of material culture. Cultural foundations of this kind are mainly visible on the level of the rich conceptual structures of the source domains. Some of the idioms quoted in section 10.3 have already illustrated that physical objects based on "achievements" of material culture, such as tools (*ladder*) or clothes (*trousers, sleeves*), can be part of the literal reading of CFUs. As the idioms show, these objects are for the most part reinterpreted, i.e. either used like a symbol (LADDER standing for 'social hierarchy', TROUSERS for 'masculinity') or involved in semiotised gestures (cf. SLEEVE).

The material objects themselves and their foundation in culture are of no interest to our study. It would be trivial to describe every kind of commonplace realia item, and the various "culture-based" artefacts or frames which can be found as image components of CFUs (possibly even the artefact *bucket*, as it emerges in the idiom *to kick the bucket*).

If we refer back to the distinguishing feature of "culture-specifics", however, we will be able to reveal cognitively relevant information about conventional figurative language. Fine-grained cross-linguistic analyses can uncover the ways in which speech communities make use of (everyday) material culture. For the languages analysed in this study, we have found some idiosyncratic aspects of material culture as well as a large number of similarities in the conventional figurative units.

First of all let us point to the great uniformity of the culture-based imagery in CFUs of contemporary Western standard languages. There are figurative widespread idioms such as English *to be on the same wavelength as someone*, which has equivalents in many other languages, e.g. German *auf der gleichen Wellenlänge liegen* "to lie on the same wavelength", French *être sur la même longueur d'onde* "to be on the same wavelength", Finnish *olla samalla aaltopituudella (jkn. kanssa)* "to be on the same wavelength (with someone)" or Greek *εκπέμπουν στο ίδιο μήκος κύματος* "they are on the same wavelength", etc., all meaning 'to have similar ideas and opinions (to another person's), to understand each other very well'.

The similarity of such idioms cannot be due to areal contact, since they are common from northernmost Europe (Finland) to southernmost Europe (Greece). Furthermore, the genetic affiliation or linguistic typology is of no importance here, as one example comes from Finnish, which is not related to the other Indo-European languages. Rather, the uniformity of these idioms is grounded in aspects of modern material culture ('radio and telecommunication'). The great similarity of the culture-based imagery in conventional figurative language is a result of the convergence of contemporary standard languages in Europe. As far as their imagery is concerned, they tend to grow closer together, irrespective of their genetic relationship. This is paralleled by the extent to which the cultures of modern urban societies in Europe are converging.

While this fact as such is not of primary interest to our study, it has to be emphasised that there are linguistic varieties, even in Central Europe, where there is no place for such "achievements of material culture" as source concepts. One such variety is the Low German dialect WML. When asked if it was possible to use an expression like "to be on the same wavelength" to signify 'to have similar ideas and opinions (to another person's), to understand each other very well', the large number of speakers of this dialect responded that this was absolutely impossible. Undeniably, most of these dialect speakers are familiar with radio and telecommunication. Nevertheless, WAVELENGTH is a feature of the contemporary material culture, and there is no place for elements of modern culture in conventional figurative units of this Low German dialect.

10.4.2 Culture-specific artefacts

In this section we want to approach material culture by means of "culture-specifics". We could enumerate many CFUs that, on the level of the image components, refer to specific physical objects of a given cultural community. This is the case with such basic artefacts (people's most elementary necessities) as, for example, traditional food, clothing and housing, where cross-cultural differences or specifics of a traditional culture may emerge. English idioms containing the word *apple-pie*[17] may serve as an example (22–23).

(22) *(to be) in apple-pie order*
'(to be) in very good order, organised very well'

(23) *as easy as apple-pie*
'very easy'

Idiom (22) seems to be motivated by fragments of knowledge about the production of apple-pies, which has to take place in some order, or about the appearance

---

[17] According to Gulland and Hinds-Howell (2001: 183) the idiom *(to be) in apple-pie order* traces back to French *nappe pliée en ordre* 'neatly folded linen'. Speake (1999: 9) lists the idiom *(as) American as apple pie* 'typically American in character'.

of apple-pies (since they are usually kept in some order, e.g. in lines or rows). In idiom (23), no clear motivation can be found, but there is a specific organisation of the lexical structure, namely the vocalic alliteration (all components begin with a vowel, and even if they are not pronounced alike there is a graphic alliteration). This means that the reason for the choice of the component *apple-pie* does not lie in its semantics but, at least partly, in its form. Possibly this is the reason why there are no equivalents of *apple-pie* in CFUs other than English.

The same holds for Finnish expressions with the word *palttu* 'blood-pudding', a typical traditional Finnish dish (24). *Palttu* is a kind of big, thick pancake made of blood-batter, baked on the baking sheet in the oven.

(24) Finnish *antaa palttua* "to give blood pudding"
'to be very indifferent, not to care about anything'

The motivational link here seems to be the large quantity of an undifferentiated ("indifferent") mixture of blood and flour. Obviously, special knowledge about this foodstuff is required for the processing of idiom (24). Despite the fact that the European standard languages are coming closer together, examples of this kind can be found in CFUs of every individual language, not to mention non-European languages or rural basic dialects.

The ways people dress are also converging in modern Western societies. Therefore, most idioms containing words for garments, parts of clothes or footwear do not reveal culture-specific images. Let us reconsider the above-quoted idioms containing the word for "sleeves" ((11) *to roll up one's sleeves*) or CFUs with *collar* or *shoes* like the English *(to be) hot under the collar* '(to be) embarrassed' or '(to be) very angry', or *to put oneself in someone's shoes* 'to put oneself in someone's position (how one would feel or act if one were in someone else's situation)'.

A relic of former footwear seems to emerge in British English *to pop one's clogs*, a very colloquial expression meaning 'to die'. Several idioms with 'clog' can also be found in Dutch conventional figurative language (25–26).

(25) Dutch *dat kun je op je klompen aanvoelen* "that you can feel on your clogs"
'that is easy to understand, it is obvious, it was to be expected'

(26) Dutch *nou breekt mijn klomp* "now my clog breaks"
'I am very surprised, I am stunned'

Both idioms (25–26) are still very much in use, with the latter also belonging to young people's language. Although young people do not wear clogs, specifics of the former Dutch material culture (different from other European cultures) are still mentally present and handed down by using these CFUs. Admittedly, clogs are not only worn in some Dutch rural areas up to the present but are also a kind of symbol for the Netherlands, for instance in the field of tourism.

Certainly, the farther one moves away from the (relatively unified) European cultures, the more elements of culture-specific artefacts can be found in figurative language. As has been illustrated by examples (12–14), idioms with literal readings that evoke the image of the well-known Japanese *kimono* with its large sleeves are more or less restricted to the cultural area of Japan. This culturally bound artefact repeatedly emerges in Japanese figurative language. Similar image components appear in idioms (27–28).

(27)　Japanese 袖を分かつ (*sode wo wakatsu*) "to split a kimono sleeve/kimono sleeves"
　　　'to break with someone, to break off a relation or a friendship'

(28)　Japanese 袖の下に (*sode no shita ni*) "under (the) kimono sleeve"
　　　'bribe, (involved in) bribery'

The well-known idiom (28) is often quoted in connection with practices of the modern Japanese male business community and politics (notably bribery and corruption, which have been a feature of Japanese post-war politics).[18] The kimono's long, expansive sleeves make an ideal place to hide money or hand it on. The literal reading refers to the past: in the Edo period (1615–1868), people used to wear kimonos with large sleeves, which made it easy to hide a gift. In order to influence government officials, people let a gift slip to them from under their sleeves (Sasaki 1993: 235). Although Japanese men seldom wear kimonos today, and almost never when conducting business, idiom (28) is still very familiar, and the concept of the long kimono sleeves is still present.

In English, a concept similar to that of idiom (28) would be verbalised by using quite different image components, e.g. expressions like *money under the table, to pass something under the table*. These idioms are also grounded in material culture (evoking the image of a Western-style room with a table). The underlying idea, however (to do something out of the public eye, e.g. to pass on money that must not be seen by others), is the same. Obviously, the material culture of home furnishing and dwelling style also leaves traces in conventional figurative language. This leads us to the following point of discussion.

---

[18] See, for example, https://www.globalsecurity.org/military/world/japan/politics-corruption.htm.

Parts of the house

Let us consider a Finnish idiom mentioned in section 9.2.2 that reflects elements of the former traditional dwelling house in Finland (29) and its counterpart in German (30). Both idioms serve to illustrate the interaction between conventional figurative language and aspects of material culture. Both idioms are commands which have to be interpreted as 'Out with you! Leave my home immediately!' However, in contrast to the uniformity of their actual meanings, the two idioms differ considerably with regard to their mental images. Their image components originate in quite different concepts, which can be traced back to different specifics of the material culture.

(29) Finnish *tuosta on viisi hirttä poikki!* "there, five logs (unhewn beams) are cut off!"

(30) German *da hat der Maurer das Loch gelassen!* "there the bricklayer has left the hole!"
both meaning something like 'Out with you, leave my home immediately!'

Expressions (29–30) are figurative in the sense that they do not point to "five logs in pieces" or "a hole in the wall". The two idioms reveal a clear difference in the source-frame. The "doorway" is a specific element in both expressions, but the doorway in (29) is not expressed by a word for 'door' but by the word string for "five logs (unhewn beams) are in pieces" – five logs on top of one another are approximately the same height as a standard doorway. Here we are dealing with a special concept of HOUSE. This is the traditional wooden house, built of logs or rough pieces of timber, as it existed in the rural areas and villages throughout the Finland of former times (see Paulaharju 2003 for details). This concept is evoked by the word *hirsi* (partitive *hirttä*)[19] 'log, beam'. The main elements of this HOUSE-frame are the unhewn beams.

Quite a different concept of HOUSE underlies the German example (30). The word string *da hat der Maurer das Loch gelassen* evokes the idea of a house made of stone and brickwork. This idea is mainly conveyed by the word *Maurer* 'bricklayer'. The word *Loch* refers to the 'doorway' and provides a motivating link to the actual meaning, namely the pointing to the door in an indirect speech act of command.

Thus, the concept HOUSE evokes different frames in different cultures. On the one hand, these frames are comparable and have many identical slots. On the

---

[19] In Finnish, a noun that follows a numeral is inflected into the partitive singular. Due to the numeral *viisi* 'five', the noun *hirsi* is inflected as *hirttä* here.

other hand, these slots have different contents, such as 'material', 'shape', 'type of construction', etc. Accordingly, metaphors composed of elements of the HOUSE concept as their source domain also differ in the two idioms. The cultural knowledge in both idioms applies to the frame HOUSE with the doorway as a salient feature, but we are dealing with two significantly different frames of house here. The Finnish wooden house lost its significance long ago. The concept of this traditional house-type is present in the idiom (29), but we have to stress that only one single CFU in standard Finnish has been found which reflects elements of the former traditional dwelling house in Finland.[20]

These examples illustrate the dichotomy between "culture-specific" and "culture-based", which is significant to the study of culture in conventional figurative language. Intuitively, only the Finnish idiom (29) would be regarded as culture-specific, because of *hirsi* 'log, beam', a very specific part of material culture. Living in houses built of stone and brickwork seems to be widespread and unspecific in terms of modern urban life. However, the juxtaposition of the two idioms (30) and (29) reveals that the concept of a 'house made of stone and brickwork' in CFL is also "culture-specific" from the perspective of cultures other than the contemporary urban cultures of Europe and North America. Other quite different concepts of HOUSE can come to light in conventional figurative language. Cultural-specific concepts of HOUSE in language and culture have been analysed systematically in chapter 9.

Hatchet/axe

Looking at aspects of material culture as they emerge on the level of rich images in CFUs, we may discover some more subtle cross-linguistic and cross-cultural differences. As an example, let us take an object of everyday material culture, a common tool, such as an axe or a hatchet, as it is fixed in CFUs. For most people there is no significant difference between the concept AXE and the concept HATCHET. Consider, however, the following idioms, which at first glance seem to be almost equivalent as far as their image components are concerned. The idioms are from Finnish (31) and Dutch (32). Although the figurative imageries of both languages, which belong to the same European cultural area, have many points in common, the two languages and cultures differ in view of their material traditions. A subtle analysis of these CFUs (or, to be more precise, of their different source-frames) may reveal nontrivial findings that are relevant to Cognitive Linguistics.

---

[20] Finnish dialects provide numerous figurative units based on the concept of the traditional house type; this has been illustrated by a North Karelian basic dialect (Piirainen 2004c).

(31) Finnish *heittää kirveensä järveen/kaivoon* "to throw one's hatchet into the lake/into the well"

(32) Dutch *het bijltje erbij neergooien* "to throw one's (little) hatchet down there" both meaning something like 'to give up in despair, to stop doing something (for good) because of discouragement, not to feel like doing something any more'

Of the ten standard languages whose CFUs have been analysed in detail (cf. 1.2), two languages emerged as possessing an above-average number of CFUs with words denoting 'hatchet' or 'axe',[21] namely Finnish and Dutch.

For Finnish, this fact is immediately comprehensible. Finland is, to a large extent, situated in an area of forests. Throughout the centuries, Finland has been a densely wooded country; forestry was one of the main national economic resources. The hatchet or axe was the prototypical tool of woodcutters, wood and forestry workers, and it was used in many other daily tasks. Thus, HATCHET/AXE was a salient concept in Finland in former days; it is not surprising that this concept has left traces in conventional figurative language. Here are some further examples: *iskeä kirveensä kiveen* "to beat one's hatchet onto a stone" 'to be severely mistaken'; *minua ei saa kirveelläkään tekemään sitä* "even a hatchet would not make me do it" 'I will never do it; no one can make me do it, not even by force'; *kirveellä olisi töitä* "the hatchet would have work" 'affairs which are in disorder should be put right".

Although the Netherlands has not been tree-covered for centuries, Dutch also has many CFUs with *bijl(tje)* 'hatchet', for example: *al vaker met dat bijltje gehakt hebben* "to have chopped more often with that small hatchet" 'to have extensive experience in a certain field'; *met de botte bijl hakken* "to chop with the blunt hatchet" 'to act rigorously, without sensitivity, without taking any precautions; to proceed in an overly generalised way, and the like'; *onherroepelijk voor de bijl gaan* "to irrevocably go before the hatchet" 'just have to cop it; have one's turn at last; to make bad experiences although one tried to avoid it'.

When we look at the history of this small fragment of material culture, it becomes evident that the concept HATCHET/AXE in Dutch conventional figurative

---

[21] One expression of biblical origin (Matthew 3:10), which is common in several languages can be left aside, cf. Finnish *kirves on pantu puun juurelle* "the hatchet is laid on the root of the tree", Dutch *de bijl aan de wortel* "the hatchet at the root" or German *die Axt an etwas legen* "to lay the axe at something". The same holds for idioms like German *das Kriegsbeil ausgraben/begraben* or French *déterrer/ enterrer la hache de guerre* "to dig up/bury the hatchet of war", etc. which can be traced back to American Indian stories.

language is of other origin than that in Finnish conventional figurative language. The Netherlands (or in former centuries the United Provinces) is known as a famous seafaring and shipbuilding nation whose big ocean-going sailing boats were shaped by Dutch shipbuilding specialists. In the time of Tsar Peter the Great, there was an active trade with boles and tree trunks from Russia. The wooden sailing ships were constructed on a building berth, around which timbers and planking were cut and shaped, joined on the berth to form the hull, and then equipped with the big masts.

The hatchet or axe was the prototypical tool of all the workers occupied with shipbuilding. The word *biltje* '((small) hatchet)' has also been used metonymically, since the ship builders themselves were called *bijltjes* 'hatchets' (Van Dale IW 1999: 62). Thus, from a cognitive point of view, HATCHET/AXE can be regarded as a relevant concept in the material cultural of the Netherlands of the past which has left traces in Dutch figurative language on the level of rich conceptual structures from the source domain.

Whether 'hatchet' or 'axe' in Finnish and Dutch culture are different material objects is not the point here, but it is important that these objects belong to different conceptual areas, as can be proved by an analysis of the figurative languages – Dutch idioms and proverbs with *bijl* or *bijltje* are connected with the large conceptual source domains of seafaring and overseas trade, which has produced an abundance of other Dutch CFUs. These source domains clearly differ from the domains 'wood' and 'forestry' as salient cognitive structures which underlie Finnish idioms with *kirves* 'hatchet', but also many further Finnish CFUs.

Seafaring and island
One culturally bound frame is 'seafaring', which clearly has left traces in languages such as Dutch, English, and above all, Icelandic. All of these languages are spoken in countries or by people of nations with links to a former culture of seafaring and sailing. As Sverrisdóttir (1987) has demonstrated, Icelandic conventional figurative language has an abundance of CFUs that contain words for vessels, masts and rigging, for navigation and steering, for harbour, coast, tides, and so on. Although English CFL also has idioms and proverbs with, e.g. *ship, sail, board, anchor, coast, sea*, etc., the number of these is far exceeded by those in Icelandic conventional figurative language (which also has many correspondences of e.g. 'boat', 'mast', 'harbour', 'rock', and so on). 'Seafaring' in Iceland was an even more salient concept than in England or in other seafaring nations, and has manifested itself in an above-average quantitiy of such CFUs up to the present time.

Let us look at some CFUs, partly connected with the frame 'seafaring'. Examples (33–35), a Japanese, a Dutch and a German idiom, contain the same frame, namely ISLAND, as the source concept. As the examples show, this frame can be used for denoting quite different target concepts. The reason for this is that, in different cultural contexts, the frame ISLAND is embedded in different conceptual domains. These different embeddings are not only grounded in the natural environment but also, and above all, in aspects of the given material culture.

(33) Dutch *we zitten hier niet op een eiland* "we do not sit here on an island"
'we are fine, we are doing quite well'

(34) Japanese 取りつく島もない (*tori tsuku shima mo nai*) "there is no island to arrive"
'to be helpless, to be left to one's own devices'

(35) German *reif für die Insel* "ripe for the island"
'ready for a holiday, weary of modern civilisation'

The Netherlands is an old seafaring nation. If a sailor were driven onto an island far from their native mainland, this would be tantamount to a feeling of desolation and hopelessness. Idiom (33) conveys world experiences of members of this former seafaring culture. In this case, the frame ISLAND is part of the frame SEAFARING. What is linguistically and cross-linguistically relevant is the fact that the concept ISLAND in Dutch conventional figurative language is not identical to the concept of ISLAND in other languages whose speakers do not belong to a seafaring nation. Associations of this kind should be part of a full-fledged semantic and pragmatic description, because such associations are unique to this culture and cannot be inferred even with the help of regular implicatures.

The opposite concept of island emerges in idiom (34). Japan is an island country, consisting of four main islands and a number of smaller ones. The Japanese saying 島国根性 (*shimaguni konjō*) "island country-mentality" is used self-mockingly in order to denote narrow-mindedness, and a kind of insularity.[22] In idiom (34) ISLAND (島 *shima*) appears as the place where one feels safe. The

---

22 The opposite to this is the outdated expression 大陸的な (*tairiku-teki na*), which literally means "continental" and refers to peoples who are generous of spirit and who do not fuss about trifles (Garrison et al. 2002: 505).

island is the home that gives a sense of security amidst the hostile surroundings of the sea. Here, the frame ISLAND is part of the frame HOMELAND, HOME.

Yet another view of ISLAND is apparent in the German idiom (35), which is a relatively young expression. The concept ISLAND has generally no significance in the German culture. Nevertheless, some present-day aspects of material culture seem to surface here. The literal reading of idiom (35) seems to refer to modern mass tourism, where people may spend their holidays on the beach of an exotic island. In this example, the frame ISLAND is part of the frames HOLIDAYS and RELAXING. Nevertheless, the idiom originates from the titles of a popular song and a novel. Thus, the lexical structure of the idiom is based on textual knowledge, which will be further explored in the following section.

To sum up, aspects of material culture play a considerable role in CFUs. A cross-linguistic and cross-cultural approach to conventional figurative language can reveal some subtle differences in the conceptions that underlie the material culture.

10.5 Textual dependence

10.5.1 Preliminary remarks

A large number of CFUs can be classified as belonging to type (iii), textual dependence or "intertextual phenomena". The term *intertextuality* was coined by Julia Kristeva in the 1960s and developed mainly within literary studies (cf. e.g. Moi 1986; Allen 2011). It is applied here in the broader sense of text linguistics (cf. De Beaugrande and Dressler 1981). In the present study, we use the term *textual dependence* to refer to the intertextual relation between CFUs and texts that can be identified as their sources.[23]

The cultural foundation of many CFUs can be ascribed to intertextual phenomena, although the average speaker is not conscious of this fact in most cases. We are dealing with quite a heterogeneous amount of CFUs, extending from connections with various kinds of texts, e.g. stories of foreign cultures such as Native American culture (*to bury the hatchet* 'to stop fighting or arguing; to end old resentments') or classic antiquity with its myths, dramas or fables (*between Scylla and Charybdis* 'between two great dangers of which the attempt to avoid one increases the risk of

---

[23] For the notion of *intertexuality* in the field of phraseology, see Burger (1991: 17–18). By this term the author mainly understands the availability of well-known, recognisable text fragments (like metaphoric phrasemes, aphorisms, titles of books or films etc.) for producing other small texts, e.g. advertising slogans, headlines, etc. Similar phenomena are subsumed under the term *Antizitat* in Mieder (1975, 1985).

the other', from Homer's "Odyssey" XII: 85–87) to historical events (e.g. *to cross the Rubicon* 'to do something irrevocable', ascribed to Caesar), etc.

Two groups of CFUs are apparent. Firstly, there may be direct references to particular (written) texts, more or less word-for-word quotations from works of belles-lettres, the Bible, advertising material, etc. Secondly, there may be allusions to an entire text or a large section of it. The relation between fables or similar narratives and CFUs is a special case of textual dependence. What CFUs of this type have in common is that they have an identifiable textual source.

10.5.2 Quotations

Many CFUs came into being on the basis of well-known texts or passages of texts. This means that the motivating links between the lexical structure of the CFU and its actual meaning were provided by knowledge about the text in question and its role in the cultural tradition. Many idioms, proverbs, and compounds are direct references to works of belles-lettres and poetry, folk tales, national epics, the Bible, and even titles of films, books or songs.

Let us go back to the German idiom (35) *reif für die Insel*. This idiom shows several stages of textual dependence. First, "Reif für die Insel" was the title of a popular song (1982), written by the Austrian songwriter Peter Cornelius. Second, Bill Bryson's novel "Notes from a Small Island" (1995) was published in German under precisely the same title "Reif für die Insel" (1997). Finally, a German travel agency chose this text fragment, which was popular at the time, as an advertising slogan, provided with a question mark, *Reif für die Insel?*, which greatly contributed to establishing this new idiom.

These phenomena have often been the topic of phraseological (and/or etymological) research.[24] A few apt examples should be sufficient here. It does not matter whether the average speaker knows that a given CFU is a quotation or whether this special knowledge about the source has been lost. One example has been given in section 4.9 (36), the familiar German idiom *das (also) ist/war des Pudels Kern*, which can be traced back to a quotation from Goethe's drama "Faust". There are many text fragments of literary works that were initially used as citations (clearly related to the author and an identifiable text passage) before they gradually developed into CFUs. Great significance must be attached to the

---

[24] The inverse process of textual dependence can be observed when a CFU is used as a title. The English (AmE) idiom *like a cat on a hot tin roof*, for example, became established in the title of Tennessee Williams' play "Cat on a Hot Tin Roof" (1955), which was later filmed. There are many examples of this kind, but we will not go into this topic here.

theatre as a mediator. The metrical form of the classic verse drama had a beneficial effect on the lexicalisation of certain expressions. Some hundred German CFUs are related to works of the poets Goethe and Schiller. The same holds for English idioms originating in Shakespeare's plays.

Another extensive group consists of "biblicisms", idioms and proverbs that directly or indirectly can be traced back to identifiable verses or chapters of the Bible. Most biblical idioms are unobtrusive, have no special "biblical" contents and are so familiar that they are used with no conscious reference to the original context. Here are some examples, directly relatable to the Bible: *to swim against the tide* 'to have opinions or ideas that are opposite to most people's at the time' (Sirach 4:31); *to pour out one's heart to someone* 'to confide all one's sorrows, fears, anxieties, etc. to another person' (Psalm 42:5); *built on sand* 'without secure foundation; liable to collapse' (Matthew 7:26); *the scales fall from someone's eyes* 'someone is no longer deceived' (Acts 9:18); *to take someone under one's wing* 'to help and protect someone, especially someone who is younger or less experienced' (Psalm 91:4); or *to separate/sort the wheat from the chaff* 'to distinguish valuable people or things from worthless ones' (Matthew 3:17).

These biblical idioms are widespread in many European languages and, in the main, familiar. For example, more than 120 still very common "biblicisms" belong to German phraseology (Parad 2003). For a long time after the invention of letterpress printing, the Bible was the only book in many families; it was read aloud every day, and many passages were learnt by heart. In view of the Bible's importance, it is not surprising that such a large amount of fixed word strings entered the lexicons of various European languages. A wealth of studies are concerned with specific aspects of biblical phrasemes or with the more general impact of Bible translations on individual languages (e.g. Gak 1998; van Dalen-Oskam and Mooijaart 2000; Parad 2003).

Many other CFUs were influenced by similar intertextual phenomena. A special case is idiom (36), which came into being in Australian English.

(36) a. *a possum up a gum tree*
 b. *up a gum tree*
 c. *up a tree*
  all meaning 1. 'in a predicament, in great difficulties; a difficult situation without escape', 2. 'unable to make any further progress'

The motivation of version (36a) seems to be clear. Most probably, the literal reading refers to the flight behaviour of possums in dangerous situations, when they climb up gum trees.²⁵ Although, to our knowledge, the origin of this idiom has not been established, it has also appeared in British and American English. The phrase *up a gum tree* was recorded in the US at the beginning of the 19th century (Speake 1999: 162), where "Possum up a gum tree" was the title of a song.²⁶ Due to this kind of textual dependence, the use of the idiom has extended to other varieties of English.

What is interesting to note in reading the reduced version (36c) is that it has no obvious motivation in itself. This example illustrates the "irregularity" of figurative language, or the "accidental nature" of how CFUs can come into being, especially in the realm of textual dependence (cf. also 4.8.4). No regularity or metaphoric "rule" can be found to explain why an image evoked by the word chain *up a tree* should be used for denoting 'a difficult situation without escape'. The construction of a metaphor like DIFFICULTY IS UP would make no sense. However, there are several "CFU false friends" (see chapter 5) where a very similar mental image leads to completely different but comprehensible metaphors, cf. English *(at) the top of the tree* '(in) the highest rank of a profession etc.' (SUCCESSFUL IS UP) or the Low German (WML) idiom *bowwen in de Bööme* ("up in the trees") 'extremely happy' (HAPPY IS UP). Even if speakers of English have an idea of how to process idiom (36c) (perhaps by analogy with a cat up in a tree, unable to climb down on its own), the existence of this idiom (with this precise lexical structure and actual meaning) is not due to certain cognitive structures but to the more or less accidental factor of textual dependence.

As idiom (37) shows, a well-known quiz show may provide a similar case of textual dependence:

(37) a. *the sixty-four thousand dollar question*
      b. American English *the million dollar question*
         both meaning 'the crucial issue; a very important question, but difficult to answer; a dilemma'

Idiom (37a) comes from the name of a television game show from the 1950s called "The 64,000 Dollar Question". The top prize offered for solving the final question was $ 64000. No symbolic meaning can be ascribed to the number *sixty-four thousand* (cf. case studies on number symbols in chapter 12). The reverse is the case with *million* in the later variant (37b), since the concept MILLION as a 'very high', round number contains symbolic connotations such as 'intensification'. However, a modern TV quiz show ("Who Wants to Be a Millionaire") may have

---

25 By contrast, Peters (2007: 239) mentions the Australian phraseme *like a possum up a gumtree* as indicating happiness with a situation.
26 The earliest citation for this phraseme is 1829 in the Oxford English Dictionary, where the phraseme is listed as an American expression.

influenced version (37b). This show has been adapted in many countries outside of the USA and demonstrates the significance of the concept MILLION: the top prize is always "a million", regardless of the respective currency. However, there is no reason to connect the number *sixty-four thousand* to a very important but difficult question, other than referring to a former TV entertainment program.

The intertextual phenomena discussed here may illustrate the difference between "textual dependence" and "cultural symbols". Compare, for example, the German idiom *Eulen nach Athen tragen* "to carry owls to Athens" discussed in 3.1. There is an equivalent of this idiom in many different languages. In some of them it is obsolete or belongs to a very elevated language style (e.g. English *to send owls to Athens*, French *apporter des chouettes à Athènes*, Finnish *viedä pöllöjä Ateenaan* "to bring owls to Athens"); in others it is quite well known and familiar, as in German or in Dutch *uilen naar Athene dragen*, Swedish *bära ugglor til Aten*, Slovakian *nosiť sovy do Atén*, Polish *nosić sowy do Aten* "to carry owls to Athens", etc.

Although these idioms may be motivated only for some well-educated people and seem to be opaque to the majority of speakers, the cultural knowledge which is implicitly present in the plane of content of this idiom cannot be neglected. The idioms originate from Aristophanes' satirical comedy "The Birds" (414 BC; Greek "Ornithes"), verse 301. The Ancient Greek expression γλαυκ' Ἀθήναζε (ἄγειν)/ γλαυκ' εἰς Ἀθήνας was used almost with the same meaning as the German idiom *Eulen nach Athen tragen*, and still is alive in the Modern Greek κομίζω γλαύκα εἰς Ἀθήνας "to send owls to Athens" (maybe as a learned quotation).

Thus, the idiom *Eulen nach Athen tragen* is based on references to an identifiable passage in a literary text, no matter whether only a few speakers of contemporary German are aware of this. In addition to that, the underlying text of Aristophanes' "The Birds" is culturally based in its turn. The motivating basis is provided by knowledge about the status and the function of the OWL in classical Athens (not about the OWL as a symbol, see below). The owl was not only a bird that flourished in Athens, but was also the emblem of *Athene*, the protective goddess of Athens. The coin of Athens bore an owl on the reverse. So there were plenty of owls in Athens (in the form of all sorts of pictures), and it would have been superfluous and unnecessary to bring more of them.

This example shows that the underlying cultural knowledge extends to the whole idiom rather than to one single constituent. No "symbolic knowledge" is required for the interpretation of this idiom. In contrast, the English simile *as wise as an owl* 'very wise' is based on the knowledge that the OWL is symbolically connected with 'intelligence' and 'wisdom' in western cultures. Finally, the idiom illustrates once more that CFUs with a particular textual source may not be fully motivated via their lexical structure. Attempts to interpret idioms such as *Eulen nach Athen tragen* on the level of the conceptual metaphor are doomed to failure. What remains a motivational link on the level of "rich imagery" is only the cognitive schema "to bring something to a certain place", whereas the functions of "owls" and "Athens" remain unclear without textual knowledge. This is due to the fact that German *Eulen nach Athen tragen* "to carry owls to Athens" has remained a quotation throughout the centuries, unlike e.g. the idiom *to carry coals to Newcastle*, which is not a quotation (cf. examples (1–3) in chapter 3).

10.5.3 Allusions

Another kind of textual dependence is the reference to an entire text, or a large passage of a text, summarising a certain situation described in that text. In such "allusions", some more or less vague knowledge of a text establishes the motivational link. Idiom (38), for example, is based on knowledge about *Adam* as the biblical first man. This idiom is not a word-for-word borrowing or approximate quotation of a biblical verse like the biblicisms named above (*to swim against the tide*), but it reflects some knowledge about biblical stories.

(38) *not to know someone from Adam*
      'not to know or be completely unable to recognise the person in question; not to know someone at all or never have seen him/her before'

Fables and similar narratives are another culturally important complex of texts, and their significance as educational subject matter started to decrease as late as in the last century. The relationship between phrasemes and fables has been a topic of intensive semiotic research using the term "intertext" (see e.g. Carnes 1988, 1991; Dolby-Stahl 1988; Grzybek 1988, 1994a, 1994b). Most CFUs related to fables were originally proverbs (simple texts themselves) that have partly been transformed into idioms. There are a number of proverb/fable complexes that share a common motif. Let us consider idioms (39–40).

(39) a. English *sour grapes*
      b. French *les raisins sont trop verts* "the grapes are too green"

(40) a. Swedish *surt, sa räven (om rönnbären)* "sour, said the fox (about the rowanberries)"
      b. Finnish *happamia, sanoi kettu pihlajanmarjoista* "sour, said the fox about the rowanberries"
      all meaning roughly 'someone is only pretending not to desire something that they actually desire but are unable to reach'

Idioms (39–40) summarise Aesop's fable "The Fox and the Grapes",[27] in which the fox, unable to reach the grapes, disparages them as being sour. In idiom (40), the realia have been adapted to the natural environment. Grapes are not native to Sweden and Finland, so rowanberries, which occur abundantly and are used for various purposes, take their place. The examples show that "textual dependence" here does not mean a "direct" quotation from the fable text but an allusion to the essential point of the story. Furthermore, the symbolic evaluations of animals in culture and conventional figurative language are to a large extent coined by narrative traditions.

This type of textual dependence largely contributes to the similarity of culture-based imagery in CFUs from many European standard languages. The uniformity of CFUs in Western standard languages is often attributed to Europe's common cultural heritage, with its literary traditions, ranging from Greek antiquity, through Medieval Latin literature, the Renaissance and Humanism (when Latin was the scholarly lingua franca) to many other literary contacts in Europe over the centuries. It is the common cultural possession of literary texts such as the Bible, fables, and classic works of literature that causes this uniformity of European figurative language, which can be connected to the term "SAE" (cf. 1.2.3).

Two contrasting language varieties are considered in the present study. In view of textual dependence, conventional figurative units of the Low German basic dialect WML, on the one hand, do not reveal direct references to other texts; there are neither biblicisms[28] nor allusions to fables, legends, or other works of poetry and literature. For CFUs of the Japanese standard language, on the other hand, textual dependence is of great significance. Of course the starting point here is not the same assemblage of texts as those mentioned above, but includes also works of traditional culture.

Hence, other cultural areas with long literary traditions show similar tendencies towards a uniformity of CFUs through works of the cultural heritage. This is the case, for instance, in those East Asian areas where languages have been strongly

---

[27] For the handing down of this fable from Greek and Latin versions to many popular and poetic works, up to La Fontaine's "Le renard et les raisins" and other variants (see e.g. Aarne and Thompson 1961: no. 59).

[28] One single "corrupted" example can be named: WML *he mäck van sien Hatte kinne Moddekuhle* "he doesn't make a mud-pit (marsh hole) of his heart", which seems to be an adaptation of the Standard German idiom (coined by Martin Luther in his translation of the Bible, 1522) *aus seinem Herzen keine Mördergrube machen* "not to make a murderer pit of one's heart" 'to speak freely, frankly about what one is thinking or feeling', where German *Mörder* 'murderer' has been replaced by the dialectal word *Modde* 'mud' (Piirainen 2000, 1: 71–72).

influenced by Classical Chinese. Paczolay (1994: 11–13) gives several examples of CFUs originating from Chinese literature that have spread equally into Korean, Japanese and Vietnamese conventional figurative language. Thus, many Japanese idioms and proverbs originate from ancient Chinese tales. Example (41) is a very familiar Japanese idiom, which can be traced back to a Chinese anecdote of the period of the "Warring States" (403–221 BC). The image component of idiom (41) summarises the essential points of the story[29] in a very condensed way – since the snake has no legs or feet, it is unnecessary to draw legs on it.

(41)   Japanese 蛇足 (*da-soku*) "snake-leg [snake's leg/legs/feet]"
'unnecessary, extraneous, superfluous'

For Chinese and Korean correspondences of idiom (41) see Paczolay (1994: 40). The Chinese idiom 畫蛇添足 (*huà shé tiān zú*) "drawing a snake (and) adding feet" is also very familiar. It has developed a second actual meaning: 'to overreach the mark, to ruin something by meddling with it; ruining a venture by doing unnecesary and surplus things' (cf. HCI 1999: 42; Lin and Leonard 2000: 61; Chang 2003: 107–108). By analogy with the far-reaching phenomena of textual dependence within "Standard Average European" languages, it is apparent that such complexes of textually related figurative units often also exist in the East Asian cultural group of languages.

10.6 Fictive conceptual domains

Many conventional figurative units with image components traceable to concepts of unreal, fictive worlds can be subsumed under the label "fictive conceptual domains" [type (iv)]. By this label we primarily understand fragments of knowledge about relevant non-material, virtual cultural creations or pre-scientific "edifices of ideas". Folk theories of ancient times and pre-scientific conceptions of the world (including religion, superstition, common belief, etc.) are important components of the cultural foundation of conventional figurative language. However, they have never been explored as systematically as have the

---

[29] The story is about some friends who bet a round of drinks on who can draw a snake the fastest. They agree that the one who finishes a good picture of a snake first will have a pot of wine. One solves the task much quicker than the others and, at his leisure, decides to add some legs to his snake. Upon seeing this, one of the other men asks how he could put legs on a reptile that originally had none. In the meantime, this man finishes his picture and takes the wine (Garrison et al. 2002: 55).

links between conventional figurative units and texts like the Bible, fables, or works of literature. Whenever linguistic studies mention the "naive world-view" with which language invariably provides all human beings, the example *sunset/ sunrise* is almost exclusively used. Although speakers know that the sun does not circle the earth, they use words reflecting pre-Copernican views. Conventional figurative language provides a wealth of comparable expressions that can be traced back to such older world-views.

An ancient folk model with a great deal of influence on the European conventional figurative language is Hippocrates' "humoural pathology" (mentioned already in section 6.2.1). This theory states that combinations of the four fluid humours of the body, yellow bile, black bile, blood, and phlegm, determine the four prototypical temperaments, namely the choleric, the melancholic, the sanguine, and the phlegmatic temperament. This doctrine was effective from antiquity and medieval times up to the 18th century, before it became outdated as a result of modern medical science. Although most average speakers have no knowledge of the doctrine, CFUs maintaining traces of it in their lexical structure are still familiar (e.g. French *se faire du mauvais sang; se faire de la bile* 'to be worried'). Anger was seen as an overproduction of yellow bile (cf. example (1) in chapter 6: German *jmdm. läuft die Galle über*). Connections between colours and emotions can also be traced back to tacit knowledge of this doctrine, which ascribed GREEN or YELLOW to ANGER (cf. Italian *diventare verde* "to become green", Russian *позеленеть от злости* "to become green with anger" 'to get very angry') as well as to 'jealousy, envy' (cf. German *gelb vor Neid* "yellow with envy", or Finnish *olla vihreänä kateudesta* "to be green because of envy"). The English idiom *the green-eyed monster* meaning 'extreme jealousy' is a quotation from Shakespeare's tragedy "Othello, the Moor of Venice" III, 3, 166, which shows that the existence of the concept GREEN ENVY in English is also supported by phenomena of textual dependence. In Shakespeare's days, the humoural doctrine was still alive, and it appears throughout his popular dramas.

Another strand of pre-scientific folk theories with long cultural traditions is connected with the LIVER. In the medicine of classical antiquity and the Middle Ages, the liver was seen as the organ of vital energy and emotions, especially of wrath. Numerous idioms reveal specifics of this semiotised concept of the LIVER, e.g. the Italian *mangiarsi il fegato* "to eat the liver" 'to be very angry' or the Hungarian *nagy mája van* "his liver is big" 'he is very angry' (see sections 6.2.1 and 11.4.3 for details). The equivalents *to lose heart, to be disheartened* or Dutch *geen hart in zijn lijf hebben* "to have no heart in one's body" 'to have no courage' reveal a related folk model, namely the semiotisation of the concept HEART, which is strongly effective in European CFL. The cultural specifics of these idioms are even more comprehensible when we turn to languages of distant cultural areas, such as East Asia. In traditional Chinese medicine (and in many Chinese CFUs) the GALLBLADDER is the seat of COURAGE (Yu 2003). For the concept HARA/BELLY in Japanese culture see section 6.2.3.

Although innumerable phraseological studies have looked at "somatisms" (cf. footnote 11 in chapter 5), there has not been, as yet, any systematic and comprehensive investigation. In view of their intensive cultural semiotic foundations, conventional figurative units based on concepts like GALL, LIVER, HEART (or HARA/BELLY in Japanese) cannot be described merely in terms of "somatic constituents" or abstract "body-based" conceptual metaphors. Many conventional figurative units are conceptually based on ancient sets of ideas later rejected in the course of scientific developments. Nowadays they may be interpreted in terms of culture, because the old world-views are still part of the particular cultural memory.

Similar virtual constructions of the world are, for example, conceptions of ancient myths, religions, folk belief, superstitions, and so on. Fictive conceptual domains like ANGELS, DEVIL or HELL are strongly elaborated in the CFUs of European languages (cf. *enough to make the angels weep; it hurts like hell*, and many similar idioms from other languages), which suggests that these fictive concepts are alive even in modern times. Let us consider some CFUs whose image components are related to the concept DEVIL. The interpretation of idiom (42) is based on knowledge about certain traditions of Christian ideas, according to which the devil is afraid of holy water. Therefore, the devil's fear of holy water can be used as an intensification of 'fear':

(42) German *etwas fürchten wie der Teufel das Weihwasser* "to fear something like the devil (fears) the holy water"
'to fear something greatly, to be very afraid of something'

European languages have many CFUs with DEVIL as a constituent part (cf. colloquial expressions like *the devil knows, there will be the devil to pay, to go to the devil*, etc.). Not only verbal texts but also pictures may have contributed to the creation of CFUs. Compare idioms (43–44).

(43) English *a cloven hoof*
'a (hidden) disadvantage, a defect'

(44) German *das hat einen Pferdefuß* "that has a horse's foot"
'there is a (at first glance hidden) disadvantage'

Idiom (43) is motivated by some vague fragments of cultural knowledge. Traditional pictures of the devil show him with the head and torso of a man but the legs and cloven feet of a goat. Thus a cloven hoof is a giveaway sign of the devil. According to another folk belief, the devil has a horse's hoof, which he cannot hide completely. In some contexts, the devil is portrayed with horse's hooves (or, to symbolise his divided nature, with one hoof and one human foot). Wherever this horse's hoof is seen, the devil is involved, and malice or disadvantage occurs, cf. the German idiom (44).

Such half-belief or half-religious images are quite productive in conventional figurative language. There are, for example, many idioms with the concept HELL, which is a fictive and non-scientific concept that can also be traced back to a kind of mythological textual dependence (45–46).

(45) *until hell freezes over*
 'for an extremely long time; forever'

(46) *come hell or high water*
 'whatever the obstacles are; when someone is determined to do something in spite of any problems or difficulties'

Idioms (45–46) are considered to be motivated and understood on the basis of shared cultural knowledge about HELL. They show how different fragments of knowledge about this frame are involved in conventional figurative language. Idiom (45) indicates the knowledge that the mythological hell is a warm or hot place, where it never freezes. With the help of this knowledge, a word string like *when hell freezes over* can be decoded as 'never'. Other idioms such as (46) demonstrate the knowledge that hell is an unpleasant place, where one is exposed to great difficulties. In view of the large number of colloquial CFUs with the concept HELL, such half-religious cultural concepts, remote in time, seem to be active in contemporary conventional figurative language. Using these CFUs "contradicts" modern scientific knowledge in the same way as using the words *sunrise* and *sunset* does.

Let us consider the contrast between the cultural foundation of types (iii) and (iv), on the one hand, and that of type (v) "cultural symbolism" (see the following section), on the other. The CFUs treated in the two sections 10.5 and 10.6 are motivated by various phenomena of mental culture, by intellectual ideas and traditions. They are, for the most part, anchored in cultural codes such as literature, fairy tales, myths, the Bible, religion, and so on, which is a point in common with expressions of type (v). Nevertheless, two linguistically relevant differences have to be stressed.

First, the motivation of types (iii) and (iv) affects the CFU as a whole rather than one single constituent. Secondly, the words in question that can be separated are interpreted based on one of their literal meanings before the whole complex is reinterpreted metaphorically or metonymically, and they have no autonomous figurative meaning of their own. The word *Teufel* 'devil' in (42) and the more or less euphemistic circumlocutions of the devil in (43–44) must be interpreted in their primary meaning, denoting just this mythological figure.

There is a significant difference in the semantic structure of conventional figurative units of type (v), because their "key constituents" are used with a secondary, symbolic meaning. For interpreting CFUs like *Peter is an old fox* or *Barbara is a snake*, it is another kind of cultural knowledge that is required. Here the "symbolic knowledge" of FOX or SNAKE must be activated, together with the knowledge of their secondary meanings 'wiliness, cunning' or 'falseness', respectively, and the knowledge of the interrelation with other codes of culture containing the symbols FOX or SNAKE. These differences will be outlined in more detail in section 11.4.

10.7 Cultural symbols

It has been shown in the previous sections how varied the cultural phenomena are that underlie CFUs. These phenomena can be related to social interactions and material objects or to various intellectual ideas and traditions. Most of them manifest themselves on the level of the rich conceptual structures of the source domains. Within our classification of the principal cultural phenomena in conventional figurative language (10.2), there remains the fifth type, *cultural symbols in figurative language*. This type is central with regard to the issues investigated in our study in view of the role of culture in figurative language. A detailed description of this type, preceded by the notion of *symbol* favoured here, will be given in chapter 11.

The term *cultural symbol in figurative language* should be touched upon here only in brief, prior to discussing the combination of cultural phenomena in CFUs. In the next section (10.8), we will examine some cases where different types of cultural phenomena are combined in one figurative unit, among them cultural symbols such as colour, flower or animal symbols (e.g. BLACK, WHITE, LILY, WOLF). For this purpose, we will anticipate here the main procedures needed to separate symbol-based CFUs from other kinds. A precondition is the analysability of the figurative unit; the element that is suspected of being a symbol is normally one single constituent that must be separable. The main criteria for a cultural symbol in figurative language are, first, that the given unit of conventional figurative language corresponds to other codes of culture, and second, that the given concept is used recurrently in this secondary function.

The first CFU that will be discussed in section 10.8 contains the symbol BLACK (in combination with other types of cultural phenomena). Let us at this point consider another expression with the constituent *black* in order to illustrate and explain the notions *symbol* and *symbolic function* which will be used here as a part of the metalinguistic apparatus.

(47)　*a black day*
　　　'a day that has disastrous consequences, a day of great unhappiness; a disaster'

The prerequisite of analysability is fulfilled because the element that is likely to be a symbol (the word *black*) can be singled out without destroying the semantic structure of the idiom and reveals an autonomous meaning (cf. a paraphrase like 'a bad day'). The constituent *black* is a sign that in the primary reading refers to a colour. In this special phraseological context, however, the second meaning must be activated. The first meaning must be reinterpreted as 'bad, unhappy'. We call this reinterpreted meaning the *symbolic function* of BLACK, not just because it is secondary to the first meaning of this word, 'a colour', but because this interpretation of BLACK is encountered in many other linguistic expressions as well as in cultural codes other than natural languages. The interpretation of the colour BLACK as 'bad, unhappy' is a cultural fact. BLACK taken as a physical entity (not only as a word, a colour term) symbolises these properties.

The main criteria for a cultural symbol in figurative language are also fulfilled. First, the symbolic function of BLACK 'bad, unhappy' is supported by cultural knowledge about the colour. As will be demonstrated in more detail in section 11.4.1, BLACK is a very strong symbol in culture. Symbolic functions like 'badness', 'unhappiness' etc. are established in various codes of culture and in many other CFUs. The knowledge about the link between the symbol BLACK in language and culture ensures that the "right" reading is activated. Hence, in view of the first criterion, BLACK in idiom (47) is a cultural symbol in a conventional figurative unit. The second criterion is also fulfilled, since the secondary function of BLACK as 'bad, unhappy' has become conventionalised in many further figurative units.

Inadvertent activation of the primary reading 'black colour' can more or less be excluded in idiom (47). However, the processing of the following idiom (48) may be temporarily disrupted if the symbolic function ('bad, unhappy') is activated first:

(48)　*to be in the black*
　　　'to have money in the bank account; to be solvent, be in credit'

The motivation of idiom (48) is not constituted by the symbolic function of BLACK. Rather, a particular fragment of world knowledge must be activated in order to ensure "switching" to the adequate reading. This fragment pertains to the former custom of banks in recording amounts on the credit side in black type and amounts overdrawn in red type (or knowledge about the graphic presentation of former balance reports, where positive numbers were written in black and negative ones in red). Thus, *black* refers to nothing more than its primary reading (black type or black ink). Furthermore, this reading is not supported by any cultural code (the role of culture here is restricted to material and social aspects), nor is it autonomous, as was the case in idiom (47) above. See section 11.4.1 for more details.

10.8 Combining of cultural phenomena in figurative units

The five main types of cultural phenomena that make up the image components of CFUs have been examined in the previous sections. There are, however, several forms of combination among these types. This means that two or more types are embodied in one single conventional figurative unit. Sometimes the types of cultural knowledge fixed in conventional figurative units correlate with the types of their motivation.

There are many CFUs that are based on a combined understanding of social interactions, material culture, and cultural symbolism. Let us look at an example where these three types act together (49). *Schwarzer Peter* (*Black Peter*) is the name of a card game in Germany. It is quite a simple children's game, similar to the game "old maid" in England, but with a card representing a black cat or a black person (a black bogyman or chimney sweeper) instead of an old maid. This game is known in several European cultures and has similar names in e.g. Dutch *zwartepiet*,[30] Swedish *svarte Petter*, and Finnish *musta Pekka*, meaning "black Peter".

(49) German *jmdm. den schwarzen Peter zuschieben/zuspielen* "to slip/pass someone the black Peter"
'to blame someone else for one's own failure, to shift the responsibility for something to someone else'

Playing cards in a given social community, at a given time, according to the rules of the game, is a matter of "social interaction" (i). Two other types of cultural

---

[30] Things are a little different in Dutch, because the word *zwartepiet* means 'scapegoat' as well; in addition, *Zwarte Piet* "Black Peter" is thought of as a bogyman and companion to St. Nicholas.

knowledge are also present in this idiom. Game cards are artefacts; as such, they belong to "material culture" [type (ii)]. Furthermore, type (v) is also apparent, since BLACK occurs in its symbolic function. BLACK is a strong symbol in many cultural codes, denoting various aspects of BAD (see 11.4.1).

BLACK in conventional figurative language is in no way inferior to BLACK in culture. All the languages analysed in this study have a large number of CFLs with BLACK in its symbolic functions such as 'evil', 'bad character', 'bad luck, misfortune', 'pessimistic views' or 'illegality' (Dobrovol'skij and Piirainen 1997: 241–252). Within the game of *Schwarzer Peter*, understood as a semiotic system, BLACK has precisely these symbolic functions. The black card is 'bad' in itself (in contrast to all the other cards); the last player to hold it has 'bad luck' and loses the game. What is crucial is not the black colour itself but the culturally relevant knowledge about the function of BLACK in the semiotic context of the game.

Idiom (50) is another example where these three features of cultural phenomena occur together in one CFU. The idiom has equivalents in many other standard languages. To understand it in its figurative sense, some "everyday" cultural knowledge about the situation at a crossroads is required. It is part of shared knowledge that cars may go when the traffic lights turn green, so the motivating link responsible for the inference is based on the similarity of two situations, namely being allowed to proceed at a crossroads and being allowed to do something that you want to do.

(50) *to give someone the green light*
'to encourage or allow to proceed, to give someone permission to do something that they were planning to do or have asked to do'

The image component of this idiom is grounded in the regulation of traffic lights. Road users have to know and follow the rules [type (i)]. As artefacts, traffic lights also belong to the material culture of modern urban communities [type (ii)]. Furthermore, traffic lights constitute a "classic" semiotic system, consisting of the three members GREEN, YELLOW and RED. The meanings of these three signs are conventional: the functions of the colours were established at the beginning of the 20th century (cf. Gamst 1980 for historical details). Nevertheless, the choice of GREEN as the colour of permission is not arbitrary but motivated on another level.[31] It continues a long cultural tradition [type (v)] of symbolic knowledge about this colour.

---

31 In communist China at the end of the nineteen-fifties, a reversal of the symbolic values of the traffic lights was seriously considered. It was argued that RED, as the colour of revolution

The semiotic function of GREEN ('to have a clear run, to be allowed to proceed') in the sign system 'traffic lights' corresponds to the symbolic function of the colour in various cultural codes. The main symbolic meaning of GREEN in the Western cultural area is HOPE. This symbolic meaning came into being by perceiving GREEN as the most important colour in nature, as a sign of the renewal of the vegetation in spring and the growing of all kinds of flora, which has been associated with hope and eternal life. There are various parallelisms to Christian symbolism; GREEN is the colour of the resurrection; in liturgies, the colour green symbolises the Holy Spirit. Therefore, traces of cultural symbolism provided by the semiotic system 'traffic lights' can be recognised in idiom (50).

The correlation of type (iv), culture-specific beliefs, with type (iii), textual dependence, has been mentioned with the help of the English idiom *the green-eyed monster* (10.6). The concept GREEN ENVY can be traced back to the humoural doctrine, but it has been "mediated" by Shakespeare's tragedy; the concrete idiom originally is a quotation from "Othello". In some cases, a cultural symbol [type (v)] can be traced back directly to elements of an ancient folk theory [type iv]. This is assumed for YELLOW in English conventional figurative units providing the symbolic meaning 'cowardice'; cf. examples (23–24) in chapter 11.

Type (v), cultural symbols in CFUs, often occurs in combination with type (iii), textual dependence. The interrelation between fables and animal symbolism has already been mentioned. The image of many animals has been formed by fables and beast epics. The symbolic meanings of FOX, WOLF or SNAKE, for example, were coined by a long tradition of fables dating from classical antiquity.[32] CFUs that are quotations from or allusions to fables and handed down throughout the centuries also play a part in the symbolic estimation of animals. The SNAKE, for instance, is generally considered a symbol of 'evil, maliciousness', 'deceitfulness' or 'danger' in the western cultural area. These symbolic meanings are particularly obvious in some idioms that are more or less literal quotations themselves: *to nourish a viper in one's bosom* 'to have one's kindness repaid with spite or ingratitude' (a quotation

---

and progress, must not be allowed to indicate 'stop'. However, this idea did not gain acceptance. Contemporary Chinese even has an idiom corresponding to (50), probably a borrowing from English: *kāi lǜ dēng* "to give green light (to someone)" meaning 'to give someone the permission for something' (Wenliang 1991: 108; Fan 1996: 277; Piirainen 2016).

[32] Compare Idström and Piirainen (2012b). Among other things, this work points to the differences between animal concepts prominent in languages with a literary tradition, and Inari Saami. While Inari Saami metaphors typically draw their motivation from the concrete life experience of the people, the widespread idioms are to a large extent based on literary traditions. In both cases motivating links are encountered that are drawn from or supported by folklore: fairy tales, mythology and superstition.

from the 97th Aesopic fable) or *a snake in the grass* 'a secret enemy, a person who cannot be trusted' (from Virgil's "Eclogues" III: 93).

The same holds for a number of CFUs that seem to display significant cultural symbols but can in turn be traced back to other texts, e.g. to the Bible, to belles-lettres, or to modern advertisements, like example (51).

(51) *whiter than white*
 'very honest, morally beyond reproach; law-abiding; very pure, too pure or good to be believed'

The symbolic character of idiom (51) is obvious. The colour WHITE is not used in its literal sense but in its symbolic meaning alone, which fits the culture symbolism of WHITE in general. Symbolic meanings such as 'purity' and 'innocence' play a role in many relevant cultural codes (e.g. in the biblical exegesis and liturgical allegory, in fairy tales or popular modern symbolism) along the same lines. There is also a wide spectrum of positive meanings connected with WHITE in conventional figurative language, such as 'good', 'true', 'morally pure', 'innocent', as emerges, for example, in the compound *whitewash* in its figurative sense 'embellishment' (see Dobrovol'skij and Piirainen 1997: 232–240 for details).

However, idiom (51) is characterised not only by symbolism but also by textual dependence. The text "Whiter than white" has been an advertising slogan since the nineteen fifties when it extolled Persil soap powder. This slogan left traces in the English language as it became popular and was adopted as a lexical unit. It does not matter whether speakers of English are conscious of the textual link of this idiom to an old advertisement.

As has been mentioned, "animal symbolism" is a large complex topic, both in culture and conventional figurative language. "Flower symbolism" is a complex cultural topic, too. There was a vast "flower symbology" during the last few centuries, which ascribed meanings to almost all flowers and their different colours and appearances (examples of this "overwrought code" are listed in Biedermann 1994: 136–138). Conventional figurative language, however, did not adopt much of it. Apart from a few idioms and proverbs with ROSE, there is one familiar English idiom with LILY in a symbolic meaning (52). It is also a quotation:

(52) a. *to gild the lily*
 b. American English *to paint the lily*
 'to try to improve what is already beautiful or excellent; to try to make perfection more perfect; to mask natural beauty or a good quality by over-decorating it'

The symbolic meanings of LILY clearly emerge in idioms (52); they can be described as 'natural beauty' and 'perfection, excellence'. These meanings correspond to "the lily of the field" in the verse of Matthew 4:29, where we read "that even Solomon in all his glory was not arrayed like one of these", but they differ from the cultural symbolism ascribed to the lily since the Christian Middle Ages. The most salient symbolic qualities of the lily, particularly of the white lily as a Christian symbol, are 'innocence', 'purity', and 'chastity, virginity'. The lily is the flower of the Virgin Mary (Gabriel, the Angel of the Annunciation, is usually portrayed holding a lily) and became a symbol of pure, virginal love (Hall 1994: 149; Biedermann 1994: 207–208).

Moreover, two symbols come together in idiom (52). As version (52a) shows, the symbolic function of GOLD 'something very valuable' (evoked by the verb *gild*) must also be taken into account. Covering the lily (which is considered beautiful enough as it is) with gold means overdoing it. There are different symbolic interpretations of idiom (52a) such as 'to add ornament or decoration to something that is pleasing in its original state' or 'to attempt to improve something that is already good (and to spoil it by doing so)'. The idiom shows that the cultural symbols LILY and GOLD are alive in conventional figurative units of the English language, but they are only a part of the cultural features here. The textual dependence of idioms (52a) and (52b) also plays an important role. It is an adaptation from Shakespeare's words in "King John" (IV, 2) "To gild refined gold, to paint the lily [...] Is wasteful and ridiculous excess".

There are many CFUs that contain a cultural symbol and are at the same time connected with literary texts or narrative traditions, for example, *a wolf in sheep's clothing* (initially from the Bible, Matthew 7:14, but also adopted by fables and other literary texts; WOLF is symbolically connected with 'evil', 'danger') and *to cry wolf (too often)* 'to cry for help (even when there is no danger involved), to raise a false alarm' (from the Aesopian fable and many other fables, WOLF in the symbolic meaning 'danger'); or *to kill the goose that lays the golden eggs* 'to destroy a reliable and valuable source of income' (with allusion to a fable by Aesop, with GOLD being a symbol of 'something very precious, highly valued'). The idiom *to be in seventh heaven* and its equivalents in other languages stand out by combining several types of cultural knowledge.

Finally, several CFUs mainly based on type (i) "social interaction" are actually references to other texts [type (iii)]. As has been outlined above, expressions that are traceable to the conceptual metaphor TIME IS MONEY embody social aspects of a given cultural area. Nevertheless, even this prominent metaphor became established in language originally by means of a quotation, i.e. via textual dependence. The proverb *Time is money* began to gain popularity after Benjamin Franklin's comment "Remember that Time is Money". Thus, the corresponding concept of the metaphor TIME IS MONEY introduced in Lakoff and Johnson (1980) is actually based on this quotation. Compare also section 10.3.1.

Further aspects of "social interactions in figurative units" include gestures fixed in certain idioms. The relation between an idiom like *to tear one's hair out* and traditional forms of behaviour in antiquity has been outlined above (example (15) in 10.3.3). There are several idioms the image components of which reveal particular gestures that were customary in bygone times, probably once performed in biblical times. Some idioms can be traced back directly to verses of the Bible, as for example *to beat one's breast* 'to make a great show of sorrow or regret' (Luke 18:13 and 23:48).

Several binomials can be traced back to gestures performed in medieval legal practice, together with ancient wordings of a law, cf. German *Stein und Bein schwören* "to swear stone and bone" 'to swear blind': the defendant had to swear the oath by the altar (*Stein*) and the relic (*Bein*). Thus, different aspects of culture are also involved here.

In sum, many CFUs are grounded in more than one cultural domain. In several cases, no sharp line can be drawn between the different types of cultural phenomena that have mainly contributed to the existence of a given figurative unit. The combination of "social culture", "material culture" and "symbols", as well as the links between "symbols" and "textual dependence", are the most dominant kinds of blending.

10.9 Cultural connotations

10.9.1 Preliminary notes

The main topics in the last sections were culture-specifics of figurative language (in the domains of social and material culture, textual dependence and cultural symbolism). One suitable tool for revealing these specifics was the *cross-linguistic* approach: the culture-specifics of a given language were defined in relation to other languages. There is, however, yet another type of culture-specific CFU, which is accessible without juxtaposing it with other languages. This type consists of expressions that native speakers themselves see as marked by their traditional culture.[33]

---

[33] Wierzbicka's (1997) propositions that the "Russian national character" can be captured by means of, among other things, the Russian lexicon, have been assessed as follows: "Each of these propositions, taken one by one, is highly dubious, if not downright false. Put them together, and we are likely to get a very strange cocktail!" (Mondry and Taylor 1998: 30). Similarly

Speakers of a language perceive certain figurative units as "their own and only their own". In these cases, the notion of *culture* is used in the sense of *cultural connotation*.[34] We use the term *traditional culture* here instead of *national culture*, which is widely used in studies on cultural aspects of language.

No cross-linguistic contrast is needed to perceive a lexical unit as being culturally connoted. Rather, it is the specific properties of these lexical units that native speakers consider to be grounded in their traditional culture, in texts of folklore, folk beliefs, national history and the like. These properties lead to *culture-specific usage restrictions*. The lexical units in question are for the most part untranslatable. The cultural connotations manifest themselves in restrictions of usage of a given lexical unit, which can be explained only on the basis of associations with certain motifs, subjects and other knowledge structures belonging to the culture in question. CFUs of this type can be discovered by turning to the language intuition of the speakers (i.e. by the introspective approach).

Linguistic items that are singled out as marked in the framework of the contrastive approach need not have anything in common with items singled out in the framework of the introspective approach. What is perceived as being specific from the perspective of another language or another culture (i.e. from an "outer" point of view) may be perceived as trivial from an "inner" perspective.

The domain of cultural connotations includes very different elements. Some of the most important things for example, are

- the presence of national names and their derivatives in the lexical structure of an expression (cf. Russian *коломенская верста* "the verst (an old length unit) of Kolomna" 'a very tall man', evoking associations with the town of *Kolomna*); the correct etymology of the expression is traced back to extremely tall mileposts set on the road between Moscow and the royal residence of *Kolomenskoe* in the 18th century (for details on culture-specific proper nouns, see 10.9.2);
- characters of "folk mythology" (cf. Finnish *hiisi vieköön* "(the) *Hiisi* may take (it) away" 'it is all the same, it makes no difference', *Hiisi* being the big Evil in Finnish mythology);

---

unproven assertions of a national-cultural specificity come from Teliya et al. (1998: 59): "Thus, *правда* denotes truth as an ethical phenomenon with no direct counterpart in English. This is a case of linguistic/cultural lacuna. Similarly, *совесть*, 'conscience', is a case of partial overlap". Assumptions of this kind are mostly based on the authors' intuitions and cannot be verified in general.

34 Compare the discussion of the notion of *cultural connotations* in Teliya et al. (1998: 59–61). In the authors' opinion, *cultural connotations* are associative relations between the image and the cultural pattern. It remains unclear what is meant by "cultural pattern". There is not much in common with the notion of cultural connotations favoured in our study.

– words denoting idioethnic realia (cf. Teliya et al. 1998) (e.g. *щи* 'cabbage soup' and *лапоть* 'bast shoe' in the Russian idiom *не лаптем щи хлебать* "to not eat the cabbage soup with a bast shoe" 'to be a civilised, socially experienced person; to be not so rurally naive, behind the times or uncultivated as has been assumed' (see 10.9.3).

Further elements that can pertain to this domain are CFUs with unique constituents (cf. English *kith and kin* 'one's relations', *kith* being unique to this expression) and irregular morphological forms of the constituents. The use of these irregular forms can be based on word play, with an intentional form of distortion, e.g. Russian *с таком* '(of some food, dish, baked goods etc.) without any sauce, dressing, filling etc.: (just) plain)' in contexts such as *Конфеты кончились и пришлось пить чай с таком* 'Sweets had run out of stock and we had to drink tea with tak_{instr}' (*tak* is a particle meaning 'so'; it does not allow for inflection; hence, its use in the instrumental case violates the grammar norms).

The irregularity of a morphological form of the constituent may be explained by its archaicness (German *fröhliche Urständ feiern* 'to revive something, to come to life again'; Russian *ничтоже сумняшеся* 'without any doubt', *темна вода во облацех* "dark water in the clouds" '≈ something is absolutely unclear or unpredictable'. Both parts of the expression, *ничтоже сумняшеся* and the form *облацех* in *темна вода во облацех*, come from Old Church Slavonic. Both expressions can be traced back to the Bible.

No matter how much of a paradox it may seem, language speakers are prone to consider units containing elements that are not fully understandable as "native folk" units (that is to claim them as "their own"), although quite often these elements are not native etymologically (for example, German *jmdm. pomade sein* "to be *pomade* to someone" 'to be a matter of complete indifference to someone, to be all the same to someone'). This phenomenon is akin to the "process of sacralisation of incomprehensible texts" (cf. Lotman and Pjatigorskij 2000: 437).

Finally, factors of form complication (rhyming, alliteration, onomatopoeia etc.) can also be pertinent to the domain of cultural connotations, cf. English *to and fro*, *hum and haw* (BrE), *hem and haw* (AmE) 'to keep pausing before you speak'. The Finnish language provides numerous such expressions, e.g. *mullin mallin* and *vinksin vonksin*, both meaning 'completely chaotic, a great muddle'. These expressions are perceived as a unique property of Finnish, as specific language traditions and "their own and only their own".

In the following sections we want to look at some of these phenomena in more detail. We will discuss some examples from the domains of proper nouns and idioethnic realia. Finally, we will look at some CFUs referring to culture-specific entities. This means that it is not the source concept but the target concept that is responsible for the culture-specifics. If such expressions contain additional elements that speakers interpret as pointing to cultural uniqueness, they may also reveal cultural connotations.

10.9.2 Proper nouns

In some cases, speakers perceive conventional figurative units that contain a proper noun typical of a given traditional culture as being culturally connoted. The onymic element of such expressions may be a toponym, e.g. names of towns and rivers or anthroponym. Compare idioms with the city names *Newcastle* and *Tula* (53–54).

(53) English *to carry/sell/take coals to Newcastle*
'to bring or send certain objects to a place where there are already many objects of that kind; to present certain ideas, artistic achievements, etc. as being new if they are already well-known in a given place'

(54) Russian *ездить в Тулу со своим самоваром* "to go to Tula with one's one samovar"
'to bring or send certain objects to a place where there are already many objects of that kind; to bring somebody to a place where there are many people of that kind'

Chapter 3 included an analysis of idioms (53) and (54) and their quasi-equivalent German *Eulen nach Athen tragen* in view of the fine-grained differences in their semantic interpretation, which are grounded in the different lexical structure (image component) of the idioms. These expressions may illustrate the phenomenon of cultural connotation here. Because of the city names *Newcastle* and *Tula*, the idioms are set in the cultural contexts of England[35] and Russia, respectively. In addition to that, idiom (54) is culturally connoted by means of the word *samovar*, which denotes a significant object of traditional Russian culture.

There are a number of idioms with river names in the colloquial or vernacular varieties of German. For the most part the names of the rivers are interchangeable – according to the particular river of a given region of the German-speaking countries. Compare German *mit Spreewasser getauft sein* "to be baptised with water from the Spree" 'to be a native of Berlin' and *mit Alsterwasser getauft sein*

---

[35] There is also a Newcastle in Australia, and it too is in a coalmining area.

"to be baptised with water from the Alster" 'to be a native of Hamburg' (*Spree* and *Alster* being the rivers of Berlin and Hamburg, respectively).

Another idiom type, *Wasser in den Fluss gießen/schütten/tragen* "to pour/carry water into the river" 'to bring or send something to a place where these entities already exist; to do unnecessary work, to do senseless things', has about 20 adaptations to particular regions through the varying river names (e.g. *Wasser in den Rhein/in die Donau/Saar/Spree/ . . . tragen* "to carry water into the Rhine/Danube/Saar/Spree/ . . .", cf. Piirainen 2016). These idioms are culturally connoted with regard to each particular area.

A special case is the microtoponyms in CFUs. Because of the restricted areas where field names are known, they cannot, by their nature, occur in national standard languages. In dialectal CFL, however, they occur in the same way as other toponyms and evoke the same kind of cultural connotations as place names in standard languages.

Another group of onymic culture-specific CFUs are those containing anthroponyms (first names and family names). A good example is the Russian *мамаево побоище* "Mamai's slaughter". This used to refer to a bloody fight among many people, an allusion to a medieval battle between Russians and Tartars. This idiom is strongly culturally connoted. This property can be proved by means of text corpora as well as by the inner form – the idiom is a direct reference to the history of Russia. With the help of this idiom, the average Russian speaker knows who Mamai was, although many other Khans of the Tartars soon fell into oblivion (for more about this idiom see e.g. Teliya et al. 1998: 60).

A pseudo-name can also provide cultural connotations. *Koivuniemi* in idiom (55) is a construction that resembles a real toponym. In Finland, *Koivuniemi* is also a common and frequent name for a peninsula (*koivu* meaning 'birch' and *niemi* 'peninsula').

(55) Finnish *antaa Koivuniemen herra jklle* "to give sir/master of (the) *Koivuniemi* (*Birch-peninsula*) to someone"
'to give someone a thrashing; to beat someone with a rod'

Nowadays the idiom is used jokingly. In former times, however, it was said to children as a threat to beat them with a birch rod. Thus, it is originally a euphemistic saying – the master of the birch-peninsula provides the link to "beating, punishment" only by virtue of the element "birch"; the rods that were used to thrash children came from this tree.

CFUs with anthroponyms can also be perceived as being culturally connoted. Idioms with Christian names and surnames include, for example, English *a Jack of all trades* 'a man who knows a little of many jobs or can do many different types of work, but none properly' or German *Lieschen Müller* 'the average girl/woman'.

The specific cultural connotations become particularly clear in idiom (56). It is restricted to the cultural area of Germany because of the name *Adam Riese*, a man who is known throughout Germany yet almost completely unknown elsewhere. Adam Riese (1492–1559) was a master of arithmetic and published several popular textbooks on mathematics, which influenced German school curricula for a long time.

(56) German *nach Adam Riese* "according to *Adam Riese*"
'quite correct; it is (considered) right according to the most basic arithmetic principles'

The phenomenon of cultural connotations can be illustrated by very similar idioms from other languages, which also contain names of historical people who are well known due to their studies on arithmetic and are therefore prominent in their countries. There is a Dutch idiom (57) and a Finnish one (58), each as familiar as the German idiom (56) in their respective languages, whereas the English and Russian equivalents (59–60) are less familiar. Idioms (58–60) mean exactly the same as idiom (56) but refer to people who are known mainly in their respective countries.

(57) Dutch *volgens Bartjens* "according to *Bartjens*"

(58) Finnish *Elon laskuopin mukaan* "according to the calculating schoolbook of *Elo*"

(59) English (outdated) *according to Cocker*

(60) Russian (outdated) *по Малинину и Буренину* "according to *Malinin* and *Burenin*"

What idioms (56–60) have in common is that they are mostly used jokingly or ironically. The people referred to are famous because of their impact on arithmetic. All of them had great influence on the teaching of mathematics in their countries. *Willem Bartjens* (1569–1638) was a schoolmaster whose book on arithmetic "Cijfferinge" was published first in 1604 and republished repeatedly until 1839. *Efraim Elo* lived in the early 19th century and was a teacher in Joensuu (Finland). His well-known arithmetic textbook was used in the elementary schools in Finland between World War I and World War II. *Edward Cocker* (1631–1675) is the reputed author of the popular textbook "Cocker's Arithmetic", published in 1678, which has gone through more than 100 editions. Aleksandr F. Malinin (1834– 1888) and Konstantin P. Burenin (died 1882) were teachers and famous authors of mathematics and physics textbooks. Their books went through large numbers of editions as well.

10.9.3 Idioethnic realia

Another large group of culturally connoted conventional figurative units are those with words denoting "idioethnic realia". Russian *самовар* 'samovar', *щи* 'cabbage soup' or *лапти* 'bast shoes' named above are such words that denote culturally connoted objects. These words evoke associations with a concept of the traditional culture of Russia. Thus, the cultural connotation is grounded in the realia item itself. A comparable word is *sauna* in Finnish, which also denotes a culturally connoted concept. In Finland, The SAUNA is an essential part of the national tradition; most Finnish people can identify with the sauna. SAUNA is not only a relevant concept in the Finnish culture but also a relevant source-frame in some CFUs.

(61) Finnish *mennä syyhymättä saunaan* "to go to the sauna, although it does not itch [although one does not feel very dirty]"
'to interfere, unasked, in things that do not concern one; to show too much interest in someone else's affairs, so that they become annoyed or angry'

(62) Finnish *lisätä löylyä/lyödä lisää löylyä* "to increase (sauna-)steam/pour more (sauna)-steam"
'to make a bad situation much worse than it is, to cause a conflict to become more intense'

Finnish native speakers will not hesitate to connect expression (62) with the sauna steam bath. There are two words for 'steam' in Finnish: *höyry* 'steam produced by boiling water' and *löyly* 'steam from water thrown on heated stones (of the sauna stove)'. The two words are not interchangeable because they denote different kinds of steam. Thus idioms (61–62) are firmly embedded in the traditional culture and, therefore, reveal cultural connotations.

Sometimes such expressions contain elements that are relevant from the point of view of the "material culture". Whereas they were considered from the perspective of their nontrivial cross-cultural specifics in section 10.4, expressions of this kind are a matter of linguistic interest here, as bearers of specific pragmatic features, i.e. of cultural connotations.

10.9 Cultural connotations — 321

Finally, the coining of new CFUs can reveal cultural connotations. Let us consider some idioms that came into being at the time of the former GDR and were in circulation only in that part of Germany, containing GDR peculiarities in their source domains (63–65).[36]

(63) German *er/sie sieht kein Westfernsehen mehr* "he/she does not watch West German TV channels anymore"
'he/she died'

(64) German *er/sie hat das Neue Deutschland abbestellt* "he/she cancelled the "Neues Deutschland"
'he/she died'

(65) German *das ist wie ein innerer/innerlicher Parteitag* "that is like an inner party conference"
'when one is very glad and pleased about something'

These idioms have significant presuppositions which were comprehensible only in the former GDR, where it was forbidden to watch West German TV programs (63), though most people still watched them. In fact, watching West German TV channels was a salient activity; only the deceased did not watch them anymore. The "Neues Deutschland" (65) was a GDR daily newspaper. GDR citizens loyal to the party line were obliged to subscribe to this paper; "dying" was the only excuse for cancelling it. A party conference (66) was propagated as a festival or holiday.

Idioms (63–65) also contain "social aspects" of culture, because they appeal to the particular knowledge encoded in the underlying frames. Other GDR-specifics are grounded in the target domain rather than in the source domain of some idioms, for example the matter of elections (66), since voting was no more than folding a piece of paper:

(66) German *(Zettel) falten gehen* "to go to fold (a slip/slips of paper)"
'to go to vote'

---

[36] These idioms came to light during the project "Survey on the Common Knowledge of Idioms in Colloquial German". This empirical study was started in order to make an inventory of the common knowledge of idioms in individual regions of Germany, primarily focusing on regional differences. During that study, several hundred idioms emerged that had not been listed in dictionaries before (see Piirainen 2001b, 2002, 2003a for detail).

Although these idioms seem to be short lived, they were felt as their own because of the allusions to cultural specifics in this former state.

10.9.4 Culture-specifics in the target concept

In cases like SAMOVAR or SAUNA, the culturally connoted concepts are centred on one single constituent of the CFU. There are also CFUs whose whole word string signifies culture specific objects, such as (67).

(67) Russian *чёрный ворон* "a black raven"
'a police vehicle for the transportation of prisoners and arrested people'

Being an idiom with identifying semantics, i.e. one that allows concrete-referential use, this idiom denotes a target concept which evokes a lot of cultural and historical associations. In this sense, the referent itself is unique and culturally marked. On the other hand, the image component of the meaning of the idiom corresponds to a concept that plays an important role in Russian folklore, i.e. to the concept RAVEN. The RAVEN (*ворон* – *вран*) is an important symbol in Russian (and Proto-Slavonic) culture. It symbolises a connection between the world of the living and the world of the dead. Puškin regards the RAVEN as a symbol of execution (Pen'kovskij 2005: 187–224). This allows us to consider the idiom *чёрный ворон* as a culture-specific phenomenon of the Russian language, both in terms of cultural connotations and with regard to other languages. The same kind of police vehicle exists, for example, in Germany or England. For comparison, we can take a look at the almost semantically equivalent English and German idioms (68–69).

(68) English *Black Maria*

(69) German *die grüne Minna* "the green Minna"
both meaning 'a police vehicle for the transportation of prisoners and arrested people'

The idioms also have cultural connotations because of the personal names *Maria* or *Minna*. *Minna* was a very popular first name in 19th century Germany; domestic servants or maids, for instance, were often called "Minna". The word *grün* 'green' in (69) originates not only from the green colour of the transport van but also from a "Rotwelsch" (thieves' cant, underworld jargon) word meaning 'unpleasant, eerie' (Duden 2013: 293). The actual meaning itself is culture-specific, not only the image. The same holds for the English *Black Maria*; however, the symbolic meaning of BLACK, which has, of course, nothing to do with cultural connotations, should be noticed in this case. Compare also the idioms (49–50) mentioned in chapter 3: Spanish *el chino de la esquina* and German *Tante-Emma-Laden* both meaning 'a small shop of traditional type'.

Finally, there are conventional figurative units whose whole word string denotes culture specific objects (which have just as few counterparts in other cultural communities). Idiom (70) itself is a proper noun, a specific cultural target concept.

(70)   Russian *Матросская тишина* "sailor's silence"
       'a well-known prison in Moscow'

The actual meanings of idioms like Russian (70) are unique. In order to explain this uniqueness, there is no need to involve the category of cultural connotations. From the viewpoint of the semantic function, idioms of this kind are proper nouns, that is to say, they are unique by definition.

Furthermore, this example shows that historical and cultural associations evoked by an idiom on the one hand and its cultural specifics on the other hand are not identical. Of course, they are parts of culture. However, it is not necessary to turn to culture-specific cognitive structures in order to explain their motivation, i.e. the relevant links between the phonological structure and the actual meaning (the conceptual bridge between them). In other words, expressions of this kind are culturally specific because they refer to a unique denotatum which is part of the traditional culture. Thus, the target concept is culturally specific, while the source concept is not. The culture-specific features are grounded in denotations rather than in connotations.

10.10 Concluding remarks

The importance of culture to conventional figurative language has been demonstrated in detail. It has been noticed that the vast majority of CFUs are affected by culture in one way or another. We have put forward some relevant distinctions between five main types of shared cultural knowledge that underlie conventional figurative units: (more or less tacit) knowledge (i) of social interactions and patterns of behaviour, (ii) of given parts of the material culture, such as artefacts, (iii) of the textual dependence of CFUs, (iv) of references to fictive conceptual domains and pre-scientific models of the world, and (v) of cultural symbols in language, i.e. semiotic knowledge about the interrelation between items in conventional figurative language and other relevant codes of culture. Besides these, there are several kinds of combinations of these cultural phenomena in conventional figurative language. Finally, "cultural connotations" (aspects of traditional culture in CFUs) are involved in conventional figurative language.

This classification can be seen as a tool that could make it possible to compare the cultural foundation of different languages. The typology of the principal cultural phenomena enables us to compare given parts of conventional figurative language across many languages and find similarities and contrasts based on a great variety of linguistic data (including standard languages and dialects).

In traditional linguistic research, no differentiation of types of cultural knowledge underlying conventional figurative language existed. All cultural phenomena expounded here were generally subsumed under "culture", with the consequence that the notion of "culture" in this undifferentiated form could not be used in linguistic analyses proper. The classification proposed here enables us to decide which concrete cultural phenomenon is concerned in every single case. Each of these phenomena requires its own methods of analysis.

Aspects of social interactions and material culture, can for the most part, be described in terms of semantics, i.e. by explicating the image components of the conventional figurative units in question. Social aspects of figurative language such as restrictions on speaking, euphemisms or gender-specifics belong to the domain of pragmatics. Text-related conventional figurative units cannot be interpreted merely on the basis of their imagery; rather, a change of direction towards text analysis is required, since they are part of the large domain of intertextuality in language. The same holds for CFUs originating from fictive domains and ancient folk theories later rejected in the course of scientific developments. Cultural symbols in language, i.e. the symbolic interpretation of certain concepts, can be described most adequately within the framework of semiotics of culture. Finally, cultural connotations have to be explicated as components of pragmatics.

Conventional figurative units tend to absorb and accumulate cultural elements; permanent use of the CFUs hands these elements down and impresses them in the cultural memory. There can be no adequate description of conventional figurative units and the way they function in a language without regard to culture, since in many cases culturally based concepts govern the inference from literal to figurative. Investigations into conventional figurative language from a cultural-semiotic perspective have so far been restricted to single fields and to a small number of languages. While there are some well-investigated sub-areas of cultural foundation, such as the textual dependence of many CFUs or the connection between gestures and idioms, a lot of basic research on cultural foundations is still lacking. Wide areas are still far from clear, such as the actual part that former pre-scientific conceptual domains plays in the overall inventory of conventional figurative units and the extent to which cultural models appear in conventional figurative language.

11 Cultural symbolism in figurative language

In this chapter we will look at conventional figurative units that are based on a very special kind of cultural knowledge, i.e. on the knowledge of *cultural symbols*. This concept can, in some respects, be considered a part of the *semiotics of culture* (in the sense of the Moscow-Tartu School). Therefore, we will give a brief outline of the main ideas of this school and of those theoretical issues that are useful for the aims of our study (11.1).

We will also go into the term *symbol* in more detail. The *symbol* is a key concept in linguistics as well as in many other academic disciplines, but it is used in different, even conflicting senses. We will give a short overview of the complex notion of "symbols in culture and language". First we will have a cursory look at concepts of the *symbol* in some disciplines other than linguistics (11.2). After that, we will consider more closely some linguistic and semiotic concepts of the symbol (11.3). Against this background, we want to develop our working concept of *cultural symbols in language*. This will then be illustrated by additional examples (11.4).

11.1 The semiotics of culture

In order to investigate *cultural symbolism in figurative language*, we need a metalinguistic apparatus that enables us to describe the phenomena of different semiotic systems along the same lines. A consistent terminology is necessary to describe certain culturally based phenomena (*symbols*) in conventional figurative language, on the one hand, and in other cultural codes such as mythology, religions, popular customs, etc., on the other. These aims comply with the theories of culture connected with semioticians such as Jurij M. Lotman, Boris A. Uspenskij and their circle, known as the *Moscow-Tartu School* (cf. Lotman and Uspenskij 1971; Lotman 1971 1974, 1990; Uspenskij et al. 1973; Eimermacher 1974; Shukman 1977, 1986; Chernov 1988; Sebeok 1988; Portis-Winner 1994: 114–115; Torop 2002; Winner 2002; Semenenko 2012; Pilshchikov and Trunin 2016). The semiotic tradition developed by the Moscow-Tartu School is called *the semiotics of culture*.

Semioticians of this provenance put forward some promising heuristics which can be used as a foundation for developing relevant methods of analysis. However, the theoretical framework of cultural semiotics cannot be fully compared with theories such as the Cognitive Theory of Metaphor. No institutionalisation or doctrine comparable to those theories has been formed in the field of the semiotics of culture. Rather, the semiotics of culture is regarded as an accumulation of interdisciplinary research on cultural phenomena, extending from the analysis of language and literature to all other culturally relevant phenomena.

11.1.1 The Moscow-Tartu School

In this section we give a brief outline of the main ideas of the Moscow-Tartu semiotic school. According to this semiotic tradition, culture can be regarded as the totality of all non-inherited information and the ways by which it is organised and preserved. In the view of the Moscow-Tartu School, culture is the totality of semiotic systems by means of which mankind or a particular human group maintains its coherence. There is a hierarchical ordering of different semiotic systems. In the terminology of the Moscow-Tartu School, natural language is labelled as the *primary modelling system*, contrasting with all other semiotic systems, referred to as *secondary modelling systems*. Literature, art, etc., or cultural sign systems in general, are considered secondary modelling systems in relation to the primary system of language, because they are constructed on the basis of *natural language*.

> As a system of systems based in the final analysis on a natural language (this is implied in the term "secondary modelling systems", which are contrasted with the "primary system", that is to say, the natural language), culture may be regarded as a hierarchy of semiotic systems correlated in pairs, the correlation between them being to a considerable extent realized through correlation with the system of the natural language. This connection appears especially clearly in the reconstruction of Proto-Slavic antiquities on account of the greater syncretism of archaic cultures (cf. the connection between certain rhythmic and melodic types and metrical ones, which in their turn are conditioned by rules of syntactic prosody; the direct reflection of ritual functions in the linguistic denotations of such elements of ritual texts as the names of ceremonial foods). (Uspenskij et al. 1973: 21)

At this point it has to be mentioned that, during the time of totalitarianism in Russia, terms like *primary modelling system* and *secondary modelling systems* served as a means of camouflage. This intentionally complicated metalanguage allowed scholars to continue their research on culture in Russia before the revolution, above all their research on the culture of Russian aristocracy in the 18th and 19th century, unnoticed by the prevailing censorship (cf. e.g. Lotman 1974). Although the terms *primary modelling system* and *secondary modelling systems* seem to be "exotic" from a contemporary point of view and are now little used, we regard the basic idea of the Moscow-Tartu School as applicable to our aims. Its basic idea is a complete translatability of all cultural codes by means of natural language (see below). The idea that natural language underlies all other cultural codes is the most important one.

The umbrella term *secondary modelling systems* created in the framework of the Moscow-Tartu School covers a variety of cultural codes, including, besides literature and arts, religions, rituals, myths, fairy tales and popular beliefs, as well as architecture, music, film, and the like (see 11.4.4). All of these are seen as supplementary superstructures based on *natural language*, which is considered the only means by which secondary (cultural) systems can be interpreted, memorised, and taken into the collective memory.

In a further development of this theory, the concept of *texts* (in a general semiotic sense of this word) has replaced the position of *language* as of prime importance. Since all cultural processes are semiotic – i.e. sign-based – processes, all cultural products are "texts". This means that human culture is seen as the totality of texts and their functions. Seen from the synchronic viewpoint, human culture is a system of texts, whereas from the diachronic viewpoint, culture is made up of the production, transmission, storing, reception, and interpretation of "texts" (in the semiotic sense). Culture is understood as

> a hierarchy of semiotic systems composed of texts, as the sum of the texts and the set of functions correlated with them, or as a certain mechanism which generates these texts [...], culture may be understood by analogy with the individual mechanism of memory as a certain collective mechanism for the storage and processing of information.
> (Uspenskij et al. 1973: 17)

According to Lotman and Uspenskij (1971: 857–858), culture generates various heterogeneous semiotic systems, which the authors call "multilingualism in principle". Culture is considered a complex of "polyglot" semiotic systems with its own memory and self-regulatory mechanisms. It constitutes a *hierarchy of special semiotic systems* and the sum of all texts. Compared to individual memory, culture is described as collective memory, which is constantly storing and processing information. The adoption of an element into the cultural code means its adoption into the "text" of memory. This kind of adoption shows all the characteristics of translation from one language into another.

11.1.2 Semiotics of culture and figurative language

For the purposes of our study, it is not necessary to deal with all the details of the theory of the Moscow-Tartu School outlined above. However, some elements of this theory will be adopted as a theoretical framework for the analysis of cultural symbols in conventional figurative language. These elements of cultural semiotics will be integrated into the Conventional Figurative Language Theory that we develop here.

What remains crucial to the analysis and description of *cultural symbols in figurative language* is the basic idea of the connection between "symbols in natural language" and "symbols (symbolisations) outside language". This theoretical framework should make it possible to relate very different occurrences of symbols to each other. One of the most important consequences for the aims of our study is the idea that phenomena of natural language, such as conventional figurative units, can be compared with similar phenomena in other codes ("secondary cultural codes" or "texts"). The mutual translatability from one code into another is possible via natural language, which forms a universal foundation for all secondary codes. This means that similar linguistic and/or semiotic methodologies can be used for the study of all cultural phenomena.

In addition, the Moscow-Tartu semioticians differentiated between "paradigmatic" and "syntagmatic" culture, resulting from the "hierarchical ordering" of the semiotic codes and entailing consequences for research on symbols in language. This dichotomy is summarised in Shukman (1986: 167):

> Cultures may be classified as "paradigmatic" (all phenomena are signs of some higher reality), or "syntagmatic" (meaning arises by relationships between individual phenomena, not by reference to a higher Meaning): the high degree of semioticization in medieval culture is an example of the former, while the eighteenth century Enlightenment, with its desemioticizing tendencies (preference of nature over convention), is an example of the latter.

The hypothesis of a hierarchical ordering of semiotic codes has consequences for the study of *cultural symbols in figurative language*. Symbols are created (or originate) in "paradigmatic" stages of development of the cultures in question. Contemporary cultures tend to be "syntagmatic", whereas "paradigmatic remains" exist only in the form of some traces in conventional figurative language, hardly recognisable from a synchronic point of view. Our aim is to describe these traces because they reveal cultural, semiotic and, to some extent, linguistic dimensions. In this sense, our study also has a diachronic dimension.

We will now focus on some ideas of the Moscow-Tartu semiotic school concerning the symbol, mainly postulated by Lotman (1990, 1992). The symbol is regarded as a significant mechanism of cultural memory. An overview of the main features of the symbol is given in Lotman (1990: 103):

> A symbol, as commonly understood, involves the idea of a content which in its turn serves as expression level for another content, one which is as a rule more highly valued in that culture. We must distinguish a symbol from a reminiscence or quotation since in them the 'outer' level of content-expression is not independent but rather a kind of index-sign pointing to a larger text with which it is in a metonymic relationship. Whereas a symbol both in expression level and in content level is always a text, i.e. it has a single, self-contained

meaning value and a clearly demarcated boundary, which makes it possible to isolate it from the surrounding semiotic context. We believe that this latter circumstance is especially important for the ability to be a symbol.

The properties of the symbol named here are applicable to the notion of the symbol in conventional figurative language (see 11.4). Firstly, the symbol is a sign whose content serves to express another content. This second content of the symbol is generally of a higher value in the hierarchy of cultural values than the primary content. "Higher value" means 'higher density' or 'higher degree of abstraction'. Secondly, the semantic potentials of the symbol are always greater than any of their realisations. Thirdly, the symbol is independent from the given context; it can be isolated semantically.

Lotman points to a further feature of the symbol, which is also significant for the symbol in figurative language, namely its ability to "enter a new textual context" when separated from its former semiotic context.

> Symbols have preserved this ability to store up long and important texts in condensed form. But even more interesting is another feature, also an archaic one: a symbol, being a finalized text, does not have to be included in a syntagmatic chain, and if it is included in one, it preserves its own semantic and structural independence. It can readily be picked out from its semiotic context and just as readily enter a new textual context. (Lotman 1990: 103)

The ability of the symbol to enter a new context is a prerequisite for comparing symbols in language and in other cultural codes: the same symbol can occur in a myth, a legend, a work of art, a piece of music, a figurative expression, or other manifestations, and still remain the same entity, containing the same symbolic meaning.

According to Lotman, one result of this is that the symbol always contains an archaic layer, referring back to as far as preliterate times. "[A] symbol never belongs only to one synchronic section of a culture, it always cuts across that section vertically, coming from the past and passing on into the future. A symbol's memory is always more ancient than the memory of its non-symbolic text-context" (Lotman 1990: 103). However, the symbol correlates with its cultural context. It can be transformed under the influence of this context and can transform the context for its part.

Being "condensed memory", the symbol is positioned between similarity and convention. Lotman (1992: 192–193) compares the symbol with iconography in the Orthodox Church in order to make clear that symbols stand between iconicity and arbitrariness. Sacred icons in Orthodoxy differ from secular paintings in the same way as the "symbol" differs from an "icon": the sacred icon paintings refer to their content without aspiring to a portrayal-like depiction. Orthodox iconography is based on tradition; every depiction is of the same kind, as tradition demands and prescribes. To interpret these icons, some knowledge of the tradition and the kind of conventionalisation is required.

11.2 Concepts of the symbol in non-linguistic paradigms

The ubiquity of *symbols* has often been pointed out. The function of the symbol as a key concept has been emphasised in various academic disciplines concerned with man and culture (e.g. Nöth 1995: 115). Research in this field includes quite different scientific disciplines. Symbols are studied by theologians, psychoanalysts, ethnologists and anthropologists, as well as by fairy tale researchers, literature specialists, art historians, musicologists and representatives of other aesthetic and cultural domains. There is a long tradition of symbol research in many other disciplines, such as painting, or baroque poetry, or traditional folk culture.[1]

The reason for this is the central position of symbols in all areas of human culture. In this section we will discuss the notions of the *symbol* in some non-linguistic paradigms. We will start with remarks on the correlations between interdisciplinary symbol research in general and CFUs (11.2.1). After that, we will consider the complexity of the term *symbol* and the difficulties scholars have defining it (11.2.2). Finally, four main concepts of the *symbol* in the history of symbol studies will be examined (11.2.3).

11.2.1 Symbol research and research on conventional figurative units

Symbols occur in religions, myths, fairy tales, iconography and liturgy, as well as in customs, superstition (or rather, popular beliefs) and similar domains. They are used more or less consciously, or, rather, intuitively, in sacred or secular fine arts and architecture, literature, art performance, films, music, and many other fields. All these areas can be categorised as semiotic systems, which, in their entirety, make up a culture. In line with the terminology of the Moscow-Tartu School (see 11.1), we call them *codes of culture* or *cultural codes*.

Natural language is another semiotic system in which symbols play an important role. The language that forms the "primary modelling system" shows, in principle, the same symbolic phenomena as those in the codes of culture mentioned above. Whatever different schools and disciplines understand by

---

[1] Compare for the Slavic folk tradition, among others, Afanas'ev ([1865–1869] 1994), Sumcov (1996), Zelenin (1994), Tolstoj (1995), and Stepanov (1997).

symbol, linguistics and interdisciplinary symbol studies have a great deal in common. Symbol studies and linguistics could mutually supplement and enrich each other, even though they have failed to do so thus far.

Until recently, languages have not been analysed for symbolic phenomena, even though they could provide important data needed for a cultural-semiotic investigation into symbols. Symbol researchers, on the one hand, and linguists, on the other, have hardly noticed each other. It has to be stressed, however, that the few points of contact between them are to be found in the area of conventional figurative language, first of all in the area of idioms and proverbs, and then to some degree in the area of figurative compounds.

The results of general symbolic studies have been taken into account primarily in the historical and etymological explanations of some idioms and proverbs, for instance, in etymologically oriented phraseological dictionaries. Let us look at the entry for *Gold* in Röhrich's "Dictionary of proverbial expressions":

> Gold wurde urspr. mit göttlichen, heiligen und königlichen Werten in Beziehung gesetzt. Als edles Metall war es vor allem *ein Symbol* für innere Werte. Daher auch u.a. *der Vergleich* 'treu wie Gold', d.h. ein Inbegriff der Treue sein. (Röhrich 1991: 566) [emphasis ours]

> [Originally, gold was brought into relation with divine, sacred, and royal values. As a precious metal, it was above all *a symbol* of inner qualities. Hence also *the simile* 'true as gold', i.e. to be an epitome of faithfulness.]

Röhrich relates several figurative units containing a word such as *Gold, golden* to GOLD as a cultural symbol, so that the secondary readings (symbolic functions) of *Gold, golden* in these expressions, i.e. 'of high value, valuable, estimable', can be derived. Similar observations have been made in other dictionaries of proverbial sayings. For example, FOX is considered a symbol of intelligence and cunning, and ROSE is thought to be a symbol of beauty or purity – in this regard, CFUs correspond to cultural codes.

Treatises on certain culturally important symbols tend to cite idioms or proverbs containing a word that corresponds to the symbol in question. We can demonstrate this with the entries WOLF, LYNX, NINE and BREAD in Biedermann's "Dictionary of symbolism" (1994) [emphasis ours]:

WOLF:

> [. . .] *English idioms* preserve the image of the wolf as ravenous, a menace, a predator. "To keep the wolf from the door" is to earn sufficient money to avert starvation; "to cry wolf" is to raise a false alarm; and a human "wolf" (distinguished not by his howl but by his "whistle") is a man who relentlessly pursues large numbers of women for sexual gratification. (Biedermann 1994: 388)

LYNX:

[. . .] The beast of prey known for its acuity of vision (as in *the expression* "lynx-eyed") is relegated in Christian iconography to the realm of the devil.   (Biedermann 1994: 213–214)

NINE:

[. . .] In the Occident there were nine orders of angels, nine cosmic spheres in medieval cosmology, nine muses. *We say that* a cat has nine lives, and a person who is "dressed to the nines" is wearing his or her most elaborate finery.   (Biedermann 1994: 239)

BREAD:

[. . .] *Countless idioms* reflect the figurative importance of bread ("to take the bread out of someone's mouth," "that's my bread and butter").   (Biedermann 1994: 48)

Furthermore, let us look at the entry BREAD (*Brot*) in the original German version of Biedermann's dictionary "Lexikon der Symbole" (1989: 75), where, similarly, only two of many figurative expressions with *Brot* are quoted: *das bittere Brot der Verbannung essen* "to eat the bitter bread of banishment" and *jemandem Brot anbieten, aber Steine geben* "to offer bread to someone, but give him stones". By naming these two idioms, the author intends to illustrate the paramount status of BREAD as a symbol in culture. From the linguistic point of view, however, this approach has some weaknesses.

On the one hand, the choice of the examples is rather accidental; one should not look at two isolated idioms but at conventional figurative expressions in a larger framework. On the other hand, the degree of familiarity of the idioms has not been taken into account. Both German idioms have become obsolete, and neither can be said to represent units of contemporary German. Moreover, both idioms are direct references to other texts, and thus belong to the realm of textual dependence (see 10.5): the first idiom is a literary quotation (from Shakespeare's "King Richard" II, III, 2: *Eating the bitter bread of banishment*), and the second one is a biblical saying (Matthew 7:9). Finally, it should be pointed out that there are differences between the symbolic functions of BREAD in language and in culture. If all contemporary German idioms with BREAD had been taken into account, Biedermann would have come to a different result.[2] The symbolic function of BREAD in CFUs is, for the most part, restricted to 'the money one earns,

---

[2] The English version of Biedermann's dictionary (1994: 48) does no better in this regard. In connection with the idiom *that's my bread and butter* quoted above, the figurative meaning of BUTTER should have been mentioned, too.

livelihood', whereas in cultural codes, in various manifestations of Christian belief, BREAD is a holy and sacred symbol (see 4.6).

To sum up, one can say that a *systematic* investigation into the correlations between symbols in language and in other cultural codes does not yet exist. The inclusion of natural language into studies on symbols, especially conventional figurative language, as a sign system, could be a valuable addition to the aforementioned interdisciplinary symbol research. Conversely, we expect a systematic investigation into symbols in CFL and a comparison with symbols in other codes of culture to yield relevant results for linguistics. In this study, the question of the relations between symbols in language and symbols in culture is to the fore. Cross-cultural studies may serve as an instrument of research along these lines.

A basic requirement for a reliable study on symbols in language and culture is a possibly complete list of symbols occurring in certain symbolic fields [cf. the term *symbolic domain* in 11.3.5 (f)], a systematic compilation of an inventory of the CFUs of the languages in question. Research of this kind should be carried out in as many languages as possible. In an attempt to make a first step in this direction, we will present the complete linguistic material of certain symbolic domains (numbers and animals) in some case studies; see also Dobrovol'skij and Piirainen (1997).

11.2.2 Attempts to define "symbol"

Considering the diverse research areas in which symbols are an object of study, one should not be surprised that there is no universal interdisciplinary concept of the *symbol*. Each field of research includes its own theoretical background influencing the terminology. Various scientific fields involved in researching symbols, such as religious studies, mythology, ethnology and anthropology, literary studies, history of art, and musicology (as well as the areas of linguistics and semiotics) have elaborated their own conceptions of the *symbol*. Different attempts to define it can even be contradictory.

The question of how *symbol* should be defined and understood depends on the theoretical framework in which it is considered. There cannot be any universal definition of the *symbol* suitable for all theoretical paradigms. The word *symbol* has a long and diverse history. Some philosophers have maintained that *symbol* is the same as *sign*, or *emblem, allegory* or *metaphor*. Others insist that they are all different. An overview of the understandings of symbolic phenomena from antiquity to the present is given in Todorov (1977).

Eco (1984: 130) points to the vagueness and openness of the symbol: "What is frequently appreciated in many so-called symbols is exactly their vagueness, their openness, their fruitful ineffectiveness to express a 'final' meaning, so that

with symbols and by symbols one indicates what is always 'beyond' one's reach."
Similar ideas come, among others, from Firth (1973: 66–67):

> But in the interpretation of a symbol the conditions of its presentation are such that the interpreter ordinarily has much scope for exercise of his own judgment – the alternatives in the situation may be much less circumscribed. He may be left to 'get out of it' what he can by the fabricator of the symbol, who may be concerned primarily with his own mode of expression. Hence one way of distinguishing broadly between signal and symbol may be to class as symbols those presentations where there is much greater lack of fit – even perhaps intentionally – in the attribution of the fabricator and the interpreter.

Eco (1984: 153–154) illustrates the impossibility of defining the symbol by means of an anecdote. He labels as "one of the most pathetic moments in the history of philosophical terminology" the time when the collaborators of the *Dictionnaire de philosophie* of Lalande (1902–1923) gathered to discuss the definition of *symbol*. Let us cite this anecdotic event verbatim, in place of further examples of terminological confusion.

> After a first definition according to which a symbol is something representing something else by virtue of an analogical correspondence (for example: the scepter, symbol of royalty – where it is not clear where the analogy lies, because this is a paramount case of metonymical *contiguity*), a second definition is proposed, namely, that symbols concern a continued system of terms, each of which represents an element of another system. It is a good definition for the Morse code; unfortunately the illustrative citation [from Jules Lemaitre] following it speaks of a system of uninterrupted metaphors, and the Morse code seems hardy definable as a metaphorical system. At this point Lalande adds that a symbol is also a "formulary of orthodoxy", and he quotes the *Credo*. A discussion follows: Delacroix insists on the analogy, Lalande claims to have received from O. Karmin the proposal to define as a symbol every conventional representation; Brunschvicq speaks of an "internal" representational power and mentions the archetypical circular image of the serpent biting its own tail; van Biéma reminds the party that the fish was the symbol of Christ only for acronymic reasons; Lalande wonders how a piece of paper can become the symbol for a given amount of gold, while a mathematician speaks of symbols for the signs of the square root; Delacroix is caught by the suspicion that there is no relation between the sign for square root and the fox as a symbol of cunning; someone else distinguishes between intellectual and emotional symbols; and the entry fortunately stops at this point. The effort of Lalande has not been fruitless; it has suggested that a symbol can be everything and nothing. What a shame!
> (Eco 1984: 130–131)

Attempts at *symbol* definitions frequently refer back to the etymology of the word *symbol*, to Greek σύμβολον (*sýmbolon*), which comes from the Greek verb συμβαλλῶ (*symballō*) 'to throw together, to make something coincide with something else, to put together'. The noun σύμβολον, related to it, means 'contract, token, insignia' or 'a means of identification', thus a kind of 'sign'.

A symbol was originally an identification mark made up of two halves of a coin or a medal. The part guaranteed the presence of the whole and indicated the larger context. They represented two halves of the same thing, either one standing for the other, both becoming, however, fully effective only when matched to make up the original whole. Thus, parties to a contract, or guests and their host, could identify each other with the help of the parts of the σύμβολον. Therefore, the *symbol* is, at least etymologically, based on the principle of complementarity.

11.2.3 Concepts of the symbol in various disciplines

Varying semantic specifics ascribed to the symbol are to the fore in different disciplines concerned with symbols. Let us have a look at concepts of the symbol in non-linguistic paradigms. Nöth (1995: 119) divides the concepts found in various symbol studies into four categories. At the same time, he emphasises the common feature of a "connotative surplus": "What is the semantic nature of the connotative "surplus" by which the symbol is characterized? At the risk of oversimplification, four major interpretations will be distinguished which seem to have dominated in the history of symbol studies: the *essential, the cryptic, the irrational, and the unconscious meaning*". [emphasis ours]

(i) The interpretation of the symbol as an *essential meaning* assumes that the main feature of the symbol is its "connotative meaning". In this context, the term *connotative* is used in a very special way, not in the sense of a linguistic theory (as an addition to the primary denotative meaning, cf. section 11.3.4). In contrast to its denotative meaning, the *connotation* of the symbol is fundamental ("essential"), expressing some deeper layers of content as opposed to its less important surface meaning. The symbol primarily has a connotative meaning and only in the second place a denotative one. Accordingly, the secondary meaning is its real, central feature. The connotative, distinguishing characteristic of the symbol becomes evident when, for example, an everyday object, used as a symbol, points to something more significant or abstract and requires a corresponding interpretation (for example "hammer and sickle" used as a symbol for "communism").

(ii) Furthermore, we will take a brief look at the *cryptic meaning* of the symbol, which can be found in various interpretations of the symbol outside of linguistics and semiotics – mainly in psychoanalysis, but also, for instance, in theological exegesis. This understanding of the symbol postulates a hidden, invisible meaning of the symbol, which has to be discovered. A very general description of the cryptic characteristics of the symbol is Carl Gustav Jung's often quoted formulation at the beginning of his work "Man and his Symbols":

> Das, was wir Symbol nennen, ist ein Ausdruck, ein Name oder auch ein Bild, das uns im täglichen Leben vertraut sein kann, das aber zusätzlich zu seinem konventionellen Sinn noch besondere Nebenbedeutungen hat. Es enthält etwas Unbestimmtes, Unbekanntes oder für uns Unsichtbares. [. . .] Ein Wort oder Bild ist symbolisch, wenn es mehr enthält, als man auf den ersten Blick erkennen kann. Es hat dann einen weiteren „unbewussten" Aspekt, den man wohl nie ganz genau definieren kann. (Jung 1968: 20–21)
>
> [What we call a symbol is a term, a name, or even a picture that may be familiar in daily life, yet that possesses specific connotations in addition to its conventional and obvious meaning. It implies something vague, unknown, or hidden from us. [. . .] Thus a word or an image is symbolic when it implies something more than its obvious and immediate meaning. It has a wider "unconscious" aspect that is never precisely defined or fully explained.]

According to Jung, a symbol is beyond rationality and cannot be adequately expressed in the familiar words of our language. It refers to a meaning that can be intuitively perceived but not intellectually understood. In view of this interpretation, a whole myth, a medieval monastery complex, a poem or a dream can be labelled a *symbol* because it conveys a meaningful message that would not be accessible in any other way. Far-reaching symbolic interpretations of mythology in this cryptic sense can be found in the studies of Mircea Eliade (e.g. Eliade 1952, 1957). It was one of C.G. Jung's findings that alchemistic-like symbols could frequently be found in dreams (i.e. in the dreams of his patients). He concluded that these "cryptic" symbols were manifestations of archetypal elements of the collective unconscious (see also iv). In the course of the following discussion, this notion of the symbol (in the psychotherapeutic tradition) can be left out of consideration.

(iii) The *irrational meaning* of the symbol mainly affects internal discussions within 19th century ethnology and earlier cultural anthropology (e.g. Tylor 1871). Controversial discussions were held about the question of whether there can be symbolism without rationalism and whether or not symbolism is a semiological cognitive system. Those discussions are no longer topical; therefore, the "irrational" understanding of the symbol is of no relevance to current research.

(iv) The *unconscious meaning* has to be looked at in connection with Sigmund Freud's dream symbols. Freud (1921: 125–127) regarded symbols as an "indirect method of representation". Dream symbols are, above all, symbolic contents that do not permeate someone's consciousness. This unconscious meaning might be raised into one's consciousness for therapeutic reasons. The notion of "unconscious symbolism" has some aspects in common with the "cryptic" and the "irrational" understanding of the symbol – all of them regard the symbol as a picture or sign charged with a significant meaning that refers to deeper, hidden, coherent contexts (German "Sinnzusammenhänge").

The symbol is considered a visible sign of something invisible that goes beyond the perceptible world or serves as a bridge between the rational world and a mystical one. St. Paul's formulation "Per visibilia ad invisibilia" ("through the visible to the invisible" (Romans 1:20) has often been quoted by symbol researchers. It is a maxim that is accepted to a great extent by all supporters of these versions of the symbol (e.g. Cirlot 1962: xvi). According to Florenskij (1922), symbols do not fit into the plane of reason; their structure is filled with antinomies. But this feature of symbols is not an objection to them; on the contrary, it is a guarantee that they are real.

The three latter interpretations of the symbol are not relevant for developing our concept of *cultural symbols in figurative language*. What remains for the theoretical framework of this study are the aspects of connotation (i), which are related to our concept of cultural symbolism. We will look at them in more detail in section 11.4.

11.3 Concepts of the symbol in linguistics and semiotics

11.3.1 Introduction

As has been shown in the last section, there is no unique, interdisciplinarily accepted concept of the *symbol* in non-linguistic academic fields. However, even linguists, philosophers of language, and semioticians use the term *symbol* in different senses. (Let us recall Eco's quotation about the lexicographers' attempts to describe the meanings of the word *symbol*, Eco 1984: 130–131.) The differentiation between *sign* and *symbol* is often vague in linguistics and semiotics – both terms are used in the same sense in some conceptions (for example, Saussure's *sign* means the same as Peirce's *symbol*), whereas other researchers use one term as a hyponym of the other.

In Sebeok's opinion (1986b: 1029), the various contrasting positions can be summarised in full with the following alternative: either *symbol* is the semiotic genus and all other semiotic phenomena, including signs, are species of it, or there is a semiotic genus *sign* and symbols are one of its species. In fact, however, things are more complicated. There is not only the relationship *sign* → *symbol* or *symbol* → *sign*. There is also a relationship of quasi-synonymy: *sign* ≈ *symbol*, as well as a relationship of quasi-antonymy: *sign* ↔ *symbol*.

Even if *symbol* is understood as a hyponym of *sign* (the relationship *sign* → *symbol*), there can be quite different interpretations of the two terms. For example, according to Saussure *signs* include all arbitrary signs, among them linguistic signs, whereas *symbols* are only secondary readings. Peirce's understanding of *symbols* differs considerably from this. *Symbol*, as in the theory of Saussure, is a hyponym of *sign*, but for Peirce (in contrast to Saussure), symbols are conventional arbitrary signs. This is to say that symbols are entities of a natural or artificial language, while *signs* also include non-arbitrary *symptoms* (see below).

For the purposes of our study, it is not necessary to look at these issues in more detail. However, some of the most prominent readings of the term *symbol* supported by linguists, philosophers of language, and semioticians should be considered here in order to take stock of the status of the symbol favoured in this study. In this section, we will discuss the following three understandings of the term *symbol*:

(i) The *symbol* is everything connected with analogical thinking, including metaphors (Cassirer)
(ii) The *symbol* is an arbitrary sign in contrast to the *index* and the *icon* (Peirce)
(iii) The *symbol* is never arbitrary; its outstanding feature is its *connotation* (Saussure)

11.3.2 The symbol as analogical thinking

Ernst Cassirer, in the tradition of Immanuel Kant, supports a broad concept of *symbol* in the fields of language theory and language philosophy. He groups non-differentiated terms like *image, parable, metaphor* and *allegory* under the umbrella term *symbolisation*. The human being is viewed as "animal symbolicum", a creature that is able to think and to structure the world through symbols (i.e. through analogy). The entire human experience is, according to Cassirer and his followers, of a symbolic nature, and all cultural accomplishments are versions of the symbol-creating ability of the human mind ("Ausprägungen einer symbolbildenden Kraft des menschlichen Geistes", Cassirer 1944: 26).

In his major work "The philosophy of symbolic forms" (1923–1929), Cassirer examined the functions of the mind and mental images that underlie every manifestation of human culture. In his view, people are essentially characterised by their unique ability to use "symbolic forms" as a means of structuring their experiences and understanding the world. According to Cassirer, symbols manifest themselves in various forms of our intellectual creation and cultural expression, such as language, myth, religion, arts and science, including logic, mathematics and technology, though they are based on different structural principles.

Such a broad conception of *symbol* would be of no use for the present study, as it would not enable us to investigate phenomena of cultural symbolism in conventional figurative language. If every human activity and the entire perception of the world were of a symbolic nature, there would no longer be a need for a special linguistic topic of research in the field of symbolic entities.

11.3.3 The symbol as an arbitrary sign

Cassirer's interpretation of symbols is a clear contrast to the interpretation of symbols as arbitrary signs, to which Charles Sanders Peirce's prominent semiotic approach belongs. For Peirce and his supporters, the symbol can be equated to the *sign* in Ferdinand de Saussure's tradition, but with a different notion of *symbol* to that held by Saussure.[3] In accordance with Peirce's semiotic theory, the relationship between the *signifier* and the *signified* of a symbol is not based on similarity but rather on convention. *Sign* is used as a generic term for all semiotic entities.

For Peirce, signs manifest themselves as "trivalent elements". He divides signs into three types, depending on their relation to the respective objects: *icon* (defined as a sign which represents an object mainly by its similarity to that object), *index* (a sign which represents its object by its existential relation to the object in spatial, temporal and causal contiguity), and *symbol* (a sign which signifies this object by law or convention):

> According to the second trichotomy, a Sign may be termed an *Icon*, an *Index*, or a *Symbol*. An *Icon* is a sign which refers to the Object that it denotes merely by virtue of characters of its own, and which it processes just the same, whether any such Object actually exists or not. [...] An *Index* is a sign which refers to the Object that it denotes by virtue of being really affected by that object. [...] A *Symbol* is a sign which refers to the Object that it denotes by virtue of a law, usually an association of general ideas, which operates to cause the Symbol to be interpreted as referring to that Object. (Peirce 1960: 247–249)

Symbols, again, are trivalent; they are divided into *terms*, *propositions*, and *arguments* (Peirce 1960: 249). Thus, for Peirce, all linguistic signs are symbols. The

---

[3] Saussure (1916: 66) defines the linguistic *sign* as that which unites not a thing and a name, but a concept and a sound-image. The latter is not the material sound, a purely physical thing, but the psychological imprint of the sound, the impression that it makes on our senses.

term *symbol*, or *linguistic symbol*, is used in many linguistic studies with this sense of an arbitrary sign, or, with regard to Peirce, as a kind of synonym for *word*.

There are many more linguists who favour this notion of the symbol. Langacker (2002: 82–83), for instance, takes the view that "a linguistic symbol is bipolar, defined by a semantic structure standing in correspondence to a phonological structure." According to Langacker, all words, roots or affixes are verbal symbols because they are conventional phonological units having conventional meanings. In short, *symbol* in this version is reduced to the "signifier".

The interpretation of *symbol* favoured in our study differs fundamentally from this understanding. Indeed, such a notion of *symbol* would be useless for our theoretical framework. Since one of the aims of our study is to uncover the relevant specific features of cultural symbols in the semantic motivation of conventional figurative units, we do not need such a broad and generalised understanding of the symbol. If every linguistic sign is a symbol, no specific properties of certain lexical units can be called *symbolic functions*. What we need is an understanding of *symbol* as an entity that corresponds to similar entities in other cultural codes (see below).

11.3.4 The symbol as connotative meaning

There is a third interpretation of *symbol* which – in addition to relationships of similarity and conventionalisation – points out the main semantic feature of the symbol, namely the secondary, derived meaning, or, in Saussure's terms, the *connotative meaning* (cf. also the interpretation of the symbol as *essential meaning* in non-linguistic paradigms [11.2.3 (i)], which stresses that the main feature of the symbol is its "connotative meaning"). This concept of *symbol* was mainly presented by Ferdinand de Saussure. His well-known example explains why a *pair of scales* can symbolise 'justice', and a *chariot* cannot.

> Le symbole a pour caractère de n'être jamais tout à fait arbitraire; il n'est pas vide, il y a un rudiment de lien naturel entre le signifiant et le signifié. Le symbole de la justice, la balance, ne pourrait pas être remplacé par n'importe quoi, un char, par exemple. (Saussure 1916: 101)

> [One of the characters of the symbol is that it is never wholly arbitrary; it is not empty, for there is the rudiment of a natural bond between the signifier and the signified. The symbol of justice, a pair of scales, could not be replaced by just any symbol, such as a chariot.]

What Saussure calls the *connotative meaning* of a symbol is its secondary, derived signification. In other words, the connotational conception of symbol stresses its secondary nature. This interpretation defines the symbol as a sign to whose primary *signified* a secondary meaning is added. Semantic reinterpretation is a necessary precondition of symbolisation. Without a secondary meaning, the word and the concept behind it cannot be regarded as a symbol. Being culturally dependent, this secondary meaning is not fully conventional or arbitrary (unlike the symbol in Peirce's theory) but clearly derived from the primary meaning of the corresponding concept.

Saussure's concept does not contradict the concept of *symbol* favoured in this present study (our working concept of *cultural symbol* in language), but it is quite vague. A clear line between *metaphor* and *symbol* cannot be found. However, a sharp boundary between these two terms – applied to occurrences in conventional figurative language – is crucial for our purposes (see 11.4.1).

11.3.5 The symbol as a culture-semiotic phenomenon

Having touched on some prominent linguistic and semiotic concepts of the symbol (identified as a way of analogical thinking, as an arbitrary sign, and as connotative meaning), we will now discuss our working concept of the *cultural symbol in figurative language* and explain it with some examples. Among the concepts of the symbol outlined above, the Saussurian view is closest to our understanding of this semiotised category. In addition, within the framework of the Moscow-Tartu School of cultural semiotics there are several remarks on symbols that we find ourselves in agreement with. Although neither Saussure nor the members of the Moscow-Tartu School explicitly refer to figurative language, there are some correspondences between their conception of the symbol and our theory of cultural symbolism in language.

In what follows, we develop the semiotic foundations of the theory of cultural symbols in language, which is one of the central tenets of the Conventional Figurative Language Theory. Here the main features of the cultural symbol in language will be briefly described and exemplified.

(a) The symbol is seen as a sign whose primary meaning serves as a form for expressing a different content. The symbolic meaning is therefore a result of metonymic shift. In the hierarchy of cultural values, the second content of the symbol is considered to be of higher value (of a higher density or a higher degree of abstraction) than the primary content. This may be illustrated by Saussure's well-known example of the SCALES. The primary content, 'weighing instrument', is used to denote a second content, 'justice'. This second content is, from a cultural perspective, obviously more significant than the 'scale as an item of everyday use'. The same holds for cultural symbols fixed in a given language. Let us look at the expressions *whiter than white* and *whitewash* (10.8) once again – the primary meaning, 'the colour white', has metonymically shifted to meanings such as 'honest', 'true' or 'morally pure'. These second meanings are of "higher value" than the primary one. Nevertheless, the symbol WHITE in language preserves connotations of the colour 'white'.

(b) Many symbols show a kind of polysemy or even homonymy. As far as conventional figurative language is concerned, we speak of different *symbolic functions* of one figurative unit. In CFUs of contemporary English, for example, WOLF reveals the symbolic functions 'malice', 'aggressiveness', 'danger', 'poverty', or 'economic despair'. All these symbolic functions are recurrent in CFL and supported by other codes of culture (the image of the wolf as a greedy, people devouring demon in narrative traditions; see chapter 13 for details).

Furthermore, what was originally one and the same symbolic function can be modified according to the semiotic code in question – SEVEN as a sacred number in various cultural codes and meaning 'much, many' in CFUs, or BREAD as a sacrament in religious codes, meaning 'livelihood' in conventional figurative language. Linguistic figurative expressions, as a rule, do not signify something solemn or sacred. Therefore, corresponding semantic components in the symbolic meaning in question are suppressed. In principle, this can be called a semantic derivation, which does not take place within one code, but cross-semiotically, across the borders of semiotic codes [see (d)]. In this sense, we are dealing with homology of symbolic functions in such cases. The result of such a derivation across the borders of semiotic codes is a kind of polysemy.

(c) The symbol is semantically independent of the given context. What is important for cultural symbols in language is the fact that symbols can be isolated semantically; they can be separated from other elements of the word string in question (in the phraseological research known as *semantic analysability* or *semantic decomposability*, see 11.4.1). Examples are sentences like *She is pure gold* and CFUs like *to have a heart of gold*. The constituent *gold* (i.e. the concept GOLD) can be singled out, and a separate (independent, autonomous) meaning – 'someone or something extremely good and valuable' – can be attributed to it. In contrast to this, an idiom like *out of a clear (blue) sky* 'as a complete surprise, totally unexpected' is not decomposable in the sense that the constituents *clear* or *sky* could be separated from the other constituents of this idiom; no autonomous figurative meaning could be ascribed to them.

(d) A further relevant property of symbols is their semiotic constancy. That is to say that a symbol may enter a new semiotic context when separated from its former context. The ability to adapt to another text is a precondition for the com-

11.3 Concepts of the symbol in linguistics and semiotics — 343

parability of a linguistic symbol and its correspondences in other cultural codes, such as literature, fine arts or films. For example, OWL as a symbol of 'intelligence, wisdom' is known in philosophy (Hegel) just as well as in modern advertising, as the logo of an academic publishing house, as the emblem of a university, as a prize in an intellectual quiz show, or as an idiom constituent (e.g. in the simile *as wise as an owl*), and still remains the same symbol containing the same symbolic meaning.

(e) The symbol is seen as standing between iconicity and convention. There is only a gradual difference between the *pictorial* and the *symbolic*. Consistent with Averincev's (2001) explanation, every symbol is a pictorial image and every image is (at least to some extent) a symbol. The symbol can be characterised as a faded image with a concentrated sense, so that the relation between form and meaning is conventional rather than pictorially comprehensible. Symbols, in Arutjunova's (1988) opinion, stand between metaphors and signs (in the sense of an arbitrary semiotic entity). Symbols are not primarily interpreted on the basis of iconicity but on the basis of "agreement", i.e. of conventionalisation. Symbols do not merely originate from "similarity". As a consequence, symbols demand a higher semiotic status than metaphors (Arutjunova 1988: 157–158; see also Stepanov 1997).

Let us illustrate this conventionalisation by two examples. The meaning of HAMMER AND SICKLE can be recognised easily as a symbol of communism. The meanings of the names for both tools have thus shifted metonymically, denoting entities of a "higher value": a SICKLE has been a symbol of 'harvest' and 'agriculture' since prehistoric times, whereas a HAMMER, rich in tradition as well, symbolises the work of a blacksmith, miner, craftsman or worker in general. The two metonymic symbols were combined in the revolutionary tradition and reinterpreted once more, as a symbol of the workers' and farmers' power. By contrast, the FISH as a symbol of early Christianity and Christian confession seems to be opaque and accidental. Its origin is supposed to be due to the Greek acronym ΙΧΘΥΣ for "Jesus Christ, God's Son, Saviour", which leads to the word *ichthys* 'fish', although there are other biblical references to FISH, such as the Apostles being called "fishers of men" (cf. 11.4.2).

(f) Some symbols show a tendency to occur in groups or fields. We have termed these kinds of symbolic complexes *symbolic domains*. Let us take some examples from the domain of colour symbolism. The concept WHITE, for instance, can be evoked by the antonymous concept BLACK, cf. Russian *выдавать черное за белое* "to make black look white" 'to make something bad look good'. The concept BLACK, however, is used not only in contrast with WHITE, but also with other colour concepts. GREEN, for example, stood in contrast to BLACK in heraldry. The underlying cause of this was a confrontation between the symbolism of

GRASS and STONE, from which the cultural antithesis between country and town, field and house, nature and culture was developed (Lotman 1995: 80). There are also the oppositions BLACK, GREY and WHITE, cf. expressions like *the black market* 'illegal buying and selling of products' and *the grey market* 'business conducted in the form of shares or goods before they are traded officially'. Finally, the concept BLACK can be evoked by the antonymous concept ROSE, cf. idioms like *to look through rose-coloured spectacles* 'to think of only the good things in a situation and pretend that the bad things do not exist; to see things too optimistically', antonymous to e.g. *to look on the black side*.

The concept WHITE can in turn be in opposition to the concept RED. This contrast of WHITE and RED can be found in various cultural areas, e.g. in the Old Testament (RED as the colour of sin, WHITE as the colour of innocence, cf. Isaiah 1:18), in Indian Buddhist texts ("The female and the male principles are each linked with a number of paired concepts, some of which may be regarded as 'red' and 'white'", Slavik 1994: 206–207), in the history of the Russian revolution, or in fairy tales like the German "Schneeweißchen und Rosenrot". The contrast of WHITE and RED also occurs in the conventional figurative language of different cultural areas. WHITE and RED are opposites in the Lithuanian CFU *ar baltas, ar raudonas – vis tiek malonus* "whether white or red – it is equally pleasant/agreeable" (Grigas 2000: no. 1089). In Japanese, the two colours are attributed to two different kinds of lies: 白々しい嘘 (*shirajirashii uso*) "a white-white lie (a pure white, very clear lie)" 'a lie that is easy to see through",[4] and 真っ赤な嘘 (*makka na uso*) "a deep red lie" 'an impertinent, impudent lie'.

Together, these concepts form the domain of colour symbols. Symbols occurring in groups are related to each other and can reveal a kind of intrinsic order within a given symbolic domain.

(g) A further relevant feature of symbols is their cultural embedding. Symbols exist within their cultural area and are connected with the social community to which they belong. Although symbols have a high degree of consistency in their internal cultural logic, their meanings can undergo transformations under the impact of the cultural context and in accordance with the change of the culture in question.

An illustrative example of how a symbol can be transformed according to social change in the course of history is the MONKEY in Japanese culture. Ohnuki-Tier-

---

[4] CFUs like English *white lie* and Finnish *valkoinen valhe* "white lie" 'evasive lie' can be labeled "false friends" with respect to this Japanese idiom (see chapter 5).

ney (1987, 1990: 14–16) developed a theory of semiotic change in the Japanese national identity over a long period, studying the perception of the MONKEY over the course of a millennium. During the medieval period, the MONKEY was believed to have the healing power of a mediator of the sacred, moving between humans and deities, bringing the power of purity from the deities to the Japanese people. Later on, this highly estimated symbol took on a contrasting meaning. During the Early Modern period, the MONKEY increasingly became a devalued scapegoat who was believed to take impurity from the Japanese. In the present day, the MONKEY is seen as a clown who is the target of laughter (see also Handelman 1998). This example shows how contrary aspects (the positive power of the animal most similar to humans and its ugly appearance) can become alternately dominant in constituting a symbol.

Our linguistic data include only figurative expressions of present-day languages (rather than historic varieties of those languages), making it difficult to give examples of historical changes in the symbolic meanings of a language's conventional figurative units. One example, however, is the obsolete English simile *as wise as a serpent* 'very wise' (very probably referring to the biblical saying "Be as clever as the snakes", Matthew 10:16). This stands in contrast to the conceptualisation of the SNAKE as a symbol of falseness and danger in contemporary English, for instance in a sentence like *She is a real snake* 'She is false, evil, treacherous' or in the idiom *a snake in the grass* 'a hidden, treacherous enemy; a lurking peril' (see section 13.2).

It is well known that the symbolic value of animals can also differ considerably in different cultural areas. For example, the RAT is conceptualised predominantly with negative symbolic associations in the West, whereas it is highly esteemed in some East Asian cultures. In Japan, the RAT and the MOUSE (there is no linguistic distinction between these two animals) are associated with wealth and diligence. When a rat nibbles, it is said to be counting money. The absence of rats from a household used to give cause for concern in former times. Moreover, in popular Japanese religion, RATS are thought to be messengers of *Daikokuten*, one of the seven gods of luck.

These symbolic evaluations have consequences for the conventional figurative language of the cultural communities in question. A derogative use of RAT as in English, where it denotes an unpleasant person or a traitor (a *political rat* meaning 'a renegade, deserter, turncoat'), would not be comprehensible in other cultural areas. The same holds for CFUs such as *to rat on someone* 'to inform on someone behind his or her back' or *to smell a rat* 'to suspect that something is not quite right, to begin to suspect trickery or deception'.

Another good example is the BAT, "an animal of multiple symbolic significance, whose dual nature (as a winged mammal) has attracted attention in many cultures" (Biedermann 1994: 29). In China, the BAT is believed to live for a long time. It is a symbol of longevity and joy, attributed to *Fu Hsing*, one of the five gods of luck, whereas the West sees it primarily as an eerie creature. This has an effect on conventional figurative language, too. Expressions like *an old bat*, said of an elderly woman in a derogatory way, *to go/become batty* 'to go crazy' or *to have bats in one's belfry* 'to be slightly mad or strange' would have no place in cultures where BAT is a positively connoted symbol.

The last example here is the WOLF. Germanic mythology associated it with light and force, and such positive connotations were handed down via Germanic names (like *the Ulfilas, Beowulf* or *Wolfgang*, a German given name). The symbolic value of the WOLF, however, changed more and more to a "terrible devouring demon", mainly due to well-known fairy tales and other narrative traditions (cf. section 13.3.3).

11.3.6 Summary

Of all the diverse notions of *symbol* in various research areas, that supported by Ferdinand de Saussure and members of the Moscow-Tartu School is closest to our concept of symbols in conventional figurative language. Some correspondences between the cultural semiotic view of symbols and our own approach have been expounded. Let us summarise the main features of the symbol that are relevant for our theory and for analysing our empirical data.

(a) A symbol has undergone a semantic reinterpretation (often, a metonymic shift). It is a sign whose content is used as a sign for denoting other content.
(b) A symbol may develop divergent meanings, i.e. different *symbolic functions*.
(c) A symbol is semantically autonomous; it can be isolated from a given context.
(d) A symbol is semiotically constant; it may gain entry into a new semiotic context and still preserve its symbolic functions.
(e) A symbol stands between iconicity and convention. The relation between its form and meaning is conventional.
(f) Symbols can occur in groups, i.e. in *symbolic domains*.
(g) Symbols are embedded in culture; their meanings may change in accordance with changes of the culture in question.

In the following section, the main emphasis will lie on refining the notion of symbols in language by means of more concrete linguistic data.

11.4 Cultural symbols in figurative language

The main aspects of *cultural symbols* have been sketched out above, mainly from the vantage point of cultural semiotics. In this chapter, we will examine in more detail *cultural symbols in figurative language* from a linguistic point of view.[5] First of all, we will work out the operational criteria that make it possible to differentiate metaphors from symbols in conventional figurative language (11.4.1). The second topic will then be the motivation of symbols in language (11.4.2). Finally, we will look more thoroughly at the effects that the cultural context has on these symbols (11.4.3) and at cultural codes relevant to symbols in CFL (11.4.4).

11.4.1 Metaphor vs. symbol

Operational criteria
Conventional figurative language has both metaphors and symbols. Since these two phenomena have different linguistic properties, it is necessary to develop an instrument that will enable us to distinguish them. We will turn again to the criteria for singling out symbols in language, expounded briefly in section 10.7. Let us consider two idioms which both contain the constituent *dog*. There is a significant difference in the semantic structure of idioms (1) and (2). In idiom (1), the constituent *dog* is taken in its primary meaning before the whole expression is semantically reinterpreted. In idiom (2), by contrast, *dog* has a symbolic meaning.

(1) *to call off the dogs*
 'to abandon an investigation when it is leading nowhere, to stop threatening or chasing somebody'

(2) *to lead a dog's life*
 'to lead a completely miserable life, an unhappy existence full of problems or unfair treatment'

The first difference between idioms (1) and (2) is that the semantic structure of (1) is not decomposable, whereas the semantic structure of (2) is. The constituents of (1) do not have autonomous meanings; they cannot be isolated from the lexical

---

[5] The term *cultural symbol* has also been used by other linguists in a sense that is obviously different from our understanding of this term (cf. e.g. Teliya et al. 1998: 63). According to those authors, a figurative expression such as Russian *глупая баба* "a silly common female", a stereotype of the low intellectual capacity of women, is a "cultural symbol".

and semantic structure of the idiom without destroying its figurative meaning. It is only when taken as a whole that the idiom can be interpreted in a meaningful way. This non-analysability makes it impossible to define the exact meaning of the constituent *dogs* in this context. Consequently, this constituent cannot be understood as a symbol.

The constituent *dog* in idiom (2), however, has a relatively autonomous meaning, i.e. 'someone miserable and pitiful', and can therefore be isolated without destroying the semantic structure of the idiom. It is motivated by cultural knowledge about the symbolic interpretation of the concept DOG (see below). Thus, we can formulate the prerequisite for detecting cultural symbols in CFUs. The figurative expression in question must be analysable with regard to the element suspected of being a symbol. Figurative units that consist of only one element, of course, do not need to fulfil this requirement by definition. In order to be able to qualify certain elements of CFUs as symbols, it is necessary to be able to isolate these elements without destroying the expression semantically. The semantic structure of a given figurative unit must allow the separation of single constituents in principle, i.e. the expression must be analysable. See section 4.2.1 for the term *analysability* in regard to the semantic structure of CFUs.

As has been outlined briefly in section 10.7, there are two main criteria for ascertaining cultural symbols in conventional figurative language: first, the given CFL unit must be supported by other cultural codes, and secondly, the given unit must occur often in its secondary function.

The first, most relevant criterion for selecting symbols is grounded in the kind of motivation exhibited by the given CFU. Since symbols are meaningful by definition, non-motivated figurative expressions can be ignored here. Two main types of CFUs have to be distinguished. Expressions of the first type are connected with fragments of world knowledge. Expressions of the second type are connected with knowledge of cultural conventions. The symbol is viewed as a sign with content that is used as a sign for denoting other content which, from a cultural perspective, is more important than the primary content.

Idiom (1) as a whole is motivated by the knowledge of a fragment of reality, namely the role of dogs in the prototypical scenario of 'a hunt'. Hunters call off their dogs when they follow a wrong scent. Therefore, the concept DOG evoked by the word *dog* is a part of the HUNT-scenario, i.e. a cognitive structure which, taken as a whole, provides the relevant motivating link in this case.

The word *dog* in idiom (2), however, cannot primarily be interpreted on the basis of world knowledge: neither on knowledge about hunting with dogs nor about any biological feature connected with dogs. The interpretation of the linguistic sign is not based on nature, but rather on specific cultural knowledge, which we call *symbolic knowledge*. Only those linguistic units that correspond to other cultural codes are symbols. This characteristic of symbols is accompanied by a high degree of culture-based conventionalisation and a lower degree of iconicity. Therefore, we call these linguistic units *cultural symbols*. The concept DOG is connected with a rich symbolic tradition in various cultural codes. One strong symbolic strand of interpretation of the DOG is 'impurity' and 'inferiority'. This interpretation originated in the Middle East and the Old Testament, and partly also in the New Testament and biblical exegeses (Lurker 1973: 160–161). The DOG was seen as a pitiful, miserable and inferior creature on the lowest level of a hierarchy of values. From this comes the meaning of *a dog's life* as an 'inferior existence'.

The connection of the imagery of idiom (2) with this symbolic tradition (even if this connection is not always perceived by the speakers) allows us to consider the concept DOG here to be a cultural symbol, at least from the point of view of the first criterion, in that it has correspondences with other cultural codes. It is not sufficient to explain the relation between the word *dog* and 'inferiority' in CFUs like *I was treated like a dog* by means of "the stereotypical social place of dogs in our society" (Murphy 2002: 271), especially since this is not the concept of a DOG most people have at present (in contemporary society dogs tend to be pampered rather than treated badly).[6] The concept of the DOG as an inferior creature rather traces back to bygone times, to biblical or medieval conceptions. This concept is handed down, above all, by such conventionalised figurative units.

There are many other CFUs with the same symbolic function of DOG, for example English *to go to the dogs* 'to ruin oneself due to a licentious or degenerate lifestyle', *to treat someone like a dog* 'to treat someone very badly', *dog-Latin* 'inferior or degenerate Latin', or even *dog rose* 'wild rose, briar rose' and *dog violet* 'wild violet', "inferior" flowers compared with the cultivated garden flowers. This recurrence of DOG with the symbolic function of 'inferiority' allows us to conclude that the second requirement is also satisfied.

A useful example comes from Makkai (1978: 412–413), who discusses the "idiomatic" use of DOG. He considers the retention of the original meaning of *dog* 'canis familiaris' in the idiom *to be in the doghouse* as entirely different from the meaning of *dog* in the compound *dogwood* 'a kind of blossoming shrub or tree of the genus Cornus' (i.e. a thorny shrub the wood of which is worthless). "The original meaning retains its metaphorical translucence in the former and has none in the latter. (To be out of favour is easily likened to having to live in an actual

---

[6] In present times, people normally would not treat a dog badly; the dog is even called "man's best friend". In urban society, dogs and other pets are rather treated as fellow humans; pet owners even relate to the pets as if they were their children (cf. Rakusan 2000: 278).

doghouse, whereas the shrubs of the species *Cornus* have nothing associative or metaphorical about them to dogs)" (Makkai 1978: 412). This problem can be solved by applying the dichotomy between "iconic" and "symbolic" motivation. On one hand we have the iconically (metaphorically) motivated idiom, and the symbolic meaning of DOG 'inferior, worthless' in the compound, on the other. This symbolic meaning may be "inactive", synchronically not comprehensible; it came into being via "agreement" (convention). Within botanic nomenclature, "worthless" plants have been denoted by the Latin word *canis* 'dog', for which the botanists referred back to the traditional symbolic meaning of DOG 'inferior, worthless creature'. The element *dog* in *dogwood* is thus grounded on (former) specific symbolic knowledge of the concept DOG.

The knowledge by which these CFUs have to be interpreted can be traced back to the concept 'inferiority' as a symbolic function of DOG. It is of little importance whether speakers actually know the cultural codes or certain parts of them (e.g. passages of the Bible). What is crucial for the "symbolic interpretation" is the knowledge that there is a potential link between the symbol in conventional figurative language and that same symbol in other cultural codes. The knowledge of this link has the effect that idiom (2) is interpreted not on the basis of world knowledge about dogs but on the basis of cultural knowledge of the symbol DOG.

The actual presence of a certain cultural knowledge can vary according to the circumstances of the handing down of the cultural codes in question. For example, the knowledge that the WOLF is a 'terrible, devouring beast' will be alive as long as children are told fairy tales that convey this impression. The knowledge that NINE was an outstanding symbol in former times, however, has been lost almost completely. Nevertheless, there must be some knowledge of the link between the symbolic cultural function of NINE and the use of NINE in English CFUs (see section 12.3.4).

The same holds for the concept LYNX in CFUs like *to be lynx-eyed* 'to have good eyesight' (see (25–26) below). The knowledge of the cultural codes that handed down the symbolic meanings of the LYNX ('sharp-sighted; perspicacious' and 'watchful; vigilant') may be entirely lost. Nevertheless, some tacit knowledge that there is a link between such former symbolisations and conventional figurative language causes the symbolic reading to be more salient than the literal one. As long as people know and use such figurative units, they are somehow interpreting the inner form of the units. Thus, speakers not only reproduce a CFU with its actual meaning but also reproduce the link between its lexical structure taken literally and its actual meaning.

A secondary semiotisation is a characteristic of all idioms and other CFUs that provide two readings. The difference between metaphors and symbols is the feature of cultural relevance: it is the cultural (and not only the linguistic) relevance of the linguistically encoded symbols. These questions will be discussed in more detail in chapters 12 and 13.

Testing for the criteria
Let us consider another idiom in order to make the notion of *symbolic function* more precise.

(3) *someone cannot see the wood* (AmE *the forest*) *for the trees*
'someone does not notice what is important about a situation because they are paying too much attention to small details; to fail to grasp the essential point because of over-attention to detail'

We can now try to decide whether or not this idiom is symbolically motivated. Both noun constituents, *wood* (or *forest*) and *trees*, have relatively autonomous figurative meanings: *wood/forest* stands for 'the whole' and *trees* for 'the details' (the prerequisite of analysability is fulfilled). From this point of view, the expression could be both metaphor and symbol. In a further step, we have to decide whether these concepts are motivated by world knowledge or by symbolic knowledge. In order to answer this question, we have to return to the cultural facts. We must check whether there are other cultural codes in which WOOD/FOREST has the symbolic meaning 'the whole' or TREE the symbolic meaning 'detail'. There are none. Neither WOOD/FOREST meaning 'the whole' nor TREES meaning 'details' has an equivalent in other cultural codes. The first criterion by which a symbol can be determined is therefore not fulfilled, and it is thus unnecessary to test the second criterion, recurrence of a given symbolic function in CFUs.

This conclusion does not imply that WOOD/FOREST or TREE cannot be relevant symbols in cultural codes. The TREE is, for example, a significant symbol in Old Germanic cosmogony (the world-tree Yggdrasil in Norse mythology is thought of as the axis of the world, symbolising the universe). The forbidden tree, the TREE OF KNOWLEDGE, is a well-known symbol from the Old Testament and is believed to have provided the wood for Jesus' cross, to have been transformed into the Tree of Life. There is a rich TREE symbolism also in anthropology (cf. Rival 1998). However, none of the constituents of idiom (3) is a cultural symbol, because idiom-internal meanings do not correspond to symbols in cultural codes. This procedure makes it possible to approach the description of semantically analysable idioms in a more precise way.

This method can be tested on every CFU in which a constituent is suspected of carrying a symbolic function. Let us look at a pair of idioms, (4) and (5), which are quite similar on the level of their lexical structure, but differ fundamentally in their motivation:

(4) *to see (things/everything) in black and white*
'to characterise everything as either very good or very bad, without intermediate levels; to consider moral matters etc. only in terms of absolutely wrong or right, without recognising subtler differences'

(5) *in black and white*
'reduced to writing; official, in writing or print'

Only idiom (4) includes symbolic functions of the concepts BLACK and WHITE. Only in (4) do the constituents *black* and *white* present a relative semantic autonomy (the prerequisite for determining a symbol), whereas they are not autonomous in (5). Only the motivation of idiom (4) is based on the symbolic knowledge about BLACK and WHITE, the symbolic function of BLACK being 'bad, evil, and insincere', that of WHITE being 'good, correct, true'. In contrast to that, the two colour adjectives in idiom (5) must be interpreted in their literal meaning, on the basis of a fragment of world knowledge. They refer to black printing ink and white paper. Thus, the motivation is based on knowledge about print products.

Some further CFUs containing BLACK in symbolic functions have already been discussed in 10.7, revealing a wide spectrum of negative meanings. These symbolic functions of BLACK are supported by cultural knowledge about the colour. BLACK is a well-known symbol of badness or unhappiness in various cultural codes. It is the colour of death, funerals, and mourning. In popular belief, black animals (like a black cat or a black spider) are bringers of bad tidings. The devil is believed to be black.[7] Almost all aesthetic genres (the fine arts, literature, the performing arts, film, etc.) use, consciously or intuitively, these symbolic functions of BLACK. Thus, the criterion of cultural significance is fulfilled.

This interpretation of BLACK has also become conventionalised in many further CFUs (e.g. *things are looking black* 'the prospects are very bad'; *not as black as it is painted* 'not as bad as one is claimed to be'; *to be in a black mood* 'to be very depressed'; *to look on the black side* 'to see everything pessimistically'; *to blacken someone's character* 'to make someone appear worse than they really are by exaggerating their faults'; *to blackmail someone* 'to obtain money by threats and extortion'; *the pot calls the kettle black* 'someone accuses someone of faults that they themselves have'; *a black mark* 'a flaw'; *blackguard* 'rogue; villain' or

---

[7] A lot of English cartoons portray the devil as red, perhaps because of flames.

the black sheep (of the family) and *a black day*. It is linguistically significant that the idiom *a black day* cannot be substituted by *a dark day* without changing the meaning. It is obvious that *black* in its symbolic reading has a semantic function that is different from that of *dark*, which can be interpreted on the basis of direct experience (the world knowledge about darkness being connected with unpleasant sensations). Thus, BLACK in (4) is a cultural symbol in a figurative expression that fits in well with a broad cultural context.

The same holds for WHITE in idiom (4). This symbol in conventional figurative language is also supported by a strong cultural symbol; various cultural codes include the symbol WHITE. Most of its symbolic functions are diametrically opposed to the function of BLACK (functions like 'honesty', 'truthfulness', or 'innocence'). In addition to that, there are many CFUs with similar symbolic functions of WHITE; cf. the figurative units *whiter than white, to whitewash*, mentioned in 10.8, and idioms like *a whited sepulchre* 'innocent and pure in appearance, but dirty and corrupt within' or German *eine weiße Weste haben* "to have a white waistcoat" 'to have not done anything dishonourable, to have a good record'.

There are several CFUs like (4), where the contrast between BLACK and WHITE symbolises the contrast between BAD and GOOD. Against this background, it is evident that BLACK and WHITE are cultural symbols in the following Russian CFUs as well (6–7):

(6) *черная зависть* "black envy"
    'very strong envy'

(7) *белая зависть* "white envy"
    'appreciative attitude towards someone who is successful; the person who feels "white envy" wishes a comparable success for himself without having negative feelings about the person who is successful'

Obviously, BLACK in (6) contains a very negative symbolic function. ENVY is a bad emotion in itself, and it may cause negative behaviour patterns. The concept BLACK intensifies the negative aspects of being envious of someone or something. In contrast to this, the "white envy" in (7) is not envy at all, but a kind of pleasure in the fact that the other is well and the desire to be in their place – without wishing them ill or taking away their fortune. The concept WHITE is so strong that it not only moderates the negative meaning of ENVY, but changes it fundamentally and even converts the negative aspects into positive ones.

11.4.2 Symbols: Transparent vs. opaque

As has been outlined in section 11.3.5 (e), the symbol stands between two poles, namely the pole of *iconicity* and the pole of *arbitrariness*. The symbol is always conventional; otherwise it would not be a symbol. However, many symbols can be transparent or opaque to a certain degree. Let us go back to the examples HAMMER AND SICKLE, standing for 'the workers' and farmers' power', and FISH, standing for 'early Christianity'. The former is more transparent than the latter. The same applies to cultural symbols in conventional figurative language, where gradual differences between the two poles can also be observed.

As an example of a high degree of transparency let us consider the symbol GOLD in CFL and culture. Gold is a precious metal that is used in many ways. It is considered to be very valuable in many cultures. This esteem, however, is based on convention. In reality, steel and iron, for example, are much more useful, and platinum is more expensive (see below). The symbolic meaning of GOLD in CFL and other cultural codes is almost identical with the conventionalised meaning of 'very valuable'. Therefore, CFUs with the concept GOLD can be easily decoded due to the knowledge of the conventionalised meaning of GOLD. This case is quite close to Saussure's notion of the symbol, which emphasises its *connotative meaning* (the symbol as a sign to whose primary signified a secondary meaning is added).

There are two main symbolic functions of GOLD in CFUs (in the European languages analysed here): 'something very good, excellent or valuable', cf. idiom (8), and 'a vast amount of money, a great capital' (example 9). However, these two symbolic functions often overlap, as idiom (10) shows.

(8) English *to have a heart of gold*
'to be a friendly, generous, forgiving person whose qualities are much appreciated'

(9) English *a golden handshake* 'a lump sum of money paid to a retiring director or manager, or to a redundant worker'

(10) German *Gold in der Kehle haben* "to have gold in the throat"
'to have a very beautiful voice, to have a great talent for singing and to be able to earn money by means of this talent'

The complete idioms cannot be understood as metaphors because it is not possible to imagine that someone's heart is really made of gold (8), that someone shakes hands 'in a golden way' (9) or that someone has gold in their throat, enabling them to sing beautifully (10). What is meant is that the speaker or hearer is able to activate a special component of his or her cultural knowledge, namely the knowledge of certain non-literal functions of the concept GOLD. The symbolic meanings 'something very positive, valuable' etc. are fixed in both language and culture.

The significance of GOLD is rooted in the old traditions of numerous cultural codes. Its high value is dominant in ancient myths (e.g. the gold of Agamemnon), in fairy tales (e.g. GOLD as a buried treasure), or, most obviously, in alchemy. As a Christian symbol, GOLD is thought of as the pure light of heaven. It also has an outstanding symbolic function in the fine arts. Gold pigment is used in painting for the aureoles of God and the saints. In Orthodox Christianity, GOLD symbolises perfection and the light of heaven, as the golden backgrounds of medieval panels and Byzantine icons suggest. Even in our modern society, GOLD is a well-known symbol, for example in sport, where *Olympic gold*, the gold medal, is the most valuable prize. This coherence throughout many different cultural codes has to be emphasised. Against this cultural background, the symbolic function of GOLD in figurative units such as (8–10) is easily comprehensible.

The symbolic functions of GOLD in CFUs are intelligible because of their high degree of transparency, supported by cultural knowledge. However, this should not obscure the fact that the symbol GOLD is in itself arbitrary. There is a much more valuable precious metal, namely platinum. Hardly any cultural code has raised platinum to the status of a symbol. There is a lack of cultural tradition in the Euro-American cultural area according to which the concept PLATINUM could be used in a symbolic function (except for some objects of the modern culture such as Platinum Records or Platinum Credit Cards), in contrast to the concept GOLD as a very strong cultural symbol throughout the centuries. Other valuable objects like PEARLS or DIAMONDS do not come anywhere near the prominence of GOLD in language and culture. In sum, one can say that GOLD came into the figurative language merely by cultural convention.

There are other symbols in culture and conventional figurative units that are very opaque, at least for people not involved in cultural studies. In these cases, additional knowledge about the conventionalisation is required. This does not contradict the Saussurian notion of the symbol ("le symbole a pour caractère de n'être jamais tout à fait arbitraire", see 11.3.3), because the symbol, once conventionalised, can lose its iconic motivation in the course of history.

Number symbols can illustrate how the "transparency" of bygone times can become completely darkened. The notion of certain numbers as being more significant than others can often be traced back to astronomic observations in a distant past. It is presumed that the number NINE, once an outstanding symbol in the North European cultural spheres, achieved this status through people observing the lunar system in ancient times. However, the knowledge of NINE as a significant number in the lunar calendar has been lost entirely over the centuries.

Hence, number symbols in conventional figurative language generally belong to this group. This is also connected with the status of numbers in language. They are very abstract and never figurative themselves. All symbolic functions of numerals in CFUs must be considered arbitrary. There is no objective reason why certain numerals should occur in the symbolic functions of an outstanding or positively connoted number (such as SEVEN in many European languages and EIGHT in Japanese) or in the symbolic function of a 'bad number', other than cultural constructs in the course of history. Numbers are neither good nor bad from an objective point of view. The role of culture in conventionalising the symbolic functions of numerals in CFL will be examined in detail in chapter 12.

Idioms (11) serve to exemplify this high degree of arbitrariness and culture-based conventionalisation. The notion of THIRTEEN as a 'bad number' is totally arbitrary. Nevertheless, THIRTEEN is 'bad' in various cultural codes, as it exceeds the sacred number TWELVE.

(11) a. Russian *чертова дюжина*
"the devil's dozen"
b. Finnish *pirun tusina*
"the devil's dozen"
both meaning 'thirteen (thirteen pieces, specimens of something)'<?>

From an objective point of view, THIRTEEN is a number like any other, neither better nor worse. In traditional European folk belief (and, of course, in cultures derived from European traditions, e.g. those of North America and Australia), however, THIRTEEN is considered to be an evil number. It is seen as the number of disaster in various cultural codes, standing in contrast to the sacred and perfect number TWELVE in the Old and New Testament, biblical exegesis and medieval Christian allegory. Popular belief had it that the devil would accompany a coven of twelve witches as their thirteenth member. The same holds for fairy tales, e.g. the German "Dornröschen" ("Little Briar Rose"), where the thirteenth Wise Woman wishes to avenge herself and wreaks havoc on the king's party (cf. Böklen 1913; Schuppener 1996).

There exists even in the modern enlightened society a fear of the number thirteen, called *triskaidekaphobia*. Examples from Opie and Tatem (1995: 398–399) include cases where the number THIRTEEN is missing in hotels and where people are afraid to go out with 13 pounds in their pockets.[8] Thus, THIRTEEN is a very active symbol strongly represented in various cultural domains.

---

8 There is a special fear concerning the date Friday the 13th. In an extensive article in "USA Today" from Friday, April 13, 2001, advice was given as to how "today's dark forces potentially can be offset."

This superstition, which is connected with other semiotic codes as part of a traditional number symbolism in European folk culture, provides a motivational link between the actual meaning of idioms (11) and the meaning of their constituent parts. The reference to the devil fixed in the lexical structure of idioms (11) seems to be highly arbitrary. It makes sense only if one knows that THIRTEEN is the number of bad luck. The number constituent DOZEN, which has a symbolic function itself, changes its symbolic meaning to the opposite because of the combination with the DEVIL, which is also a culturally relevant concept. However, the concept THIRTEEN is infrequent in CFUs, of which there are only a few obsolete examples (e.g. Dutch *hij is nummer dertien* "he is number thirteen" 'he is unbearable, one does not want to have anything to do with him').

Other CFUs involve gradual differences between transparency and opaqueness. They can be viewed as located on a scale, either closer to the end of "intelligible" iconicity or closer to the end of mere convention, being no longer comprehensible.

Some of the conventional figurative units can be interpreted metaphorically as a whole, but one outstanding constituent must be interpreted in its symbolic function at the same time. Let us look at a German idiom with the numeral THIRTEEN. The motivation of the idiom is metaphoric rather than symbolic:

(12) German *jetzt schlägt's dreizehn* "now it strikes thirteen"
 'that is going too far; that is just incredible; that is enough of that'

The negative connotations of THIRTEEN as a very bad and unfortunate number are obvious, maybe influencing the actual meaning of the idiom to a certain extent. Nonetheless, the entire idiom is not motivated by this number symbol but by the metaphoric inference. Special knowledge of the frame CLOCK is required. A clock strikes up to a maximum of twelve times. The content 'twelve times' is replaced in the slot "clock strikes" by the uncharacteristic content 'thirteen times'. When a clock strikes thirteen times, this is 'very unusual, against the norm', which is the basis of the actual meaning of this idiom. This "blending" of world knowledge and certain connotations based on symbolic knowledge is similar to those cases mentioned in section 10.8.

The same phenomenon arises especially in the field of animal symbolism. Several CFUs with animal constituents reveal symbolic readings but preserve some iconic characteristics of the real animal. The case studies on animal names in conventional figurative language (chapter 13) will examine these problems in more detail. There we try to distinguish between symbolically and iconically determined conventional figurative units. However, a clear differentiation is not possible in some cases. The symbolic interpretations of animals (as they manifest themselves in various cultural codes) can often be traced back to real observation.

Some idioms and proverbs based on the concept of the SNAKE, for example, lie somewhere between arbitrariness and similarity. Symbolic readings like 'evil', 'maliciousness', 'falseness' are to a great extent culturally based and conventional. Nevertheless, some iconic aspects, traces of the animal's actual appearance or behaviour, can be present at the same time. The idiom *a snake in the grass*, meaning 'a hidden, treacherous enemy', preserves such iconic aspects of the snake. Not only does the animal "live in the grass" but there are, above all, common negative experiences people have had with snakes (such as a snake's sudden and painful bite). However, the idiom belongs to the complex of intertextual phenomena (see 10.5).

The same can be assumed for the proverb *one must howl with the wolves* 'people should adapt themselves to the habits and customs of the society they find themselves in (even to the extent of accepting bad habits and customs)'. This proverb can be interpreted metaphorically, based on the outstanding characteristic of the WOLF as a pack animal which almost never appears alone but within a "howling pack". At the same time, WOLF is a symbol of 'malice, aggressiveness', connected with WOLF in other cultural codes (see 11.4.4). Iconicity and convention play an almost equal role in motivating this type of CFU.

As a concluding example, let us look at the CRANE, a weighty and highly esteemed symbol in Japanese culture. The CRANE, Japanese 鶴 (*tsuru*), was revered as a sacred bird, symbolising the eminence of the island nation and believed to embody a divine spirit that it brought to Japan's shores from distant regions. Folk legends also tell of the crane bringing rice cultivation to Japan from the north (Garrison et al. 2002: 593). The CRANE is traditionally thought to live for a thousand years, and it is therefore a symbol of good luck and longevity. Old age, for its part, stands for prudence, noble character and dignity. Older people are treated with great respect in East Asia (unlike in many Euro-American areas). This symbolic esteem of the CRANE can be recognised in idiom (13):

(13) Japanese 鶴の一声 (*tsuru no hitokoe*) "a crane's one voice [the single cry of the crane]"
'a word from on high, the voice of authority, an unchallengeable order (especially when children or young persons are squabbling or not able to reach a required decision)'

Idiom (13) is deeply anchored in the cultural traditions of Japan. Authority has the last word in Japan when children or young people are not able to reach a required decision. It is obvious that CRANE in (13) must be interpreted in its symbolic function, 'a wise person who enjoys a high reputation, confidence and authority'. Nevertheless, the iconic aspects should not be overlooked. It is the voice of the crane that distinguishes it from other birds. The crane's voice is more powerful and can be interpreted as standing above the voices of other birds. This "iconic" quality of the crane in nature is present at the same time. Its powerful voice can be compared with the voice of authority that can override or resolve differences of opinion among less powerful people (cf. Sasaki 1993: 275). Thus, CRANE is a very active cultural symbol.

At this point we would like to mention the so-called *poetic symbols*, such as FIRE as a symbol of strong emotion, especially love. Poetic symbols are strongly conventionalised and, at the same time, very transparent. They are entrenched both in culture and conventional figurative language and are mostly bound to special types of text, i.e. to poetic texts.

The example of FIRE as a symbol of strong emotion and love emerges in many Russian CFUs, e.g. *огонь любви* "(the) fire of love" 'strong love' and *огонь в груди* "(the) fire in the breast" 'strong emotion'. These expressions are very familiar, as their high frequency on the Internet shows. FIRE with the symbolic meaning 'strong emotion, love' is supported by various cultural codes, mainly poetic works. There is a long tradition of studying poetic symbols of this kind in Russian semiotics and linguistics (compare e.g. Levin 1969; Tolstaja 2002; Pen'kovskij 2005).

In sum, not all symbols in figurative language are conventionalised along the same lines. At one end of the scale, there is complete arbitrariness, based on cultural symbolisations that are no longer understandable. At the other end is culturally based symbolisation through "iconic" realisations, i.e. through a certain similarity between the concept underlying the literal meaning of the figurative unit and the concept that it symbolises.

11.4.3 Cultural context of symbols

The scope of a symbol is determined by its cultural area, as has been shown in section 11.3.5 (g). We have already mentioned examples of divergent, even opposite symbolic interpretations of certain animal symbols in different cultural areas. One example is the negative image of the BAT in the West, producing idioms with derogatory meanings that would be inconceivable in regions where the BAT is well regarded. There are several examples of this kind in the field of animal symbolism.

HARE and 'cowardice'

The potential polysemy of symbols has been mentioned above. The concept HARE in the conventional figurative language of different cultural communities may serve as an example. In some European languages it has developed the symbolic function 'cowardice, timorousness' (cf. examples 14–18), and speakers of these languages may be convinced that this is a natural or ubiquitous quality of hares and rabbits. However, 'cowardice' as a symbolic attribute of hares is completely unknown outside Western cultural areas. Allusions to HARE implying 'coward' would not be understandable, for instance, in traditional Asian or African cultures, and could not be translated by the equivalent words meaning 'hare'. Let us look at some CFUs [compounds and restricted collocations (14–18)] meaning 'a very cowardly or anxious person'.

(14) German *Angsthase* "fear-hare"; *Hasenfuß* "harefoot"

(15) Dutch *hazehart* "hare-heart"

(16) Swedish *harhjärtad människa* "hare-heart-like man"

(17) Russian *заячья душа* "hare-soul"

(18) Finnish *jänishousu* "hare-trousers"

Apart from 'cowardice', however, further symbolic functions are ascribed to the HARE in various European languages, namely 'speed', which is connected with 'cleverness'. All these symbolic functions are supported by cultural codes, e.g. by narrative traditions such as fables and fairy tales, but also by current comic strips or animated cartoons. Traces of the animal's natural behaviour (its ability to flee very quickly) can be recognised, too.

What seems to be of an accidental nature is which of the possible symbolic readings becomes dominant in conventional figurative units of a given language. According to our empirical data drawn from various languages, the symbolic function 'cowardice' can be definitely established for German, Dutch, Swedish, Russian and Finnish CFUs, but hardly at all for French or English. For example, the similes German *ängstlich wie ein Hase*, Dutch *bang als een haas* or Russian *трусливый как заяц* "anxious/timorous as a hare", meaning 'very anxious or frightened' have no equivalents in French or English. CFUs in contemporary Finnish show the symbolic function 'cowardice' very clearly (19–20), whereas most expressions with this meaning of HARE have become obsolete in other languages, such as (21–22). See also Dobrovol'skij and Piirainen (1997: 187–193) for more details.

(19) Finnish *hänellä on jänis housuissa* "he has the/a hare in the trousers"
 'he is very afraid'

(20) Finnish *turvautua jäniksen passiin* "to seek shelter in the hare's passport"
 'to run away cowardly'

(21) Dutch (dated) *haas vreten* "to eat hare"

(22) Dutch (dated) *hazebloed hebben* "to have hare-blood"
 both meaning 'to be very anxious and frightened'

YELLOW LIVER and 'cowardice'
Further expressions from the semantic field 'cowardice' can be used for comparison. The CFUs listed in Roget (1992: no. 491) show that the English language prefers images and symbols that are quite different from those connected with the concept HARE. First, other small animals are associated with a cowardly person (*chicken, mouse* or *jellyfish* as well as *fraidy-cat, scaredy-cat*), and are also used attributively with *hearted* (*chicken-hearted, henhearted, pigeonhearted*). Second, there is a concept of YELLOW (or PALE) in combination with LIVER that manifests itself in several expressions in the field 'cowardice' (23–24).

(23) *to be yellow/yellow-bellied/yellow-livered, to be a yellow-belly, to show a yellow streak*, etc.

(24) *to be white-livered/milk-livered, to be a white liver/a lily-liver*, etc.
 'to be very cowardly, to be a coward'

These expressions are indirectly influenced by pre-scientific medical traditions related to "humoural pathology", which dates back to classical antiquity and was passed on in European folk beliefs from medieval times up to the 18th century (cf. section 6.2.1). Certain combinations of the four fluid humours of the body were thought to determine human temperament and human features. From antiquity, the liver was regarded as the seat of various temperaments and according to pre-scientific anatomy it was believed to play the major role in the production of blood. The red liver, supplied with blood, was associated with 'courage'. The liver lacking blood, the "white liver", was connected with 'cowardice' (the Ancient Greek λευκ-ηπατίας "white-livered" means 'anxious, discouraged').

Strangely enough, this strand of medical folk belief, once wide-spread in Europe, left traces in only a few European languages. There are some expressions in French, though they are not very familiar, e.g. *avoir les foies rouges* "to have the red livers" 'to be courageous', *avoir les foies blancs* "to have the white livers" 'to have a terrible fear, be terribly worried'. There are also some more familiar variants like *avoir les foies bleus/verts* "to have blue/green livers" (colours that are not "red" but contrast with it) or even, as a play on words (a punning cliché), *avoir les foies tricolore* "to have 'tricolour' livers", i.e. 'blue, white, not only red', meaning 'to have fear' (Rey and Chantreau 2003: 425).

The old pre-scientific theory that the liver of a coward contained no blood is preserved in English conventional figurative units, even though it may be completely obsolete today. The "bloodless liver" is imagined to be yellow (in to red) (23) or to be white, which led to circumlocutions like *lily-livered*, (24). Thus, members of English linguistic communities, where these idioms are well known,[9] would attach the symbolic meaning 'cowardice' to YELLOW, as if it was a natural or ever-present symbol of cowardice (cf. e.g. Bennett 1988: 66; Biedermann 1994: 74).[10]

This existence of the concept YELLOW LIVER in English is possibly supported by the phenomenon of textual dependence (10.5). In Shakespeare's days, for example, these popular doctrines were still alive and they appear throughout his popular dramas.

The expression *lily-livered* is probably a direct quotation from Shakespeare's "Macbeth" V,3 (*Stand up and fight, you lily-livered scoundrel!*). There are other passages in his texts where the ancient folk doctrine becomes apparent, such as in Sir Toby's remark in "Twelfth Night" III,2: "For Andrew, if he were opened, and you find so much blood in his liver as will clog the foot of a fear, I'll eat the rest of the anatomy."[11] Nevertheless, may be only a coincidence that fragments of this old folk theory are strongly present in CFUs of one language, namely English, but completely unknown in other languages. This is one of the irregularities of conventional figurative language that has not yet been explained.

This example leads us to the impact of history on symbols in language. It can be established that interpretations of one and the same symbol in figurative units can vary in different historical phases. The obsolete English simile *as wise as a*

---

[9] Maybe some of the expressions (23–24) are colloquial or slang and are not known throughout the area of distribution of the English language.

[10] In culturally related areas, however, for example in Germany or in Finland, this symbolic value of YELLOW is completely incomprehensible, leading to some mistakes in its use. For instance, *yellow* has been used in advertising without knowledge of the fact that it evokes negative associations with 'cowardice'. A private German electricity supplier chose the name *Yello Strom* and advertised: *Strom ist gelb* ("Current is yellow"). A slogan of the FDP, Liberal German Party, was: *Wählt gelb!* ("Elect yellow!"). A Finnish newspaper advertisement, extolling "Chiquita" bananas, reads *Feeling blue? Söy keltainen* (a mixture of English and Finnish: When you "feel blue", meaning 'depressed', "eat yellow").

[11] This is, of course, also true for other poets and dramas of the time. Molière's "Le Malade imaginaire" ("The Hypochondriac" 1674), for example, deals with the theory of "humoural pathology" to a great extent.

serpent is an example, as it reflects esteem held for the SNAKE in past cultures (see 13.2).

Lynx in language and culture

As has been mentioned above, the significance of symbols can change in the course of history. The development of different codes (in this case, of natural language and secondary cultural codes) does not necessarily proceed in a parallel way. Culturally relevant codes can change over time, just as languages change. Languages can follow the change of symbols in cultural codes and develop its symbols in the same way (as in the case of SEVEN in many European languages), but they can also hold on to former phases in historical processes, as is assumed for NINE in English, Lithuanian and Finnish (see 12.3 for details).

Let us look at the concept LYNX in CFUs and in various cultural codes, as this is a special case. The secondary readings of the concept LYNX are present in CFUs of some European languages (though not in all of them), e.g. in English, Dutch, French and German. Let us look at some German CFUs.

(25) *Augen haben wie ein Luchs, Luchsaugen haben, luchsäugig sein* "to have eyes like a lynx/to have the eyes of a lynx/to be lynx-eyed"
'to have very sharp eyesight, to have good powers of vision'

(26) *aufpassen wie ein Luchs* "to watch (out) like a lynx"
'to be very attentive, observant, to pay keen attention (to something)'

Expressions (25–26) cannot be interpreted iconically on the basis of world knowledge, e.g. on knowledge of the outward appearance, behaviour or other features of the LYNX (as is the case when interpreting the idiom *to have eyes like a hawk* 'to have very sharp eyesight, to have good powers of vision'). It is impossible for anyone to have any experience of the alleged sharp eyesight of the lynx. The animal is not remarkable in this respect; its eyes are no sharper than those of other animals of the Felidae. Besides, the lynx has been extinct in most parts of Central Europe for some time and plays almost no role in everyday life. Therefore, it can be assumed that idioms (25–26) are motivated by symbolic knowledge.

According to our concept of cultural symbolism in conventional figurative language, two criteria should be fulfilled in order to prove that LYNX is a symbol: firstly, correspondences in cultural codes other than language, and secondly, recurrence of the given symbolic function in CFL. The second criterion can be regarded as fulfilled in view of the repeated occurrence of the secondary meaning of LYNX in the German idioms (25–26).

As far as the first criterion is concerned, LYNX as a symbol of 'sight' and 'vigilance' is a construct established over a short period of time. The symbolic functions ascribed to the LYNX are neither correct from a zoological point of view nor supported by later cultural traditions. Cultural codes like fairy tales, fables, poetry, and religious traditions or popular beliefs that are known today do not support this symbolic interpretation of the LYNX.

Rather, LYNX as a symbol came into being due to a number of historical "accidences". In Greek mythology, good powers of vision were ascribed to *Lynkeos*, one of the Argonauts. It is recorded in Horace's I. Epistle (1:28) that he was so sharp-sighted that he could see through the earth and distinguish objects that were miles away. *Lynkeos*' name has been connected with the similarly sounding Greek word λύγξ 'lynx'. Referring to this ancient tradition, the LYNX was considered a symbol of 'watchfulness, vigilance' in some cultural codes that were important in the Middle Ages. Konrad von Megenburg praises the lynx's acuity of vision and hearing in his influential "Buch der Natur" ("Book of Nature", 1350). He attributes to the lynx the quality of being able to see through a thick stone wall, as this was attributed to *Lynkeos* in Greek mythology. This supposed yet conventionalised "symbolic knowledge" was spread by other authors, among them Martin Luther, and resulted in CFUs such as (25–26).

In Christian medieval symbolic codes, LYNX referred to 'vigilance, watchful alertness'; it was connected with both Jesus and the devil and had the same symbolic function in iconography and heraldry (Röhrich 1991: 977–978; Biedermann 1994: 213). This symbolic knowledge has been almost completely lost in the course of the following centuries. It is only due to a few CFUs that certain conceptual and linguistic traces of this former knowledge are preserved. LYNX continues to be a symbol in the cultures in question only thanks to conventional figurative language. Still, there may be some tacit symbolic knowledge that has an effect on the usage of words in the symbolic meaning. It is not possible to use the word *Luchs* 'lynx' symbolically in free word combinations without reference to expressions (25–26). An utterance like German *unsere Sekretärin ist ein Luchs* ("our secretary is a lynx") in the sense 'she is very attentive' or 'she has very sharp eyes' can only be understood if the context makes reference to the above-mentioned CFUs. Such restrictions have a clear nature: if relevant cultural knowledge has been lost and does not play any role synchronically, it can only be handed down via fixed linguistic structures that were developed earlier and are now used as "prefabricated" conventional expressions. LYNX as a symbol was active at the time when the idioms in question came into being, but in contemporary culture it has lost its activity. Therefore, we may call it an "inactive" or "dead" symbol.

In summary, cultural domains bring the symbols in conventional figurative language into existence. Some asymmetries have been observed in conventional figurative language. Different semiotic domains can undergo different developments in the course of history. Thus, a symbol may exist in contemporary CFL while its counterpart in other cultural codes may have been lost. Furthermore, there are differences even between related languages belonging to the same cultural area. This confirms the suggestion that many factors in the domain of conventional figurative language are unpredictable in principle.

11.4.4 Cultural codes

Numbers and animal constituents are suitable domains to demonstrate the significant correspondence between conventional figurative language and culture. We will present two detailed case studies – one concerned with numbers and one with animals – in the following chapters (12 and 13). For the time being, we will take a brief look at the main cultural codes that are relevant to these case studies.

Religions: Christian traditions, the Old and New Testaments, and centuries of biblical exegesis have contributed to the development of number symbols like SEVEN or TWELVE and animal symbols such as SNAKE, LAMB, or WOLF. The Bible has had a lasting influence on the CFUs of all European languages analysed in this study. Likewise, the Japanese religious traditions of Shintoism and Buddhism, as well as "Shinbutsukonkō", a modern form of syncretism, have created number symbols (cf. the significance of EIGHT in Japanese language and culture) and symbolic animal concepts (such as FOX, DOG, or SNAKE), which are significant in conventional figurative language.

Myths, national epics: The symbolic elements of classical myths continued to exist in later occidental traditions. There is a symbolic significance of the number NINE and symbolic characteristics ascribed to animals such as HORSES or WOLVES in Germanic mythology (in the tradition of the Anglo-Saxon epic poem "Beowulf" or the "Edda", the myths about the gods). FOUR, as a symbol, can be reconstructed for the Indo-European period and is related to the mythic image of the four winds and to ancient astronomy. The Finnish national epic poem "Kalevala", with its myths, which was recorded by Elias Lönnrot around 1834, is also significant with regard to symbolic interpretations (e.g. NINE and BEAR). Similarly, Japanese mythology and cosmogony are documented in Japan's oldest scripts, the "Kojiki" (712 AD) and the "Nihonshoki" (720 AD), which enables us to detect important symbols (the number EIGHT and the SNAKE).

Fairy tales: Some of the fairy tales collected by Jacob and Wilhelm Grimm at the beginning of the 19th century have made their way into contemporary culture. Well-known fairy tales like "Little Red Riding Hood" contributed to the symbolisation of the WOLF. It is not only the telling or reading of fairy tales that pass on symbolic traditions, but also film animation and comic adaptations, such as Walt Disney's "The Story of the Three Little Pigs" (1933), a cartoon version of the British fairy tale of the same name. Japanese fairy tales, too, have symbolic contents, which today are passed on via children's books, comics, and movies.

Fables, beast epics: Animal symbolism came into being through rich narrative traditions. Fables and beast epics have shaped the symbolic image of certain animals (e.g. FOX, LION, BEAR, WOLF). In the Middle Ages, the bestiary was a popular literary form with various popular adaptations. The majority of the symbolic meanings of animals were handed down via Aesop's fables, or the fables of La Fontaine, Gellert, Lessing, or Krylov, but also via other literary works such as Rudyard Kipling's "Jungle Books" (1894–1895) or George Orwell's "Animal Farm" (1945).

Popular belief, popular customs, ethnic traditions: There is a snake cult in ancient Baltic traditions. According to Lithuanian folk beliefs, the SNAKE was a demon and protectress of the house, and it was considered good luck to have a snake in the house. Relics of popular customs connected with the once outstanding number NINE can be recognised in Lithuanian folk traditions up to the present day, whereas comparable ancient agricultural customs in Finland have fallen into oblivion. Customs to do with the seasons are connected with symbolisations (e.g. ELEVEN in the Rhineland carnival). Popular beliefs and customs have contributed to contemporary symbolism – even today, people in Western cultural areas believe that the number THIRTEEN can bring bad luck. Similar properties are ascribed to the numbers FOUR and NINE in Japan.

Philosophy, literature, arts, music, etc.: Number symbolism can be related to philosophical traditions, such as the Pythagorean teaching in the ancient world, or to number mysticism, for instance in the Middle Ages or in ancient China. Philosophy also contributed to the symbolisation of the OWL. Finally, literature, the fine and performing arts, architecture, film and music productions contain many symbols similar to those found in conventional figurative language, cf. e.g. Russian symbolism in painting and literature at the beginning of the 20th century or the number symbolism in compositions of the Baroque Age.

12 Numeral words and number symbols in culture and language: Case studies

12.1 General remarks

12.1.1 Linguistic aspects of numerals and number symbols

Numbers as linguistic signs

Numbers are, on the one hand, elements of a sign system of their own, of the numerical code, and as such they are independent of language. On the other hand, as numerals, they are tied to language, which means that they are integrated into a completely different semiotic system. Numerals have, in many respects, a special status in language. Their meanings are stable but restricted to denoting definite quantities; they cannot be used figuratively. There is in principle no kind of metaphoric use of numbers, and the following conventional figurative units are no exceptions:

(1) German *stehen wie eine Eins* "to stand like a one"
 'to stand straight and tight'

(2) Finnish *yks – kaks* "one – two"
 'very quick, in great haste'

The numeral in idiom (1) is not used metaphorically, but the graphic form of the sign 1 is used as an icon (like *ramrod* in the English simile *to stand straight as a ramrod*). The motivation for idiom (2) is of an indexical nature (see 4.10). The numerals *yks* 'one' and *kaks* 'two' (shortened from *yksi* and *kaksi*) are not used with a secondary meaning. It is the speed at which these words are pronounced or at which a counting function can be carried out that points to the actual meaning 'very quick'. No iconic or symbolic functions can be attributed to these number constituents.

Whenever a numeral seems to be used metaphorically, it is in fact connected to another element that constitutes the metaphor, as in a word string like *two diamonds* 'two eyes'. As Revzina (1995) shows, with the example of the literary work of Marina Cvetaeva, numerals are special linguistic signs that are not suitable as signs of poetic language. When, in a special context, a number deviates from merely expressing a quantity, this has to be taken as an indicator of a symbolic function.

Thus, one characteristic of most numerals as linguistic signs is their semantic poverty. Synonymy and antonymy are impossible in principle. One numeral cannot denote two or more different quantities, as one quantity cannot be expressed by two different numerals.[1] Furthermore, the distribution of numerals is heavily restricted. There are no combinations of numerals and abstract or mass nouns (*three heights, *five prudences, *six waters) unless the nouns in question lose their abstract meanings or are used in specific contexts; compare *the Three Universal Truths* 'the three basic ideas of Buddhism'.

Stability of form is another feature of numerals. Stylistically, numerals are less differentiated than other lexical units; there are neither slang words nor elevated expressions for numbers, but at best some dialectal or archaic variants (e.g. German *fuffzig* vs. *fünfzig* 'fifty' or *siebenzig* vs. *siebzig* 'seventy') or modernisms for practical reasons (the use of French *huitante* and *novante* in Switzerland or *octante* and *nonante* in Belgium, instead of standard French *quatre-vingt(s)* '80' and *quatre-vingt dix* '90', respectively).

The number ONE is an exception in many respects; it has a special status among the numerals of a language. The characteristics of most other numerals, such as semantic poverty and stability, do not apply to ONE. In some languages, the cardinal number ONE shares its form and/or semantic properties with other parts of speech (article, pronoun or adjective), which also affects conventional figurative units.

(3) English *there is one born every minute*
'someone was stupid to believe or trust something or someone'

(4) German *ein Mann, ein Wort* "one man, one word" or "a man, a word"
'a trustworthy man always does what he has promised to do'

In many English idioms and proverbs, the numeral *one* coincides with the indefinite pronoun *one* ('one', 'someone, anyone'). Thus, the secondary reading of *one* in example (3) cannot clearly be ascribed to a numeral. In some other languages, the numeral cannot be distinguished from the indefinite article, as in the German example (4). Cf. also Harweg (1973), Givón (1981), and Schmidt (1994).

---

[1] However, it is possible to express the same numerical concept using a numeral and a paraphrastic description; compare *six* and *half a dozen*.

Numbers as symbols
Numerals as symbols in language behave completely differently. They can develop indirect (symbolic) meanings in conventional figurative expressions like idioms, proverbs or figurative compounds. As has already been mentioned, synonymy and antonymy of numbers or numerals are impossible. Nevertheless, numbers that are part of figurative expressions can occur with antonymous meanings. An example is the number FOUR in French, which has the symbolic function of 'much, many' in numerous conventional figurative units but also occurs, in some idioms, with just the opposite meaning, 'few, less'. Let us look at idioms (5–6), where FOUR stands for 'many, much', and idiom (7), where the very same number means 'few'.

(5) French *ne pas y aller par quatre chemins* "not to go there by four ways"
    'to express one's opinion or view very directly, to be straightforward'

(6) French *(monter/descendre) quatre à quatre* "(to go up/down the stairs) four by four"
    'to take several steps of the stairs at once'

(7) French *à quatre pas d'ici* "four steps from here"
    'only a few steps from here, quite near'

The non-literal, symbolic function of *quatre* is obvious here, since the literal meaning of one linguistic unit cannot express 'many' and 'few' at the same time. Similarly, (cross-linguistic) synonymy can also be found. Different numerals may become synonyms in conventional figurative units in various languages. For example, THREE does not contrast with FOUR in the following examples (8–9).

(8) a. Russian *есть за троих* "to eat for three"
    b. German *essen für drei* "to eat for three"
       'to eat a lot'

(9) French *manger comme quatre* "to eat like four"
    'to eat a lot'

The meanings of the expressions (8) "to eat for three" and (9) "to eat for four" are synonymous, both meaning 'to eat as much as if one were eating the portions of several people'. Thus, the numbers THREE and FOUR reveal that only a symbolic reading, i.e. 'many', is possible here.

A corollary of this synonymy is the interchangeability. A number in its primary reading is never replaceable by another number. In symbolic readings, however, this is not unusual. Proverb research has revealed that the choice of numerals sometimes seems to be arbitrary (cf. the variants of the expression *a dozen trades, thirteen miseries* in section 12.3.2). Another example is the pair of idioms (10–11). The symbolic function of the number SEVEN in (10) and TWO (more than one) in (11) is 'very much' in an intensifying sense. The Dutch correspondence shows the quantifier *all* instead of a number symbol (12).

(10) German *in sieben Sprachen schweigen* "in seven languages to keep silent/to say nothing"

(11) Finnish *vaieta kahdella kielellä* "to keep silent/to say nothing in two languages"

(12) Dutch *in alle talen zwijgen* "in all languages to keep silent/to say nothing" all meaning 'to answer to nothing, to not comment on anything'

The cross-linguistic approach reveals several cases of a relation "symbol vs. non-symbol" like (11–12): German *ein Buch mit sieben Siegeln* "a book with seven seals" (of biblical origin) vs. English *a closed book* (or *a sealed book*) 'a subject about which one knows nothing, a mystery'.

Another interesting example of a number symbol is FORTY. Schimmel (1987: 18) emphasises the significance of FORTY in the cultures of the Middle East. FORTY meaning 'very many' is an important number in Islamic lore (cf. Ali Baba's forty thieves). The number is very popular in Turkey, where major festivities last for 40 days and 40 nights. Ancient rites connected with death and purification are based on the number FORTY. The Bible and Christian traditions are full of entities that include the number FORTY (spans of forty days are of particular significance); see Roscher (1909) for details.

FORTY was also an important round number in the Greek-Byzantine region, and remnants of that usage can still be found. The forty days' period of mourning plays a role in both Greek and Russian culture to the present day. Forty days after a death, a funeral repast is held, and it is believed that the immortal soul finally leaves this world on that day. Among the languages analysed here, only Russian provides idioms using FORTY to express 'many, much', cf. *сорок сороков* "forty by forty" 'the many churches of Moscow', which became the symbolic name for the city of Moscow, and *наговорить/наплести сорок бочек (арестантов)* "to narrate forty barrels (arrested people)" 'to tell stories that are not true'. Forty is the highest number that occurs in independent Russian CFUs. In a historical context, a correlation between linguistic and cultural symbols can thus be assumed.

"Sacred numbers" have another quality. They are cultural symbols that exist outside of language (e.g. THREE, SEVEN). However, these "sacred numbers" can occur in conventional figurative units. As linguistic units, they receive additional symbolic functions with regard to the cultural codes with which they are connected. Seen from the semiotic perspective, these numbers are polyfunctional signs.

In the course of history, symbols may undergo different developments in a given language and in cultural codes. The numbers SEVEN and NINE are such examples of divergent developments: NINE is an important number symbol in conventional figurative units in English, Lithuanian and Finnish, but the number has no symbolic relevance in contemporary culture (or in the cultural areas where English, Lithuanian or Finnish are spoken). Furthermore, it has to be emphasised that NINE enjoys this special status in only a few European languages, in contrast to many other languages that clearly prefer SEVEN as a significant number symbol, in accordance with the dominant general status of SEVEN in both earlier and contemporary culture. The genetic relationship is not important here, since Estonian, closely related to Finnish, clearly prefers SEVEN in a number of conventional figurative units. The same holds for Dutch, German or Swedish, languages that rarely use NINE with a symbolic function, although they are closely related to English.

A similar example is the above-mentioned FOUR in French (as well as in other Romance languages, e.g. Italian). As far as conventional figurative language is concerned, FOUR clearly surpasses the status of THREE (cf. examples (6–7) and (9) above). THREE is relatively insignificant in French conventional figurative language, and whereas FOUR is not a central symbol within French culture, THREE is definitely more important. Figurative language and culture do not always coincide.

12.1.2 Cultural aspects of number symbols

It can be assumed that most cultures pay attention to numerical relations, countable entities and mathematical principles, and that numerical units are often dealt with symbolically. Numbers, numerical proportions and ratios are significant for the cosmic order; they play a large role in structuring space and time, in observing the sun, the moon and the stars, and in calculating the courses of the celestial bodies and planets (cf. the lunar number NINE in the distant past). Since the earliest testimonies, all advanced civilisations have correlated macrocosm and microcosm on the basis of numbers. Numerical units and ratios have been interpreted as symbols, and were used to organise the world of the demons and gods, to describe the inner structure of man, and to systematise mythology and theology.

Number symbolism plays an important role in several philosophical and ideological schools, e.g. in Pythagoreanism (6th century BC). Pythagoras' number symbolism influenced various subsequent schools of mystic thought. To the Pythagoreans, numbers were a matter of cosmic concern; they were symbols of a divine world order that consisted of the principle of pairs of opposites: the unlimited (represented by the even numbers) and the limited (represented by the odd numbers), the latter regarded as an active force that effects order and harmony (cf. Bindel 1962; Butler 1970: 4–6). The Pythagoreans discovered that numbers and ratios could explain certain relations in music, geometry and astronomy. They discovered that vibrating strings whose length could be expressed in simple numerical ratios produced enjoyable chords. This led to the development of their influential theory of harmony. Later, it is thought that Pythagoreans discovered that the distances between the heavenly bodies and the Earth, as well as the formation of crystals, corresponded to musical intervals.

The Pythagoreans also developed a cosmogonical theory that explained the generation of numbers with a concept of limited odd numbers and unlimited even numbers. According to this theory, every form can be expressed in numbers. Things are numbers, or resemble numbers. Even abstract entities are associated with numbers (e.g. justice with the number four, marriage with the number five, etc.). Pythagorean number speculation, as well their cosmology and its associated aesthetic of harmony, were incorporated into Plato's philosophy and then passed on to the scholars of the Middle Ages.

Another example of the symbolic significance of numbers comes from ancient Chinese philosophy and religion, in which the categorical formation of the numbers ONE to NINE was one of the most important principles. In the Taoist tradition and in the ideas of Confucius, China's most famous and influential philosopher, the entire conception of the world was number-based. The numbers were related to the cosmos, not so much to quantify things as to indicate their quality, their position and their place within the cosmos.

The polarity of *Yin* and *Yang* is the idea that two complementary forces form all aspects of life. They are depicted as a light and a dark half of a circle. *Yin* is present in the even numbers and thought of as earth, female, dark, passive, etc. *Yang* is present in the odd numbers and thought of as heaven, male, light, active, etc. The same polarity appears in the two different kinds of lines (solid/broken) that are used in the oracle of "I Ching" ("The Book of Changes", the guide to "reading the sticks"), an influential ancient Chinese text originally used for divination (Granet 1963: 106–108).

From the union of the polar forces *Yin* and *Yang* arises the idea of the "five elements" or "five phases" (*wu-hsing*: earth, water, fire, metal, wood), which bring forth "ten thousand things", i.e. a countless number of things. The five phases are also conceptualised as "breaths", as active energies, which enabled philosophers to construct a coherent system of correspondences and participations, linking all phenomena of the macrocosm and the microcosm. Associated with spatial directions, seasons of the year, colours, musical notes and animals, they also correspond to the five inner organs of the human body (Granet 1963: 156; Nowotny 1969: 127–129).

Number symbolism is also of great importance in Christian theology and exegesis, particularly in mediaeval mysticism. This tradition regards certain numbers as "sacred". Early Christian systems of cosmology were based on the number THREE, the number of perfection, which referred to the doctrine of the Trinity. The immense effect that numerology has had on Christian thought can be touched upon only briefly here. Another two very significant and sacred numbers are SEVEN and TWELVE, whereas ELEVEN and THIRTEEN are regarded as "bad" numbers (e.g. Lurker 1973: 179).

Number symbolism has been discovered in medieval literature and arts, especially in ecclesiastical architecture such as Gothic church buildings. Number symbolism and music is also a wide field. A notable example of number symbolism can be found in the compositions of Johann Sebastian Bach. In his "St. Matthew Passion", for instance, almost any number and numeric ratio may be called "symbolic" (cf. e.g. Blankenburg and Endres 1979; Jung 1988).

As these examples show, number symbolism and numerology were of far-reaching significance in bygone times, in the traditions of philosophy, religions, mysticism, aesthetics, and so on. The phenomenon of number symbolism has been described in numerous monographs and encyclopaedias (e.g. Endres and Schimmel 1985; for the cultural history of numbers see, among others, Ifrah 1986; Posner 1984). All these studies deal with numbers as cultural symbols.

12.1.3 Numbers in conventional figurative units and culture: Special cases

Conventional figurative units that contain number constituents drawn from the ten standard languages and one dialect analysed in this study constitute a very large complex. Apart from the number ONE, which is an exception, the linguistic data concerning the numbers TWO, THREE and SEVEN alone would offer some hundreds of examples. In view of the vast amount of idioms, proverbs and figurative compounds with a number constituent, not all of them can be examined in detail here. Detailed and exhaustive analyses of these numbers in figurative language and culture have already been presented in Dobrovol'skij and Piirainen (1997). A choice had to be made for the purposes of the present study, in order to illustrate the links between numerals in figurative expressions and cultural knowledge.

The following case studies will exemplify some of the more obvious characteristics of numerals in languages and cultures:
– FOUR: the special case of French (12.2)
– NINE in figurative language and culture: Finnish, Lithuanian and English (12.3)
– ELEVEN: the "crazy number" in Dutch figurative units (12.4)

12.2 FOUR: The special case of French

This section deals with conventional figurative units containing the concept FOUR. First, we will present some CFUs from various languages. The purpose of discussing these examples is to illustrate different functions of FOUR in CFUs (12.2.1). Unlike the other chapters of this study, this section will then concentrate on one single language, namely French. This exception is due to the fact that the number FOUR is found abundantly only in French CFUs, where it mostly has a symbolic meaning (12.2.2). This peculiarity of French, which sets it apart from all other languages analysed in this study, has to be emphasised. Possibly, there are cultural reasons for this distinctive feature (12.2.3).

12.2.1 FOUR in conventional figurative units of different languages

With the exception of French, the languages considered here show only a small number of idioms and figurative compounds with the number FOUR. These few expressions can be grouped according to the semantics of their image component. The concept FOUR is closely connected to concepts like the "four limbs of the body" (13–15), the "four eyes" of two people having a private conversation (16), or the "four walls" of a building and the "four boards" of a coffin (17). Furthermore, FOUR can be the result of a simple calculation (18–21) or the number of letters of certain words. Let us start with the rather "body-based" expressions (13), found in various languages.

(13) a. English *(to be/crawl/move) on all fours*
 b. German *auf allen vieren* "on all fours"
 c. French *à quatre pattes* "on four paws"

d. Russian *на четвереньках* "on fours"
e. Lithuanian *visomis keturiomis* "with (one's) four (limbs) [on all fours]"
f. Greek *στα τέσσερα* "on fours"
g. Finnish *nelin kontin* "four-crawling [crawling with (one's) four (limbs)]"
all meaning 'on one's hands and feet, (to be/crawl/move) on hands and knees'

These expressions are quite clear and regularly motivated; they may be seen as borderline cases of figurative units. The Russian expression can be regarded as an idiom because of the unique constituent *четвереньках* "(on) fours [suffix-dim and final ablative-pl]". The semantic relations in the following expressions (14) are also quite regular. It should be noted that their literal and figurative readings are not too far apart.

(14) a. German *alle viere von sich strecken* "to stretch all four (limbs) out"[2]
b. Japanese 四肢を延ばす (*shishi wo nobasu*) "four limbs to extend [to stretch (the/one's) four limbs]"
both meaning 'to stretch arms and legs out wide (while lying down), to put one's feet up'

The number FOUR in examples (13–14) refers to the shape of the human body with its four limbs, two arms, and two legs. Because of this naturalness and independence of culture, we can find great similarities between non-related languages here, including an almost complete equivalent of the German idiom (14a) in Japanese (14b). By contrast, the French idiom (15) provides a different image component from (14). The person in question is compared to a horse lying on the ground, extending its legs into the air. The concept HORSE is indicated by the word *fers* 'irons/horseshoes'.

(15) French *(tomber) les quatre fers en l'air* "(to fall) the four irons/horseshoes into the air" '(to fall) flat on one's back'

For the sake of completeness, we can also quote the French idiom *je n'ai pas quatre bras* "I do not have four arms" 'I cannot do more than is within my power', where FOUR also refers literally to the limbs (the arms in the function of 'help' or 'work'). The idioms below (16) are "body-based" in a wider sense since two people, taken

---

[2] Idiom (14a) is an elliptic construction where *viere* 'four' stands for 'four limbs'.

together, have four eyes.³ These idioms can be used in order to avoid saying directly that one wants to have a private or quiet word with someone, without any witness. Therefore, they are slightly euphemistic.

(16) German *unter vier Augen (mit jmdm. sprechen)*; Dutch *onder vier ogen (spreken met iemand)*; French *(parler à qn.) entre quatre yeux/entre quat'zyeux* "(to talk to someone) between four eyes"
all meaning '(to talk to someone) in private, without the presence of other people'

One could ask why the situation of a face-to-face communication is encoded by word strings like "between four eyes" rather than, for example, "two mouths" or "two tongues", images that would seem even more suitable to verbal communication. However, using the image "between four eyes" for this denotatum is not purely coincidental but culturally based. In Western cultures, people usually look into their partner's eyes when speaking. This is an important gesture and one of the "aspects of social interactions", which belong to the types of cultural foundation of figurative language (cf. 10.3.3). Our observation can be proved by cross-linguistic comparison. Russian, for example, does not have an idiom of the sort discussed above.⁴ This explains why iconic images of this kind lead to lexical units which are perceived as figurative.

Furthermore, the concept FOUR occurs repeatedly in connection with rooms, houses, or other kinds of buildings, the "four walls" of which constitute the boundaries. This concept is culturally based in the sense of "material culture" (10.4) insofar as buildings in Western cultures are usually rectangular and have four walls (in contrast to, for instance, yurts, tepees or igloos).⁵ Some idioms whose underlying image refers to the concept 'within the four walls' have been discussed in chapter 5 (31–33), e.g. German *in den eigenen vier Wänden* "within one's own four walls" 'in the privacy of one's (own) home, at home; in an atmosphere of confidence', French *rester entre quatre murs* "to remain between four walls" 'to always stay at home, never go out, be isolated, be bored' and Dutch *tussen de vier muren zitten* "to sit between the four walls" 'to be in prison', the

---

3 Certain proverbs show the same idea of "four eyes" referring to two people, e.g. German *Vier Augen sehen mehr als zwei*, French *Quatre yeux voient plus que deux* "Four eyes see more than two" 'It is better that two people work together in order to avoid mistakes'.
4 In Japan, eye-contact during conversation has to be avoided. So there would be no place for such idioms in Japanese (cf. Tohyama 1991: 206; Hasada 1997: 87–89).
5 However, the concept 'four walls of a single room' has no place in the (Western) WML dialect, cf. chapter 9.

latter being a euphemistic circumlocution used to avoid saying directly that someone is serving a sentence of imprisonment.

There are further comparable euphemistic expressions in Dutch, French, and Finnish (17). Here, the concept FOUR is related to the boards of a coffin, for which the "four boards" are figurative euphemisms.

(17) a. Dutch *tussen de vier planken liggen* "to lie between the four boards"
b. French *être entre quatre planches* "to be between four boards"
c. Finnish *olla neljän laudan välissä* "to be between the four planks"
all meaning 'to be dead (to be lying in the coffin)'

Finally, FOUR can be the result of a very simple mathematical equation (18–21). Any multiplication or addition of the small number two is so easy that the result is obvious. Thus, the concept FOUR can be evoked by using the concept TWO twice. The reference to such a simple calculation is a link to the actual meanings 'very simple' (18), 'very clear' (19–20), or 'very sure' (21).

(18) a. English *as simple as two and two*
b. Russian *просто как дважды два четыре* "as simple as (the fact that) two times two are four"
'very simple'

(19) a. English *to put two and two together*[6]
'to draw an obvious conclusion from what is known or evident'
b. English *two and two make four*
'an obvious conclusion'

(20) Russian *ясно как дважды два четыре* "as obvious as (the fact that) two times two (are four)"
'very clear'

(21) a. German *so sicher wie zwei mal zwei vier ist* "as sure as two times two are four"
b. Dutch *zo zeker als twee keer twee vier is* "as sure as two times two are four"

---

[6] A jocular extension of this idiom is to *put two and two together and make five* meaning 'to draw a plausible but incorrect conclusion from what is known or evident'.

c. French *(être) aussi sûr que deux et deux font quatre* "(to be) as sure as two and two are four"
all meaning '(to be) very certain or sure'

The choice of the numbers TWO and FOUR in (21) seems to be arbitrary; no cultural-semiotic knowledge about these numbers is necessary. This is evident when we consider an almost equivalent Spanish expression, where the use of different small numbers (THREE, TWO and FIVE) leads to the same semantic result: *seguro como tres y dos son cinco* "as sure as three and two are five".

We should also mention some CFUs referring to "four letters" at this point, e.g. the jocular and somewhat euphemistic German idiom *sich auf seine vier Buchstaben setzen* "to sit on one's four letters" 'to sit down (on one's backside)'. The "four letters" refer to the harmless nursery language word *Popo* 'bottom'. There is also the English *four-letter word*, a circumlocution for the traditional "dirty" or "swear" word, many of which consist of four letters and some of which are known worldwide (e.g. *cock, cunt, fuck, piss, shit, turd*, cf. Spears 1991: 166).

In order to process the above-mentioned CFUs, speakers do not need any symbolic knowledge about the number FOUR. The number has to be interpreted literally, on the basis of world knowledge, indicating four entities. The following Dutch idiom (22) is a borderline case: although the iconic reading seems to be primary, a symbolic function cannot be excluded completely.

(22) Dutch (outdated) *door zijn geweten kan wel een koets met vier paarden rondrijden* "a carriage drawn by four horses could drive around in his conscience"
'he has a large conscience; he is very dishonest'

The iconic (non-symbolic) interpretation of FOUR makes sense because carriages drawn by four horses are well-known objects in the real world. However, a symbolic reading of FOUR is also possible. The image of the horse-drawn carriage driving around indicates space, which is the imagery basis for 'large conscience, extreme dishonesty'. Within this image, the symbolic function of intensifying is attached to the number FOUR: four horses require a larger radius of movement than, for example, two horses. Hence, the actual meaning of idiom (22): the person in question is "very dishonest".

Other types of borderline cases are "the four corners of the world" (23) or "the four directions from where the wind blows" (24). Here the iconic and the symbolic functions of FOUR cannot be separated from each other. The conception of space in terms of four entities (four directions, four (principal) points of the compass, etc.) seems to be natural or universal, if not even "body-based": FOUR refers to the space in front of a person, behind him/her, and on both the left and the right hand side of the person. This "fourfold" conception of space is deeply anchored in culture (see section 12.2.3).

(23) a. English *(from/to) the four corners of the world/earth/globe*
'(from/to) all parts of the world'
b. French *aux quatre coins du monde* "to the four corners of the world"
'to all parts of the world, everywhere'[7]

(24) a. English *to the four winds*
b. German *in alle vier Winde* "in all four winds"
c. French *aux quatre vents* "at/to the four winds"
d. Finnish *kaikkiin neljään tuuleen* "into all four winds"
all meaning 'in all directions, everywhere'

The concept FOUR can be interpreted in its secondary function as 'many, all' ('everywhere, in all directions'). In the German and Finnish idioms (24), this secondary reading is supported by the constituent *alle* and *kaikkiin* 'all', respectively.[8]

In Finland, the traditional headdress of the Sámi, the former nomadic population of Lapland, is still known as a cultural symbol of the four directions of the wind. The hat, formed with four corners, is called *neljän tuulen lakki* "four wind hat [the hat of the four winds]". A less symbolic reading of the expression "the four winds" can be found in the French *ouvert aux quatre vents* "open to the four winds" (also: *ouvert à tous les vent* "open to all the winds"), which means a house is badly protected on all sides (Rey and Chantreau 2003: 904).

Let us consider another idiom, in which the concept FOUR can possibly be interpreted as 'much', 'intensifying'.

(25) Swedish *äta så att magen står i fyra hörn/att magen blir fyrkantig* "to eat so that the stomach stands in four corners/that the stomach becomes quadrilateral"
'to eat excessively'

---

[7] There is a jocular extension of this idiom: *courir les quatre coins et le milieu de la ville* "to run the four corners of the world and the centre of the town" 'to exhaust oneself by running around looking for something'.
[8] Compare CFUs with 'all' and 'far' carrying the same function as FOUR: Finnish *kaikkiin ilmansuuntiin* "into all wind directions [i.e. the compass directions]", Dutch *uit alle windstreken* "from all wind-directions", English *the far corners of the world* 'places that are far away from each other'.

As far as the "four corners" are concerned, we would like to call to mind the idioms given above (23). The Swedish idiom (25) has a variant with the number FIFTEEN as well: *äta så att magen står i femton hörn* "to eat so that the stomach stands in fifteen corners", which shows the intensifying function of the numbers. In fact, FIFTEEN may be a quintessential number.

12.2.2 FOUR in French conventional figurative units

So far, we have mentioned several French CFUs with the number FOUR. Most of them have equivalents in other languages. In addition to that, French provides more than a dozen conventional figurative units with FOUR that do not have equivalents in other languages. In all these cases, FOUR has to be interpreted symbolically. This calls attention to the fact that we are dealing with a salient concept in the conventional figurative language of French. The following two French idioms seem to emphasise FOUR as a quintessential number (26–27). Its symbolic meaning is neither 'much' nor 'few' but 'the best possible number'.

(26) *quatre à quatre (et le reste en gros)* "four by four (and the rest wholesale)"
 'at random, on the off-chance'

(27) *un de ces quatre matins* "one of these four mornings"
 'in near future, at some time, soon'

There is a variant of (27) without *matins*: *un de ces quatre*, and a salutation formula *bon, à un de ces quatre!* "well, to one of these four" 'see you (soon); good bye'.

In most French CFUs, FOUR has the symbolic functions of 'much, many' or 'very, intense'. We mentioned some of these idioms with FOUR in section 12.1.1 above. "Four ways" in idiom (5), *ne pas y aller par quatre chemins* "to not go there by four ways", stands for 'many ways', which forms a contrast to "one single direct way", the figurative reading of which is 'to express one's opinion or view directly'. Another French idiom, which uses almost the same constituents (*chemins* 'ways' in a more literal reading), leads to a different semantic result: *être toujours sur les quatre chemins* "to be always on the four ways" 'to travel a lot, to be always on the road, to be away often'.

Idiom (6), *(monter/descendre) quatre à quatre* "(to go upstairs/downstairs) four by four", refers to a concrete situation. Normally, one walks upstairs by putting one foot in front of the other, but if one runs upstairs in a hurry, sometimes two or three steps are taken at a time. The French language uses a CFU with FOUR to express this, whereas the other languages examined here do not have such an idiomatic expression. As far as idiom (9) is concerned (*manger comme quatre* "to eat like four"), we have shown that other languages prefer THREE here ("to eat for three" meaning 'to eat a lot'). There are some further French similes with *comme quatre* "like four", such as *travailler comme quatre* "to work like four" 'to work very hard', but *manger comme quatre* is the most frequent one. The following idiom also shows FOUR with the symbolic meaning of 'many, much'.

(28) *couper/scier/fendre les cheveux/un cheveu en quatre* "to cut/saw/split a hair into four"[9]
'to talk about small, unimportant differences between things as if they were important; to waste one's time on trifles'

Idiom (28) corresponds to the English *to split hairs* or *hair-splitting*, with approximately the same actual meaning. To split a hair "into four" ('into many parts') seems to be an intensification of "to split a hair" (suggesting only two parts). The same function of *en quatre* "into four" can be observed in (28–30).

(29) *avoir la tête (fendue) en quatre* "to have the head (split) into four"
'to have a dazed head, to feel dizzy'

(30) *se mettre en quatre pour qn.* "to put oneself into four for someone"
'to make every effort to help someone; to unselfishly lend aid to someone; to nearly ruin oneself (for someone, in order to help someone)'

While "to split a hair" already seems absurd, referring to something which would not be done in reality, the absurdity goes even further in idiom (29). The function of FOUR remains the same. The imagination of a head split into four (i.e. 'many') pieces serves as the basis of the relevant meaning 'to have a dazed head, to feel dizzy'. Similarly, one cannot really divide oneself "into four" in order to do one's utmost for somebody else (30). Once more the significance of FOUR in French conventional figurative language becomes apparent, while other languages prefer the number THREE. There is a colloquial German idiom, *ich könnte mich wohl in drei Teile zerreißen* "I could well tear myself into three pieces", meaning 'I have a lot to do, I have a lot of work to do' (cf. also the French *je n'ais pas quatre bras* "I do not have four arms", mentioned above).

---

9 There is a Polish idiom, *dzielić włos na cworo* "to divide a hair in four parts", with the same meaning. Presumably, this idiom is a borrowing from French.

Let us look at some other CFUs where FOUR has the symbolic functions 'many, much' and 'very, intense'. These functions cannot always be separated from each other. Idiom (31) is used in contexts such as 'to control oneself in order not to laugh' or 'to do everything to control one's bad temper', 'to calm down, to pull oneself together'. Idioms (32–33) connect the equivalents of "truth" and "will" with the symbolic functions of FOUR.

(31) tenir/retenir à quatre "to hold oneself to four"
'to control oneself (with effort)'

(32) dire à quelqu'un ses quatre vérités "to tell someone his/her four truths"
'to tell everything to someone frankly, without circumlocutions'

(33) faire les quatre volontés de qqn "to make the four wills of someone"
'to get one's (own) way; to act according to one's moods'

There are few French conventional figurative units that contain the number FOUR with the opposite function, i.e. 'few' or 'less'. One idiom has already been mentioned above: (7) à quatre pas d'ici "at four steps from here". The interpretation of "four steps" as '(only) a few steps' results from the actual meaning of the idiom, 'quite near, not far from here'. Presumably, other languages would prefer the number THREE here. Thus, one can say in German das ist doch nur drei Schritte von hier "it is only three (i.e. 'very few') steps from here", although this is not a conventionalised expression. The same holds for (34), where the meaning 'only a few' is supported by ne – que 'only':

(34) (il n'y avait que) quatre pelés et un tondu "(there were only) four baldheads and one shaven head"
'hardly anyone was there, only some unimportant people were there'

We may notice some linguistic consequences of quatre with the symbolic function 'few' here: the number quatre was chosen to translate German drei 'three' to mean 'few, a small amount' in the title of Bert Brecht's play Die Dreigroschenoper ("The Threepenny Opera", 1928): L'opera à quatre sous "the four cent opera". The word string quatre sous "four cents" points to something small, worthless, a very small amount of money, which corresponds to the drei Groschen 'three ten-pfennig pieces' in the title of Brecht's play.

12.2.3 FOUR in culture

According to Schimmel (1987: 15), FOUR is a material and cosmic number that "brings order into the chaos". In comparison to the number THREE, a sacred number in various contexts, the qualities ascribed to FOUR are more "earthly". FOUR was a central symbol in ancient cultures. Gamkrelidze and Ivanov (1995, 1: 749–750) have reconstructed an important symbolism of FOUR in Indo-European times, which is related to the mythic image of the four winds associated with the four compass directions. The fourfold division of heaven and earth belongs to this Indo-European symbolism, which has links to ancient astronomy.

The number FOUR primarily structures space, as with the four cardinal points of the earth. The Romans, as well as the Celts, imagined the world to be square-shaped, having four "world corners". The city, as a mirror of the world, used to be square as well; the city of Rome was named *Roma quadrata* after its design (Siebs 1969: 40–41; Endres and Schimmel 1985: 116). Housing conditions also make reference to the number FOUR: ground plans are normally rectangular, and houses usually have four walls and four corners. Since the Middle Ages, the expression *the four posts of a house* has been a German legal term, and special laws and protection rules apply within these posts.

As a number of cosmic order, FOUR also divides time. Especially well known are the examples of the four periods of the day, the four phases of the moon, and the four seasons of the year.

FOUR has also played a role in other ways. Since antique philosophy, the four elements (fire, earth, air, and water) have been thought to symbolise order and harmony. The ancient "humoural pathology" is a semiotic system in which the concept FOUR plays a notable role. The four human temperaments were believed to be governed by four kinds of bodily fluids, in accordance with four colours and many other fourfold entities (cf. section 6.2.1).

In Christianity, FOUR is mainly connected with the cross. With its four right angles, it is "the rightest figure of all", extending to the four corners of the world (Schimmel 1987: 15). Groups of four in Christian symbolism include, for example, the four Evangelists, the four rivers in paradise, the four cherubs, and the four cardinal virtues (Hall 1994: 184). By contrast, the number FOUR is of no significance in fairy tales, folk beliefs, folk customs, or similar domains.

In many cultures, FOUR was the upper limit of counting as well as a unit of measure. The Roman FOUR (IV, originally a pictograph of a hand without a thumb) still indicates its origin from the quadruple system. Numbers such as French *quatre-vingt(s)* ("four-twenty"), Danish *firs* for 'eighty' are relics of this system that break the "normal" numerical order (cf. also the "irregular" numbers Russian *сорок* or Modern Greek *σαράντα* meaning 'forty').

12.2.4 Conclusions

Except for its appearance in French conventional figurative units, the number FOUR appears only rarely with a symbolic function in CFUs of the languages analysed here. The symbolic significance of FOUR in French conventional figurative language is clearly exceeded by THREE as a symbol in culture. Parallels between the symbolic function of FOUR in culture and language are restricted to the dominant reference to space.

In French CFUs, FOUR clearly surpasses THREE with regard to its symbolic function (similar examples can be found in other Romance languages, e.g. Italian). THREE is almost insignificant in French figurative language. Nevertheless, FOUR is not a central symbol in French culture, where THREE is definitely more important. With regard to FOUR in French, a historico-cultural context points to links that are much older than ancient history. This number was an important symbol in Indo-European culture; presumably, it achieved its status through astronomy in the distant past. However, FOUR is of no importance in CFUs of other European language families, which, for their part, prefer THREE as a relevant symbol. In the current French conventional figurative language, FOUR may be regarded as an inactive symbol.

12.3 NINE in figurative language and culture: Finnish, Lithuanian and English

Among the languages analysed in this study, there are only three that provide numerous conventional figurative units with the numeral NINE in symbolic functions and culture-based contexts. These languages are Finnish, Lithuanian and English. There are great differences between those languages that are closely related to English, insofar as Dutch and Swedish do not possess familiar idioms, proverbs or compounds containing NINE, whereas Standard German and the Low German dialect WML have only a few CFUs with NINE. The same applies to French, where NINE is of no importance, as well as to Russian, where it is only rarely that NINE appears in conventional figurative units.

This phenomenon should not be looked at separately from the occurrence of SEVEN in CFUs. Whereas SEVEN is infrequent in Finnish, Lithuanian and English figurative language, it stands out as a numeral in German, Low German, Dutch, Swedish, French and Russian conventional figurative units. In Japanese, CFUs with NINE are also infrequent, but the situation in Japanese is different and more complex.

To start with, we will take a look at those languages where the numeral NINE is of marginal importance (12.3.1). In the next sections, the data basis of Finnish (12.3.2), Lithuanian (12.3.3) and English (12.3.4) will be presented; these sections will also attempt to answer the question of the extent to which CFUs with NINE possibly reflect cultural traces. Finally, we will compare NINE and SEVEN in conventional figurative language and in culture (12.4.5).

There are only a few expressions where the numeral NINE appears with a literal interpretation. Some idioms include NINE as part of a percentage calculation, representing a high amount in relation to TEN, cf. English *nine times out of ten* or Dutch *in negen van de tien gevallen* "in nine of the ten cases", both meaning 'in general, in most cases, nearly always'. 'Nine out of ten parts' is also the concept that underlies the expression *Possession is nine points of the law* 'Actually being in possession of something is the greatest possible advantage in establishing one's right'.

In other cases, NINE refers to the time of day, to the typical office hours from nine a.m. to five p.m.: English *a nine-to-five-job; a nine-to-fiver; the nine-to-five world; the nine-to-five mentality* referring to a 'regular eight hour day' or, somewhat ironically, to an 'employee mentality' shaped by routine and predictability. No symbolic knowledge about NINE is required in processing these expressions, and they can be disregarded here.

12.3.1 NINE as a marginal numeral in some languages

In most of the other conventional figurative units with NINE in the languages considered here, this numeral has to be interpreted in figurative readings, above all in the function of a large but indefinite quantity (something like 'many' or 'much'), often connected with an intensifying function, and, more seldom, in the function of 'few'. As has been mentioned, languages other than Finnish, Lithuanian and English provide many expressions with SEVEN in secondary functions (in Japanese it is the EIGHT that occupies this position), whereas they reveal only some traces of NINE. Thus, the following units represent isolated occurrences within the languages in question.

There is only one monolexical expression containing NINE in Standard German in which the intensifying function of NINE is clear (35). This German adjective has a multi-word equivalent in the WML dialect (36).

(35) German *neunmalklug/neunmalgescheit* "nine-times-clever"
       'smart-aleck, know-all'

(36) WML *ne neggenmaol Klooken* "a nine times clever (person)"
'a smart-aleck person, a very clever person'

In general, these expressions are used ironically or derogatorily, in the sense that someone thinks themselves to be very clever or superior, always knowing better. The numeral NINE is completely isolated in German conventional figurative language and restricted to the adjective compound (35). However, the adjective *neunmalklug* or *neunmalgescheit* has a variant (in colloquial Southern German) *siebengescheit* "seven-times clever" (Röhrich 1991: 1473), which demonstrates the former rivalry between NINE and SEVEN in German and/or Germanic languages and culture (see below).

The WML dialect possesses another expression with NINE in the symbolic reading 'many' (37). As in some other cases, NINE occurs in relation to the "big" round number TEN, which stands for 'a great many'. The image component of (37), 'to take off nine skins', emerges also in the Lithuanian idiom (49), although it carries quite a different actual meaning.

(37) WML *ne Buur häff tien Felle, neggen kann he sik uuttrecken* "a farmer has ten furs/skins, he can take off nine"
'farmers are less affected by poverty, as they can first sell (their land/ property)'

The Russian language has only one CFU with NINE, which is still familiar (38).

(38) Russian *за тридевять земель* "(remote from) three times nine countries"
'very remote, at the back of beyond'

In this idiom, the number NINE is intensified by the number THREE. The arithmetical operation "three times nine" provides the idea of 'very', which contributes to the semantic result 'very remote'. Some knowledge about NINE in its secondary meaning 'much, many' has to be activated in the processing of this idiom.

12.3.2 NINE in Finnish conventional figurative language and culture

Finnish conventional figurative units

The presentation of the empirical data will follow the sequence of languages mentioned above, and we will begin with Finnish. There are many Finnish conventional figurative units that contain the word NINE. In all cases, this numeral has to be interpreted in the secondary function 'much, many'. Alliteration or

12.3 NINE in figurative language and culture: Finnish, Lithuanian and English

other poetic characteristics such as rhythm and rhyme are often significant at the same time. In some proverbs, NINE is in contrast to the number ONE, symbolising something 'small, trivial', as ONE and NINE together make the round number TEN (39–40).

(39) *yksi synti varkahalla, yhdeksän luulijalla* "one misdeed (is made) by the thief, NINE (are made) by him who suspects"
'it is worse to suspect someone of stealing than to steal'

(40) *yksi tyhmä/hullu kysyy enemmän kuin yhdeksän viisasta ehtii/jaksaa vastata* "one fool/mad person asks more than nine clever people can answer"
1. 'a stupid person can ask very intelligent questions', 2. 'used when someone asks too many or too difficult questions'

The idea of proverb (39) is that theft is only a small misdeed (figuratively only "one misdeed") compared to suspicion (figuratively "nine misdeeds"). The same applies to (40), where "one stupid person" forms a contrast to "nine clever people", all together making TEN, the number of totality. Example (40) is a proverb that was once spread throughout various languages but now seems to be familiar only in Finnish. There are different variants, such as the Dutch proverb that provides a contrast between ONE and SEVEN or TEN: *een gek kan meer vragen dan zeven/tien wijzen kunnen beantwoorden* "one fool can ask more (questions) than seven/ten wise persons can answer". In an English variant, the contrast consists of "one hour" against "seven years": *a fool may ask more questions in an hour than a wise man can answer in seven years* (cf. Cox 1988: no. 1009).

The same juxtaposition of NINE 'many, a large quantity' and ONE 'very few' can be found in the following proverbs (41–42). Proverb (42), an extension of (41), does not seem to be familiar any more (cf. NSS 1992, 1: 517).

(41) *hukalla on yhdeksän miehen mieli* "the wolf has the mind of nine men"
'the wolf is very sly and cunning'

(42) *karhulla on yhden miehen mieli ja yhdeksän miehen voima, sudella yhdeksän miehen mieli ja yhden miehen voima* "the bear has the mind of one man and the force of nine men, the wolf has the mind of nine men and the force of one man"
'the bear is strong but stupid, whereas the wolf is cunning but weak'

Other Finnish conventional figurative units contrast NINE with EIGHT or TEN. EIGHT in idiom (43) occurs in the symbolic function 'almost as much as' the large quantity of NINE, with which it is compared.

(43) *luvata yhdeksän hyvää ja kahdeksan kaunista* "to promise nine good things and eight beautiful things"
'to promise anything and everything (and not keep it)'

It can be assumed that the alliteration in (43) (*kahdeksan kaunista*) and other peculiarities of the form, such as the parallelism and the vowel harmony, have influenced the choice of words in this idiom. The same applies to (44), where NINE is in juxtaposition to TEN, the number of totality.

(44) *yhdeksän virkaa, kymmenen nälkää* "nine trades, ten hungers"
'said about a person who has many occupations but is not able to earn his living'

The large quantity indicated by the numeral NINE ('very many trades') in example (44) is still exceeded by TEN, expressing 'very many hungers'. This should be interpreted as 'great hardship, need and poverty', experienced by someone who changes jobs frequently, tries many careers but does not get anywhere. Expression (44) has an equivalent in Lithuanian (see (48), below), whereas equivalents in some languages in which NINE does not play a role contain other numerals, for example TWELVE and THIRTEEN: English *a dozen trades, thirteen miseries*, Dutch *twaalf ambachten, dertien ongelukken* and French *douze métiers, treize malheurs* "twelve trades, thirteen misfortunes". Here, TWELVE also represents a large, round and symbolically significant number, in contrast to THIRTEEN, the number of evil and misfortune. Other number combinations may be accidental, such as THIRTEEN and FIFTEEN in German *dreizehn Handwerke, fünfzehn Ungelücke* "thirteen crafts/trades, fifteen misfortunes". The examples show that the choice of the numerals may be arbitrary. Different numbers with the reading 'many, much' plus 1 or 2 can occur, like a formula "N occupations = N + 1 or N + 2 misfortunes", but options are not unlimited: not every N can be conventionalised, only NINE, TWELVE and THIRTEEN for diverse cultural reasons.

In the following CFUs (45–47), we will deal only with NINE. Some world knowledge is needed for the interpretation of example (45), apart from symbolic knowledge about NINE.

(45) *syksyinen yö ajaa yhdeksällä hevosella* "the autumnal night rides with nine horses"
'during an autumn night the weather changes very often'

During strenuous and difficult journeys by horse-drawn carriage, the horses had to be changed frequently. So the word group "nine horses" means 'horses changed nine times', i.e. 'very often'. Finally, this scenario was mapped onto the 'very changeful weather' in autumnal nights. The same intensifying function of the numeral NINE is obvious in idiom (46).

(46) *siellä on kahavi/kahvi että se puhuu yhdeksän kieltä* "there is coffee (of such kind) that it speaks nine languages"
'the coffee is very strong'

Although there are some further Finnish idioms and proverbs with NINE in figurative readings, most of them are rather out of date, for example the proverb *Laki luetaan yhdeksällä tavalla ja aina oikein* "The law is read in nine ways but always (interpreted) in the correct way" 'The law is always interpreted in the right way', which can be ignored. There is also a popular belief in Finland that cats have nine lives: *kissalla on yhdeksän henkeä* "a/the cat has nine lives" meaning something like 'a cat has unusual powers of survival, stays alive in the most unbelievable situations' [cf. the English idiom (60)].

Myths and folklore of Finland

The importance of NINE in Finnish conventional figurative units corresponds to former cultural codes in Finland that preserve traces of old pre-Christian number symbolism, where NINE was more important than SEVEN. Units of nine objects constantly recur in myths that were handed down by the Finnish national epic poem Kalevala, various folk traditions, magic spells or folk medicine. No other number reaches the significance of NINE.

Let us first consider the epos Kalevala, whose myths are significant with regard to NINE as a symbol. Units of nine objects are repeatedly connected with an indefinite large number. There is some mention of the *nine seas*. Young Lemminkäinen escapes to an island beyond the *nine seas*. The symbolic function of NINE seems to be an intensification "beyond very many seas, i.e. extremely far away". In the same way, NINE has an intensifying effect in scene 39 (Kalevala 39:17–19), when Smith Ilmarinen narrates how *Sampo* is hidden: "There the Sampo's been taken [...] inside the slope of copper/ locked behind *nine locks*;/ in their roots have been rooted/ to a depth of *nine fathoms*."[10]

---

[10] There is a similarly structured idiom with SEVEN: Finnish *jtk on seitsemän lukon takana* "something is behind seven locks" 'something is closely guarded'.

Furthermore, a magic ointment of *nine herbs* is prepared, which has to boil for *nine hours*.[11] Pohjola's old landlady, who gave birth to *nine sons*, plays an important role. This evil woman, together with her sons, brings exceptional diseases to people, called the *nine illnesses*, *nine pains* or *nine evils (demons)* (Kalevala 45:153–155). Only the "great magic spell of the origin of the nine illnesses" can be used against these nine evils, as it was supposed to have an adverse effect on disasters (Haavio 1967: 336–337 and 391–393).

Entities of nine are also preferred in Finnish folk traditions. A magician often had to use nine things (cf. Sirelius 1921: 568–569). Up to the present day, the predilection for NINE is attributed to the *nine dark months* of winter (September to May). In the popular belief in rural areas, *nine days* were also significant.

The number NINE also appears in popular agricultural customs in Finland – in order to protect turnips against caterpillars, farmers used to spread salt and ash on the turnip field *nine days* after sowing. *Nine hands* full of salt had to be put into a vessel, a bat was put next to it for *nine days*, and it was kept in a dark place until the time of sowing (Bächtold-Stäubli and Hoffmann-Krayer 1927–1942, 8: 647).

Furthermore, the NINE was supposed to have an adverse effect on disasters. The house god *Tontu* was called to protect the house against disasters by walking around the kitchen *nine times* (Endres and Schimmel 1985: 192–194). In the West of Finland, there was a tradition that if young girls put *nine flowers* under their pillow on Midsummer Eve they would see their future fiancés.

The number SEVEN has no significance whatsoever in any cultural domain of Finnish mythology and folklore, although it clearly exceeds the importance of NINE in Finland's present culture. Clearly, there is a parallel between the role of NINE in conventional figurative language and in former cultural traditions.

12.3.3 NINE in Lithuanian conventional figurative language and culture

Lithuanian conventional figurative units
The conventional figurative expressions from Lithuanian show similarities with the Finnish figurative expressions analysed above. In view of idiom (47), once more the rivalry between SEVEN and NINE should be noticed.

---

[11] "He put in some extra hay/ many kinds of grass/ which had been brought from elsewhere/ brought back from a hundred trips/ from *nine* soothsayers/ from eight who treat ills./ He cooked three nights more/ for *nine* nights on end." (Kalevala 9:456–458).

(47) *devintas vanduo nuo kisieliaus* "the ninth water on the fruit pudding"
 'a distant relative'

There is a similar idiom in Russian corresponding to (47), namely *седьмая вода на киселе* "the seventh water on the fruit pudding" 'a distant relative'. It is remarkable in the context of the present discussion that Russian takes SEVEN where Lithuanian takes NINE. The same applies to idiom (48), which has NINE in Lithuanian, but SEVEN in corresponding idioms in other languages (see below). With regard to expression (48), see the Finnish equivalent (44).

(48) *devyni amatai, dešimtas badas* "nine trades, the tenth (is) hunger"
 'said about someone who has many occupations but is not able to earn his living'

As has been mentioned, there is a similarity between the image component of idiom (49) and the WML proverb (37), although both expressions provide different semantic results (both CFUs are related to each other like "false friends", cf. chapter 5).

(49) *devynis kailius (nu)lupti* "to take off nine skins"
 'to urge someone to work hard, to push someone to work and exploit them'

Compare the similar Russian idiom *драть/содрать три шкуры с кого-л.* "to take off three skins from someone" (example (48) in chapter 3) with THREE in the same symbolic function as NINE in the Lithuanian idiom (49). In the following CFUs, the central function of NINE is intensification, as the paraphrases 'violently' in (50) and 'very' in (51–52) show.

(50) *devyni dangūs galvoj(e) pasidarė* "to have nine heavens made in the head"
 'said about a person who has bumped his/her head violently and became dizzy'

(51) *devynios galybės* "nine quantities"
 'very many'

(52) *devintą prakaitą braukti* "to wipe off the ninth sweat from one's forehead"
 'to be exhausted from work'

The following idiom (53) is a special case that contains the numeral NINE in Lithuanian but SEVEN in semantically corresponding idioms in many other languages.

This Lithuanian idiom has to be assessed within the framework of textual dependence (cf. 10.5). Presumably, this is an ancient biblical idiom that was adapted to the earlier Lithuanian vernacular. Two different cultures met in one idiom and left their traces – the ancient Semitic-biblical conception of the world with many (i.e. seven) heavens and the former Baltic folk tradition, where NINE is a more important number than SEVEN.

(53) *devintam(e) danguj(e) būti/pasijusti* "to be/to feel in the ninth heaven"
      'to be in a state of perfect bliss, extreme happiness and satisfaction'

The widespread idiom type with the numeral SEVEN ("to be in seventh heaven") can be found, for example, in Germanic languages like German *im siebten Himmel sein*, Dutch *in de zevende hemel zijn* and Swedish *vara i sjunde himlen*, but also in Romance languages, e.g. French *être au septième ciel*, and Slavonic languages, e.g. Slovakian *byt' (ako) v siedmom nebi* "to be (as) in seventh heaven", Russian *быть на седьмом небе* "to be in seventh heaven" or Greek *είμαι στον έβδομον ουρανό* "to be in the seventh heaven". All of them mean 'to be extremely happy because something good has happened to you recently'. This idiom type is a special case, mainly in view of Finnish and English – whereas both languages prefer NINE in many other expressions, they follow the biblical version with SEVEN here. Finnish *olla (kuin) seitsemännessä taivaassa* "to be (as) in the seventh heaven" (cf. also Estonian *seitsmendas taevas olema* "to be in seventh heaven") and English *to be in seventh heaven (of delight)*. Another case is English *to be on cloud nine* (see (59) below). Some peculiarities of Lithuanian (in comparison with the other European languages) may also be ascribed to these parameters, i.e. to the late development of the written language.

The idiom type "to be in seventh heaven" originates from different cultural traditions. On the one hand, it is connected with ancient cosmogony, in which the universe was thought to consist of several concentric spheres (the exact number varying from seven to eleven). On the other hand, the cabbalists maintained that there were seven heavens, rising one above the other, with the seventh being the abode of God and the highest class of angels. The seventh heaven, first mentioned in the Apocrypha, is also described in the Talmud (cf. e.g. Brewer 1992: 490; Röhrich 1991: 715). Thus, the idiom *to be in seventh heaven* can only be interpreted by means of three different types of knowledge: the conceptual metaphor HAPPY IS UP, number symbolism and intertextual connections.

Let us consider some further Lithuanian CFUs. There are many figurative compounds with NINE as the first component meaning 'many' or 'much', cf. (54).

(54) *devynliežuvė* "nine tongues"
      'very mendacious, lying frequently'

Other figurative compounds with NINE are less familiar or even unknown in contemporary Lithuanian, for example *devyngerklė*, a poetic name for the nightingale (based on the idea of "nine throats"), *devynmoterius* 'adulterer' (literally meaning "nine women"), *devyniatėvis* 'illegitimate child' (literally referring to "having nine fathers"). Cf. also (Grigas 2000: 486–488).

The former Baltic cultural area

As has been shown in Finnish conventional figurative units and former Finnish cultural codes, there are clear connections between language and culture as far as the symbolic functions of NINE are concerned. What the Finnish and the Baltic cultural areas have in common is the former relevance of NINE.

Lithuanian folklore tells us about *nine goddesses*, the rulers of human lives. The "nine lakes and the nine seas" (Lithuanian *už devynių jūrų ir marių*) are known in Lithuanian fairy tales. They should be seen in connection with the "nine seas" in the above-mentioned Kalevala and, in contrast to this, the "seven seas" in cultural traditions of classical antiquity. Furthermore, the *devyngalvis*, the "nine-headed" dragon, is of importance in Lithuanian mythology.

There are also many rituals in the Lithuanian ethnic tradition that contain NINE as a symbolic number. For example, the baking of the *Vėlinių pyragas* (the All Saint's Day pie) was a ritual where three spoonfuls of flour were taken from each of *nine cups*. Another example is the *Devintinės*, the commemorative ceremony of the deceased, held *nine days* after their death.

However, Lithuanian sources about aspects of pre-Christian cosmogony are insufficient. More details about the importance of NINE in the former Baltic religion are handed down via Latvian folk traditions and mythology. Latvian folk tales mention the *nine horses* that draw the sun carriage of *Dievs* (Lithuanian *Dievas*), the god of heaven.[12] The god of thunder (Latvian *Pērkons*) had *nine sons*, and a verse from a folktale shows the significant number NINE in relation to THREE: *Pērkoṇa tēvam Deviņi dēli: trīs spēra, trīs rūca, trīs zibināja* ("Father Pērkons has nine sons: three struck, three were thunder, three were lightning", cf. Bauer 1972: 168).

The status of NINE in Lithuanian figurative language and culture is very similar to its status in Finnish. The important position of NINE can be observed in ancient

---

[12] Bauer (1972) gives some examples: a folktale says that "God [diminutive] drove over the hill on pebbles, with nine horses" (*Dieviņš brauca oļu kalnu, Div'dzelteni kumeļim*), or that there are "the nine brothers" (*deviņi bāleliņi*), see Bauer (1972: 148, 166). For more details about the Baltic religion and its ethnic culture, see Ström and Biezais (1975), Biezais (1987), and Luven (2001: 24–60).

cultural codes such as fairy tales and folk customs; obviously, the preference for this number has parallels in conventional figurative language. The number SEVEN is not known in Lithuanian conventional figurative language, though it is important in many other cultural domains, above all in the realm of Christianity. Although Catholicism had a great deal of influence on the culture of Lithuania, Lithuanian figurative language did not adopt SEVEN as a relevant number symbol but followed earlier folk traditions that preferred NINE as a symbol.

12.3.4 NINE in English conventional figurative language and culture

English conventional figurative units

The symbolic functions of the numeral NINE in Finnish and Lithuanian figurative expressions are 'much, many (a large, indefinite quantity)' and 'intensification'. However, there is one English idiom in which NINE appears in the opposite reading of 'few, a small amount' (55). Antonymic readings within such a "large" number as NINE are an interesting phenomenon.[13]

(55) British English *a nine days' wonder / nine-day wonder*
'something very sensational or scandalous that will be forgotten after a short time; a person or thing that attracts a lot of notice and is the subject of much talk for a short time but soon forgotten'

The combination of *nine* and *days* is noteworthy. The words *seven* and *days* are normally connected to form the concept of 'one week'. The combination *nine days* reminds one of the Old Germanic week, which consisted of nine days (see below), even though this does not belong to the knowledge of the average English speaker. Nevertheless, *nine days* has to be interpreted as '(only) a very short period'. There is a corresponding English (AmE) proverb with SEVEN: *a dead person is wept/mourned for seven days, a fool all his life*, where *seven days*, 'a very short time', contrasts with *all his life*. Further conventional figurative units (56–60) show NINE with the symbolic function of 'much, many', mostly with an intensifying function, cf. the interpretation 'extremely' in idiom (57).

---

[13] This kind of antonymy can also be encountered, in many languages, in CFUs containing the number THREE. This is understandable, because THREE can be considered to be neither 'few' nor 'many'.

12.3 NINE in figurative language and culture: Finnish, Lithuanian and English — 395

(56) *a stitch in time saves nine*
'if one spends a little time or effort dealing with a problem when it first appears, one will probably prevent it from turning into a bigger problem that is more difficult to deal with'

(57) *to be dressed (up) to the nines*
'to be dressed very smartly or in an extremely fine manner'

Proverb (56) is well known in British and American English. The symbolic meaning 'much, more' (cf. the paraphrase 'a bigger problem') can be ascribed to NINE in contrast with *A stitch* ("one stitch" 'a little time or effort'). Speake (1999: 339) points to a matter of textual dependence, to an old couplet that goes "a stitch in time saves nine". This proverb can even be extended by another rhyming expression: *A stitch in time saves nine and sometimes ninety-nine* (Mieder 1992: 564). However, *time* is a kind of rhyme (or assonance) with *nine*, so the word *time* might have influenced the occurrence of this number constituent, which qualifies the assumed symbolic function. The same may be true for idiom (57), since the word string *up to the nines* is considered to be a corruption of medieval English *up to the eyne* "up to the eyes" (Gulland and Hinds-Howell 2001: 260).

The secondary meaning of NINE ('many') can clearly be discovered in the following proverb (58), which now seems to be out of date.

(58) British English *nine tailors make a man*
'a gentleman must select his attire from various sources'[14]

Special attention should be paid to idiom (59). It is familiar in modern British and American English, although it has a variant *to be on cloud seven*. However, this variant is outdated and not nearly as common as (59).

(59) *to be on cloud nine*
'to be in a state of perfect bliss, extreme happiness and satisfaction; to be very happy and joyful'

The number NINE has to be interpreted in the function of intensification. Thus, *cloud nine* is almost the highest conceivable cloud. As in (56–57), NINE denotes

---

[14] There is quite a well-known detective novel by Dorothy Sayers called *The Nine Tailors*. The book's title is taken from the expression *Nine tailors make a man*, which Sayers quotes at the end of the novel.

'much, many'. There is a corresponding idiom with the number SEVEN in the same function (German *auf Wolke sieben schweben* "to be floating on cloud seven"). Compare the remarks about the equivalents of idiom (53) above. Further conventional figurative units include:

(60) a. *a cat with nine lives*
'a cat seems to escape being killed many times'
b. *like a cat with nine lives*
'possessing unusual powers of survival; fortunate in one's escape(s) from accident(s) or death'

An old and widespread popular belief is handed down in the two expressions (60). Even today it is presumed that cats have nine lives, which forms the basis for the actual meaning of (60b). The same folk belief in Finnish culture has already been mentioned above (12.3.2). According to this popular belief, a cat, which has nine lives, can turn into a witch at the age of nine.[15] Simpson (1992: 196) offers another folk belief, which manifests itself in a proverb: *Parsley seed goes nine times to the devil* ('Parsley seed is very delicate and does not always succeed in thriving'). Such kinds of folk belief lead us to the next section, on the relevance of the number NINE in culture.

Old Germanic cultural codes

The number NINE was a significant symbol in various cultural codes of Old Germanic culture, with a clear difference to SEVEN, which did not play a vital role in the Northern Europe of ancient times. Only a few traces of this symbolism can be found in Anglo-Saxon literature, particularly in the epic poem "Beowulf". There is, for example, a passage in which Beowulf kills the *nine sea monsters*. Another example is an Old English charm in which the gradual disappearance of *nine sisters* corresponds to the disappearance of *nine diseases* (Nöth 1990: 156).

Old Germanic mythology is full of NINE symbolism. The Northern Germanic cosmogony postulates the existence of *nine worlds* with *Nieflhem* being the lowest. There were *nine earths*, *Hel* being the goddess of the ninth. The songs of the Nordic "Voluspá" show an abundance of NINE: there were *nine Valkyries* and *nine-fold sacrifices* at rituals in which nine or a nine-fold number of men had to

---

[15] Cf. the word *cat-o'-nine-tails*: a whip with nine lashes used for punishing offenders, known as the "cat" for flogging. Popular superstition says that the nine tails were because flogging by "a trinity of trinities" would be more efficient (Brewer 1992: 185).

participate. A rich compilation of units of nine objects in Old Nordic literature is given in Schuppener (1998: 18–20).

The number NINE is also linked to the conception of time, as the period of *nine days* was of special importance. For example, according to the myth, Odin was hanging on a windy tree for nine days, trying to gain possession of the Runes. Nine days and nights also made up a period of time that was legally significant, and it is assumed that the week in the Germanic world had nine days, based on astronomic observations and on the lunar system (Weinhold 1897: 47). Idiom (55) contains an allusion to the nine-day week.

The system of measurement in the Germanic cultural area, which used *nine steps* or *nine feet*, was equally important and symbolically relevant. After the world snake had fatally wounded him, Thor still walked nine steps (cf. Weinhold 1897; Schimmel 1987: 16).

The significant status of NINE in number symbolism continues in the popular belief and folk custom of the middle and northern European area. There are many examples of the dominance of NINE in all folkloristic areas: its magic significance in incantations, sacrificial plants (such as nine-herb dish, bunch of nine herbs, crown of nine flowers) or in the magic of healing, which was only supposed to work if nine ingredients were involved and if the incantation was repeated nine times (Bächtold-Stäubli and Hoffmann-Krayer 1927–1942, 6: 1057–1059; Weinhold 1897; Weinreich 1916).

Finally it should be mentioned that the Celts had the same interpretation of NINE as a significant number. The Celtic native inhabitants of Wales, for example, used NINE in customs as well as in law making, where nine steps, nine days or nine generations were legally significant. The Celtic-Germanic legends of King Arthur also contain a number of units of nine objects (Endres and Schimmel 1985: 188–189; Schimmel 1987: 16–17).

12.3.5 The rivalry of NINE and SEVEN in languages and cultures

Among the languages analysed here, a complementary distribution of the numbers SEVEN and NINE in conventional figurative units can be observed. NINE is a significant number in Finnish, Lithuanian and English, where SEVEN hardly ever appears as a relevant number constituent. However, NINE is of no importance in the other languages, which prefer SEVEN as a significant number symbol (the role of EIGHT in Japanese is a different case). The genetic relationship is irrelevant in this case. German, Dutch and Swedish, closely related to English, do not use NINE as a symbol in their systems of conventional figurative language but offer an abundance of expressions with SEVEN in symbolic functions. The same holds for Finnish, preferring NINE, in contrast to the closely related Estonian, which favours SEVEN in a number of conventional figurative units.

An explanation for the different status of NINE in different languages should be viewed within the framework of historical and cultural semiotics. The divergence of NINE and SEVEN is rooted in a historical context. A problem we face here is the fact that the significance of symbols can change in the course of history, or, more precisely, can change in different cultural codes of a given cultural community. The development of different codes (in this case, natural language and secondary codes of culture) does not necessarily proceed in a parallel way. Currently, the number SEVEN plays the same role in the numerical symbolism of European cultures in question and has obviously surpassed NINE. However, this was not always so. The number NINE was a significant symbol in various cultural codes in Old Germanic and North European cultures, in clear contrast to SEVEN, which did not play a vital role there.

The number SEVEN is a special number in Western cultures. Its relevance originates from long-held Jewish-Semitic and Christian symbolic traditions, from symbolism in the Old and New Testament, in biblical exegesis and other codes connected to Christian religions throughout the centuries. Böklen (1913) and Weinhold (1897) speak of a "competition" between NINE, which in former times was dominant in the northern Germanic cultural area, and SEVEN, in those days dominant in Christian biblical number symbolism. They consider this "rivalry" between both numbers as a superseding of the Indo-Germanic ("Aryan") NINE with the "Babylonian" SEVEN.

Against this background, it is clear why NINE and SEVEN are used with the same symbolic function across languages and why some languages prefer SEVEN whereas other languages prefer NINE. The relevant explanation must be given in terms of culture. It is a matter of a semiotic, culturally based divergence among genetically related or non-related languages.

12.4 ELEVEN: The "crazy number" in Dutch figurative units

12.4.1 Iconic functions and textual dependence

ELEVEN as a number constituent of conventional figurative units seems to be quite rare in the languages analysed in this study. In Lithuanian, Russian and Japanese no familiar expressions with this numeral have been found. In the other languages, apart from Dutch, ELEVEN occurs in only a few CFUs, where it rarely has a symbolic function.

12.4 ELEVEN: The "crazy number" in Dutch figurative units — 399

English, Dutch and Swedish provide one well-known idiom with the number ELEVEN. It originates from Jesus' parable of the labourers hired right at the end of the day, "at the eleventh hour", to work the vineyard (Matthew 20:1–3). In the historical context this means "at five o'clock in the afternoon", i.e. 'one hour before the end of the working day':

(61) a. English *at the eleventh hour*
 b. Dutch *te elfder ure* "at the eleventh hour"
 c. Swedish *i elfte timmen* "at the eleventh hour"
    all meaning 'at the last possible moment before it is too late'

The idiom (61a) seems to be productive in English in view of derivations like *an eleventh-hour decision* 'a decision at the last possible moment' or *an eleventh-hour change of plan* 'a change of plan at the last minute'. However, the textual origin is still visible, particularly in the archaic lexical structure of the Dutch *te elfder ure*. The constituents denoting 'hour' in (61), English *hour*, Dutch *ure* and Swedish *timme* respectively, indicate the predominance of the frame 'last but one, penultimate number to a temporal limit (i.e. twelve o'clock)'. We can assume that the average speaker has no historical or etymological knowledge of the "eleventh hour" in biblical times. The Finnish idiom (62) is derived from the same biblical source, but there is no word for 'hour' in this idiom, so that ELEVEN could more likely be interpreted in a function such as 'very much, (more than) much', going beyond the large round number TEN.

(62) Finnish *(tehdä jtk) yhdennellätoista hetkellä* "(to do something) at the eleventh moment"
 'to do something at the last possible time before it is too late'

Idioms (61–62) are derived from "intertextuality" and that explains why they elude a "regular" motivation, be it on the level of "rich imagery" (e.g. frame knowledge of the time of day) or by means of cultural symbolism. Without textual knowledge, the function of ELEVEN remains unclear. Except for the aforementioned quotation from the Bible there are hardly any relevant equivalents of ELEVEN meaning 'very much' in other cultural codes. Besides, it is not the number ELEVEN itself that is a kind of culturally significant entity in (61) and (62), but the idea of the ELEVENTH HOUR or ELEVENTH MOMENT.

In contrast, iconic functions seem to predominate in the WML dialect idiom (63).

(63) WML *se*[16] *weet, dat sess un sess mähr is as elf* "she knows that six and six makes more than eleven"
'she is very efficient, energetic and clever'

The idea underlying idiom (63) is a mental arithmetical operation (6 plus 6 makes 12, not eleven). Nevertheless, a symbolic connotation of ELEVEN cannot be completely ruled out. In this idiom, ELEVEN is oriented towards TWELVE. In various cultural codes TWELVE is the number of perfection – it is the sacred number in the Old and New Testament, in biblical exegesis and medieval Christian allegory. In this sense ELEVEN in (63) can be interpreted symbolically.

12.4.2 Symbolic functions

The important position of ELEVEN in conventional figurative units in Dutch has already been mentioned. ELEVEN is regarded as a 'crazy number'. Several CFUs with ELEVEN show the symbolic function of 'craziness, madness'. The expressions (64–65) can be uttered jocularly when there are eleven people together.

(64) Dutch *elf is het gekkengetal* "eleven is the number of fools"
'eleven is the crazy number'

(65) Dutch *elf is de gek zelf* "eleven is the fool himself"
'eleven is a crazy number'

In the idioms (66–67) ELEVEN is also connected with 'craziness'. Both idioms are euphemistic circumlocutions. They can be used as an inconspicuous reference when one wants to point out someone's negative behaviour patterns without mentioning them directly: when someone behaves in a crazy way (66) or absolutely wants to get his/her word in (67). "Number eleven" in (66) is an allusion to an institution for mentally ill or deranged people. "Hose eleven" in (67) seems to be superfluous and unnecessary.

(66) Dutch *hij behoorde in nummer elf te zitten* "he should sit in number eleven"
'he is mad or behaves crazily'

---

16 Our informants, competent speakers of the WML dialect, maintained that there is a gender-specific restriction to this idiom; it can refer only to females. Therefore, the form of the entry with *she* was chosen. The same holds for example (70).

(67) Dutch *spuit elf geeft ook modder* "hose eleven also gives mud"
     'used when someone absolutely wants to get their word in'

There is an artificial and jocular number in conventional figurative units in Dutch and the WML dialect which also seems to be 'crazy': Dutch *elfendertig, elf en dertig* (68–69) and WML *elf-un-dattig* "eleven thirty", cf. idioms like (70–71).

(68) Dutch *op z'n elfendertigste* "on his/its eleven thirties"
     'very slowly and in an involved, roundabout way'

(69) Dutch *voor de elfendertigste keer* "for the eleven thirtieth time"
     'for the umpteenth time, repeatedly, much too often'

(70) WML *se häff alls up't Elf-un-dattigste* "she has everything at the eleven-and-thirtieth"
     'she has everything perfectly in order; she is excessively neat and tidy'

(71) WML *et bruukt nich alls up't Elf-un-dattigste (feddig) weern* "there is no need to have everything (ready) at the eleven-and-thirtieth"
     'it doesn't need to be perfect, it does not need to be of the finest quality'

To sum up, the secondary function of ELEVEN, 'craziness, madness', is often seen in Dutch conventional figurative units. Moreover, this special function is definitely supported by other cultural codes (see 12.4.3). This function of ELEVEN is unique, firstly within the entire symbolism of numbers and secondly among the languages analysed here. Dutch has a unique position in this regard. The other closely related West Germanic languages do not provide ELEVEN as a 'crazy number' (apart from the artificial and jocular number "eleven-and-thirtieth" in the WML dialect).

There is also one French idiom with the constituent *onze* 'eleven' (72). The actual meaning of (72) reflects the very negative connotation of ELEVEN that emerges in other cultural codes (see below) so that the symbolic function 'bad, evil' here can be singled out. The number ELEVEN does not refer to a particular frame [like the time of the day in (61)], but is connected to the period of "eleven hours".

(72) French *bouillon d'onze heures* "bouillon of eleven hours"
     'a poisoned beverage'

Although ELEVEN is seen as a bad and evil number in various cultural codes other than language, the numeral in idiom (72) cannot be labelled a cultural symbol in language, because this function is not used recurrently in French conventional figurative language.

12.4.3 ELEVEN in culture

ELEVEN is located between the two numbers of perfection, the round number TEN and the round number TWELVE, i.e. between the two important numbers that constitute the decimal system and the duodecimal system respectively. ELEVEN consistently has a negative symbolic content in the teachings of the Early Fathers and in medieval Christian allegory, where it is seen as a number of transgression, being beyond the perfect TEN (exceeding the TEN of the Ten Commandments) and as an incomplete number, being under the equally perfect TWELVE (falling short of the TWELVE in the number of the Apostles). Therefore ELEVEN was thought to be the number of sin and misfortune (Meyer 1975: 146; Schimmel 1987: 17). There are many references in Christian exegesis where ELEVEN is interpreted as a warning of the Last Judgement. One example is the biblical *eleventh hour* as the last hour mentioned above (61). Later Christian depictions of a clock in which the hand points to eleven symbolise transience and death. Even until the beginning of the 19th century, not only theologians and other specialists but also the upper class recognised the very negative evaluation of the number ELEVEN (Moser 1986: 175).

In present-day popular symbolism, ELEVEN plays a role on various occasions. In football, for instance, ELEVEN is an important number (a team consists of eleven players, the penalty is taken eleven metres from the goal, cf. German *Elfmeter* 'penalty'). Likewise, ELEVEN is associated with 'something foolish or crazy'. Numbers which are multiplied by ELEVEN are considered to be funny or crazy. In German such numbers in which all the digits are the same (22, 33, 44 etc.) are called *Schnapszahl* 'schnapps number' (cf. Endres and Schimmel 1985: 206–208).

The association with 'craziness' appears particularly in the Rhineland carnival (German *Karneval*). In Cologne and the Rhineland, where the festivities are the most elaborate, the official beginning is marked on the eleventh hour (eleven minutes past eleven) of the eleventh day of the eleventh month of the year. The carnival committee consists of eleven members (German *Elferrat*). According to Moser (1982–1983: 348–349), the contemporary popularity of ELEVEN as 'the number of fools' can be traced back to the reformation of the Cologne carnival after 1823, the customs of which swiftly spread to other regions.

Historically, though, the use of ELEVEN as the fools' number goes farther back in time. It is derived from a deliberate disregard of the law, a violation of the Ten

Commandments during carnival or Shrovetide respectively, which is little known today. Carnival served to display an alternative universe in which the common rules did not apply or were violated (Moser 1986: 171). Therefore, during carnival time the rules and order of daily life were subverted. This gave rise to such customs as handing over the keys of the city to a council of fools. It also inspired fancy-dress parades and masked balls, satirical plays, carnival speeches, and generally silly and excessive behaviour, all of which are still common elements of contemporary carnival celebrations.

In Dutch consciousness, ELEVEN is still strongly anchored as the 'crazy number', as the number of fools, even without concrete links to carnival customs.

12.4.4 Results

In most of the languages investigated in this study, ELEVEN as a number constituent is of no symbolic significance. However, in a few cases some symbolic functions of ELEVEN have emerged: there is one French idiom that provides negative connotations of the number, and there are several Dutch CFUs in which negative functions of ELEVEN are clearly apparent and ELEVEN is seen to be the number of fools and craziness. In cultural codes other than language, ELEVEN is a 'bad' number, seen as the number of sin, exceeding the round and perfect number TEN. Thus, in a broad cultural framework, number symbols in figurative language (above all in Dutch conventional figurative language) and in other cultural codes are closely connected. It remains uncertain, however, why this cultural symbolism should be passed on in Dutch, but not in other languages.

13 Animal metaphors and animal symbols: Case studies

13.1 Animals in conventional figurative language

Words denoting animals play an important role in conventional figurative language. Every language analysed in this respect contains a group of idiom or proverb constituents denoting animals – domestic animals as well as wild animals, birds, fish, insects, etc. (cf. e.g. Fleischer 1997: 184). In what follows, we will use the shorter term *animal constituents* for this special kind of CFU constituent. Various studies have been carried out in this field, for instance on animal constituents in Swedish proverbs (Rooth 1968), Russian and German idioms (Stephan 1989), German and Spanish similes (Piñel López 1997), German and French idioms (Moncharmont 1998), Russian and Italian phrasemes (Büchler 1998), Greek and German idioms (Chrissou 2000), Czech and English similes (Rakusan 2000), Slovene phrasemes (Schauer-Trampusch 2002) and Chinese and German phrasemes (Chang 2003). In most of these studies, however, no attention has been paid to the significant peculiarity of animal constituents regarding the function that they have in the semantic structure of the CFU as a whole. This peculiarity is connected with the different types of motivation, especially with the *iconic* and *symbolic functions* of certain animal constituents in conventional figurative units (or the concepts behind them).

In view of the difficulties that words denoting animals pose for cross-linguistic examination (see below), only the animal concepts SNAKE, WOLF and BEAR will be addressed here. In the course of extensive preliminary research, all CFUs containing these animal concepts were identified in dictionaries and by asking native speakers. From a total of more than 300 CFUs selected in this first step, the most significant examples, which allow us to demonstrate relevant specifics, were chosen for presentation.[1]

---

[1] This chapter is not only a contribution to the research into the phenomenon of semantic motivation, but also an empirical analysis of CFUs from different languages containing animal constituents. Since units of this kind are a traditional subject of research in the fields of phraseology and paremiology, an empirical analysis may evoke the interest of linguists working in this area. What we try to achieve by means of this analysis is, from a purely linguistic point of view, a description of the languages under consideration which is aimed at discovering both cross-linguistic and cross-cultural parallels and contrasts.

Before delving into an empirical analysis of CFUs containing animal constituents, we will discuss some of the problems which have arisen in the course of these case studies.

(i) The first problem, the fragmentation of the world, is typical of cross-linguistic studies of all kinds. Every language structures the world in an idiosyncratic way. To name just one example from the realm of animals, let us look at the Japanese word 鼠 (*nezumi*), denoting both MOUSE and RAT. Whereas these two animals have different names in all European languages and, therefore, are usually perceived as different creatures, MOUSE and RAT are practically the same animal for Japanese speakers.

Even between closely related languages, non-trivial differences can be found. In Swedish figurative units, for example, the word *råtta* 'rat' often occurs where related languages use the word meaning 'mouse', cf. English *to play cat and mouse (with someone)* vs. Swedish *leka (med ngn.) som katten med råtten* "to play (with someone) like the cat with the rat". As a linguistic consequence, the title *Katt och råtta* was chosen in the Swedish translation of the title of Günter Grass's novella *Katz und Maus*, although there exists the Swedish word *mus* as a (quasi-) equivalent of the German *Maus* (cf. Blume 2001).

By contrast, in the following case Japanese has two different words, whereas German has only one. The German word *Schildkröte*, denoting both 'turtle' and 'tortoise' (just like Russian *черепаха*), corresponds to two different words in Japanese, which distinguish between different types of TURTLE, namely between 鼈 (*suppon*), a lowly mud turtle or snapping turtle, i.e. a freshwater terrapin, and 亀 (*kame*), a sea turtle or tortoise (cf. the terms *diversification* or *neutralisation* for these phenomena in translation studies).

This problem becomes even more complicated if we compare not only animal names from different languages but also conventional figurative units containing such names. If animals have several alternative names, and even if all of them are used in a parallel way in the language analysis, it may be possible that only one of them is used as a CFU constituent in language L1, while in language L2 the corresponding expressions contain different names for this animal.

For example, in a comparison of conventional figurative units with the names for HORSE, even in languages as closely related as German, English, Dutch, and Swedish, it is impossible to simply take all German CFUs with the constituent *Pferd* 'horse' and compare them with all English, Dutch and Swedish expressions containing the words *horse, paard* or *häst*. This is because *Gaul* 'old and weak horse' or *Ross* 'horse (elevated)' may also appear in German CFUs instead of *Pferd*, while the English, Dutch and Swedish expressions with corresponding meanings contain only *horse, paard* and *häst* respectively.

Here are some examples: German *auf dem hohen Ross sitzen* "to sit on the high horse" vs. English *to be on one's high horse*, Dutch *hoog te paard zitten* "to sit high on the horse" vs. Swedish *sitta på sina höga hästar* "to sit on one's high horses", all meaning 'to behave in an arrogant manner, to be in a supercilious mood; to be proud and haughty' [cf. example (25) in chapter 5]. Compare also the German *Ross und Reiter nennen* "to name horse and rider" and the Dutch *man en paard noemen* "to name man and horse" 'to say clearly who is meant' or the proverbs: German *einem geschenkten Gaul sieht man nicht ins Maul* "one does not look into the mouth of a given horse", Dutch *een gegeven paard moet men niet in de bek zien* and Swedish *man ska inte skåda given häst i munnen* "one should not look a gift horse in the mouth", all meaning 'one should not complain about, or look for faults in, something that is freely offered or received as a gift'.

With regard to Russian conventional figurative language, we must consider different constituents denoting 'horse', i.e. лошадь ('horse (in general)', конь 'horse, riding horse', мерин 'gelding', and кобыла 'mare, female horse'. Among the two Greek words meaning 'horse' – the vernacular άλογο and ίππος, a learned loan from Ancient Greek – only the first appears in conventional figurative units; cf. *(και) πράσινα άλογα* "(and) green horses" 'something not existing, swindle, fantasy'.

Another example comes from Finnish, where different words can be used for RABBIT: the usual word *jänis* and a word used only in children's language, *pupu*. Both words occur in conventional figurative units. Cf. the idioms *hänellä on jänis housuissa* "he has the/a hare in the trousers" [example (19) in chapter 11] and *jollakulla menee pupu housuun* "a little hare goes into someone's trousers" both meaning 'someone is very afraid, gets very scared'.

In Swedish conventional figurative units, there are two constituents used for WOLF – the literary and outdated word *varg* (denoting WOLF e.g. in fairy tales, cf. Swedish *Rödluvan och varg* "Little Ridinghood and the Wolf") and *ulv* (the wolf as it appears in nature). There is no semantic difference between these two words as CFU constituents, cf. *tjuta/yla med vargarna/med ulvarna* "to howl with the wolves" 'to adapt oneself to the habits and customs of the surrounding society' [see (24) below], *vara hungrig som en varg* "to be hungry as a wolf" and *en ulv i fårakläder* "a wolf in sheep's clothing" [see (40) below]. The SNAKE concept (as we use it here) is an umbrella notion which also covers concepts such as ADDER or VIPER (see 13.2).

(ii) The next problem to be discussed here is related to the degree of familiarity of the conventional figurative units that are to be compared. Finding CFUs with the same meaning and the same image basis in different languages does not automatically mean that one is dealing with absolute equivalents. If a CFU is very familiar in language L1 and out of date in language L2, this fact will have to be accounted for (cf. section 3.4.3). For example, while analysing CFUs with the word denoting FOX, we found several English proverbs which (as all the native speakers asked about their usage confirmed) were obsolete. Many informants did not know them at all, e.g. the following examples, all containing *fox* with the symbolic function 'slyness': *when the fox preaches, beware your geese; the sleepy fox has seldom feathered breakfasts; an old fox is not easily snared; old foxes want no tutors.*

If these proverbs were the only expressions where the word *fox* occurred with this symbolic function, it would be quite risky to claim that this symbolic function is represented in English conventional figurative language. It is the same when a certain symbolic function can only be found in one idiom. In such cases, it is not quite clear whether the symbolic function in question is really entrenched in figurative language (cf. the criteria for singling out symbols in figurative language, section 11.4.1).

(iii) In our attempt to distinguish between different types of motivation (i.e. mainly between iconic and symbolic motivation), the domain of animals as constituents of conventional figurative units has additional difficulties, compared to the domain of number constituents (cf. 12.1). The semiotisation (cultural interpretation) of animals is often based on observation of their behaviour in real life. This can lead us to think that some cases of symbolic usage are motivated by direct experience. In section 11.3.5 (g), we have already highlighted this problem in connection with idioms like English *a snake in the grass* 'a great danger; a very evil person' (see (15) below). In addition, this idiom displays textual dependence. Originally, it is a quotation going back to an aphorism from Virgil's "Eclogues", III:93: *latet anguis in herba* "there is a snake hiding in the grass". To a well-educated person, this means that there is a clear connection between this idiom and the relevant text, and that the word *snake* could be regarded as a symbol of 'danger' and 'malice' within this textual source. For most people, however, the origin of this idiom does not play any role in its interpretation. They are more likely to perceive the idiom as being motivated by observation from nature. In this study, we are trying to uncover the links between language and cultural codes. Therefore, it is crucial to point out any cultural basis for the motivation of such CFUs. However, we also realise that alternative interpretations are possible and that the psychological reality of these alternatives can only be described in terms of individual linguistic and cultural competence.

(iv) Another difficulty lies in the fact that similes differ from other types of idioms in so far as they display no real meaning shift because they are based on an explicit comparison. Therefore, the semantic contribution of the animal constituent is of a different nature. Similes are motivated by their structure – in most cases, the "right part" of the simile, i.e. the comparandum with the particles *as* or *like* – expresses intensification, to be interpreted semantically as 'very', 'much', or 'big' (that is to say, as the lexical function MAGN in the Meaning-Text-Theory, cf. Žolkovskij and Mel'čuk 1967).

Strictly speaking, it is not possible to refer to the semantic function of the animal constituent in similes as either an iconic or a symbolic function. As we have said, the meaning of the "right part" of a simile is in most cases just an intensification of the meaning of the "left part". However, if the "left part" of a simile expresses a feature of the animal in question which is supported by cultural traditions, we can assume that the given animal constituent corresponds to its symbolic, i.e. culturally based, conceptualisation. The conceptualisation of the wolf as a greedy, always hungry animal emerges, for instance, in the Dutch simile *honger hebben als een wolf* "to have hunger as a wolf" 'to be very hungry'. *Wolf* is to be understood as a perfect example of a hungry being; its semantic function contributes to the intensification of 'hunger', but since 'hunger' agrees with the symbolic function of WOLF in cultural codes (such as fairy tales, folk-beliefs, etc.), we regard the semantic function of *wolf* as symbolically relevant.

Other similes, however, should be interpreted according to the iconic features of the animals in question. BEAR appears neither in cultural codes nor in nature as a "devouring demon" (as is the case with WOLF). Accordingly, there is no correspondence between conventional figurative language and culture in an idiom like English *as hungry as a bear* 'very hungry' (cf. also the German compound *Bärenhunger* "bear's-hunger"). It would not be correct to consider the semantic function of *bear* as symbolically relevant.

Since Dutch *honger hebben als een wolf* "to have hunger as a wolf" and English *to be as hungry as a bear* mean the same – and it would be difficult to find any significant difference in their usage – it seems unreasonable to postulate distinctions with regard to the function of animal constituents, at least from the linguistic point of view. On the other hand, there are similes like German *leben wie ein Hund* "to live like a dog" 'to lead a miserable life', where the animal constituent with the particle does not intensify the meaning of the "left part", but has its own semantic function, which can be interpreted either iconically or symbolically.

(v) In some cases, the concept of an animal can be evoked by a CFU without being based on a single word in the lexical structure of that CFU. A concept can be evoked not only by referring to the animal directly, but also by giving semantically related words. Let us begin with examples in which the animal concepts evoked have iconic functions: *to bark up the wrong tree* 'to make the wrong choice; to ask the wrong person; to follow the wrong course' and *to have one's tail between one's legs* 'to be frightened'. In these idioms, the concept DOG is evoked not by an animal constituent but by the word *bark* or by the whole word string, which literally refers to a frightened dog. In the same way, the concept HORSE in the German idiom *jmdm. die Steigbügel halten* "to hold someone the stirrups" is activated not by an animal constituent but by the word *Steigbügel* (the Dutch equivalent is *iemand op zijn paard helpen* "to help someone onto his or her horse" containing the word *paard*).

Let us also consider the Russian idiom *распустить/распушить хвост* "to unfold the tail" 'to think oneself to be important, trying to get the attention of other people and to impress them, to behave in a pompous and vain manner', for which a symbolic interpretation is required. To interpret the links between the literal meanings of the constituents and the actual meaning of the idiom, i.e. to trace the inference back, we have to include the concept PEACOCK in our interpretation. The action explicitly denoted by the idiom, namely 'unfolding the tail', is clearly bound to this bird, and hearing or using the idiom will evoke the corresponding associations for Russian native speakers. Even without being named explicitly, PEACOCK is present in the conceptual structure of the idiom because there is no action without an actor. It is important from the perspective of our study that this implicit part of the conceptual structure requires a symbolic interpretation. In order to explain why the idiom, which literally denotes the peacock's behaviour, means what it does, we have to know that the peacock is considered a symbol of vanity in European culture (cf. also the English simile *vain as a peacock*).

Although cases like this are infrequent, they have to be taken into consideration in analysing the iconic and symbolic functions of an animal concept in conventional figurative language.

13.2 Snake

The SNAKE concept is represented in conventional figurative units of all the languages considered in this study, apart from the WML dialect, although it is not used extensively. The majority of figurative units provide this concept in symbolic functions, whereas only a few expressions with SNAKE are to be interpreted iconically.

13.2.1 Iconic functions of SNAKE

The iconic function of the snake in conventional figurative units is its references to the outward figure and appearance of the animal, above all to the windings and the curves of the snake's body, cf. (1).

(1) French *serpent monétaire (européen)* "(European) monetary snake"
    'margin of fluctuation of (European) currency'

Idiom (1) is based on the metaphoric models MORE IS UP and LESS IS DOWN which are evoked by the wavy line, the windings (like "ups" and "downs") of the snake's body. There is a comparable English slang expression *the snake* 'the monetary snake'. Some adjectives, verbs and nouns with this element – English *snak(e)-*, German *schlang(e)-*, French/Latin *serpent-* – can be found with the same iconic function: English (BrE) *snaky* 'winding' (in contrast to American slang *snaky* 'false, evil; sly' in symbolic meaning, cf. 5.3); German *schlängelig* 'winding'; English *to snake* (in a sentence like *The river snakes through the town*), German *sich schlängeln* 'to wind one's way', *eine geschlängelte Linie* 'a wavy line'; French *serpenter* 'to wind (a way, road, etc.)'; German *Serpentinen* 'zigzag mountain road (with numerous hairpin bends)'; German *Schlangenlinie* 'wavy line'.

Another iconic aspect of the snake is its length, which is a basis for metaphoric interpretation. The German idiom (2) is based on the resemblance between a line of people and the body of a snake. To understand this idiom, no cultural knowledge of the SNAKE concept is required.

(2) German *Schlange stehen* "to stand snake"
    'to queue up, to stand in line'

This idea appears in similar compounds: German *Menschenschlange* "man-snake" 'queue' or *Autoschlange* "car-snake" 'tailback'.

The snake's sudden and painful bite also provides an iconic basis for CFUs, cf. (3–4). The bite makes the person jump with pain (a quasi-equivalent German idiom is *wie von der Tarantel gestochen* "as if bitten by the tarantula").

(3) Dutch *als door een adder gebeten* "as if bitten by a snake"
    'to be struck unpleasantly and, therefore, to react negatively'

(4) Swedish *fara upp som biten av en orm* "to be startled as if bitten by a snake"
    'to be startled'

(5) Lithuanian *kaip gyvatės įgeltas* "as bitten by a snake"
    'when someone jumps up from his/her seat very quickly'

The English idiom *to scotch the snake* 'to spoil a plan' seems to be a borderline case between iconic and symbolic interpretations. The idiom is not decomposable; only when taken as a whole can it be interpreted meaningfully. Nevertheless, the SNAKE concept has negative connotations. The Dutch simile *kronkelen als een slang* "to wind one's way like a snake" 'to use all kinds of cunning means so as to achieve one's goals or to escape from an unpleasant situation' shows how iconic properties (the winding snake) and semiotisation (SNAKE connected with 'ruse' and 'maliciousness') can be combined.

13.2.2 Symbolic functions of SNAKE

To interpret most figurative units containing the SNAKE concept, symbolic knowledge is required. The predominant functions are (i) 'falseness' and 'malice, evil' to which the function (ii) 'danger' also pertains. In a few CFUs, however, the symbolic meaning (iii) 'cleverness, wisdom' can be found.

(i) *'Falsity, malice, evil'*: The symbolic meanings 'falseness' and 'malice, evil' are clearly apparent in idiom (6). The idiom is a matter of textual dependence, as it can be traced back to Aesop's 97th fable. The fable deals with a farmer who finds a snake frozen stiff, feels compassion towards it and picks it up. The farmer warms the snake under his vest, but is later bitten by it (Dicke and Grubmüller 1987: no. 431). Idiom (6) summarises the essential points of the fable in a very concise form (i.e. the idea that a kind-hearted person warming a snake in his/her bosom is likely to be bitten by the false and evil creature).

(6) *to warm/nurture a viper in one's bosom, to cherish a snake in one's bosom*
 'to lavish attention, care on a person who later turns out to be ungrateful, treacherous; to have one's kindness repaid with spite or ingratitude'

The SNAKE concept here can be labelled as a symbol. First, a relatively autonomous meaning can be attached to it: SNAKE means something like 'a traitor, a false and malicious person'. This meaning is even more obvious in the reduced version *a viper in one's bosom* 'someone who injures or betrays a benefactor'. Second, the symbolic function is supported by culture. SNAKE is a powerful symbol of 'falsity, maliciousness' in various cultural codes (see 13.2.3).

Idiom (6) exists in many European languages and is rich in lexical variations (nouns denoting 'snake', 'adder' or 'viper' and verbs meaning 'warm', 'cherish', 'feed' and the like), e.g. German *eine Schlange/Natter am Busen nähren* "to feed a snake/an adder on one's bosom"; Dutch *een adder/een slang aan zijn borst koesteren* "to warm an adder/a snake on one's bosom"; Swedish *nära en orm vid sin barm* "to feed a snake at one's bosom"; French (obsolete) *réchauffer/nourrir un serpent dans/sur son sein* "to warm/feed a snake on one's bosom"; Russian *пригреть змею на груди* "to warm a snake on one's bosom"; Lithuanian *gyvatę maitinti užantyje* "to feed a snake/an adder on one's bosom"; Greek *ζεσταίνω/έχω φίδι στον κόρφο μου* "to warm/to have a snake in one's bosom", Finnish *elättää käärmettä/kyytä povellaan* "to feed a snake/a viper on one's bosom". Some of these expressions may be obsolete. The average person using these idioms is probably not familiar with the reference to the fable (or to the Latin expressions *viperam nutricare sub ala; tu viperam sub ala nutricas; in sinu viperam habere*), and will interpret SNAKE as symbolically as referring to 'falsity' is, although the function 'danger' cannot be excluded.

The examples show that more common words for 'snake', e.g. German *Schlange* and Dutch *slang*, can alternate with more specific ones, especially in cases of textual dependence, due to different translations and adaptations of the textual source. German *Natter* and Dutch *adder* denote smaller kinds of snakes, most of them non-poisonous and harmless. In these idioms, however, *Natter* and *adder* belong more to the literary, elevated lexical level. By contrast, the Finnish *käärme* is a common word for 'snake', whereas *kyy* denotes a viper, which is a very dangerous venomous snake in Finland.

Other figurative units with varying words for 'snake' are related to biblical texts. Correspondences of the English *brood of vipers* or *nest of vipers* 'deceitful, malicious people' appear in other European languages. The same concept emerges e.g. in the German *Otternbrut, Otterngezücht*, the Dutch *adderengebroed*, or the Finnish *käärmeensikiö* "adderbrood", originating from Matthew 12:34. Cf. also the English adjective *viperish* 'venomous, sharp, spiteful' or the German colloquial word *Schlangenfraß* "snake-food" 'muck'.

There are some other idioms where the SNAKE concept has the negative symbolic functions of falsity and malice. Let us consider some Greek and Lithuanian expressions.

(7) Greek *φίδι κολοβό* "clipped/docked snake"
 'a false, deceitful person'

(8) Greek *χύνω σαν το φίδι το φαρμάκι μου* "to spray one's poison like the snake"
 'to be very malicious, venomous'

(9) Greek (outdated) *το αυγό του φιδιού* "the egg of the snake"
 'a false person; something treacherous'

(10) Lithuanian *gyvatės kiaušinyje perėtas* '(a person) born in the egg of a snake'
 'a bad, despicable person'

(11) Lithuanian *kiaušinį išprašytų iš gyvatės* "(someone) would ask for snake-eggs"
'said when someone is begging for something obstinately, in an overbearing manner'

Interestingly, the Greek and Lithuanian idioms (9–11) present "the egg of a snake" or "snake-eggs" in terms of the same negative qualities as the snake itself.

Similes with SNAKE can be found in all the languages under consideration, in most cases as an intensifier of 'falsity', cf. (12–13).

(12) German *falsch wie eine Schlange* "false as a snake"
'very false'

(13) a. Finnish *kavala kuin käärme* "crafty, deceitful as a snake"
b. Finnish *notkea kuin käärme* "smooth, adroit as a snake"
both meaning 'very false, crafty, deceitful'

There is another Finnish idiom with the SNAKE concept which has very negative symbolic functions:

(14) Finnish *olla käärmeissään* "to be in one's snakes"
'to be very angry, to be furious'

(ii) *'Danger':* The symbolic function 'danger' is quite close to the former 'malice' and 'evil'. 'Danger' seems to be predominant in idiom (15). The content plane of this idiom also reveals intertextual features. As has been mentioned in 13.1, it originates from an aphorism from Virgil's Eclogues.

(15) *a snake in the grass*
'a hidden, treacherous enemy; lurking peril'

Like many well-known aphorisms and literary quotations, the expression exists in many other European standard languages, cf. e.g. the Dutch *er schuilt een addertje onder het gras* "there is a little snake hiding under the grass" 'there is danger or a cunning trick lurking' or the French (outdated) *un serpent caché sous des fleurs* "a snake hidden under the flowers" 'a danger hidden beneath external enticements, temptations'. 'Danger' is also the symbolic meaning of SNAKE in the Russian idiom (16), which, presumably, originated independently of the type of idiom mentioned in (15).

(16) Russian *змея подколодная* "a snake (living) under the well"
'(often used when addressing a person, usually a woman) an insidious, dangerous person'

Russian *подколодная* "(living) under the well" is a word which is linked to the idiom (a unique constituent); it only occurs in connection with *змея*, the feminine for 'snake'.

Further CFUs with SNAKE having the symbolic function of 'danger' come from Greek (17–18).

(17) Greek *με ζώνουν τα φίδια* "(being) surrounded by snakes"
'foreseeing a coming danger, being worried, suspicious'

(18) Greek *βγάζω το φίδι απ' την τρύπα* "to take the snake out of the hole"
'to get someone out of a predicament, often at some risk to oneself'

Alcoholism and alcohol abuse are dangers, too. Therefore, vodka can be symbolically connected with the snake,[2] cf. (19–20).

(19) Russian *зеленый змий/змей* "green snake"
'vodka'

(20) Russian *в объятиях зеленого змия/змея* "in the embrace of the green snake"
'completely drunk; terribly drunk'

The word string "green snake" should be regarded symbolically in these CFUs. In processing the expressions, the actual background – the fact that vodka or wine was poured into green bottles and vodka was called "green wine" (*зеленое вино*) – plays only a very small role. The Russian *змий/змей* is an outdated word, now only used with figurative meanings. The original meaning of the word is not 'snake' but 'dragon', which is no longer common knowledge among present-day speakers of Russian (see (21) below).

(iii) *'Cleverness, wisdom'*: There is still another symbolic function of SNAKE in conventional figurative units which differs from the former negative functions,

---

[2] The connection between SNAKE (in negative symbolic functions) and 'alcoholic drink' is not restricted to Russian. There is an English expression *snake-bite* for a mixture of cider and lager, which is a very strong drink. Some public houses forbid the sale of snake-bite because of the effect it has on some people. There is also a Greek simile *πίνω σαν νερόφιδο* "to drink like (a) watersnake" meaning 'to drink a lot'.

namely 'cleverness, wisdom'. This symbolic function is of only marginal importance, as in the Russian idiom (21).

(21) Russian *мудрый змий* "a wise snake"
      'a very clever and knowledgeable person (man)'

Russian *змий* is a male variant of *змея*, which is a common and stylistically neutral word for 'snake'. *Змий*, on the other hand, is an outdated, elevated word with biblical associations. In addition, there is another male word, *змей*, which is a popular word associated with fairy tales. Nowadays, idiom (21) could occur in the variant *мудрый змей* if the archaic connotations of *змий* were to be toned down. The male gender, however, is constant; only the male forms are symbolically connected with 'wisdom', in contrast to *змея* standing symbolically for 'evil person'. Thus, in the symbolic area *змий* and *змей* respectively and *змея* are two different beings. Obviously, this originates from the old, historical meaning of *змий/змей*.

The English language makes the same distinction regarding the concepts of SNAKE, but this does not manifest itself in conventional figurative units that are still familiar today. Cf. the outdated English simile *as wise as a serpent* 'very wise'. *Serpent* is a word found in literature and the Bible, whereas *snake* is a common word for the animal found in nature.

The symbolic meaning 'wisdom' also occurs in the Finnish simile (13a) *kavala kuin käärme* "crafty, deceitful as a snake". Another Finnish idiom should be mentioned here (22).

(22) Finnish *hänellä on käärmeen kieli* "he/she has the tongue of a snake"
      'he/she is a good, eloquent speaker'

This idiom deals with SNAKE not only as a symbol, but as a combination of symbols. The Finnish constituent *kieli* 'tongue' is involved in the meaning 'to speak', so the word string *käärmeen kieli* "the tongue of a snake" forms a complexity of symbols. Similar functions of the snake can be noticed in similes, e.g. in the Dutch *listig als een slang* "cunning as a snake" 'very cunning'.

13.2.3 SNAKE in cultural codes

In general representations of animal symbolism, for example in dictionaries of symbols, entries on SNAKE take up the most space (e.g. Biedermann 1994; Hall 1994). Numerous articles and monographs are concerned with the SNAKE concept and its symbolic interpretations (e.g. Egli 1994). This exceedingly abundant, often ambivalent symbolism can only be shown here in a broad outline. The strand of symbols most known in European culture characterises the snake as an embodiment of evil. In Indo-European mythology, the SNAKE is the most significant being of the underworld, the most important adversary of the gods. The masculine word form of the snake is equated with 'dragon' (though the actual animal corresponds more to the feminine form, cf. above with regard to Russian). This creature is regarded as prototypically evil (Gamkrelidze and Ivanov 1995).

In Finnish mythology the snake is an animal of the underworld too, and the omnivorous monster *Mana-caterpillar* is mentioned in the epic poem Kalevala.

Ancient Baltic and Slavic traditions have a cult of the snake, traces of which can be found in Latvian folk songs. According to folk beliefs in Lithuania, *gyvatė*, the snake, was a demon and protectress of the house. It was also considered good luck to have a *zaltys* (a harmless green snake) in the house and cowshed (under the threshold) and bad luck to kill one. *Zaltys* was also the companion of the sun goddess *Saule* (cf. Eckert 1998; Luven 2001).

From the biblical point of view, the snake or serpent is a symbol of original sin, of seduction, deception, disobedience and expulsion from Paradise, and the embodiment of Satan, God's antagonist. As a sign of its humiliation, it has to eat dust. Behind this extremely negative picture of the mythological and biblical snake are real, biologically linked characteristic features. The snake crawls on its belly, disappears into a hole – which is interpreted as being solely related to earthly life or underground – and hatches out of an egg. The strongest negative symbolism of the snake, however, results from its very quick, poisonous bite, which can be deadly.

Further symbolic treatment of the snake in biblical contexts demonstrates how closely connected different symbolic meanings can be. The snake can also become a symbol of intelligence, a mediator of knowledge, as there is – besides the story of the Fall of Man – evidence for this in other passages of the Old Testament. "And the snake was more intelligent than all animals in the world, which Jehovah has created", says Genesis 3:1, as well as "Be as clever as serpents and as guileless as the doves" (Matthew 10:16). The same applies to the serpent of brass which Moses put upon a pole in the desert as a sign of salvation. It became a symbol of Christ crucified and a symbol of knowledge and cognition. The snakes on Byzantine Episcopal staves are also to be interpreted in this way.

However, the snake as a symbol of knowledge is not restricted to the Bible. In many ancient cultures the snake was an oracular animal, a symbol of supernatural knowledge. The most famous one is the oracular snake of the Aesculapian cult in Epidauros. The sick were treated according to the prophecies of the snake; in this connection the poison was considered to be curative. The snake's annual shedding of its skin contributed to the fact that it became a symbol of life and health. The cult was taken over by the Romans as the medical art of Aesculapius. The Aesculapian snake wound around a staff remains a sign of the medical profession and pharmacy even today (cf. e.g. Lurker 1973: 268–270; Miquel 1991: 251–253).

The snake's shedding of its skin, its ability to rejuvenate, is connoted positively in other contexts, too. It has become a symbol of renewal, eternal life, immortality and reincarnation.

As is the case in many cultures, the snake also shows an ambivalent, complex symbolism in Japan. Snakes are fairly common in Japan, but seldom poisonous. Only the *mamushi*, a kind of pit viper, is widespread and feared. Therefore, snakes are commonly held to be mysterious and fearsome. By contrast, concepts of a field deity in the shape of a snake were widespread. The connection of the snake with life-giving water, which is especially important for the humid cultivation of rice, is also of symbolic character. Notwithstanding the perilousness and the destructive power of the snake, the positive traits have predominated as a symbol of water and fertility (cf. Pretzell 1970).

In Shintoistic popular belief, the snake has been of importance from ancient times to the present day. The myths of the Kojiki, Japan's oldest literary document, tell of the eight-headed and eight-tailed snake *Yamata-no-Orochi* as a divine being and of the storm god *Susano-wo* who slays this giant snake and discovers a sacred sword in its tail (Kojiki I:19). Ozawa (1991) points out that this myth deals with a snake, not a dragon-like creature. Likewise, in Japanese fairy tales the snake appears (particularly in the motif of the "snake-groom") as a deity that can take on human shape. In the "Dojoji", the most famous play of the Kabuki- and Noh-Theatre, there is a girl who turns into a dangerous snake.

The white snake is regarded as a sacred animal, as a messenger of the gods and as a symbol of luck. Because of the shedding of its skin it is considered immortal, a symbol of the circle of death and rebirth. Today, Shintoistic places of worship in which snakes are venerated and worshipped as divine beings – the so-called snake-god shrines – are widespread. Moreover, according to a popular belief, it will bring immense bad luck if one hurts a snake which has nested under one's house. In the past, it was considered a good deed to liberate a captured snake, and snake deities were often represented in folk art. A snake pattern on the sword symbolised the warrior's ability to strike his opponent quickly.

13.2.4 Results

Non-symbolic functions of the SNAKE concept in conventional figurative language are quite rare. Some iconic properties of the snake emerge in conventional figurative units, such as its coils and length, or its sudden, painful bite. In figurative language, the snake is particularly prominent with negative symbolic functions, which range from 'false' through 'malicious, malevolent' to 'dangerous'. The negative symbolic meanings in the European standard languages examined here and in Japanese coincide to a large extent. Ancient positive estimations of the snake, e.g. as a house-protectress in Lithuanian folk belief, have not left any traces in Lithuanian conventional figurative language.

There is only scant evidence for the symbolic meaning 'wisdom' in CFUs in the contemporary European languages. The positive symbolism of the snake in Japanese culture as a sacred, divine being and a symbol of luck is not found in Japanese conventional figurative units. The SNAKE concept is exclusively a symbol of evil and danger in Japanese idioms and proverbs.

13.3 WOLF

The WOLF concept manifests itself in a number of conventional figurative units in all the languages analysed here. Non-symbolic functions of the WOLF concept in conventional figurative language are quite rare. Idioms like the German *jmdn. durch den Wolf drehen* "to put someone through the mincer" 'to subject someone to a very stressful experience, to put great pressure on someone in order to make him or her act as one desires' do not belong to this field because *Wolf* in this phraseological context does not mean the animal WOLF. On the other hand, even in this case we are dealing, indirectly, with a symbolic reading of *Wolf*. Although this word appears in the idiom with a "non-animalistic" meaning and thus seems to be irrelevant to our discussion, one may ask why a mincer is called a *Wolf*. Certainly, a kind of symbolic function (something like 'dangerous' or 'destructive') lies behind this naming. It can also be interpreted metaphorically: an instrument for chopping up meat was called a *Wolf* because it is commonly believed that hungry wolves can consume enormous quantities of meat and tear apart their prey.

13.3.1 Iconic functions of WOLF

There are only a few CFUs with WOLF which are motivated iconically, such as the French idiom (23). The literal reading of the idiom refers to one of the wolf's external features, i.e. to its stealthy way of walking.[3]

---

[3] Cf. idiom (51) below referring literally to the bear's way of walking.

(23) French *à pas de loup* "by wolf's step(s)"
'(walking) very carefully, with gentle steps'

In the image components of some expressions, the wolf occurs as a pack animal, as in the cross-linguistically widespread conventional figurative unit (24).

(24) *one must howl with the wolves*

Most expressions corresponding to the English proverb (24) are idioms in other standard languages, e.g. the German *mit den Wölfen heulen* "to howl with the wolves"; Dutch *met de wolven (in het bos) huilen* "to howl with the wolves (in the wood)"; Swedish *tjuta/yla med vargarna/med ulvarna* "to howl with the wolves"; French *hurler avec les loups* "to howl with the wolves"; Russian *с волками жить – по-волчьи выть*; "to live with the wolves – to howl with the wolves"; Finnish *ulvoa susien mukana/kanssa* "to howl with the wolves".[4] All these conventional figurative units mean something like 'people should adapt themselves to the habits and customs of the society that they belong to'. With regard to their motivation, these expressions are borderline cases – they can be interpreted metaphorically, based on the mental image of a howling pack of wolves, but at the same time WOLF is a symbol of 'malice, aggressiveness', connected with WOLF in other cultural codes (see 13.3.3 below). Let us consider idioms (25).

(25) a. English *lone wolf*
 b. Russian *одинокий волк* "lone wolf"

The idioms are derived from the same image as (24), the wolf as a pack animal. Here we prefer to highlight the iconic function of WOLF, because a meaning such as 'a loner, a person who shuns the company of other people' does not belong to the dominant symbolic functions of WOLF in other cultural codes.

---

[4] The WML dialect provides a parallel idiom in which DOG, one of the common domestic animals on a farm, assumes the negative function of WOLF: *met de Hunde hüülen, waor man met in'n Busk is* "to howl with the dogs that one is with in the forest".

13.3.2 Symbolic functions of WOLF

Most other conventional figurative units with the WOLF concept seem to be symbolically motivated. The predominant functions include (i) 'malice, aggressiveness', (ii) 'danger', (iii) 'poverty, economic despair', and (iv) 'inferiority'.[5]

(i) *'Malice, aggressiveness, evil'*: With proverb (24) *one must howl with the wolves*, an example of the symbolic function of 'malice, something bad' has already been given, although we have predominantly considered the iconic function of the wolf as a pack animal. In other cases, the symbolic functions 'danger' and 'malice' cannot be clearly separated, as in the idioms subsumed under (40), "a wolf in sheep's clothing". The majority of CFUs with the WOLF concept are based on the symbolic function 'malice, aggressiveness, something bad'. In most cases, they concern the 'malice' of a person's character, in some cases also evil itself. This symbolic function can be illustrated by CFU (26).

(26) Russian *как волка ни корми, он все в лес смотрит* "no matter how you try to feed the wolf, it looks to the forest anyway"
'no matter how you try to change someone or win someone over, their true nature, feelings, habits, etc. will always remain the same'

According to this expression, the wolf's "true nature" is evil and malicious, and this character is unchangeable. Various proverbs with animal constituents like (26) convey the idea that a bad character can never change. Cf. the Finnish proverbs *susilla (on) suden pojatkin* "wolves have sons of the wolf as well" and *kyllä susi poikansa ulvomaan opettaa* "of course, the wolf teaches its son to howl" meaning 'Certain (bad) qualities are transferred or inherited' (both are not very common proverbs). Another Finnish proverb has been mentioned in chapter 12 (41): *hukalla on yhdeksän miehen mieli* "the wolf has the mind of nine men" 'the wolf is very sly and cunning'.

There is yet another proverb providing this symbolic function of the wolf. This proverb used to be more widespread in European languages, but nowadays it is most likely to be found in French (27a). The German version *der Wolf frisst auch gezählte Schafe* "the wolf even eats counted sheep" still has a counterpart in the WML dialect (27b).

---

[5] For the conventional figurative conceptualisation of the wolf in an endangered language in contrast to widespread idioms see (Idström and Piirainen 2012b).

(27) a. French *brebis comptées, le loup les mange* "(although) sheep (are) counted, the wolf eats them"
 b. WML *de Wulf frett ook getällte Schaope* "the wolf even eats counted sheep"
 'it is hardly possible to protect oneself against evil'

In these CFUs, the wolf is seen as the embodiment of 'evil', although there are iconic aspects, too (wolves eat sheep). Repeatedly, WOLF and SHEEP occur symbolically as opponents of 'evil' and 'innocent', as in the Russian idiom (28) and the Finnish idiom (29).

(28) Russian *и волки сыты и овцы целы* "the wolves are full, and the sheep are unhurt"
 'a peaceful compromise'

(29) Finnish *hän ei halua asettua suden eikä lampaan puolelle* "he/she doesn't want to place him/herself neither on the wolf's side nor on the sheep's' side"
 'he/she wants to be independent, not attached to any of the parties'

Whereas in (28–29) SHEEP and WOLF are contrasting symbols of 'good' and 'evil' respectively, MAN and WOLF are antagonists of good and evil in the following idiom:

(30) Finnish *vaikka sukuni sutena juoksisi, kun minä itse ihminen olen* "even though my relatives would run like a wolf, the main thing is I am a human being myself"
 'I am a good person'

WOLF means something like 'malice, damage' in idioms (31), (32), and (33). It is remarkable that this specific symbolic function only occurs in Swedish and Finnish:[6]

(31) Swedish *blir en varg* "to become a wolf"
 'to fail, to go wrong'

---

[6] Compare the same function of SHARK in the Dutch idiom *het is naar de haaien* "it is to the sharks" 'it has failed, it has been hopelessly spoilt'.

(32) Finnish *susi tuli* "the wolf came"
'it has failed, it has gone wrong (e.g. projects), it has been hopelessly spoilt'

(33) Finnish *susi söi eväät* "the wolf has eaten the food for the journey"
'nothing will come of this project, journey; the plans have been ruined'

(ii) *'Danger'*: 'Danger' is one of the central symbolic functions of the WOLF concept in conventional figurative language. This function partially overlaps with the above-named symbolic functions.

(34) *to cry wolf (too often)*
'to cry for help (even when there is no danger involved); to raise a false alarm'

People say, particularly to children: *Don't cry wolf!* This is to teach the children that they should not cry for help just for fun, in situations where there is no danger. Certainly, the wolf presents no real danger to people in present-day England. Therefore, since it appears in this phraseological context as one of the greatest dangers, its symbolic character is evident. Idiom (34) cannot be immediately traced back to an expression that could be taken literally – the noun *wolf*, taken in its primary meaning, cannot be combined with the verb *to cry*.

Presumably, not all English speakers are familiar with the origin of this idiom, which goes back to Aesop's fable of the shepherd boy who so often shouted out "Wolf!", just to make fun of his neighbours, that when at last the wolf came, no one would believe him (Brewer 1992: 1104).

In some further conventional figurative units from different languages carrying this function, the word groups *the wolf's mouth* (35), *la gueule du loup* (36) and *suden suu* (37) "the mouth of the wolf" symbolically stand for 'great danger'.

(35) English *to put one's head into the wolf's mouth*
'to expose oneself to needless danger'

(36) French *se mettre dans la gueule du loup* "to betake oneself/to go into the mouth of the wolf"
'to go into great danger, to be racing towards one's own destruction'

(37) Finnish *mennä/joutua (suoraan) suden suuhun* "to be led/to go (directly) into the wolf's mouth"
'to be in great danger, to be racing towards one's own destruction'

The allusion is to Aesop's fable of the crane that put its head into a wolf's (or fox's) mouth in order to get a bone out (Brewer 1992: 1103). There is a comparable Greek CFU:

(38) Greek *γλιτώνω από του λύκου τα δόντια/το στόμα* "to escape from the teeth/the mouth of the wolf"
'to escape from a dangerous situation just in time'

Two great dangers are compared in the following Russian CFU, though the wolf presents a smaller danger than does the bear. The bear used to be an existential threat in Northern Europe in former times (i.e. hunting the bear); it was much more dangerous than the wolf. Idiom (39) is outdated. A Finnish equivalent will be discussed below (53).

(39) Russian *бежит от волка, а попадает медведю в зубы* "he flees from the wolf but gets/falls into the teeth of the bear"

The idiom means 'he gets out of the way of a small danger only to get into a bigger one; he is in a hopeless situation'.

In some idioms, the symbolic functions 'danger' and 'maliciousness' cannot be clearly distinguished from each other. The following examples illustrate this. Some of them are internationally widespread, such as (40), which also goes back to the Bible and to an Aesopean fable. Jesus' admonition "Beware of false prophets, which come to you in sheep's clothing, but inwardly they are ravening wolves" (Matthew 7:14) has become established in animal fables and other literary texts (cf. Dicke and Grubmüller 1987: no. 642).

(40) *(to be) a wolf in sheep's clothing*

Equivalents in other European standard languages include the German *ein Wolf im Schafspelz Schafsfell* "a wolf in sheepskin/sheep's fleece"; Dutch *een wolf in schaapskleren* "a wolf in sheep's clothing"; Swedish *en ulv i fårakläder* "a wolf in sheep's clothing"; Russian *волк в овечьей шкуре* "a wolf in sheep fleece"; Lithuanian *vilkas avies kaily(je)* "a wolf in sheep fleece"; Greek *λύκος με μορφή προβάτου* "wolf with sheep's shape"; Finnish *susi lampaan/lammasten vaatteissa* "a wolf in sheep's clothing". The actual meaning of these idioms can be described as 'a person who pretends to be good but is bad in reality; a person who has evil intentions but conceals them and appears harmless or friendly; an enemy pretending to be a friend'. Here, the symbolic function of WOLF is 'danger', on the one hand, and 'wickedness' on the other – the latter in contrast to 'goodness' and 'innocence', which are the symbolic functions of SHEEP in the biblical sense.

The same applies to the Greek βάζω το λύκο να φυλάει τα πρόβατα "to engage the wolf to guard the sheep", named in chapter 3, footnote 9. The contrast between WOLF and SHEEP also emerges in the Greek idiom (41), which has a German equivalent without SHEEP (42).

(41) Greek ως πρόβατα εν μέσω λύκων "like sheep in the midst of wolves"

(42) German *unter die Wölfe geraten* "to get among the wolves"
both meaning 'to be treated inconsiderately; to be cheated, exploited'

Let us consider the book title "Nackt unter Wölfen" ["Naked among wolves"] (1958), which Bruno Apitz chose in view of the idiom *unter die Wölfe geraten*. The widespread idiom-type (43) also reveals the symbolic function 'danger' together with 'malice, evil'.

(43) a. English *to throw someone to the wolves*
   b. Dutch *iemand voor de wolven gooien* "to throw someone to the wolves"
   c. Finnish *heittää jk susille* "to throw someone to the wolves"
   all meaning 'to sacrifice someone such as a companion, a friend, or a subordinate to their enemies in order to avert danger or difficulties from oneself or a group of people'

Russian conventional figurative language provides another example of WOLF having the symbolic function 'danger' (44). At the same time there are some iconic aspects (the wolf as an animal living in the wood):

(44) Russian *волков бояться – в лес не ходить* "fearing the wolves, do not go into the forest"
'once you are determined to do something, you must not let impending difficulties or risks deter you'

In idiom (44), too, the symbolic meaning 'danger' cannot be separated from the interpretation of WOLF as a 'malicious, wicked person'.

(iii) *'Poverty, economic despair'*: The symbolic functions 'economic despair' and 'poverty' appear in current English in idiom (45), whereas proverb (46), which also contains this symbol, is outdated.

(45) *to keep the wolf from the door*
'to earn enough money to avert hunger or starvation; to maintain oneself at a minimal level; to have sufficient funds to pay one's bills and keep the bailiffs out'

(46) *when the wolf comes in at the door, love creeps out of the window*
'love must have a secure financial basis; it ends in case of poverty'

The common English proverb *when poverty comes in at the door, love flies out of the window* serves as evidence that WOLF in (46) does not denote the animal but provides the symbolic function 'poverty'. The symbolic functions 'poverty' and 'economic despair' agree with WOLF's symbolic functions 'hunger' and 'greediness' in cultural codes (such as fairy tales, folk beliefs, etc.).

The conceptualisation of the wolf as a greedy animal that is always hungry is also found in expressions like *to have a wolf in one's stomach* 'to be a ravenous person' or *to wolf (down) one's food, to wolf (food) down* 'to eat voraciously, to swallow up one's food without chewing' or the Dutch verb *wolven* 'to devour, swallow'. The German compound *Wolfsgesellschaft* "wolf's-society" 'society in which one pursues one's own goals without consideration for others', where 'aggressiveness' is the symbolic function of WOLF, also pertains to this domain.

Nevertheless, the conventional figurative units of the languages under research do not primarily provide examples of WOLF carrying the symbolic functions 'hunger' or 'greediness'. By contrast, there are several similes and compounds in which WOLF is to be understood as a perfect example of a hungry being. Its semantic function is to contribute to the intensification of 'hunger' and 'greediness'. Compare similes like German *hungrig wie ein Wolf*, Swedish *hungrig som en varg*, Finnish *nälkäinen kuin susi* "hungry as a wolf" 'very hungry', Dutch *honger hebben als een wolf* "to have hunger as a wolf" 'to be very hungry', German *fressen wie ein Wolf*, Dutch *eten als een wolf*, French *manger comme un loup*, Greek πεινάω/τρώω σα λύκο, Finnish *syödä kuin susi* "to eat like a wolf" 'to eat very much and in a greedy manner, to eat voraciously', compounds like German *Wolfshunger*, Dutch *wolfshonger*, Finnish *sudennälkä* "wolf's-hunger", and word groups like French *faim de loup* "hunger of wolf" 'a violent hunger', Russian *волчий аппетит* "wolf-like appetite" 'a very large appetite'.

(iv) *'Inferiority':* WOLF as a symbol of 'inferiority' only occurs in Finnish conventional figurative units, cf. (47).

(47) Finnish *sinne ei mene susikaan* "not even a/the wolf would go there"
'a remote, out-of-the way, and usually undesirable place'

The wolf is seen as an inferior creature, on the lowest level of a hierarchy of values. Hence, not even the most inferior being would make their way to such an undesirable place (47). 'Inferiority' is also the symbolic meaning of WOLF in the Finnish compound *sudenilma* "wolf's weather" 'very bad weather'. Other languages provide the concept DOG in the same function, e.g. German *Hundewetter* "dog's weather" 'very bad weather'; see also section 11.4.1). This symbolic function of WOLF must be separated from the function 'bad, malicious' (in connection with a person's character). The meaning 'inferiority' is not bound to a person as a bearer of this feature.

13.3.3 WOLF in cultural codes

In the past, the wolf was indigenous to different parts of Europe and Asia. The symbolic interpretations of the wolf are mainly based on two biological peculiarities:
(i) The wolf is able to see in the dark; its eyes shine at night.
(ii) The wolf is a predator that attacks not only bigger animals but also people, though only when it is starving.[7]

Moreover, hungry wolves can consume enormous quantities of meat. They also bury parts of their prey, which gives the impression that the prey disappears overnight. The deeply rooted image of the wolf's dangerousness and its insatiable greed can be traced back to these peculiarities. Nevertheless, the negative image of the wolf in culture is not primarily based on physical experiences with the real animal as an existential danger. In Central Europe as well as in Japan, the wolf has been extinct for about a hundred years. In Japan, the last wolf was shot and killed in 1905 (Garrison et al. 2002: 462).

Despite the fact that it is no longer physically present, the wolf is well known even today because of its semiotisations. People often become familiar with a certain image of the wolf from their early childhood on. Various cultural codes are involved in the symbolisation of the wolf, of which fairy tales are the most well-known, such as "Little Red Riding Hood" and "The Wolf and the Seven Little Goats" collected by the Grimm Brothers, or the British fairy tale "The Story of the Three Little Pigs", where the wolf appears as a greedy and people-devouring killer (cf. Scherf 1987).

---

[7] The bear, however, was much more dangerous to mankind. It is superior in close combat because of its force.

These associations are alive due to many adaptations of famous fairy tales in children's books, comics, and animated cartoons, among them Walt Disney's worldwide popular adaptations of the evil wolf. Before this, there were numerous fantastic stories about the "Beast Wolf". Schenda (1993: 392) deals with examples of wolf fables since the 12th century. The effects of the "horrifying children's fairy tales" and narrative traditions of the "terrible devouring demon" ("der schreckliche Freß- und Verschlingungsdämon", Scherf 1987: 83) should not be underestimated. Children's verses and games like "Who is afraid of the Big Bad Wolf". Thus, the ideas of the wolf's greed and gluttony have been handed down up to the present and have become firmly established in the collective memory (see also Ross 1988; Gura 1997).

The idea of the dangerous, people-devouring wolf can be found as early as the Latin proverb *homo homini lupus* "Man is a Wolf to Man", which goes back to Plautus and was popularised by the English philosopher Thomas Hobbes (1588–1679).

In some fables, the wolf symbolises cunning and treachery (cf. the fables "The wolf preaching to the sheep" and "The wolf and the crane"). By contrast, in other beast epics and fables, the character of the wolf *Ysengrin/Isegrim* or Finnish *susi hukkanen* (originally these were taboo names for the wolf) appears as rather simple-minded, competing for slyness with the fox but eventually losing.[8] In Russian folk tales, the wolf is for the most part greedy, evil and dangerous as well, but sometimes also simple-minded or even helpful. In Russian fairy tales, it often appears as a foolish or evil person, who is punished together with the evil vixen.

Despite these negative interpretations, WOLF has been a highly ambivalent symbol. It was seen not only as a devouring and bloodthirsty beast but also, e.g. in old Indo-European traditions, as a sacred being, endowed with superior, even supernatural, qualities. The wolf was connected with the greatest deities in Greek, Roman and Germanic mythology, *Zeus, Apollo*, and *Odin*, respectively (Gamkrelidze and Ivanov 1995: 413–415). Because of its great ability to see in the dark, it also appears as a solar symbol in Northern Europe, as well as in classical Greek antiquity. For the Romans, the wolf was associated with Mars, the god of war.

In Germanic mythology, the ambivalence of the symbolism is fully developed. The wolf is connected with light and provided with special powers (cf. Ward 1987: 211–213). These positive connotations are handed down, for instance, through name giving in Germanic languages. Personal names such as *Wolf, Wolfgang* or even *Beowulf* and the *Ulfilas* were believed to transfer the magic of the wolf to

---

[8] The stories follow this pattern: the wolf threatens the fox and forces him to get food. The fox escapes and does harm to the wolf. In nature, however, these animals are not rivals with respect to food (Eggenberger 1991: 192).

humans. In the majority of cultural codes used today, however, negative characteristics of the wolf are dominant.

In Old Nordic mythology and folk stories, for example, the mighty wolf *Fenrir* is a dangerous demon, an evil spirit. *Fenrir* swallows the sun and is then killed by Odin. In this strand of tradition, wolves pursue the sun and the moon in order to devour them. Images of the wolf's magical properties and supernatural power have been preserved in the medieval belief in werewolves, an image of the "enemy in animal form". There are legends of bloodthirsty humans turning into wolves as well as more recent popular beliefs that wolves, as well as witches, can be understood as incarnations of the devil. Nowadays, the werewolf belief forms the plot of different stories (cf. Mike Nicholas' film "Wolf", 1994, and Antony Waller's film "American Werewolf in Paris", 1997).

The symbolic interpretation of the wolf is also supported by the Bible and Christian exegesis, where the wolf appears as the embodiment of evil, meanness, and destructive forces. Biblical symbolism is characterised by the relationship between WOLF and SHEEP/ LAMB (feigned kindness, connected with danger, as opposed to devout innocence, cf. the above-named passage from Matthew 7:14). In Christian iconography, the wolf is primarily a diabolical enemy that threatens a flock of the faithful (lambs). The wolf in sheep's clothing serves as a symbol of the seductive false prophet, whose goal is to corrupt the innocent. False prophets and pagans who persecute the Christian community are called "wolves". Of the seven deadly sins, the hungry and greedy wolf symbolises gluttony and avarice.

Even in pieces of music, the WOLF concept manifests itself as a symbol of evil. The tritone (the augmented fourth) was called *lupus in musica* "wolf in music". Throughout the history of music, the tritone occurs as a symbol of the powers of darkness and evil. Up to the 19th century, use of the tritone was not allowed in compositions, except for the expression of EVIL. Thus, the term *lupus in musica* clearly points to the correspondence between WOLF and EVIL; cf. also the use of the tritone in Carl Maria von Weber's opera "Der Freischütz", 1821, especially in the "Wolfsschluchtszene" ("scene of the wolf's-gorge"). Similar estimations of the WOLF can be found in Sergej Prokof'ev's "Peter and the Wolf".

The semiotisation of the wolf was ambivalent in Japan, too. In Japan, it was previously believed that the wolf was a divine creature capable of protecting humans from a variety of misfortunes.[9] In Japanese fairy tales, the wolf (also

---

9 Folk practices related to this belief included the use of a wolf's skull to guard against a form of mental illness known as fox possession, possibly a reflection of the fact that the wolf was a natural enemy of the fox.

tora-ōkami "tigerwolf") plays a role as a dangerous predator on the one hand, and as a helpful creature on the other hand (cf. Ikeda 1971: 169). Since tigers are not indigenous to Japan, the wolf takes the role of the tiger in Japanese folk tales originating from Chinese or Korean narrative traditions (Rumpf 1938: 12–13; Ashiya 1939: 18–19). Japanese folk beliefs about wolves are often related to childbirth since the mountain god, whom some folk tales depict as turning into a wolf, was held to be the guardian god of childbirth.

13.3.4 Results

To sum up, we can stress that language (the conventional figurative units of all languages under consideration) and cultural codes are congruent to a high degree. Conventional figurative language predominantly provides a symbolic version of the WOLF concept; the "real" wolf hardly plays any role at all. Our cross-cultural analysis has revealed that all the languages in question hand down only negative symbolic meanings of WOLF; of these, the North European languages Swedish and Finnish provide even more negative connotations.

13.4 Bear

Among the languages analysed in this study, words meaning 'bear' are frequent only in Swedish and Finnish, and less frequent in Russian, French and Greek conventional figurative units. In some languages, the occurrence of the BEAR concept is more or less restricted to similes or simile-like compounds such as the German *stark wie ein Bär*, Dutch *zo sterk als een beer* "as strong as a bear", Greek δυνατός σαν αρκούδα "strong as bear" 'very strong',[10] or the English *as hungry as a bear* and German *einen Bärenhunger haben* "to have a bear's hunger" '(to be) very hungry, to be famished, starving'. This meaning has parallels with WOLF (see 13.3). Similes with BEAR, however, only refer to specific hunger, or the greedy behaviour of a person while eating, but not to the secondary function 'economic despair and poverty'.

The WML dialect does not provide any conventional figurative units containing the BEAR concept.

---

10 Cf. the Finnish proverb (42) in chapter 12: *Karhulla on yhden miehen mieli ja yhdeksän miehen voima, sudella yhdeksän miehen mieli ja yhden miehen voima* 'The bear is strong but stupid, whereas the wolf is cunning but weak'.

13.4.1 Iconic functions of BEAR

Only a few conventional figurative units containing the BEAR concept should be interpreted on the basis of iconicity. Metaphoric reading is required for idiom (48); its literal meaning refers to bears in the wild, to a landscape where bears can exist up to the present day. Another iconic motive is BEAR as an attraction in the circus, in the zoo, etc. (49).

(48)   Russian *медвежий угол* "bear corner"
       'a remote, out-of-the-way, and usually undesirable place'

(49)   French *faire l'ours en cage/tourner comme un ours en cage* "to make the bear in the cage/to turn like a bear in the cage"
       'to walk to and fro in a room'

Idioms like German *da ist der Bär los* "there the bear is off", Dutch *de beer is los* "the bear is off" meaning 'there is a lot going on, one can get it up there' are connected to the scenario of a funfair with dancing bears. The 'hungry bear' and the 'dancing bear' come together in a Greek idiom: *νηστικό τ'αρκούδι δεν χορεύει* "(being) hungry, the bear does not dance" 'if certain preconditions are not fulfilled, the task cannot be carried out'. The English CFU *a bear garden* 'a place or gathering where there is noise and unruly or coarse behavior' is ascribed to the scenario of public amusement, where bear baiting took place (Cowie, Mackin, and McCaig 1993: 57).

Likewise, the following figurative unit (50) is motivated metaphorically. The image goes back to bear hunting. This is an idiom or proverb widespread in European languages, which is also a case of textual dependence. It is an allusion to an Aesopian fable (Fables V:20).

(50)   *to sell the skin before you have caught the bear*
       'to count on future benefits that may never materialize; to distribute expected profits etc. from a job not yet accomplished'

Various parallels in other standard languages can be listed here, e.g. Swedish *sälja skinnet innan björnen är skjuten* "to sell the skin before the bear is shot"; French *Il ne faut pas vendre la peau de l'ours (avant qu'on ne l'ait pris/avant de l'avoir tué)* (a local proverb) "One must not sell the skin of the bear (before one has it/before one has killed it)" or Russian *делить шкуру неубитого медведя* "to deal out the skin of the not-killed bear". Cf. also (51–52).

(51) Dutch *een beer op sokken* "a bear on socks"
'a person who walks awkwardly'

(52) Russian *медведь на ухо наступил кому-л.* "a bear has stepped on someone's ear"
'someone has absolutely no ear for music'

The semantic function of BEAR in (51) and (52) can be understood as an iconic one, based on significant external features of the animal, i.e. on its clumsy way of walking, its ungainliness and heaviness. Idiom (51) is restricted to males; this restriction is caused by the mental image of an ungainly bear in conjunction with the constituent *sokken* 'socks', a garment for men.

13.4.2 Symbolic functions of BEAR

In what follows, we will concentrate mainly on Swedish and Finnish, which provide examples of the symbolic functions of BEAR. The predominant functions include (i) 'danger' and (ii) 'malice, aggressiveness', which can partly overlap with each other.

(i) *'Danger'*: Let us look at conventional figurative units in which BEAR has the symbolic meaning 'danger'. WOLF and BEAR as two great dangers have already been established in the Russian idiom (39) *бежит от волка, а попадает медведю в зубы* "he flees from the wolf but gets/falls into the teeth of the bear" above. There is a similar Finnish idiom, where BEAR also proves to be the more serious danger of the two. Unlike the Russian idiom, the Finnish expression (53) is still quite well known.

(53) Finnish *hän menee sutta karkuun/pakoon ja karhu tulee vastaan* "he/she flees/escapes from the wolf and faces the bear"
'he/she gets out of the way of a small danger but gets into a bigger one; he/she is in a hopeless situation'

The symbolic functions 'danger' and 'aggressiveness' occur together. Symbolic and iconic functions cannot be strictly separated in the following examples:

(54) Swedish *man ska inte väcka den björn som sover* "one must not wake up the bear that sleeps"

'one must not cause trouble or danger if one does not have to; one must not talk about things which have caused trouble in the past'

(55) Finnish *herättää nukkuva karhu* "to wake up the sleeping bear"
'to cause unnecessary trouble'

(56) Finnish *älä karhua vitsalla lyö* "do not beat the bear with the whip"
'do not cause unnecessary trouble'

The same symbolic meanings 'danger' and 'aggressiveness' are connected with DOG in other languages, cf. English *let sleeping dogs lie* or German *(man soll nicht) schlafende Hunde wecken* "(one should not) wake up sleeping dogs" with similar meanings.

(ii) *'Malice, aggressiveness'*: The central symbolic meaning of BEAR, especially in Finnish idioms and proverbs, is 'malice, aggressiveness'.

(57) Finnish *he käyvät toistensa kimppuun kuin kaksi karhua* "they attack each other like two bears"
'they quarrel violently'

(58) Finnish *kuin takapuoleen/perseeseen ammuttu karhu; kuin ammuttu karhu* "like a bear which is shot in the bottom/like a shot (and wounded) bear"
'very angry and irritated'

'Bad character' is a symbolic meaning in the following proverb. The idea that bad character is inherited and can never change underlies different proverbs with animal constituents:

(59) Finnish *karhulla on karhun pojat* "the bear has sons of the bear"
'certain (bad) characteristics are inherited'

It should be stressed again that only Swedish and Finnish figurative units connect such symbolic functions as 'danger', 'aggressiveness', 'malice', or 'evil character' with the BEAR.

13.4.3 Bear in cultural codes

In Indo-European mythology, the bear was generally of less importance than the wolf. In the Germanic tradition, however, the bear was a sacred animal, a symbol of strength and power besides the wolf. The fact that the bear was placed under a taboo and that pseudonyms such as *Bruin* "the Brown" (cf. also Russian *медведь* "the one that knows honey") were applied to this animal points to its cultic-mythological significance.

For inhabitants of the northern regions of the world, the bear used to be of existential importance (as well as a threat). Bear hunting, on the one hand, was the most important basis of existence, while fighting with the wild animal, on the other hand, was dangerous and life threatening. Among the northern nations of Europe and Asia – from the Finns to the Ainu, the aboriginal population of the northern island of Hokkaido, – the bear was an important cultic symbol, a progenitor, totem or divine being, and, accordingly, cults and celebrations of the bear were common. Among several arctic and subarctic populations, rituals connected with bear hunting, gutting and eating the bear meat, as well as ceremonies worshipping the victim, are still alive today.

In Finland, ursine cults continued to exist far into the 20th century (cf. Haavio 1967: 18–37; Pentikäinen 1987: 207–210). A vivid description of the bear hunt and the archaic ceremony of the bear can be found in the 46th canto of the Finnish epic poem Kalevala. The bear is approached with deference in order to conciliate him. Flattering names such as 'broad forehead' ('apple of the forest') (Kalevala 46:63), 'chunky honey-paw' (46:73) or 'golden forest cuckoo' (46:117) are applied to him. It is said that the bear is not killed but falls down (46:111–112); after that, the hunter invites him to his house for the ceremony of the bear.

The teeth of a bear were often used as instruments of magic and amulets; special reverence was paid to the long teeth and the skull. Bear fat is a common remedy in folk medicine; for this reason, the bear has also become a symbol of healing.

In the more southern regions of Europe and Asia, the bear is of minor importance. However, in the cult of the ancient goddess Artemis, the bear plays a certain part, and the Greek name for the North star is ἄρκτος 'bear'. In Christian symbolism, the bear (as well as the wolf) could be classified together with the devil as "the dangerous, evil one" (Forstner 1982: 267). According to the bestiaries, bear cubs are born formless and 'licked into shape' by their mother, symbolising Christian conversion of the heathen.

Central European fairy tales present the bear in quite a different light: For the most part, it appears as a good-natured and helpful animal, an enchanted prince (e.g. in the German fairy tale "Schneeweißchen und Rosenrot"). In Russian fairy tales, the bear often represents an important person who has power and can punish others (e.g. the bad fox and the evil wolf); generally, the bear is connoted positively here. In contemporary Russian folklore, the bear – in a minimised and harmless form – appears as a good-natured animal; it is neither greedy nor threatening but only wants to sleep and lick honey. Again, there is a symbol of a different kind, known as the "Russian bear" (in the ideological discussion of the recent past it is portrayed as an aggressor).

Modern symbolic concepts of the bear are connected with a good-natured shaggy animal or with the teddy bear. Literary characters from children's books such as "Paddington" (1958–1966 by Michael Bond and Peggy Fortune) or "Winnie-the-Pooh" (1928 by A. A. Milne and E. H. Shepard) have contributed to this image.

In European culture, the consciousness of symbols has been levelled in the course of the centuries. Thus, nowadays, for the "average" Finn or Russian, as well as for other Europeans, the bear is 'strong' on the one hand, but 'clumsy' and 'cute' on the other hand (which can also be explained by the polarity of the teddy bear as a toy). The archaic threatening component of the bear is completely blurred.

In Japan, too, the bear was once an animal to be afraid of (Schwind 1967: 438). However, in contrast to the Ainu, where the bear was venerated as a deity (see above), the bear is of minor importance in Japanese cultural traditions. Neither fairy tales nor religious concepts ascribe a substantial role to the bear.

13.4.4 Results

The symbolic functions of BEAR in conventional figurative units coincide only partly with cultural codes. It is only in the Finnish conventional figurative language that BEAR is abundantly represented, namely as a symbol of danger, malevolence and aggressiveness. The archaic threatening component of the bear which has emerged in cultural traditions (e.g. ursine cults) over the centuries, is – on the basis of the linguistic data – still ascertainable; direct reflections of Finland's subarctic natural conditions can also be recognised. At present, there is a levelling of symbolism – the bear is not understood as a threat but rather as a good-natured, pudgy, teddy bear-like being. The bear occurs as a clumsy, awkward being in present Finnish culture, just as in other European cultural areas.

Neither in cultural codes nor in nature does the bear appear as a "devouring demon" (in contrast to the wolf). When BEAR is associated with 'hunger, greed' in similes in some Central European languages, this can only be very loosely related to the former threat that the bear once presented.

14 Conclusions

In this study, we have analysed a large amount of empirical data on conventional figurative units (CFUs) from various languages. We have examined the data from both a cross-linguistic and a cross-cultural perspective, which means that we have described and compared not only linguistic structures – the figurative expressions themselves – but also cultural phenomena whose traces are encoded in these figurative units.

By analysing the empirical data along these lines, we have been able to develop a new, coherent approach, to create a theory of conventional figurative language.

One of the fundamental principles of our approach is the differentiation between conventional and novel figurative expressions. These two types of figurative expressions have different functions and different cognitive and communicative values. What they have in common is the general principle of their formation, i.e. they often use the same cognitive strategies to create a figurative reading on the basis of a literal one. However, their value in conceptualising a given situation is not identical, a fact that has not received enough attention so far. Conventional figurative units contribute much less to the structuring of barely structured concepts than do novel metaphors. Rather, conventional figurative units convey different kinds of knowledge, accumulated in the course of their existence in the language. This observation calls for a theory that is specially designed to describe conventional figurative language (CFL). Thus, this study has concentrated on CFL, as opposed to novel individual figurative expressions, and we call the theoretical framework developed here the Conventional Figurative Language Theory (CFLT).

This theory arose from the necessity of establishing basic principles and operational criteria in order to make data from different languages fundamentally comparable. In order to find such principles and criteria, we had to review certain well-known approaches and positions. The primary aim of this discussion was to clarify our own position and justify the path of analysis we have chosen. At the same time, discussing the various theories and approaches and testing them against our empirical data helped us to formulate some general postulates regarding the theoretical foundations of figurative language analysis. In general, we have not analysed our empirical data with the goal of verifying or falsifying existing theories but in order to gain new insights into the specific linguistic properties and the cognitive and cultural foundations of CFL. The theoretical postulates, heuristics, and hypotheses formulated in the course of the analysis are the core of CFLT. We would now like to summarise briefly the principal ideas of our proposed theory.

14.1 Basic principles of the Conventional Figurative Language Theory

The basic assumption of the theory proposed here is that the image component, i.e. a specific conceptual structure mediating between the lexical structure and the actual meaning of a figurative unit, is an important element of its content plane. In other words, the mental image underlying the actual meaning of a given conventional figurative unit is not only an etymological phenomenon but also of synchronic relevance, at least to a certain extent. The underlying mental image, which is in general an individual psychological phenomenon, possesses certain elements that are more or less stable and intersubjective in the sense that they leave traces in the lexicalised figurative meaning of a CFU (i.e. in its actual meaning) or in those parts of its content plane that are traditionally attributed to pragmatics. These elements of the mental image make up the image component of a CFU. The image component provides motivating links.

From this basic assumption, we have derived a number of linguistic hypotheses. In the course of analysis, these hypotheses have been tested against rich empirical data. The results achieved by verifying these hypotheses can be considered the principal findings of our study and the basic postulates of CFLT. Thus, we can systematise them according to the corresponding hypotheses (cf. section 1.1).

14.1.1 Basic postulates of the Conventional Figurative Language Theory

1. Many relevant restrictions on the use of figurative units are due to the specifics of their image components.
2. Semantic and/or pragmatic differences between figurative expressions with similar actual meanings often originate from the specifics of the image component.

    These two postulates do not imply that image components necessarily influence the semantic and/or pragmatic properties of conventional figurative units.
3. Near-equivalent conventional figurative units from different languages are never identical with regard to their semantic and/or pragmatic properties if their image components reveal substantial differences.
4. Although the image component does not immediately influence the way a given figurative unit is used, it is still potentially a part of its content plane, which can be activated in specific contexts such as plays on words.
5. Since the specifics of the image component are often historically grounded (i.e. the image component preserves knowledge structures relevant at the time

14.1 Basic principles of the Conventional Figurative Language Theory — **437**

when the figurative unit originated), some elements of the user's etymological knowledge may influence the image component's semantic and/or pragmatic properties.

This postulate does not imply that etymological knowledge necessarily influences the semantic and/or pragmatic properties of conventional figurative units.

6. Since the specific features of the image component are often culturally grounded, the specifics of a given culture can influence the structures of conventional figurative language. The linguistic relevance of cultural phenomena manifests itself not only in the combinatorial and discursive behaviour of CFUs (e.g. culturally grounded usage restrictions), but also in cross-linguistic differences that can only be explained via cultural specifics.

This does not mean that all relevant cross-linguistic differences in this area can be explained in cross-cultural terms.

As these postulates show, most of our study's findings concern aspects of motivation. Motivation, understood as a conceptual bridge between "literal" and "figurative", has been a central guideline for our analysis. There is a clear reason for the fact that motivation is central to our study – the most striking feature of conventional figurative language is that CFUs have an additional conceptual layer, as compared to non-figurative lexical items.

Perhaps the most important theoretical question in this connection, determining all other heuristics and procedures of analysis, is whether or not the motivational phenomena are regular.

Generally speaking, the production of figurative expressions is based on the human ability to conceptualise certain elements of the world in terms of other domains of experience. In this sense, the relationships between the primary, initial reading of a lexical item and its secondary, figurative reading can be seen as a special kind of semantic derivation, revealing systematic features. In other words, the principles that govern the generation of figurative units on the basis of literal expressions are partly regular (cf. cognitive operations discovered in Cognitive Modelling, conceptual correspondences uncovered by the Cognitive Theory of Metaphor (CTM), or semiotic mechanisms of symbolisation described by the semiotics of culture).

However, these regularities concern the interpretation of a given semantic result (i.e. a given CFU with its lexicalised actual meaning in relation to the underlying source concept), rather than the actual production of CFUs, because the semantic results cannot be predicted. All that can be realistically expected in the domain of conventional figurative language are *ex post factum* explanations. Thus, we can normally explain why X was figuratively reinterpreted as Y, but it could also, in principle, be reinterpreted as Z, and this is actually often the case; there are CFUs in different languages with (nearly) the same source-frame structure (X) but different actual meanings (Y and Z).

We are therefore not dealing with causal relations here. As far as conventional figurative language is concerned, it is only possible to predict some general tendencies, such as which semantic domains tend to provide source material for figurative reinterpretations, and what target domains are likely to attract figurative expressions. These are, however, only more or less evident tendencies, with exceptions which cannot always be explained. We cannot even rule out certain correspondences between the underlying image and the semantic result (the actual meaning) as impossible in principle. This is not a peculiarity of conventional figurative language – relations between units of the lexicon are generally only partly predictable and sometimes even only partly explicable.

Central to our approach is the idea that even if the production of CFUs is governed by some general principles of human cognition, they remain, above all, irregular units of the lexicon. Thus, the most salient features of their semantic structure and discursive behaviour cannot be captured by metalinguistic tools aimed exclusively at discovering regular characteristics. Large portions of CFL came into being under the influence of certain culture-specific phenomena; they may also be historically determined or just accidental developments. Hence the primary task of a linguistic theory designed to shed light on this domain is to provide appropriate tools for both a description of general principles of CFL and a fine-grained analysis and description of the semantic and pragmatic specifics of every single figurative expression, as well as for contrasting semantically similar expressions in different languages.

In order to analyse the empirical data from different languages in the proposed theoretical framework, various tools of analysis have been developed in this study, including, among other things, selection criteria, classifications and typologies of relevant phenomena, and metalanguages for describing these phenomena. These tools represent the metalinguistic component of the proposed theory.

14.1.2 Tools of the Conventional Figurative Language Theory

1. A set of criteria for retrieving conventional figurative units from the lexicon

In order to distinguish between conventional figurative units and non-figurative lexical items, we propose two criteria, namely (a) *image requirement*, and (b) *additional naming*. For example, the expression *to tighten one's belt*, meaning 'to spend less than before because one has less money', possesses an image (evoked by the lexical structure "to tighten one's belt") and is at the same time an additional naming because there are alternative expressions such as *to cut back on one's spending*. These two criteria enable us to exclude phenomena that do not belong to the field of conventional figurative language (e.g. indirect speech acts, irony, non-figurative metaphors and metonymies) from the scope of our study.

2. A set of criteria for classifying CFUs according to their linguistically relevant properties

The three main classes of CFUs are most idioms (including idiomatic similes), figurative proverbs, and figurative words (both compounds and simplexes). For example, the expression *to throw in the towel/sponge*, meaning 'to give up or lose all hope, esp. in a challenging or conflict situation', is a typical idiom because it is, firstly, figurative (i.e. it fulfils both the criterion of image requirement and the criterion of additional naming), secondly, fully reinterpreted semantically and, thirdly, not absolutely transparent. The expression *Every dog has its day* is a figurative proverb because it meets not only the criteria of idiomaticity, but also the following three additional requirements: (i) a universal quantifier is included in the semantic structure, in this case the word *every*, (ii) it has the illocutionary force of "recommendation", and (iii) it has discursive autonomy.

As for some restricted collocations, they are only weakly figurative. For example, the expression *a busy bee* is a figurative collocation because its lexical structure is fixed (as is the case with all other phraseme types) but, in contrast to idioms, only one constituent is reinterpreted, namely *bee*. Some non-idiomatic similes, such as *(as) white as snow*, are also weakly figurative, because they may provide certain image-based associations.

3. Typology of the motivating links between the lexical structure of CFUs and their actual meanings

The four main types of motivation are *semantic motivation*, *syntactic motivation*, *motivation based on textual knowledge*, and *index-based motivation*. Most CFUs are *semantically* motivated. Within this motivation type, three subtypes can be distinguished: *metaphors* (based on conceptual mapping), *symbols* (based on semiotic conventions), and *coercion* (based on a meaning shift).

Syntactic motivation is based on the fact that certain syntactic structures have typical (almost default) conceptual interpretations. The syntactically motivated CFUs come close to the notion of *construction* in the sense of Construction Grammar, more precisely to the postulate that certain syntactic patterns themselves have a kind of lexical meaning.

In every language studied here, there are a number of conventional figurative lexical units that partly escape semantic motivation based on metaphoric or symbolic elements. The image component of this type connects the CFU with a well-known text or text passage. There are two basic requirements for the realisation of this motivation type. Firstly, the lexical structure of a given CFU is derived from an already existing text. Secondly, the speaker/hearer must have appropriate information about the text (i.e. a quotation, an allusion) in order to connect the text with the CFU. We call this type of motivation *textual dependence* or *text-based motivation*.

As for *index-based motivation*, here we are dealing with CFUs whose motivating links are provided on the level of phonetic associations between parts of a given CFU and words pointing to its actual meaning, or on the level of the knowledge of certain general principles of pragmatics. That is, motivating links of this type do not take place on the semantic or syntactic level. Within this type, we must distinguish between *phonetic indexation* and *conceptual indexation*. In the case of phonetic indexation, some features of the sound structure point to the corresponding features of the actual meaning. In the case of conceptual indexation, it is the conceptual organisation of the given expression as a whole that underlies the actual meaning and influences the pragmatic aspects of the utterance.

4. Typology of linguistically relevant cultural phenomena

Different types of cultural knowledge are involved in establishing motivational links between "literal" and "figurative". The five main types of cultural phenomena relevant to conventional figurative language are (i) *social interaction*, (ii) *aspects of material culture*, (iii) *textual dependence*, (iv) *fictive conceptual domains*, and (v) *cultural symbols*. This typology enables us to compare the cultural foundations of different languages. Moreover, different kinds of *cultural connotations* also play an important role in the contextual behaviour of CFUs.

5. Instruments for analysing the image component

The specifics of the image component can mainly be explained either in terms of conceptual metaphors (metaphoric mapping at the superordinate level of categorisation), corresponding frames (metaphoric mapping at the level of rich images, focussing on the individual properties of the figurative units in question), or the symbolic functions of certain lexical elements. According to these approaches, the following three sets of metalinguistic instruments can be put forward:

5.1. A set of metalinguistic tools based on the Cognitive Theory of Metaphor (CTM), including notions such as *source domain, target domain, mapping, conceptual metaphor, metaphoric model, basic-level metaphor, rich image*, etc.

5.2. A set of metalinguistic tools based on the Theory of Cognitive Modelling, including notions such as *source frame, target frame, slot, filler, cognitive operation*, etc.

5.3. A set of metalinguistic tools based on the ideas of the semiotics of culture, including notions such as *cultural symbol, cultural convention, cultural codes, symbolic function, symbolic domain, (tacit) symbolic knowledge*, as well as a set of criteria for retrieving symbols from the domain of conventional figurative language.

6. Tools for cross-linguistic analysis of CFUs
These tools are based on the three semiotic dimensions of *semantics, syntactics* and *pragmatics*, and they include notions such as *functional equivalence, cross-linguistic contrast, idiomatic "false friends", cross-linguistic near-synonyms, "asymmetrical polysemy", cultural connotations*, etc.

14.2 The essence of the Conventional Figurative Language Theory

Let us now briefly characterise the essence of the CFLT. Our proposed theory is
- cognitively based,
- open to relevant ideas from the traditional philological approach to figurative language, and
- culturally oriented.

We will summarise these principles in more detail in the following paragraphs.

1. The Conventional Figurative Language Theory is cognitive in nature
Our goal is not only to describe conventional figurative language, but also to explain it. The cognitive approach to the analysis of linguistic phenomena seems to be appropriate for achieving this goal. One reason for the significance of the cognitive approach is the salience of the image component in the content plane of CFUs. Traditional methods of describing lexical semantics and pragmatics take no account of the image component. Therefore, there is no suitable metalinguistic apparatus available in traditional conceptions of CFL. One of the aims of the cognitive approach is to integrate conceptual entities (among them conceptual structures encoded in the inner form of figurative units) into the linguistic analysis. In cognitive semantics, metalanguages are being developed that are able

to capture not only linguistic features proper but also linguistically relevant knowledge structures.

The cognitive nature of the proposed theory lies in the fact that it requires the uncovering of all relevant kinds of knowledge standing behind the linguistic expressions under consideration (cf. the "cognitive commitment" as one of the basic principles of Cognitive Linguistics). Uncovering relevant knowledge structures contributes to a more precise analysis of the linguistic behaviour of CFUs. For example, the fact that CFUs are often difficult or impossible to translate into other languages can be explained in cognitive terms. Conventional figurative units are structurally rather complicated from both a semantic and a pragmatic viewpoint because they are based on several heterogeneous knowledge structures. Certain traces of knowledge structures that were constitutive at the point of origin of a given CFU continue to influence its semantic, pragmatic, and, to a certain extent, even syntactic behaviour.

One of the tasks of the CFLT is, therefore, classifying these knowledge structures and designing metalinguistic tools to analyse and describe them. The specific advantage of our metalinguistic apparatus is that it permits the use of the conceptual structures that stand behind the linguistic signs in question as explanations for the linguistic behaviour of these signs.

Addressing different kinds of knowledge while describing figurative expressions is not an invention of Cognitive Linguistics but an integral part of the traditional philological approach to figurative language. Cognitive Linguistics, however, has rediscovered this tradition.

2. The CFLT has inherited relevant heuristics and methods from the traditional philological approach to figurative language

The most important theory module coming from the philological tradition is the etymological analysis of conventional figurative units, along with the idea that etymology is (at least in some cases) an indispensable part of the accurate description of a figurative phenomenon. In this respect, the CFLT stands in clear contrast to the CTM and similar approaches. One postulate of the CTM points to the irrelevance of "true etymology" for cognitively oriented linguistic research. The argument against "true etymology" in favour of "folk etymology" is based on the assumption that speakers address only the latter while activating motivating links. It is hard to verify or falsify this assumption in the framework of linguistics; only more or less plausible hypotheses are possible. Testing them is the proper task of psycholinguistic experiments, which produce contradictory results partly because different speakers may address different knowledge structures while processing figurative units.

14.2 The essence of the Conventional Figurative Language Theory — 443

Thus, all knowledge structures that could turn out to be relevant and become salient in different types of contexts have to be included in the analyses. We attempt to provide an intersubjectively oriented description of CFUs which includes historical and cultural elements. In this sense, we let ourselves be guided by the well-known philological tradition, with its interest in "true etymologies" and cultural backgrounds.

3. The Conventional Figurative Language Theory is strongly oriented towards cultural phenomena

Considering cultural phenomena while describing figurative language can be important from a cross-linguistic perspective. Different languages often use different "literal" material to denote a given concept figuratively. On the other hand, different languages sometimes reinterpret the same "literal" material in very different ways, with the result that the actual meanings of lexically corresponding figurative units do not coincide. Adequate explanations for this cannot be given in terms of universal cognitive principles. The reasons often lie in cross-cultural differences. Languages do not just take conceptual material based on "biological entities" to denote abstract concepts; rather, they make use of a kind of cultural filter, which allows only a few "biological features" from a relevant set to pass through to the conceptual target domain.

Moreover, within a given language, the motivating links (the conceptual links between the lexical structure and the actual meaning of a CFU) can often be explained only by addressing cultural phenomena. Many of these phenomena go back to aspects of social and material culture, others to symbols, i.e. conventional signs originating from semiotic systems other than natural language. Then again, some CFUs were once quotations from other textual sources and still preserve "irregular elements" in their lexical structure, inherited from the sources. Finally, ancient beliefs, and fictive, pre-scientific conceptions of the world have left more traces in conventional figurative language than has been assumed so far.

Addressing various types of cultural phenomena has enabled us to explain some of the nontrivial facts that we discovered in the course of our analysis. In fact, there are significant cross-linguistic contrasts in the choice of imagery that serves as a basis for figurative expressions, i.e. in the way that certain concepts are linguistically fixed in conventional figurative units. These contrasts do not exist between languages that reveal significant genetic and typological differences (e.g. German vs. Finnish), as they do between languages which are very closely related both genetically and typologically but belong to different domains in terms of material and/or social culture, intertextual preferences and the like (e.g. standard language vs. basic dialects). The European standard languages considered here reveal a remarkable uniformity, since many aspects of their conventional figurative units can be ascribed to either "the common cultural heritage" or the convergence of modern societies. The most different cultural features underlying CFUs can be found not only in languages spoken far from the occidental cultural area (such as Japanese), but also in archaic non-standard dialectal varieties that are almost unaffected by the cultural foundations of the standard languages.

***

In summary, the Conventional Figurative Language Theory is a theory designed to analyse certain parts of the lexicon, rather than a grammar-like theory. It has certain similarities to the approaches within Construction Grammar. It provides principles and methods of analysis, reasonable heuristics, and ways of description, rather than productive rules. This, of course, does not mean that generalisations are impossible within the CFLT. Every valid theory must allow generalisations. The question is, which status is claimed for these generalisations? In the framework of the CFLT, generalisations have the status of *ex post factum* explanations and/or plausible tendencies, which provide insights into possible semantic developments but cannot predict concrete semantic results.

References

Aarne, Antti & Stith Thompson. 1961. *The types of the folktale. A classification and bibliography.* Helsinki: Academia Scientiarum Fennica.

Abaev, Vasilij I. 1948. Ponjatie ideosemantiki [On the notion of ideosemantics]. *Jazyk i myšlenie* XI, 13–28.

Abel, Beate. 2003. *Sprecherurteile zur Dekomponierbarkeit englischer Idiome.* Tübingen: Max Niemeyer.

Abelson, Robert P. 1973. The structure of belief systems. In Roger C. Schank & Kenneth Mark Colby (eds.), *Computer models of thought and language*, 287–339. San Francisco: Freeman.

Abraham, Werner. 1989. Idioms in contrastive and in universally based typological research: Toward distinctions of relevance. In Martin Everaert & Erik-Jan van der Linden (eds.), *Proceedings of the first Tilburg workshop on idioms*, 1–22. Tilburg: ITK.

Afanas'ev, Aleksandr N. 1994 [1865–1869]. *Poètičeskie vozzrenija slavjan na prirodu* [Poetic views of the Slavs on nature]. Moscow: Indrik.

Akiyama, Nobuo & Carol Akiyama. 1996. *2001 Japanese and English idioms.* Hauppauge & New York: Barron's.

Allen, Graham. 2011. *Intertextuality.* 2nd edn. London & New York: Routledge.

Alverson, Hoyt. 1991. Metaphor and experience. Looking over the notion of image schema. In James W. Fernandez (ed.), *Beyond metaphor. The theory of tropes in anthropology*, 94–117. Stanford, CA: Stanford University Press.

Ammer, Christine. 1997. *The American heritage dictionary of idioms.* Boston & New York: Houghton Mifflin Company.

Amosova, Natalija N. 1963. *Osnovy anglijskoj frazeologii* [Basics of English phraseology]. Leningrad: Nauka.

Antoniadou, Christina & Petra Kaltsas. 1994. *Lexikon der idiomatischen Redewendungen griechisch-deutsch / deutsch-griechisch.* Thessaloniki: Romiosini, Köln & Vanias.

Apresjan, Jurij D. 1974a. *Leksičeskaja semantika. Sinonimičeskie sredstva jazyka* [Lexical semantics. synonymous means of language]. Moscow: Nauka.

Apresjan, Jurij D. 1974b. Regular polysemy. *Linguistics. An International Review* 142, 5–32.

Apresjan, Jurij D. 1995. Konnotacii kak čast' pragmatiki slova [Connotations as part of the pragmatics of the word]. In Jurij D. Apresjan, *Izbrannye trudy* [Selected works], vol. 2: *Integral'noe oposanie jazyka i sistemnaja leksikografija* [Integral description of language and systematic lexicography], 156–177. Moscow: Škola "Jazyki russkoj kul'tury," Izd. "Vostochnaja literatura", RAN.

Apresjan, Jurij D. 2004. O semantičeskoj nepustote i motivirovannosti glagol'nyx leksičeskix funkcij [On semantic non-emptiness and motivation of verbal lexical functions]. *Voprosy jazykoznanija* 4. 3–18.

Apresjan, Jurij D. 2009. *Issledovanija po semantike i leksikografii: Paradigmatika* [Studies in semantics and lexicography: Paradigmatics] Moscow: Jazyki slavjanskix kul'tur.

Apresjan, Valentina J. 1997. 'Fear' and 'pity' in Russian and English from a lexicographic perspective. *International Journal of Lexicography* 10. 85–111.

Apresjan, Valentina. 2019. Metaphor in grammar: Mapping across syntactic domains. In Ignasi Navarro i Ferrando (ed.), *Current approaches to metaphor analysis in discourse*, 111–130. Berlin & Boston: Mouton de Gruyter.

Apresjan, Valentina J. & Jurij D. Apresjan. 1993. Metafora v semantičeskom predstavlenii emocij [Metaphor in the semantic representation of emotions]. *Voprosy jazykoznanija* 3. 27–35.

Arutjunova, Nina D. 1988. Ot obraza k znaku [From image to sign]. In V. V. Petrov (ed.), *Myšlenie. Kognitivnye nauki. Iskusstvennyj intellekt* [Thinking. Cognitive sciences. Artificial intelligence], 147–162. Moscow: AN SSSR.

Ashiya, Mizuyo. 1939. *Japanische und Deutsche Tiermärchen, besonders Fuchsmärchen, in ihrem Wesen und nach ihrer volkstumskundlichen Grundlage*. Köln: Orthen.

Athanasiadou, Angeliki & Herbert L. Colston (eds.). 2017. *Irony in language use and communication*. Amsterdam & Philadelphia: John Benjamins.

Athanasopoulos, Panos, Steven Samuel & Emanuel Bylund. 2017. The psychological reality of spatio-temporal metaphors. In Angeliki Athanasiadou (ed.), *Studies in figurative thought and language*, 295–321. Amsterdam: John Benjamins.

Atkins, Sue, Charles J. Fillmore & Christopher R. Johnson. 2003. Lexicographic relevance: Selecting information from corpus evidence. *International Journal of Lexicography* 16. 251–280.

Attardo, Salvatore. 2019. Humor in language. In Mark Aronoff (ed.), *Oxford research encyclopedia of linguistics*. Oxford: Oxford University Press.

Austin, John L. 1962. *How to do things with words*. Cambridge, MA: Harvard University Press.

Averincev, Sergej S. 2001. Simvol [Symbol]. In Aleksandr N. Nikoljukin (ed.), *Literaturnaja ènciklopedija terminov i ponjatij* [Literary encyclopedia of terms and concepts], 976–978. Moscow: Intelvak.

Bächtold-Stäubli, Hanns & Eduard Hoffmann-Krayer (eds.). 1927-1942. *Handwörterbuch des deutschen Aberglaubens*, 10 Bände. Berlin & Leipzig: Walter de Gruyter.

Baldauf, Christa. 1997. *Metapher und Kognition: Grundlagen einer neuen Theorie der Alltags-metapher*. Frankfurt am Main etc.: Peter Lang.

Baldauf, Christa. 2003. On the mixing of conceptual metaphors. In Cornelia Zelinsky-Wibbelt (ed.), *Text, context, concepts*, 47–63. Berlin & New York: Mouton de Gruyter.

Bally, Charles. 1932. *Linguistique générale et linguistique française*. Paris: Klincksieck.

Bally, Charles. 1951 [1909]. *Traité de stylistique français*. Genève: Georg & Cie.

Baran, Anneli. 2015. Gender in Estonian older phraseology. In Joanna Szerszunowicz & Boguslaw Nowowiejski (eds.), *Linguo-cultural research on phraseology*, vol. 3, 315–336. Bialystok: University of Bialystok Publishing House.

Baranov, Anatolij N. & Dmitrij O. Dobrovol'skij. 1996. Cognitive modeling of actual meaning in the field of phraseology. *Journal of Pragmatics* 25. 409–429.

Baranov, Anatolij N. & Dmitrij O. Dobrovol'skij. 2005. Zum Idiombegriff. In Evelyn Breiteneder & Dmitrij O. Dobrovol'skij (eds.), *Textlexikographie und Phraseologie: Fedor M. Dostoevskij*, 28–91. Wien: Verlag der Österreichischen Akademie der Wissenschaften.

Baranov, Anatolij N. & Dmitrij O. Dobrovol'skij (eds.). 2007. *Slovar'-tezaurus sovremennoj russkoj idiomatiki* [Thesaurus of modern Russian idioms]. Moscow: Mir ènciklopedij Avanta+.

Baranov, Anatolij N. & Dmitrij O. Dobrovol'skij. 2008. *Aspekty teorii frazeologii* [Aspects of the theory of phraseology]. Moscow: Znak.

Baranov, Anatolij N. & Dmitrij O. Dobrovol'skij. 2013. *Osnovy frazeologii (kratkij kurs)* [Fundamentals of phraseology (short course)]. Moscow: Flinta, Nauka.

Baranov, Anatolij N. & Dmitrij O. Dobrovol'skij (eds.). 2018. *Tezaurus russkix idiom: semantičeskie gruppy i konteksty* [Thesaurus of Russian idioms: Semantic groups and contexts]. 2nd edn. Moscow: Leksrus.

Baranov, Anatolij N. & Dmitrij O. Dobrovol'skij (eds.). 2020. *Akademičeskij slovar' russkoj frazeologii* [Academy dictionary of Russian phraseology]. 3rd edn., revised and enlarged. Moscow: Leksrus.

Barcelona, Antonio (ed.). 2000. *Metaphor and metonymy at the crossroads: A cognitive perspective*. Berlin & New York: Mouton de Gruyter.

Bauer, Gerhard. 1972. *Gesellschaft und Weltbild im baltischen Traditionsmilieu. Eine soziologisch-volkskundliche Untersuchung über die Gesellschaft und Mythologie bei den baltischen Völkern, dargestellt anhand historischer und volkskundlicher Quellen*. Heidelberg: Heidelberg University dissertation.

Bennett, Thomas J. A. 1988. *Aspects of English colour collocations and idioms*. Heidelberg: Universitätsverlag Winter.

Bergen, Benjamin. 2007. Mental simulation in literal and figurative language understanding. In Seana Coulson & Barbara Lewandowska-Tomaszczyk (eds.), *The literal and nonliteral in language and thought*, 255-280. Berlin: Peter Lang.

Bergenholtz, Henning. 1980. *Das Wortfeld „Angst". Eine lexikographische Untersuchung mit Vorschlägen für ein großes interdisziplinäres Wörterbuch der deutschen Sprache*. Stuttgart: Klett-Cotta.

Biedermann, Hans. 1989. *Knaurs Lexikon der Symbole*. München: Droemer Knaur.

Biedermann, Hans. 1994. *Dictionary of symbolism. Cultural icons and the meanings behind them*. New York: Meridian.

Bierwisch, Manfred. 1983. Psychologische Aspekte der Semantik natürlicher Sprachen. In Wolfgang Motsch & Dieter Viehweger (eds.), *Richtungen der modernen Semantikforschung*, 15–34. Berlin: Akademie-Verlag.

Biezais, Haralds. 1987. Baltic religion. In Mircea Eliade (ed.), *The encyclopedia of religion*, vol. 2, 49–55. New York & London: Macmillan Publishing.

Bindel, Ernst. 1962. *Pythagoras. Leben und Lehre in Wirklichkeit und Legende*. Stuttgart: Verlag Freies Geistesleben.

Binovič, Leonid È. & Nikolaj N. Grišin. 1975. *Nemecko-russkij frazeologičeskij slovar' = Deutsch-russisches phraseologisches Wörterbuch*. Moscow: Russkij jazyk.

Birix, Aleksandr K., Valerij M. Mokienko & Ljudmila I. Stepanova. 2005. *Slovar' russkoj frazeologii. Istoriko-ètimologičeskij spravočnik*. [Dictionary of Russian phraseology. Historical and etymological reference book]. 3rd edn. Moscow: Astrel'.

Black, Max. 1955. Metaphor. *Proceedings of the Aristotelian Society* 55 (1). 273–294.

Black, Max. 1962. *Models and metaphors. Studies in language and philosophy*. Ithaca, NY: Cornell University Press.

Black, Max. 1993. More about metaphor. In Andrew Ortony (ed.), *Metaphor and thought*, 2nd edn., 19–44. Cambridge: Cambridge University Press.

Blankenburg, Walter & W. Endres. 1979. Zahlensymbolik. In Friedrich Blume (ed.), *Musik in Geschichte und Gegenwart (MGG)*, Ergänzungsband, 1971–1978. Basel: Bärenreiter Verlag.

Blume, Herbert. 2001. Katt och råtta, Katz und Maus. Ungleiche lexikalisch-semantische Strukturen im Schwedischen und Deutschen. In Armin Burkhardt & Dieter Cherubim (eds.), *Sprache im Leben der Zeit. Beiträge zur Theorie, Analyse und Kritik der deutschen Sprache in Vergangenheit und Gegenwart. Helmut Henne zum 65. Geburtstag*, 389–399. Tübingen: Max Niemeyer.

Bobrow, Samuel A. & Susan M. Bell. 1973. On catching on to idiomatic expressions. *Memory and Cognition* 1. 343–346.

Böklen, Ernst. 1913. *"Unglückszahl" Dreizehn und ihre mythische Bedeutung*. Leipzig: J. C. Hinrichs.

Booij, Geert. 2002. Constructional idioms, morphology, and the Dutch lexicon. *Journal of Germanic Linguistics* 14. 301–329.
Boroditsky, Lera. 2000. Metaphoric structuring: Understanding time through spatial metaphors. *Cognition* 75 (1). 1–28.
Boroditsky, Lera. 2001. Does language shape thought? Mandarin and English speakers' conceptions of time. *Cognitive Psychology* 43 (1). 1–22.
Brewer, Ebenezer Cobham. 1992. *Brewer's concise dictionary of phrase and fable*. Ed. by Betty Kirkpatrick. Helicon, Oxford: Orion Publishing.
Brillouët, Georges & Anna Kokkinidou-Maxime. 2008. *7000 Expressions, locutions, proverbes du Grec Moderne*. 2nd edn. Paris: Éditions Rue d'Ulm.
Büchler, Marianne. 1998. Kontrastive Analyse phraseologischer Einheiten mit Tierbezeichnungen. In Wolfgang Eismann (ed.), *EUROPHRAS 95. Europäische Phraseologie im Vergleich: Gemeinsames Erbe und kulturelle Vielfalt*, 67–78. Bochum: Brockmeyer.
Budvytyte, Aina. 2003. Der axiologische Aspekt der deutschen und litauischen Somatismen. In Harald Burger, Gertrud Gréciano & Annelies Häcki Buhofer (eds.), *Flut von Texten – Vielfalt der Kulturen. Ascona 2001 zur Methodologie und Kulturspezifik der Phraseologie*, 255–265. Baltmannsweiler: Schneider.
Burger, Harald. 1973. *Idiomatik des Deutschen*. Unter Mitarbeit von Harald Jakske. Tübingen: Max Niemeyer.
Burger, Harald. 1976. Die Achseln zucken. Zur sprachlichen Kodierung nicht-sprachlicher Kommunikation. *Wirkendes Wort* 26. 311–334.
Burger, Harald. 1979. Phraseologie und gesprochene Sprache. In Heinrich Löffler, Karl Pestalozzi & Martin Stern, (eds.), *Standard und Dialekt. Studien zur gesprochenen und geschriebenen Sprache. Festschrift für Heinz Rupp zum 60. Geburtstag*, 89–103. Bern & München: Francke.
Burger, Harald. 1991. Phraseologie und Intertextualität. In Christine Palm (ed.), *EUROPHRAS 90: Akten der internationalen Tagung der germanistischen Phraseologieforschung in Aske (Schweden), 12.-15. Juni 1990*, 13–27. Uppsala: Univ. Uppsala.
Burger, Harald. 1992. Phraseologie im Wörterbuch. Überlegungen aus germanistischer Perspektive. In Wolfgang Eismann & Jürgen Petermann (eds.), *Studia Phraseologica et alia. Festschrift für Josip Matešic zum 65. Geburtstag*, 33–51. München: Otto Sagner Verlag.
Burger, Harald. 1998. Idiom and metaphor. Their relation in theory and text. In Peter Ďurčo (ed.), *EUROPHRAS 97. September 2-5, 1997, Liptovský Ján: Phraseology and paremiology*, 30–36. Bratislava: Akadémia PZ.
Burger, Harald. 2015. *Phraseologie. Eine Einführung am Beispiel des Deutschen*. 5., neu bearbeitete Auflage. Berlin: Erich Schmidt Verlag.
Burger, Harald, Annelies Buhofer & Ambros Sialm. 1982. *Handbuch der Phraseologie*. Berlin: Walter de Gruyter.
Burger, Harald, Dmitrij Dobrovol'skij, Peter Kühn & Neal R. Norrick. (eds.). 2007a. *Phraseologie: Ein internationales Handbuch zeitgenössischer Forschung = Phraseology: An international handbook of contemporary research*. Berlin & New York: Walter de Gruyter.
Burger, Harald, Dmitrij Dobrovol'skij, Peter Kühn, Neal R. Norrick. 2007b. Phraseology: Subject area, terminology and research topics. In Harald Burger, Dmitrij Dobrovol'skij, Peter Kühn & Neal R. Norrick (eds.), *Phraseologie: Ein internationales Handbuch zeitgenössischer Forschung = Phraseology: An international handbook of contemporary research*, vol. 1, 10–19. Berlin & New York: Walter de Gruyter.
Butler, Christopher. 1970. *Number symbolism*. London: Routledge & Kegan Paul.

Cacciari, Cristina. 1993. The place of idioms in a literal and metaphorical world. In Cacciari, Cristina & Patrizia Tabossi (eds.), *Idioms: processing, structure, and interpretation*, 27–55. Hillsdale, NJ: Lawrence Erlbaum.
Cacciari, Cristina. 2014. Processing multiword idiomatic strings: many words in one? *Mental Lexicon* 9. 267–293.
Cacciari, Cristina & Sam Glucksberg. 1991. Understanding idiomatic expressions: The contribution of word meanings. In Gregory B. Simpson (ed.), *Understanding word and sentence*, 217–240. Amsterdam & New York: North-Holland.
Cacciari, Cristina & Sam Glucksberg. 1994. Understanding figurative language. In Morton Ann Gernsbacher (eds.), *Handbook of psycholinguistics*, 447–477. New York: Academic Press.
Cacciari, Cristina, Raffaella Ida Rumiati & Sam Glucksberg. 1992. The role of word meanings, transparency and familiarity in the mental images of idioms. In Martin Everaert, Erik-Jan van der Linden, André Schenk & Robert Schreuder (eds.), *Proceedings of IDIOMS*, 1–9. Tilburg: ITK.
Cacciari, Cristina & Patrizia Tabossi. 1988. The comprehension of idioms. *Journal of Memory and Language* 27. 668–683.
Cacciari, Cristina & Patrizia Tabossi (eds.). 1993. *Idioms: processing, structure, and interpretation*. Hillsdale, NJ: Lawrence Erlbaum.
Cameron, Lynne J & Juup Stelma. 2004. Metaphor clusters in discourse. *Journal of Applied Linguistics* 1 (2). 107–136.
Cameron, Lynne J. 2008. Metaphor and talk. In Raymond W. Gibbs (ed.), *The Cambridge handbook of metaphor and thought*, 197–211. Cambridge: Cambridge University Press.
Campbell, John D. & Albert N. Katz. 2006. On reversing the topics and vehicles of metaphor. *Metaphor and Symbol* 21 (1). 1–22.
Carnes, Pack (ed.). 1988. *Proverbia in fabula. Essays on the relationship of the proverb and the fable*. Bern & New York: Peter Lang.
Carnes, Pack. 1991. The fable and the proverb: Intertexts and reception. *Proverbium. Yearbook of International Proverb Scholarship* 8. 55–76.
Casasanto, Danel & Lera Boroditsky. 2008. Time in the mind: Using space to think about time. *Cognition* 106. 579–593.
Cassirer, Ernst. 1923–1929. *The philosophy of symbolic forms*. New Haven: Yale University Press.
Cassirer, Ernst. 1944. *An essay on man: An introduction to a philosophy of human culture*. New Haven: Yale University Press.
Čermák, František. 1998. Somatic idioms revisited. In Wolfgang Eismann (ed.), *EUROPHRAS 95. Europäische Phraseologie im Vergleich: Gemeinsames Erbe und kulturelle Vielfalt*, 109–119. Bochum: Brockmeyer.
Černyševa, Irina I. 1975. Phraseologie. In Marija D. Stepanova & Irina I. Černyševa (eds.), *Lexikologie der deutschen Gegenwartsdsprache*, 198–261. Moscow: Vysšaja škola.
Černyševa, Irina I. 1980. *Feste Wortkomplexe des Deutschen in Sprache und Rede*. Moscow: Vysšaja škola.
Chamizo Domínguez, Pedro J. & Brigitte Nerlich. 2002. False friends: Their origin and semantics in some selected languages. *Journal of Pragmatics* 34. 1833-1849.
Chang, Hsiu-chuan. 2003. *Chinesische und deutsche sprichwörtliche Redensarten. Eine kontrastive Betrachtung unter sprachlichen, funktionellen und kulturhistorischen Aspekten am Beispiel von Tierbildern*. Hamburg: Kovač.
Charteris-Black, Jonathan. 2004. *Corpus approaches to critical metaphor analysis*. Basingstoke: Palgrave Macmillan.

Chernov, Igor. 1988. Historical survey of Tartu-Moscow Semiotic School. In Henri Broms, Rebecca Kaufmann (eds.), *Semiotics of culture. Proceedings of the 25th symposium of the Tartu-Moscow School of Semiotics, Imatra, Finland, 27th-29th July, 1987*, 7–16. Helsinki: Arator.

Chiappe, Dan L. & John M. Kennedy. 2000. Are metaphors elliptical similes? *Journal of Psycholinguistic Research* 29. 371–398.

Chiappe, Dan L. & John M. Kennedy. 2001. Literal bases for metaphor and simile. *Metaphor and Symbol* 16. 249–276.

Chomsky, Noam. 1965. *Aspects of the theory of syntax*. Cambridge, MA: MIT Press.

Chrissou, Marios. 2000. *Kontrastive Untersuchungen zu deutschen und neugriechischen Phraseologismen mit animalitischer Lexik*. Essen: Clemon-Verlag.

Cirlot, Juan Eduardo. 1962. *A dictionary of symbols*. Translated by Jack Sage. London: Routledge & Kegan Paul.

Coates, Jennifer. 2016. *Women, men and language: A sociolinguistic account of gender differences in language*. 3rd edn. London & New York: Routledge.

Colson, Jean-Pierre. 2003. Corpus linguistics and phraseological statistics: A few hypotheses and examples. In Harald Burger, Gertrud Gréciano & Annelies Häcki Buhofer (eds.), *Flut von Texten – Vielfalt der Kulturen. Ascona 2001 zur Methodologie und Kulturspezifik der Phraseologie*, 47–59. Baltmannsweiler: Schneider.

Colston, Herbert L. 1997. "I've never seen anything like it": Overstatement, understatement, and irony. *Metaphor and Symbol* 12. 43–58.

Colston, Herbert L. 2002. Contrast and assimilation in verbal irony. *Journal of Pragmatics* 34. 111–142.

Colston, Herbert L. & Raymond W. Gibbs. 2002. Are irony and metaphor understood differently? *Metaphor and Symbol* 17. 57–70.

Colston, Herbert L. & Raymond W. Gibbs. 2007. A brief history of irony. In Raymond W. Gibbs & Herbert L. Colston (eds.), *Irony in language and thought: A cognitive science reader*, 3–21. London & New York: Routledge.

Corwin, Charles (ed.). 1994. *A dictionary of Japanese and English idiomatic equivalents*. Tokyo: Kodansha International.

Cotta Ramusino, Paola & Fabio Mollica (eds.). 2020. *Contrastive phraseology: Languages and cultures in comparison*. Cambridge: Cambridge Scholars Publishing.

Coulmas, Florian. 1981. *Routine im Gespräch. Zur pragmatischen Fundierung der Idiomatik*. Wiesbaden: Akademische Verlagsgesellschaft Athenaion.

Coulson, Seana & Todd Oakley. 2000. Blending basis. *Cognitive Linguistics* 11. 175–196.

Coulson, Seana & Todd Oakley. 2005. Blending and coded meaning: Literal and figurative meaning in cognitive semantics. *Journal of Pragmatics* 37. 1510–1536.

Cowie, Anthony P. 1998a. Introduction. In Anthony P. Cowie (ed.), *Phraseology. Theory, analysis, and applications*, 1–20. New York & Oxford: Oxford University Press.

Cowie, Anthony P. 1998b. Semantic frame theory and the analysis of phraseology. *Moscow State University Bulletin* 19. 40–50.

Cowie, Anthony P. & Ronald Mackin. 1998. *Oxford dictionary of phrasal verbs*. Oxford: Oxford University Press.

Cowie, Anthony P., Ronald Mackin & Isabel R. McCaig. 1993. *Oxford dictionary of English idioms*. Oxford: Oxford University Press.

Cox, Heinrich Leonhard. 1988. *Spreekwoordenboek in vier talen. Nederlands Frans Duits Engels* [Proverb dictionary in four languages. Dutch French German English]. Antwerpen & Utrecht: Van Dale Lexicografie.

Cram, D. 1983. The linguistic status of the proverb. *Cahiers de lexicologie* 43. 53–71.
Croft, William. 1993. The role of domains in the interpretation of metaphors and metonymies. *Cognitive Linguistics* 4. 335–370.
Croft, William & D. Alan Cruse. 2004. *Cognitive linguistics*. Cambridge & New York: Cambridge University Press.
Crowther, Jonathan, Sheila Dignen & Diana Lea (eds). 2002. *Oxford collocations dictionary for students of English*. Oxford: Oxford University Press.
Cserép, Attila. 2009. The interaction of metaphor and metonymy in idioms of *brain*, *head* and *mind*. In Csaba Földes (ed.), *Phraseologie disziplinär und interdisziplinär*, 87–98. Tübingen: Gunter Narr.
Cserép Attila. 2017a. Idiom variation and decomposability. Part I: Verbal variation. *Yearbook of Phraseology* 8. 95–122.
Cserép Attila. 2017b. Idiom variation and decomposability. Part II: Variation in the noun phrase. *Yearbook of Phraseology* 8. 123–144.
Cuccio, Valentina. 2018. *Attention to metaphor. From neurons to representations*. Amsterdam & Philadelphia: John Benjamins.
Dahl, Östen. 1990. Standard Average European as an exotic language. In Johannes Bechert, Giuliano Bernini & Claude Buridant (eds.), *Toward a typology of European languages*, 3–8. Berlin & New York: Mouton de Gruyter.
Dahl, Östen. 2001. Principles of areal typology. In Martin Haspelmath, Ekkehard König, W. Oesterreicher & W. Raible (eds.), *Language typology and language universals. An international handbook*, vol. 2, 1456–1470. Berlin & New York: Walter de Gruyter.
Dancygier, Barbara & Eve Sweetser. 2014. *Figurative language*. Cambridge: University Press.
David, Oana Alexandra. 2016. *Metaphor in the grammar of argument realization*. Berkeley: University of California dissertation.
Davidou, Aliki. 1998. *Kontrastive Untersuchungen zur griechischen und deutschen Phraseologie: mit einem zweisprachigen Lexikon somatischer Phraseologismen*. Erlangen & Jena: Palm & Enke.
De Beaugrande, Robert A. & Wolfgang U. Dressler. 1981. *Introduction to textlinguistics*. London & New York: Longman.
Deignan, Alice. 2005. *Metaphor and corpus linguistics*. Amsterdam & Philadelphia: John Benjamins.
Deignan, Alice. 2007. The grammar of linguistic metaphors: In Anatol Stefanowitsch & Stefan Th. Gries (eds.), *Corpus-based approaches to metaphor and metonymy*, 106–122. Berlin & New York: Mouton de Gruyter.
Deignan, Alice. 2009. Searching for metaphorical patterns in corpora. In Paul Baker (ed.), *Contemporary corpus linguistics*, 9–30. London: Continuum.
Deignan, Alice, Jeanette Littlemore & Elena Semino. 2013. *Figurative language, genre and register*. Cambridge: Cambridge University Press.
Dews, Shelly & Ellen Winner. 1999. Obligatory processing of literal and nonliteral meanings in verbal irony. *Journal of Pragmatics* 31. 1579–1599.
Dicke, Gerd & Klaus Grubmüller. 1987. *Die Fabeln des Mittelalters und der frühen Neuzeit. Ein Katalog der deutschen Versionen und ihrer lateinischen Entsprechungen*. München: Fink.
Dirven, René. 2002. Structuring of word meaning III: Figurative use of language. In D. Alan Cruse, Franz Hundsnurscher, Michael Job & Peter Rolf Lutzeier (eds.), *Lexicology. An international handbook on the nature and structure of words and vocabularies*, vol. 1, 337–342. Berlin & New York: Walter de Gruyter.

Dirven, René & Ralf Pörings (eds.). 2002. *Metaphor and metonymy in comparison and contrast*. Berlin & New York: Mouton de Gruyter.

Dobrovol'skij, Dmitrij. 1982. Zum Problem der phraseologisch gebundenen Bedeutung. *Beiträge zur Erforschung der deutschen Sprache* 2. 52–67.

Dobrovol'skij, Dmitrij. 1988. *Phraseologie als Objekt der Universalienlinguistik*. Leipzig: Enzyklopädie.

Dobrovol'skij, Dmitrij. 1992. Phraseological universals: theoretical and applied aspects. In Michel Kefer & Johan van der Auwera (eds.), *Meaning and grammar. Cross-linguistic perspectives*, 279–301. Berlin & New York: Mouton de Gruyter.

Dobrovol'skij, Dmitrij O. 1997. Nacional'no-kul'turnaja specifika vo frazeologii [National and cultural specificity in phraseology]. *Voprosy jazykoznanija* 6. 37–48.

Dobrovol'skij, Dmitrij. 1998. On cultural component in the semantic structure of idioms. In Peter Ďurčo (ed.), *EUROPHRAS 97: International symposium. September 2-5, 1997, Liptovský Jan. Phraseology and paremiology*, 55–61. Bratislava: Akademia PZ.

Dobrovol'skij, Dmitrij. 1999a. On the cross-linguistic equivalence of idioms. In Christopher Beedham (ed.), *"Langue" and "parole" in synchronic and diachronic perspective. Selected proceedings of the XXXIst annual meeting of the Societas Linguistica Europeae, St. Andrews, 1998*, 203–219. Amsterdam & Oxford: Elsevier.

Dobrovol'skij, Dmitrij. 1999b. Phraseologische Wörterbücher Deutsch-Russisch und Russisch-Deutsch. Stand und Perspektiven. In Herbert Ernst Wiegand (ed.), *Germanistische Linguistik. Studien zur zweisprachigen Lexikographie mit Deutsch IV*, 141–175. Hildesheim & New York: Georg Olms.

Dobrovol'skij, Dmitrij. 2001. Pragmatische Konventionen aus kontrastiver Sicht. In Hartmut Schröder, Petra Kumschlies & María González (eds.), *Linguistik als Kulturwissenschaft. Festschrift für Bernd Spillner zum 60. Geburtstag*, 31–41, Frankfurt am Main etc.: Peter Lang.

Dobrovol'skij, Dmitrij. 2002. Phraseologismen in kontrastiver Sicht. In D. Alan Cruse, Franz Hundsnurscher, Michael Job & Peter Rolf Lutzeier (eds.), *Lexicology. An international handbook on the nature and structure of words and vocabularies*, vol. 1, 442–451. Berlin & New York: Walter de Gruyter.

Dobrovol'skij, Dmitrij O. 2004. Reguljarnaja mnogoznačnost' v sfere idiomatiki [Regular polysemy in the domain of idioms]. In Jurij D. Apresjan (ed.), *Sokrovennye smzsly. Slovo. Tekst. Kul'tura* [Innermost meanings. Word. Text, Culture], 204–218. Moscow: Jazyki slavjanskoj kul'tury.

Dobrovol'skij, Dmitrij. 2006. Reguläre Polysemie und verwandte Erscheinungen. In Kristel Proost & Edeltraud Winkler (eds.), *Von Intentionaltät zur Bedeutung konventionalisierter Zeichen. FS für Gisela Harras zum 65. Geburtstag*, 29–64. Tübingen: Gunter Narr.

Dobrovol'skij, Dmitrij. 2007. Cognitive approaches to idiom analysis. In Harald Burger, Dmitrij Dobrovol'skij, Peter Kühn & Neal R. Norrick. (eds.), *Phraseologie: Ein internationales Handbuch zeitgenössischer Forschung = Phraseology: An international handbook of contemporary research*, vol. 2, 789–818. Berlin & New York: Walter de Gruyter.

Dobrovol'skij, Dmitrij 2011a. Criteria for distinguishing between proverbs and sentential phrasemes of other types. In Rui J. B. Soares & Outi Lauhakangas (eds.), *Proceedings of the 4th interdisciplinary colloquium on proverbs*, 97–105. Tavira: International Association of Paremiology.

Dobrovol'skij, Dmitrij 2011b. Phraseologie und Konstruktionsgrammatik. In Alexander Lasch & Alexander Ziem (eds.), *Konstruktionsgrammatik III. Aktuelle Fragen und Lösungsansätze*, 111–130. Tübingen: Stauffenburg.

Dobrovol'skij, Dmitrij 2011c. The structure of metaphor and idiom semantics (a cognitive approach). In Sandra Handl & Hans-Jörg Schmid (eds.), *Windows to the mind: Metaphor, metonymy and conceptual blending*, 41–62. Berlin & New York: Mouton de Gruyter.

Dobrovol'skij, Dmitrij. 2013. Phraseologie im Wörterbuch. *Zeitschrift für angewandte Linguistik* 58 (1). 41–74.

Dobrovol'skij, Dmitrij. 2014. On the semantic structure of idioms. In Vanda Durante (ed.), *Fraseología y paremiología: enfoques y aplicaciones*, 23–32. Madrid: Instituto Cervantes.

Dobrovol'skij, Dmitrij (ed.). 2015. Phraseology and dictionaries [Special issue]. *International Journal of Lexicography* 28 (3).

Dobrovol'skij, Dmitrij. 2016a. *Kognitive Aspekte der Idiom-Semantik. Studien zum Thesaurus deutscher Idiome*. 2., aktualisierte und erweiterte Auflage. Tübingen: Stauffenburg.

Dobrovol'skij, Dmitrij. 2016b. The notion of "inner form" and idiom semantics. *Études et travaux d'Eur'ORBEM 1* [Special issue: *Proverbes et stéréotypes: forme, formes et contextes*]. 21–36.

Dobrovol'skij, Dmitrij. 2016c. Grammatika konstrukcij i frazeologija [Construction Grammar and phraseology]. *Voprosy jazykoznanija* 3. 7–21.

Dobrovol'skij, Dmitrij. In press. Deutsche Phrasem-Konstruktion [X hin, X her]. In Carmen Mellado Blanco, Fabio Mollica & Elmar Schafroth (eds.), *Konstruktionen zwischen Lexikon und Grammatik. Phrasem-Konstruktionen monolingual, bilingial, multilingual*. Berlin: Walter de Gruyter.

Dobrovol'skij, Dmitrij & Elisabeth Piirainen. 1994. Sprachliche Unikalia im Deutschen: Zum Phänomen phraseologisch gebundener Formative. *Folia Linguistica* 28. 449–473.

Dobrovol'skij, Dmitrij & Elisabeth Piirainen. 1997. *Symbole in Sprache und Kultur. Studien zur Phraseologie aus kultursemiotischer Perspektive*. Bochum: Brockmeyer.

Dobrovol'skij, Dmitrij & Elisabeth Piirainen. 1998. On symbols. Cognitive and cultural aspects of figurative language. *Lexicology* 4 (2). 1–34.

Dobrovol'skij, Dmitrij & Elisabeth Piirainen. 2005. Cognitive theory of metaphor and idiom analysis. *Jezikoslovlje* 6 (1). 7–35.

Dobrovol'skij, Dmitrij & Elisabeth Piirainen. 2009. *Zur Theorie der Phraseologie: Kognitive und kulturelle Aspekte*. Tübingen: Stauffenburg.

Dobrovol'skij, Dmitrij & Elisabeth Piirainen. 2010. Idioms: Motivation and etymology. *Yearbook of Phraseology* 1. 73–96.

Dmitrij Dobrovol'skij & Elisabeth Piirainen. 2017. Konstruktionspatterns in der Idiomatik und ihre kognitiven Grundlagen. *Yearbook of Phraseology* 8. 31–58.

Dobrovol'skij, Dmitrij & Elisabeth Piirainen. 2018. Conventional Figurative Language Theory and idiom motivation. *Yearbook of Phraseology* 9. 5–30.

Dobrovol'skij, Dmitrij & Elisabeth Piirainen. 2019. Kognitive Grundlagen der Idiom-Motivation. In Maurice Kauffer & Yvon Keromnes (eds.), *Theorie und Empirie in der Phraseologie – Approches théoretiques et empiriques en phraséologie*, 19–31. Tübingen: Stauffenburg.

Doherty, Monika. 1996. Information structure: A key concept for translation theory. *Linguistics* 34. 441–457.

Dolby-Stahl, Sandra K. 1988. Sour grapes: Fable, proverb, unripe fruit. In Pack Carnes (ed.), *Proverbia in fabula. Essays on the relationship of the proverb and the fable*, 295–309. Bern & New York: Peter Lang.

Dölling, Johannes. 2021. Systematic polysemy. In Daniel Gutzmann, Lisa Matthewson, Cécile Meier, Hotze Rullmann & Thomas Ede Zimmermann (eds.), *The Wiley Blackwell companion to semantics*. Oxford: John Wiley & Sons.

Doyle, Charles C. 2008. Is the Pope still Catholic?: Historical observations on sarcastic interrogatives. *Western Folklore* 67 (1). 5–33.

Drewer, Petra. 2003. *Die kognitive Metapher als Werkzeug des Denkens. Zur Rolle der Analogie bei der Gewinnung und Vermittlung wissenschaftlicher Erkenntnisse*. Tübingen: Gunter Narr.

Duden. 2013 = *Duden Redewendungen. Wörterbuch der deutschen Idiomatik*. 4., neu bearb. und aktualisierte Auflage. Berlin: Bibliographisches Institut, Dudenverlag.

Duden. 2015 = *Duden. Deutsches Universalwörterbuch*. 8., überarbeitete und erweiterte Auflage. Berlin: Bibliographisches Institut, Dudenverlag.

Duranti, Alessandro. 1997. *Linguistic anthropology*. Cambridge & New York: Cambridge University Press.

Dürckheim, Karlfried Graf von. 1956. *Hara: die Erdmitte des Menschen*. München-Planegg: Otto Wilhelm Barth-Verlag.

Ďurčo, Peter. 1994. *Probleme der allgemeinen und kontrastiven Phraseologie: Am Beispiel Deutsch und Slowakisch*. Heidelberg: Julius Groos.

Ďurčo, Peter, Kathrin Steyer & Katrin Hein. 2017. *Sprichwörter im Gebrauch*. Unveränderter Wiederabdruck der 2015 in Trnava erschienenen Erstausgabe. Mannheim: Institut für Deutsche Sprache.

Dynel, Marta (ed.). 2013. *Developments in linguistic humour theory*. Amsterdam & Philadelphia: John Benjamins.

Eckert, Rainer. 1998. On the cult of the snake in ancient Baltic and Slavic tradition (based on language material from the Latvian folksongs). *Zeitschrift für Slawistik* 43. 97–100.

Eckert, Rainer & Kurt Günther. 1992. *Die Phraseologie der russischen Sprache*. Leipzig, Berlin, München, Wien, Zürich & New York: Langenscheidt & Enzyklopädie.

Eco, Umberto. 1984. *Semiotics and the philosophy of language*. London: Macmillan.

Edličko, Marija I. & Aleksandt I. Rubinštejn. 1959. *Sbornik frazeologičeskix vyraženij v nemeckom jazyke = Deutsche Redensarten*. 2. Auflage. Moscow: Učpedgiz.

Eggenberger, Christoph. 1991. Tierfriede, Tierkampf: Gallus und der Bär. In Paul Michel (ed.), *Tiersymbolik*, 91–109. Bern: Peter Lang.

Egli, Hans. 1994. *Das Schlangensymbol. Geschichte Märchen Mythos*. 3. Auflage. Düsseldorf: Patmos.

Eimermacher, Kurt. 1974. Ju. M. Lotman. Bemerkungen zu einer Semiotik als integrativer Kulturwissenschaft. In Kurt Eimermacher (ed.), *Ju. M. Lotman, Aufsätze zur Theorie und Methodologie der Literatur und Kultur*, vii–xxv. Kronberg Ts.: Scriptor.

Eiynck, Andreas. 1996. *Damals bei uns in Westfalen. Alles unter Dach und Fach. Bauen und Wohnen in altem Fachwerk auf dem Lande*. Münster: Landwirtschaftsverlag.

Ekman, Paul, Robert W. Levenson & Wallace V. Friesen. 1983. Autonomic nervous system activity distinguishes among emotions. *Science* 221. 1208–1210.

Eliade, Mircea. 1952. *Images et symboles*. Paris: Gallimard.

Eliade, Mircea. 1957. *Myths, dreams, and mysteries*. New York: Harper.

Endres, Franz C. & Annemarie Schimmel. 1985. *Das Mysterium der Zahl. Zahlensymbolik im Kulturvergleich*. Köln: Diederichs.

Engstrøm, Anders. 1999. The contemporary theory of metaphor revisited. *Metaphor and Symbol* 14. 53–61.

Ettinger, Stefan. 1994. Phraseologische faux amis des Sprachenpaares Französisch-Deutsch. In Barbara Sandig (ed.), *EUROPHRAS 92. Tendenzen der Phraseologieforschung*, 109–136. Bochum: Brockmeyer.

Ettinger, Stefan. 2012. Phraseologische Faux Amis des Sprachenpaares Französisch-Deutsch unter phraseographischen und translatorischen Gesichtspunkten. In Michael Prinz & Ulrike Richter-Vapaatalo (eds.), *Idiome, Konstruktionen, „verblümte rede". Beiträge zur Geschichte der germanistischen Phraseologieforschung*, 357–374. Stuttgart: Hirzel.

Evans, Vyvyan. 2013. *Language and time: A cognitive linguistics approach*. Cambridge: Cambridge University Press.

Fan, Yanqian. 1996. *Farbnomenklatur im Deutschen und im Chinesischen. Eine kontrastive Analyse unter psycholinguistischen, semantischen und kulturellen Aspekten*. Frankfurt am Main etc.: Peter Lang.

Farø, Ken. 2002. Somatismen als Problem der dänischen und deutschen Lexikographie. In Henrik Gottlieb, Jens Erik Mogensen & Arne Zettersten, *Symposium on lexicography X. Proceedings of the tenth international symposium on lexicography May 4-6, 2000 at the University of Copenhagen*, 107–124. Tübingen: Max Niemeyer.

Fass, Dan. 1997. *Processing metonymy and metaphor*. Greenwich, CT: Ablex Publishing.

Fauconnier, Gilles. 1997. *Mappings in thought and language*. Cambridge: Cambridge University Press.

Fauconnier, Gilles & Mark Turner. 1998. Conceptual integration network. *Cognitive Science* 2. 133–187.

Fauconnier, Gilles & Mark Turner. 2002. *The way we think. Conceptual blending and the mind's hidden complexities*. New York: Perseus Books Group.

Fellbaum, Christiane (ed.). 2007. *Idioms and collocations. Corpus-based linguistic and lexicographic studies*. London: Continuum.

Feyaerts, Kurt. 1994. Zur lexikalisch-semantischen Komplexität der Phraseologismen mit phraseologisch gebundenen Formativen. In Christoph Chlosta, Peter Grzybek & Elisabeth Piirainen (eds.), *Sprachbilder zwischen Theorie und Praxis. Akten des Westfälischen Arbeitskreises "Phraseologie/Parömiologie"*, 133–162. Bochum: Brockmeyer.

Filatkina, Natalia. 2002. Zum kulturellen Aspekt der Phraseologie des Lëtzebuergeschen. In Elisabeth Piirainen & Ilpo T. Piirainen (eds.), *Phraseologie in Raum und Zeit. Akten der 10. Tagung des Westfälischen Arbeitskreises „Phraseologie/Parömiologie" Münster 2001*, 32–56. Baltmannsweiler: Schneider.

Filatkina, Natalia. 2005. *Phraseologie des Lëtzebuergeschen. Empirische Untersuchungen zu strukturellen, semantischen, pragmatischen und bildlichen Besonderheiten der jüngsten westgermanischen Sprache*. Heidelberg: Universitätsverlag Winter.

Filatkina, Natalia. 2018. *Historische formelhafte Sprache. Theoretische Grundlagen und methodische Herausforderungen*. Berlin & Boston: Walter de Gruyter.

Fillmore, Charles J. 1977. Scenes-and-frames semantics. In Antonio Zampolli (ed.), *Linguistic structures processing*, 55–81. Amsterdam & New York: North-Holland.

Fillmore, Charles J. 1985. Frames and the semantics of understanding. *Quaderni di semantica* 6. 222–254.

Fillmore, Charles J. 1990. *Construction Grammar. Course reader for linguistics 120 A*. Berkeley: University of California.

Fillmore, Charles J. 2008. Border conflicts: FrameNet meets Construction Grammar. In Elisenda Bernal & Janet DeCesaris (eds.), *Proceedings of the XIII Euralex international congress*, 49–68. Barcelona: IULA.

Fillmore, Charles J. & Beryl T. Atkins. 1992. Towards a frame-based lexicon: The semantics of RISK and its neighbors. In Adrienne Lehrer, Eva Feder Kittay & Richard Lehrer (eds.), *Frames, fields, and contrasts*, 75–102. Hillsdale, NJ: Lawrence Erlbaum.

Fillmore, Charles J., Christopher R. Johnson & Miriam R. L. Petruck. 2003. Background to FrameNet. *International Journal of Lexicography* 16. 235–250.

Fillmore, Charles J., Paul Kay & Mary Catherine O'Connor. 1988. Regularity and idiomaticity in grammatical constructions. The case of 'let alone'. *Language* 64 (3). 501–538.

Fillmore, Charles J., Miriam R. L. Petruck, Josef Ruppenhofer & A. Wright. 2003. FrameNet in Action: The case of attaching. *International Journal of Lexicography* 16 (3). 297–332.

Finkbeiner, Rita & Barbara Schlücker. 2019. Compounds and multi-word expressions in the languages of Europe. In Barbara Schlücker (ed.), *Complex lexical units*, 1–44. Berlin & Boston: Walter de Gruyter.

Firth, Raymond. 1973. *Symbols: Public and private*. London: George Allen & Unwin.

Fleischer, Wolfgang. 1997. *Phraseologie der deutschen Gegenwartssprache*. 2. Neuauflage. Tübingen: Max Niemeyer.

Florenskij, Pavel. 1922. Nebesnye znamenija (razmyšlenie o simvolike cvetov) [Heavenly signs (reflections on the symbolism of flowers)]. *Makovec* 2. 14–16.

Fogelin, Robert J. 1994. Metaphors, similes and similarity. In Jaakko Hintikka (ed.), *Aspects of metaphor*, 23–39. Dordrecht, Boston & London: Kluwer Academic Publishers.

Földes, Csaba. 1996. *Deutsche Phraseologie kontrastiv: intra- und interlinguale Zugänge*. Heidelberg: Julius Groos.

Fontenelle, Thierry. 1998. Discovering significant lexical functions in dictionary entries. In Anthony P. Cowie, (ed.), *Phraseology. Theory, analysis, and applications*, 189–207. New York & Oxford: Oxford University Press.

Foolen, Ad. 2008. The heart as a source of semiosis: The case of Dutch. In Farzad Sharifian, René Dirven, Ning Yu & Susanne Niemeier (eds.), *Culture, body, and language. Conceptualizations of internal body organs across cultures and languages*, 373–394. Berlin: Mouton de Gruyter.

Forstner, Dorothea. 1982. *Die Welt der christlichen Symbole*. Innsbruck: Tyrolia.

Freud, Sigmund. 1921. *Introductory lectures on psychoanalysis. A course of twenty-eight lectures delivered at the University of Vienna*. Authorized English translation by Joan Riviere. London: George Allen & Unwin.

Friederich, Wolf. 1966. *Moderne deutsche Idiomatik*. München: Max Hueber.

Fusaroli, Riccardo & Simone Morgagni. 2013. Introduction: Thirty years after. In: Riccardo Fusaroli & Simone Morgagni (eds.), *Conceptual Metaphors Theory: Thirty years after*, 1-13. Berlin & Boston: Mouton de Gruyter.

Gak, Vladimir G. 1998. Probleme der kontrastiven Phraseologie. Biblische Phraseologismen in der russischen und in der französischen Sprache. In Wolfgang Eismann (ed.), *EUROPHRAS 95. Europäische Phraseologie im Vergleich: Gemeinsames Erbe und kulturelle Vielfalt*, 237–246. Bochum: Brockmeyer.

Galnaitytė, Elzė, J. Pikčilingis & M. Sivickienė. 1989. *Mokyklinis Lietuvių-Rusų kalbų frazeologijos žodynas*. Kaunas: Šdviesa.

Gamkrelidze, Thomas V. & Vjačeslav V. Ivanov. 1995. *Indo-European and the Indo-Europeans. A reconstruction and historical analysis of a proto-language and proto-culture*. Berlin & New York: Mouton de Gruyter.

Gamst, Frederick C. 1980. Rethinking Leach's structural analysis of color and instructional categories in traffic control signals. In Eric B. Ross (ed.), *Beyond the myths of culture. Essays in cultural materialism*, 359–392. New York: Academic Press.

Garrison, Jeff & Masahiko Goshi. 1996. *Animal idioms*. Tokyo: Kodansha International.

Garrison, Jeff, Kayoko Kimiya, George Wallace & Masahiko Goshi. 2002. *Kodansha's dictionary of basic Japanese idioms*. Tokyo: Kodansha International.

Gavins, Joanna & Gerard Steen (eds.). 2003. *Cognitive poetics in practice*. London & New York: Routledge.

Geeraerts, Dirk. 1997. *Diachronic prototype semantics. A contribution to historical lexicology*. Oxford: Clarendon Press.

Geeraerts, Dirk. 2002. The interaction of metaphor and metonymy in composite expressions. In René Dirven & Ralf Pörings (eds.), *Metaphor and metonymy in comparison and contrast*, 435–465. Berlin & New York: Mouton de Gruyter.

Geeraerts, Dirk. 2006. Meaning and culture. In Dirk Geeraerts, *Words and other wonders. Papers on lexical and semantic topics*, 227–324. Berlin & New York: Mouton der Gruyter.

Geeraerts, Dirk & Caroline Gevaert. 2008. Hearts and (angry) minds in Old English. In Farzad Sharifian, René Dirven, Ning Yu & Susanne Niemeier (eds.), *Culture, body, and language: Conceptualizations of internal body organs across cultures and languages*, 319–347. Berlin & New York: Mouton de Gruyter.

Geeraerts, Dirk & Stefan Grondelaers. 1995. Looking back at anger: Cultural traditions and metaphorical patterns. In John R. Taylor & Robert E. MacLaury (eds.), *Language and the cognitive construal of the world*, 155–179. Berlin & New York: Mouton de Gruyter.

Geertz, Clifford. 1973. Thick description: Towards an interpretative theory of culture. In Clifford Geertz (ed.), *The interpretation of cultures. Selected essays*, 3–30. New York: Basic Books,

Gibbs, Raymond W. 1980. Spilling the beans on understanding and memory for idioms in conversation. *Memory and Cognition* 8. 149–156.

Gibbs, Raymond W. 1986. Skating on thin ice: Literal meaning and understanding idioms in conversation. *Discourse Processes* 9. 17–30.

Gibbs, Raymond W. 1990. Psycholinguistic studies on the conceptual basis of idiomaticity. *Cognitive Linguistics* 1. 417–451.

Gibbs, Raymond W. 1993. Why idioms are not dead metaphors. In Cristina Cacciari & Patrizia Tabossi (eds.), *Idioms: Processing, structure, and interpretation*, 57–77. Hillsdale, NJ: Lawrence Erlbaum.

Gibbs, Raymond W. 1994. *The poetics of mind. Figurative thought, language, and understanding*. Cambridge: Cambridge University Press.

Gibbs, Raymond W. 1996. Why many concepts are metaphorical. *Cognition* 61. 309–319.

Gibbs, Raymond W. 2000. Making good psychology out of blending theory. *Cognitive Linguistics* 11. 347–358.

Gibbs, Raymond W. 2001a. Evaluating contemporary models of figurative language understanding. *Metaphor and Symbol* 16. 317–333.

Gibbs, Raymond W. 2001b. Proverbial themes we live by. *Poetics* 29. 167–188.

Gibbs, Raymond W. 2002. A new look at literal meaning in understanding what is said and implicated. *Journal of Pragmatics* 34. 457–486.

Gibbs Raymond W. 2006. Metaphor interpretation as embodied simulation. *Mind and Language* 21 (3). 434–458.

Gibbs, Raymond W. (ed.). 2008. *The Cambridge handbook of metaphor and thought*. Cambridge: Cambridge University Press.

Gibbs, Raymond W. 2011. Are deliberate metaphors really deliberate? A question of human consciousness and action. *Metaphor and the Social World* 1 (1). 26–52.

Gibbs, Raymond W. 2015. Do pragmatic signals affect conventional metaphor understanding? A failed test of deliberate metaphor theory. *Journal of Pragmatics* 90. 77–87.

Gibbs, Raymond W. & Diñara Beitel. 1995. What proverb understanding reveals about how people think. *Psychological Bulletin* 118. 133–154.
Gibbs, Raymond W., Herbert L. Colston & Michael D. Johnson. 1996. Proverbs and the metaphorical mind. *Metaphor and Symbolic Activity* 11. 207–216.
Gibbs, Raymond W. & Herbert L. Colston. 2012. *Interpreting figurative meaning*. Cambridge & New York: Cambridge University Press.
Gibbs, Raymond W., Nandini P. Nayak & Copper Cutting. 1989. How to kick the bucket and not decompose: Analyzability and idiom processing. *Journal of Memory and Language* 28. 576–593.
Gibbs, Raymond W. & Jennifer E. O'Brien. 1990. Idioms and mental imagery: The metaphorical motivation for idiomatic meaning. *Cognition* 36. 3–68.
Giora, Rachel. 1995. On irony and negation. *Discourse Processes* 19. 239–264.
Giora, Rachel. 1997. Understanding figurative and literal language: The graded salience hypothesis. *Cognitive Linguistics* 8. 183–206.
Giora, Rachel. 1999. On the priority of salient meanings: Studies of literal and figurative language. *Journal of Pragmatics* 31. 919–929.
Giora, Rachel. 2002. Literal vs. figurative language: Different or equal? *Journal of Pragmatics* 34. 487–506.
Giora, Rachel & Ofer Fein. 1999a. Irony: Context and salience. *Metaphor and Symbol* 14. 241–257.
Giora, Rachel & Ofer Fein. 1999b. On understanding familiar and less-familiar figurative language. *Journal of Pragmatics* 31. 1601–1618.
Giora, Rachel, Ofer Fein & Tamir Schwartz. 1998. Irony. Graded salience and indirect negation. *Metaphor and Symbol* 13. 83–101.
Givón, Talmy. 1981. On the development of the numeral 'one' as an indefinite marker. *Folia Linguistica Historica* 2. 35–53.
Givón, Talmy. 1995. *Functionalism and grammar*. Amsterdam & Philadelphia: John Benjamins.
Glucksberg, Sam (ed.). 2001. *Understanding figurative language: From metaphors to idioms*. Oxford: Oxford University Press.
Glucksberg, Sam & Boaz Keysar. 1993. How metaphors work. In Andrew Ortony (ed.), *Metaphor and thought*, 2nd edn., 401–424. Cambridge: Cambridge University Press.
Glucksberg, Sam, Marry Brown & Matthew S. McGlone. 1993. Conceptual metaphors are not automatically accessed during idiom comprehension. *Memory and Cognition* 21. 711–719.
Goldberg, Adele E. 1995. *Constructions: A Construction Grammar approach to argument structure*. Chicago: The University of Chicago Press.
Goldberg, Adele E. 2006. *Constructions at work: The nature of generalization in language*. Oxford: Oxford University Press.
Goossens, Louis. 1990. Metaphtonomy: The interaction of metaphor and metonymy in expressions for linguistic action. *Cognitive Linguistics* 1 (3). 323–340.
Goossens, Louis, Paul Pauwels, Brygida Rudzka-Ostyn, Anne-Marie Simon-Vandenbergen & Johan Vanparys (eds.). 1995. *By word of mouth: Metaphor, metonymy and linguistic action in a cognitive perspective*. Amsterdam & Philadelphia: John Benjamins.
Gorbahn-Orme, Adeline & Franz Josef Hausmann. 1991. The dictionary of false friends. In Franz Josef Hausmann, O. Reichmann, H. E. Wiegand, L. Zgusta (eds.), *Wörterbücher. Dictionaries. Dictionnaires. Ein internationales Handbuch zur Lexikographie*, 2882–2888. Berlin & New York: Walter de Gruyter.

Grady, Joseph E., Todd Oakley & Seana Coulson. 1999. Blending and metaphor. In Raymond W. Gibbs & Gerard Steen (eds.), *Metaphor in cognitive linguistics: Selected papers from the fifth international cognitive linguistics conference in Amsterdam*, 101–124. Amsterdam & Philadelphia: John Benjamins.

Graf, Adolf Eduard. 1954. *Idiomatische Redewendungen der russischen und deutschen Sprache*. Berlin: Deutscher Verlag der Wissenschaften.

Granet, Marcel. 1963. *Das chinesische Denken. Inhalt. Form. Charakter*. München: R. Piper & Co Verlag.

Gréciano, Gertrud. 1983. *Signification et dénotation en allemand. La sémantique des expressions idiomatique*. Paris: Klincksieck.

Gréciano, Gertrud (ed.). 1989. *EUROPHRAS 88: Phraséologie Contrastive. Actes du Colloque International Klingenthal-Strasbourg, 12-16 mai 1988*. Strasbourg: USHS.

Gréciano, Gertrud. 1993. Zur Motiviertheit der Idiome. In Christoph Küper (ed.), *Motiviertheit im sprachlichen und im poetischen Kode*, 51–60. Tübingen: Stauffenburg.

Gréciano, Gertrud. 1997. Deutsch-Französische Konvergenzen. In Gertrud Gréciano & Annely Rothkegel (eds.), *Phraseme in Kontext und Kontrast*, 99–115. Bochum: Brockmeyer.

Gréciano, Gertrud. 2002. Semantik und Herkunftserklärungen von Phraseologismen. In D. Alan Cruse, Franz Hundsnurscher, Michael Job & Peter Rolf Lutzeier (eds.), *Lexicology. An international handbook on the nature and structure of words and vocabularies*, vol. 1, 433–441. Berlin & New York: Walter de Gruyter.

Grice, H. Paul. 1975. Logic and conversation. In Peter Cole & Jerry L. Morgan (eds.), *Syntax and semantics*, vol. 3: *Speech acts*, 41–58. New York: Academic Press.

Grigas, Kazys. 2000. *Lietuvių patarlės ir priežodžiai* [Lithuanian proverbs and sayings], vol. 1: *A-D*. Vilnius: Lietuvių literatūros ir tautosakos institutas.

Grigas, Kazys. 2008. *Lietuvių patarlės ir priežodžiai* [Lithuanian proverbs and sayings], vol. 2: *E-J*. Vilnius: Lietuvių literatūros ir tautosakos institutas.

Grzybek, Peter. 1988. Sprichwort und Fabel: Überlegungen zur Beschreibung von Sinnstrukturen in Texten. *Proverbium. Yearbook of International Proverb Scholarship* 5. 39–65.

Grzybek, Peter. 1994a. Proverb. In Walter A. Koch (ed.), *Simple forms. An encyclopaedia of simple text-types in lore and literature*, 227–241. Bochum: Brockmeyer.

Grzybek, Peter. 1994b. Foundations of semiotic proverb study. In Wolfgang Mieder (ed.), *Wise words. Essays on the proverb*, 31–97. New York & London: Garland Publishing.

Grzybek, Peter. 1994c. Comparison. In Walter A. Koch (ed.), *Simple forms. An encyclopaedia of simple text-types in lore and literature*, 68–74. Bochum: Brockmeyer.

Gulland, Daphne M. & David Hinds-Howell (eds.). 2001. *The Penguin dictionary of English idioms*. 2nd edn. London: Penguin Books.

Gura, Aleksandr V. 1997. *Simvolika životnyx v slavjanskoj narodnoj tradicii* [Animal symbolism in the Slavic folk tradition]. Moscow: Indrik.

Gurevič, Valerij V. & Žanna A. Dozorec. 1995. *Kratkij russko-anglijskij frazeologičeskij slovar'* [Concise Russian-English phraseological dictionary]. Moscow: Vlados.

Haas, Heather A. 2013. If it walks like a proverb and talks like a question: Proverbial and other formulaic interrogatives. *Proverbium. Yearbook of International Proverb Scholarship* 30. 19–50.

Haavio, Martti. 1967. *Suomalainen mytologia* [Finnish mythology]. Porvo & Helsinki: Werner Söderström Osakeyhtiö.

Häcki Buhofer, Annelies. 2004. Spielräume des Sprachverstehens. Psycholinguistische Zugänge zum individuellen Umgang mit Phraseologismen. In Kathrin Steyer (ed.), *Wortverbindungen – mehr oder weniger fest*, 144–164. Berlin & New York: Walter de Gruyter.

Häcki Buhofer, Annelies & Harald Burger. 1994. Phraseologismen im Urteil von Sprecherinnen und Sprechern. In Barbara Sandig (ed.), *EUROPHRAS 92: Tendenzen der Phraseologieforschung*, 1–33. Bochum: Brockmeyer.

Häcki Buhofer, Annelies, Stefanie Meier, Marcel Dräger & Tobias Roth. 2014. *Feste Wortverbindungen des Deutschen: Kollokationenwörterbuch für den Alltag*. Tübingen: Narr Francke Attempto.

Haiman, John. 1982. Discussion: Dictionaries and encyclopaedias again. *Lingua* 56. 353–355.

Hall, James. 1994. *Illustrated dictionary of symbols in Eastern and Western art*. Illustrated by Chris Puleston. New York: IconEditions.

Handelman, Don. 1998. Review article: The transformation of symbolic structures through history and the rhythms of time. *Semiotica* 119. 403–425.

Hanks, Patrick. 2004. The syntagmatics of metaphor and idiom. *International Journal of Lexicography* 17 (3). 245–274.

Hanks, Patrick. 2007. Metaphoricity is gradable. In Anatol Stefanowitsch and Stefan Th. Gries (eds.), *Corpus-based approaches to metaphor and metonymy*, 17–35. Berlin & New York: Mouton de Gruyter.

Hanks, Patrick. 2010. Nine issues in metaphor theory and analysis. *International Journal of Corpus Linguistics* 15(1). 133–150.

Hanks, Patrick. 2016. Three kinds of semantic resonance. In Tinatin Margalitadze & George Meladze (eds.), *Proceedings of the XVII Euralex international congress: Lexicography and linguistic diversity*, 37–48. Tbilisi: Ivane Javakhishvili Tbilisi State University.

Harkins, Jean & Anna Wierzbicka (eds.). 2001. *Emotions in crosslinguistic perspective*. Berlin & New York: Mouton de Gruyter.

Harré, Rom (ed.). 1986. *The social construction of emotions*. Oxford & New York: Basil Blackwell.

Harris, Richard Jackson, Brien M. Friel & Nolan Rett Mickelson. 2006. Attribution of discourse goals for using concrete- and abstract-tenor metaphors and similes with or without discourse context. *Journal of Pragmatics* 38 (6). 863–879.

Harweg, Roland. 1973. Grundzahlwort und unbestimmter Artikel. *Zeitschrift für Phonetik, Sprachwissenschaft und Kommunikationsforschung* 26. 320–327.

Hasada, Rie. 1997. Some aspects of Japanese cultural ethos embedded in nonverbal communicative behavior. In Fernando Poyatos (ed.), *Nonverbal communication and translation. New perspectives and challenges in literature, interpretation and the media*, 83–103. Amsterdam & Philadelphia: John Benjamin.

Hasada, Rie. 2002. 'Body part' terms and emotion in Japanese. *Pragmatics & Cognition* 10 (1–2). 107–128.

Hashimoto, Fumio. 1953. Wesenszüge des östlichen Denkens. In Klaus Piper (ed.), *Offener Horizont. Festschrift für Karl Jaspers*, 36–43. München: Piper.

Haspelmath, Martin & Ekkehard König. 2001. The European linguistic area: Standard Average European. In Martin Haspelmath, Ekkehard König, Wulf Oesterreicher & Wolfgang Raible (eds.), *Language typology and language universals. An international handbook*, vol. 2, 1492–1509. Berlin & New York: Walter de Gruyter.

Haught, Catrinel. 2013. A tale of two tropes: How metaphor and simile differ. *Metaphor and Symbol* 28 (4). 254–274.

Häusermann, Jörg. 1977. *Phraseologie. Hauptprobleme der deutschen Phraseologie auf der Basis sowjetischer Forschungsergebnisse*. Tübingen: Max Niemeyer.
Hausmann, Franz Josef. 2004. Was sind eigentlich Kollokationen? In Kathrin Steyer (ed.), *Wortverbindungen – mehr oder weniger fest*, 309–334. Berlin & New York: Walter de Gruyter.
HCI. 1999. *Hundred common Chinese idioms and set phrases*. Beijing: Sinolingua.
Hessky, Regina. 1987. *Phraseologie. Linguistische Grundlagen und kontrastives Modell deutsch-ungarisch*. Tübingen: Max Niemeyer.
Hidalgo-Downing, Laura & Blanca Kraljevic Mujic (eds.). 2020. *Performing metaphoric creativity across modes and contexts*. Amsterdam & Philadelphia: John Benjamins.
Hoffmann, Thomas & Graeme Trousdale (eds.). 2013. *The Oxford handbook of Construction Grammar*. Oxford: Oxford University Press.
Holland, Dorothy & Naomi Quinn (eds.). 1987. *Cultural models in language and thought*. Cambridge: Cambridge University Press.
Holzinger, Herbert J. 2018. Unikale Elemente oder phraseologisch gebundene Wörter? Antworten aus korpuslinguistischer Sicht. *Revista de Filología Alemana* 26. 199–213.
Honeck, Richard P. & Jon G. Temple. 1996. Proverbs and the complete mind. *Metaphor and Symbolic Activity* 11. 217–232.
Hrisztova-Gotthardt, Hrisztalina & Melita Aleksa Varga (eds.). 2015. *Introduction to paremiology. A comprehensive guide to proverb studies*. Warsaw & Berlin: De Gryuter Open.
Huang, Shuanfan. 2002. Tsou is different: A cognitive perspective on language, emotion, and body. *Cognitive Linguistics* 13 (2). 167–186.
Huizinga, Albertus. 1994. *Huizinga's spreekwoorden en gezegden. Herkomst, verklaring en vergelijking met Frans, Duits en Engels* [Huizinga's proverbs and sayings. Origin, explanation and comparison with French, German and English]. Baarn: Tirion.
Humboldt, Wilhelm von. 1979 [1836]. Über die Verschiedenheit des menschlichen Sprachbaues und ihren Einfluss auf die geistige Entwicklung des Menschengeschlechts. In Andreas Flitner & Klaus Giel (eds.), *Wilhelm von Humboldt, Werke in fünf Bänden*, Band 3: *Schriften zur Sprachphilosophie*, 386–756. Darmstadt: Wissenschaftliche Buchgesellschaft.
Hüning, Matthias & Barbara Schlücker. 2016. Multi-word expressions. In Peter O. Müller, Ingeborg Ohnheiser, Susan Olsen & Franz Rainer (eds.), *Word-formation. An international handbook of the languages of Europe in word-formation*, vol. 5, 450–466. Berlin & Boston& Mouton de Gruyter.
Ibarretxe-Antuñano, Iraide. 2008. Vision metaphors for the intellect: Are they really crosslinguistic? *Atlantis* 30 (1). 15–33.
Ibarretxe-Antuñano, Iraide. 2012. The importance of unveiling conceptual metaphors in a minority language: The case of Basque. In Anna Idström & Elisabeth Piirainen (eds.), *Endangered metaphors*, 253–273. Amsterdam & Philadelphia: John Benjamins.
Idström, Anna. 2012. Antlers as a metaphor of pride – What idioms reveal about the relationship between human and animal in Inari Saami conceptual system. In Anna Idström & Elisabeth Piirainen (eds.), *Endangered metaphors*, 275–292. Amsterdam & Philadelphia: John Benjamins.
Idström, Anna & Elisabeth Piirainen (eds.). 2012a. *Endangered metaphors*. Amsterdam & Philadelphia: John Benjamins.
Idström, Anna & Elisabeth Piirainen. 2012b. The wolf – an evil and ever-hungry beast or a nasty thief? Conventional Inari Saami metaphors and widespread idioms in contrast. *Metaphor and the Social World* 2-1. 87–113.

Ifrah, Georges. 1986. *Universalgeschichte der Zahlen*. Frankfurt am Main & New York: Campus.

Ikeda, Hiroko. 1971. *A type and motif index of Japanese folk-literature*. Helsinki. Suomalainen Tiedeakatemia.

Ikegami, Yoshihiko. 1985. From the Sapir-Whorf hypothesis to cultural semiotics – Some considerations on the "language-culture problem". In Kurt R. Jankowsky (ed.), *Scientific and humanistic dimensions of language. Festschrift for Robert Lado on the occasion of his 70th birthday on May 31, 1985*, 215–222. Amsterdam & Philadelphia: John Benjamins.

Ikegami, Yoshihiko. 1989. Culture and semiotics. In Walter A. Koch (ed.), *Culture and semiotics*, 13–26. Bochum: Brockmeyer.

Ikegami, Yoshihiko. 1991. Introduction: Semiotics and culture. In Yoshihiko Ikegami (ed.), *The empire of signs. Semiotic essays on Japanese culture*, 1–24. Amsterdam & Philadelphia: John Benjamins.

Iordanskaja, Lidija N. 1973. Tentative lexicographic definitions for a group of Russian words denoting emotions. In Ferenc Kiefer (ed.), *Trends in Soviet theoretical linguistics*, 389–410. Dordrecht: Reidel.

Iordanskaja, Lidija N. & Igor A. Mel'čuk. 1990. Semantics of two emotion verbs in Russian: *bojat'sja* 'to be afraid' and *nadejat'sja* 'to hope'. *Australian Journal of Linguistics* 10. 307–357.

Irvine, Judith T. (ed.). 1994. *Edward Sapir. The psychology of culture: A course of lectures*. Berlin & New York: Mouton de Gruyter.

Jackendoff, Ray S. 2002. *Foundations of language. Brain, meaning, grammar, evolution*. Oxford: Oxford University Press.

Jackendoff, Ray S. & David Aaron. 1991. Review article: More than cool reason: A field guide to poetic metaphor, by George Lakoff & Mark Turner. *Language. Journal of the Linguistic Society of America* 67. 320–338.

Jäkel, Olaf. 1988. Der handgreifliche Intellekt: zur Metaphorik geistiger Tätigkeiten. *Grazer Linguistische Studien* 30. 5–19.

Jäkel, Olaf. 1999. Kant, Blumenberg, Weinrich. Some forgotten contributions to the cognitive theory of metaphor. In Raymond W. Gibbs & Gerard Steen (eds.), *Metaphor in cognitive linguistics: Selected papers from the fifth international cognitive linguistics conference in Amsterdam*, 9–27. Amsterdam & Philadelphia: John Benjamins.

Jäkel, Olaf. 2003. *Wie Metaphern Wissen schaffen. Die kognitive Metapherntheorie und ihre Anwendung in Modell-Analysen der Diskursbereiche Geistestätigkeit, Wirtschaft, Wissenschaft und Religion*. 2. Auflage. Hamburg: Kovač.

Jaki, Sylvia. 2014. The explanatory power of Conceptual Integration Theory in the analysis of phraseological substitutions. In Vida Jesenšek & Dmitrij Dobrovol'skij (eds.), *Phraseologie und Kultur = Phraseology and culture*, 193–206. Budapet, Kansas, Maribor, Praha: Zora.

Jakobson, Roman. 1959. On linguistic aspects of translation. In Reuben Arthur Brower (ed.), *On translation*, 232–239. Cambridge, MA: Harvard University Press.

Jaksche, Harald, Ambros Sialm & Harald Burger (eds.). 1981. *Reader zur sowjetischen Phraseologie*. Berlin & New York: Walter de Gruyter.

Johnson, Mark (ed.). 1981. *Philosophical perspectives on metaphor*. Minneapolis: University of Minnesota Press.

Johnson, Mark. 1987. *The body in the mind. The bodily basis of meaning, imagination, and reason*. Chicago & London: The University of Chicago Press.

Jung, Carl Gustav. 1968. *Der Mensch und seine Symbole*. Olten & Freiburg i.B.: Walter Verlag.

Jung, Hermann. 1988. Zahlen und Zahlensymbolik in der Musik. Ein Forschungsbericht. In Werner Bies & Hermann Jung (eds.), *Mnemosyne. Festschrift für Manfred Lurker zum 60. Geburtstag*, 179–20. Baden-Baden: Koerner.

Kalevala = *The Kalevala. An epic poem after oral tradition by Elias Lönnrot*. Translated from the Finnish with an introduction and notes by K. Bossley and a foreword by A. B. Lord. New York & Oxford: Oxford University Press.

Kari, Erkki. 1993. *Naulan kantaan. Nykysuomen idiomisanakirja* [Nail on the head. Modern Finnish idiom dictionary]. Helsinki: Otava.

Katz, Albert N. 1998. Figurative language and figurative thought: A review. In Albert N. Katz, Cristina Cacciari, Raymond W. Gibbs & Mark Turner (eds.), *Figurative language and thought*, 3–43. New York & Oxford: Oxford University Press.

Katz, Albert N. 2000. Introduction to the special issue: The uses and processing of irony and sarcasm. *Metaphor and Symbol* 15. 1–3.

Katz, Albert N. & Todd R. Feretti. 2001. Moment-by-moment reading of proverbs in literal and nonliteral contexts. *Metaphor and Symbol* 16. 193–221.

Kennedy, John M. & Dan L. Chiappe. 1999. What makes a metaphor stronger than a simile? *Metaphor and Symbol* 12. 63–69.

Kessler, Stephan. 2013. *Theories of metaphor revised. Against a Cognitive Theory of Metaphor: An advocacy of classical metaphor*. Berlin: Logos.

Keysar, Boaz & Bridget M. Bly 1999. Swimming against the current: Do idioms reflect conceptual structure? *Journal of Pragmatics* 31. 1559–1578.

Keysar, Boaz, Yeshayahu Shen, Sam Glucksberg & William S. Horton. 2000. Conventional language: How metaphorical is it? *Journal of Memory and Language* 43. 576–593.

Kiefer, Ferenc. 1990. Linguistic, conceptual and encyclopedic knowledge: some implications for lexicography. In Tamás Magay & J. Zigány (eds.), *BudaLEX '88 Proceedings. Papers from the 3rd international Euralex congress, Budapest, 4-9 September 1988*, 1–10. Budapest: Akadémiai Kiadó.

Kim-Werner, Samhwa. 1996. *Phraseologisches Wörterbuch: Deutsch-Koreanisch. Am Beispiel der somatischen Phraseologismen*. Seoul: Yulin-Madang.

Kispál, Tamás. 2004. Leben ist eine Reise mit dem rollenden Stein und dem Moos. Sprichwörter in der kognitiven Metapherntheorie. In Csaba Földes (ed.), *Res humanae proverbiorum et sententiarum. Ad honorem Wolfgangi Mieder*, 129–139. Tübingen: Gunter Narr.

Kleiber, Georges. 1989. Sur la définition du proverbe. In Gertrud Gréciano (ed.), *EUROPHRAS 88: Phraséologie Contrastive. Actes du Colloque International Klingenthal-Strasbourg, 12-16 mai 1988*, 233–252. Strasbourg: USHS.

Kleiber, Georges. 1999. Les proverbes antinomiques: une grosse pierre "logique" dans le jardin toujours "universel" des proverbes. *Bulletin de la Société de linguistique de Paris* 94. 185–208.

Koch, Walter A. (ed.). 1989. *Culture and semiotics*. Bochum: Brockmeyer.

Kochman-Haładyj, Bożena. 2020. The vexing problem of gender stereotyping in world proverbs. *SKASE Journal of Theoretical Linguistics* 17 (1), 73+. https://www.academia.edu/43348958/The_vexing_problem_of_gender_stereotyping_in_world_proverbs (accessed 12 May 2021).

Koerner, E. F. Konrad (ed.). 1984. *Edward Sapir. Appraisals of his life and work*. Amsterdam & Philadelphia: John Benjamins.

Konerding, Klaus Peter. 1993. *Frames und lexikalisches Bedeutungswissen. Untersuchungen zur linguistischen Grundlegung einer Frametheorie und zu ihrer Anwendung in der Lexikographie*. Tübingen: Max Niemeyer.

König, Ekkehard & Martin Haspelmath. 1999. Der europäische Sprachbund. In Norbert Reiter (ed.), *Eurolinguistik: Ein Schritt in die Zukunft. Beiträge zum Symposion vom 24. bis 27. März 1997 im Jagdschloß Glienicke (bei Berlin)*, 111–127. Wiesbaden: Harrassowitz.

Korhonen, Jarmo. 1995. *Studien zur Phraseologie des Deutschen und des Finnischen I*. Bochum: Brockmeyer.

Korhonen, Jarmo (ed.). 1996. *Studien zur Phraseologie des Deutschen und des Finnischen II*. Bochum: Brockmeyer.

Korhonen, Jarmo. 2001. *Alles im Griff. Homma hanskassa. Saksa-suomi-idiomisanakirja. Idiomwörterbuch Deutsch-Finnisch*. Helsinki: Werner Söderström Oy.

Korhonen, Jarmo (ed.). 2008. *Saksa-suomi-suursanakirja. Großwörterbuch Deutsch-Finnisch*. Helsinki: Werner Söderström Oy.

Korhonen, Jarmo. 2007. Probleme der kontrastiven Phraseologie. In Harald Burger, Dmitrij Dobrovol'skij, Peter Kühn & Neal R. Norrick (eds.), *Phraseologie: Ein internationales Handbuch zeitgenössischer Forschung = Phraseology: An international handbook of contemporary research*, vol. 1, 574–589. Berlin & New York: Walter de Gruyter.

Kotb, Sigrun. 2002. *Körperteilbezogene Phraseologismen im Ägyptisch-Arabischen*. Wiesbaden: Reichert Verlag.

Kövecses, Zoltán. 1986. *Metaphors of anger, pride, and love: A lexical approach to the structure of concepts*. Amsterdam & Philadelphia: John Benjamins.

Kövecses, Zoltán. 1990. *Emotion concepts*. New York et al: Springer.

Kövecses, Zoltán. 1995a. The "container" metaphor of anger in English, Chinese, Japanese and Hungarian. In Zdravko Radman (ed.), *From a metaphorical point of view. A multidisciplinary approach to the cognitive content of metaphor*, 117–145. Berlin & New York: Walter de Gruyter.

Kövecses, Zoltán. 1995b. Anger: Its language, conceptualization, and physiology in the light of cross-cultural evidence. In John R. Taylor, Robert E. MacLaury (eds.), *Language and the cognitive construal of the world*, 181–196. Berlin & New York: Mouton de Gruyter.

Kövecses, Zoltán. 1995c. Metaphor and the folk understanding of anger. In James A. Russell, José-Miguel Fernández-Dols, Anthony S. Manstead & Jane C. Wellenkamp (eds.), *Everyday conceptions of emotion. An introduction to the psychology, anthropology and linguistics of emotion*, 49–71. Dordrecht, Boston & London: Kluwer Academic Publishers.

Kövecses, Zoltán 1998. Are there any emotion-specific metaphors? In Angeliki Athanasiadou & Elzbieta Tabakowska (eds.), *Speaking of emotions: Conceptualisation and expression*, 127–151. Berlin & New York: Mouton de Gruyter.

Kövecses, Zoltán. 2010. *Metaphor: A practical introduction*. 2nd edn. Oxford & New York: Oxford University Press.

Kövecses, Zoltán 2011. Methodological issues in conceptual metaphor theory. In Sandra Handl & Hans-Jörg Schmid (eds.), *Windows to the mind: Metaphor, metonymy and conceptual blending*, 23–39. Berlin & New York: Mouton de Gruyter.

Kövecses, Zoltán & Günter Radden. 1998. Metonymy: Developing a cognitive linguistic view. *Cognitive Linguistics* 9. 37–77.

Kremer, Ludger (ed.). 1993. *Diglossiestudien. Dialekt und Hochsprache im niederländisch-deutschen Grenzland*. Vreden: Landeskundliches Institut.

Kremer, Ludger. 1996. Standardisierungstendenzen und die Entstehung sprachlicher Bruchstellen am Beispiel der niederländisch-deutschen Kontaktzone. *Niederdeutsches Wort* 36. 59–74.

Kreuz, Roger J. & Sam Glucksberg. 1989. How to be sarcastic: The echoic reminder theory of verbal irony. *Journal of Experimental Psychology: General* 118. 374–386.

Kreuz, Roger J., M. A. Kassler, L. Coppenrath & B. McLain Allen. 1999. Tag question and common ground effects in the perception of verbal irony. *Journal of Pragmatics* 31. 1685–1700.

Kroeber, Alfred & Clyde Kluckhohn. 1952. *Culture: A critical review of concepts and definitions.* Papers of the Peabody Museum of Archaeology and Ethnology. 47 (1). Harvard: Harvard University.

Krohn, Karin. 1994. *Hand und Fuß. Eine konstrastive Analyse von Phraseologismen im Deutschen und Schwedischen.* Göteborg: Acta Universitatis Gothoburgensis.

Kroschewski, Annette. 2000. *False friends und true friends. Ein Beitrag zur Klassifizierung des Phänomens der intersprachlich-heterogenen Referenz und zu deren fremdsprachendidaktischen Implikationen.* Frankfurt am Main etc.: Peter Lang.

Kunin, Aleksandr V. 1984. *Anglo-russkij frazeologičeskij slovar' = English-Russian phraseological dictionary.* 4th edn., revised and enlarged. Moscow: Russkij jazyk.

Kustova, Galina I. 2002. O tipax proizvodnyx značenij s èksperiencial'noj semantikoj [On types of derived meanings with experiential semantics]. *Voprosy jazykoznanija* 2. 16–34.

Kutas, Marta & Kara D. Federmeier. 2000. Electrophysiology reveals semantic memory use in language comprehension. *Trends in Cognitive Sciences* 4 (12). 463–470.

Lai, Vicky Tzuyin, Tim Curran & Lise Menn. 2009. Comprehending conventional and novel metaphors: An ERP study. In *Brain Research* 1284. 145–155.

Lakoff, George. 1987a. Position paper on metaphor. In *Proceedings of the 1987 workshop on theoretical issues in natural language processing*, 194–197. Stroudsburg, PA: Association for Computational Linguistics.

Lakoff, George. 1987b. *Women, fire, and dangerous things: What categories reveal about the mind.* Chicago & London: The University of Chicago Press.

Lakoff, George. 1990. The Invariance Hypothesis: Is abstract reason based on image-schemas? *Cognitive Linguistics* 1. 39–74.

Lakoff, George. 1993. The contemporary theory of metaphor. In Andrew Ortony (ed.), *Metaphor and thought*, 2nd edn., 202–251. Cambridge: Cambridge University Press.

Lakoff, George. 2008. The neural theory of metaphor. In Raymond W. Gibbs (ed.), *The Cambridge handbook of metaphor and thought*, 17–38. Cambridge: Cambridge University Press.

Lakoff, George & Mark Johnson. 1980. *Metaphors we live by.* Chicago: The University of Chicago Press.

Lakoff, George & Mark Johnson. 1999. *Philosophy in the flesh. The embodied mind and its challenge to Western thought.* New York: Basic Books.

Lakoff, George & Zoltán Kövecses. 1987. The cognitive model of anger inherent in American English. In Dorothy Holland & Naomi Quinn (eds.), *Cultural models in language and thought*, 195–221. Cambridge: Cambridge University Press.

Lakoff, George & Mark Turner. 1989. *More than cool reason: A field guide to poetic metaphor.* Chicago & London: The University of Chicago Press.

Lakoff, Robin. 1975. *Language and woman's place.* New York: Harper & Row.

Langacker, Ronald W. 1987. *Foundations of Cognitive Grammar: Theoretical prerequisites.* Stanford: Stanford University Press.

Langacker, Ronald W. 2002. *Concept, image and symbol. The cognitive basis of grammar.* Berlin & New York: Mouton de Gruyter.

Langlotz, Andreas. 2006. *Idiomatic creativity. A cognitive-linguistic model of idiom-representation and idiom-variation in English*. Amsterdam & Philadelphia: John Benjamins.

Laurent, Jean-Paul, Guy Denhiéres, Christine Passerieus, Galina Iakimova & Marie-Christine Hardy-Baylé. 2006. On understanding idiomatic language: The salience hypothesis assessed by ERPs. *Brain Research* 1068, 151–160.

Lee, Christopher. J. & Albert N. Katz. 1998. The Differential Role of Ridicule in Sarcasm and Irony. *Metaphor and Symbol* 13. 1–15.

Leezenberg, Michiel. 2001. *Contexts of metaphor*. Amsterdam & London: Elsevier.

Levin, Viktor D. (ed.). 1969. *Poétičeskaja frazeologija Puškina*. [Pushkin's poetic phraseology] Moscow: Nauka.

Liebert, Wolf-Andreas. 1992. *Metaphernbereiche der deutschen Alltagssprache. Kognitive Linguistik und die Perspektiven einer Kognitiven Lexikographie*. Frankfurt am Main etc.: Peter Lang.

Lin, Marjorie & Schalk Leonard. 2000. *Dictionary of 1000 Chinese idioms*. New York: Hippocrene Books.

Lindner, Susan Jean. 1983. *A lexico-semantic analysis of English verb particle constructions*. Bloomington, Ind.: Indiana University Linguistics Club.

Lloyd, Geoffrey E. R. 2003. The problem of metaphor: Chinese reflections. In George R. Boys-Stones (ed.), *Metaphor, allegory, and the classical tradition. Ancient thought and modern revision*, 101–114. Oxford: Oxford University Press.

Long, Tomas Hill & Della Summers (eds.). 1979. *Longman dictionary of English idioms*. Harlow & London: Longman.

Longman ID. 1998 = *Longman idioms dictionary*. Harlow: Longman.

Lotman, Jurij M. 1971. Problèmes de la typologie des cultures. In Julia Kristeva, Josette Rey-Debove & Donna Umiker (eds.), *Essays in semiotics. Essais de sémiotique*, 46–56. The Hague & Paris: Mouton.

Lotman, Jurij M. 1974. *Aufsätze zur Theorie und Methodologie der Literatur und Kultur*. Kronberg Ts.: Scriptor.

Lotman, Yuri [Jurij] M. 1990. *Universe of the mind. A semiotic theory of culture*. Translated by Ann Shukman. Introduction by Umberto Eco. London & New York: I. B. Tauris Publishers.

Lotman, Jurij M. 1992. Simvol v sisteme kul'tury [Symbol in the cultural system]. In Jurij M. Lotman, *Izbrannye stat'i v trex tomax* [Selected articles in three volumes], vol. 1, 191–199. Tallinn: Alexandra.

Lotman, Jurij M. 1995. Kamen' i trava [Stone and grass]. In Mixail L. Gasparov (ed.), *Lotmanovskij sbornik*, 79–84. Moscow: IC-Garant.

Lotman, Jurij M. & Aleksandr M. Pjatigorskij. 2000. Tekst i funkcija [Text and function]. In Jurij M. Lotman (ed.), *Semiosfera* [Semiosphere], 434–442. S.-Peterburg: Iskusstvo–SPB.

Lotman, Jurij M.& Boris A. Uspenskij. 1971. O semiotičeskom mexanizme kul'tury [On the semiotic mechanism of culture]. *Trudy po znakovym sistemam* V. 144–166. [German translation: *Zum semiotischen Mechanismus der Kultur*. 1986. In Kurt Eimermacher, (ed.), *Semiotica Sovietica. Sowjetische Arbeiten der Moskauer und Tartuer Schule zu sekundären modellbildenden Zeichensystemen (1962-1973)*, 853–880. Aachen: Rader.]

Lowie, Robert Harry. 1934. *An introduction to cultural anthropology*. London: George G. Harrap & Co.

Lubensky, Sophia. 2013. *Russian-English dictionary of idioms*. Revised edn. New Haven & London: Yale University Press.

Lurker, Manfred. 1973. *Wörterbuch biblischer Bilder und Symbole*. München: Kösel.

Lutz, Catherine A. 1987. Goals, events, and understanding in Ifaluk emotion theory. In Dorothy Holland & Naomi Quinn (eds.), *Cultural models in language and thought*, 290–311. Cambridge: Cambridge University Press.

Lutz, Catherine A. 1988. *Unnatural emotions: Everyday sentiments on a Micronesian Atoll and their challenge to Western theory*. Chicago: The University of Chicago Press.

Luven, Yvonne. 2001. *Der Kult der Hausschlange. Eine Studie zur Religionsgeschichte der Letten und Litauer*. Köln: Böhlau Verlag.

Lyanda-Geller, Olga. 2018. From language to word-concept: Gustav Shpet's variations on inner form. *Slavic and East European Journal*. 62 (1). 60–76.

Makkai, Adam. 1972. *Idiom structure in English*. The Hague & Paris: Mouton.

Makkai, Adam. 1978. Idiomaticity as a language universal. In Joseph H. Greenberg (ed.), *Universals of human language*, vol. 3: *Word structure*, 401–448. Stanford, CA: Stanford University Press.

Makkai, Adam, Maxine Tull Boatner & J. E. Gates. 1995. *A dictionary of American idioms*. New York: Barron's.

Mal'ceva, Dina G. 2011. *Nemecko-russkij slovar' sovremennyx frazeologizmov = Aktuelle idiomatische Redensarten: Deutsch-russisches Wörterbuch*. Moscow: Russkij jazyk-Media.

Malotki, Ekkehart. 1983. *Hopi time. A linguistic analysis of the temporal concepts in the Hopi language*. Berlin, New York & Amsterdam: Mouton.

Mashal, Nira & Miriam Faust. 2009. Conventionalisation of novel metaphors: A shift in hemispheric asymmetry. *Laterality* 14 (6). 573–589.

Matsuki, Keiko. 1995. Metaphors of anger in Japanese. In John R. Taylor & Robert E. MacLaury (eds.), *Language and the cognitive construal of the world*, 137–151. Berlin & New York: Mouton de Gruyter.

Matsumoto, David. 1996. *Unmasking Japan. Myths and realities about the emotions of the Japanese*. Stanford, CA: Stanford University Press.

Matsumoto, Michihiro. 1988. *The unspoken way: Haragei: Silence in Japanese business and society*. Tokyo: Kodansha.

Mauranen, Anna & Seppo Raudaskoski. 2006. *Englannin Idiomisanakirja* [Idiom dictionary of English]. Helsinki: Otava.

Maynard, Michael L. & Senko K. Maynard. 1993. *101 Japanese idioms. Understanding Japanese language and culture through popular phrases*. Lincolnwood: Passport Books.

McCarthy, Michael. 2002. *Cambrige international dictionary of idioms*. 5th edn. Cambridge: Cambridge University Press.

McGlone, Matthew S. 1996. Conceptual metaphors and figurative language interpretation: Food for thought? *Journal of Memory and Language* 35. 544–565.

McGlone, Matthew S. 2001. Concepts as metaphors. In Sam Glucksberg (ed.), *Understanding figurative language: From metaphors to idioms*, 88–107. Oxford: Oxford University Press.

McGlone, Matthew S. 2007. What is the explanatory value of a conceptual metaphor? *Language & Communication*, 27 (2). 109–126.

McVeigh, Brian. 1996. Standing stomachs, clamoring chests and cooling livers: Metaphors in the psychological lexicon of Japanese. *Journal of Pragmatics* 26. 25–50.

Mejri, Salah. 2003. La stéréotypie du corps dans la phraséologie: approche contrastive. In Harald Burger, Gertrud Gréciano & Annelies Häcki Buhofer (eds.), *Flut von Texten – Vielfalt der Kulturen. Ascona 2001 zur Methodologie und Kulturspezifik der Phraseologie*, 203–217. Baltmannsweiler: Schneider.

Mel'čuk, Igor A. 1960. O terminax 'ustojčivost' i 'idiomatičnost' [On the terms 'stability' and 'idiomaticity']. *Voprosy jazykoznanija* 4. 73–79.

Mel'čuk, Igor. 1998. Collocations and lexical functions. In Anthony P. Cowie (ed.), *Phraseology. Theory, analysis, and applications*, 23–53. New York & Oxford: Oxford University Press.

Mel'čuk, Igor. 2012. Phraseology in the language, in the dictionary, and in the computer. *Yearbook of Phraseology* 3. 31–56.

Mel'čuk, Igor. 2015. Clichés, an understudied subclass of phrasemes. *Yearbook of Phraseology* 6. 55–85.

Mel'čuk, Igor & Tilmann Reuther. 1984. Bemerkungen zur lexikographischen Beschreibung von Phraseologismen und zum Problem unikaler Lexeme (an Beispielen aus dem Deutschen). *Wiener Linguistische Gazette* 33/34. 19–34.

Mellado Blanco, Carmen. 2015. The notion of cross-linguistic and cross-cultural equivalence in the field of phraseology. *International Journal of Lexicography* 28 (3). 385–390.

Mellado Blanco, Carmen. 2019. Phrasem-Konstruktionen kontrastiv Deutsch-Spanisch: ein korpusbasiertes Beschreibungsmodell anhand ironischer Vergleiche. *Yearbook of Phraseology* 10. 65–88.

Mellado Blanco, Carmen (ed.). 2021. *Productive patterns in phraseology and Construction Grammar. A multilingual approach*. Berlin & Boston: Walter de Gruyter.

Mellado Blanco, Carmen, Katrin Berty & Inés Olza (eds.). 2017. *Discurso repetido y fraseología textual (español y español-alemán)*. Frankfurt am Main: Iberoamericana Vervuert.

Mellado Blanco, Carmen, Fabio Mollica & Elmar Schafroth (eds.). In press. *Konstruktionen zwischen Lexikon und Grammatik. Phrasem-Konstruktionen monolingual, bilingial, multilingual*. Berlin: Walter de Gruyter.

Meunier, Fanny & Sylviane Granger (eds.). 2008. *Phraseology in foreign language learning and teaching*. Amsterdam & Philadelphia: John Benjamins.

Meyer, Heinz. 1975. *Die Zahlenallegorese im Mittelalter. Methode und Gebrauch*. München: Fink.

Mieder, Wolfgang. 1975. Buchtitel als Schlagzeile. *Sprachspiegel* 31. 36–43.

Mieder, Wolfgang. 1982-1993. *International proverb scholarship: An annotated bibliography*. New York & London: Garland Publishing.

Mieder, Wolfgang. 1985. *Sprichwort, Redensart, Zitat. Tradierte Formelsprache in der Moderne*. Bern: Peter Lang.

Mieder, Wolfgang. 1992. *A dictionary of American proverbs*. New York & Oxford: Oxford University Press.

Mieder, Wolfgang. 2009. *International bibliography of paremiology and phraseology*. Berlin: Walter de Gruyter.

Minsky, Marvin L. 1985. *The society of mind*. New York: Simon & Schuster.

Miquel, Dom Pierre. 1991. *Dictionnaire symbolique des animaux. Zoologie mystique*. Paris: Le Léopard d'Or,

Moi, Toril. 1986. *The Kristeva reader*. Oxford: Basil Blackwell.

Moncharmont, Michèle. 1998. *Les expressions figées de l'Allemand comportant un nom d'animal: élaboration d'un dictionnaire bilingue*. Aix en Provence: Université de Provence dissertation.

Mondry, Henrietta & John R. Taylor. 1998. The cultural dynamics of "national character": The case of the new Russians. In Angeliki Athanasiadou & Elzbieta Tabakowska (eds.), *Speaking of emotions: Conceptualisation and expression*, 28–48. Berlin & New York: Mouton de Gruyter.

Moon, Rosamund. 1998. *Fixed expressions and idioms in English. A corpus-based approach*. Oxford: Clarendon Press.

Moore, Kevin Ezra. 2014. *The spatial language of time: Metaphor, metonymy, and frames of reference*. Amsterdam & Philadelphia: John Benjamins.
Morgan, Jerry L. 1978. Two types of convention in indirect speech acts. In Peter Cole & Jerry L. Morgan (eds.), *Syntax and semantics*, vol. 9: *Pragmatics*, 261–280. New York: Academic Press.
Moser, Dietz-Rüdiger. 1982-1983. Elf als Zahl der Narren. Zur Funktion der Zahlenallegorese im Fastnachtsbrauch. *Jahrbuch für Volksliedforschung* 27-28. 346–363.
Moser, Dietz-Rüdiger. 1986. *Fastnacht, Fasching, Karneval. Das Fest der „verkehrten Welt"*. Graz: Styria Verlag.
Müller, Wolfgang. 1984. Zur Praxis der Bedeutungserklärung (BE) in (einsprachigen) deutschen Wörterbüchern und die semantische Umkehrprobe. In Herbert Ernst Wiegand (ed.), *Studien zur neuhochdeutschen Lexikographie V*, 359–448. Hildesheim & New York: Georg Olms.
Murakami, Mamiko. 1997. *Love, hate and everything in between. Expressing emotions in Japanese*. Translated by Ernest Reiss. Tokyo: Kodansha International.
Murphy, Gregory L. 1996. On metaphoric representation. *Cognition* 60 (2). 173–204.
Murphy, Gregory L. 1997. Reasons to doubt the present evidence for metaphoric representation. *Cognition* 62 (1). 99–108.
Murphy, Gregory L. 2002. Conceptual approaches I: An overview. In D. Alan Cruse, Franz Hundsnurscher, Michael Job & Peter Rolf Lutzeier (eds.), *Lexicology. An international handbook on the nature and structure of words and vocabularies*, vol. 1, 269–277. Berlin & New York: Walter de Gruyter.
Naciscione, Anita. 2010. *Stylistic use of phraseological units in discourse*. Amsterdam & Philadelphia: John Benjamins.
Naumann, Nelly. 1981. Haus und Gehöft. In Bruno Lewin (ed.), *Kleines Wörterbuch der Japanologie*, 132–136. Wiesbaden: Harrassowitz.
Nayak, Nandini P. & Raymond W. Gibbs. 1990. Conceptual knowledge in the interpretation of idioms. *Journal of Experimental Psychology: General* 119. 315–330.
Neuhaus, H. Joachim. 1988. False friends, Frege's sense, and word-formation. In Werner Hüllen & Rainer Schulze (eds.), *Understanding the lexicon. Meaning, sense and world knowledge in lexical semantics*, 252–257. Tübingen: Max Niemeyer.
Norrick, Neal R. 1980. Nondirect speech acts and double binds. *Poetics* 10. 33–47.
Norrick, Neal R. 1985. *How proverbs mean. Semantic studies in English proverbs*. Berlin, New York & Amsterdam: Mouton.
Norrick, Neal R. 1986. Stock similes. *Journal of Literary Semantics. An International Review* 15. 39–52.
Norrick, Neal R. 1987. Humorous proverbial comparisons. *Proverbium. Yearbook of International Proverb Scholarship* 4. 173–186.
Nöth, Winfried. 1990. Semiotics of magic. In Walter A. Koch (ed.), *Aspekte einer Kultursemiotik*, 141–163. Bochum: Brockmeyer.
Nöth, Winfried. 1995. *Handbook of semiotics*. Bloomington & Indianapolis: Indiana University Press.
Nowotny, Karl A. 1969. *Beiträge zur Geschichte des Weltbildes. Farben und Weltrichtungen*. Wien & Horn: Berger & Söhne OHG.
NSS. 1992 = *Nykysuomen sanakirja* [Dictionary of modern Finnish]. Porvoo: Söderström.
Nunberg, Geoffrey & Annie Zaenen. 1992. Systematic polysemy in lexicology and lexicography. In Hannu Tommola, Krista Varantola, Tarja-Salmi-Tolonen & Jurgen Schopp (eds.), *Proceedings of Euralex II*, 387–396. Tampere: University of Tampere.

Nunberg, Geoffrey, Ivan A. Sag & Thomas Wasow. 1994. Idioms. *Language* 70 (3). 491–538.
Núñez, Rafael E., Benjamin Motz & Ursina Teuscher. 2006. Time after time: The psychological reality of the ego-and time-reference-point distinction in metaphorical construals of time. *Metaphor and Symbol* 21 (3). 133–146.
Oakley, Todd V. 1998. Conceptual blending, narrative discourse, and rhetoric. *Cognitive Linguistics* 9 (4). 321–360.
Ōhashi, Ryōsuke. 1999. *Japan im interkulturellen Dialog*. München: Iudicium.
Ohnuki-Tierney, Emiko. 1987. *The monkey as mirror: Symbolic transformations in Japanese history and ritual*. Princeton: Princeton University Press.
Ohnuki-Tierney, Emiko. 1990. Introduction: The historicization of anthropology. In Emiko Ohnuki-Tierney (ed.), *Culture through time: Anthropological approaches*, 1–25. Stanford, CA: Stanford University Press.
Ohnuki-Tierney, Emiko. 1993. *Rice as self: Japanese identities through time*. Princeton: Princeton University Press.
Omazić, Marija. 2005. Cognitive linguistic theories in phraseology. *Jezikoslovlje* 6 (1–2). 37–56.
Omazić, Marija. 2008. Processing of idioms and idiom modifications: A view from cognitive linguistics. In Sylviane Granger & Fanny Meunier (eds.), *Phraseology: An interdisciplinary perspective*, 67–79. Amsterdam & Philadelphia: John Benjamins.
Omazić, Marija & Nihada Delibegović Džanić. 2009. Constraints to mechanisms of idiom modification. In Csaba Földes (ed.), *Phraseologie disziplinär und interdisziplinär*, 211–222. Tübingen: Gunter Narr.
Onishi, Kristine H. & Gregory L. Murphy. 1993. Metaphoric reference: When metaphors are not understood as easily as literal expressions. *Memory and Cognition* 21. 763–772.
Opie, Iona & Moira Tatem. 1995. *A dictionary of superstitions*. New York & Oxford: Oxford University Press.
Ortony, Andrew (ed.). 1993. *Metaphor and thought*. 2nd edn. Cambridge: Cambridge University Press.
Owens, Jonathan. 1996. Grammatisierung, Semantisierung und Sprachkontakt: Arabisch im Tschad-See-Gebiet. *Sprachtypologie und Universalienforschung* 49. 79–85.
Ozawa, Toshio. 1991. Die Schlange und ihre phantasierte Form Ryu. In Arnica Esterl & Wilhelm Solms (eds.), *Tiere und Tiergestaltige im Märchen*, 65–77. Regensburg: Erich Röth.
Paczolay, Gyula. 1994. *European, Far-Eastern and some Asian proverbs. A comparison of European, Chinese, Korean, Japanese, Vietnamese and other Asian proverbs*. Veszprém: University of Veszprém.
Paczolay, Gyula. 1997. *European proverbs in 55 languages with equivalents in Arabic, Persian, Sanskrit, Chinese and Japanese*. Veszprém: Nyomda.
Padučeva, Elena V. 1988. O paradigme reguljarnoj mnogoznačnosti (na primere glagolov zvuka) [On the paradigm of regular polysemy (verbs of sound)]. *Naučno-texničeskaja informacija (Serija 2)*, 4. 28–40.
Padučeva, Elena V. 2004a. *Dinamičeskie modeli v semantike leksiki* [Dynamic models in lexical semantics]. Moscow: Jazyki slavjanskoj kul'tury.
Padučeva, Elena V. 2004b. Metafora i ee rodstvenniki [Metaphor and its relatives]. In Jurij D. Apresjan (ed.), *Sokrovennye smzsly. Slovo. Tekst. Kul'tura* [Innermost meanings. Word. Text, Culture], 187–203. Moscow: Jazyki slavjanskoj kul'tury.
Palmer, Gary B. 1996. *Toward a theory of cultural linguistics*. Austin: University of Texas Press.
Pamies, Antonio. 2011. À propos de la motivation phraséologique. In Antonio Pamies & Dmitrij Dobrovol'skij (eds.), *Linguo-cultural competence and phraseological motivation*, 25–39. Baltmannsweiler: Schneider.

Pamies-Bertrán, Antonio & Wang Yuan. 2020. The spatial conceptualization of time in Spanish and Chinese. *Yearbook of Phraseology* 11. 107–138.
Panther, Klaus-Uwe & Günter Radden (eds.). 1999. *Metonymy in language and thought.* Amsterdam & Philadelphia: John Benjamins.
Papafragou, Anna. 1996. On metonymy. *Lingua* 99. 169–195.
Parad, Jouko. 2003. *Biblische Verbphraseme und ihr Verhältnis zum Urtext und zur Lutherbibel. Ein Beitrag zur historisch-kontrastiven Phraseologie am Beispiel deutscher und schwedischer Bibelübersetzungen.* Frankfurt am Main etc.: Peter Lang.
Parina, Irina. 2014. Ein Gentleman vom Scheitel bis zur Sohle: Korpusbasierte Untersuchung und lexikographische Beschreibung der phraseologischen Synonyme. In Martine Dalmas & Elisabeth Piirainen (eds.), *Figurative Sprache – Figurative Language – Langage Figuré. Festgabe für Dmitrij O. Dobrovol'skij,* 161–172. Tübingen: Stauffenburg.
Paul, Hermann. 1920 [1880]. *Prinzipien der Sprachgeschichte.* 5. Auflage. Tübingen: Max Niemeyer.
Paulaharju, Samuli. 2003. *Karjalaista rakennustaitoa. Kuvaus Pohjois- ja Itä-Karjalan rakennuksista* [Karelian building skills. Description of buildings in North and East Karelia]. Jyväskylä: Suomalaisen Kirjallisuuden Seura.
Payne, Michael. 1996. Introduction. Some versions of cultural and critical theory. In Michael Payne (ed.), *A dictionary of cultural and critical theory,* 1–12. Oxford: Blackwell Publishers.
Peirce, Charles Sanders. 1960. *Collected papers of Charles Sanders Peirce,* vol. 2: *Elements of logic.* Cambridge, MA: Harvard University Press.
Pen'kovskij, Aleksandr B. 2005. *Zagadki puškinskogo teksta i slovarja. Opyt filologičeskoj germenevtiki* [Mysteries of Pushkin's text and lexicon. Towards philological hermeneutics]. Moscow: Jazyki slavjanskoj kul'tury.
Pentikäinen, Juha. 1987. *Kalevalan mytologia* [Kalevala mythology]. Helsinki: Gaudeamus.
Petermann, Jürgen, Renate Hansen-Kokoruš & Tamara Bill. 1995. *Russisch-deutsches phraseologisches Wörterbuch.* Ed. by Josip Matešić. Leipzig, Berlin & München: Langenscheidt & Enzyklopädie.
Peters, Pam. 2007. Similes and other evaluative idioms in Australian English. In Paul Skandera (ed.), *Phraseology and culture in English,* 235–255. Berlin: Mouton de Gruyter.
Petrova, Roumyana. 2002. Gender aspects of English proverbs. *Proverbium. Yearbook of International Proverb Scholarship* 19. 337–348.
Philippi, Donald L. 1969. *Kojiki.* Translated with an introduction and notes. Princeton: Princeton University Press & Tokyo: University of Tokyo Press.
Piirainen, Elisabeth. 1999. Falsche Freunde in der Phraseologie des Sprachenpaares Deutsch-Niederländisch. In Annette Sabban (ed.), *Phraseologie und Übersetzen. Phrasematia II,* 187–204. Bielefeld: Aisthesis Verlag.
Piirainen, Elisabeth. 2000. *Phraseologie der westmünsterländischen Mundart.* Baltmannsweiler: Schneider.
Piirainen, Elisabeth. 2001a. Der hat aber Haare auf den Zähnen! Geschlechtsspezifik in der deutschen Phraseologie. In Rudolf Hoberg (ed.), *Sprache – Erotik – Sexualität,* 284–307. Berlin: Erich Schmidt Verlag.
Piirainen, Elisabeth. 2001b. Phraseologie und Arealität. *Deutsch als Fremdsprache* 38. 240–243.
Piirainen, Elisabeth. 2002. Ein Wink mit dem Scheunentor? Nochmals zur Bekanntheit von Idiomen. *Deutsch als Fremdsprache* 39. 221–225.
Piirainen, Elisabeth. 2003a. Areale Aspekte der Phraseologie: Zur Bekanntheit von Idiomen in den regionalen Umgangssprachen. In Harald Burger, Gertrud Gréciano & Annelies Häcki Buhofer (eds.), *Flut von Texten – Vielfalt der Kulturen. Ascona 2001 zur Methodologie und Kulturspezifik der Phraseologie,* 117–128. Baltmannsweiler: Schneider.

Piirainen, Elisabeth. 2003b. *Hij is naar de eeuwige jachtvelden vertrokken*: Idiome des semantischen Feldes 'sterben' im Niederländischen. *Neerlandica Wratislaviensia* 14. 109–134.
Piirainen, Elisabeth. 2004a. False friends in conventional figurative units. In Csaba Földes & Jan Wirrer (eds.), *Phraseologie als Gegenstand sprach- und kulturwissenschaftlicher Forschung*, 311–321. Baltmannsweiler: Schneider.
Piirainen, Elisabeth. 2004b. Cognitive, cultural and pragmatic aspects of dialectal phraseology – exemplified by the Low German dialect "Westmünsterländisch". *Dialectologia et Geolinguistica* 12. 46–47.
Piirainen, Elisabeth. 2004c. Culture in figurative language: "Standard Average European" vs. dialects. In T. Baccouche, Harald Burger, Annelies Haecki-Buhofer & Salah Mejri (eds.), *L'espace euro-méditerranéen: Une idiomaticité partagée. Actes du colloque international (Hammamet 19, 20 & 21 septembre 2003)*, vol. 2, 339–354. Tunis : Cahiers du CERES.
Piirainen, Elisabeth. 2007. Dialectal Phraseology – Linguistic Aspects. In Harald Burger, Dmitrij Dobrovol'skij, Peter Kühn & Neal R. Norrick. (eds.), Phraseologie: Ein internationales Handbuch zeitgenössischer Forschung = Phraseology: An international handbook of contemporary research, vol. 1, 530–540. Berlin & New York: Walter de Gruyter.
Piirainen, Elisabeth. 2012. *Widespread idioms in Europe and beyond. Toward a lexicon of common figurative units*. New York etc.: Peter Lang.
Piirainen, Elisabeth. 2016. *Lexicon of common figurative units. Widespread idioms in Europe and beyond*, vol. II. In cooperation with József Attila Balázsi. New York etc.: Peter Lang.
Piirainen, Elisabeth & Ari Sherris. 2015. *Language endangerment*. Amsterdam & Philadelphia: John Benjamins.
Pilard, Georges, Stuart Fortey, Kate Allan & Nadia Cornuau. 2012. *Harrap's dictionnaire des expressions anglaises*. Paris: Harrap.
Pilshchikov, Igor & Mikhail Trunin 2016. The Tartu-Moscow School of Semiotics: A transnational perspective. *Sign Systems Studies* 44 (3). 368–401.
Piñel López, Rosa María. 1997. El mundo animal en las expresiones alemanas y españolas y sus connotaciones socioculturales. *Revista de Filología Alemana* 5. 259–274.
Portis-Winner, Irene. 1986. Semiotics of culture. In John Deely, Brooke Williams & Felicia E. Kruse (eds.), *Frontiers in semiotics*, 181–184. Bloomington: Indiana University Press.
Portis-Winner, Irene. 1994. *Semiotics of culture: "The strange Intruder"*. Bochum: Brockmeyer.
Portis-Winner, Irene & Thomas G. Winner. 1976. The semiotics of cultural texts. *Semiotica* 18. 101–156.
Porzig, Walter. 1950. *Das Wunder der Sprache. Probleme, Methoden und Ergebnisse der modernen Sprachwissenschaft*. München: Lehnen.
Posner, Roland. 1984. Die Zahlen und ihre Zeichen. Geschichte und Ökonomie der Zahldarstellung. In Klaus Oehler (ed.), *Zeichen und Realität. Akten des 3. semiotischen Kolloquiums der Deutschen Gesellschaft für Semiotik e.V. Hamburg 1981*, 235–247. Tübingen: Stauffenburg.
Posner, Roland. 1991. Kultur als Zeichensystem. Zur semiotischen Explikation kulturwissenschaftlicher Grundbegriffe. In Aleida Assmann & Dietrich Harth (eds.), *Kultur als Lebenswelt und Monument*, 37–74. Frankfurt am Main: Fischer Taschenbuch Verlag.
Potebnja, Aleksandr A. 1892. *Mysl' i jazyk* [Thought and language]. 2nd edn. Xar'kov: T-ja Adol'fa Dorre.
Pretzell, Klaus-Albrecht. 1970. Zur Frage des Schlangenbildes im japanischen Altertum. *Nachrichten der Gesellschaft für Natur- und Völkerkunde Ostasiens. Zeitschrift für Kultur und Geschichte Ost- und Südostasiens* 107/108. 39–70.

Quinn, Naomi. 1987. Convergent evidence for a cultural model of American marriage. In Dorothy Holland & Naomi Quinn (eds.), *Cultural models in language and thought*, 173–192. Cambridge: Cambridge University Press.

Quinn, Naomi. 1991. The cultural basis of metaphor. In James W. Fernandez (ed.), *Beyond metaphor. The theory of tropes in anthropology*, 56–93. Stanford, CA: Stanford University Press.

Quinn, Naomi & Dorothy Holland. 1987. Preface. In Dorothy Holland & Naomi Quinn (eds.), *Cultural models in language and thought*, vii–x. Cambridge: Cambridge University Press.

Radden, Günter. 2002. How metonymic are metaphors? In René Dirven & Ralf Pörings (eds.), *Metaphor and metonymy in comparison and contrast*, 407–434. Berlin & New York: Mouton de Gruyter.

Radden, Günter. 2003. The metaphor TIME AS SPACE across languages. *Zeitschrift für Interkulturellen Fremdsprachenunterricht* 8 (2–3). 226–239.

Rajxštejn, Aleksandr D. 1980. *Sopostavitel'nyj analiz nemeckoj i russkoj frazeologii* [Contrastive analysis of German and Russian phraseology]. Moscow: Vysšaja škola.

Rakova, Marina. 2003. *The extent of the literal. Metaphor, polysemy and theories of concepts*. New York: Palgrave Macmillan.

Rakusan, Jaromira. 2000. Language constructs of animals and men in two cultures: Czech vs. English similes with animals in comparatum. *Multilingua. Journal of Cross-Cultural and Interlanguage Communication* 19. 265–279.

Ramiro, Christian, Mahesh Srinivasan, Barbara C. Malt & Yang Xu. 2018. Algorithms in the historical emergence of word senses. *Proceedings of the National Academy of Sciences of the USA* 115 (10). 2323–2328.

Reda, Ghsoon. 2016. Figurative meaning construction: From cognitive operations to thought and culture. *Open Linguistics* (2). 610–619.

Reddy, Michael. 1979. The conduit metaphor: A case of frame conflict in our language about language. In Andrew Ortony (ed.), *Metaphor and thought*, 284–324. Cambridge: Cambridge University Press.

Revzina, Ol'ga. G. 1995. Čislo i količestvo v poetičeskom jazyke i poetičeskom mire M. Cvetaevoj [Number and quantity in the language and poetic world of M. Cvetaeva]. *Lotmanovskij sbornik* 1. 619–641.

Rey, Alain. & Sophie Chantreau. 2003. *Dictionnaire des expressions et locutions*. 2ème éd. Paris: Les usuels du Robert.

Ritchie, David. 2003. "ARGUMENT IS WAR" – Or is it a game of chess? Multiple meanings in the analysis of implicit metaphors. *Metaphor and Symbol* 18. 125–146.

Ritchie, David. 2006. *Context and connection in metaphor*. Basingstoke: Palgrave Macmillan.

Rival, Laura (ed.). 1998. *The social life of trees: Anthropological perspectives on tree symbolism*. Oxford & New York: Berg.

Roget, Peter Mark. 1992. *Roget's international thesaurus*. 5th edition. Ed. by Rober L. Chapman. New York: Harper Perennial.

Röhrich, Lutz. 1991. *Das große Lexikon der sprichwörtlichen Redensarten*. Freiburg i.B.: Herder.

Rooth, Anna Birgitta. 1968. Domestic animals and wild animals as symbols and referents in the proverbs. *Proverbium. Yearbook of International Proverb Scholarship* 11. 286–288.

Rosch, Eleanor. 1975. Cognitive representations of semantic categories. *Journal of Experimental Psychology: General* 104. 192–233.

Rosch, Eleanor. 1978. Principles of categorization. In Eleanor Rosch & Barbara B. Lloyd (eds.), *Cognition and categorization*, 27–48. Hillsdale, NJ: Lawrence Erlbaum.

Roscher, Wilhelm Heinrich. 1909. *Die Tessarakontaden und Tesserakontadenlehren der Griechen und anderer Völker. Ein Beitrag zur vergleichenden Religionswissenschaft, Volkskunde und Zahlenmystik sowie zur Geschichte der Medizin und Biologie.* Leipzig: Königlich Sächsische Gesellschaft der Wissenschaften zu Leipzig.

Ross, Bruce. 1988. *The inheritance of animal symbols in modern literature and world culture. Essays, notes and lectures.* New York etc.: Peter Lang.

Ross, Don. 1993. *Metaphor, meaning and cognition.* New York etc.: Peter Lang.

Ruiz de Mendoza Ibañez, Francisco J. & Alicia Galera-Masegosa. 2011. Going beyond metaphtonymy: Metaphoric and metonymic complexes in phrasal verb interpretation. *Language Value* 3 (1). 1–29.

Rumpf, Fritz. 1938. *Japanische Volksmärchen.* Übersetzt, ausgewählt und eingeleitet von Fritz Rumpf. Jena: Diederichs.

Sabban, Annette. 2008. Critical observations on the culture-boundness of phraseology. In Sylviane Granger & Fanny Meunier (eds.), *Phraseology: An interdisciplinary perspective*, 229–241. Amsterdam & Philadelphia: John Benjamins.

Sanseido (ed.). 2002. *A handbook of common Japanese phrases.* Translated and adapted by John Brennan. Tokyo: Kodansha International.

Sapir, Edward. 1949. The status of linguistics as a science. In David G. Mandelbaum (ed.), *Selected writings of Edward Sapir in language, culture, and personality*, 160–166. Berkeley: University of California Press.

Sapir, Edward. 1964. Conceptual categories in primitive languages. In Dell Hymes (ed.), *Language in culture and society*, 128–150. New York: Harper & Row.

Sasaki, Mizue. 1993. *The complete Japanese expression guide.* Rutland, Vermont & Tokyo: Tuttle.

Sauermann, Dietmar. 1996. *Damals bei uns in Westfalen. Vom alten Brauch in Stadt und Land. Ländliches Brauchtum im Jahreslauf in Bildern und Berichten aus dem Archiv für westfälische Volkskunde.* Münster: Landwirtschaftsverlag.

Saussure, Ferdinand de. 1916. *Cours de linguistique generale.* Publié par Charles Bally et Albert Sechehaye. Paris: Payot.

Schank, Roger C. 1975. *Conceptual information processsing.* Amsterdam & New York: North-Holland.

Schank, Roger C. & Robert P. Abelson. 1977. *Scripts, plans, goals and understanding. An inquiry into human knowledge structures.* Hillsdale, NJ: Lawrence Erlbaum.

Schauer-Trampusch, Tatjana. 2002. Klein, aber oho! Symbole und Metaphern in der slowenischen Tierphraseologie am Beispiel der Konzepte AMEISE, BIENE, WESPE und FLIEGE. In Elisabeth Piirainen & Ilpo Tapani Piirainen (eds.), *Phraseologie in Raum und Zeit. Akten der 10. Tagung des Westfälischen Arbeitskreises "Phraseologie/Parömiologie" Münster 2001*, 57–75. Baltmannsweiler: Schneider.

Schemann, Hans. 1989. *Synonymwörterbuch der deutschen Redensarten.* Straelen: Straelener Manuskripte Verlag.

Schenda, Rudolf. 1993. *Von Mund zu Ohr: Bausteine zu einer Kulturgeschichte volkstümlichen Erzählens in Europa.* Göttingen: Vandenhoeck & Ruprecht.

Schepers, Josef. 1995. *Haus und Hof westfälischer Bauern.* Münster: Aschendorff.

Scherf, Walter. 1987. *Die Herausforderung des Dämons. Form und Funktion grausiger Kindermärchen. Eine volkskundliche und tiefenpsychologische Darstellung der Struktur, Motivik und Rezeption von 27 untereinander verwandten Erzähltypen.* München: Saur.

Schimmel, Annemarie. 1987. Numbers. An Overview. In Mircea Eliade (ed.), *The encyclopedia of religion*, vol. 11, 13–18. New York & London: Macmillan Publishing.

Schmidt, Ulrich A. 1994. Zahl und Zahlwort in Sprache und Text. In Peter Canisius, Clemens-Peter Herbermann & Gerhard Tschauder (eds.), *Text und Grammatik. Festschrift für Roland Harweg zum 60. Geburtstag*, 239–247. Bochum: Brockmeyer.

Schöner, Erich. 1964. *Das Viererschema in der antiken Humoralpathologie*. Mit einem Vorwort und einer Tafel von R. Herrlinger. Wiesbaden: Franz Steiner Verlag.

Schottmann, Hans. 2012. *Vergleichende Idiomatik des Schwedischen*. Berlin: Lit Verlag.

Schuppener, Georg. 1996. *Germanische Zahlwörter: sprach- und kulturgeschichtliche Untersuchungen insbesondere zur Zahl 12*. Leipzig: Leipziger Universitätsverlag.

Schuppener, Georg. 1998. Bedeutende Zahlen in der germanischen Mythologie. In Georg Schuppener & Reiner Tetzner (eds.), *Glaube und Mythos*. Leipzig: Arbeitskreis für Vergleichende Mythologie.

Schweigert, Wendy. A. 1986. The comprehension of familiar and less familiar idioms. *Journal of Psycholinguistic Research* 15. 33–46.

Schweigert, Wendy A. & Danny R. Moates. 1988. Familiar idiom comprehension. *Journal of Psycholinguistic Research* 17. 281–296.

Schwind, Martin. 1967. *Das japanische Inselreich*, Band 1: *Die Naturlandschaft*. Berlin: Walter de Gruyter.

Searle, John R. 1969. *Speech acts. An essay in the philosophy of language*. Cambridge: Cambridge University Press.

Searle, John R. 1975. Indirect speech acts. In Peter Cole & Jerry L. Morgan (eds.), *Syntax and semantics*, vol. 3: *Speech acts*, 59–82. New York: Academic Press.

Searle, John R. 1979. Metaphor. In Andrew Ortony (ed.), *Metaphor and thought*, 92–123. Cambridge: Cambridge University Press.

Sebeok, Thomas A. 1986a. Culture. In Thomas A. Sebeok (ed.), *Encyclopaedic dictionary of semiotics*, 163–166. Berlin & New York: Mouton de Gruyter.

Sebeok, Thomas A. 1986b. Symbol. In Thomas A. Sebeok (ed.), *Encyclopaedic dictionary of semiotics*, 1027–1030. Berlin & New York: Mouton de Gruyter.

Sebeok, Thomas A. 1988. In what sense is language a "primary modeling system?" In Henri Broms, Rebecca Kaufmann (eds.), *Semiotics of culture. Proceedings of the 25th symposium of the Tartu-Moscow School of Semiotics, Imatra, Finland, 27th-29th July, 1987*, 67–76. Helsinki: Arator.

Segura García, Blanca. 1997. Kulturspezifische Phraseologismen in literarischen Texten und ihre Interferenzen beim Übersetzen vom Spanischen ins Deutsche. In Annette Sabban (ed.), *Phraseme im Text: Beiträge aus romanistischer Sicht*, 221–236. Bochum: Brockmeyer.

Šekasjuk, Boris P. 2010. *Novyj nemecko-russkij frazeologičeskij slovar'* [A new German-Russian phraseological dictionary]. 2nd edn. Moscow: Librokom.

Semenenko, Aleksei 2012. *The texture of culture: An introduction to Yuri Lotman's semiotic theory*. New York: Palgrave Macmillan.

Semenova, O'ga A. 2011. *Russko-nemeckij, nemecko-russkij slovar' frazeologizmov* [A Russian-German and German-Russian phraseological dictionary]. Minsk: Poppuri.

Semino, Elena. 2002. A cognitive stylistic approach to mind style in narrative fiction. In Elena Semino & Jonathan V. Culpeper (eds.), *Cognitive stylistics: Language and cognition in text analysis*, 95–122. Amsterdam & Philadelphia: John Benjamins.

Semino, Elena. 2008. *Metaphor and discourse*. Cambridge: Cambridge University Press.

Shore, Bradd. 1996. *Culture in mind: Cognition, culture, and the problem of meaning*. New York & Oxford: Oxford University Press.

Shukman, Ann. 1977. *Literature and semiotics. A study of the writings of Yu. M. Lotman*. Amsterdam & New York: North-Holland.

Shukman, Ann. 1986. Moscow-Tartu School. In Thomas A. Sebeok (ed.), *Encyclopaedic dictionary of semiotics*, 166–168. Berlin & New York: Mouton de Gruyter.

Šichová, Kateřina. 2013a: Kann *er ihr* Hörner aufsetzen? Zu Geschlechtsspezifik und Restriktionen von deutschen und tschechischen somatischen Phrasemen. *Aussiger Beiträge* 7. 211–236.

Šichová, Kateřina. 2013b. *Mit Händen und Füssen reden. Verbale Phraseme im deutsch-tschechischen Vergleich*. Tübingen: Julius Groos.

Siebs, Benno Eide. 1969. *Weltbild, symbolische Zahl und Verfassung*. Aalen: Scientia.

Simpson, John. 1992. *The concise Oxford dictionary of proverbs*. 2nd edn. New York & Oxford: Oxford University Press.

Sinclair, John. 1991. *Corpus, concordance, collocation*. Oxford: Oxford University Press.

Sirelius, Uuno Taavi. 1921. *Suomen kansanomaista kulttuuria II* [Finnish folk culture II]. Helsinki: Otava.

Škljarov, Vladimir T., Rainer Eckert & Horst Engelke. 1977. *Kratkij russko-nemeckij frazeologičeskij slovar'. Okolo 800 frazeologizmov = Kurzes russisch-deutsches phraseologisches Wörterbuch mit etwa 800 Phraseologismen*. Moscow: Russkij jazyk.

Slavik, Jan. 1994. *Dance of colours. Basic patterns of colour symbolism in Mahāyāna Buddhism*. Göteborg: Etnografiska Museet.

Smith, Philip. 2001. *Cultural theory. An introduction*. Massachusetts & Oxford: Blackwell Publishers.

Speake, Jennifer (ed.). 1999. *The Oxford dictionary of idioms*. Oxford: Oxford University Press.

Spears, Richard A. 1997. *NTC's thematic dictionary of American idioms*. Lincolnwood: NTC Publishing Group.

Spears, Richard A. 1999. *Phrases and idioms. A practical guide to American English expressions*. Lincolnwood: NTC Publishing Group.

Sperber, Dan & Deirdre Wilson. 1981. Irony and the use-mention distinction. In Peter Cole (ed.), *Radical pragmatics*, 295–312. New York: Academic Press.

Sperber, Dan & Deirdre Wilson. 1986. *Relevance. Communication and cognition*. Oxford: Basil Blackwell.

Sprenger, Simone A., Willem J.M. Levelt & Gerard Kempen. 2006. Lexical access during the production of idiomatic phrases. *Journal of Memory and Language* 54. 161–184.

Steen, Gerard. 2008. The paradox of metaphor: Why we need a three-dimensional model of metaphor. *Metaphor and Symbol* 23 (4). 213–241.

Steen, Gerard. 2015. Developing, testing and interpreting deliberate metaphor theory. *Journal of Pragmatics* 90. 67–72.

Stefanowitsch, Anatol. 2007. Words and their metaphors: A corpus-based approach. In Anatol Stefanowitsch & Stefan Th. Gries (eds.), *Corpus-based approaches to metaphor and metonymy*, 63–105. Berlin & New York: Mouton de Gruyter.

Stepanov, Jurij S. 1997. *Konstanty. Slovar' russkoj kul'tury. Opyt issledovanija* [Constants. Towards a dictionary of Russian culture]. Moscow: Škola "Jazyki russkoj kul'tury.

Stephan, Brigitte. 1989. Phraseologische Einheiten mit Tierbezeichnungen. Ein Vergleich Russisch-Deutsch. *Wissenschaftliche Zeitschrift der Martin-Luther-Universität Halle-Wittenberg, Gesellschafts- und Sprachwiss. Reihe* 38. 95–98.

Stern, Josef. 2000. *Metaphor in context*. Cambridge, MA & London: MIT Press.

Steyer, Kathrin (ed.). 2012. *Sprichwörter multilingual. Theoretische, empirische und angewandte Aspekte der modernen Parömiologie*. Tübingen: Gunter Narr.
Steyer, Kathrin, 2015. Patterns. Phraseology in a state of flux. *International Journal of Lexicography* 28 (3). 279–298.
Steyer, Kathrin (ed.). 2018. *Sprachliche Verfestigung. Wortverbindungen, Muster, Phrasem-Konstruktionen*. Tübingen: Narr Francke Attempto.
Steyer, Kathrin 2019. There's no X, only Y. A corpus-based study of German and English proverb patterns. In Andreas Nolte & Dennis Mahoney (eds.), *Living by the golden rule. Mentor – scholar – world citizen. A Festschrift for Wolfgang Mieder's 75th birthday*, 125–142. Berlin, Bern & Wien: Peter Lang.
Strohner, Hans & Roselore Brose. 1992. A cognitive system approach to linguistic knowledge. *Language Sciences* 14 (1-2). 55–76.
Ström, Åke V. & Haralds Biezais. 1975. *Germanische und Baltische Religion*. Stuttgart: W. Kohlhammer.
Stumpf, Sören. 2015. *Formelhafte (Ir-)Regularitäten. Korpuslinguistische Befunde und sprachtheoretische Überlegungen*. Frankfurt am Main etc.: Peter Lang.
Stumpf, Sören. 2018. Free usage of German unique components. Corpus linguistics, psycholinguistics and lexicographical approaches. In Sabine Arndt-Lappe, Angelika Braun, Claudine Moulin & Esme Winter-Froemel (eds.), *Expanding the lexicon. Linguistic innovation, morphological productivity, and ludicity*, 67–89. Berlin & Boston: Walter de Gruyter.
Sullivan, Karen Sorensen. 2007. *Grammar in metaphor: A Construction Grammar account of metaphoric language*. Berkeley: University of California dissertation.
Sumcov, Nikolaj F. 1996. *Simvolika slavjanskix obrjadov* [Symbolism of Slavic rites]. Moscow: Vostočnaja literatura.
Sverrisdóttir, Oddný Guārún. 1987. *Land in Sicht. Eine kontrastive Untersuchung deutscher und isländischer Redensarten aus der Seemannssprache*. Frankfurt am Main etc.: Peter Lang.
Sweetser, Eve. 1990. *From etymology to pragmatics. Metaphorical and cultural aspects of semantic structure*. Cambridge: Cambridge University Press.
Sweetser, Eve. 1999. Compositionality and blending: Semantic composition in a cognitively realistic framework. In Theo Janssen & Gisela Redeker (eds.), *Cognitive linguistics: Foundations, scope and methodology*, 129–162. Berlin & New York: Mouton de Gruyter.
Sweetser, Eve. 2000. Blended spaces and performativity. *Cognitive Linguistics* 11. 305–333.
Szpila, Grzegorz. 2000. False friends in phraseology: An English-Polish contrastive study. In Elżbieta Mańczak-Wohlfeld (ed.), *Tradition and postmodernity: English and American studies and the challenge of the future*. Kraków: Jagiellonian University Press.
Takada, Mari, Kazuko Shinohara, Fumi Morizumi & Michiko Sato. 2000. A study of metaphorical mapping involving socio-cultural values: How woman is conceptualized in Japanese. In *Proceedings of the 14th Pacific Asia conference on language, information and computation*, 301–312. Tokyo: PACLIC.
Takashima, Taiji. 1981. *Kotowaza no izumi. Fountain of Japanese proverbs. Brunnen japanischer Sprichwörter, Fontaine de proverbes japonais*. Tokyo: Hokuseido Press.
Takeda, Katsuaki. 1995. Proverb studies in Japan. *Proverbium. Yearbook of International Proverb Scholarship* 12, 323–341.
Taylor, John R. 2006. Polysemy and the lexicon. In Gitte Kristiansen, Michel Achard, René Dirven, Francisco J. Ruiz de Mendoza Ibáñez (eds.), *Cognitive linguistics: Current approaches and future perspectives*, 51–80. Berlin & New York: Mouton de Gruyter.

Taylor, John R. & Thandi G. Mbense. 1998. Red dogs and rotten mealies: How Zulus talk about anger. In Angeliki Athanasiadou & Elzbieta Tabakowska (eds.), *Speaking of emotions: Conceptualisation and expression*, 191–226. Berlin & New York: Mouton de Gruyter.

Taylor, Ronald & Walter Gottschalk. 1978. *A German-English dictionary of idioms. Idiomatic and figurative expressions with English translations*. 4. Auflage. München: Max Hueber.

Telija [Teliya], Veronika N. 1996. *Russkaja frazeologija. Semantičeskij, pragmatičeskij i lingvokul'turologičeskij aspekty* [Russian phraseology. Semantic, pragmatic and linguocultural aspects]. Moscow: Škola "Jazyki russkoj kul'tury".

Teliya [Telija], Veronika N., Natalija Bragina, Elena Oparina & Irina Sandomirskaya. 1998. Phraseology as a language of culture: Its role in the representation of a collective memory. In Anthony P. Cowie (ed.), *Phraseology. Theory, analysis, and applications*, 55–57. New York & Oxford: Oxford University Press.

Thibodeau, Paul & Frank H. Durgin. 2007. Productive figurative communication: Conventional metaphors facilitate the comprehension of related novel metaphors. *Journal of Memory and Language* 58 (2). 521–542.

Titone, Debra A. & Cynthia M. Connine. 1999. On the compositional and noncompositional nature of idiomatic expressions. *Journal of Pragmatics* 31 (12), 1655–1674.

Todorov, Tzvetan. 1977. *Théories du symbole*. Paris: Éditions du Seuil.

Tohyama, Yasuko. 1991. Aspects of Japanese nonverbal behavior in relation to traditional culture. In Yoshihiko Ikegami (ed.), *The empire of signs. Semiotic essays on Japanese culture*, 181–218. Amsterdam & Philadelphia: John Benjamins.

Tolstaja, Svetlana M. 2002. Motivacionnye semantičeskie modeli i kartina mira [Motivational semantic models and picture of the world]. *Russkij jazyk v naučnom osveščenii* 1. 112–127.

Tolstoj, Nikita I. 1995. *Jazyk i narodnaja kul'tura. Očerki po slavjanskoj mifologii i ètnolingvistike* [Language and popular culture. Essays on Slavic mythology and ethnolinguistics]. Moscow: Indrik.

Torop, Peeter. 2002. Introduction: Re-reading of cultural semiotics. In Peeter Torop, Mihhail Lotman & Kalevi Kull (eds.), *Sign system studies*, vol. 30.2, 395–404. Tartu: Tartu University Press.

Traugott, Elizabeth Closs. 1978. On the expression of spatio-temporal relations in language. In Joseph H. Greenberg (ed.), *Universals of human language*, vol. 3: Word structure, 369–400. Stanford, CA: Stanford University Press.

Traugott, Elizabeth Closs. 1985. "Conventional" and "dead" metaphors revisited. In Wolf Paprotté & René Dirven (eds.), *The ubiquity of metaphor. Metaphor in language and thought*, 17–56. Amsterdam & Philadelphia: John Benjamins.

Traugott, Elizabeth Closs & Richard B. Dasher. 2002. *Regularity in semantic change*. Cambridge: Cambridge University Press.

Trier, Jost. 1931. *Der deutsche Wortschatz im Sinnbezirk des Verstandes. Die Geschichte eines sprachlichen Feldes*, Band 1: *Von den Anfängen bis zum Beginn des 13. Jahrhunderts*. Heidelberg: Winter.

Tsuji, Yukio. 1996. A note on the Cognitive Theory of Metaphor and emotive language. *Poetica* 46. 15–39.

Tsur, Reuven. 1992. *Toward a theory of cognitive poetics*. Amsterdam: Elsevier.

Tsur, Reuven. 2002. Aspects of cognitive poetics. In Elena Semino & Jonathan V. Culpeper (eds.), *Cognitive stylistics: Language and cognition in text analysis*, 279–318. Amsterdam & Philadelphia John Benjamins.

Turney, Peter D., Yair Neuman, Dan Assaf & Yohai Cohen. 2011. Literal and metaphorical sense identification through concrete and abstract context. In *Proceedings of the 2011 conference on empirical methods in natural language*, 680–690. Edinburgh: Association for Computational Linguistics.

Tylor, Edward Burnett. 1871. *Primitive culture. Researches into the development of mythology, philosophy, religion, language, art, and custom*, vol. 1. 4th edn. London: John Murray.

Uspenskij, Boris A., Vjaceslav V. Ivanov, Vladimir N. Toporov, Aleksandr M. Pjatigorskij & Jurij M. Lotman. 1973. Theses on the semiotic study of cultures (as applied to Slavic texts). In Jan van der Eng & Monéir Grygar (eds.), *Structure of texts and semiotics of culture*, 1–28. The Hague & Paris: Mouton.

Uspenskij, Vladimir A. 1979. O veščnyx konnotacijax abstraktnyx suščestvitel'nyx [On the material connotations of abstract nouns]. *Semiotika i informatika* 11. 143–148.

Van Dale GWNT. 1992 = *Van Dale groot woordenboek der Nederlandse taal* [Van Dale comprehensive dictionary of the Dutch language]. 12de druk door Guido Geerts en Hans Heestermans. 3 delen. Utrecht & Antwerpen: Van Dale Lexicografie.

Van Dale IW. 1999 = *Idioomwoordenboek. Verklaring en herkomst van uitdrukkingen en gezegden* [Idiom dictionary. Explanation and origin of expressions and sayings]. Utrecht & Antwerpen: Van Dale Lexicografie.

van Dalen-Oskam, Karina & Marijke Mooijaart. 2000. *Bijbels lexicon – Woorden en uitdrukkingen uit de bijbel in het Nederlands van nu* [Biblical lexicon – Words and expressions from the Bible in today's Dutch]. Amsterdam: Prometheus.

van der Auwera, Johan (ed.). 1998. *Adverbial constructions in the languages of Europe*. In collaboration with Dónall P. Ó Baoill. Berlin & New York: Mouton de Gruyter.

Vervaeke, John & Christopher D. Green. 1997. Women, fire, and dangerous theories: A critique of Lakoff's theory of categorization. *Metaphor and Symbol* 12. 59–80.

Vervaeke, John & John M. Kennedy. 1996. Metaphors in language and thought: Falsification and multiple meanings. *Metaphor and Symbolic Activity* 11. 273–284.

Vinogradov, Viktor V. 1977a [1947]. Ob osnovnyx tipax frazeologičeskix edinic v sovremennom russkom jazyke [On the main types of phraseological units in modern Russian]. In Viktor V. Vinogradov, *Izbrannye trudy. Leksikologija i leksikografija* [Selected works. Lexicology and lexicography], 140–162. Moscow: Nauka.

Vinogradov, Viktor V. 1977b [1946]. Osnovnye ponjatija russkoj frazeologii kak lingvističeskoj discipliny [Basic concepts of Russian phraseology as a linguistic discipline]. In Viktor V. Vinogradov, *Izbrannye trudy. Leksikologija i leksikografija* [Selected works. Lexicology and lexicography], 118–139. Moscow: Nauka.

Vinogradov, Viktor V. 1953. Osnovnye tipy leksičeskix znacenij slova [Basic types of lexical meanings of the word]. *Voprosy jazykoznanija* 5. 3–29.

Vrbinc, Marjeta & Alenka Vrbinc. 2014. Friends or foes? Phraseological false friends in English and Slovene. *AAA – Arbeiten aus Anglistik und Amerikanistik* 39 (1). 71–86.

Wallace, George & Kayoko Kimiya. 1994. *Communicating with "ki". The "spirit" in Japanese idioms*. Tokyo: Kodansha International.

Wallace, George & Kayoko Kimiya. 1995. *Kanji idioms*. Tokyo: Kodansha International.

Wandruszka, Mario. 1979. Falsche Freunde: Ein linguistisches Problem und seine Lösung. *Lebende Sprachen. Zeitschrift für fremde Sprachen in Wissenschaft und Praxis*. 24. 4–9.

Ward, Donald. 1987. The wolf: Proverbial ambivalence. *Proverbium. Yearbook of International Proverb Scholarship* 4. 211–224.

Weinhold, Karl. 1897. *Die mystische Neunzahl bei den Deutschen*. Berlin: Königliche Akademie der Wissenschaften zu Berlin.
Weinreich, Otto. 1916. *Triskaidekadische Studien. Beiträge zur Geschichte der Zahlen*. Giessen: Alfred Tölpelmann.
Weinrich, Harald. 1976. *Sprache in Texten*. Stuttgart: Klett.
Weisgerber, Leo. 1929. *Muttersprache und Geistesbildung*. Göttingen: Vandenhoeck & Ruprecht.
Weisgerber, Leo. 1961. *Grundzüge der inhaltbezogenen Grammatik*. Düsseldorf: Schwann.
Weisgerber, Leo. 1962. *Die sprachliche Gestaltung der Welt*. 3. Auflage. Düsseldorf: Schwann.
Wenliang, Yang. 1991. Chinesische und deutsche idiomatische Redewendungen. Kontrastive Betrachtungen. *Muttersprache* 101, 106–115.
Whorf, Benjamin Lee. 1956 [1941]. *Language, thought, and reality*. Ed. and with an introduction by John B. Carroll. Cambridge, MA: MIT Press.
Wierzbicka, Anna. 1985. Different cultures, different languages, different speech acts. Polish vs. English. *Journal of Pragmatics* 9. 145–178.
Wierzbicka, Anna. 1990. The semantics of emotions: *Fear* and its relatives in English. *Australian Journal of Linguistics* 10. 359–375.
Wierzbicka, Anna. 1992. *Semantics, culture, and cognition. Universal human concepts in culture-specific configurations*. New York & Oxford: Oxford University Press.
Wierzbicka, Anna. 1996. *Semantics: Primes and universals*. New York & Oxford: Oxford University Press.
Wierzbicka, Anna. 1997. *Understanding cultures through their key words. English, Russian, Polish, German, and Japanese*. New York & Oxford: Oxford University Press.
Wierzbicka, Anna. 1999. *Emotions across languages and cultures: Diversity and universals*. Cambridge: Cambridge University Press.
Wierzbicka, Anna. 2003. *Cross-cultural pragmatics. The semantics of natural language*. 2nd edn. Berlin & New York: Mouton de Gruyter.
Winner, Thomas G. 2002. How did the ideas of Juri Lotman reach the West? In Peeter Torop, Mihhail Lotman & Kalevi Kull (eds.), *Sign system studies*, vol. 30.2, 419–427. Tartu: Tartu University Press.
Wotjak, Barbara. 1992a. *Verbale Phraseolexeme in System und Text*. Tübingen: Max Niemeyer.
Wotjak, Barbara. 1992b. Mehr Fragen als Antworten? Problemskizze – (nicht nur) zur konfrontativen Phraseologie. In Csaba Földes (ed.), *Deutsche Phraseologie in Sprachsystem und Sprachverwendung*, 197–217. Wien: Edition Praesens.
Wotjak, Barbara & Manfred Richter. 1993. *Sage und schreibe. Deutsche Phraseologismen in Theorie und Praxis*. Berlin etc.: Langenscheidt & Enzyklopädie.
Wray, Alison. 2002. *Formulaic language and the lexicon*. Cambridge: Cambridge University Press.
Wray, Alison. 2013. Formulaic language. *Language Teaching* 46 (3). 316–334.
Wulff, Stefanie. 2008. *Rethinking idiomaticity: A usage-based approach*. London & New York: Continuum.
Wulff, Stefanie. 2013. Words and idioms. In Thomas Hoffmann & Graeme Trousdale (eds.), 274–289. *The Oxford handbook of Construction Grammar*. Oxford: Oxford University Press.
Yamaoka, Haruo. 1976. *Meditation gut enlightenment: The way of hara*. San Francisco, CA: International.
Yu, Ning. 1998. *The contemporary theory of metaphor: A perspective from Chinese*. Amsterdam & Philadelphia: John Benjamins.
Yu, Ning. 2003. Metaphor, body, and culture: The Chinese understanding of gallbladder and courage. *Metaphor and Symbol* 18. 13–31.

Zaliznjak, Anna. 2006. *Mnogoznačnost' v jazyke i sposoby ee predstavlenija* [Polysemy in language and ways of its representation]. Moscow: Jazyki slavjanskix kul'tur.

Zaliznjak, Anna. 2013. *Russkaja semantika v tipologičeskoj perspektive* [Russian semantics in a typological perspective]. Moscow: Jazyki slavjanskix kul'tur.

Zelenin, Dmitrij K. 1994. *Izbrannye trudy. Stat'i po duxovnoj kul'ture 1901–1913* [Selected works. Articles on spiritual culture 1901–1913]. Moscow: Indrik.

Ziem, Alexander. 2008. *Frames und sprachliches Wissen. Kognitive Aspekte der semantischen Kompetenz*. Berlin & New York: Walter de Gruyter.

Ziem, Alexander 2015. Frames of understanding in text and discourse. Theoretical foundations and descriptive applications. Amsterdam & Philadelphia: John Benjamins.

Ziem, Alexander & Alexander Lasch. 2013. *Konstruktionsgrammatik. Konzepte und Grundlagen gebrauchsbasierter Ansätze*. Berlin & Boston: Walter de Gruyter.

Zhu, Kaifu. 1998. *Lexikographische Untersuchungen somatischer Phraseologismen im Deutschen und Chinesischen*. Frankfurt am Main etc.: Peter Lang.

Zipf, George Kingsley. 1949. *Human behavior and the principle of least effort*. Cambridge, MA: Addison-Wesley.

Žolkovskij, Aleksandr K. & Igor A. Mel'čuk. 1967. O semantičeskom sinteze [On semantic synthesis]. *Problemy kibernetiki* 19. 177–238.

Žukov, Vlas P. 1978. *Semantika frazeologičeskix oborotov* [Semantics of phraseological units]. Moscow: Prosveščenie.

Abbreviations

CFL	conventional figurative language
CFLT	Conventional Figurative Language Theory
CFU	conventional figurative unit
CTM	Cognitive Theory of Metaphor
WML	Westmünsterländisch

Subject index

Actual meaning VI–VII, 1, 14, 20, 85, 89–91, 93–96, 104–106, 141, 143, 148, 164, 222–224, 227–234, 436–440, 443
Additional naming 13, 21–23, 33, 46, 438–439
Analysability 109–110, 342, 348
Animal constituent 126, 139, 357, 365, 404–405, 407–409, 420, 432
Animal metaphor 178, 404
Animal symbol 78, 307, 311, 359, 365, 404
Asymmetrical polysemy 89, 92–93, 441

Basic-level metaphor 167, 176, 218, 440
Blending (of mental spaces) 135, 176, 227–228

Coercion 114–115, 132–133, 135–136, 439
Cognitive modelling (of figurative semantics) 217, 219, 222–224, 229, 231–237, 437, 441
Cognitive Theory of Metaphor (CTM) 29, 116, 165–168, 172–173, 184–187, 189–190, 192–193, 325, 437, 440
Colour symbol 78, 344
Compound, see Figurative compound
Conceptual blending, see Blending (of mental spaces)
Conceptual indexation 141–143, 440
Conceptual metaphor 10, 12–13, 74, 80, 85, 95, 115–124, 155–156, 158–159, 163–185, 187–193, 195–197, 199–200, 217–218, 229, 231–232, 278, 440
Conventional Figurative Language Theory (CFLT) VI–VII, 177, 327, 341, 435–436, 438, 441, 443–444
Cross-linguistic idiom analysis 73–74, 77, 81–82, 85–86, 88, 101–102
Cultural anthropology 263, 336
Cultural connotations 271, 273, 275, 314–324, 440–441
Cultural knowledge VII, 53, 125–126, 173, 232, 257, 264, 273–276, 300, 305–310, 323–325, 348, 350, 355, 440
Cultural model 71, 170, 184–185, 264, 275–277, 285, 324, 337, 340–342, 347–349

Cultural symbol 66, 127–130, 233, 272–274, 300, 307–308, 311–313, 323–325, 327–328, 353–355, 371, 379, 440–441
Culture-based (phenomena/features) 127, 273–275, 278, 287–288, 292, 302, 349, 356, 384
Culture-specific (phenomena/features) 141–142, 177, 183–185, 267–271, 274–275, 278, 287–290, 292, 311, 314–318, 322–323, 438

Decomposability, see Analysability
Dialect 3–8, 39, 152, 175, 178, 239–242, 253, 258

Emotions 168–170, 172–177, 179, 181–183, 186, 201, 209, 215–216, 279, 304
Etymological memory 18–20, 95, 106, 108
Etymology 19–21, 103–109, 138, 442

False friends 89–91, 146–148, 150–156, 158–164, 441
Fictive conceptual domains 273–274, 303, 305, 323, 440
Figurative compound 43–45, 47, 71, 140, 274, 331, 369, 373–374
Folk theory 176, 181, 311, 362
Frame 19, 46, 53, 115–117, 122–128, 134, 159, 161, 219–224, 230, 232, 237, 239–248, 253–257, 291–292, 294–296, 399, 440–441
Functional equivalence 74, 98, 102, 441

Gender specifics 283–286, 324
Gesture 74, 107–108, 245, 281–283, 314, 376

Humoural doctrine 169–171, 304, 311

Iconicity 329, 343, 346, 349, 354, 357–358, 430
Idiom 31–33, 36–38, 41, 49–61, 64–71, 104–105, 109, 114, 155–163, 167–168, 191–193, 197–205, 207, 209–216, 222, 236, 439, see also Cross-linguistic idiom analysis

https://doi.org/10.1515/9783110702538-017

Idiomaticity 52, 54, 59, 439
Image component VII, 1, 13–22, 33, 85, 101, 104, 116, 127, 200, 223–226, 436–437, 440–441
Image requirement 13, 17–18, 21–22, 438–439
Index-based motivation 114–116, 140, 143, 439–440
Inner form 18–21, 107, 148, 441
Intertextual resonance, *see* Textual dependence
Irregularity 38, 52, 54–58, 60, 64–65

Lexicalised meaning, *see* Actual meaning

Material culture 287–288, 290–293, 309–310, 314, 323–324, 440, 443
Mental image V–VII, 18–21, 89–91, 96, 103–105, 148, 200, 231, 338, 436
Mental space 135, 176
Metaphor V, 9–15, 25, 28–30, 41–44, 59, 104, 114–125, 151, 164–165, 193–196, 218, 333, 338, 341, 343, 347, 350–351, 439–440, *see also* Animal metaphor, Basic-level metaphor, Cognitive Theory of Metaphor, Conceptual metaphor, Novel metaphor
Metaphoric model 55, 117–121, 165, 184, 193, 197, 204, 207, 209–210, 212, 218, 232, 440
Metaphoric motivation 62, 115–117, 217–218, 221–222
Metonymy 11, 28–31, 127, 136, 172, 203
Moscow-Tartu school 265, 325–327, 330, 341, 346
Motivation 19–21, 31, 38, 93, 103–106, 108–113, 117, 122–123, 133–135, 139, 142–143, 145–146, 155, 170–173, 192, 224, 272, 275, 289, 347, 350, 437, 439–440, *see also* Index-based motivation, Metaphoric motivation, Semantic motivation, Symbol-based motivation, Syntactic motivation, Types of motivation

Novel metaphor V, 12, 29, 121, 175, 193, 435

Number symbol 78, 355–357, 365–367, 370–373, 394, 397, 403

Opacity 33, 52–54, 56–57, 61

Phonetic indexation 141, 440
Phraseme 36–38, 42, 47–52, 54–61, 63, 65–68, 72, 103, 298, 301, 404, 439, *see also* Types of phrasemes
Phraseology 31, 36–37, 39–40, 54, 61–64, 66–67, 74, 76, 79, 82, 135, 139, 147, 165, 167, 298
Play on words 17, 24, 134–135, 276, 362, *see also* Pun, Word play
Proverb 31, 34–35, 38, 43–44, 48–49, 66–72, 128–129, 140, 150–151, 276–277, 287–298, 301, 312–313, 331, 358, 368–370, 387, 389, 391, 394–396, 404, 406–407, 420, 432, 439
Pun 21, 23, 49, 101, 271, *see also* Play on words, Word play

Regular polysemy 30, 93, 121–122
Restricted collocation 38, 49, 54–55, 62–65, 72, 151, 277, 360, 439
Rich image 20–21, 46, 80, 86, 115–118, 122–125, 155–157, 159, 164, 176–178, 196, 217–219, 221, 229–232, 292, 440

Semantic field 79, 84–85, 88, 92–93, 96, 100, 121, 197, 204, 207–208, 225, 280–281, 361
Semantic motivation 114, 132, 137–138, 340, 439–440
Semantic reinterpretation 33, 52–54, 65, 89, 148, 159, 223, 227, 244, 341, 346
Semiotics of culture VIII, 74, 78, 234, 263, 265, 324–325, 327, 437, 441
Simile 44, 49, 58–62, 72, 134–137, 151–152, 225, 404, 407–409, 413, 425, 429, 434, 439
Social convention 279–281
Social interaction 274–276, 281, 283, 286, 307, 309, 313–314, 323–324, 376, 440
Source concept 7, 14, 20, 53–54, 64, 94, 116, 150, 152–156, 158–159, 166, 186–189,

195, 227–231, 238, 242–243, 246, 255, 276, 278, 283, 285, 288, 295, 316, 323, 437
Speech formulae 25, 67–68, 250
Stability 52, 54, 59–61, 64, 67, 368
Standard language 2–6, 39, 131, 152, 240–241, 261, 285–289, 293, 302, 310, 318, 418
Symbol 45, 86, 95, 114–115, 130, 245, 257–258, 265, 275, 287, 322, 325, 328–346, 354–355, 439, *see also* Animal symbol, Colour symbol, Cultural symbol, Number symbol
Symbolic domain 333, 343–344, 346, 441
Symbol-based motivation 115, 127–128, 130, 132, 141, 143, 217, 234
Syntactic motivation 114–115, 136, 439

Target concept 15, 53–54, 116, 123, 161, 166, 185, 187–190, 195, 217, 224, 227, 230–232, 238, 255, 257, 276, 278–280, 316, 322–323
Textual dependence 138, 273–274, 296–297, 299–304, 311–314, 323–324, 332, 362, 392, 395, 398, 407, 411–412, 440
Textual knowledge 114–116, 137–138, 296, 301, 399, 439
Types of motivation 114, 116, 127–128, 132, 143, 146, 404, 407, 439
Types of phrasemes 42, 49, 51, 54–56, 58

Unique constituent 31–34, 56, 61, 64, 112, 117, 316, 375, 414

Word play 17–18, 46, 81, 316, *see also* Play on words, Pun

www.ingramcontent.com/pod-product-compliance
Lightning Source LLC
Chambersburg PA
CBHW030559230426
43661CB00053B/1777